D1383168

PERSPECTIVES OLD AND NEW ON PAUL

Perspectives Old and New on Paul

The "Lutheran" Paul and His Critics

STEPHEN WESTERHOLM

Montante Family Library
D'Youville College

WILLIAM B. EERDMANS PUBLISHING COMPANY
GRAND RAPIDS, MICHIGAN / CAMBRIDGE, U.K.

MAR 1 8 2010

© 2004 Wm. B. Eerdmans Publishing Co.
All rights reserved

Wm. B. Eerdmans Publishing Co.
2140 Oak Industrial Drive N.E., Grand Rapids, Michigan 49505 /
P.O. Box 163, Cambridge CB3 9PU U.K.

Printed in the United States of America

13 12 11 10 09 08   9 8 7 6 5 4

Library of Congress Cataloging-in-Publication Data

Westerholm, Stephen, 1949-
Perspectives old and new on Paul: the "Lutheran" Paul and his critics /
Stephen Westerholm.
p.   cm.
Includes bibliographical references and index.
ISBN 978-0-8028-4809-5 (pbk.: alk. paper)
1. Bible. N.T. Epistles of Paul — Criticism, interpretation, etc. — History.
2. Bible. N.T. Epistles of Paul — Theology.
3. Lutheran Church — Doctrines.   I. Title.

BS2651.W46   2004
335.9'2 — dc22

2003064214

www.eerdmans.com

BS
2651
.W46
2004

For Birger Gerhardsson

Contents

CONTENTS

PART TWO:
TWENTIETH-CENTURY RESPONSES
TO THE "LUTHERAN" PAUL

CONTENTS

Preface

This book began as a revision and updating of my *Israel's Law and the Church's Faith: Paul and His Recent Interpreters;* in places it retains that character. Chapters 2 through 6 of the earlier book are repeated, with minimal rewriting, in chapters 6 through 10 here. Chapter 7 of *Israel's Law,* though considerably expanded, remains the basis of chapter 16 in this study. Parts of chapters 9 and 10 of *Israel's Law* have been taken over in chapter 19 here.

Chapter 1 of *Israel's Law* was largely given to a (rather breezy) nine-page treatment of Luther, setting the stage for the summaries that followed of twentieth-century scholars who have attacked aspects of Luther's reading of Paul. That chapter has been replaced here by a new Part One in which Luther is treated more substantially and reviewers' suggestions that Augustine and Calvin merit a look have been adopted. Wesley has been added as well lest it be thought that all who understand Paul's doctrine of justification to exclude any role for human "works" also championed predestination. With the additions, Part One offers a detailed and, I hope, sympathetic portrait of the "Lutheran" Paul, the object of much twentieth-century critique; one result, however, was that a book with the subtitle *Paul and His Recent Interpreters* needed to be renamed! Part Two of this study contains three chapters (11 through 13) dealing with contributions to the debate later than my work in *Israel's Law.* Part Three looks very different from Part Two of *Israel's Law,* partly because it responds to more recent literature, partly because I have attempted to refine earlier arguments, and partly because my own thinking (I would like to believe) has matured in several respects.

A quarter-century ago — around the time E. P. Sanders was completing and publishing his monumental *Paul and Palestinian Judaism* — I pursued doctoral studies in Lund, Sweden, under the supervision of Birger Gerhardsson. Gerhardsson himself is best known for his significant contributions to Matthean scholarship and to our understanding of the formation and transmission of the Gospel tradition; I should add that his sparkling chapter on Paul in *The Ethos of the Bible* was an important stimulus for my own thinking about the apostle. Our meetings since I returned to North America have been far too few; yet Gerhardsson's commitment to meticulous historical scholarship, his conviction of its importance, and his continuing friendship have meant much to me over the years. To him, as a token of my appreciation and respect, this book is dedicated.

Whimsical Introduction

A friend and I were perusing the literature on Paul in the World's Biggest Bookstore when we were joined, rather unexpectedly, by Martin Luther himself. Surprised and flustered, I started to greet him but was cut off by the Reformer, who clearly did not want to be known. "What's new on Paul?" he asked.

I began a frantic search to see if a reprint of Ridderbos's *Paul* might still be on the shelf. My friend, however, sizing up our guest as one who could use a good introduction, seized upon the Oxford Past Masters volume on Paul, written by E. P. Sanders. My attempts at distraction were futile.

"Here's just the thing," my well-meaning friend explained. "A great scholar, Ed Sanders. *The* most influential scholar on Paul in the last quarter-century. And he sums it all up in this little book. You've got to read it."

Luther started leafing through its pages. Not surprisingly, his eyes fell first on a reference to himself: "Martin Luther, whose influence on subsequent interpreters has been enormous, made Paul's statements central to his own quite different theology."[1] "Hmm," hummed the Reformer. "I wonder what he means by that?"

He turned a couple pages and read some more. "Luther, plagued by guilt, read Paul's passages on 'righteousness by faith' as meaning that God reckoned a Christian to be righteous even though he or she was a sinner. . . . Luther's emphasis on fictional, imputed righteousness, though it has often been shown to be an incorrect interpretation of Paul, has been influential. . . . Luther sought and found relief from guilt. But Luther's problems were not Paul's, and we misunderstand him if we see him through Luther's eyes" (49).

---

1. Sanders, *Paul*, 44. Parenthetical numbers in the following text refer to pages from this work.

At this point I fully expected to hear a few samples drawn from Luther's extensive vocabulary of vituperative epithets. He said nothing, however; apparently half a millennium spent where conflicts are no more had mollified even Brother Martin. He read on, though rather subdued.

> The subject-matter [in Gal. 2–4 and Rom. 3–4] is not "how can the individual be righteous in God's sight?," but rather, "on what grounds can Gentiles participate in the people of God in the last days?" (50)

> Paul fully espoused and observed a "work-ethic," as long as the goal was the right one. His opposition to "works of the law" was not motivated by dislike of effort. . . . He did not . . . regard effort in doing good as being in any way opposed to membership in the body of Christ. (102-3)

Luther looked puzzled. My friend hastened to explain: "You see, Luther thought *Paul* thought you shouldn't do any work to become a Christian; you just had to trust Christ."

Luther looked as though he wanted to speak. He didn't, however, so my friend went on. "Sanders shows that wasn't at all what Paul meant. Look, he says so over here." My friend took the book, found a favorite passage, and handed it back to the Reformer to read: "The problem in these chapters is the concrete one of Israel's refusal to accept the grace of God as recently revealed, not the individual's effort or lack of it. The Jews have one fault, but only one: rejecting Jesus as the Christ" (122).

Again Luther looked as though he had something to say. Perhaps realizing, however, that his time for doing so had long passed, he turned back to the book.

> Guided by Luther, many scholars overlook Paul's perfectionism, but this partial list of passages shows that it was an appreciable aspect of his preaching. (101)

> Christians should live morally blameless lives. The idea of fictional, imputed righteousness had not occurred to [Paul], but had it done so he would have raged against it. (68)

"What does he mean: Paul would have raged against imputed righteousness?" wondered Martin Luther.

My friend chuckled. "Sanders is from Texas, you know. They're not known for understatement down there."

The concept of understatement seemed completely foreign to the Reformer. As an alternative to what he had just read from Sanders, however, it held some promise. "Are there any books here on Paul by people who *are* known for their understatement?" he asked.

I began a frenzied search for F. F. Bruce's *Paul: Apostle of the Heart Set Free*. Alas, without any frenzy, my friend was again faster.

"Oh, that would be the British," he replied. "Now Jimmy Dunn — he's British, you know. He's got a nice little book on justification you might like." He handed Luther a book by Dunn and Alan M. Suggate: *The Justice of God: A Fresh Look at the Old Doctrine of Justification by Faith*.

I bit my tongue.

Luther started to read. He found that he had been wrong in thinking that Paul had suffered "the same agonies of conscience about his sinfulness and inability to satisfy God" that he himself had known.[2] He had been wrong in thinking first-century Jews were like Catholics of medieval times who counted up their good works to secure salvation (14). He found that the real point of Paul's doctrine of justification by faith was that "the unconditional grace of God had Gentiles in view as much as Jews"; Jewish "exclusivism," not "legalism," was the target (25). Paul was "not hitting at people who thought they could earn God's goodwill by their achievements, or merit God's final acquittal on the basis of all their good deeds. That theological insight is true and of lasting importance. But it is not quite what Paul was saying" (27).

"What does he mean, 'Not *quite* what Paul was saying'?" wondered Martin Luther.

My friend chuckled. "Oh, that's British understatement for you. Dunn just means that's not what Paul had in mind."

Apparently understatement was not the answer. Luther tried once more. "Do you have anything here on Paul by a . . . a *preacher of the Word?*" he inquired.

This sounded promising, but it stumped me for a moment. It didn't stump my well-meaning friend.

"Tom Wright's your man. Dean of a famous cathedral in England.[3] Good scholar too. You'd enjoy his *What Saint Paul Really Said*." He handed the Reformer a copy.

I conceded defeat. Luther started reading.

"Justification by works" has nothing to do with individual Jews attempting a

---

2. Dunn and Suggate, *Justice*, 13. Parenthetical numbers in the following text refer to pages from this work.

3. At the time of our exchange, Dr. Wright was dean of Lichfield Cathedral in Staffordshire, England.

kind of proto-Pelagian pulling themselves up by their moral bootstraps, and everything to do with the definition of the true Israel.[4]

The problem Paul addresses in Galatians . . . is: should his ex-pagan converts be circumcised or not? Now this question is by no means obviously to do with the questions faced by Augustine and Pelagius, or by Luther and Erasmus. On anyone's reading, but especially within its first-century context, it has to do quite obviously with the question of how you *define the people of God:* are they to be defined by the badges of Jewish race, or in some other way? Circumcision is not a "moral" issue; it does not have to do with moral effort, or earning salvation by good deeds. (120)

Justification, in Galatians, is the doctrine which insists that all who share faith in Christ belong at the same table, no matter what their racial differences. (122)

Paul has no thought in this passage of warding off a proto-Pelagianism, of which in any case his contemporaries were not guilty. He is here, as in Galatians and Philippians, declaring that there is no road into covenant membership on the grounds of Jewish racial privilege. (129)

Luther looked around in despair. As he did so, his eyes fell on another section of the bookstore, labeled "Self-Help." "I think I'll check out those books over there," he said, leaving us to browse the literature on Paul.

Among the tragic "if only's" of history we may surely reckon the wish that Luther's visit had been thirty years earlier. How different, how positively *Protestantic,* the Pauline shelves of the World's Biggest Bookstore looked then! To be sure, various aspects of Luther's reading of the apostle had been disputed by isolated scholars; indeed, a history of protests against the "Lutheran" interpretive paradigm would include much of the significant twentieth-century literature on Paul. The centrality of justification by faith in Pauline thought was questioned already at the beginning of the century. Well before the 1970s the notion that Paul, like Luther, found in the gospel relief from the pangs of a troubled conscience was famously challenged; so, too, was the view that Paul thought Christians were doomed throughout their earthly sojourn to fall short of doing "the good that [they] would," while succumbing to "the evil that [they] would not."

---

4. Wright, *Founder,* 119. Parenthetical numbers in the following text refer to pages from this work.

Challenges there were, but a number of the greatest Paulinists were "Lutheran" to their core, and their disciples were legion. The heart of the Pauline (= Christian) gospel, in the minds of these scholars, was still the doctrine of justification by faith. Its target was thought to be the pretension that human achievement was the way to secure God's favor and a place in the blessed hereafter. Against any such notion of justification by "works" the "Lutheran" Paul protested that faith, and faith alone, was needed. God would ascribe ("impute") to believers in Christ the righteousness of the Savior, though they remained sinners after, as they were sinners before, their conversion.

The turning point, as my well-meaning friend so inauspiciously pointed out, came with E. P. Sanders's *Paul and Palestinian Judaism* (1977). Sanders's monograph begins with a massively documented attack on the "Lutheran" understanding of the Judaism in which Paul was fostered, then proceeds to make the claim that distorted views of Judaism have led to distortions of Paul's thought. Not all have been convinced. But many have, and the focus and tone of Pauline scholarship have shifted dramatically.

Part Two of this study summarizes the story of how the "Lutheran" Paul fared in twentieth-century Pauline scholarship. Friends as well as foes are treated, though the emphasis is on the latter. Part Three turns to Paul and the issues themselves, attempting to answer the strictly separate though at times (one can hope) overlapping questions of where the state of the debate, and where the truth, may lie.

We begin, however, with four portraits of the "Lutheran" Paul. Here "Lutheran" designates, not the denominational affiliation of the interpreters, but their reading of the apostle as one for whom the doctrine of justification by faith is central and deliberately excludes any role for human "works." For our initial statements of the position we turn not to the ranks of nineteenth- or twentieth-century biblical scholars, none of whom represents the source of the tradition, and none of whom (the eminence of our profession notwithstanding) can justly be labeled earthshakers or history makers; we look rather to four undisputed giants in the history of the Christian West. Their unmistakably "Lutheran" understanding of Paul affected (and continues to affect) the faith and lives of many millions: the "Lutheran" Paul is not, after all, the preserve of academics. Nor, once we have escaped the provincialism that thinks serious biblical scholarship a modern invention, should we overlook the enormous importance of Augustine, Luther, Calvin, and Wesley in the history of Pauline interpretation.

The first portrait, that of Augustine, is included because he anticipated the most striking features of the "Lutheran" understanding of the apostle. Whether, when Luther is charged with distorting Paul, Augustine should be summoned to face similar charges or to witness on the defendant's behalf may be left to those prosecuting the case; in any event, Augustine's voice should be heard in the debate. Luther comes next: enough said. Calvin and Wesley are then added because, while retaining much of Luther's thought, they departed from it in ways sufficiently influential, and significant, to merit separate attention.

With modern interpreters of Paul, we seldom need look at their wider thought and affiliations; what matters is their construction of Paul's words, his work, his world. Not so with Augustine, Luther, Calvin, and Wesley. In each case their understanding of Paul has decisively shaped their thinking as a whole and can scarcely be disentangled from it. On the other hand, the more creative the mind that adopts Paul as its mentor, the less recognizably Pauline may be the result; and the charge is frequently made that Augustine, Luther, Calvin, and Wesley, in adapting Paul's words to their own situations and thinking, were very creative. Clearly the charge can only be considered after we have some sense of how the basic tenets of their reading of Paul fit into the context of their wider thought.

In order to allow characteristic features of their positions to emerge, I have attempted to let emphases in their own writings determine the disposition of each summary rather than impose a single pattern on them all. Nonetheless, the topics that recur include the following, each important in the current Pauline debate: human nature in its "fallen" condition, the nature and function of the Mosaic law, justification by faith apart from works, the place of works in the lives of believers, the role in believers' lives of both the law and the Spirit, the possibility (or inevitability) of believers' sin, and the "election" of those who come to faith. Economy of presentation prevents us from examining in Part One how the views of our Pauline interpreters are derived from Pauline texts.[5] That should in any case become clear in Part Three, where the viability of their reading of Paul is tested by a fresh look at crucial texts in the epistles.

Augustine, Luther, Calvin, and Wesley are all eminently worthy of study in their own right — and none of them has suffered any deprivation in that regard. I have nothing new to add to existing studies, nor do I here explore several areas essential to any work of which *they* are the focus: the development of their thinking, for example, or its antecedents or rootedness in the debates of their day. Here I paint with the broadest of brushes, though still, I hope, in sufficient detail to clarify their importance for the current Pauline debate. Perhaps the at-

---

5. Augustine, Luther, Calvin, and Wesley all would of course have claimed that their views were consonant with the testimony of the sacred Scriptures as a whole. Yet, on the subjects of concern here, it is in nearly every case clear that Pauline texts bear the weight of the argument *for* their positions; and in every case it is clear that Pauline texts are construed along the lines of these positions.

tempt will serve as well to counter the tendency toward caricature of the "Lutheran" Paul that is inevitable when dismissals of the position become less the product of firsthand grappling with the issues and sources and more the accepted "wisdom" of the field, adopted without question by a new generation of students and scholars.

Some question, I believe, is still very much in order. We may well decide, in the end, that the reading of Paul reached by Augustine, Luther, Calvin, and Wesley after much wrestling with the texts, and embraced by generations of scholars who were neither appreciably dumber than we nor less conversant with the Pauline writings, requires modification in the light of later knowledge; I myself believe this is true. We may even decide that the long-accepted reading should be given up today as hopelessly wrongheaded from the start — though I myself do not think so. In any case, our own thinking will be stretched by the exercise, we will learn much of the history of Pauline scholarship in the process, and we may even discover an insight or two into the apostolic object of all the wrangling.

Part One

Portraits of the "Lutheran" Paul

Chapter 1

Augustine

For Augustine "the apostle" means Paul (*C. duas epp. Pel.* 3.3.4),[1] and Paul is the "great preacher of grace" (*De gest. Pel.* 14.35; cf. *Ench.* 9.32). Himself the target of an extraordinary display of divine grace, Paul proved "loud and eager above all" in its "defence" (*De spir. et litt.* 7.12). Against whom, Pauline scholars now muse, did grace ever need defending? Augustine affirms what they emphatically deny: against "the proud and arrogant presumers upon their own works"[2] (7.12; cf. *De pecc. mer.* 1.27.43) who "unthankfully despise [God's] grace," and "trust[ing] in [their] own strength" as sufficient to "fulfil the law," seek to "establish [their] own righteousness" (*Ep.* 145.3; cf. 82.20; *De spir. et litt.* 9.15).

In all essentials Augustine appears to represent what in many recent discussions has come to be dismissed as the "Lutheran" reading of Paul. We may perhaps forgo a demonstration that he arrived at such a reading without the liability of "Reformation spectacles." It is sufficient to note that, with his eleven-century head start on Luther, his dominance of Christian thinking throughout those years, and his demonstrable impact on the Reformers themselves, Augustine has a fair claim to be history's most influential reader of Paul. That ought to secure him a hearing in the debate.

Augustine had his own spectacles, to be sure, furnished in part by his struggles with heretics. The latter, like other perversions of the good in Augustine's universe, inevitably served useful purposes: they compelled the church to "investigate [its articles of faith] more accurately, to understand them more clearly, and to proclaim them more earnestly" (*De civ. Dei* 16.2). His mature views on

---

1. References to Augustine's works are in the text; for details see the bibliography.
2. Note that this quotation is found in the very first paragraph of Luther's *Lectures on Romans*.

3

human weakness and divine grace were essentially in place long before the Pelagian conflict erupted (indeed, Augustine's *Confessions* proved a provocation to Pelagius; *De don. pers.* 20.53) (*Ad Simpl.* 1.2.12-13; *De don. pers.* 20.52; *De praed. sanct.* 4.8); significantly, he felt constrained to adopt them by his study of Paul, though in important respects they clashed with his own prior thinking.[3] Yet he himself grants that the dispute with Pelagius enabled him to see things that other readers of Paul had missed (*De doctr. Chr.* 3.104); and certainly the radical implications of his own position were first worked out in rebutting that of his foes.

Our attention here must focus primarily on Augustine's developed stance. The tale can most simply be told as one of creation, fall, and redemption, with postscripted treatments of the law and of human dependence on divine grace.[4] The discussion will be simplified, however, if a few fundamental Augustinian theses are spelled out from the start.

1. For Augustine all human beings possess free will inasmuch as all have their own likes and dislikes, their characteristic desires and distastes, and inasmuch as their personal inclinations steer their deliberate actions (*De civ. Dei* 5.10; *De lib. arb.* 3.3.27). At times we may be compelled to act against our will, but we can never be forced to *will* against our will: our will is always our own and, in that sense, "free" (3.3.33).[5] But the pursuit of what our wills desire is a dubious path to happiness: what people want may not be (and since Adam's sin, is not by nature) what is right, good, and conducive to their own well-being (*De civ. Dei* 8.8; cf. *De Trin.* 13.8). In the end, should we even call "free" those whose misdirected desires confine them to a compulsive pursuit of goods that neither satisfy nor last, and who are cut off from their supreme good — the only good they could never lose against their will — by their own incapacity to sincerely *want* it (cf. *Ench.* 9.30)?

2. Human desire is central to Augustine's thinking in other respects as well. Though it is always better to do right than wrong (*Serm.* 156.14), one is not oneself right in doing what is right unless one delights in the right one chooses (*De spir. et litt.* 14.26). A wolf may do the right thing (from a sheep's perspective) when, frightened by the barks of dogs and shouts of shepherds, it leaves the

---

3. Cf. *Retr.* 2.27: "I, indeed, labored in defence of the free choice of the human will; but the grace of God conquered, and finally I was able to understand, with full clarity, the meaning of the Apostle: 'For who singles thee out? Or what hast thou that thou hast not received?'"

4. The condensed, (more or less) systematic nature of the following summary gives it a character very different from that of Augustine's own writings, well known for their discursive quality. It is hoped nonetheless that Augustine's views are fairly represented.

5. My colleague Dr. Travis Kroeker reminds me, however, that Augustine portrays the fallen human will as divided against itself in *Conf.* 8.9.21-24 (citing Rom. 7:17, 20).

sheep in peace. But it remains a wolf with a wolfish appetite. What the wolf needs (from a sheep's perspective) is to become a sheep (*Serm.* 169.8). So, too, with us. Fear of burning in hell may drive us to do the right — and better that than sinning. But we are only the people we ought to be when our actions are driven by love for the good, and we loathe sin no less than the flames of perdition (*Ep.* 145.4). The story of human redemption is for Augustine not simply one of sin and forgiveness, of condemnation and acquittal; it is, perhaps above all, a story of the healing of the wounded will (*De spir. et litt.* 30.52), the transformation of human desires so that we begin to love what we ought to love, and God above all.

3. In Augustine's universe all that exists is good, and all things, considered together, are very good (*Conf.* 7.12.18; 13.28.43; *Ench.* 3.10), but they are not all equally good. That the Eternal alone is supremely good does not rule out the inferior goodness of things temporal (cf. *Conf.* 4.10.15; *De civ. Dei* 12.4; *De lib. arb.* 3.15.146). Nothing could be more transitory than the words we speak; yet if in the end what we say is good, each passing word has a share in its goodness. Similarly, that which is born, lives, and passes away partakes of, because it contributes to, the goodness of all creation (*Conf.* 4.10.15). There is, moreover, among temporal goods themselves a hierarchy of goodness to be respected (*De civ. Dei* 11.16; *De doctr. Chr.* 1.17-18; *De lib. arb.* 3.5.56): sentient beings are superior to nonsentient, intelligent to nonintelligent, those capable of movement to those with no such capacity, those living to those that lack life, and so on. Yet even things (like stones) that have no life, no movement, no intelligence, and no feeling of their own are not on that account no good; they, too, have their place in the beauty and goodness of the whole. "A weeping man is better than a happy worm. And yet I could speak at great length without any falsehood in praise of the worm" (*De ver. rel.* 41.77; cf. *De civ. Dei* 11.22).

4. From these considerations emerge Augustine's characteristic definitions of virtue and vice. Virtue is appropriate ("ordinate") love: not simply loving what one ought to love, but loving most what deserves the most love and all else with a love suited to its worth. Hence the Augustinian prayer, "Order love within me" (*De civ. Dei* 15.22).[6] Vice, conversely, is inappropriate ("inordinate") love of things that nonetheless are by nature good (12.8):[7] loving more what should be loved less, and turning in the process from the God who, because of his supreme and eternal goodness, and because he is the source and sustainer of

---

6. From Cant. 2:4; cf. *De doctr. Chr.* 1.59.

7. Vice leads as well to inappropriate *dis*likes: "evil men account those things alone evil which do not make men evil. . . . It grieves them more to own a bad house than a bad life" (*De civ. Dei* 3.1). Cf. *Serm.* 297.8.

all else that is good, is alone worthy of love with all our heart, soul, and mind (*Conf.* 2.5.10; *De doctr. Chr.* 1.42-43).[8]

i. Creation

In Augustine's view the first human beings were created with mortal, animal bodies that required nourishment from food and drink (*De civ. Dei* 13.1, 24; *De pecc. mer.* 1.2.2; 1.5.5). Adam and Eve could, however, have been sustained in their mortal condition by eating of the tree of life until they proved their faithfulness to God. They would then have been rewarded with spiritual bodies and immortal life (2.21.35; cf. *De civ. Dei* 13.23).

In short, they were not unable to die, but they were able not to die.

They were also not unable to sin, but they were able not to sin (*De corr. et grat.* 12.33).

The possibility of sin, like that of doing right, requires the existence of a will that chooses to act in accordance with its wants: behavior that we do not ourselves will can be the object of neither blame nor praise (*De lib. arb.* 2.18.179; *De spir. et litt.* 5.7; *De ver. rel.* 14.27). Humans were given such a will by God. Nor should the creation of the human will be decried because the will can be misused; we do not, after all, consider it evil that human beings have hands and eyes, though these, too, can be turned to ill purpose (*De lib. arb.* 2.18.182-85). There is good that can only be achieved by creatures with a will; hence it is good that God made such creatures.

Of course, an all-knowing God knew at the outset how humans would employ the will he gave them. Again, his goodness in creation is not in question (cf. *De cat. rud.* 2.18.30). For one thing, his foreknowledge of what humans would do in no way compelled them to do it (*De civ. Dei* 14.27; *De corr. et grat.* 12.37; *De lib. arb.* 3.4.39); on the contrary, divine foreknowledge confirms the reality of human choice, since what God foreknew was precisely that humans would *choose* what was wrong (*De civ. Dei* 5.10; *De lib. arb.* 3.3.28-35). Secondly, wrongdoing leads to punishment, the punishment of evil is just, and justice is a good thing. Should God leave evil unpunished, the order and goodness of his creation would be in doubt. But he won't, and they aren't (3.9.93-95; *De nat. bon.* 37; *De ver. rel.* 23.44): "the ugliness of sin is never without the beauty of punishment" (*De lib. arb.* 3.15.152).[9] Thirdly, God foreknew from the beginning

---

8. Cf. *Conf.* 10.27.38, where Augustine confesses to have "plunged into those lovely created things which you made." Also *De civ. Dei* 12.1, 6; *De ver. rel.* 12.23. And note *De nat. bon.* 36: "Evil is making a bad use of a good thing"; *Ench.* 4.13: a "bad man" is "an evil good."

(if such time-bound language can be used of a Being beyond time) not simply the evil that would be wrought by his creatures, but also how divine resourcefulness would turn it to good account (*De civ. Dei* 11.17-18; 12.22; 14.27; 22.1; *De corr. et grat.* 10.27; *Ench.* 3.11; 26.100; 28.104).

Can God, then, be faulted for not taking steps so that humans would *not* misuse their will?

This is a thornier question for Augustine than we might think, since he believed that as long as humans pursue what they themselves want, their will is "free," even if their wants are determined for them.[10] Indeed, Augustine believes (as we shall see) that a transformation of their corrupted will is God's signal gift to his saints (*De grat. et lib. arb.* 16.32); clearly, then, a will programmed to desire only good could have been given to Adam and Eve at their creation. Still, God is not to be blamed. He gave our forebears enough grace to be able to will and do what is right. And though this is a lesser gift than one by which they necessarily *would* have willed the right, even a gift of a lower order of goodness had its appropriate time and place in the unfolding divine scheme (cf. *Ench.* 28.105).

Moreover, it must be remembered that by divine design Adam and Eve had everything in their favor (*De civ. Dei* 14.15). The creation they enjoyed was still unreservedly good. Their nature, still uncorrupted, felt no hankering for sin and had neither bad habits nor perilous precedents to overcome. The command they were given was straightforward and simple. When they nonetheless sinned under so favorable conditions, they have only themselves to blame.

How, then, did they do so?

ii. The Fall

The fruit chosen by Adam and Eve was necessarily *good* fruit, and nourishing to eat (*De pecc. mer.* 2.21.35). The prohibition of something in itself good gave Adam and Eve the opportunity to exercise their will by doing right, loving the Source of all goodness more than the goods he made.

They failed, partly because they believed the lie that their happiness lay apart from God in the pursuit of lesser goods (*De civ. Dei* 14.4),[11] and partly be-

---

9. Cf. 3.9.94: "when sinners are unhappy, the universe is perfect."

10. Cf. *De grat. et lib. arb.* 21.42: God "sets in motion even in the innermost hearts of men the movement of their will, so that He does through their agency whatsoever He wishes to perform through them."

11. Note 14.5: "to desert the Creator good, and live according to the created good, is not good."

cause they affected to live (14.15) in independence from God. This too is a lie, since the "dominion of the Almighty cannot be eluded" (11.13).

When conditions for doing right were ideal, the consequences of doing wrong were disastrous (14.12). Nor were the effects confined to Adam and Eve as individuals, for the good reason that Adam and Eve were not mere individuals but the forebears and prototypes of the race. Individualization came later; and, descended as we all are from the same prototypes, we all inherit a nature corrupted by their sin (13.14; *De nupt. et conc.* 2.5.15). Indeed, since the whole race of which we are a part was "contained" in Adam,[12] we cannot condemn him without condemning ourselves. All of us are born with a share in his guilt. What is more, all of us no sooner reach the age of our own moral accountability than we add sins of our individual choosing to our share in the original sin of the species (*C. duas epp. Pel.* 1.3.7; *De pecc. mer.* 1.10.12).

Of course, the conditions under which we make our choices are not the ideal ones enjoyed by Adam and Eve. Before their fall they were able not to die; once they sinned, they began — as, once we are born, we join — the relentless race toward death (*De civ. Dei* 13.10; *De pecc. mer.* 1.16.21). Before the fall Adam and Eve were able not to sin; their nature, once fallen — and ours, once born — suffers from a hankering for sin that neither they nor we are able to conquer. Habits built up by repeated wrongdoing become compulsive (*Conf.* 8.5.10). Our difficulty in doing right is further compounded by our ignorance of what is right — yet another consequence of, and just punishment for, humanity's refusal to acknowledge and do the right when we had the unencumbered opportunity to do so (*De lib. arb.* 3.18.178). As a result, we sin at times willfully, at other times unwillingly or even unwittingly, unable to overcome the habits and liabilities of fallen human nature. But since we bear responsibility for those habits and liabilities, we are guilty for these latter sins as well (*De lib. arb.* 3.19.183-84; *De nat. et grat.* 22.24).

We cannot, of our own, do good. If at times we appear to do so, we are merely avoiding more blatant sins by succumbing to ones less apparent: baser lusts, for example, may be restrained by a love of human praise (*De civ. Dei* 5.13; 21.16; *De nupt. et conc.* 1.2.4). We act rightly, in keeping with the reality of our own dependent nature and the ordered goodness of the universe, only when our deeds are motivated by a love of God and delight in righteousness (*De civ. Dei* 13.5; *Ench.* 32.121). Of such love fallen human nature, the captive of lesser loves, proves utterly incapable (*De Trin.* 15.31).

---

12. As is well known, Augustine understood Rom. 5:12 to mean that sin entered the world through one man, "in whom all sinned" (or, possibly, as Augustine also allowed, "in which [=Adam's] sin all sinned"); cf. *De pecc. mer.* 1.10.11.

Finally, in a universe that is just and good evil must be condemned. In that condemnation all human beings, the offspring of Adam and Eve, have their share (*De grat. Chr.* 2.29.34).

iii. Redemption

From the mass of condemned humanity God redeems a people for his kingdom. God the Son, who, as a fire's brightness is coeval with the flame that begets it, is as eternal as the Father who eternally begets him (*De Trin.* 6.1), was begotten in time as well, taking on human form to offer his life for human sin (*De grat. Chr.* 2.32.37; *Ench.* 13.41). In so doing he delivered God's children from divine retribution for their sin (*De Trin.* 13.21). The punishment is spoken of, by human analogy, as God's "wrath," though God is himself not subject to changeable emotions (*De civ. Dei* 9.5; 15.25; *Ench.* 10.33); nor dare we think that a more kindly Son reconciled a reluctant Father to his noncompliant creatures. Father and Son were one in condemning human sin, and one in providing redemption (*De Trin.* 13.15).

Apart from the faith in Christ's redemptive work by which sinners are justified, all human beings are justly condemned; there can be no other salvation. Augustine believes, however, that precisely this faith was found in individuals in Israel and even among the pagan nations (*De civ. Dei* 18.47) before Christ came as well as during his life and after his resurrection (*De grat. Chr.* 2.24.28; *De nupt. et conc.* 2.11.24; *Ep.* 102.12, 15): "Christianity" existed, in all but name, from the beginning of the world (*C. duas epp. Pel.* 3.4.11; *Retr.* 1.12.3), for when Christ's work was variously foretold, the same saving faith in Christ could be evoked as now when the gospel is proclaimed (cf. *Conf.* 10.43.68). The same faith, however, is accompanied in different ages by different sacraments: circumcision was instituted before Christ's coming, baptism has been required ever since (*De nupt. et conc.* 2.11.24; *De pecc. mer.* 2.29.47).

What is entailed in this salvation?

Though in the world to come the righteous and wicked will receive their just and distinct deserts, in this world they share alike in life's goods and ills: so the righteous learn not to treasure things that the wicked likewise enjoy, nor to fear those ills that they see even good people suffer (*De civ. Dei* 1.8).[13] More serious is their ongoing battle with sin; for though the baptized now (like the circumcised of old) are delivered at once from the guilt of original sin and of

---

13. Cf. 1.29: God exposes the righteous to adversities "either to prove [their] perfections or correct [their] imperfections." Also *De Trin.* 13.20.

whatever particular sins they have committed (*De pecc. mer.* 2.28.46; cf. *Ench.* 14.50), they are by no means delivered from the hankering for sin (or "concupiscence") that oppresses human nature since the fall (*De pecc. mer.* 1.39.70). As when a fever disappears, a patient still needs to recover strength; or as, when an arrow is removed from the flesh, the wound still needs to heal; so sin is pardoned in baptism, but the debility it caused remains to be cured (*De Trin.* 14.23). Augustine at one point thought that the "I" portrayed in Romans 7 as unable to carry out desired good must refer to unbelievers living "under law," but he came to see (*De praed. sanct.* 4.8; *Retr.* 1.22.1; 2.27) the passage as depicting the struggle of believers ("under grace"; *C. duas epp. Pel.* 1.11.24)[14] to overcome the hankering for sin ("the law of sin in my members"; *De nupt. et conc.* 1.23.25; *De pecc. mer.* 1.39.70; 2.4.4; cf. Rom. 7:23) that tempts them throughout their lives and prevents them from fulfilling the command "Thou shalt not covet." They are, to be sure, able to restrain themselves from actively pursuing what they covet (*C. duas epp. Pel.* 1.11.24; *De nat. et grat.* 61.72; *De nupt. et conc.* 1.23.25); furthermore, in those progressing in the path of holiness, the hankering for sin diminishes day by day (1.25.28; *De perf. just. hom.* 13.31). But it is never banished as long as the saints live in this body (a "body of death"; *Serm.* 151.5; cf. Rom. 7:24); and while a hankering for sin remains within them, they fail to love God "with all their soul" as they ought (*De perf. just. hom.* 8.19).

To resist this "sin in the flesh," Christians are given the gift of God's Spirit: it lives in them and infuses a love for God in their hearts (*De spir. et litt.* 3.5; 32.56). This invasion by divine grace by no means destroys the human will: rather, God's Spirit restores the will, changing it from bad to good (*De grat. et lib. arb.* 20.41; *De spir. et litt.* 9.15; 30.52). Moved by the Spirit, they themselves begin to want to do good and succeed in some measure in so doing. But life remains "a warfare, not a triumphal celebration" (*Serm.* 151.2). The conflict between "flesh"[15] and spirit is carried on without intermission (*De civ. Dei* 22.23): the flesh continues to rise up, to tickle the fancy, to give ideas, to entice, to boil over (*Serm.* 154.3). Throughout their earthly lives ("between the laver . . . and the kingdom"; *De gest. Pel.* 12.28) Christians need to pray the Lord's Prayer, asking for forgiveness for those sins into which concupiscence has enticed them

---

14. According to 1.10.22, Augustine came to think that no one "under law" could delight in the law as the speaker of Rom. 7:22 is said to do.

15. Augustine notes that the use of the term "flesh" in texts such as Gal. 5:17 might suggest that the problem is the body itself; he insists that this is a misreading. The body, though now corrupted, was created good and, once restored, will have a part in the world to come. See *De doctr. Chr.* 1.48-53; and cf. *De civ. Dei* 10.24; 13.20, 22; 14.2-3, 5; 15.7. Note also *Serm.* 30.4: "I don't want my flesh, as something foreign to me, to be separated from me for ever, but to be all healed with me for ever."

("forgive us our debts"), for ability to resist the hankering for sin that still haunts them ("lead us not into temptation"), and for ultimate deliverance from its very presence ("but deliver us from evil") (*De pecc. mer.* 2.4.4; cf. *De civ. Dei* 22.23).

In this life, then, the people of God have a kind of dual nature. Because they are God's children their sins are forgiven, they desire to be like God their Father, and they live without sin. At the same time, to the degree that they are still unlike God, they remain children of Adam[16] and are by no means without sin (*De pecc. mer.* 2.7.9–8.10; *De perf. just. hom.* 18.39).

The continuing presence of sin does not, however, excuse complacency in sinning; nor should the abundance of God's grace be thought to encourage it. To praise the benefits of the medicine (grace) by no means implies good in the diseases from which it heals (*De spir. et litt.* 6.9). Faith must be accompanied by good works — though their relationship requires careful delineation (*Ench.* 18.67).

It is not an issue on which Paul and James are in any disagreement (*De div. quaest.* 76.2). When Paul insists that we are justified by faith, not works, he excludes any role for human works done prior to our justification.[17] Of themselves (as we have seen) humans can do "absolutely no good thing" (*De corr. et grat.* 2.3). Grace is granted where no good merits can warrant it, where, indeed, evil merits must be overcome (*De grat. et lib. arb.* 6.13). It operates without human cooperation (17.33), replacing a "heart of stone" (i.e., "a will of the hardest

16. Or "children of the flesh and of the world" (*De pecc. mer.* 2.8.10).

17. This, for Augustine, is the point Paul is making when he insists that one is not justified by the works of the law. The latter works, he notes, must *not* be confined to the ceremonial observances (such as circumcision) no longer required of believers: they are rather works which "a man . . . regards . . . as his own, apart from the help and gift of God. . . . The contrast lies entirely in the point that they [i.e., the 'Israel' of Rom. 9:31] ascribed to themselves the keeping of the law 'Thou shalt not covet,' and the rest of the holy and righteous commands of God. Man's power to accomplish them is wrought in man by God through faith of Jesus Christ, who is the end unto righteousness for everyone that believeth" (*De spir. et litt.* 29.50). Cf. 13.21–14.25, where Augustine, answering those who would confine Paul's rejection of the works of the law to its ceremonial observances, cites Paul's argument that it is *the law itself* that causes sin to abound, brings an awareness of sin, represents "the letter that kills," works "wrath," etc. "Consider the whole of [Rom. 7], and see whether it has any reference at all to circumcision, sabbath or any ordinance that is a 'shadow of things to come'; or is not entirely concerned to show that the letter forbidding sin does not give life to man, but rather kills through increasing concupiscence and filling up iniquity with transgression — did not grace bring deliverance through the law of faith which is in Christ Jesus" (14.25). "The examination and discussion which we have carried out . . . has led us to conclude that man is not justified by the precepts of the good life, but only through the faith of Jesus Christ: that is, . . . not by the deserts of our actions but by grace freely given" (13.22).

kind and such as is absolutely inflexible against God") with a "heart of flesh" (14.29; cf. Ezek. 11:19). No better illustration of the truth can be found than that shown by the grace bestowed in baptism on infants. They can have no merits of their own. Furthermore, if any will is to be attributed to them, it is expressed rather in their cries and struggle to avoid the laver than in any inclination to approach it (22.44).

On the other hand, when James declares that faith without works is dead, he has in mind the good works that must be done after a sinner comes to faith (*De div. quaest.* 76.2; cf. *De fid. et op.* 14.21); and Paul too insisted that we will be judged by our works and accepted only if they are appropriate. Faith without love is vain (14.21, citing 1 Cor. 13:2; *Ench.* 31.117). If those once forgiven fail to persevere in the true faith or to produce appropriate works, they will be condemned as sinners. Conversely, the good works of Christians can be said to merit salvation, which is given to them as a fitting reward (cf. *De grat. et lib. arb.* 6.13–8.20). Yet all such works are made possible only by the gift of the Holy Spirit, who transforms the human will[18] so that erstwhile sinners delight in doing good. A further grace of perseverance is needed if even the saints are not to fall (*De corr. et grat.* 12.38; *De grat. et lib. arb.* 6.13), for without Christ they can do nothing (8.20, citing John 15:5). The principle remains: humans can do evil on their own, but they can do no good that God does not cause them to do (*C. duas epp. Pel.* 2.9.21). Before their justification God *operates* on human beings apart from their will; after justification he *cooperates* with their will, moving them to desire, and do, righteous deeds (*De grat. et lib. arb.* 17.13; cf. 5.12). When he then rewards believers for what they do, he is in effect rewarding his own gifts (6.13, 15; 9.21).

The gifts God gives Christians in this life go beyond those given to Adam and Eve but fall short of what will be theirs at the end of the age. Our first progenitors were, by divine grace, able not to sin, but it was left to their will whether they would do so (*De corr. et grat.* 11.32). Christians in this life have the Spirit's help in actually willing what is right (11.31-32; 12.38). In the age to come they will find themselves unable to sin. Concupiscence will no longer trouble them, and they will desire only good (*Ench.* 28.105). Free will, by which they freely pursue their desires, will still be theirs. But the freedom enjoyed by those who desire only what is good is far greater than that of those who must struggle with a hankering for sin that can yet bring them to misery (*De civ. Dei* 22.30).

> Then we won't sin, not only by deed, but not even by desire, when we see that face which beats and surpasses all desires. Because it is so lovely, my brothers

---

18. Such a will is "prepared by the Lord" (*De grat. et lib. arb.* 16.32, citing Prov. 8:35).

and sisters, so beautiful, that once you have seen it, nothing else can give you pleasure. It will give insatiable satisfaction of which we can never tire. (*Serm.* 170.9)

iv. The Place of the Law

Since our actions are steered by what we love, they will conform with the eternal law if our love is fixed on the supreme good, God. Those who love God will also love their neighbor, as God commands them (*De Trin.* 8.10; cf. *De doctr. Chr.* 3.52-53). The eternal law of love (*De spir. et litt.* 17.29) has been written by God on the human heart and never quite effaced by human sin (28.48; cf. *De Trin.* 14.21). Other laws and customs may change, depending on the conditions under which people live and the stage in the divine plan in which they find themselves (cf. *Conf.* 3.7.13; *Ep.* 138.2). Such diversity of laws and customs is by no means to be taken as an indication that there is no eternal, unchanging law or justice (*De doctr. Chr.* 3.52).

The Mosaic law itself combines expressions of the eternal law with prescriptions suited peculiarly to Israel in the period before Christ (*C. Faust.* 6.2). The latter, ceremonial laws foreshadowed in various ways the coming of the Messiah and his redemptive work; while during the age of anticipation it was incumbent upon Israel to observe these commandments (6.7, 9; *De gest. Pel.* 5.14), and the Maccabees rightly suffered martyrdom in their defense (*Ep.* 40.6), the fulfillment by Christ of their very raison d'être renders pointless any further fulfillment (*C. Faust.* 19.18).[19] Admittedly, many of the earliest Christians, who were Jews themselves and accustomed to their observance, continued to keep them for a time, and it was right that they should (19.17). These were not, after all, the "diabolical impieties of heathenism" (*Ep.* 82.20), but divinely given commands which, even after their lifetime had passed, were worthy of respect and "honorable burial" (82.15-16, 20). It would, however, be disastrous to believe that salvation depended on their keeping (*C. Faust.* 19.17); nor should their "ashes" now be disturbed by contemporary Christians (including Jewish converts) inclined to renew their observance (*Ep.* 82.16). The continued observance of commandments that foreshadowed Christ's work would imply that the reality to which they point is still awaited (*C. Faust.* 19.8).

But the Mosaic law also contains moral commandments: in particular, and apart from the Sabbath command, those of the Decalogue (*C. duas epp. Pel.*

---

19. The Mosaic ceremonial laws do, however, remain worthwhile objects of study for their allegorical significance (*C. Faust.* 6.2; *De util. cred.* 3.9; *De ver. rel.* 17.33).

3.4.10; *De spir. et litt.* 14.23). These are, of course, to be kept by Christians (*C. Faust.* 10.2; *De spir. et litt.* 14.23): it is inconceivable that Christians would be free to murder, commit adultery, or steal (*C. Faust.* 19.18; cf. *C. duas epp. Pel.* 3.4.10). In the Sermon on the Mount Christ added little to the moral prescriptions of the Old Testament (*C. Faust.* 19.28; *Retr.* 1.21.2), but rather interpreted and explained them, enjoining conduct that would ensure conformity with their true intention (*C. Faust.* 19.24-27). The sum and substance of all the commandments is the command to love (*De Trin.* 8.10; *Ench.* 32.121).

Far from "destroying" the law, then, Christ "fulfilled" it. The ceremonial laws were fulfilled when the significant aspect of his work which they foreshadowed became a reality. To the moral commands Christ brought fulfillment by enabling, through the gift of the Holy Spirit, that love which constitutes the law's true observance among Christians (*C. Faust.* 19.7, 18).

The Mosaic order (the "old testament" properly so called; *C. duas epp. Pel.* 3.12-13; *De gest. Pel.* 5.14) could not itself provide salvation, and was not intended to do so (*De grat. Chr.* 1.8.9; *Serm.* 152.5). The institution of its laws and threats brought fear to the hearts of the ancient Israelites (155.6; cf. Exod. 20:19), a fear that ought to have led them to seek the aid afforded only by Christ's grace (*De nat. et grat.* 1.1).[20]

The stages in history through which God's people passed have their parallels in the lives of individuals (*De civ. Dei* 10.14; *De div. quaest.* 66.3-7). The first phase is that in which, because no law has been encountered, we are ignorant of sin and submit without a struggle to its desires. The second is that "under law" when, fearing the law's sanctions, we struggle in vain to overcome sinful habits. The law thus brings knowledge of sin but not its destruction; it discovers our disease but does not cure it (*De grat. Chr.* 1.8.9; cf. *Serm.* 154.1). Those who turn to Christ for aid then live "under grace": the struggle with sin remains, but with the Spirit's help sin can be resisted and the law fulfilled.[21] This stage continues until, passing through death, we are perfected by God (*De Trin.* 14.23), the struggle with sin is over, and we live "in full and perfect peace" (*Ench.* 31.118) for all eternity.

Even before the coming of Christ there were those who used the law as it was intended (*C. Faust.* 4.2; *De doctr. Chr.* 3.30-31). They understood the reali-

---

20. Cf. *De spir. et litt.* 6.9: "Man needed to be shown the foulness of his malady. . . . 'The law entered in, that the offence might abound' [Rom. 5:20]; so that thus convicted and confounded he might see his need for God, . . . that he should flee to the help of mercy for his healing." More epigrammatically, "The law was given that grace might be sought; grace was given that the law might be fulfilled" (19.34).

21. Cf. *Ep.* 145.3: the law leads to faith, faith obtains the Spirit, the Spirit sheds love abroad in us, love fulfills the law.

ties its ceremonies foreshadowed and trusted in the promised Christ. They looked beyond its promises of earthly happiness to the spiritual and eternal goods that the promises prefigured (*De gest. Pel.* 5.14). They sought, and were aided by, God's Spirit in doing right (*C. duas epp. Pel.* 3.4.6). As stewards of the old testament, they were faithful in observing its statutes. At the same time, however, they were heirs of the new testament (3.4.6): who can deny that the psalmist who wrote, "Create in me a clean heart, O God," knew *new* testament grace (3.4.6)? So, too, did the patriarchs, Moses, and the prophets, and all the righteous in Israel: they lived before Christ, but yet, through faith in Christ, "under grace" (3.4.11; *De grat. Chr.* 2.25.29). One must not exclude the ancient saints from the grace of the Mediator (2.26.31)!

Other Jews, however, heeded only the prescribed ceremonies themselves, not the realities of which they were signs (*De doctr. Chr.* 3.23).[22] They lived "under the law" in that their motive for obeying the law's commands was fear of its sanctions rather than love of righteousness (*De spir. et litt.* 8.13). Most disastrously, they set about to "establish their own righteousness" rather than receiving that which comes from God; deeming themselves competent to fulfill the law in their own strength, they did not seek the grace to be found in Christ (*De grat. et lib. arb.* 12.24; *Serm.* 156.4). When Paul writes that they sought to attain the law of righteousness "as though by works" (Rom. 9:32), he means that they thought the law of righteousness could be "wrought . . . by themselves, not believing that God wrought it in them" (*De spir. et litt.* 29.50).

Christians who in love fulfill the law (*Ep.* 145.3; cf. *De spir. et litt.* 21.36) are not in need of the law themselves: the law is not for the righteous (10.16, citing 1 Tim. 1:9). The true function of the law applies before, not after, their justification. The justified may dispense with its use, as those who complete a journey have no further need of their vehicle (10.16). Not that they disregard the law's commands (*C. duas epp. Pel.* 3.4.10); the point is rather that love, not the sanctions of the law, now motivates their obedience (*De spir. et litt.* 29.51).

Only by grace can the law be kept (*De grat. et lib. arb.* 12.24). The law commands, "Love one another." Grace adds at once the provision for its fulfillment: "Love is of God" (18.37). "By the law of works God says, 'Do what I command': by the law of faith we say to God, 'Give what thou commandest'" (*De spir. et litt.* 13.22; cf. *Conf.* 10.29.40).

---

22. Augustine did share the belief that Jews would one day, through the work of the prophet Elijah, turn to faith in Christ (*De civ. Dei* 20.29-30).

v. Human Dependence on Grace

Dismayed by the presumption of his Corinthian converts, Paul once demanded of them, "What do you have that you have not received?" (1 Cor. 4:7). He expected, and certainly believed, the answer to be "Nothing." Augustine elevated Paul's query to an axiom in the light of which all Scripture is to be read, all doctrine to be tested, and all life lived (*De praed. sanct.* 3.7–4.8). From Paul, too, came the passion that drove Augustine in the relentless application of the principle: humans must be left with nothing of which to boast; all glory must be given to God (5.9).[23]

Prior to their creation humans can have had no merit to warrant their appearance on God's earth (*Serm.* 26.12). Creation itself must be ascribed to a divine initiative, undertaken (Augustine believed) solely out of God's own goodness (*Conf.* 13.4.5; *De civ. Dei* 11.24). In his design of the human body, for example, the love of beauty was more a factor than was strict necessity: the latter is a mere temporary consideration, the former an eternal one. Augustine writes eloquently and movingly of the goodness of human gifts and potential even in their fallen condition (22.24). All such good is a token of God's grace to humankind in creation.

Together with their free will humans were given sufficient divine assistance to be able to avoid sin (*De corr. et grat.* 11.31): as the human eye can on its own refuse to see, but needs in addition to its own powers external light for vision, so human beings can sin on their own but cannot on their own do good (*De gest. Pel.* 3.7; *De spir. et litt.* 7.11; *Ench.* 28.106). Nonetheless, it was left to the human will whether or not it would do what was right (*De civ. Dei* 14.27).

Humans sinned. Christ died for their sin. The point now for Augustine is to demonstrate not simply human dependence on divine grace for salvation, but their dependence on the particular grace associated with Christ's redemptive work. Two alternative suggestions must be rejected (*De spir. et litt.* 2.4).

First, in responding to people who excused their sinful behavior by blaming the frailties of human nature, some taught that ever since their creation human beings have possessed adequate resources to choose and do what is right (*De grat. et lib. arb.* 13.25; *De nat. et grat.* 1.1). Augustine, however, insists that God the Creator must not be honored by making Christ the Savior superfluous (34.39): if human nature is still able to choose and do what is right, then Christ died to no pur-

---

23. Cf. *Ad Simpl.* 1.2.3: Rom. 9 was written "to break and cast down the pride of men who are not grateful for the grace of God but dare to glory in their own merits." Augustine was as convinced that humans cannot contemplate God by their own powers of intellect as he was that they cannot please God by their own goodness (*De civ. Dei* 11.2; *De util. cred.* 9.21); and he scorched the pride of those who thought otherwise (*De Trin.* 1.1; 4.20).

pose (2.2). The error of Pelagius lies in his failure to recognize that human nature, created good, has been wounded, hurt, damaged, ruined (53.62). Those who proclaim the good health of the human will deter the cries for help that would lead to its healing (49.57). Better to seek the grace of Christ the Physician (23.25).

Second, some propose that humans depend for guidance on God's law, but that, so informed, they are able to do what is right. But again, if righteousness were possible through the law, Christ died to no purpose (*De grat. et lib. arb.* 13.25; cf. Gal. 2:21). The law brings the knowledge, not the overcoming, of sin (10.22, citing Rom. 3:20).

Faith in Christ, then, is necessary for salvation, and credit for such faith must itself be given to God. As a Christian, Augustine was always clear on this point, though his thinking underwent a significant shift in the details. At one time he believed that God is given sufficient credit once it is recognized that faith is evoked by the proclamation of the gospel and by divinely contrived inducements to believe; that said, it is up to humans whether they respond with faith or unbelief (cf. *De praed. sanct.* 3.7; *De spir. et litt.* 34.60). What Paul says in 1 Corinthians 4:7 is still true: all that believers have, they receive from God, though the receiving itself must be their own (34.60). At this stage in his thinking he was prepared to read in its evident sense the verse that God "desires everyone to be saved and to come to the knowledge of the truth" (1 Tim. 2:4). That not all come to faith was not thought to frustrate the divine will. Should a master desire that his servants work in the vineyard, yet add that those who refuse must grind forever in the mill, his will is not defeated if some rebels end up at the grindstone. Similarly, God wants all to be saved but has added that those who refuse to believe will perish. So long as unbelievers meet the punishment he prescribed, his will has not been frustrated (33.58).

Later, however, pressing the text "What do you have that you have not received?" to its limits, Augustine came to believe that faith itself was necessarily a gift of God (*De praed. sanct.* 3.7; 8.16); other Pauline texts, too, were cited in support (Rom. 12:3; Eph. 2:8; 6:23; Phil. 1:29; cf. *De grat. et lib. arb.* 14.28).[24] Knowing what moves each individual, God so incites the hearts and directs the circumstances of those he has chosen to be his children that they find themselves attracted to faith and freely choose it (cf. *De civ. Dei* 15.6; *De praed. sanct.* 8.15). If, however, faith only and always exists where God decides to bestow it, then it follows that God has seen fit to grant it to some and not to others; the

24. In Paul's prayers of thanksgiving to God for the faith of new believers, Augustine finds further confirmation that faith is a divine gift (*De praed. sanct.* 19.39). Conversely, if faith is deemed a precondition for divine grace, Augustine concludes that we are no longer speaking of grace, which must, by definition, be given gratuitously (*De gest. Pel.* 14.33, citing Rom. 11:6; *De praed. sanct.* 2.6).

latter are left, by divine selectivity, on the path to damnation. Augustine, of course, was aware of these implications, and they troubled him (*Serm.* 26.15). In the end, however, he felt constrained to assert and defend them.

1. In support of his position (indeed, responsible for his adopting of it), he believed, were Pauline texts. To the realization that some are saved and others not he applied the Pauline query, "Who made you to differ from one another?" The answer must be "God" (*De corr. et grat.* 7.12). Romans 9, in particular, played a key role in the development of Augustine's thinking (*Ench.* 25.98-99). God (Paul writes) chose Jacob and rejected Esau before either was born in order that his "intention of operating by means of his own election might continue, depending not on works but on the one who calls" (Rom. 9:11-12). To Moses God said, "'I will have mercy on whom I have mercy, and I will have compassion on whom I have compassion.' So it depends not on the one who wills or runs, but on God who shows mercy" (9:15-16). These verses, Augustine came to believe, allow no place for human works, already done or only anticipated, or even for anticipated responses of faith, as the basis for divine election.

2. Divine election, however, by no means implies human passivity (*Serm.* 156.11). Humans must respond to the gospel in faith, they must produce works that merit salvation, they must love God and delight in the works that please him: *their* faith, *their* works, *their* love are all required. The elect of God, after all, are not "insensate stones" but creatures with reason and will (*De pecc. mer.* 2.5.6). Moreover, the regenerate must persevere in true faith and appropriate behavior if they are to be saved: none can be assured, as long as they live, that they will gain life eternal (*Conf.* 10.32.48; *De corr. et grat.* 13.40; *De don. pers.* 1.1; 22.62). There is thus a place for prayer, preaching, exhortation, rebuke, and warning in bringing human beings to appropriate choices and actions: each plays precisely the role in converting or hardening sinners that God foreknew it would (*De civ. Dei* 5.10).

What this in effect means, however, is that all must believe, act in love, and persevere inasmuch as none can know in this life whether or not they have been predestined for salvation. In fact, none of those so predestined can fail to achieve the goal, and none not so appointed can possibly reach it (*De corr. et grat.* 7.13-16). Without divine aid fallen human beings cannot believe or love as they ought; hence those not receiving divine aid have no hope of salvation. On the other hand, since it is God who works through the circumstances and in the hearts of those predestined to salvation in such a way that they believe and behave as they ought, credit for what they do must be ascribed to divine grace (*Ench.* 9.32).[25]

---

25. And note *De grat. et lib. arb.* 16.32: "It is certain that it is we that *will* when we will, but it is He who makes us will what is good. . . . It is certain that it is we that act when we act; but it is He who makes us act, by applying efficacious powers to our will."

3. Augustine will not, of course, allow any inconsistency in the canonical Scriptures (cf. *C. Faust.* 11.5). If Scripture says God "desires everyone to be saved" (1 Tim. 2:4), that text must be harmonized with another affirming that God achieves whatever he pleases in heaven and earth (*De corr. et grat.* 14.45, citing Ps. 135:6; cf. *Ench.* 24.95). If with the latter text we know that God never fails in anything he wills, and if we know that not all come to faith, it follows that God must not *will* all to come to faith. Hence 1 Timothy 2:4 can only mean that God wants all who will be saved to be saved, or that he wants some to be saved from every type and group of people (*De corr. et grat.* 14.44; *Ench.* 27.103).

Nor is the Scripture to be denied that insists that God hates none of his creatures (*Ad Simpl.* 1.2.18, citing Wis. 11:24). But he loves what he has made in them, not the perversity of their sin. In condemning some he is condemning what they have become; in saving others he is restoring them to be the creatures of his intentions and love.

4. Augustine can offer no explanation why God chooses some and not others. Any explanation based on a difference in the human beings concerned would mean there was something in some human beings that God recognized and rewarded; their salvation would no longer depend on his grace alone.[26] If, on the other hand, the decision rests exclusively on God's sovereign will, then it must remain impenetrable for human minds.

But Augustine does insist on the justice of what God does. Blame for human sin rests on humans alone — God has not compelled them to sin[27] — and all merit condemnation. The condemned are justly condemned (*Ench.* 24.94); and since justice itself is a good thing, there is even goodness in their condemnation. Furthermore, that some are condemned reminds the forgiven of what their sins merit and of the magnitude of God's mercy (*De don. pers.* 12.28). As one to whom many owe money can decide to cancel the debts of some and exact payment from others, and it would be presumptuous of the debtors either to think the decision should be theirs or to fault their creditor for exercising a creditor's prerogative, so God is free to show mercy as he pleases without doing injustice to any (*Ad Simpl.* 1.2.16). If God displays his mercy in some and his justice in others, there is goodness in his justice and justice in his mercy (*De don. pers.* 12.28).

---

26. Note, however, Augustine's earlier thinking in *De div. quaest.* 68.4.

27. Texts that speak of God "hardening" sinners can only mean that God leaves them in their sinful ways; Augustine will not allow that God plays any *active* role in promoting sin (*Ad Simpl.* 1.2.15-16).

vi. Summary

Whether we should say that Augustine's Paul was "Lutheran" or that Luther's Paul was Augustinian is a moot point. For our purposes it is sufficient to note that Augustine and Luther construed Paul along similar lines, and that in crucial respects their interpretation has long dominated both the popular and the scholarly reading of the apostle. Our summary here is of Augustine's way of putting things.

Nothing inherently evil exists in God's creation; evil was introduced when creatures endowed with a will opted to pursue a lesser rather than their greatest good. The sinful choice of Adam and Eve was freely made. As a consequence of their sin, however, human beings now suffer from a hankering for sin, from habits of sin, and from an ignorance of what is right that we are unable of ourselves to overcome. Our wills are still "free" in the sense that we can pursue what we desire. But we cannot, on our own, either desire or do what is good.

The Son of God sacrificed his life to deliver fallen human beings from divine retribution for their sins. Those who believe in him are freed from the guilt of their sin and given the gift of God's Spirit. The Spirit begins at once to transform their corrupted wills, enabling them both to want and in some measure to do what is good. Still, throughout their earthly lives believers must struggle to overcome the hankering for sin that remains within them. And though its strength gradually decreases in the faithful, they never in this life completely fulfill the commandment "Thou shalt not covet" or that which requires that they love God with all their being. They are at the same time children of God and children of Adam.

Believers are justified by God's grace, apart from any "works" of their own. Prior to their justification their only "merits" were evil. Once justified, their faith must lead to good works, which God will reward with eternal life. Yet even these works are the product of God's grace and of his Spirit's activity. When God rewards them, he rewards his own gifts.

The ceremonial laws of Moses foreshadowed Christ's mission. Their validity ended with his appearance. The law's moral commandments serve in the first place to draw attention to our inability to fulfill them; thus made aware of our moral "disease," we turn for help to Christ the Physician. The justified are by no means free to transgress the moral commandments. On the contrary, the law, summed up in the commands to love God and our neighbor, is first fulfilled when the Spirit infuses God's love into believers' hearts. So moved, they no longer require the sanctions of the law to motivate their obedience.

The faith of believers is itself a gift of God. At one time Augustine thought that, while God must create the conditions under which a sinner comes to faith, it is up to sinners whether they respond with faith or unbelief. Later, interpreting in a more radical way Paul's claim that we have nothing that we have not received, Augustine thought God himself has predetermined who will believe and who will not, and who of the former group will persevere in their faith to the end; and God directs the circumstances of people's lives in a way that assures the results he has predetermined. In those who are damned we see God's justice; in those who are saved, his mercy.

Chapter 2

Martin Luther

Martin Luther, Reformer, is charged with misreading Paul, apostle, confusing the latter's first-century controversies with his own idiosyncratic and sixteenth-century concerns, thereby distorting for centuries the understanding of Paul held alike by undiscerning scholars, unsuspecting preachers, and the masses that know not the law. In this chapter we will venture, in spite of the magnitude of the charges and the guilty verdict already reached in many minds, to give the defendant a fair hearing.[1]

Luther is said to have called Paul's letter to the Galatians his Katy von Bora (*Table Talk*, 54:20). The reference was to his wife and, moreover, was meant as a compliment: Galatians was his most treasured epistle. Luther directed those seeking discussions of particular terms in Galatians to his commentary of 1519; his later commentary on the epistle was intended "to set forth the doctrine of justification as clearly as possible" (*Gal.*, 27:87). Since the gravamen of the charges against him relates to the latter doctrine, we will draw heavily, though not exclusively, on the Galatians commentary of 1535 for Luther's defense.

The following theses of Luther, all under attack as distorting Paul, will here be examined in the context of Luther's own thought.

1. In our relationship with God, faith in his goodness rather than the good works we do is decisive.

---

1. Apart from the catechisms, the references in the text are to the American edition of *Luther's Works.* Luther's works are cited by their (usually abbreviated) English titles followed by the relevant volume and page number from this edition. For full information see bibliography.

2. The law, like a mighty hammer, is meant to crush human self-righteousness and to drive human beings, made aware of their sinfulness, to seek mercy from the Savior.

3. We are justified by faith in Jesus Christ, not by the works we do.

4. Though believers are righteous in God's eyes, they remain sinners throughout their earthly lives.

5. The law must be banished from the thinking of believers when their relationship with God is the issue. Yet it must continue its role of identifying and judging their sin.

6. God predestined believers to salvation.

Thesis I: In our relationship with God, faith in his goodness rather than the good works we do is decisive.[2]

We may take Jack's delight in pleasing Jill as a sign of their happy marriage; not so, Dan's nervous attempts to win Dana's favor. Both Jack and Dan may buy chocolates for their spouses. Jack, however, does so joyfully and almost without reflection, assured of Jill's love and goodwill. Dan, on the other hand, fearful lest his peace offering be dismissed with contempt, sweats oceans as he ponders which box to purchase, and when, and with what words, to present it. Jack feels no compulsion to be kind, though he is so: how else would he treat the woman he loves? Dan's acts of would-be kindness carry little conviction: he sees no other way to gain his wife's approval, yet doubts the outcome, whatever he does.

What makes Jack's marriage successful and different from Dan's is evidently not the good deeds he does for his wife (Dan does the same), but the trust he has in her, the good *faith* that informs all his behavior toward her. Just so, Luther insists, is faith crucial in a proper relationship with God (cf. *Good Works*, 44:26-27).

God assures us of his goodwill and favor. Taken seriously (and how else dare we treat the word of our Maker?), such assurance should evoke our complete confidence in his goodness. God and faith *go* together: what you trust completely is your god, and God alone is worthy of complete trust (*Large Cat.*, 9). Moreover, complete faith in the goodness of God will surely be accompanied by a love for him (*Good Works*, 44:30), and heartfelt love and trust in God

2. Justification by faith, in Luther's view the "principal doctrine of Christianity" (*Gal.*, 26:106), is (for ease of presentation) here treated as thesis 3. The distinct point to be made in the first thesis is that for Luther, even apart from the central issue of justification, faith is the mark of a good relationship with God (as with others), whereas deeds done for others with no confidence in their goodwill are a sign of something less.

will inevitably direct and imbue all that we do.[3] Since for good relations with God we must take him at his word in good faith, and since acts of service may or may not be inspired by faith whereas faith will necessarily be embodied in actions, the essential and decisive factor is faith.

The proper relationship between God's word and our faith can be violated in two distinct ways.

1. Open disobedience of God's express will is clearly not compatible with trust in his goodness. If we reckon "Thou shalt not murder," "Thou shalt not commit adultery," and "Thou shalt not steal" among God's commands, and assume that murderers, adulterers, and thieves all act in their own perceived best interests, then we must conclude from their actions that they trust their own rather than God's judgment of where those interests lie. Three brief observations are in order.

a. Clearly, whatever else disobedience may show, it always reveals unbelief in the desirability of what is commanded, and hence in the goodness or wisdom of the one who commands. If sin is disobeying God, then unbelief is the root of all sin. Conversely, faith in God's goodness underlies all true fulfillment of his commands (*Pref. Rom.*, 35:369).

b. Any who believe that God has forbidden murder, adultery, and theft will have no problem recognizing the sinfulness of those who openly transgress these commands.

c. At one point Luther provocatively claimed that "God is not hostile to sinners, only to unbelievers" (*Good Works*, 44:64). What did he mean? Human nature being what it is, murder, adultery, and theft may all be acts of impulse that violate rather than reveal the wrongdoer's settled convictions. Sins they remain, and expressions of a (temporary, at least) lack of faith. But habitual unbelief in God precludes good relations with him in a way that individual lapses in judgment need not.

2. Faith in God's goodness is subverted by acts of open disobedience, but no less really (though much less obviously)[4] by those who doubt or disregard God's assurance of his favor and set out to secure divine approval by their good behavior. These "Dan's" of the world may well avoid murder, adultery, and theft; they may indeed appear to comply with *all* God's commands. But all is

3. "In [faith] all good works exist, and from faith these works receive a borrowed goodness" (*Good Works*, 44:24).

4. "Human reason does not know that unbelief and despair of God is sin. Indeed it knows nothing about man's duty to believe and trust in God. Hardened in its blindness, it goes its way and never feels this sin at all. Meanwhile it does some works that would otherwise be good, and it leads an outwardly respectable life. Then it thinks it stands well and the matter has been satisfactorily handled" (*Pref. OT*, 35:242).

not well in our relations with God when doubts of his favor steer our actions. Three brief observations are again in order.

a. Acts done by those who doubt God's favor and seek to secure it may be identical with those of people who trust in his goodness (as both Dan and Jack bought chocolates). Still, in the latter but not the former case they reflect a healthy and appropriate relationship with God.

b. Acts done to secure God's favor only appear to comply with his will. After all, God's first commandment is that we have "no other gods before [him]" (Exod. 20:3); we are, in other words, to "fear, love, and trust God above anything else,"[5] and to recognize him as the source of all goodness (*Gal.*, 26:226-27; *Good Works*, 44:30; *Large Cat.*, 9). Those who doubt God's favor but aim to secure it thus break God's first commandment even when they attempt compliance with the others. Their offense lies partly in their failure to trust God's assurance of his own goodwill; but they also fail to ascribe all goodness to him, treating their own activity rather than his love as decisive for good relations with him (*Good Works*, 44:30-31).

c. What greater contempt can we show toward God than not believing his promise, thus doubting his truthfulness (*Freedom*, 31:350)? What greater rashness than to imagine that mere creatures, made from nothing by God, can bargain with their Creator, offering their deeds for his favor (*Table Talk*, 54:429)? Indeed, at the deepest level the sin of those who depend on the merits of their own activity to please God is more insidious than that of those who blatantly transgress his will. The former sinners are of course easier to live with: the moral works[6] by which they conform (outwardly at least) with the commandments prescribing our relations with other human beings have great importance for the stability of society (cf. *Gal.*, 26:183, 249-51, 275, 308-9). In terms of their relations with God, however, their ceaseless attempts, in the face of God's assurance of his favor, to secure his approval by their own actions betray their settled unbelief more unmistakably than do the open transgressions of others.

Into this trap Luther believed the church of his day had fallen. In the first place he denounced (in his own inimitable, and not to be imitated, way) its

---

5. So *The Small Catechism* explains the first commandment of the Decalogue.

6. Luther distinguishes between "moral" and "theological" works: the same good deeds are merely moral when they are not driven by faith in God, theological when they are (*Gal.*, 26:266). In *The Small Catechism* Luther expresses the "theological" nature of true compliance with God's commands in the words with which he begins his explanations of the last nine commandments of the Decalogue (in the process, he intends to show that these commandments are all rooted in the first): "*We are to fear and love God so that* we do not use his name superstitiously . . ." (explaining "You shall not take the name of the Lord your God in vain"), or "*We are to fear and love God so that* we do not hurt our neighbor in any way . . ." (on "You shall not kill").

substitution of demands devised by humans for those prescribed by God. What God requires is clear in the Ten Commandments, and in these there is more than enough to keep us busy. If misuse of God's name is prohibited, the command can only be fulfilled by those who use God's name aright, praising and thanking him for whatever good may come their way, and calling on him whenever help is needed. Why, then, run off to seek holy places when honoring God's name is a task that will fill every moment of our lives (*Good Works*, 44:40-41)? In forbidding murder God intends that we treat kindly even our enemies. We all have those who irritate us, thereby testing our patience and goodwill, whether we can "speak well of [them], do good to [them], and not intend any evil against [them]." Now "if this is what God wants, and if God will be paid in no other coin, of what use is it then for us to run around performing great works which are not commanded, and to neglect this?" (102).

> The works which are not commanded are the building of churches, beautifying them, making pilgrimages, and all those things of which so much is written in the ecclesiastical regulations. These things have misled and burdened the world, brought it to ruin, troubled consciences, silenced and weakened faith. It is also clear that a man has enough to engage all his strength to keep the commandments of God, and even if he neglects everything else, he can never do all the good works he is commanded to do. Why then does he seek other works which are neither necessary nor commanded, and yet neglect those that are necessary and commanded? (113-14)

Still worse, however, than the substitution of human for divine commands are the pride and unbelief that provoke their performance. Pride is apparent not only in the ostentatious nature of the tasks undertaken, but still more in the presumption that our Creator will be sufficiently impressed by what we do to grant us heaven as a reward (*Large Cat.*, 11; cf. *Gal.*, 26:258). But at the bottom of these efforts to win God's approval lies unbelief in the divine assurance of his favor (*Good Works*, 44:27, 42).

Though Luther devoted much attention to the church of his day, this most pernicious error he believed to be universal. The attempt to gain God's favor by one's own good deeds is for Luther "the fundamental principle of the devil and of the world" (*Gal.*, 27:146). To it the heathen, the Jew, and the Christian heretic, despite insignificant variations in creed and practice, give united allegiance. "There is no difference at all between a papist, a Jew, a Turk, or a sectarian. Their persons, locations, rituals, religions, works, and forms of worship are, of course, diverse; but they all have the same reason, the same heart, the same opinion and idea. . . . 'If I do this or that, I have a God who is favorably disposed toward me; if I do not, I have a God who is wrathful'" (*Gal.*, 26:396).

Thesis 2: The law, like a mighty hammer, is meant to crush human self-
righteousness and to drive human beings, made aware of their sinfulness, to seek mercy from the Savior.

To this point we have spoken as though faith and unbelief were options equally
open to humankind. But Luther (no less than Augustine) believed that,
through Adam's sin (*Gal.*, 26:352; *Bondage*, 33:272)[7] and those of our own
choosing, we have already embarked on the path of unbelief — to disastrous effect. "Ignorance, hatred, and contempt of God in the heart, ingratitude, mur-
muring against God, and resistance to the will of God . . . are rooted in the nature of man" (*Gal.*, 26:125). So "corrupt" are our spiritual capacities that
"whatever is in our will is evil; whatever is in our intellect is error" (174). In the
depths of our heart there is "displeasure in what is good and pleasure in what is
bad"; but where there is "no willing pleasure in the good," even deeds that
would otherwise be good cannot be pleasing to God (*Pref. Rom.*, 35:366).

God's answer to this dilemma is of course the Christian gospel. But for Luther, before the gospel can be effective the law must do its work.

What Luther means by "law" is not always transparent. We may identify
three distinct usages.

1. In the minds of humans God has implanted an awareness that we should
do to others what we want done to ourselves. "This principle and others like it,
which we call the law of nature, are the foundation of human law and of all
good works" (*Gal.*, 27:53).

2. "Law" may also refer to the Mosaic code found in the opening books of
the Bible. In view of its importance for our study, Luther's understanding of the
Mosaic law is worth a brief digression.

Human beings bear responsibilities both toward God who gave them life
on earth and toward other human beings with whom they share it. We may
speak of two spheres of responsibility, or even (since they are differently administered) of two "kingdoms." One is temporal and visible. In it we function as
husbands and wives, children and parents, subjects and rulers, teachers and pupils, soldiers, preachers, cobblers, and farmers. Here "works" of moral and civic
righteousness are prescribed, and failure to comply with the laws is duly punished (*Gal.*, 26:95-96, 116-17). The other is a spiritual kingdom. Here our relationship with God is at stake.

Among the family of nations, the people of Israel occupy a unique position
"between these two kingdoms" (*Moses*, 35:164). Accordingly, its laws prescribe

---

7. Cf. *Faith and Law*, 34:119 (thesis 81): "Because we were all once made sinners through the
disobedience of Adam, we can never become obedient by ourselves."

conduct toward both God and other people. Though God is God of all nations, Israel's God-given laws are imposed only on Israel: readers of Scripture must note not only what God commands, but to whom his commands are given (170); and the Mosaic code is explicitly said to be given to Israel. Other individuals and nations may see in the Mosaic code a model of how good laws ought to appear, and they are of course free to adapt its principles and laws for their own use; but the code is binding only on the Jews to whom it was given (*Gal.*, 26:448; 27:15; *Moses*, 35:166-67).

Of the moral laws of the Pentateuch (and the Decalogue in particular), Luther can speak in divergent ways, though his underlying intention seems clear. On the one hand he can find in the Decalogue "a summary of divine teaching on what we are to do to make our whole life pleasing to God" (*Large Cat.*, 51). Elsewhere, however, he will insist that the moral commandments of the Mosaic law, including the Decalogue, no less than its civic and ceremonial prescriptions, were given to Jews alone and do not pertain to others — as Exodus 20:2 makes explicit (*Moses*, 35:164). What he seems to mean is this. (a) The Mosaic law, as such and in its entirety, was given to Jews and binds no others. (b) Much of the Mosaic law prohibits — and thus makes sinful for those bound by its statutes — things that otherwise would not be sinful, and which for that reason are not prohibited to non-Jews (cf. *Pref. OT*, 35:243). (c) The law of nature is written on human hearts and is valid for all. (d) The Decalogue contains commandments which perfectly express the natural law; hence these commands are binding on all, not because Moses ("an intermediary solely for the Jewish people"; *Moses*, 35:164) commanded them, but because they embody the law of nature. Given that the corruption of human reason caused by sin has distorted our understanding of the law of nature, we do well to heed its formulation in the Mosaic code (*Gal.*, 27:53; *Pref. OT*, 35:237). (e) As no one can fully isolate the spiritual from the temporal affairs of life and attend to each successively, so the laws of Moses mix requirements of the law of nature with prescriptions peculiar to Israel (241). Even in the Decalogue, interspersed with the universally valid prohibitions of murder, adultery, and theft, we find the Sabbath command and the prohibition of images, both of which pertain in their literal sense only to Israel (*Large Cat.*, 82; *Moses*, 35:172-73; *Table Talk*, 54:52).[8]

3. In his most typical references to "law," Luther has in mind neither the law of nature as such nor the Mosaic code, but Scripture wherever it places requirements on people, all that "we are to do and give to God" (*Moses*, 35:162). The whole of Scripture can be treated under two headings: command and promise

---

8. Luther's understanding of the Christian's relation to the Mosaic law will be treated below.

(*Freedom,* 31:348), or — in Luther's preferred terminology — law and gospel. The Old Testament is primarily (though by no means exclusively) "a book of laws" teaching what we "are to do and not to do," together with "examples and stories of how these laws are kept or broken." The New Testament is principally (though, again, not exclusively) the "proclamation of grace and peace through the forgiveness of sins in Christ" (*Pref. OT,* 35:236-37; cf. *Bondage,* 33:150).

Luther sees the purpose of "law" as twofold. The political laws found in Scripture were intended "to restrain those who are uncivilized and wicked" by threatening them with the sword and the executioner (*Gal.,* 26:274-75). Like chains that prevent lions and bears from ravaging what comes their way, so the restraining influence of the law by no means transforms the character of those whose wickedness it curbs (308). The good it achieves is more limited, though still essential: maintaining some semblance of public peace, lest "men . . . devour one another, and . . . the world . . . be reduced to chaos" (*Temp. Auth.,* 45:91). This is the "civil use of the Law" (*Gal.,* 26:275).

But God can hardly be content with keeping his creation a mere notch above chaos, or with controlling human beings with threats like savage beasts on chains. In the divine scheme to redeem and "justify" God's fallen creatures, "law" plays an important, though preliminary, role (315).

When the Mosaic code was imposed on Israel, the people were summoned from their tents to the foot of Mount Sinai, where "the lightning, the thunder, the dark cloud, the smoking and burning mountain, and the whole horrendous sight . . . terrified them" (313). The scene dramatically portrays the primary function of the law: to lead us out of the "tents" of our self-confidence and complacency into the presence of God. There, confronted by demands we know we have not met, and threatened with sanctions we know we have incurred, we may see the peril of our ways (148-50). The law serves as a light for the "ignorant and blind," revealing "sickness, sin, evil, death, hell, the wrath of God" — though not itself affording deliverance from any of these (*Bondage,* 33:261-62). "If someone is not a murderer, adulterer, or thief, and abstains from external sins, . . . he would swear . . . that he is a righteous man; therefore he develops the presumption of righteousness and relies on his good works. . . . Therefore the proper and absolute use of the Law is to terrify with lightning (as on Mt. Sinai), thunder, and the blare of the trumpet, with a thunderbolt to burn and crush that brute which is called the presumption of righteousness" (*Gal.,* 26:310; cf. *Bondage,* 33:130-31).

The law defines not what we can do, but what we ought to do. Nor is it strange to say that we are required to do what we cannot, since it is only the corruption of our God-given nature brought about by sin that prevents us from living as we ought. Itself merely the sum of God's requirements, the law has no capacity to effect their fulfillment. Its principal task is rather to remind us how far we have fallen, and that, in God's good creation, our sinful ways represent a pollution that must in the end be purged. Terrified by the law, and despairing of our own capacity to meet its demands, we must turn for help where help is to be found — in the gospel (*Gal.*, 26:131-32).

Thesis 3: We are justified by faith in Jesus Christ, not by the works we do.

If the law is the sum of what we must do for God, the gospel is the proclamation of what God has done for us (*Moses*, 35:162).[9] If the law reminds us of the works we do not, cannot, and yet are required to perform, the gospel is God's promise of forgiveness and grace.

Neither grace nor gospel is a New Testament discovery (*Pref. OT*, 35:237). What the Old Testament is chiefly about is the "teaching of laws, the showing up of sin, and the demanding of good"; nonetheless, it includes "promises and words of grace," and those (like Abraham) who responded with faith in God's word enjoyed his favor even before Christ came. Gentiles too (like the Ninevites who believed Jonah's prophetic message) were justified in Old Testament times by their faith in God's word (*Gal.*, 26:2,11-12). Yet the true object of their faith, even before Christ came, was necessarily Christ, inasmuch as the promise of God's grace in which they believed had its warrant and fulfillment in him (*Table Talk*, 54:63; cf. *Gal.*, 26:239). Hence Gentile and Jewish believers before Christ were "just as much Christians as we are" (*Temp. Auth.*, 45:97).

Sinners of all ages, then, are "justified by faith in Christ, and not by works of the law" (Gal. 2:16). No text was more central to Luther's understanding of Paul. Here we may look in turn at the object of faith ("in Christ"), the origin of faith, the meaning of "justification," and the conceivable path to justification here excluded ("not by works of the law").

1. *The Object of Faith:* That the faith that justifies must have Jesus Christ as its object is apparent on two grounds. First, the God whose greatness far transcends our comprehension can be known and believed in only as he chooses to reveal himself to us. The invisible, hidden God is beyond our ken, and it is fruitless and presumptuous for us to pursue him. Rather we must turn in faith to God as he has chosen to make himself visible in the word and work of Christ (*Table Talk*, 54:35). "Through Christ God announces His favor and mercy to us. In Christ we see that God is not a wrathful taskmaster and judge but a gracious and kind Father" (*Gal.*, 26:396).

---

9. Cf. *Gal.*, 26:122: "Whatever is not grace is Law, whether it be the Civil Law, the Ceremonial Law, or the Decalog."

Second, it is only through Christ that we can be delivered from the sin that otherwise would condemn us. God the Father, seeing our dilemma, sent his Son into the world, "heaped all the sins of all men upon Him, and said to Him: 'Be Peter the denier; Paul the persecutor, blasphemer, and assaulter; David the adulterer; the sinner who ate the apple in Paradise; the thief on the cross. In short, be the person of all men, the one who has committed the sin of all men'" (280). In this way Christ became "the greatest thief, murderer, adulterer, robber, desecrator, blasphemer, etc., there has ever been anywhere in the world. He is not acting in His own person now. . . . But He is a sinner, who has and bears the sin of Paul, . . . of Peter, . . . of David, . . . all the sins of all men in His body — not in the sense that He has committed them but in the sense that He took these sins, committed by us, upon His own body" (277). By thus taking all sins upon himself, Christ left the law no choice: it must condemn and curse sin, so it condemned and cursed Christ the Sinner.

But Christ the Sinner is also Christ the incarnate God. "The highest, greatest, and the only sin" converges in his person with "the highest, the greatest, and the only righteousness. Here one of them must yield and be conquered" (281). Had Christ not been God (as the heretic Arius claimed), he could never have conquered the "sin of the world, death, the curse, and the wrath of God in Himself — this is the work, not of any creature but of the divine power." Christ "conquers and destroys these monsters" so that they no longer can harm believers (282).

It is to Christ, then, that we must turn in faith if we would be delivered from our sins; to Christ, not as our example, ethical teacher, lawgiver, or prophet, but as the innocent Sinner who died under the law's condemnation: "our sin must be Christ's own sin, or we shall perish eternally" (278). In faith we approach Christ as a bride would her groom, for a marriage in which all possessions are shared: Christ, the Bridegroom, acquires our "sins, death, and damnation" while we receive his "grace, life, and salvation" (*Freedom*, 31:351). It is in fact an arranged wedding, planned by God so that when he looks at us, sinners though we are, he need see only the righteousness of Christ; and seeing us so, he can welcome us as his children into his kingdom.

2. *The Origin of Faith:* Christ, then, is the object of the faith that justifies — though indeed faith in Christ, properly understood, is not to be distinguished from faith in God, who made himself visible in Christ. In view of who Christ is and what he has done, faith is surely the appropriate response. "Faith must spring up and flow from the blood and wounds and death of Christ. If you see in these that God is so kindly disposed toward you that he even gives his own Son for you, then your heart in turn must grow sweet and disposed toward God. And in this way your confidence must grow out of pure good will and love — God's toward you, and yours toward God" (*Good Works*, 44:38).

Yet, however appropriate a response of faith may be, it is not a response that human beings are themselves able to muster. Counterfeit faith they can manage, the product of a human decision to believe that neither "reaches the depths of the heart" nor leads to real transformation; such would-be faith serves only to discredit the true (*Pref. Rom.*, 35:370). But the unbelieving, ungrateful, hostile heart of human beings will never be roused to real faith in God — and especially to so paradoxical a revelation of God as that of the incarnate Christ (*Bondage*, 33:158; cf. *Gal.*, 26:230-31) — unless God himself does the rousing. In the simple words of *The Small Catechism*:

> I believe that I cannot by my own understanding or effort
>   believe in Jesus Christ my Lord, or come to him.
> But the Holy Spirit has called me through the Gospel. . . .

"Through the Gospel": God has chosen to reveal himself in Christ; hence his Spirit does not illumine the human heart apart from the proclamation of his word in the gospel (*Gal.*, 26:73).[10] The content of God's word to us, and of the Spirit's illumination, is found in — and limited to — the sacred Scriptures; it becomes, however, God's word *to us* — his *summons* to us — when the Spirit of God takes the word externally heard and "by it . . . illumines and kindles hearts so that they grasp and accept it, cling to it, and persevere in it" (*Large Cat.*, 60). Unlike faith's counterfeit, the divine gift of true faith is effective and transformative. It "changes us and makes us to be born anew of God. It kills the old Adam and makes us altogether different men, in heart and spirit and mind and powers; and it brings with it the Holy Spirit. O it is a living, busy, active, mighty thing, this faith. It is impossible for it not to be doing good works incessantly" (*Pref. Rom.*, 35:370).

3. *Justification:* When Paul writes that "the righteousness of God is revealed in the gospel" (Rom. 1:17), the "righteousness of God" is not (as Luther once believed, to his terror) the justice and wrath with which God punishes sinners, but the gift of God to sinners by which he declares them righteous for Christ's sake and gives them new life (*Pref. Lat. Writ.*, 34:336-37).

God pronounces sinners righteous (*Gal.*, 26:137), not because he overlooks their sin, but because Christ bore it; and not because God does not require righteousness, but because, in the "marriage" that sinners enter with Christ through their faith in him, the righteousness of the divine Groom becomes theirs. From one perspective their righteousness is, and remains, an "alien" and "passive" righteousness, in that it is not the product of anything they do (6-7,

---

10. Cf. *Table Talk*, 54:97: "The devil has no better way to conquer us than by leading us away from the Word and to the Spirit." Also *Bondage*, 33:154-55.

234; *Two Kinds,* 31:297-99). Still, the marriage is divinely arranged and recognized, and Christ's righteousness really becomes their own. Now and at the judgment day the divine declaration that sinners are righteous is entirely due to the Savior. "The doctrine of justification is this, that we are pronounced righteous and are saved solely by faith in Christ, and without works" (*Gal.,* 26:223).

Yet this is not the whole story. Without faith we are not righteous and can no more produce righteous, God-pleasing works than make apples out of wood or mud (255). But things are very different for those who come to true faith in God. It takes a tree to produce apples, but apple trees do produce them; in the same way, though we could do no righteous deeds until we were made righteous, now that we are, we do (169, 255).[11] Our standing with God begins and ends with the "justification" by which God declares us righteous for Christ's sake; but justification brings with it a new and different life.

4. *"Not by Works of the Law":* The words refer to the deeds required by the Mosaic law, but they imply that nothing we do can gain our justification. After all, God's "law" is by definition the sum of what we are required to do for God. Faith, conversely, is not a matter of what *we* do, but of trusting *God* to do what he has promised. In essence, then, Paul lists all conceivable paths to justification when he contrasts our accepting what God has done for us ("justified by faith in Christ") with our performing something for him ("not by works of the law"). The latter option he here excludes: if the works that God commands in his law cannot justify, neither can any of our own devising. "For if, according to the testimony of the apostle, no one is justified by the works of the divine Law, much less will anyone be justified by the rule of Benedict, Francis, etc., in which there is not a syllable about faith in Christ but only the insistence that whoever observes these things has eternal life" (140). That Paul, with "works of the law," means to exclude any works of our own as the path to justification is apparent from other texts in which works in general are ruled out for this purpose so that we may be justified by grace: "grace would not be grace if it were earned by works" (*Bondage,* 33:268-69, referring to Rom. 4:4; 11:6). The point is underlined again in Romans 9:30, where grace is shown to be "given freely to those without merits and the most undeserving, and is not obtained by any efforts, endeavors, or works, whether small or great, even of the best and most virtuous of men, though they seek and pursue righteousness with burning zeal" (276-77; cf. 257-58).

---

11. Using a different illustration, Luther notes that a man who is not a bishop is not made a bishop by doing a bishop's tasks; once made a bishop, however, the man will do the job of a bishop (*Freedom,* 31:360-61).

Two misunderstandings of Paul's meaning merit special mention. The first Luther opposes together with Augustine; in the second he opposes Augustine.

Some see Paul's rejection of works of the law as targeting only its ceremonial commands. Luther rejects such an interpretation as an intolerable trivialization of Paul's meaning, a single error by itself "pestilent and potent enough to make havoc of the gospel" (258-59). Why single out the ceremonial commands of the law for exclusion from justification when they, no less than the other demands, were imposed by God (259; Gal., 26:123)? Why single them out for attention when, if we are to be justified by *any* part of the law, Christ died to no purpose (Gal., 26:181)? Galatians 3:21 makes it clear that no law can give life to the dead (330). Paul's point is not that the ceremonial law has been abrogated, but that the whole "bundle" of law cannot justify (121; cf. Bondage, 33:259-60). If Christ's liberation is only from the ceremonial law and from the guilt of its transgression, then Jews and Gentiles alike are left to perish in the guilt of their *moral* sins; but Christ died for *all* their sin (Faith and Law, 34:114-16 [theses 4-34 on law]).

In the second misunderstanding Augustine himself is implicated (Table Talk, 54:10). Here the true gospel (we are justified by faith in Christ without works) is corrupted into the claim that we are justified by faith in Christ *with* works. The necessity of faith is granted, but God's approval in the end is given only to those whose faith leads to love and good deeds, and it is on the basis of the latter that they are justified.

Luther's opposition to such a view may appear only semantic. Whereas others[12] distinguish faith that does not love or lead to good works from faith that does, Luther draws the line between a counterfeit faith that neither loves nor works and true faith that does. In the latter insistence he is unrelenting. True faith is a divine and transforming gift. It brings to the believer the power of God's Holy Spirit, who "does not permit a man to be idle but drives him to all the exercises of devotion, to the love of God, to patience in affliction, to prayer, to thanksgiving, and to the practice of love toward all men" (Gal., 26:155). Those who show no works of love are not true believers, whatever they may say; nor, lacking true faith, will they be justified (Gal., 27:30).[13]

Nonetheless, Luther finds it important to insist that faith in Christ, not the

---

12. Like, to be sure, the author of James 2 — whom Luther will not allow to have been an apostle. No apostle could have said that works justify (Pref. James, 35:395-96).

13. Cf. Pref. Ep. John, 35:393; also Gal., 26:155: "We, too, say that faith without works is worthless and useless. The papists and the fanatics take this to mean that faith without works does not justify, or that if faith does not have works, it is of no avail, no matter how true it is. That is false. But faith without works — that is, a fantastic idea and mere vanity and a dream of the heart — is a false faith and does not justify."

works we do after we have come to faith, is the sole ground of our justification. Otherwise the redemptive work of Christ is deemed insufficient ("Christ leaves us in our sins"; *Gal.*, 26:146; cf. 268-69) until it is supplemented by deeds of our own. We can neither be assured of salvation (377-78) nor confident in our faith in Christ if we believe God's approval at the last will depend on the adequacy of our deeds.

Why can one not be justified by "works"? Luther is never more eager or eloquent than when he tackles this question.

a. The power, wisdom, and majesty of God exceed by far what the human mind can understand and what human nature can endure. Any attempt to approach or comprehend him on one's own leads inevitably to a fall, to despair and death. This is why God came to us in the person of Jesus. "Take hold of [Jesus Christ]; cling to Him with all your heart. . . . When you do this, you will see the love, the goodness, and the sweetness of God. You will see His wisdom, His power, and His majesty sweetened and mitigated to your ability to stand it" (29-30). But since righteousness by faith in Christ is God's appointed path to himself, to approach him with one's own righteousness is to deny God's righteousness, to infringe on his prerogative of telling us how we may come to him, and to vainly imagine that our puny works are sufficient to bridge the chasm between God and humanity.

b. Only the doctrine of justification by faith gives glory where glory is due. If God is to be acknowledged as God, we must cling to him as the source of every good, our help in every need. This, the substance of the first commandment of the Decalogue, is fulfilled by faith alone, which places all its trust in God, relies exclusively on his grace, believes and rejoices in his promises in the gospel, and so gives glory to God (227-29, 253-54). Those who attempt to justify themselves, free themselves from sin and death, overcome Satan, and gain heaven by force are taking upon themselves roles which belong exclusively to God and robbing him of his glory (66, 127, 257).

c. The law requires perfect obedience; yet such obedience is nowhere to be found (273-74, 398). In this context Luther frequently emphasizes that God demands perfection in one's innermost heart. From his own experience he knew how an outward "cover" of sanctity could conceal inner attitudes of mistrust, fear, even blasphemy (70). Nor is that all. Experience told Luther that those who try to please God by their own deeds can never be certain whether God's standards have been met. Thus they end up multiplying sins of doubt, despair, and blasphemy in their hearts. "When I was a monk, I made a great effort to live according to the requirements of the monastic rule. . . . Nevertheless, my conscience could never achieve certainty but was always in doubt and said: 'You have not done this correctly. You were not contrite enough. You omitted this in your confession.' Therefore the longer I tried to heal my uncertain, weak, and troubled conscience with human traditions, the more uncertain, weak, and troubled I continually made it" (*Gal.*, 27:13; cf. 26:387-88, 404-6).

d. In fact, all such efforts are doomed at the outset, for it is not only our patent sins but even our so-called good works that are unacceptable apart from faith. Truly good deeds, that is, deeds God can approve, simply cannot come from sinful people (cf. *Bondage*, 33:264, 274). To try to please God with one's "good works" thus amounts to adding sins to sins (*Gal.*, 26:126). Luther makes a similar point by citing John's Gospel: "That which is born of the flesh is flesh" (John 3:6). "Flesh" includes not simply gross sins but the highest morality, wisdom, and religion of which the world is capable (139-40, 216); all this, apart from the faith that acknowledges God's righteousness and gives him his due, remains the work of the flesh and is unacceptable to God.

e. Humankind must be redeemed from the "present evil age" (Gal. 1:4), from bondage to the devil (39-40). Whatever works we may do, we remain in the present evil age. And the devil for his part does not "stoop down one handbreadth" for all the works and righteousness we may accomplish (40-41; cf. *Bondage*, 33:287-88). Only God through Christ is able to deliver us from his grasp.

f. That the Son of God died for us is proof in itself that our sins cannot be covered by our works; to claim that they can is to commit the idolatry of giving glory to ourselves that belongs to Christ (*Gal.*, 26:145), the blasphemy of making the death of Christ useless (176, 185). This reminder should keep us, on the one hand, from trivializing our sins and, on the other hand, from despairing because of them. Surely those who believe God's Son died for their sin cannot regard such sin as "something trivial, a mere nothing," of "so little weight and force that some little work or merit of ours will remove it" (33). But neither should they succumb to the temptation to despair, for to Satan's mention of their many sins they can simply reply that Christ died, not for righteous people, but for sinners (35-37).

Thesis 4: Though believers are righteous in God's eyes, they remain sinners throughout their earthly lives.

This thesis merely renders in sentence form one of Luther's most famous formulas: *simul iustus et peccator*, "(the believer is) at the same time righteous and a sinner" (*Gal.*, 26:232; cf. 27:68).

Christians are not people without sin, but those against whom, because of their faith in Christ, God does not count their sin. "Sin is always present, and the godly feel it. But it is ignored and hidden in the sight of God, because Christ the Mediator stands between" (*Gal.,* 26:133). Christians, then, are sinners *and* righteous at the same time.

And such they remain throughout their earthly lives (235): Luther allows neither complacency in sin nor pretensions of sinless sanctity. Faith has begun a transformation, though vice remains. "Many things are indeed cleansed, especially the head of the serpent — that is, unbelief and ignorance of God are cut off and crushed (Gen. 3:15) — but the scaly body and the remnants of sin still remain in us" (189). Already we have received the Spirit and begin to love, but our beginnings are painfully feeble (*Gal.,* 27:64-65). The best of us find our neighbors at times irritating (66). Even a devout married man finds himself liking "the form or the manner of some other woman" more than his wife's — on the principle that "what a man has, he despises; what he does not have, he loves" (67). The struggle Paul describes between flesh and Spirit is known to all believers, even the most saintly: the latter are no "stumps and stones" but human beings subject to the desires of the flesh (75-76). All Christians must "strive to avoid the works of the flesh; they cannot avoid its desires" (85).

> **Thesis 5:** The law must be banished from the thinking of believers when their relationship with God is the issue. Yet it must continue its role of identifying and judging their sin.

How does the Christian relate to the Mosaic law? Certain distinctions must be drawn.

1. The political laws of Moses never applied to non-Jews. Christians must remember, however, that they (like all other people) are subject to the laws of their own land, as Jews were subject to the Mosaic code (*Gal.,* 26:448).

2. The ceremonial laws of Moses were, again, binding only on Jews. They do not bind Christians — though we should bear in mind that life on earth entirely without ceremonies and rituals is inconceivable, and that "the Gospel permits ordinances to be established in the church regarding festivals, prescribed times, prescribed places, etc., so that the people may know on what day, at what time, and in what place they should gather to hear the Word of God. . . . It permits such things to be established with the purpose that all things should be done decently and in order (1 Cor. 14:40), not that those who observe such ordinances should merit the forgiveness of sins" (448; cf. 411).

In the case of Jews, the need to observe the ceremonial laws of Moses ended with the coming of Christ (317; cf. *Pref. OT,* 35:244). Thereafter observance of those laws was in itself a matter of indifference: one's purpose in observing them determined the character of one's deed (*Gal.,* 26:111, 118). Jewish Christians, long accustomed to Mosaic ceremonies, could continue these practices without sin, provided they did not see observance as required for salvation (80). On the other hand, they were free to ignore Mosaic rituals — unless by so doing they gave offense to others.

Luther saw parallels in his own day. In principle there was no sin in putting on a cowl or taking it off, entering a monastery or leaving it, fasting or eating meats and vegetables, and so on (84-86). Provided one did not link salvation to the observance of particular pious practices, one was free to continue them: Luther himself repeatedly stressed his willingness to observe whatever Rome might prescribe, as long as it was agreed that such observances did not atone for sin or gain God's grace (90, 225). Conversely he heaped scorn on those who imagined that Christian liberty could only be shown "by despising and finding fault with ceremonies, traditions, and human laws; as if they were Christians because on stated days they do not fast or eat meat when others fast, or because they do not use the accustomed prayers, and with upturned nose scoff at the precepts of men, although they utterly disregard all else that pertains to the Christian religion" (*Freedom*, 31:372).

3. When Paul rejects the "works" and the "righteousness" of the law, he has in mind the entire law, but particularly its moral commands (*Gal.*, 26:446-47). He means that their observance cannot secure God's approval, nor can the sanctions attached to disobedience of these commands threaten believers: "the Law of the Decalog has no right to accuse and terrify the conscience in which Christ reigns through grace, for Christ has made this right obsolete" (447; cf. *Pref. OT*, 35:244).

But though the conscience of believers is free from the law, their bodies are still subject to the temptations and desires of the "flesh": they remain sinners throughout their earthly lives, and as such they need the knowledge, the discipline,[14] and even the warnings that come from the law.[15] The view of those radicals

---

14. As long as the Christian lives on earth, there will be need for the law, like a "custodian," to "discipline and torment the flesh, that powerful jackass, so that by this discipline sins may be diminished" (*Gal.*, 26:350).

15. Note, however, that at times Luther can speak with surprising optimism of the righteousness of true believers: the righteous need no law to admonish and constrain them, but do spontaneously what the law requires (*Gal.*, 27:96); if all had faith, there would be no need for laws (*Good Works*, 44:34-35); "if all the world were composed of real Christians, that is, true believers, there would be no need for or benefits from prince, king, lord, sword, or law . . . , since Christians have in their heart the Holy Spirit, who both teaches and makes them to do injustice to no one, to love everyone, and to suffer injustice and even death willingly and cheerfully at the hands of anyone" (*Temp. Auth.*, 45:89). So, at least, the ideal. A page or so later, however, Luther concedes that without laws people would devour each other, "seeing that the whole world is evil and that among thousands there is scarcely a single true Christian. . . . If anyone attempted to rule the world by the gospel and to abolish all temporal law and sword on the plea that all are baptized

must be rejected who confuse Christian liberty with a "carnal license to do whatever they please" (*Gal.*, 26:343-44). In view of the dual nature of Christian existence, there is in every believer's life a time for law as well as a time for grace (341).

Complacency in sin requires the former. When, however, the law has done its work and the conscience of Christians is troubled, the time for grace has come. In the conscience, where the Christian's relationship with God is the issue, grace, not law, must prevail (349). Here is the bridal chamber for the believing bride and the divine Groom; law, with its demands and threats, must not be allowed to intrude (120).

Can the law be fulfilled? Not, of course, without faith; but with faith and the gift of the Holy Spirit, Christians can be said to fulfill it. They themselves begin to observe its demands; and in whatever respect they fail to do so, their failures are not counted against them but forgiven for the sake of Christ (260; cf. 274; also *Pref. Rom.*, 35:368-69).

Thesis 6: God predestined believers to salvation.

Like Augustine, Luther believed not only that faith itself is a gift from God but also that God has predetermined those to whom he will grant it. In part, Luther (again, like Augustine) was convinced that divine predestination to salvation is needed because human nature has been so corrupted by sin that humans can contribute not a thing to their salvation: salvation must "be taken entirely out of our hands and put in the hand of God alone" (*Pref. Rom.*, 35:378; cf. *Bondage*, 33:61-62). In Luther's *Bondage of the Will*, however, an added factor is his understanding of divine omnipotence (175, 189), according to which God is the effective cause of all that happens in his creation: if God "works all in all" (210, quoting 1 Cor. 12:6),[16] then the coming to faith of believers must have its predetermined place in his plan.

---

and Christian, . . . he would be loosing the ropes and chains of the savage wild beasts. . . . The world and the masses are and always will be un-Christian, even if they are all baptized and Christian in name. . . . A man who would venture to govern an entire country or the world with the gospel would be like a shepherd who should put together in one fold wolves, lions, eagles, and sheep, and let them freely mingle with one another. . . . The sheep would doubtless keep the peace and allow themselves to be fed and governed peacefully, but they would not live long" (91-92).

16. Of course Luther believed that human beings have their own will ("heaven . . . was not made for geese" [*Bondage*, 33:67]), and furthermore that, though God is the effective agent in all that humans do, he does not compel them to act *against* their will: "when a man is without the Spirit of God he does not do evil against his will, as if he were taken by the scruff of the neck and forced to it, . . . but he does it of his own accord and with a ready will"; in believers the Spirit of God has changed the will so that "it goes on willing and delighting in and loving the good, just as before it willed and delighted in and loved evil" (64-65; cf. 184-85). But people have the "sort

For both Augustine and Luther a great mystery surrounds predestination. Augustine's great concern is to demonstrate that divine predestination is fully compatible with divine justice: all merit the damnation to which some are rightly doomed, though others are graciously delivered. Here the mystery lies in the selectivity God exercises. In *The Bondage of the Will* Luther is not concerned to demonstrate divine justice, but he summons people to believe in it, appearances notwithstanding: here is a real task for faith (62-63)! The mystery, in Luther's understanding of predestination, lies primarily in the tension between the God who reveals himself as offering grace and salvation to all on the one hand, and on the other the hidden God whose salvific purposes are more limited.

> It is this that God as he is preached is concerned with, namely, that sin and death should be taken away and we should be saved. . . . But God hidden in his majesty neither deplores nor takes away death, but works life, death, and all in all. For there he has not bound himself by his word, but has kept himself free over all things. (140)

> It is likewise the part of this incarnate God to weep, wail, and groan over the perdition of the ungodly, when the will of the Divine Majesty purposely abandons and reprobates some to perish. And it is not for us to ask why he does so, but to stand in awe of God who both can do and wills to do such things. (146)

But the God who hides himself, Luther insists, is not to be our concern.[17] Nor need believers doubt their salvation. "I have been baptized and I have the

---

of will" that God has given them "and that God carries along by his own momentum" (233). God "works all in all, even in the ungodly, inasmuch as he alone moves, actuates, and carries along by the motion of his omnipotence all things, . . . and this motion the creatures can neither avoid nor alter, but they necessarily follow and obey it" (242).

Such reasoning certainly suggests that God is the effective agent even when people do evil. Here Luther insists that, though God moves people to act in whatever they do, the nature of their action is determined by their character: evil people, driven to act, inevitably commit evil (175-77). The argument cannot account for how human beings, created good, *became* evil; but in Gen. 3 (Luther reminds us), "man became evil when he was deserted by God and left to himself. From this man, thus corrupted, all are born ungodly" (174). If Adam was "left to himself" to sin, this would, of course, appear to be an exception to Luther's understanding of divine omnipotence, by which God "works all in all"; Luther does not, however, address the issue.

17. Indeed, predestination is barely hinted at in the great commentary on Galatians of 1535. Elsewhere Luther noted that Paul raised the issue in Romans only to repudiate the righteousness of the law and insist that salvation is by grace (*Table Talk*, 54:90-91), and he repeatedly emphasized the "ungodly and dangerous" folly of searching out the "hidden mysteries of God" (249; cf. 399-400).

Word, and so I have no doubt about my salvation as long as I continue to cling to the Word. When we take our eyes off Christ we come upon predestination and start to dispute. Our Lord God says, 'Why don't you believe me? Yet you hear me when I say that you are beloved by me and your sins are forgiven.' This is our nature, that we are always running away from the Word" (*Table Talk*, 54:57-58).

Summary

Faith in God's goodness is crucial to our relationship with him. God assures us of his goodwill and favor. The sin of unbelief is expressed both by open disobedience of God's commands and by acts of service to God when they are intended, in spite of the assurances God has already given, to secure his approval.

Human nature has been corrupted by sin. God's law (which includes all that, according to Scripture, we are to do and give to God) is designed primarily to awaken us to the peril of our condition as sinners threatened by divine judgment.

Christ, when crucified, took upon himself the sin of humankind. He then overcame sin and death. Those who trust in Christ receive from him grace, life, and salvation. Their faith is itself a gift of God roused in their hearts by God's Holy Spirit, who enables them to believe the gospel when they hear it. God pronounces believers righteous and enables them to do righteous deeds. On the other hand, sinners can never secure God's approval by their "works." Those who attempt to do so are guilty of folly, presumption, idolatry, and blasphemy, among other sins. They are also embarking on a path that can only lead to disillusionment and despair.

Believers are at the same time righteous and sinners. God counts them righteous because of their faith in Christ; and once justified, they begin to do what is right. But the task of resisting sin remains a struggle, never entirely successful, throughout their earthly lives.

Believers have been delivered from the sanctions of the law. Nonetheless, inasmuch as they remain beset by temptations, the law still serves to guide their actions and warn them of sin's peril. The law is not, however, the basis of their relationship with God. There grace alone prevails.

Those who believe in Christ were predestined by God to faith and salvation. This is but one area in which God shows his omnipotence as the unseen but real Actor in all that transpires in his creation. It is, moreover, a particularly essential area of divine activity, since sinful human beings can contribute not a thing to their salvation.

Chapter 3

John Calvin

According to Calvin, God decreed, before he created the universe, that you would read my words at this moment. It is thus God's will that you do so. Alas, it by no means follows that that is what you *ought* to be doing.

How can it be God's will that we do what we ought *not* to do? We may address the question by reflecting on what the biblical story of Joseph, as read by Calvin (cf. *Inst.* 1.17.8; also *Defence*, 298-99), reveals about God's rule of human affairs.[1]

i. Divine Providence and Human Responsibility

Joseph's brothers, motivated by hatred, sell Joseph as a slave. He is taken to Egypt where, in time, he becomes the effective ruler of the land. As such he is able to preserve his family through a period of famine. Looking back at what happened, he tells his brothers, "You meant evil against me; but God meant it for good, to bring about the saving of many lives" (Gen. 50:20).

In Calvin's world punch lines do not come any better than that. The whole story is a paradigm case by which we can grasp the nature of, and the relationship between, divine providence and human responsibility.

God decreed, before there was a world, that Joseph's brothers, motivated by hatred, would sell Joseph as a slave. God would not be God if he were not in control of all that happens. For Calvin divine control of events means their divine predetermination: "all events are governed by God's secret plan" (*Inst.* 1.16.2); "nothing happens except what is knowingly and willingly decreed by

---

1. For full information on Calvin's works that are cited in abbreviated forms in the text, see bibliography.

him" (1.16.3). Divine *omnipotence,* for Calvin, is not an unexercised power by which God *could* do anything he pleases, but his active and sovereign determination of "all things by his will" (*Cat. Gen.,* 93; cf. *Inst.* 1.16.3). God's *providence* "pertains no less to his hands than to his eyes" (1.16.4; cf. *Defence,* 224). He does not simply observe what human beings do, leaving them to act in keeping with their own nature and the free choice of their will; rather, he "regulates" all things so that they proceed according to "his set plan" (*Inst.* 1.16.4). It is absurd to say that unsavory events are merely *permitted* by God: "they babble and talk absurdly who, in place of God's providence, substitute bare permission — as if God sat in a watchtower awaiting chance events, and his judgments thus depended upon human will" (1.18.1). Nothing happens by chance (1.16.2; 1.17.6). On the contrary, God's will is the "principal and all-high *cause* of all things in heaven and earth" (*Defence,* 246).

Joseph, sold into slavery by his brothers, should thus see the hand of God in his experience and rest in God's protection (*Inst.* 1.17.8; cf. 1.16.3). Such should be the posture of all believers in every situation, knowing that every situation is divinely controlled. The winds and the rain have their own natural properties, but they proceed only as "directed by God's ever-present hand" (1.16.2, 5, 7). The rising and setting of the sun represent much more than nature's inevitable course: they, too, are divinely governed, so that each new day represents a fresh, and "special, providence of God" (1.16.2). Human beings for their part may seem to rush about "like brute beasts confined by no chains, . . . yet God by His secret bridle so holds and governs them, that they cannot move even one of their fingers without accomplishing the work of God much more than their own" (*Defence,* 238). The wicked, and even Satan and his demons, though pursuing their own plans, inevitably do "the work of God" (239-40; cf. *Inst.* 1.14.17; 1.17.5, 8, 11; 2.4.3).[2] Joseph's brothers are no exception to this rule.

But ours is a thoughtful Joseph. Divine providence brings comfort for which he is grateful, but it also provokes questions that he cannot but ponder. How can the God he trusts have decreed that his brothers, motivated by hatred, would sell him as a slave? Is God the author of evil? How can an event in which Joseph's brothers transgressed God's commands nonetheless represent God's will? Does God have one will when he plans and another when he commands?

Guided by the *Institutes, our* Joseph would resolve these issues somewhat as follows.

He would remember, first, that among the natural endowments given to humankind are two faculties of the human soul: understanding and will. By the

---

2. Also *Comm.* Eph. 2:2: "What is Satan but God's executioner to punish man's ingratitude?"

former, human beings distinguish good from evil, right from wrong; by the latter they choose which to pursue (1.15.7-8). To be sure, the human will is not for Calvin the one area of the universe exempt from divine control: God "governs the hearts of men, bends their wills this way and that in accordance with his choice" (*BLW*, 2.257).[3] Still, to be human is to have a will (*Inst.* 2.3.5). Humans sin both necessarily and voluntarily (2.5.1): necessarily, because God decrees what they do and they cannot do otherwise (*BLW*, 4.335); voluntarily, because they are not "dragged unwillingly into sinning" but themselves *choose* (admittedly, by divine decree) to commit (admittedly, divinely decreed) deeds that are wrong (2.280).[4]

Secondly, Joseph would recall the important distinction between principal and secondary causes. Just as a violin sounds *both* because a violinist is playing a sonata *and* because the bow crosses the strings, and neither explanation rules out the other because they operate on different levels, so Joseph's brothers sell him as a slave *both* because God decreed that they would do so *and* because they hate Joseph and want to be rid of him.

Joseph would realize, thirdly, that the purpose underlying an act is crucial to its moral assessment. We condemn the wanton cruelty of those who torture animals but praise a judge who administers punishment (*Defence*, 249). Similarly, though Joseph's brothers are rightly blamed for their sin in hating and selling their brother, God's intention in using their evil to preserve his people from starvation is righteous and good. Here the principal and secondary causes of the same action are subject to contrary moral assessments: "those things which are vainly or unrighteously done by men are, rightly and righteously, the works of God" (233).[5] Thus God, though the author of the event in which Joseph's brothers committed evil, is not himself the author of their evil (303-4; *Inst.* 2.4.2).

Joseph would conclude as well that a distinction must be drawn between God's precepts and his plan (1.18.4): Joseph's brothers transgressed God's commands, though in so doing they carried out God's plan to save his people. Still, both precept and plan are good, and we must not imagine that God has two "wills" pitted against each other when he uses the breaking of his precepts to promote his purposes (*Defence*, 306-10).

Our Joseph, however, is still uneasy. That God uses human evil for good

3. Cf. *Defence*, 243: God "performs not by the hands of men the things which He has decreed, without first working in their hearts the very will which precedes the acts they are to perform." Also *Inst.* 2.4.6-7.

4. Note Calvin's insistence in *Comm.* Rom. 7:14 that humans do not sin by "compulsion . . . for we sin of our own free will. It would not be sin if it were not voluntary." Cf. *Inst.* 2.3.5.

5. Cf. 255: "God willeth righteously those things which men do wickedly."

purposes is one thing. But why would God plan for his brothers to do evil in the first place? And why would he then steer their hearts and wills in such a way that they commit it? Must his brothers' cruelty not be excused in the light of its place in God's "secret plan"?

In responding to the latter question, Calvin has a question of his own: Did Joseph's brothers act against their will or with it? Since they sinned *with* their will, they are responsible for what they did. If people "find the source of evil within themselves, why do they strain after external causes so as not to seem the authors of their own destruction?" (*Inst.* 2.5.11; cf. *Defence,* 318). We sin, by God's design, in such a way that we ourselves are to blame for our sinning (cf. *Inst.* 3.23.8).

But to the question why God would will what he has evidently willed, there can, in the very nature of things, be no answer. We can explain *x* by referring to *y,* and *y* by referring to *z,* and proceed as long as wit and patience permit. In the end, however, the will of God must be the ultimate (or better, the first and primary) cause of what happens: there can be no cause higher than the will of God by which the latter can be explained (3.23.2), nor is God subject to a higher law. And though he is a "law to himself" in the sense that he consistently acts according to his character, and though his power and justice are as inseparable as the sun and its heat (*Defence,* 248), yet we cannot expect his secret ways to be penetrable by our understanding. Moreover, we do well to remember that God is not required to account for his deeds to us, nor dare we presume ourselves competent to judge them. "We must always at last return to the sole decision of God's will, the cause of which is hidden in him" (*Inst.* 3.23.4).

But enough of these musings. Joseph has jobs to do. Divine providence seldom meets us "in its naked form" (1.17.4); most often we encounter it clothed in commands and obligations, cautions and warnings, resources and opportunities, and these must be put to good effect. The future may be decreed by God's secret plan, but for us it is uncertain (1.16.9). The neglect or diligence, folly or prudence that we show will be rewarded according to God's promise at the same time as we in fact carry out God's hidden counsel by what we do (*Defence,* 235-36).

So much we may glean from the story of Joseph about divine sovereignty and human responsibility, God's secret plan and our duty. Where does it leave the question with which we began?

If you are (still) reading my words, God must have decreed that you would do so, since all that happens has been divinely predetermined. It is thus part of God's plan, and promotes the achievement of God's good purposes, that you do so. Yet it is not impossible that you ought now to be apologizing to your spouse, visiting your mother-in-law, or listening sympathetically to the complaints of an ornery neighbor. If that is the case, you ought not to be reading and are to blame for doing so (you chose, after all, to shirk your duty by reading) — even though God, to achieve good ends, decreed that that is what you would do. Should my words prod you to return to your responsibilities, then that too — rest assured! — was divinely ordained.

We turn now to the decisive players in the divine script for human history — to Adam, Christ, Abraham, and Moses — before concluding with a look at (Calvin's understanding of) the life of the redeemed.

ii. Adam

Any discussion of human nature must distinguish between its condition as created on the one hand and as fallen on the other (*Inst.* 1.15.1). The goodness of the former state requires no elaboration here, though the provisions by which humanity could know its Creator are worth mentioning. God has "implanted" in the human mind an awareness of his divinity that can never be completely effaced and that accounts for the presence of religion wherever human beings are found. Clever people have certainly used religion to bring the simple under their power; still, human awareness of God is not the product of such exploitation, but what precedes and makes it possible (1.3.1-3). Confirming this inner human conviction of the reality of God is the testimony of "the whole workmanship of the universe" (1.5.1), "this most beautiful theater" in which God's majesty is on display (1.14.20).

Those who grasp something of God's greatness must sense that honor is due him (1.2.1). Indeed, as our Creator he has the right to be revered as our Father and Lord; his will, prescribing that he "be worshiped by us all, and that we love one another," should be our law (1.2.2; 2.8.2; 4.20.15). Since God is the source of our every good, our desire should be to "cleave to him and trust in him" (1.2.2). "It would be monstrous for us to want to withdraw from his rule when we cannot exist apart from him" (2.8.13). Yet that is what Adam, and we, have done.

Adam sinned by his own free will: in his case (though not in that of his descendants) his will had the inherent capacity to choose good *or* evil (1.15.8). Unfaithfulness, ambition, pride, and ungratefulness were all expressed when he turned from God to falsehood (2.1.4). For that sin he alone is culpable (1.15.8).

Yet it remains true that he sinned as well by divine decree (*Defence,* 267).[6]

---

6. An analogy may illustrate how Adam's will had the inherent capacity to do either good or evil though, by divine decree, he necessarily did the latter. Jesus' bones were human bones, and as such were inherently breakable. But not a bone of his could be broken because God so decreed it (*Inst.* 1.16.9, referring to John 19:36).

Scripture may not say so explicitly, but for Calvin, that God could have left undecided the destiny of the "noblest of his creatures" is inconceivable to begin with and incompatible with the omnipotence by which God determines all things (*Inst.* 3.23.7). "The first man fell because the Lord had judged it to be expedient; why he so judged is hidden from us. Yet it is certain that he so judged because he saw that thereby the glory of his name is duly revealed. . . . We should contemplate the evident cause of condemnation in the corrupt nature of humanity — which is closer to us — rather than seek a hidden and utterly incomprehensible cause in God's predestination" (3.23.8).

With Adam's sin human nature was corrupted. Paul can speak of the corruption itself as "sin" (it is what is meant by "original sin"); from it flow the particular evil deeds that we do (2.1.5, 8; *Comm.* Rom. 5:12; 6:12). The transmission, from Adam to succeeding generations, of a corrupted human nature is entirely appropriate: Adam was not only the "progenitor" of humankind but also the "root" of human nature. Those who share his nature partake of its corruption (*Inst.* 2.1.6). Put differently, the Lord entrusted "gifts" to Adam to be conferred on humankind; when Adam lost those gifts, we all share in the loss (2.1.7). Yet, though appropriate, Calvin insists that the transmission of Adam's guilt and corruption was not merely given "in the nature of things"; rather, it, too, is the result of a divine decree (*Defence*, 269; cf. *Inst.* 3.23.7).

What is entailed in the corruption of our nature? Philosophers of all ages have conceded the proneness of human sensuality to evil; the remedy, as they commonly see it, is for the human will to follow the guidance of human reason rather than succumb to sensual desires. The will, though tempted by sensuality, is deemed able to choose the good (2.2.3-4). Calvin counters this depiction with one of the corruption of human nature in its "every part" (2.1.8), laying special emphasis on that of the reason and will: we are both fools and knaves.

Contemplation of the "magnificent theater of heaven and earth" ought to have led us to piety and, hence, to eternal life and blessedness (2.6.1). But it is "in vain that so many burning lamps shine for us in the workmanship of the universe to show forth the glory of its Author" (1.5.14). Such is our folly that we grow increasingly indifferent to the wonders of creation, attribute them to "nature" so that we need not mention God, and turn from the living God to our own "prodigious trifles" (1.5.4-5, 11). The books of philosophers may be "sprinkled" with "droplets of truth" about the divinity, but these are found mingled with "monstrous lies" (2.2.18). A longing for truth remains in humankind, but its pursuit is easily turned aside to vanity. Human reason "cannot hold to the right path, but wanders through various errors and stumbles repeatedly" (2.12.2).

Nor do we foster the awareness of God planted in our hearts (1.4.1). A "vague general veneration of God" is everywhere attested (1.2.2), but humans persist in pleasing themselves. Not that they live without a semblance of religion; but whereas they owe God consistent obedience, all they render is "a few paltry sacrifices," hoping thus to induce him to overlook their rebellion (1.4.4).

Where true knowledge of God is lacking, so necessarily is a proper understanding of ourselves. Had we raised our thoughts to God, we could not but sense our own wickedness. But surrounded as we are by "great immorality," we deem "most pure" whatever is "a little less vile," and see ourselves as models of uprightness (1.1.2).

Our minds are thus corrupted by sin; so is our will, disposed as it is to neglect God and pursue its own pleasure (2.2.12). The human will remains "self-determined" in the sense that it eagerly embraces the promptings of our sinful desires (*BLW*, 2.280; *Inst.* 2.3.5). Some would call a will that does what it likes "free," but Calvin finds the term misleading. "Free will" suggests that we are capable of choosing either good or evil, whereas Calvin thinks the human will a captive of evil (2.2.7, 12). We consent to our captivity, but a captivity it remains as long as the sphere of our activity is confined (necessarily) to that of sin.

In short, as a result of sin humans have been stripped of the supernatural gifts that bring eternal life and bliss (faith, true love of God and neighbor), while their natural endowments (the human mind and heart) have been corrupted (2.2.12; 2.5.19). Corruption is not extinction, to be sure. Something of God's gifts and image remains in humankind and is not to be despised (2.2.13-17). We see remnants of former virtues wherever humans acquiesce in rule by law and political order, in notions of justice and equitable laws, in perceptive observations of the natural order, in the development of medicine and the mathematical sciences, in artistic talent and vocational skills. Nor dare we deny the "difference between the justice, moderation, and equity of Titus and Trajan and the madness, intemperance, and savagery of Caligula or Nero or Domitian, or . . . between observance and contempt of right and of laws" (3.14.2; cf. 2.3.3). All that is praiseworthy in humankind comes from God; its goodness ought to be acknowledged. Yet human depravity remains. The motives of even the most zealous pursuers of virtue are never free from sin (2.3.3). Nor can there be true righteousness without that true religion by which God our Maker is given his due. Of such worship fallen humanity is incapable (2.3.4; 2.8.11; 3.14.3).

iii. Christ

"Christ" means "anointed one." The work of Christ can be summed up in the three offices with which the Scriptures associate anointing with oil: Christ is king, prophet, and priest (2.15.1-2).

As *king* of a spiritual realm, Christ provides for the needs of his people throughout their earthly lives and leads them to the life eternal (*Cat. Gen.*, 95; *Inst.* 2.15.4).

As *prophet*, Christ brings us divine truth.

Not that Christ was the first through whom God's word addressed human beings. God spoke to the patriarchs of Israel and, through Moses and the prophets, to Israel as a whole. Why did he do so? Neither the awareness of himself that God has placed in human hearts nor the contemplation of his created works led humankind to true knowledge of the Creator; so God added "the light of his word" (1.6.1-4). Moreover, given humanity's proclivity for forgetfulness and error, God provided his people with that word in written form. Creation is itself a kind of "book" in which God's majesty can be read, but humanity's weak vision proved incapable of deciphering it without the "spectacles" of Scripture (1.6.1).

God spoke through prophets before Christ only intermittently and even obscurely. The "prophetic dignity" of Christ's office means that his teaching contains "all parts of perfect wisdom" (2.15.2). The "dim light" of earlier prophecies is outshone by "the perfect radiance of divine truth" brought by the "Sun of Righteousness" (4.8.7). By "fully declaring the Father's will," Christ "put an end to all revelations and prophecies" (*Cat. Gen.*, 95; cf. *Inst.* 2.15.2; *Comm. Rom.* 12:6). "The mouths of all men should be closed when once he has spoken, in whom the Heavenly Father willed all the treasures of knowledge and wisdom to be hid" (*Inst.* 4.8.7).

As *priest*, Christ's task was to reconcile his people to God. Neither we nor our prayers can have access to God while our sins block the way: the "disagreement" between righteousness and unrighteousness is "perpetual and irreconcilable" (2.16.3). But "all cause for enmity" is removed when Christ intervenes as both offering priest and offered sacrifice, dying to expiate our sins and obtain for us God's favor (2.16.3; cf. 2.15.6).

iv. Abraham and Moses

Here three topics may be explored: the covenant with Abraham, the Mosaic religion, and the election of God's people.

1. *The Abrahamic Covenant:* All Adam's offspring suffer under the same bondage to sin and corruption, all can obtain God's favor only through his mercy, and that mercy is mediated for all only through Christ. "The original adoption of the chosen people depended upon the Mediator's grace. . . . God cannot without the Mediator be propitious toward the human race" (2.6.2; cf.

2.7.1). Hence the promises of God's favor given to Abraham and his descendants hinged for their validity upon the (at their time, still future) priestly work of Christ, and it was toward him that the faith of the patriarchs and of all God's true people was, however inchoately, directed (2.6.3-4).[7]

The faith of the faithful in Israel[8] was thus, in essence, the same as that of believers today, a response to the same promises of God's "mercy and fatherly favor" (2.9.2; 2.10.20; 2.11.1). In short, believers of all ages know a "common salvation" (2.10.1), communicated through a common covenant based not on human merit but on the mercy of God and the mediation of Christ (2.10.2, 4). "The covenant which the Lord once made with Abraham [cf. Gen. 17:14] is no less in force today for Christians than it was of old for the Jewish people" (4.16.6; cf. 2.11.4); it "could in no way be made void" (4.16.14). In ancient Israel the church was in its childhood, but it was the same church as that of our day (2.11.2).

2. *The Mosaic Religion:* "Law" is at times used by Calvin (and in Calvin's understanding, by Paul) of the righteous requirements God makes of human beings and the promises and sanctions accompanying these demands. This law was revealed to Moses on Mount Sinai and may be contrasted with the gospel of God's mercy (2.9.4; cf. 2.11.7). But "law" may also refer more broadly to the whole "form of religion handed down by God through Moses" (2.7.1; cf. *Comm.* Rom. 10:5). This Mosaic religion was a reminder (or renewal) rather than a replacement of the covenant of mercy God made with Abraham (*Inst.* 2.7.1; *Comm.* Rom. 9:4). Thus, when the "entire law" is in view, the gospel itself must be seen as confirming, not supplanting, it (*Inst.* 2.9.4).

After all, the covenant with Abraham depended for its efficacy on the mediating work of Christ between God and humankind; the same must be said of the Mosaic religion. Its ceremonies foreshadowed the work of Christ and directed the minds of worshipers toward him. Apart from their reference to Christ, these ceremonies would have been empty, even ridiculous, and no better than the rites of paganism (3.2.32; 4.14.25): how could "loathsome stench from the fat of cattle" ever reconcile people to God, or a "sprinkling of water and blood" ever cleanse the filth of their sin (2.7.1)? "Even though atonement for sins had been truly promised in the ancient sacrifices, . . . all this would have been but shadow had it not been grounded in the grace of Christ" (2.7.16).

---

7. When Paul talks of faith as first "coming" with the appearance of Christ, he is speaking "relatively, not absolutely": a "full revelation" was made by Christ of things hitherto "not so openly manifested." But the "fathers" too had faith, and the "doctrine of faith" is "attested by Moses and all the prophets" (*Comm.* Gal. 3:23).

8. Though God entered a covenant with the "children of Abraham," not all were "children of God" because "few continued firm in the faith of the covenant" (*Comm.* Rom. 9:6).

The coming of Christ, then, "gave substance to the shadows" of the Mosaic ceremonies (2.9.4). It also, to be sure, did away with the point of their observance, though rather by honoring and confirming them than by depriving them of their sanctity: "just as the ceremonies would have provided the people of the Old Covenant with an empty show if the power of Christ's death and resurrection had not been displayed therein; so, if they had not ceased, we would be unable today to discern for what purpose they were established" (2.7.16; *Comm.* Col. 2:11, 17).

The change in the "outward form and manner" (*Inst.* 2.11.13) in which God's covenant is observed[9] is reflected in the biblical language of an "old" covenant (or "testament") and a "new." The ancient sacraments are now replaced by baptism and the Lord's Supper, which more clearly represent the cleansing and redemption made possible through Christ (4.14.22; *Comm.* Col. 2:17). Still, the purpose of the sacraments has always been to represent Christ's work and direct thoughts to him (*Inst.* 4.14.20).

What, then, is to be said of "law" in the more limited sense of the righteous requirements of God?

The first thing to be insisted upon is that law, so understood, is an abstraction from the full "doctrine taught by Moses" as we encounter it in Scripture. Between law in its fullest sense and the gospel there can be no conflict, for they have the same divine Source, and God cannot be "unlike Himself" (*Comm.* Gal. 3:12, 21). Thus the ministries of Moses and Christ are both based on the righteousness of faith, and God's grace and Spirit are at work in both. But since God's justification of sinners and the operation, among sinners, of grace and God's Spirit depend on the work of Christ, Paul may at times distinguish the "law" (or the "letter") from Christ and mean by the former only "what belonged peculiarly to the law": the commands and prohibitions, revealed to Moses, that define the way of life acceptable to God, with their accompanying promises and threats.[10] The (full) law, "an-

---

9. Cf. *Comm.* Gal. 4:1: "the difference between us and the ancient fathers lies not in substance but in accidents. In all the chief points of the testament or covenant we agree. The ceremonies and all that régime in which we differ are, so to say, appendages."

10. So *Comm.* Rom. 8:15: "Although the covenant of grace is contained in the law, yet Paul removes it from there, for in opposing the Gospel to the law he regards only what was peculiar to the law itself, viz. command and prohibition, and the restraining of transgressors by the threat of death. He assigns to the law its own quality, by which it differs from the Gospel." Cf. also *Inst.* 2.11.7, 10; *Comm.* Rom. 10:5; 2 Cor. 3:6, 7; Gal. 3:19. In *Inst.* 2.7.2 Calvin notes Paul's use of the term "law" to refer to "the bare law in a narrow sense." The apostle was compelled to adopt this usage in refuting those who failed to see Christ as the "fulfillment or end of the law" and taught that we, by the works of the law, may "merit righteousness." Paul pointed out in these contexts what the law (apart from Christ) requires for righteousness, and how its demands can only lead to the condemnation of sinners.

imated by Christ," is the subject of encomiums in Scripture, such as that pronounced by David in Psalm 19. On the other hand, the law that Paul can call "the ministry of sin and death" is the law considered *apart* from Christ, lifeless as a body from which the soul has been removed (*Comm.* 2 Cor. 3:17; Phil. 3:6).

Secondly, we should note that the law, in promising life to those who fully meet its demands and cursing its transgressors, sets forth a pathway to righteousness and life that is conditional on human works, and thus very different from the "righteousness of faith" offered freely to sinners by God's grace (*Comm.* Rom. 2:13; 10:4; Gal. 3:12, 18; Phil. 3:9). The pathway of the law is nonetheless divinely instituted and valid, and would prove efficacious among human beings of "virtue and integrity" — though clearly it cannot bring life to the "sinful and corrupt" (*Comm.* Rom. 4:15; 7:16). That the law proves lethal to human beings is thus by no means inherent in *its* nature, but rather the result of an "accident" in human history; now, however, the law's curse on corrupted human nature is "perpetual and inseparable" (*Comm.* Rom. 7:10; Gal. 3:10).

Thirdly, we must see the righteousness of faith as God's answer to the dilemma brought about by our rebellion against his moral law (*Comm.* Gal. 2:21; 3:6; Phil. 3:9). Furthermore, the statement — to *sinners* — of the "righteousness of works" in the Mosaic law was meant to provoke an awareness on our part of our need for a different righteousness, and thus point us to Christ. "Blinded and drunk" as we are with "self-love," the law's requirements serve to show us our weakness, our iniquity, and our need for divine mercy (*Inst.* 2.7.6-7). Hence the real goal of the moral (no less than of the ceremonial) demands of the Mosaic law is to point to Christ (*Comm.* Rom. 3:21, 31; 5:20; Gal. 3:24); and those who set about to gain God's acceptance by fulfilling his law's demands pervert its true nature and purpose (*Comm.* Rom. 3:21; 10:4).

The first "use" of the moral law is thus, by setting forth God's righteousness, to warn and convict human beings of their own *un*righteousness and drive them to seek mercy in Christ (*Inst.* 2.7.6-9). It performs a second function in restraining with its threats the activities of the wicked and thus preserving a measure of peace in human society (2.7.10-11). Its third use, however, is the "principal" one: to guide and motivate believers in doing what is right (2.7.12).

The moral law is, after all, "the true and eternal rule of righteousness, prescribed for men of all nations and times, who wish to conform their lives to God's will" (4.20.15). Just as the promises, the faith, and the grace that mark the people of God are the same in all ages, so is there "one everlasting and unchangeable rule to live by" (2.7.13). Indeed, God has "engraved" the requirements of his rule in every human heart, and every human being retains an "inner witness" of what we owe God, of the "difference between good and evil," and of our own failure to fulfill our duties. Proof of human awareness of the real difference between virtue and vice is furnished whenever people accuse each other of wrongdoing or set out to defend the innocence of their ways (*Comm.* Rom. 2:14; 5:13). Still, in view of human dullness and arrogance, God has seen fit to provide us with a clear and unambiguous witness of his demands in the two tablets (i.e., the Ten Commandments) of the law (*Inst.* 2.8.1).

Christ neither set aside nor supplemented the commands of the Decalogue. Instead he pointed to their correct interpretation, restoring the law "to its integrity," "free[ing] and cleans[ing] it" of falsehoods (2.8.7). Rightly understood, the commands of the Decalogue each embrace a whole category of human behavior. Extreme examples, such as murder and adultery, are cited to rouse our minds to a "greater detestation of every sort of sin"; but the prohibition of murder rules out harm to others in *any* form, and with adultery must be reckoned seductive behavior of *any* kind, in dress, gesture, or speech (2.8.10, 44). Indeed, murder includes even anger, and adultery, impure thoughts, since the divine Lawgiver sees the heart as well as outward appearances and requires inner purity that matches outward conformity with his demands (2.8.6). Moreover, the forbidding of vices implies an obligation to show the opposing virtue (2.8.9): not only are we not to profane the divine name, but we are positively to display zeal and care in honoring it with reverence (2.8.22); not only are we not to kill, but we are positively to "give our neighbor's life all the help we can" (2.8.9). Seen in this way, the Decalogue represents a comprehensive statement of our duty toward God and other human beings.[11] Nor should we exclude the Sabbath commandment from our responsibilities. Though its "ceremonial part" has been done away with and (marking the difference) the day of its observance has shifted to the first day of the week (on which Christ rose),[12] two other reasons for the Sabbath command still apply today: Christians, too, must assemble to hear God's word and for public prayers, and workers today need rest no less than did the Jews of old (2.8.31-34).

Christians must not, then, believe they can disregard God's eternal law and merely "follow the Spirit as their guide," imagining that "under [the Spirit's] impulsion they can never go astray." The Spirit of Christ is also the Spirit of the law and the prophets, and Christians are to "seek a knowledge of him from the

11. Cf. *Comm.* Rom. 7:2: "We must never imagine that the law is in any way abrogated in regard to the Ten Commandments, in which God has taught us what is right and has ordered our life, because the will of God must stand for ever." Also *Comm.* Gal. 3:25.

12. Calvin insists, however, that Christians have been set free from the "outward observances" of the Mosaic law and that they do not regard one day as more holy than another. That a particular day of the week has been set aside as the Christian "Sabbath" is merely intended to maintain order and harmony in the church (*Inst.* 2.8.33; *Comm.* Gal. 4:10).

Scriptures." There they will learn that he "distinguishes between lawful and un-lawful" and teaches us "to keep measure and temperance." The Spirit is given not to replace God's commandments, but to enable believers to fulfill them (3.3.14).

What, then, is meant by Christian "freedom" from the law? First and fore-most, Christians are delivered from the law's demand for perfect righteousness and its condemnation of all transgressors (2.7.14; 3.19.2; *Comm.* Rom. 6:14; 7:2; Gal. 3:25). Freed from that dread, they can willingly and cheerfully obey God's will (*Inst.* 3.19.4), knowing that their services, "however small, rude, and imper-fect these may be," are accepted by their heavenly Father (3.19.5; *Comm.* Gal. 5:18). The same freedom of spirit, to be sure, was already enjoyed by "Moses and Daniel, all the godly kings, priests and prophets and the whole company of be-lievers" before Christ: "they had been taught about the free pardon of sins, and their consciences were delivered from the tyranny of sin and death" (*Comm.* Gal. 4:1). Israel before Christ was, however, bound by the yoke of its ceremonial laws: these oppressed the shoulders but hardly the spirits of those who saw in them a foreshadowing of the Savior, but amounted to a true slavery for those who adhered to the "bare law" without discerning its significance as a "school-master to bring them to Christ" (*Comm.* Gal. 4:1, 24). By way of contrast, Chris-tians are now "free as to all outward matters," with a freedom that must be stoutly maintained: such observances can quickly degenerate into superstitions that trouble the conscience (*Inst.* 3.19.7-8; *Comm.* Gal. 4:1). Christian freedom is not, however, an excuse for indulging sinful desires or giving offense to others (*Inst.* 3.19.9).

We began our look at "law narrowly defined" with a reference to the prom-ise attached to the "righteousness of the law": perfect obedience would be re-warded with eternal salvation. Such obedience, we noted, is not to be found.[13] Yet even this divine promise Calvin will not allow to have been empty. When we embrace the gospel, our obedience remains imperfect; yet God "suppl[ies] what is lacking to complete it" and so "causes us to receive the benefit of the promises of the law as if we had fulfilled their condition" (2.7.4; cf. 3.17.3; *Comm.* Rom. 3:22).

3. *The Election of God's People:* Divine predestination follows inevitably from (Calvin's understanding of) divine providence: if all that happens has been decreed by God, then God has determined those who will come to faith.

---

13. Not even among Christians. Calvin insists that Rom. 8:4 does not mean that believers "make such progress that the righteousness of the law is full or complete in them." The verse re-fers rather to the forgiveness of their sins, by which they are accounted just and the law's de-mand is satisfied (*Comm.* Rom. 8:4).

God's people are thus his "elect." But (as a simple matter of observation) not all come to faith. This too, then, must have been divinely decreed: "eternal life is foreordained for some, eternal damnation for others" (*Inst.* 3.21.5).

The pattern is clear already with Abraham: "one people is peculiarly chosen, while the others are rejected" (3.21.5). Indeed, God's election immediately becomes more limited still, in that not all of Abraham's race itself are chosen: Ishmael and Esau may stand for those descendants of Abraham excluded from God's people (3.21.6). The confinement of God's covenant to a single nation has, since Christ, been done away with and salvation offered to all (2.11.11-12; 3.24.17); but election remains. This "general call, by which God invites all equally to himself through the outward preaching of the word," is not to be confused with the "special" call by which the Spirit of God so illumines the human heart that the preached word is received with faith (3.24.8). The latter call is directed specifically to the elect. "God Himself exhorts all men to repentance by His voice," but he "draw[s] His elect by the secret operation of His Spirit" (*Defence*, 277).[14]

Does God not love the whole human race? He does, with a love that is apparent in the gifts he has given to all. His general love does not prevent him, however, from directing his "especial or peculiar love to a few, whom he has . . . been pleased to choose out of the rest" (268). No law requires him to embrace all humankind with an equal love, and his adoption of the family of Abraham and not that of others, of Jacob and not Esau, demonstrates that he has not done so (268; cf. *Inst.* 3.22.6, 10). That the gift of eternal life is not bestowed indiscriminately upon all serves to emphasize the generosity and mercy shown to the elect (3.21.1).

Not that the reprobate have reason to complain: their own guilt, the result of willful sin, is the cause of their condemnation (3.23.3).

But in the end, since all are guilty, and since the elect can claim no merits of their own to set them apart from the reprobate, the election of some and not of others rests with God alone (3.24.12). God the Creator is naturally free to make some creatures oxen, others asses, and still others human beings; he has the same right, as their Creator, to designate some human beings for life, others for condemnation (3.22.1; *Comm.* Rom. 9:20, 21). "When it is said that God hardens or shows mercy to whom he wills, men are warned by this to seek no cause outside his will" (*Inst.* 3.22.11).

---

14. Cf. *Inst.* 3.22.10: "Although the voice of the gospel addresses all in general, yet the gift of faith is rare."

v. The Life of the Redeemed

Here we look at the *justification* by which sinners gain favor with God, and the *sanctification* by which they are progressively remade into his image.

1. *Justification by Faith:* Those who are accused and summoned before a judge are then "justified" if they are found innocent and acquitted of the charges brought against them. Thus in Romans 8:33 Paul can contrast "justification," by which the justified are absolved from charges brought against them, with "accusation" (*Comm.* Rom. 8:33). The justified in God's eyes are those found righteous and approved by his judgment; justification amounts to the "acceptance with which God receives us into his favor as righteous" (*Inst.* 3.11.2). What complicates the picture is the sinfulness, guilt, and corruption found in every human being, making it impossible for God to pronounce us righteous as we are (3.11.21). For sinners (and we all are sinners) justification must consist of the remission of sins and the crediting (or imputation) to us of a righteousness not found in ourselves, the righteousness of Christ (3.11.2): note how in Romans 4:6-7 Paul identifies justification with the forgiveness of sins (*Comm.* Rom. 4:6). That Paul in Romans does not use "justification" to refer to a quality (righteousness) found in believers themselves is clear as well from 3:24: if we are said to be "justified" (or "accounted righteous before God") "because we are redeemed at a price, we certainly borrow from some other source what we do not have" (*Comm.* Rom. 3:24).

Theoretically we could be justified by works if the purity and holiness of our lives measured up to the standards of God's judgment (*Inst.* 3.11.2), but this cannot happen with sinners (3.17.2). Even in "the case of believers, the best of their works is always spotted and corrupted with some impurity of the flesh. . . . Let a holy servant of God . . . choose from the whole course of his life what of an especially noteworthy character he thinks he has done. Let him well turn over in his mind its several parts. Undoubtedly he will somewhere perceive that it savors of the rottenness of the flesh, since our eagerness for well-doing is never what it ought to be" (3.14.9; cf. *Comm.* Gal. 6:8). Moreover, should individual deeds be deemed righteous, they would immediately be offset by sin that follows (*Inst.* 3.14.10): not even Christians pass a single day without falling "time and again" (3.4.28). Thus our works — whether done before or after we come to faith — can have no part in our being deemed righteous (3.11.15). "Oil will sooner be pressed from a stone than any good works from us" (3.14.5).

Some may object that when Paul excludes "works" from any role in justification, his concern is not with works in general but with the works of the law; even more specifically, it is the law's ceremonial demands (in particular, that of circumcision) that are at issue in his epistles. Calvin grants the point only to dismiss its relevance: "Of course I admit that Paul is there [= in Galatians] discussing ceremonies, for his quarrel is with false apostles who were trying to reintroduce into the Christian church the old shadows of the law that had been abolished by Christ's coming. But for the discussion of this question, the higher topics upon which the whole controversy rested had to be considered" (3.19.3; cf. *Comm.* Gal. 2:15). Paul's rejection of circumcision, the food laws, and the like rests upon fundamental considerations. Only the "mad" would think that Paul, in saying that life was promised to those who do the law's works, intended only its ceremonial requirements, or that the transgression of the latter is what brings the curse of Galatians 3:10. Elsewhere Paul says that the law brings the knowledge of sin and effects God's wrath (Rom. 3:20; 4:15). He says that justification is "not the reward of works but is given unearned [Rom. 4:4-5]"; that if a law could have imparted life, then righteousness would have been by the law (Gal. 3:21). "Let them now babble, if they dare, that these statements apply to ceremonies, not to morals. Even schoolboys would hoot at such impudence. Therefore, let us hold as certain that when the ability to justify is denied to the law, these words refer to the whole law" (*Inst.* 3.11.19).

Indeed, *no* works of our own can contribute to our justification: there are texts in which Paul excludes works without any further qualification. That, moreover, is the point of his insistence that righteousness is freely given (3.11.17) and that the law differs from faith in that the former (but not the latter) requires works (3.11.18, referring to Gal. 3:11-12). Therefore, the general principle stands: works of any sort have no place in a believer's justification (3.11.20; cf. *Sadolet, 235; Comm.* Eph. 2:9).

When our righteousness is not based on our works, we are left with no "occasion for boasting" (*Inst.* 3.11.13). Our eyes must turn from ourselves and our deeds to God's mercy and Christ's perfection (3.11.16). It is right that they do so: "man cannot without sacrilege claim for himself even a crumb of righteousness, for just so much is plucked and taken away from the glory of God's righteousness" (3.13.2). It is also reassuring: if our works were the criterion at the judgment of God, we would be plagued by doubts about its outcome (3.13.3; *Comm.* Rom. 4:14).

Before we leave the topic of justification and works, a paradox must be noted: "we are justified not without works yet not through works" (*Inst.* 3.16.1).[15] On the one hand (as we have seen), believers can never be justified by their works; they are "justified by free imputation" (3.11.11, citing 2 Cor. 5:19, 21; Rom. 4:7). Christ does not, however, remain "outside" those to whom his righ-

---

15. Alternatively, we may say that faith alone justifies, but that the faith that justifies is not alone (*Comm.* Gal. 5:6).

teousness is imputed: they become "one with him," "put on Christ and are engrafted into his body" (3.11.10). And "Christ justifies no one whom he does not at the same time sanctify" (3.16.1): forgiveness of sins and acceptance with God are only the beginning of a life in which the character of the sinner is increasingly transformed and God-pleasing works are produced.[16] Justification and sanctification must be distinguished as we distinguish the sun's light from its heat: we do not "say that the earth is warmed by its light, or lighted by its heat" (3.11.6). Still, the two are inseparable: Christ "contains both of them inseparably in himself" (3.16.1), and those who share in Christ cannot have one without the other.[17] "We dream neither of a faith devoid of good works nor of a justification that stands without them. This alone is of importance: having admitted that faith and good works must cleave together, we still lodge justification in faith, not in works" (3.16.1).

It is, then, through faith, not works, that believers are justified. But what is "faith"?

Faith is necessarily faith *in* something or someone, a trusting response *to* something or someone we encounter. In this case our faith must be in God as we encounter him in his word: there is "a permanent relationship between faith and the Word" (3.2.6). Yet God's word inspires our trust only if it assures us of God's mercy and goodness; and God's mercy and goodness are given only in Christ. Hence faith is our response of trust in God's benevolence toward us as revealed in the gospel message about Christ.

Yet true faith is much more than the belief that the gospel story is true (3.2.1); it is an "inward persuasion" that can be effected only by God's Holy Spirit (cf. 1.8.13). Not that God's Spirit operates independently of God's word, "inventing new and unheard-of revelations" or "forging a new kind of doctrine" (1.9.1): we recognize that a conviction is brought by God's Spirit precisely by its conformity to God's word (1.9.2). But God's word can have no effect on us unless it is "confirmed by the testimony of the Spirit" (1.9.3). "Without the illumination of the Holy Spirit, the Word can do nothing" (3.2.33).

Faith's assurance of God's benevolence allows believers to face God's judgment with confidence (3.2.15). They are by no means presumptuous in doing so: who "will not despise such beasts, who declare that a man is acting rashly

16. The latter works may simply be called "good," though, as we have seen, they are not, even at their best, untouched by sin that requires God's pardon.

17. Cf. *Sadolet*, 68: "If you would duly understand how inseparable faith and works are, look to Christ, who, as the Apostle teaches (I Cor. 1:30), has been given to us for justification and for sanctification. Wherever, therefore, that righteousness of faith which we maintain to be gratuitous is, there too Christ is; and where Christ is, there too is the spirit of holiness who regenerates the soul to newness of life." See also *Comm.* Rom. 6:1.

and presumptuously if he trust that God is true? For, though the Lord wills that we await all things from his goodness, they say that it is presumption to lean and rest upon it" (3.2.43). Not that faith is without its struggles with doubt and anxiety; the latter, in this life, are inevitable. But where true, God-given faith is found, "the end of the conflict is always this: that faith ultimately triumphs over those difficulties which besiege and seem to imperil it" (3.2.18).

This, then, is Calvin's definition of faith: "a firm and certain knowledge of God's benevolence toward us, founded upon the truth of the freely given promise in Christ, both revealed to our minds and sealed upon our hearts through the Holy Spirit" (3.2.7).

It remains only to be emphasized that human faith does not originate with humans as an initiative on *our* part to which God then responds with mercy; nor does it represent the human contribution (however minimal) to our justification (2.3.6-7). It is itself a "singular gift of God" (3.2.33) — why else would Paul thank God for believers' faith (*Comm.* Rom. 1:8)? — and the "principal work of the Holy Spirit" (*Inst.* 3.1.4). Finally, faith must not be misconstrued as the *cause* of justification: it is "only the instrument for receiving righteousness." Christ is "the material cause and at the same time the Author and Minister of this great benefit" (3.11.7).

How important is justification by faith for Calvin? He names it "the main hinge on which religion turns. . . . Unless you first of all grasp what your relationship to God is, and the nature of his judgment concerning you, you have neither a foundation on which to establish your salvation nor one on which to build piety toward God" (3.11.1). "Wherever the knowledge of [justification by faith] is taken away, the glory of Christ is extinguished, religion abolished, the Church destroyed, and the hope of salvation utterly overthrown" (*Sadolet,* 234).

2. *Sanctification:* Sanctification, for Calvin, is the transformation of believers by which the image of God, long "disfigured and all but obliterated through Adam's transgression," is restored (*Inst.* 3.3.9; cf. 1.15.4). "This restoration does not take place in one moment or one day or one year; but through continual and sometimes even slow advances God wipes out in his elect the corruptions of the flesh, cleanses them of guilt, consecrates them to himself as temples renewing all their minds to true purity" (3.3.9).

When justified, believers are delivered from the guilt of their sin, but the corruption of the nature inherited from Adam still remains (3.3.11; 4.15.10). Paul does indeed pray that his converts will be "blameless" on the Day of the Lord. But such perfection is the goal to which the godly must aspire; the path toward the goal is necessarily one of progression, and the end is not reached in this life (3.17.15). Sin's perversity is not fully done away with, nor do sinful desires cease, until believers are freed by death from their "warfare" (3.3.9; 4.15.11; *Comm.*

59

Rom. 7:25). Nonetheless, sin is not to "dominate or rule" in their lives,[18] and the traces of sin that remain are pardoned by God's mercy (*Inst.* 3.3.11; 3.4.28; 4.15.11).

The believer's struggle with sin is depicted in Romans 7. The struggle is not even known to those who know nothing of the sanctification of God's Spirit; without the Spirit they are not moved to resist the sinful urges of the "flesh." Believers are so moved, and thus find within themselves a conflict between the corruption of their nature and the renewing impulses of God's Spirit: "they fight against their own nature and find their own nature fighting against them." Their (Spirit-inspired) desires for good are by no means without some efficacy; still, as long as something of sin's corruption remains, the goodness that believers do is never done with wholehearted fervency, and hence always falls short of what they desire: "the good which I *would* I do not" (*Comm.* Rom. 7:14-20).

In view of their continuing failures, Christians remain dependent throughout their lives on the grace of divine forgiveness. They are equally dependent on God's grace and Spirit for any victories they achieve over the flesh (*Inst.* 3.14.9) and for any good works they may do. The works believers do are, in one sense, their own: no *outside* force impels Christians' actions, but they act as moved by their own heart and will (2.3.14); and God, having pardoned the imperfections that remain attached to all they do, is pleased to reward them (3.15.3-4). Still, believers' readiness to do good is itself a product of divine grace, an *inner* work of the Spirit that shapes their wills: "Does not the Spirit of God . . . nourish the very inclination to obedience that he first engendered, and strengthen its constancy to persevere?" (2.3.11). Grace "forms both choice and will in the heart, so that whatever good works then follow are the fruit and effect of grace" (2.3.13).

And it is only by grace that the elect persevere to the end. The faith of some is transitory — even though its beginnings are the product of the Spirit's working, they are granted "a momentary awareness of [God's] grace," and they appear to differ in no way from the elect (3.2.10-11). "It daily happens that those who seemed to be Christ's, fall away from him again, and hasten to destruction" (3.24.7). In the end the only explanation why some persevere and others do not is that the former, though not the latter, have been given the gift of perseverance (2.5.3).

Finally, we should note that God, in giving believers the grace they need, uses human and visible means to communicate it, and these must not be neglected. The visible church is a "school" for believers in their weakness, and they are to remain its "pupils" all their lives: "it is always disastrous to leave the church" (4.1.4).

---

18. Sin "ceases only to reign" — it "does not also cease to dwell" — in believers (*Inst.* 3.3.11).

How is a church of God to be recognized? Not by the perfection of its people, doctrine, or practice. Those who spurn "association with all men in whom they discern any remnant of human nature" are surely possessed of a "false conviction of their own perfect sanctity" (4.1.13); and "since all men are somewhat beclouded with ignorance, either we must leave no church remaining, or we must condone delusion in those matters which can go unknown without harm to the sum of religion and without loss of salvation" (4.1.12). The distinguishing marks of a church of God are that the word of God is "purely preached and heard, and the sacraments administered according to Christ's institution" (4.1.9; *Comm.* Gal. 1:2).

Both preaching and the sacraments are divinely given aids for believers' faith. God has appointed pastors for his people, and Christians are to "allow themselves to be governed by teachers appointed to this function." It is God's will that believers be taught "through human means"; those who "deem preaching superfluous," imagining that "they can profit enough from private reading and meditation," cannot escape the penalty of falling into "pestilent errors and foulest delusions" (*Inst.* 4.1.5).

Yet the preaching and practice of the church have authority only when grounded in Scripture. The foundation of the church is the "apostles and prophets" (Eph. 2:20), and the revelations given to them are contained in the Scriptures (*Sadolet,* 229-30; *Inst.* 4.8.13). Through them God's Spirit spoke. And though the preached word can bear no fruit unless the Spirit illumines its hearers to perceive its truth, those who boast of the Spirit's leading *apart* from God's word inevitably fall prey to "strange doctrines" (4.8.13-14). "It is no less unreasonable to boast of the Spirit without the Word, than it would be absurd to bring forward the Word itself without the Spirit" (*Sadolet,* 231).

The sacraments (baptism, the Lord's Supper), too, are a divinely ordained aid to faith and gift to God's church. As their administration was first entrusted to the apostles, so today they are to be administered within the church by those appointed to the ministry (*Inst.* 4.15.20). And indeed, the sacraments must always be related to the preaching and promises of the gospel, without which they are devoid of meaning (4.14.3-4). Their function is the same as that of God's word: "to offer and set forth Christ to us, and in him the treasures of heavenly grace" (4.14.17). What they add to the preaching of the word is a visible representation of God's promises (4.14.5). So understood, they "serve our faith before God" at the same time as they "attest our confession before men" (4.14.13).

vi. Summary

God has decreed all that takes place in his creation, and by his omnipotence he brings it to pass. God is the cause even of events in which wrong is committed. The evil itself is to be ascribed to the human being who acts in defiance of God's commands (though, inevitably, the will that defies has also been steered by God to do so). God's own purposes, even when he uses human evil to achieve them, are good.

God implanted in the human mind an awareness of his divinity. The reality and majesty of God are confirmed by the display of his workmanship in creation. A recognition of God's greatness and of our dependence on him should lead human beings to trust him and obey his commands. But Adam sinned, and human nature — including human reason and will — has been corrupted. Of true righteousness fallen humanity is incapable.

Christ, the "anointed one," does the work of the three offices with which Scripture associates anointing with oil. As king, he guides and provides for his people on their way to eternal life. As prophet, he fully declared the Father's will. As priest, he offered himself to expiate our sins and obtain for sinners God's favor.

Those in every age who respond to the mercy offered in Christ belong to the covenant God made with Abraham. The Mosaic religion itself was but a reminder of that covenant of grace, its ceremonies and sacraments all pointing to Christ: "law," when understood as the whole Mosaic order, in no way conflicts with the gospel. The law of Moses contained ceremonial and judicial elements whose observance was required only of ancient Israel. Its moral component, however, is a clear and unambiguous statement of God's will for all people everywhere. When detached from the covenant of God's grace, the "bare" (moral) law makes demands for righteousness that contrast sharply with the gospel of God's freely offered mercy. Yet Christ is the goal of the moral law as well: it serves to draw attention to our weakness and need of divine mercy, drives us to seek that mercy in Christ, then provides direction for the conduct of Christians. Though the Spirit is given to enable believers to fulfill God's commandments, it does not replace the guiding role of the law.

The gospel offers salvation to all. But God enables only those he has elected for salvation to respond with saving faith. When the latter hear the gospel, the Spirit illumines their minds and persuades them of its truth.

Believers are "justified" when their sins are forgiven and they are credited with the righteousness of Christ. Human "works" have no place in justification, for nothing we do is free of sin. "Justification" is to be distinguished from "sanctification," the gradual transformation of believers by which the image of

God in them is restored. The transformation, which is never complete in this life, is, again, the work of the Spirit, who inclines the will of believers to desire what is good and enables them to do it. Preaching grounded in Scripture and sacraments understood to visibly represent God's promises in the gospel are marks of the true church of God; they are also aids God uses to communicate his grace to believers.

Chapter 4

John Wesley

Pelagius, John Wesley suspected, was one of the "holiest men" of his age; his reputation as "the arch-heretic" Wesley attributed to the slander and abuse of an angry Augustine (*Sermons*, 2:555-56).[1] Luther's celebrated *Commentary on Galatians* Wesley deemed an excellent book until he read it; then it struck him as "shallow," "muddy and confused," irresponsible in its denunciation of reason and blasphemous in its dismissal of good works and God's law (*JWJ*, June 15, 1741). The God of Calvin he thought worse than the devil: why should the latter even bother going about like a roaring lion seeking whom he might devour if God, by his own unchangeable decrees, achieves the devil's end more efficiently by compelling humans to sin their way to damnation (cf. *Sermons*, 3:556-57)?[2]

Can Wesley, then, be added to Augustine, Luther, and Calvin as a further proponent of the "Lutheran" Paul? Clearly the boundaries of the category will need to be extended if it is to include the Methodist preacher; just as clearly, they should. Wesley's tireless proclamation of justification by faith without works breathed vitality into the "Lutheran" message and brought throngs of

1. The abbreviations and short forms used to identify Wesley's works in the text are spelled out in the bibliography.

2. Wesley identified with the moral earnestness of Pelagius. Note, however, that he thought Pelagius had been misrepresented; no affinity for the heresy commonly known as Pelagianism is to be inferred. Wesley's comments on Luther's *Galatians* are revealing (cf. also *Sermons*, 3:505), but should be balanced with a reminder that, on a famous May evening in 1738, Wesley's heart was "strangely warmed," he felt he trusted Christ alone for salvation, and he was given assurance that even *his* sins had been pardoned while listening to a reading of Luther's "Preface to the Epistle to the Romans" (*JWJ*, May 24, 1738); and Luther's *Galatians* led to his brother Charles's conversion. Calvinist notions of predestination Wesley found profoundly horrifying; on justification by faith (the primary criterion by which we are defining the "Lutheran" Paul), however, Wesley insisted that he differed from Calvin not "an hair's breadth" (*JWJ*, May 14, 1765).

staggering proportions to its hearing for more than half a century; the effects are still abundantly with us. That Wesley departed from Augustine, Luther, and Calvin in significant ways only increases his value for our study. In several respects his views represent better than theirs how many who espouse the "Lutheran" dogma understand both it and, of course, the Pauline texts on which it rests.

Here we will trace Wesley's retelling of the story of redemption, take up his views of the law and the Spirit, then allow Wesley to address, with the breathtaking candor for which he is renowned, the issues of providence and the "divine decrees."

i. Of Human Nature and the Covenant of Works

In Wesley's day "many laboured panegyrics" could be read and heard on the "dignity of human nature": on the wisdom, virtue, and felicity thought generally to prevail among human beings. One "ingenious gentleman" thought the Bible the "finest book" he had ever read — apart from its "mediatorial scheme." None but sinners, after all, could need a mediator, and the gentleman in question did not see how that opprobrious designation could pertain to so worthy a fellow as himself. "It is true, I often act wrong for want of more understanding. And I frequently *feel* wrong tempers, particularly proneness to anger. But I cannot allow this to be a sin; for it depends on the motion of my blood and spirits, which I cannot help. Therefore it cannot be a sin. Or if it be, the blame must fall, not on *me,* but on him that made me." Wesley comments wryly: "Some years ago a charitable woman discovered that there was no sinner in the world but the devil. 'For,' said she, 'he *forces* men to act as they do.' . . . But these more enlightened gentlemen have discovered that 'there is no sinner in the world but God'" (4:151).

If Wesley argues by way of contrast that human nature is entirely corrupt (2:190), that human beings, left to their own resources, are as incapable of doing or even thinking anything good as they are of creating themselves (1:404), he also insists that the Creator bears none of the blame. At their creation humans were able to live in a perfectly holy, perfectly happy manner — indeed, they were "capable of God" (4:153): endowed with a capacity, that is, for living in communion with God, made to be "happy in God," though "nothing else can make [us] happy" (4:64). Human nature was not immutable, however; rather, humanity was placed in a "state of trial," competent to continue in, but liable to lose, God's favor and their bliss (2:189).

Just as, if I know the sun is shining, then it must necessarily be shining, but my knowledge does not make it shine, so God (according to Wesley) in eternity knows all that his creatures of time will do, and they necessarily act in accordance with God's knowledge of their actions, without that knowledge being the *cause* of what they do (2:417). On the contrary, when God created human beings in his own image and endued them with understanding and will, he also gave them liberty (2:540-41): "a power of directing [their] own affections and actions, a capacity of determining [themselves], of choosing good or evil" (2:401). In short, God created human beings as free agents, "and he deals with [them] as free agents from first to last" (2:531). Were God to compel our actions or the movements of our will, "man would be man no longer; his inmost nature would be changed. He would no longer be a moral agent, any more than the sun or the wind" (2:488).[3] God would thus be opposing, even destroying, his own work (2:531). "Therefore (with reverence be it spoken) the Almighty himself cannot do this thing. He cannot thus contradict himself, or undo what he has done" (2:541).

The liberty inherent in human nature is, moreover, essential to human virtue — and vice. It is not enough, for Wesley, to say that the actions of human beings are "voluntary," the product of their own will, if the will itself is "irresistibly impelled" by God to choose what he has predetermined for them; for then people would be "no more blamable for that will, than for the actions which follow it. There is no blame if they are under a necessity of willing."[4] The choices we make must not be orchestrated by God if we are to bear their responsibility.

Also inherent in the human condition is our subjection to the divine law — the *moral* law — that is written on our hearts. There is nothing arbitrary about it (2:12). The law to which we must submit is "coeval" with our nature (2:7) and "must remain in force, upon all mankind, and in all ages; as not depending either on time or place, or any other circumstances liable to change, but on the nature of God and the nature of man, and their unchangeable relation to each other" (1:552). "In every particular case God wills this or this (suppose that men should honour their parents) because it is right, agreeable to the fitness of things, to the relation wherein they stand" (2:13). The various divine requirements are summed up in (though not replaced by) the command to love both God and our neighbor (1:542; 2:38).

"To the entire law of love which was written in [Adam's] heart (against

---

3. Cf. also *Sermons*, 2:475: "Without liberty man had been so far from being a *free agent* that he could have been no *agent* at all. . . . He that is not free is not an *agent*, but a *patient*."

4. *Necessity*, 467 (the argument, incidentally, is made in response to the work of Jonathan Edwards); cf. *Sermons*, 2:417-18.

which, perhaps, he could not sin directly) it seemed good to the sovereign wisdom of God to superadd one positive law" (1:184). Adam's obedience to the God who made him was to be tested by the command not to eat of the tree of the knowledge of good and evil. The "covenant" with God to which Adam in paradise was thus subject was one of "works": perfect obedience was required if he was to continue in "the holiness and happiness wherein he was created" (1:204). Paul has this covenant in mind when in Romans 10:5 he sums up the "righteousness of the law" in the words "Do this and live" (1:202-4). The test confronting Adam was real, but also realistic: he was created "equal to the task assigned, and thoroughly furnished for every good word and work" (1:184).

Adam sinned, flatly declaring that he "would no longer have God to rule over him" (2:189), and losing in the process the favor and image of God. The nature that humans inherit from Adam has been entirely corrupted. In Romans 6:6 Paul refers to it as "our old man": a "strong and beautiful expression for that entire depravity and corruption which by nature spreads itself over the whole man, leaving no part uninfected" (*Notes,* on Rom. 6:6). Elsewhere he calls it the "flesh," and it is clear from Paul's list of the flesh's "works" (Gal. 5:19-21) that the term does not mean "the body or sensual appetites and inclinations only, but the corruption of human nature as it spreads through all the powers of the soul, as well as all the members of the body" (*Notes,* on Gal. 5:21). Left to ourselves, though we may of course do what is "good and profitable" to others, we are incapable of works that are "good in themselves, or good in the sight of God" (*Sermons,* 1:192). True human goodness must truly reflect humanity's position in God's universe; it must express perfect faith in God and that love for him that "produces love to all mankind" (1:193; cf. *Farther Appeal,* 106). Such faith and love are foreign to fallen humanity.

Yet humanity was created that we "might know, and love, and enjoy, and serve [our] great Creator to all eternity" (*Sermons,* 4:26). The task of religion, then, must be "to renew our hearts in the image of God, to repair that total loss of righteousness and true holiness which we sustained by the sin of our first parents" (2:185). The religion of Jesus Christ is in effect "God's method of healing a soul which is *thus diseased*" (2:184).

ii. The Covenant of Grace and the Path to Faith

Adam alone lived under the "covenant of works." It was designed to enable him to continue in holiness and happiness but was by no means suited to restoring bliss to sinful humankind (1:210). After Adam's sin the covenant of works was immediately replaced by one of grace. "This covenant saith not to sinful man,

'Perform unsinning obedience and live.' . . . Indeed, strictly speaking, the covenant of *grace* doth not require us to *do* anything at all . . . but only to *believe*" (1:207). It depends for its validity on the "merits and mediation" of God's own Son (1:206), who sacrificed himself to atone for the sins of the whole world. Reconciled to sinners by the death of his Son, God offers "on one only condition (which himself also enables us to perform) both to remit the punishment due to our sins, to reinstate us in his favour, and to restore our dead souls to spiritual life, as the earnest of life eternal" (1:186).

The new covenant was offered, somewhat obscurely, as a promise already to Adam (Gen. 3:15); "a little more clearly" to Abraham (Gen. 22:16-18; cf. *JWJ*, Oct. 9, 1777); then more fully still to Moses, David, and the prophets that followed — and "through them to many of the people of God in their respective generations" (*Sermons*, 1:206-7). Now this "covenant of forgiveness, of unmerited love, of pardoning mercy" is freely proclaimed to all: "Believe in the Lord Jesus Christ, and thou shalt be saved" (1:208; cf. Acts 16:31).

This is good news, of course. But it provokes at least two sweeping concerns that Wesley needs to allay. The first pertains to the billions who have never heard of the Lord Jesus Christ: unable to believe in him, have they no possibility of salvation? The second is even more universal: if humans, left to themselves, are too sinful to muster a single good thought, how can any summon up the faith necessary for salvation?

That human beings, left to their own resources, are incapable of good is an important but purely theoretical point, since God does not leave us to our "own resources" (cf. 3:207). The Son of God brings light to everyone who comes into the world; to this supernatural enlightenment may be ascribed the knowledge of God, and the awareness of the difference between moral good and evil, found even among the heathen (3:199-200, 482; cf. John 1:9). The Spirit of God "strives" with human hearts, prompting desires for good, inwardly "checking" evil desires, creating unease in those who sin against the light they have been given (2:175; 3:482; cf. Gen. 6:3). The divine Father "draws" people by planting desires for God in their hearts; if we yield to them, they "increase more and more" (2:156-57; cf. John 6:44). The ability to respond to these visitations of God's "preventing" grace itself lies in a supernatural restoration of a measure of free will to fallen human hearts (*Predestination*, 229-30).

Yet these stirrings of divine grace are not irresistible; or if for a time they overpower human resistance, yet before and after such moments God's grace may be refused (*JWJ*, Aug. 24, 1743; *Predestination*, 204; *Sermons*, 2:490). God wants all to be saved, but he forces no one: not, of course, because he lacks the resources, but because compulsion would destroy human nature as he himself made it. He wants all to be saved, "yet not as trees or stones, but as men, as reasonable creatures, endued with understanding to discern what is good, and liberty either to accept or reject it" (*Predestination*, 232). Alas, the subtle promptings of God's Spirit are often stifled and forgotten (*Sermons*, 2:157). The human being does not live who has not many times resisted the Holy Spirit. Yet every human being "has at some time 'life and death set before him,' eternal life and eternal death, and has in himself the casting vote" (2:490; cf. Deut. 30:19; *JWJ*, Aug. 24, 1743). Those who lose their own soul have chosen their own destiny (*Sermons*, 3:188).

What about the heathen? The dictum "He that believeth not shall be damned" applies only to those to whom the gospel has been preached (3:295; cf. Mark 16:16). If those who are without the law are judged without the law (so Rom. 2:12), the same principle must apply to those without the proclamation of the gospel. "Inasmuch as to them little is given, of them little will be required. . . . No more, therefore, will be expected of them than the living up to the light they had": such light, that is, as is given them by the promptings of divine grace, though some may well have been inwardly taught by God "all the essentials of true religion" (3:494; cf. Luke 12:48; John 6:45). In any case, judgment must be left to God. "But this we know, that he is not the God of the Christians only, but the God of the heathens also; that he is 'rich in mercy to all that call upon him,' 'according to the light they have'; and that 'in every nation he that feareth God and worketh righteousness is accepted of him'" (3:296; cf. Rom. 10:12; 2 Cor. 8:12; Acts 10:35).

How can saving faith be found in any sinful human being? Only as a gift of resistible grace. Faith is by no means to be reduced to orthodox beliefs: the devils themselves believe all the truths of Scripture and the creeds, but they are not saved (1:138-39, 230, 418).[5] "Over and above" such belief, faith is a "sure trust in the mercy of God through Christ Jesus. It is a confidence in a pardoning God" (1:230); and only God himself can give us assurance of his pardon. He "calls" faith into existence not with the "outward call" of the preached gospel alone, but also with the "inward call" of God's Spirit "applying his Word, enabling [the hearer] to believe in the only-begotten Son of God" (2:419). Yet even here the divine "enablement" is not compulsive; God "assist[s] . . . without depriving any . . . of that liberty which is essential to a moral agent" (2:489).

Normally those led by God on the path to faith pass through three stages: the natural, the legal, and the evangelical. A word is in order on each.

1. On reading *The Life of Sir William Penn*, Wesley thought the subject a "wise and good man" but was confounded by a remark attributed to Penn's first wife shortly before her death: "I bless God I never did any thing wrong in my

---

5. The allusion is of course to James 2:19.

life!" "Was she then," Wesley wondered, "ever convinced of sin? And if not, could she be saved on any other footing than a *heathen?*" (*JWJ*, Jan. 9, 1786).[6]

Had Wesley seen Mrs. Penn in the crowd at one of his 5:00 A.M. sermons,[7] we may be certain that he would not have preached on justification by faith: "it is absurd . . . to offer a physician to them that are whole, or that at least imagine themselves so to be" (*Sermons*, 2:23). Those in an "unawakened" *natural* state need first to hear the law.[8] They may well be happy, ignorant as they are of the pit on whose brink they stand. They serve sin willingly without being troubled or feeling condemned, content in the claim that all have their infirmities (1:251-54). They neither fear nor love God (1:263).

2. The transition to the *legal* state begins when "God touches the heart of him that lay asleep" (1:255). Conviction of sin is aroused by the Holy Spirit, whose "ordinary" tool for the task is the law (2:15). Sinners now sense the true meaning and extent of God's law; they see God as punishing its transgression, and they fear him (1:255-57). A desire is kindled in them to break free from sin: they struggle but cannot prevail (1:258, 263). Now, with a "lively" sense of their "inward and outward sin," they recognize and lament their "utter guiltiness and helplessness" (1:229).

Such repentance, such knowledge of oneself as a sinner, is a necessary prelude to faith: "Does not all experience as well as Scripture prove that no man ever yet truly 'believed the gospel' who did not first *repent?*" (*Farther Appeal*, 116). The whole process is powerfully portrayed by Paul in Romans 7 (*Sermons*, 1:258-60). Though he writes in the first person, Paul (as he sometimes does) is "assuming another character (Rom. 3:5; 1 Cor. 10:30; 4:6)" to depict "in the most lively manner" how one "ignorant of the law" comes under its sway, then "sin-

---

6. As we have seen, Wesley did not in fact rule out the salvation of the heathen. The point here, however, is that in Wesley's eyes Mrs. Penn could not have been a true *Christian* without ever having been convinced of her own sin.

7. So, for half a century, Wesley began each day. The early start provided a perfect alibi to charges that Wesley's preaching kept people from their work. For his own part Wesley believed that among the factors contributing to his longevity and physical well-being must be reckoned the regimen of "constant preaching at five in the morning, for above fifty years" (*JWJ*, June 28, 1788). When Methodists no longer gathered for 5:00 A.M. sermons, he could only lament the decline in their spiritual condition (*JWJ*, Mar. 15 and Apr. 5, 1784).

8. Cf. *JWJ*, Mar. 23, 1777: "I preached at St. Ewen's Church, but not upon justification by faith. I do not find this to be a profitable subject to an unawakened congregation. I explained here, and strongly applied, that awful word, 'It is appointed unto men once to die.'" Cf. also Wesley's reflections on when to "preach the law" and when to "preach the gospel" in his letter "to an Evangelical Layman" (London, Dec. 20, 1751; *Letters*, 2:482-89). Note that here he defines "preaching the law" as "explaining and enforcing the commands of Christ, briefly comprised in the Sermon on the Mount" (482). Also *Sermons*, 2:22-26.

cerely but ineffectually" strives to serve God (*Notes,* on Rom. 7:7).[9] Similarly, the "spirit of bondage" in Romans 8:15 refers to the operation of the Holy Spirit by which the soul comes to perceive its enslavement to sin and liability to God's wrath (*Notes,* on Rom. 8:15).

3. To some the gift of faith is granted as soon as they call upon God; others "equally athirst for salvation" may be left to mourn for months, even years. We cannot know why this is so (*Sermons,* 2:584). The coming of faith is itself unmistakable:

> a man . . . "is not to think well of his own state, till he experiences something within himself which he has not yet experienced," but "which he may be beforehand assured he shall," if the promises of God are true. That "something" is a living faith: "a sure trust and confidence in God, that by the merits of Christ his sins are forgiven, and he reconciled to the favour of God." And from this will spring many other things which till then he experienced not, as the love of God, shed abroad in his heart, that peace of God which passeth all understanding, and joy in the Holy Ghost. . . . These are some of those *inward* "fruits of the Spirit," which must be *felt,* wheresoever they are. (*JWJ,* July 31, 1739; cf. Aug. 14, 1771)[10]

9. Wesley insists that the thrust of the whole passage is missed if it is thought to depict the experience of Paul himself or of any true believer; he points to Rom. 8:2 as showing that the believer has been delivered from the fruitless struggle of the preceding verses. See also *Sermons,* 1:341.

10. Wesley's journal tells of his own surprise and discomfiture when he was asked directly, "Does the Spirit of God bear witness with your spirit that you are a child of God?" "Do you know [Christ] has saved you?" (*JWJ,* Feb. 7, 1736). Unable to give a forthright positive response, Wesley came to believe that he had served God with great rigor for years while still lacking saving faith (*JWJ,* Feb. 1, 1738; Mar. 5, 1738; May 24, 1738). He realized that "true faith in Christ" should be accompanied by "constant peace from a sense of forgiveness," that "no one could (in the nature of things) have such a sense of forgiveness and not *feel* it. But I felt it not." He was told that "this faith was the gift, the free gift of God, and that he would surely bestow it upon every soul who earnestly and perseveringly sought it. . . . I resolved to seek it unto the end" — and "continued thus to seek it . . . till Wednesday, May 24" (*JWJ,* May 24, 1738; see n. 2 above).

Wesley came to believe, however, that *"degrees of faith"* should be acknowledged, that "a man may have *some degree* of it before all things in him are become new; before he has the full assurance of faith, the abiding witness of the Spirit, or the clear perception that Christ dwelleth in him" (*JWJ,* Dec. 31, 1739). A distinction must be drawn (Wesley had not earlier done so) between the "servant" and the "child" of God. God's "servants" have been granted the faith to "fear God and work righteousness," and they are accepted by God; but they are not God's "children" until they know the "witness of the Spirit" in their heart assuring them of their adoption into God's family. Yet servants, unless they "halt by the way," will one day receive such adoption, and they must be encouraged "to expect it every moment": "Rest not till that Spirit clearly witnesses with your spirit that you are a child of God" (*Sermons,* 3:497-98; cf. 4:35-36).

That God in his own good time will grant faith is certain: "to all who see, and feel, and own their wants, and their utter inability to remove them, God freely gives faith, for the sake of him 'in whom he is always well pleased'" (*Earnest Appeal*, 48-49). In the meantime, those seeking God's favor are not to be idle. Christ has "ordained certain outward means, for conveying His grace into the souls of men" (*Sermons*, 1:378; cf. *JWJ*, Dec. 31, 1739; *Letters*, 2:27-28). These "means of grace" include prayer, searching the Scriptures, and receiving the Lord's Supper (*Sermons*, 1:381). God is not bound to use any of these means in granting faith to sinners; nor is there any "inherent power" in them apart from the work of God's Spirit (1:382). Above all, we must not "trust" in anything we do — including our observance of the means of grace — as though it were able to atone for a single sin or merit the least of God's favor (1:382-83). Yet we are not seeking salvation by works when we wait for God's promise in the way he has ordained. "I do expect that he will fulfil his Word, that he will meet and bless me in this way. Yet not for the sake of any works which I have done, nor for the merit of my righteousness; but merely through the merits and sufferings and love of his Son" (1:391).

Faith is the only condition for justification (2:162). Though the latter term is occasionally used in "so wide a sense as to include sanctification," both "St. Paul and the other inspired writers" generally employ it to mean the pardoning, or remission, of sins and — as a result of their sins' forgiveness — the acceptance of sinners by God. Nor should the nature of their pardoning be misconstrued: "justification" does not mean that "God is *deceived* in those whom he justifies," that he "believes us righteous when we are unrighteous," still less that he approves us because he "confounds" us with Christ. It is simply the act of God the Father by which, "for the sake of the propitiation made by the blood of his Son," he pardons the sins of the ungodly who believe (1:187-90). That pardoning is a present reality. Though "justification" sometimes refers to "our acquittal at the last day," at the final judgment (*Farther Appeal*, 105), more normally it denotes present forgiveness and the change of a sinner's relation with God. The divine "favor" that Adam forfeited by his sin is restored to justified sinners (*Sermons*, 1:431-32).

It remains to be noted that when Paul declares that justification is "by faith," he adds that it is not "by the works of the law" (Rom. 3:28). Deeds demanded by the *moral* law are intended: Paul cannot have been thinking of the "ritual" or "ceremonial" law of Moses, since he goes on to insist that "we establish the law" (Rom. 3:31); and the law that is affirmed by faith is not, of course, that prescribing ceremonial observances, but "the great, unchangeable law of love, the holy love of God and of our neighbour" (1:194; cf. 2:21).

Yet even obedience to the law of love cannot be a condition for justification, since the "ungodly" whom God justifies are incapable of such obedience (1:194; cf. *JWJ*, Sept. 13, 1739; Dec. 13, 1739; *Predestination*, 205). When Paul redundantly asserts that believers are justified "freely by [God's] grace" (Rom. 3:24), he could not find words that "more absolutely exclude all consideration of our own works and obedience, or more emphatically ascribe the whole of our justification to free, unmerited goodness" (*Notes*, on Rom. 3:24). Later in Romans (11:6) Paul points out that justification by grace and justification by works necessarily exclude each other. "For what is given to works is the payment of a debt; whereas grace implies an unmerited favor. So that the same benefit cannot, in the very nature of things, be derived from both" (*Notes*, on Rom. 11:6). We are here dealing with the "very foundation of Christianity," that "a man can merit nothing of God" but that we are justified "not for any of our works or of our deservings, but by faith in the blood of the covenant" ("Protestant," 188). None can truly trust in "the merits of Christ till he has utterly renounced his own" (*Sermons*, 1:127; cf. 1:418-19, 458). Indeed, the faith that God has "fixed" as the "condition of justification" is "peculiarly fitted" to humble the proud:

> for he that cometh unto God by this faith must fix his eye singly on his own wickedness, on his guilt and helplessness, without having the least regard to any supposed good in himself, to any virtue or righteousness whatsoever. He must come as a *mere sinner* inwardly and outwardly, self-destroyed and self-condemned, bringing nothing to God but ungodliness only, pleading nothing of his own but sin and misery. Thus it is, and thus alone, when his "mouth is stopped," and he stands utterly "guilty before God," that he can "look unto Jesus" as the whole and sole "propitiation for his sins." (1:197-98)

iii. The New Birth and the Path to Sanctification

Though justification is logically prior to the new birth (or "regeneration"), the two take place simultaneously (1:431; 2:187). Justification is something God does *for* us; the new birth he brings about *in* us. Justification restores us to God's favor; the new birth, to his image. Justification changes our outward relationship to God; the new birth effects a real inward change from wickedness to goodness, from the love of creatures to the love of the Creator (*JWJ*, Sept. 13, 1739). Justification removes the guilt of sin, the new birth banishes sin's power (*Sermons*, 1:431-32). Since the new birth involves a new creation (2 Cor. 5:17), God our Creator must be its agent: "only the power that makes a world can make a Christian" (*Notes*, on 2 Cor. 5:17). And he does so in a moment, just as "in a moment, or at least in a very short time," a child is "born of a woman" (*Sermons,* 2:198).[11]

Those in a "legal" state struggle with sin but cannot conquer it; not so, those who are born again.

> An immediate and constant fruit of this faith whereby we are born of God, a fruit which can in no wise be separated from it, no, not for an hour, is power over sin: power over outward sin of every kind; over every evil word and work; . . . and over inward sin; for it "purifieth the heart" from every unholy desire and temper. This fruit of faith St. Paul has largely described in the sixth chapter of his Epistle to the Romans. "How shall we (saith he) who" by faith "are dead to sin, live any longer therein?" . . . Though ye were in the time past the servants of sin, yet now . . . "being free from sin, ye are become the servants of righteousness." (1:419-20)

Indeed, in the wake of their new life believers seem at first so completely triumphant over sin that they easily imagine themselves done with it. They feel nothing of it; temptation itself, for a time, may be absent. But the euphoria does not last. Temptation returns, and with it believers discover that a "proneness to evil" persists in their hearts (1:336-37, 483-84; 2:158-59, 165; 4:157). Paul indicates that all "newborn" Christians are "(in a degree) 'carnal'" (or "*fleshly*") (1:322, referring to 1 Cor. 3:1). Nearly all the exhortations to believers in Paul's writings and the rest of the Scriptures presuppose that nature and the flesh contend with grace and the Spirit in believers' lives (1:322; 2:159); and though, as long as they "are in Christ Jesus," believers will "walk after the Spirit" and neither will nor can yield to temptation,[12] they do not prevail without a struggle. Christ "can-

---

11. Cf. *Farther Appeal,* 107; also "Mr. Downes," 360: "We likewise believe that the spiritual life which commences when we are born again must, in the nature of the thing, have a *first moment,* as well as the natural." Still, Wesley is not prepared to "contend" with those who think the new birth takes place gradually: "I contend not for a circumstance, but the substance; if you can attain it another way, do. Only see that you do attain it; for if you fall short, you perish everlastingly" (*Farther Appeal,* 107).

12. Cf. 1 John 3:6, 9. "A Christian is so far perfect, as not to commit sin. [Note: by 'sin' Wesley here means 'a voluntary transgression of a known law' (*Perfection,* 396; *Sermons,* 3:79).] This is the glorious privilege of every Christian, yea, though he be but a babe in Christ" (*Perfection,* 376). To the objection "But sometimes a believer in Christ may lose his sight of the mercy of God," Wesley responds: "Supposing it so to be, supposing him not to see the mercy of God, then he is not a believer; for faith implies light, the light of God shining upon the soul. So far therefore as anyone loses this light, he for the time loses his faith. And no doubt a true believer in Christ may lose the light of faith. And so far as this is lost he may for a time fall again into condemnation. But this is not the case of them who now 'are in Christ Jesus,' who now believe in His name" (*Sermons,* 1:238).

not *reign* where sin *reigns;* neither will he *dwell* where any sin is *allowed.* But he *is* and *dwells* in the heart of every believer who is fighting against all sin" (1:323).

Nor is a proneness to evil that must be resisted the full extent of sin's continuing presence. Though as children of God believers cannot commit "voluntary" sin, they soon discover that something of sin "cleaves" to even the good they do: something of pride, self-will, unbelief, or idolatry (2:165). They sense that they do not love God as they ought, that their thoughts wander even in their times of intimacy with God, that their affections are but dull (1:240). This conviction of residual sin — a conviction again brought by God's Holy Spirit — constitutes a second repentance. Unlike the repentance that precedes justification, this one "implies no guilt, no sense of condemnation, no consciousness of the wrath of God" (2:164); nonetheless, believers "convinced of the deep corruption of their hearts . . . groan for deliverance from it" (1:351).

The path to sanctification — to holiness and total deliverance from sin — begins with regeneration (2:158, 198); the new believer sets about at once to overcome (to "put to death") the deeds inspired by the evil nature (2:160). A gradual progression may continue for years, but it need not (*Perfection,* 387, 446). God has promised complete victory over sin and perfection in love, and he is more than ready to grant what he has promised to those who believe and expect it (*Sermons,* 2:167-68). As they once waited for the faith of justification, so they must wait for "full salvation from all [their] sins," for their "entire sanctification" (2:160), expecting it "every day, every hour, every moment" (2:169). As they practiced the means of grace while waiting for saving faith, so now they should "wait" for entire sanctification "in vigorous, universal obedience" (*Perfection,* 402), performing appropriate works: prayer, receiving the Lord's Supper, searching the Scriptures, "using such a measure of fasting or abstinence as [their] bodily health allows," and doing works of mercy. "This is the way wherein God hath appointed his children to wait for complete salvation" (*Sermons,* 2:166). Still, the only condition for sanctification is faith (2:163), and to faith God will certainly grant it.

The perfection God grants his children is a perfection in love: they now love God with all their heart, mind, soul, and strength, and love their neighbor as they ought. All their "thoughts, words, and actions" are now "governed by pure love," and hence are free of sin (*Perfection,* 393-94; cf. *Sermons,* 3:74). Many can testify that such deliverance is received in a moment and perceived accordingly (3:176-78): they are able to give "a distinct account of the time and manner wherein the change was wrought" (*Perfection,* 398). Moreover, as the Spirit bears witness to their adoption as God's children, so it does of their entire sanctification (402, 420-21). Though one must not boast of the gift but speak of it "with the deepest humility and reverence, giving all the glory to God," it is by no means to be hidden "under a bushel"; telling of God's grace brings encouragement to others (397-98).[13]

Christian perfection is not absolute, however. It does not bring freedom from ignorance, from mistakes (in matters of fact, judgments of the character of others, or even the interpretation of Scripture), or from infirmities (such as slowness in understanding, incoherence in thought, or unretentiveness in memory) (*Sermons*, 2:100-105). It does not mean exemption from temptation; indeed, no state of perfection can be reached in this life from which the believer is not liable to fall (*Perfection*, 422, 426; *JWJ*, July 25, 1774). Even those "perfected in love" still need teaching, for possession of "much grace" need not be matched by "much light" (*Perfection*, 427-28). Nor is their perfection ever such that it does not admit of further growth in grace and in the "knowledge and love of God [our] Saviour" (*Sermons*, 2:104-5). "When God has . . . enabled you to love him with all your heart and with all your soul, think not of resting there. That is impossible. You cannot stand still; you must either rise or fall — rise higher or fall lower" (3:501).

iv. The Law and the Spirit

The Mosaic law, as such, was not a subject to which Wesley devoted much attention. He did wonder whether "the yoke of the ceremonial law" may not have been imposed as a punishment on Israel "for the national sin of idolatry (Exod. 32:1)" (*Notes*, on Gal. 3:19).[14] In any case, its ceremonies "pointed" to the mission of Christ (*Notes*, on Gal. 3:24); when he came, Christ "utterly abolish[ed]" it (*Sermons*, 1:551).

Not so the "moral law." Though one of three components of the Mosaic dispensation (*Perfection*, 414),[15] the moral law did not begin with Moses but was "coeval with [human] nature," written by the Creator on the human heart

---

13. Wesley's journal has many accounts of those who testify to such deliverance. Clearly its inception and possession are deemed eminently specifiable: "I rode to Methrose, near St. Austell, where we had the Quarterly Meeting for the eastern circuit. . . . This society has eighty-six members, and *all* rejoicing in the love of God. Fifty-five or fifty-six of these believe he has saved them from all sin. And their life no way contradicts their profession" (Sep. 17, 1765). "I returned to London and, Sunday 11, buried the remains of Eleanor Lee. I believe she received the great promise of God, entire sanctification, fifteen or sixteen years ago and that she never lost it for an hour" (Oct. 9 and 11, 1778).

14. Cf. *Sermons*, 1:551: "the ceremonial or ritual law . . . was only designed for a temporary restraint upon a disobedient and stiff-necked people." Similarly 2:511-12, though here Wesley notes that "many excellent moral precepts are interspersed among these ceremonial laws."

15. The others were its "political" and "ceremonial" parts.

(*Sermons*, 2:6-7). The corruption that followed Adam's sin all but effaced this inner engraving, but a kind of "reinscription" takes place thanks to the Son of God himself, who "enlightens every man that cometh into the world" with a measure of knowledge of what is good (2:7).[16] Still, God saw fit to give "more perfect knowledge of his law" to Israel; its chief requirements he wrote on two tablets of stone and commanded that they be taught to succeeding generations (2:7-8).[17]

The moral law, then, did not begin with Moses; nor was it revoked by Christ. On the contrary, God's law[18] was "never so fully explained nor so throughly understood till the great Author of it himself condescended to give mankind this authentic comment [the Sermon on the Mount] on all the essential branches of it; at the same time declaring it should never be changed, but remain in force to the end of the world" (1:553). Those who in spite of Christ's own words insist that he abolished the law and that there is now "but one duty, which is that of believing," are "withstanding our Lord to the face, and telling him that he understood not how to deliver the message on which he was sent." Surprisingly, such people "really believe that they honour Christ by overthrowing his law, and that they are magnifying his office while they are destroying his doctrine!" But "it is no other than betraying him with a kiss . . . to set light by any part of his law under pretence of advancing his gospel" (1:559).

The law's function is in part (as we have seen) to bring unawakened sinners to that "legal" state in which they are convinced of their guilt, helplessness, and need of redemption; but it continues to play a role in the lives of those who pass from the legal state to the "evangelical." At no point is the law superseded by the gospel. On the contrary, the two "agree perfectly well together," even using the "very same words," though what constitutes a commandment in the law becomes, through the gospel, a promise (1:554). The law prohibits murder, for example, thereby forbidding also (as Christ teaches) "every unkind word or thought" (cf. Matt. 5:21-22). The more I ponder this law, the more I feel my shortcomings and need, not only of Christ's blood to atone for my sin, but also of his Spirit to enable me to do what God has commanded (2:17-18). But such an enablement God has promised in the gospel. The salvation effected by the gospel, after all, is "not barely (according to the vulgar notion) deliverance from

16. Cf. John 1:9; also *Sermons*, 3:199-200.

17. Note that for Wesley the moral law includes the command to hallow the Sabbath. Inasmuch as Wesley took with utmost seriousness the injunction "Thou shalt in any wise rebuke thy neighbour, and not suffer sin upon him" (Lev. 19:17; cf. *Sermons*, 2:511-20), he found himself repeatedly constrained to offer a word of charitable admonition to "Sabbath-breakers." Cf. "Sabbath-Breaker," 164-66.

18. Note that the moral law is "often called 'the law' by way of eminence" (*Sermons*, 2:6).

hell, or going to heaven, but a present deliverance from sin, . . . the renewal of our souls after the image of God in righteousness and true holiness, in justice, mercy, and truth" (*Farther Appeal*, 106). Thus while the law sends me to Christ for forgiveness of my failings, Christ sends me to the law so that I may know, love, and carry out his will. Christ "endears" the law to me, "seeing I know every part of it is a gracious promise, which my Lord will fulfil in its season" (*Sermons*, 2:18).[19]

The goal of the gospel is thus to restore to believers the happiness and holiness forfeited by Adam's sin: happiness *and* holiness, for the one cannot be had without the other. Nor is the required holiness something merely "imputed" to believers so that they can count on God's creative bookkeeping to enable them to meet standards they otherwise ignore. "Scripture holiness is the image of God; the mind which was in Christ; the love of God and man; lowliness, gentleness, temperance, patience, chastity. And do you coolly affirm, that this is only imputed to a believer, and that he has none at all of this holiness in him? Is temperance imputed only to him that is a drunkard still; or chastity, to her that goes on in whoredom? Nay, but a believer is really chaste and temperate. And if so, he is thus far holy in himself" ("Moravian Brethren," 203; cf. *Sermons*, 1:462).

Such "inherent" holiness is not the "*ground* of our acceptance with God," but it is its "*fruit.*" "God *implants* righteousness in every one to whom he has *imputed* it. . . . God sanctifies, as well as justifies, all them that believe in [Christ]" (1:458-59). Only by a "device of Satan" have "faith and works" been deemed to oppose each other, with the result that some exclude good works not only from being the cause of justification, but also from being its "necessary fruit" (1:592-93). Wesley found it crucial to preach on the text "Without holiness no man can see the Lord" (Heb. 12:14) to all who expected to be "saved by faith," lest any should "dream of going to heaven by any faith which does not produce holiness" (*JWJ*, Apr. 7, 1777).[20] So he meant to counter the false prophets, "of whatever denomination," who encourage the sinful and slack to imagine themselves on the way to heaven (*Sermons*, 1:678). The "hottest place in the lake of fire" is reserved for "Methodists that do not fulfil all righteousness" (*JWJ*, Nov. 20, 1767).

What role does God's Spirit play in the life of the believer? Clearly Wesley could entertain no suggestion that the Spirit's guidance replaces that of the law. But the whole issue was a sensitive one. Wesley believed (as we have seen) that

---

19. Cf. *Sermons*, 1:554: "On the one hand the law continually makes way for and points us to the gospel; on the other the gospel continually leads us to a more exact fulfilling of the law."

20. Cf. *Perfection*, 431: "Beware of Solifidianism; crying nothing but, 'Believe, believe!' and condemning those as ignorant or legal who speak in a more scriptural way."

the witness of God's Spirit (Rom. 8:16) is experienced by all who are God's children (*Sermons*, 3:497-98) and that, if real, such fruit of the Spirit as love, joy, and peace must be felt (cf. *JWJ*, Aug. 14, 1771; *Notes*, on Phil. 1:9). Furthermore, his journal (particularly its earlier sections) contains many accounts of how listeners to his sermons responded with "sudden outcries and strong bodily convulsions"; and these responses Wesley, though granting that they may be "mimicked" by Satan, was inclined to see as natural consequences of the conviction of their sin aroused in sinners by God's Spirit (*JWJ*, Nov. 25, 1759).[21] Not surprisingly, then, Methodists were suspected of claiming to possess "extraordinary gifts" from the Spirit and of taking their guidance from inner "impulses" naively ascribed to him.

These accusations Wesley persistently denied. The crucial mark of the Spirit's presence in the lives of believers, he observed, is not extraordinary gifts but ordinary fruit. Guidance is to be derived, not from impulses that one attributes to the Spirit, but by a process of inquiry, assisted throughout by the Spirit, involving Scripture, reason, and experience.

1. Wesley shared the view that the extraordinary gifts had been withdrawn from the church in the early centuries,[22] and insisted that the Methodists claimed none ("Mr. Potter," 91; "Mr. Downes," 354; cf. *Sermons*, 2:52-53). The only "signs and wonders" they sought were the "conviction of sinners, . . . the turning men from darkness to light, from the power of Satan unto God" ("Mr. Potter," 91-92). The only sense in which Wesley would allow that there were "prophets" among the Methodists was that by which "every minister is a prophet"; "for we do speak in the name of God. . . . But we declare . . . nothing else as the will of God but what is evidently contained in his written Word, as explained by our own Church" (*Farther Appeal*, 173-74).[23] Wesley warned his followers of despising reason while "suppos[ing] the dreams of their own imaginations to be revelations from God" (*Sermons*, 2:587), of heeding "private revelations" rather than the written word of God (*JWJ*, Sept. 3, 1740; *Perfection*, 429), of imagining that they had the gift of prophecy or of "discerning of spirits" ("which I do not believe one of you has; no, nor ever had yet") (*Perfection*,

---

21. Cf. *JWJ*, Aug. 6, 1759: "I have generally observed more or [fewer] of these outward symptoms to attend the beginning of a general work of God. So it was in New England, Scotland, Holland, Ireland, and many parts of England. But after a time they gradually decrease, and the work goes on more quietly and silently."

22. Note, however, that Wesley attributed the loss of such gifts to the growing coldness of the church rather than to its diminished need for supernatural support of its claims (*Sermons*, 3:263-64; cf. *Notes*, on 1 Cor. 12:9; *JWJ*, Aug. 15, 1750).

23. Cf. *Notes*, on 1 Cor. 14:1: "*Prophecy* . . . here does not mean foretelling things to come; but rather opening and applying the Scripture."

430; cf. 406-7), of seeking any other "blessing" than love (430). His journal repeatedly draws attention to the banality,[24] perversity,[25] or simple falsity (cf. *Sermons*, 2:52-53)[26] of the "revelations" claimed by would-be prophets.

> Two of those who are called "prophets" desired to speak with me. They told me they were sent from God with a message to me, which was that very shortly I should be "borned" again. One of them added that they would stay in the house till it was done, unless I turned them out. I answered gravely, "I will not turn you out," and showed them down into the society room. It was tolerably cold, and they had neither meat nor drink. However there they sat from morning to evening. They then went quietly away, and I have heard nothing from them since. (*JWJ*, Nov. 3, 1742)

But Wesley discounted claims to "*extraordinary* gifts" of the Spirit only to emphasize "his *ordinary* fruits" (*Sermons*, 1:161). Of themselves, believers are no more able to think, desire, speak, or do any good than they were before they were justified (1:345). It is the Spirit who rouses in them love for God and their neighbor, who inspires their "every holy desire," who guides them to speak what promotes others' good and do what pleases God. "Being filled with faith and with the Holy Ghost, they possess in their hearts, and show forth in their lives, in the whole course of their words and actions, the genuine fruits of the Spirit of God" (1:236-37).

2. Wesley flatly denied that Methodists took guidance from "impulses and impressions" or followed any other directives than those of the word of God ("Bishop of London," 337). The danger he acknowledged: "if these *impressions* be received as the rule of action instead of the *written Word*, I know nothing so wicked or absurd but we may fall into, and that without remedy" (*JWJ*, July 13, 1741; cf. *JWJ*, June 22, 1742). To those who thought they must be "moved by the Spirit" before they should act, he pointed out that "God moves man, whom he

---

24. "The same words any person of a good understanding and well versed in the Scriptures might have spoken" (*JWJ*, Jan. 28, 1739).

25. The Reverend Westley Hall declared that God had revealed to him that he was to marry Wesley's youngest sister. She gave her consent. A few days later he claimed to have received a "counter-revelation" indicating that he was not to marry her, but her older sister. The jilted younger sister "fell into a lingering illness, which terminated in her death. And doth not her blood still cry unto God from the earth?" (*JWJ*, Dec. 22, 1747; also *Letters*, 2:269-73).

26. Wesley was told by a number of "prophets" over several years that the current year would be the last year of his life (*JWJ*, Jan. 1, 1789). Cf. also his reference to prophecies of "many terrible things" that failed to materialize, in *JWJ*, Dec. 31, 1788; also Jan. 16, 1760. Conversely, in *Sermons*, 3:302-3 Wesley recorded the remarkable accuracy with which one "prophet" foretold the future, only to note that the man so gifted later succumbed to (literal) insanity.

has made a reasonable creature, according to the reason which he has given him. He moves him by his understanding, as well as his affections; by light, as well as by heat" ("Quaker," 181; cf. *Farther Appeal,* 258-59; *Sermons,* 2:54, 592). To those who expected God to guide them in extraordinary ways (by "visions or dreams, by strong impressions or sudden impulses on the mind"), Wesley insisted that, though God may "in some very rare instances" reveal his will in such a manner, far more frequently people are misled by their pride and imagination to ascribe to God what is unworthy of him (2:54). Those who would know God's will should turn to the Scriptures. In particular cases, where the choice is not between good and evil and where Scripture does not offer specific direction, God's word nonetheless makes clear that we should choose that course of action deemed best to promote our own holiness and others' good. Reason and experience must decide between the alternatives, while the assistance of God's Spirit is basic to "the whole process of the inquiry." "This is the plain, scriptural, rational way to know what is the will of God in a particular case." Alas, the very phrase "the will of God" is so often abused by those who seek it in "unscriptural, irrational ways" that one could wish "the expression itself were far more sparingly used" (2:54-55).

v. Providence and the "Divine Decrees"

Wesley's journal records the following incident on June 15, 1782, just days before his eightieth birthday.

> As I was coming down stairs, the carpet slipped from under my feet, which, I know not how, turned me round, and pitched me back with my head foremost for six or seven stairs. It was impossible to recover myself, till I came to the bottom. My head rebounded once or twice from the edge of the stone stairs; but it felt to me exactly as if I had fallen on a cushion or a pillow. Dr. Douglas ran out sufficiently affrighted; but he needed not, for I rose as well as ever, having received no damage, but the loss of a little skin from one or two of my fingers. Doth not God "give his angels charge over us, to keep us in all our ways?"

The account is typical of many in the journal in which Wesley saw God's providential care at work in his life. If others thought it presumptuous to attribute to providence "things . . . which are not owing thereto," Wesley could only wonder what things the latter might be (*Sermons,* 2:56), since nothing is so trivial "as not to be an object of the care and providence of God" (2:537). Nor could he see any point in allowing a "general" but denying a "particular" providence. "Do you mean when you assert a general providence distinct from a particular one that God regards only some parts of the world, and does not regard others? . . . Which parts? Only those within the temperate zones? . . . Nay, rather say, 'The Lord is loving to every man,' and his care is 'over all his works'" (2:547; cf. Ps. 145:9).

But though, for Wesley, God manages wisely "all the affairs of his creation for the good of all his creatures" (2:540), God has not decreed all that happens, nor does he direct the doings of his creatures with irresistible power. Were he to do so, God would be the only real Agent in the universe and its governance would require little wisdom (cf. 2:541); at the same time, it is not clear, on such an understanding, how God's goodness could be affirmed in the face of the evil that is everywhere apparent (*JWJ*, Jan. 3, 1771; cf. *Necessity*, 466). But God has given liberty to his rational creatures, and though he "strongly and sweetly" influences all, he does not destroy what he has made (*Sermons*, 4:42-43). He governs "man as man; not as a stock or a stone, but as an intelligent and free spirit, capable of choosing either good or evil. . . . The whole frame of divine providence is so constituted as to afford man every possible help, in order to his doing good and eschewing evil, which can be done without turning man into a machine; without making him incapable of virtue or vice, reward or punishment" (2:541).

The notion that God has unconditionally and irresistibly elected some human beings for salvation while appointing others for damnation is thus incompatible with his purposes in creation and the modes of his providence. It is also "irreconcilable to the whole scope and tenor both of the Old and New Testament" (*Predestination*, 211). When Scripture speaks of election, it refers either to God's designation of particular people to particular tasks or to his unalterable decree that those who believe will find eternal happiness, while all who persist in unbelief will be reprobate: "He that believeth shall be saved; he that believeth not shall be damned" (209-10, citing Mark 16:16).[27] If the Bible speaks of those who are "elect from the foundation of the world," it does so because God knows from all eternity who will truly believe (210; cf. *Sermons*, 2:417). Indeed, God ac-

---

27. When Rom. 9:18, then, speaks of God showing mercy to "whom he will," it means that he "show[s] mercy on his own terms, namely, on them who believe," while he "leaves to the hardness of their hearts" those "whom he will," namely, "them that believe not" (*Notes*, on Rom. 9:18). Eph. 1:5 speaks of how God "foreordained that all who afterwards believed should enjoy the dignity of being sons of God, and joint-heirs with Christ"; the "good pleasure of his will" in this verse refers to "his free, fixed, unalterable purpose to confer this blessing on all those who should believe in Christ, and those only" (*Notes*, on Eph. 1:5). The topic of Rom. 9, however, is not "personal election or reprobation," but a demonstration "that God's rejecting the Jews and receiving the Gentiles was consistent with his word" (*Notes*, on Rom. 9:1).

commodates himself to our weak understanding whenever he speaks of his "purpose," "counsel," "plan," or "foreknowledge": "not that God has any need of 'counsel,' of 'purpose,' or of 'planning' his work beforehand" (2:421). He knows and works in ways we cannot conceive.

But we do know that he does not infringe on our liberty, for if he compelled our actions, or even the will with which we choose them, there could be no virtue or vice, moral good or evil, conduct rewardable or punishable by God (2:417-18; cf. *Necessity,* 463-69). Moreover, Scripture itself insists on countless occasions that God's grace is not irresistible, while it laments the stubbornness and folly of those who turn from him (*Predestination,* 254-55, citing, among other texts, Matt. 22:3; Luke 7:30; 13:34; Acts 7:51; 13:46; Heb. 3:8, 12; 12:25). Scripture indicates that "one who is a true believer, or, in other words, one who is holy or righteous in the judgment of God himself, may nevertheless fall finally from grace" (242). Indeed, 1 Corinthians 9:27 by itself refutes any notion of absolute and unconditional predestination, for the apostle Paul ("certainly an elect person if ever there was one") allows that he might become a "reprobate" (*Notes,* on 1 Cor. 9:27). And what are we to make of Scripture's insistence that Christ came to save all, that he died for all, and atoned for the sins of all? "Taken in their plain, easy, and obvious sense," these verses "abundantly prove, that there is not, cannot be, any such thing as unconditional reprobation" (*Predestination,* 215-16, citing, among other texts, John 1:29; 3:17; 12:47; 2 Cor. 5:14; 1 Tim. 2:6; Heb. 2:9; 1 John 2:1-2).

Some, to be sure, believe that if human free will is given any foothold, then God is robbed of "his glory in man's salvation." Wesley cannot see why this should be so, when it is God himself who must supernaturally restore to fallen human beings a measure of free will before they can respond to him, and when "it is the work of God alone to justify, to sanctify, to glorify" (229-30). And "how is it more for the glory of God to save man irresistibly, than to save him as a free agent?" (231). If God's glory is seen where his attributes are displayed, then we may well ask whether his wisdom, justice, mercy, and truth are more in evidence if salvation is by irresistible or by resistible grace. (The former alternative, it must be remembered, entails the inevitable damnation of all who are not irresistibly appointed for salvation.)

God's wisdom in the "whole economy of man's salvation" is gloriously evident "if man be in some measure free": God treats human beings as "reasonable creatures" who are both able to discern the good and free to accept or refuse it. He enlightens the understanding of all human beings, secretly reproves their wrongdoing, gently woos them to "walk in the light," instills good desires in their hearts. He appeals to their understanding as well as their emotions, mixes promises with threats. "Now, what wisdom is seen in all this, if man may indeed choose life or death!" On the other hand, if all are "unalterably consigned to heaven or hell" before they are born, where is the wisdom in dealing with them as though they were free when they are not? What are God's promises and threats "but empty farce, but mere grimace, sounding words, that mean just nothing? . . . To what end does all this apparatus serve? If you say, 'To insure his damnation'; alas, what needeth that, seeing this was insured before the foundation of the world! Let all mankind then judge, which of these accounts is more for the glory of God's wisdom!" (232-33).

What of God's justice? Those whose will is irresistibly steered by God are machines, not moral agents. They sin as God has foreordained. They lack saving grace as God has decreed. "And shall this man, for not doing what he never could do, and for doing what he never could avoid, be sentenced to depart into everlasting fire . . . ? 'Yes, because it is the sovereign will of God.' Then 'you have either found a new God, or made one!' This is not the God of the Christians" (234).

What of God's love and goodness? Scripture declares that "'the Lord is loving' (or good) 'to every man, and his mercy is over all his works'" (227; cf. Ps. 145:9). But "how is God good or loving to a reprobate?" Gifts of nature and of providence may indeed be his, but "at the price he is to pay for them, every one of them also is a curse. Every one of these comforts is, by an eternal decree, to cost him a thousand pangs in hell." Since God knew, and designed, that "this would be the fruit of whatsoever he should enjoy, . . . God is, in truth and reality, only fatting the ox for the slaughter." Whatever grace the reprobate is given may properly be termed "damning grace; since it is not only such in the event, but in the intention. . . . It was given, not to convert thee, but only to convince; not to make thee without sin, but without excuse; not to destroy but to arm the worm that never dieth, and to blow up the fire that never shall be quenched" (227-29).

God's love is certainly shown to the elect. "But why will he have mercy on these alone, and leave all those to inevitable destruction? 'He will — because he will!' . . . Then, would I ask, What would the universal voice of mankind pronounce of the man that should act thus? that being able to deliver millions of men from death with a single breath of his mouth, should refuse to save any more than one in a hundred, and say, 'I will not, because I will not!' How then do you exalt the mercy of God, when you ascribe such a proceeding to him?" Is not the mercy of God more gloriously shown "in offering salvation to every creature, actually saving all that consent thereto, and doing for the rest all that infinite wisdom, almighty power, and boundless love can do, without forcing them to be saved, which would be to destroy the very nature that he had given them" (234-35)?

What, finally, of God's truth? How are we to vindicate the sincerity of a God who protests that he takes no pleasure in the death of the wicked (Ezek. 18:23; 33:11), who pleads for his people to heed his voice and live (Deut. 5:29; Ps. 81:11), if "all this time" he has "unchangeably ordained" that they should behave as they do (224-26)? This doctrine

> represents our Blessed Lord . . . as an hypocrite, a deceiver of the people, a man void of common sincerity. For it cannot be denied that he everywhere speaks *as if he was* willing that all men should be saved. . . . You cannot deny that he says, "Come unto me, all ye that are weary and heavy laden." If then you say he calls those that cannot come, those whom he knows to be unable to come, those whom he can make able to come but will not, how is it possible to describe greater insincerity? . . . You describe him as saying one thing and meaning another; as pretending the love which he had not. . . . Then especially, when drawing nigh the city, "he wept over it," and said, "O Jerusalem, Jerusalem, . . . how often *would* I have gathered thy children together . . . and *ye would not.*" . . . You represent him (which who could hear?) as weeping crocodile's tears, weeping over the prey which himself had doomed to destruction. (*Sermons*, 3:554-55, citing Matt. 11:28; Luke 19:41; Matt. 23:37)

In short, the "horrible decree" of predestination

> represents the most Holy God as worse than the devil. . . . More false; because the devil, liar as he is, hath never said he "willeth all men to be saved." More unjust; because the devil cannot, if he would, be guilty of such injustice as you ascribe to God when you say that God condemned millions of souls to everlasting fire . . . for continuing in sin, which . . . they cannot avoid. And more cruel; because that unhappy spirit "seeketh rest and findeth none"; so that his own restless misery is a kind of temptation to him to tempt others. But God "resteth in his high and holy place"; so that to suppose him of his own mere motion, of his pure will and pleasure, happy as he is, to doom his creatures, whether they will or no, to endless misery, is to impute such cruelty to him as we cannot impute even to the great enemy of God and man. (3:555-56, citing 1 Tim. 2:4; Matt. 12:43; Isa. 57:15)

If some would attempt to prove such a doctrine from Scripture, one can only wonder what they would prove. "That God is worse than the devil? It cannot be. Whatever that Scripture proves, it never can prove this. . . . It cannot mean, whatever it mean besides, that the God of truth is a liar. Let it mean what it will, it cannot mean that the Judge of all the world is unjust. No Scripture can mean that God is not love, or that his mercy is not over all his works. That is, whatever it prove beside, no Scripture can prove predestination" (3:556).

God's eternal decree is this: "'I will set before' the sons of men 'life and death, blessing and cursing'; and the soul that chooseth life shall live, as the soul that chooseth death shall die." This is

> worthy of God. It is every way consistent with all the perfections of his nature. It gives us the noblest view both of his justice, mercy, and truth. To this agrees the whole scope of the Christian revelation, as well as all the parts thereof. . . . Thus our blessed Lord: "If any man thirst, let him come to me and drink." Thus his great Apostle, St. Paul: "God commandeth all men everywhere to repent." . . . Thus St. Peter: "The Lord is . . . not willing that any should perish, but that all should come to repentance." O hear ye this, ye that forget God! Ye cannot charge your death upon him. . . . "Turn ye, turn ye from your evil ways; for why will ye die?" (3:558-59, citing Deut. 30:19; Ezek. 33:11; John 7:37; Acts 17:30; 2 Pet. 3:9)

vi. Summary

God governs creation wisely for the good of all his creatures. He made people to be "happy in him." Indeed, he made them in his own image, with understanding, will, and liberty. As free moral agents, human beings are able to discern and choose between good and evil. God prompts and prods them to do what is right, but he respects human choices.

God wrote his law (the *moral* law) on human hearts, a law that mirrors and defines our nature and place in God's universe. Human continuance in God's favor and image was contingent on human conformity with God's law. Adam sinned, and human nature has consequently been corrupted. Left to ourselves, we are not capable of doing good.

God does not leave us to ourselves. Because his Son has atoned for human sins, God offers salvation to all who will put their trust in him. The Spirit of God uses God's law to awaken in sinful human beings an awareness of their guilt and helplessness. No "works" they do can atone for their sin or merit God's favor. When they recognize this and cry to God for help, he grants them saving faith: faith to believe that Christ died for *their* sins, and that they are "justified" — pardoned and accepted by God — for Christ's sake. At the same time as they are justified, they are also born again into God's family, a reality to which the Spirit of God gives confirmation ("witness") in their hearts.

Justification frees them from the guilt of their sin; their new birth as God's children gives them power over sin. As long as they retain their faith in Christ, they neither will nor can commit deliberate sin. Still, there remains in their hearts a proneness to evil that must be resisted; and even the good that new believers do is tinged with something of evil. Their "regeneration" (the new birth) is merely their entrance to the path that leads to sanctification. Progress is for a time gradual, but God is ready to grant "entire sanctification" and a "full salvation" to those who trust him for it. As instantaneously as they earlier were brought into God's family, they find themselves so governed by God's love that they are delivered from all sin (though not, to be sure, from ignorance, mistakes, or infirmities). Yet no state of sanctity can be achieved in this life from which the believer is unable to fall.

The ceremonial aspects of the Mosaic law were abolished by Christ. Its moral demands, however, spell out the details of the eternal law of love written in human hearts, and believers, too, are to be guided by it: without "holiness" they will not see the Lord. The Spirit inspires and enables them to do good. He also guides them in their discernment of God's will, though normally the words of Scripture and the judgment of human reason, informed by experience, are his tools for the purpose.

Predestination is a bad idea. It cannot be supported from Scripture. God wills the good of all his creatures and offers salvation to every human being. But he offers it to them *as* human beings, the moral agents that he made them. They must themselves choose between good and evil, life and death.

Chapter 5

A Portrait of the "Lutheran" Paul

My goal in the preceding chapters has been to allow Augustine, Luther, Calvin, and Wesley to speak on subjects crucial to our study, though in a context that fairly represented emphases inherent in their own writings. For our purposes each of them may be regarded as a "Lutheran" reader of Paul; and of the influence of each on other readers there can be no doubt. The task that remains to this chapter is to sketch a composite picture of the "Lutheran" Paul, to the extent that Augustine, Luther, Calvin, and Wesley can be said to represent it.

The following theses, I suggest, sum up essential features of the "Lutheran" Paul. The first five mark areas of significance in which the "Lutherans" we have studied show broad agreement (different nuances will be noted). The final two represent areas of concern that grow out of "Lutheran" emphases, though the disagreements that must be registered here prove that no *one* position in these matters follows inevitably from the "Lutheran" convictions they share.

> **Thesis 1:** Human nature, created good, has been so corrupted by sin that human beings are incapable of God-pleasing action. They are rightly subject to God's condemnation.

God is good, and he made us good. That we are not now good is not his fault, though a consequence of his endowment of human beings with wills of their own. All was well as long as Adam and Eve, the forebears and prototypes of our race, trusted their Creator and were content to live in harmony with his creation. Disaster followed, however, when they defied their Maker, distrusting his goodness and embarking on a path where perceived self-interest rather than love governed their behavior. Human beings pursue it still, to our own, and creation's, detriment.

All four of our "Lutheran" Paulinists recognized that we are responsible only for behavior that we ourselves will. They all believed, too, that God foreknew how Adam would use the will he had been given; Calvin went further, however, in claiming that God, the first Cause of all that happens in his creation, determined and directed Adam's choice. God's goodness is not in question, for he designed great good to follow from Adam's sin. The fault lies with Adam. He willed to disobey God; and he was moved by pride and ambition, and proved faithless and ungrateful, when he did so. So far Calvin. Wesley, responding to the Calvinists, insisted that human beings would not and could not be held responsible for actions done with their wills if those wills themselves were irresistibly steered by God. But they were (and are) not. God made human beings free moral agents, and he respects the choices they make. When Adam freely chose to disobey God, his culpability was clear.

Adam passed on to his descendants a nature that has been corrupted by sin. The corruption affects not only human sensual desires but our reason and wills as well. We cannot rightly know God after we have turned from him, the supreme Good, to pursue our own "prodigious trifles." We cannot rightly know ourselves when we assess our moral conduct, not by the standards we were made to live by, but by comparison with the conduct of other sinners. As for our wills, we may call them "free" if we mean that our deliberate actions are governed by our own likes and dislikes, our characteristic desires and distastes; but the human will is decidedly not free if the term implies a capacity to choose and do what is truly good as well as what is evil. On our own, human beings are incapable of doing, speaking, or even thinking anything truly good.

Before we dismiss Augustine, Luther, Calvin, and Wesley as curmudgeons who cannot bring themselves to acknowledge even the decency of their grocers, we should at least be clear about what they are saying. In an imperfect world they are perfectly prepared to recognize and value the relative goodness of particular actions and human beings. Augustine allows that people do right things, though never (he maintains) for entirely the right reasons. Luther acknowledges that people are capable of "moral" deeds that, as far as the actions themselves are concerned, conform to God's commandments. If he thinks such works are not *truly* good unless they are driven by faith in God, he warmly endorses the worth of "moral" behavior for the stability of society. Calvin grants the enormous difference between the justice of Trajan and the savagery of Caligula, between observance and contempt of laws; he is ungrudging in his praise of good laws and their keeping, as well as of human science, artistry, and vocational skills. Wesley knows that people do much that is good and profitable in their dealings with each other, though their deeds necessarily fall short of goodness in God's sight. There is much, then, that is relatively good — together with much that is unquestionably evil — in God's creation yet.

But nothing we do can be truly good while our relationship with our Creator is not what it should be: while we ignore or deny our dependence on him and allow his goodness to pass unrecognized. Human beings, for our "Lutheran" Paulinists, are living a lie in feigning independence from their Maker. And though the relative good that we do for each other makes our fallen lot more bearable, it does not begin to approximate the goodness for which we were intended. As human beings we are not as wicked as we *could* be; but a fatal flaw distorts all our thinking, every judgment, all our desires, every choice. The flaw is apparent in the horrendous deeds of which human beings have proven all too capable. It is also present in all the *relatively* good things we do, in that they evidence less than heartfelt trust and unstinted joy in the goodness of our God.

Thesis 2: Human beings must be justified by divine grace, responded to in faith, and *not* by any works of their own.

The first characteristic feature of the "Lutheran" Paul is presupposed in the second: the convictions that human nature is "fallen" and that human beings are incapable of doing what is good in God's sight are taken for granted in the "Lutheran" understanding of justification by grace, through faith, and apart from "works." It is because sinful human beings can do no works to gain God's favor that God must take the initiative and justify them on other terms.

Any and every work is excluded. Our "Lutheran" Paulinists were well aware that Paul's debate in Galatians was with those who advocated circumcision for his Gentile converts; but that, they contended, was only the starting point of his discussion. Paul quickly moves on to examine the nature, role, and limits of the Mosaic law as a whole; hence, when he rules out "the works of the law," compliance with its demands as a whole must be meant. And if the works demanded by the God-given Mosaic law cannot justify, neither can any of our own devising. The point is clearest when Paul contrasts justification by grace with a supposed justification based on works and finds the two exclusive alternatives: if by divine grace, then not by human activities. (Romans 4:4-5 and 11:6, together with Ephesians 2:8-10, are of course the primary basis for this argument.) God's grace rules out anything we might do as a basis for our justification.

"Justification," for all our "Lutheran" Paulinists, means at least the acceptance of sinners as righteous by God because their sins have been forgiven. Calvin and Wesley make a sharp distinction between justification and sanctification, while holding that the two are inseparable: justification restores sinners to

God's favor because their sins have been forgiven; sanctification is the process by which God's image is restored in them as they increasingly overcome sin and exhibit appropriate virtues (the "fruit of the Spirit"). In Augustine and Luther this careful distinction in terminology is not observed. But they too attribute God's forgiveness and acceptance of sinners solely to divine grace.

If humans furnish nothing for their own justification, then faith itself cannot be considered their contribution. Rather, for all our "Lutheran" Paulinists faith is a gift of God, whose Spirit illumines the hearts of hearers of the gospel and enables them to trust Christ as *their* Savior. For (the later) Augustine, Luther, and Calvin the work of the Spirit is irresistible; for Wesley (and the early Augustine) it is not, but human faith is still to be ascribed solely to God's grace since, without the Spirit's work, humans cannot evoke faith within themselves. Those who seek God's favor must, in Wesley's understanding, look to him expectantly for the gift of faith, not neglecting the means of grace that Scripture ordains. In God's own time the gift will be given perceptibly and unmistakably, accompanied as it is by a constant peace and sense of forgiveness.

Though all acknowledge the necessity of grace in justification, Augustine, taking his cue from the claim that humans have nothing that they have not received (1 Cor. 4:7), gives grace a distinctive emphasis. Though all regard faith as essential, Luther stresses its fundamental importance in any healthy relationship, and particularly that of humans with God. Though Augustine, Luther, and Calvin all think God has chosen those on whom he bestows the gift of faith, Calvin characteristically presses the logic of election to its most rigorous conclusions. Wesley alone attributes solely to the hearer of the gospel the decisive choice between faith and unbelief, life and death, though (to repeat) he too believes that the former option is made possible only by the illumination of God's Spirit.

The faith that justifies is, for all our Paulinists, faith in Christ, God's Son and our Savior. No *distinctive* understanding of redemption is shared by them all; but that the death of Christ atoned for sins and that his resurrection makes possible new life for believers are the common convictions of all. Faith merely appropriates for the believer the benefits of what Christ has done.

All since Adam have inherited Adam's sinful nature. And all must be justified in the same way: through no works of their own, but through faith in the redemptive work of Christ. This, the message of the Christian gospel, has been freely proclaimed ever since the first Easter. But its substance was suggested already in the promises made to Israel's patriarchs, and it was foreshadowed in the ceremonies instituted by the Mosaic law; all who responded in faith to these adumbrations of the gospel were justified. Augustine and Luther call such Old Testament believers "Christians before Christ." Calvin declares them members of the church, and maintains that believers today belong to the Abrahamic covenant no less than the faithful in ancient Israel. For Wesley believers of all ages are a part of the covenant of grace that, once Adam sinned, replaced the covenant of works to which he had been subject.

> Thesis 3: Justification by grace through faith leaves human beings with nothing of which they may boast in God's presence. The (false) notion that human beings *can* contribute to their justification opens the door to a presumption that ill suits creatures in the presence of their Creator.

For Augustine Paul championed divine grace against arrogant people who "presumed" on their own good works and despised God's grace. Human beings must be brought to realize that they have nothing they have not received: all glory must be given to God. For Luther the primary purpose of the law is to disabuse human beings of the illusion that they may be justified on the basis of their deeds and to compel them to give glory to God alone. Calvin insists that since righteousness is not based on our works, we have no occasion for boasting: were we to claim for ourselves even a "crumb" of righteousness, we would be depriving God of his due glory. Wesley suggests that God has defined faith as the "condition of justification" specifically to humble proud sinners: they must fix their eyes on their own wickedness, guilt, and helplessness if they are to find in Jesus the "propitiation" for their sins. On no point are representatives of the "Lutheran" Paul more emphatic or united than in their conviction that divine grace excludes any pretensions of human merit and any grounds for human boasting.

> Thesis 4: Those justified by faith *apart* from works must nonetheless *do* good works as believers.

Contrary to popular opinion, our "Lutheran" Paulinists do not think good works a bad thing. They do claim that no works done by unjustified sinners can be truly good, and they insist that God's grace, not human activity, is the basis of justification. That said, all are adamant that good works must follow justification: as Calvin put it, though we are not justified "through works," we are not justified "without" them either. Modern scholars who point to passages in Paul's writings where he demands effort in doing good must not imagine that they thereby refute our "Lutheran" Paulinists; the latter cite the same passages in opposing their "antinomian" foes.

For Wesley the task of religion is "to renew our hearts in the image of God, to repair that total loss of righteousness and true holiness which we sustained by the sin of our first parent." Forgiveness of sins is only the first step in that process. Though Wesley distinguished a justification that restores sinners to God's favor from a regeneration that restores them to God's image, he insisted that the two take place simultaneously and inseparably. All who are justified are also born again, and the new birth effects a real inward change: from wickedness to goodness, from the love of creatures to the love of the Creator. Regeneration in turn marks the beginning of the path to sanctification: believers now gain victory over temptations that once overpowered them, and they find themselves moved by love to do good works never before possible. Thus, though good works are by no means the basis of justification, they are its inevitable result, and those who do not produce them have no claim to be justified. Without the "holiness" that is the goal of sanctification, no one will "see the Lord."

So argued Wesley. Calvin was in essential agreement. He too distinguished sanctification from justification, defined sanctification as the restoration of God's image in the believer, and insisted that Christ sanctifies all he justifies. Those who show no God-pleasing works are not among the justified — though, again, their works evidence rather than provide the basis for their justification. Augustine went further, claiming that faith that does not lead to love and good works is vain, and that God rewards believers' good works with eternal life. Here, however, Luther drew a line: faith does not need to be supplemented by love to earn God's approval, for any faith that does not lead to love and good works is counterfeit rather than real. Those to whom God gives the gift of true faith are also the recipients of his Spirit, and that Spirit will not allow them to be idle. Good works will follow — but they must never be deemed the basis on which God grants salvation. That remains the redemptive work of Christ.

Far from opposing effort and good works, then, our "Lutheran" Paulinists thought Paul regarded them as essential marks of true faith. Does it follow that they thought that, while believers are initially "saved" by grace, they maintain their status as God's people by their works?

Given our Paulinists' insistence on the presence of "good works" in the lives of believers, it might appear so; but they are equally firm in declaring believers' utter dependence on divine grace for all the good they do. Before human beings come to faith, they can do no (truly) good thing: God, operating solely on his own initiative, must provide redemption in Christ and must awaken faith in their hearts by the inner promptings of his Holy Spirit. After their justification God's Spirit begins the process of restoring God's image in believers: he transforms their wills so that they begin to desire to do good. The good they then do is really their own, the product of their own will; but (again!) it has only been made possible by the work of God's Spirit, transforming the human faculties of the believer. When God then rewards believers' good works, he rewards his own gift. So runs the pithy formula of Augustine, who went further than the others in suggesting that eternal life itself is a recompense for the grace-inspired deeds of believers. The others retained the formula but not the suggestion: even the good works of believers are never the criterion of their standing with God.

> Thesis 5: The Mosaic law was given, in part, to awaken in human beings an awareness of their need of divine grace. Believers are delivered from its condemnation and need not observe its ceremonial prescriptions. The gift of God's Spirit enables them (in some measure) to fulfill its moral demands.

Here our Paulinists show remarkable uniformity. In view of the complexity of the subject matter, their agreement clearly signifies adherence to a common tradition. All believe that the ceremonial demands of the Mosaic law foreshadowed Christ's redemptive work but were annulled by his appearance. All believe that the moral demands of the Mosaic law spell out the eternal law of God for all people, and that Christians, too, must conform with it. All believe that God's demands in Scripture are beyond the capacity of fallen humankind to fulfill; God made these demands in part to arouse in sinners an awareness of their guilt and liability for divine judgment. All believe that the justified are delivered from the law's condemnation and God's wrath. All believe that the Spirit has been given to Christians and makes possible, at least in some measure, the fulfillment of God's commands.

Some differences there are. Neither Augustine nor Luther thinks the Sabbath law binds believers; for Calvin and Wesley, however, the Sabbath commandment is part of the moral law that is valid for all people everywhere. Augustine and Luther at times speak as though the Spirit-filled believer no longer needs the law's direction but spontaneously does what is right: whereas fallen human beings can no more do good than bad trees can produce good fruit, believers indwelt by the Spirit will, like good trees, inevitably produce what is good. On the other hand, neither imagines that believers are free to violate the moral law, and both concede that believers, in doing good, must contend with a "flesh" that desires differently. With that in mind, they are prepared to allow that God's law continues to play a role in guiding, encouraging, and even warning believers to do right. For their part Calvin and Wesley give special prominence to this latter role of the law when they list its functions.

Most famously, Luther sharply separates "law" (what God requires of us) from "gospel" (what God offers to us), and makes their differentiation the key to understanding Scripture. Calvin often draws a similar distinction, though he is careful to add that the term "law" is being used narrowly ("apart from Christ"); when the whole Mosaic order is in view, Calvin insists, the law cannot conflict with the gospel, since both have the same divine Source. Luther, having made his point, does not trouble to add the fine print, but the difference from Calvin should not be exaggerated. In those respects in which Calvin saw continuity between law and gospel (the ceremonial law foreshadowed Christ's work in the gospel, though, once fulfilled by Christ, it need no longer be observed; the moral law makes sinners aware of their need for the gospel, and remains the standard for Christian behavior; like believers today, the righteous in Israel owed their acceptability before God not to the merits of their works, but to their faith in God's goodness and to the redemptive work of Christ as proclaimed in the gospel), Luther would certainly agree.

> **Thesis 6:** Whether sin remains a reality in the lives of justified believers is an issue that "Lutherans" cannot but confront, though they disagree in their assessment of it.

Here, and on the following topic, Wesley marches to a different drummer; yet it would be unwise to disregard his views. On the matter of sin in believers' lives, both Wesley's optimism and his interpretation of Romans 7 anticipate the position of twentieth-century critics of the "Lutheran" Paul. Conversely, on election many contemporary proponents of the "Lutheran" Paul are closer to Wesley than to any of the predestinationists in the tradition.

As we have just seen, all our Paulinists contend that a real transformation accompanies the justification of believers and makes possible in some measure their fulfillment of God's commands. At the same time, all affirm that the sinful, fallen nature that human beings inherit from Adam (the "flesh") is not destroyed when people come to faith. Augustine, Luther, and Calvin insist that believers must struggle with the flesh throughout their earthly sojourn, and that they never in this life completely overcome it. While a hankering for sin remains, Augustine notes, believers are not free of covetousness, nor do they love God with all their being. Children of God though they are, they remain children of Adam as well. For Luther Christians are at the same time both righteous and sinners. The righteousness for which God accepts them is "alien" and "passive" rather than the product of their own activity: it is, in its essence, the righteousness of Christ, shared with those who belong to him. And while with the Spirit's help they begin to do what is right (indeed, true faith must do so), vice remains a troublesome reality. Calvin remarks that sin continues to dwell in believers, though it does not rule them. Even the good that they do is always soiled by sin, and they never pass a single day without falling time and again.

Wesley speaks very differently. The children of God cannot commit voluntary sin: they cannot deliberately transgress known commandments. Every believer is freed from sin's power as well as its guilt. To be sure, a proneness to sin initially remains in the hearts of the justified, but it is consistently overcome in their actions. For a time, too, believers sense that they do not love God as they ought, and that something of pride or self-will still taints their activities; but the goal of sanctification is to conquer and banish these remnants of the flesh. Moreover, God has promised complete sanctification to the faithful, and those who believe his promise and expect its fulfillment need not wait until death to experience this blessing. As perceptibly as they once felt the coming of faith, they will find themselves perfected in love and governed by it in all they do.

Thesis 7:   Whether the divine grace to which salvation is to be attributed must be deemed the irresistible source of the believer's faith is an issue that "Lutherans" cannot but confront, though they disagree in their assessment of it.

Convinced that humans are completely dependent on divine grace, Augustine came to think that those who believe must have been enabled by God to do so; moreover, those who persevere in faith must have been further empowered to remain steadfast. Since God never acts on a whim, he must have predetermined the recipients of these gifts. It follows that those who were not so blessed have been left by God to their own damnation. Augustine insisted on the justice of God in the predestination of his creatures. Those who are damned are justly damned for sins they have freely chosen. Those who are saved experience God's mercy.

Luther, too, in affirming that fallen human beings can contribute nothing to their salvation, concluded that God must predetermine who will believe. For that matter, divine omnipotence (for Luther) means that God is the effective cause of all that happens in his creation. The coming to faith of believers must be included.

For Calvin divine sovereignty is a still more central conviction. The notion that God's plans or activities are in any way contingent on human choices Calvin finds utterly preposterous. He cannot conceive how puny human beings, utterly dependent on God for all they are and have, could initiate anything that God had not predetermined, still less that they could ever in the slightest degree frustrate or alter the divine will. Everything that happens has been planned by God, including the sins of human beings — though God, whose purpose in orchestrating human sins is always good, is not to be blamed for the evil. If some human beings believe and are saved while others do not and are damned, then divine predestination lies behind the destiny of both. If the New Testament offers salvation to all, that is true only of God's "general" call, which is never sufficient in itself to rouse faith in a sinner. Faith is found only where God's general call is accompanied by the "special" call of God's Spirit, extended only to the elect and enabling them to believe. The reprobate are condemned because they sinned willingly, though it is true that God predetermined the direction of their wills. It is only right, after all, that a sovereign Creator should be free to dispose of his creatures as he sees fit and for his own glory.

If Calvin was appalled by the suggestion that human decisions could have any impact on the plans of a sovereign God, Wesley responded with visceral horror to portraits of a sovereign God who predetermined the sin, guilt, and damnation of his creatures. God's goodness was for Wesley fundamental, and, the protests of the Calvinists notwithstanding, he could find no recognizable trace of such an attribute in their dogma. If there is evil in God's creation, it cannot be by divine decree, but only as the result of choices freely made by human beings (and angels) whom God made independent moral agents. God's sovereignty is displayed, not in predetermining every event in the universe, including the sins of his creatures, but in providentially turning even the freely chosen sins of his creatures to good purposes. Furthermore, God's love and salvation are offered to all human beings, and only those who freely refuse will come to damnation. Is God's will then frustrated by that of these creatures? Not at all, for God himself chose to make them moral agents, and in allowing them to determine their own destiny, he remains true to his design in their creation.

Our study has enabled us to define certain characteristic features of the "Lutheran" Paul as well as other emphases in the writings of Augustine, Luther, Calvin, and Wesley that, though not the subject of agreement by all four, arise out of "Lutheran" concerns. That these features and concerns owe more to Luther (or, as some have duly noted, to Augustine) than to Paul has been a common theme in much Pauline scholarship of the last century or so. To its assessment of our subject we now turn.

Part Two

Twentieth-Century Responses to the "Lutheran" Paul

Chapter 6

Paul's "Polemical Doctrine": Wrede and Schweitzer

The names of William Wrede and Albert Schweitzer figure largely in reviews of New Testament scholarship; not quite coincidentally, Schweitzer himself wrote the best-known reviews. Perhaps, too, the nature of the genre, with its somewhat artificial stress on distinctive periods of scholarship and the "turning points" between them, is weighted in favor of writers at the turn of a century who determined the direction in which research would move. In any case, a modern "quest of the historical Jesus" could begin at no better place than where the old quest left off, in a review of Wrede and Schweitzer. That the same two scholars should be allowed to monopolize the first chapter of a discussion of modern Pauline scholarship seems hardly fair. But there are other criteria than fairness to be considered.

Concise, provocative, and popular in its appeal, Wrede's *Paul* remains to this day an excellent introduction to aspects of the contemporary study of Paul. Though for our purposes his importance lies primarily in his displacement of the doctrine of justification from the center of Pauline thought, that particular insistence represents only one of several ways in which Wrede anticipates recent emphases in the scholarly literature. As for Schweitzer, not only do his Pauline studies mark a foretaste of things to come (he, too, downplays the significance of Paul's "justification" language); even in translation his prose is inimitable in its imagery, spirit, and force — and eminently quotable. When competing for attention with claims like these, a plea for fairness is bound to go unheard. We begin, then, with Wrede and Schweitzer.

Since Paul's view of the law cannot be isolated from other areas of his thought, I have tried to avoid too narrow a focusing of the issue. The broader canvas should also serve to bring what is distinctive about the approaches of the scholars discussed into better perspective. And finally, a caveat to protect the innocent: what follows immediately is intended to represent, not my own views, but those of Wrede and Schweitzer. Many of the questions raised will be taken up in due course; but — it is a rule too seldom observed — fair reporting must precede scholarly assessment.

i. William Wrede

Fundamental to Wrede's presentation of Paul is his insistence that Paul was a man of his day, not ours. Paul's thinking was determined by laws we know not to be valid. He believed in beings that only children and poets speak of today. Where we see abstract terms, Paul, like all the ancients, tended to see real and effective powers. If, in spite of all this, countless of our contemporaries still believe they share the views of the apostle, this is only because they misinterpret him. They spiritualize and psychologize, they read as metaphor what Paul took to be real, they make fundamental what is secondary and miss what is basic altogether. To present the true Paul to such readers is no easy task: "it is harder to interpret Paul's doctrine to one who half understands him than to one who knows nothing about him."[1]

Redemption

The distance between Paul and his modern would-be interpreters is nowhere greater than on the subject of redemption. Three questions must be answered if we are to understand his views: "(1) Wherein lies the misery from which the redemption releases us? (2) How and by what means does Christ bring the redemption to pass? (3) In what does the benefit of this redemption consist?" (92).

1. The popular view of Paul sees the problem of men and women outside of Christ as sin, and understands sin as the moral failings of the individual will. Any scheme of redemption must therefore address the issue of how I, who have committed sins, can be made acceptable to a holy God; the answer is commonly found to lie in the atoning death of Christ, paying the penalty for, and thus freeing me from, my sins. Attention is focused on the subjective peace of heart, purity of conscience, and assurance of grace felt by the "redeemed" individual. But this is grossly inadequate as a representation of what Paul means by redemption; his statements are general, sweeping, and objective. In a nutshell, Pauline

---

1. Wrede, *Paul*, 85. All parenthetical page numbers in this section refer to this book.

redemption consists of "release from the misery of this whole present world" (92, referring to Gal. 1:4). Not deliverance from the torment experienced by a guilty soul, but "a change in the very nature and conditions of existence" is the essence of redemption (112).

Why do the conditions of humanity need changing? Again, it would be too narrow an answer to speak simply of our ingrained propensity for sin. For Paul life in "the present evil age" is characterized by bondage to "dark and evil powers" such as the flesh, sin, the law, and death (92). To our way of thinking these are abstract terms, but the ancients attributed personality to such abstractions — after all, for them Love was a goddess! Similarly, Paul thinks of the law, sin, and the like as real and effective forces. He can speak of how "*sin*, finding opportunity in the commandment, deceived me and by it killed me" (Rom. 7:11), or of how "death" is one of many "enemies" that have to be destroyed (1 Cor. 15:26). As a result, redemption in Paul's mind must involve deliverance from the evil powers that enslave us.

Of these powers, the "flesh" represents the limitations — indeed, the enslavement — imposed on us by our "finite, sensuous existence" (93) in a physical body on this earth. "Sin" must not be reduced to the sum of human wrongdoings, nor is our bondage to sin simply a metaphorical way of referring to our habit of "sinning." Sin is an active, enslaving power that accompanies the flesh. "Sin clings indissolubly to the flesh, 'dwells' in the flesh, originates indeed in the flesh and its impulses" (93; cf. Rom. 7:17-20). We are slaves of sin simply because we live in the flesh, the sphere where sin holds sway. Hence redemption must bring, not simply forgiveness for sins, but a change in the very conditions of an existence marked by bondage to sin and the flesh.

Human misery is made more bitter still by the law. Without law there may be wrongdoing, but there can be no transgression, no violation of concrete commands (Rom. 4:15); in this respect the presence of law aggravates human guilt. Moreover, the very command that prohibits lawless desires is used by sin to stimulate those desires within us (7:7-13). Hence the law, too, is a hostile power keeping humanity in bondage (7:4). And inevitably, where the flesh, sin, and the law are present, death reigns as well (5:12-21); it, too, must be vanquished if we are to be redeemed.

And even this is not the full, dismal picture. "Angels, in our time, belong to children and to poets; to Paul and his age they were a real and serious quantity." And "Paul believes that mankind without Christ is under the sway of mighty spirits, demons, and angelic powers" (95). His letters are sprinkled with references to these "powers," "dominions," "principalities," and "authorities" (1 Cor. 15:24; Col. 1:16; 2:10, 15). Men and women are "slaves to the elemental spirits of the universe" (Gal. 4:3; cf. v. 9; Col. 2:8, 20). Such forces govern this age, they are its "rulers" (1 Cor. 2:6, 8), and they separate humanity from God (cf. Rom. 8:38-39). And, of course, these angelic beings stand behind sin, the flesh, death, and (perhaps surprisingly) even the law (cf. Gal. 3:19).

Such are the conditions of human existence before the intervention of the Christ. A redemption that means merely the forgiveness of sins and acceptance by God is too narrowly conceived; what is needed is a release from the whole present world and the evil forces that control it.

2. A change is brought about by the death and resurrection of God's Son. Christ, a superhuman, celestial being, "empties" himself of his heavenly status and enters the state of misery just described. He comes under the power of the law, "wears the flesh of sin," and subjects himself to the dominion of the spirits, who ultimately crucify him (98; cf. Rom. 8:3; Gal. 4:4; 1 Cor. 2:8). But by dying Christ leaves the sphere of these powers. "He no longer wears flesh, and therefore has nothing more in common with sin, law, and death" (99). Christ "died to sin" (Rom. 6:10); "death no longer has dominion over him" (v. 9). "Through his resurrection he enters upon a new existence, which is not subject" to these evil powers (99). He is thus the means by which God "disarmed the principalities and powers . . . , triumphing over them" (Col. 2:15).

Only such a view of Christ's death provides an adequate basis for understanding redemption. The evil forces enslaving humankind had to be overcome, and it is such a victory that Paul understands Christ to have achieved in his death and resurrection. Again, if we are to grasp how Paul thought this benefited us, the vicarious understanding of Christ's death (he died *instead* of us, as a substitute for us) is too narrow. Christ represents the human race in such a real way that what happened to him happened — in Paul's view, literally and objectively — to all. It is not just that all have derived benefits from his death; "one has died for all; therefore *all have died*" (2 Cor. 5:14). And if all die with him, then they also triumph with him over the evil powers. "We know that our old self was *crucified with him* so that the sinful body might be destroyed, and we might no longer be enslaved to sin. For he who has died is freed from sin" (Rom. 6:6-7).

Thus "from the moment of [Christ's] death all men are redeemed, as fully as he himself, from the hostile powers" (100). Such is the "change in the very nature and conditions of existence" brought about by Christ (112).

3. In popular piety the "doctrine of salvation" is concerned with "what happens in the individual man." Since faith is seen as the means, its nature is carefully defined, and a vast literature is devoted to the "signs by which true and false, normal and defective faith can be distinguished" (113). But such a subjective, introspective, and psychological approach, Wrede says, has little support in Paul. Paul's concern is not with the individual but with the race, with humanity

as a whole. Salvation is indeed individually appropriated by faith and baptism. But faith here refers simply to the acceptance of the message of redemption; no attempt is made to define the psychological state of the believer. Similarly, baptism is effective objectively; the thoughts or feelings of the one baptized are of no interest to Paul. Nor is baptism to be understood in a "purely spiritual or symbolic" way (120). For Paul baptism makes the believer actually and literally a participant in the death and resurrection of Christ. With Christ the baptized die to sin, to the law, and to the world, and with Christ they rise to a new existence (Rom. 6:3-11; 7:4-6; Gal. 2:19; 6:14; Col. 3:1, 3).

All this is true in the present of the Christian. Of course the believer still bears a physical body and lives in the world. But a real, objective transformation has taken place, and only its *"outward realization . . . is reserved for the future"* (104). All will be complete with the speedy coming again of Christ. Proof that the powers of the new age are already active among believers is found in the presence of the Spirit of God.

Justification by Faith

The broad understanding of redemption outlined above is the heart of Pauline theology. What is frequently regarded as its foundation — the doctrine of justification by faith — is quite secondary by comparison, a polemical doctrine developed out of, and intended solely for, Paul's controversy with Judaism and Jewish Christianity. Only in the context of this debate is the doctrine of justification by faith referred to in the epistles, and the references are few. To make the doctrine of justification the center of Pauline thought is to distort the whole picture.

According to the popular view, the doctrine of justification by faith arose full-blown out of Paul's conversion experience. His preconversion condition is interpreted in the light of Romans 7: "I do not do the good I want, but the evil I do not want is what I do" (v. 19). Hence it is commonly thought that Paul before his conversion was "continually and vainly wrestling for righteousness before God. Instead of moral progress he suffered defeat after defeat, and ever increasing despair" (143). His vision on the road to Damascus of the risen Christ marked a watershed. Now he realized that "only grace, and never human conduct, could lead to salvation" (144). Thus the doctrine of justification is taken to be the "immediate fruit" of Paul's conversion (144).

The truth of the matter is that "the soul-strivings of Luther have stood as model for the portrait of Paul" (146). Paul paints quite a different picture of his own preconversion experience in Philippians 3:6: his life under the law had been blameless. Nor should Romans 7 be taken as a "real personal confession" of moral failings (144). The "I" of this chapter is not Paul the individual; indeed, Romans 7:9 simply cannot be taken as a true description of what Paul personally had experienced. Romans 7 is to be read as a typical, general statement of the human condition under the law before redemption, seen from the perspective gained by one who has been redeemed. Finally, it is true that Paul's life was "cut clean in two" by his Damascus vision (6), that he became convinced that Jesus was indeed the Christ; but such a conviction by itself hardly implies that circumcision and other "works of the law" are useless. Paul later said they were. But this view was forced upon him, not by the vision of the risen Christ, but by developments in his mission to the Gentiles. Practice determined theory rather than the other way around.

The doctrine of justification was designed to meet a double challenge. First, a problem was created by those who insisted that Gentile believers should adopt a Jewish way of life. This was clearly impractical. After all, to pagans circumcision and the laws about clean and unclean foods not only appeared "bizarre and childish"; they constituted "real burdens in the social life, exposed people to mockery, and made divisions in families" (64). It was therefore clear to Paul that Jewish customs simply could not be made a condition for Gentiles to enter the church. Since, however, such a conclusion was anything but self-evident to others in the early church, Paul was forced to define what in fact makes a person a Christian. Obviously Christians are distinguished from others by their faith in Jesus Christ. Thus, out of the controversy that followed Paul's missionary endeavor, the formula arose: *"not the Law with its works, but faith"* (125). A further consequence was that Paul was then compelled to demonstrate "the superfluity, perhaps harmfulness, of the Mosaic ceremonial" (125).

Second, Paul was confronted by the Jewish alternative to Christian faith. It, too, claimed to lead to salvation, but the path to that goal was seen to lie in keeping the commandments. Paul was thus faced with the task of showing how the Jewish way of salvation was in error, and he did this through the formula *"not the works of men, but grace"* (126). To be sure, the alternatives thus baldly stated involve a slight caricature of the Jewish religion, which, after all, was not ignorant of grace. But its dominant feature was nonetheless the observance of the law as a means to salvation, and this provided a sufficient base for the Pauline tenet.

The Law

The essential points in Wrede's view of Paul's understanding of the law have already been touched upon. According to Paul's view of redemption, the law is one of the hostile forces from which humanity must be redeemed. Deliverance from the law is granted to those who, by faith and baptism, are united with the Christ who himself died to the law. In Paul's polemical doctrine of justification by faith, the works of the law are seen as the opposite of faith, a false path taken by Jews in pursuit of salvation. Such a position was first developed by Paul in the course of his missionary endeavors.

Two further points require attention.

1. Paul's rejection of the law is radical and complete. "In the fullest sense 'Christ is the end of the Law'" (125, referring to Rom. 10:4). Not even the moral commandments of the law are exempted. "Certainly Paul never dreams that the *content* of the moral precepts, such as the ten commandments, is false. But he denies the right of the Law to *demand* their fulfilment; he declares that every 'thou shalt' is done away" (125-26). There is "something artificial" about all this, for "no ethical religion can dispense with the thought that God gives commandments to men" (136). Paul himself repeatedly enforces the moral commandments on his readers. The directives he gives bear "splendid witness to the circumspection, sobriety, and tact of the apostle" (59) — but not to his logical consistency. Paul can even say — in spite of his doctrine of justification — that God will judge according to works. The contradiction is apparent to us, but Paul himself may not have perceived it. In the interest of polemics, he formulated a position impossible to maintain in all its implications.

2. Paul's view of the law bears no relation to Jesus' own. Here as elsewhere the judgment must apply: "If we do not wish to deprive both figures of all historical distinctness the name 'disciple of Jesus' has little applicability to Paul, if it is used to denote an historical relation" (165). Paul never appeals to the practice of Jesus in his polemic against the law. He could not, for his view of redemption required that Jesus was born under the law and strictly fulfilled its demands. Paul's motives, too, are different. Jesus attacks the institutions of the law "when and because they slay the moral sense, rob the soul of piety, substitute appearance for reality. Where in Paul's work do we find such an ethical criticism of legalism? He fights against the Law as a missionary, and as the advocate of redemption in Christ. That is another matter" (160).

A hostile force enslaving men and women before their redemption by the Son of God; a false path to salvation in the polemical doctrine of justification by faith; a radically, though somewhat artificially, rejected element in Pauline ethics: such is the law in William Wrede's *Paul*.

ii. Albert Schweitzer

Albert Schweitzer — missionary doctor in Lambaréné, philosopher, organist and musicologist, the "greatest man in the world" in the eyes of no less an authority than *Life* magazine, winner of the Nobel Peace Prize, and much more besides — wrote two books about Paul. Unaccountably, they are classics.

The first draft of *The Mysticism of Paul the Apostle* dates back to 1906, though pressures on Schweitzer's time prevented its publication for several decades. The delay meant of course that Schweitzer was able to take later literature into account, though its prime significance is perhaps as circumstantial evidence that Schweitzer's days may after all have been limited to twenty-four hours. In 1906 the thirty-one-year-old Schweitzer was just beginning medical studies after having served for three years as principal of a theological college in Strasbourg. He had already written a dissertation on Immanuel Kant, a fine study of J. S. Bach in French, a short work on organ construction, an important monograph on the Last Supper, and the German original of *The Quest of the Historical Jesus.* During his years in medical school he kept his hand in the activities of the Paris Bach Society (which he had helped found), in organ performances, as well as in preaching and lecturing; he prepared a second, expanded edition of *The Quest* and an extended German version of his *J. S. Bach;* began editing the Bach organ works; and published the German original of *Paul and His Interpreters* (1911). Under the circumstances, if any justice prevailed among fallen humanity, Schweitzer's Pauline studies would neither bear scrutiny nor merit attention today. For once we may be thankful there is no justice.

Those familiar with *The Quest* will recognize the works on Paul at once as vintage Schweitzer: incisive, intimidating, and preoccupied with eschatology. His history of research on Jesus presented us with three inescapable choices: *either* purely historical *or* purely supernatural, *either* synoptic *or* Johannine, *either* eschatological *or* noneschatological. Readers who thought the choices too sharply put were left in no doubt about their place in the history of scholarship. "Progress always consists in taking one or other of two alternatives, in abandoning the attempt to combine them. The pioneers of progress have therefore always to reckon with the law of mental inertia which manifests itself in the majority — who always go on believing that it is possible to combine that which can no longer be combined. . . . One must just let them be, till their time is over."[2]

---

2. Schweitzer, *Quest,* 238-39. References to this work of Schweitzer, as well as to *The Mysticism of Paul the Apostle* and *Paul and His Interpreters,* will be noted in the text of the chapter by the short forms of the titles. For details see bibliography.

The correct (read: Schweitzerean) answer to the third alternative, of course, is that Jesus can only be understood in terms of eschatology. Dogmatic eschatological convictions occupied Jesus' thinking and dictated his course of action: the cataclysmic end of this world was at hand, God's kingdom would replace it, and he — Jesus — would reign as Messiah and king. Schweitzer finds the rest of the world misguided when it "seeks . . . to find in the teaching of Jesus thoughts which force their way out of the frame of the Jewish eschatological conceptions and have the character of universal religion. . . . The Gospel is at its starting-point exclusively Jewish-eschatological" (*Interpreters,* ix). Of course Christianity could not remain Jewish and eschatological. Somehow the transition to the outside world of Hellenism had to be made if the fledgling faith was to survive. "When and how the Gospel was Hellenised" thus becomes "the fundamental problem of the history of dogma" (viii).

We cannot here trace Schweitzer's broader solution to the problem, but it is important to note his insistence that the process of hellenizing did not begin with Paul. The alternatives, as always, are clear-cut: "We must now consider either a purely eschatological or a purely Hellenistic explanation of his teaching" (*Mysticism,* viii). The issue, as always, is not in doubt: "Whatever views and conceptions are brought up for comparison, the result is always the same — that Paulinism and Greek thought have nothing, absolutely nothing, in common" (*Interpreters,* 99). Opposing views, as usual, are scarcely worth consideration: "Since all [Paul's] conceptions and thoughts are rooted in eschatology, those who labour to explain him on the basis of Hellenism, are like a man who should bring water from a long distance in leaky watering-cans in order to water a garden lying beside a stream" (*Mysticism,* 140).

The stage is now set for a typically Schweitzerean tour de force: every single aspect of Pauline thought will be explained as a consistent, logical deduction from early Christian eschatological convictions. Readers willingly suspend their disbelief as long as the master is at work, effortlessly fitting together the pieces of the intricate puzzle, providing an assured explanation for each apparent anomaly that arises. Never has Paul appeared more consistent: "And how totally wrong are those who refuse to admit that Paul was a logical thinker, and proclaim as the highest outcome of their wisdom the discovery that he has no system!" (139). Schweitzer at least found a system.

What follow are the views of Schweitzer. The presentation takes its structure from three different doctrines of redemption that, according to Schweitzer, appear side by side in Paul's epistles: eschatological, mystical, and juridical.

The Eschatological Doctrine of Redemption

Like Wrede, Schweitzer believes the Pauline doctrine of redemption consists in humanity's deliverance from the rule of angelic powers who dominate this world.

According to the view current in Jewish eschatology, evil in the world derives ultimately from the demons, who "have, with God's permission, established themselves between Him and mankind" (55). Since in the eschatological timetable this state of affairs is destined to end when God's kingdom is established, the evil powers spend the final days of their hegemony wreaking their rage on those called to the kingdom. At the same time, this premessianic suffering of the elect is the means by which the latter atone for their sins. It is a necessary precondition for the coming of the kingdom.

This Jewish eschatological worldview was shared by both Jesus and Paul. Indeed, Jesus deliberately brought on his own death in an attempt to hasten the drama, to turn the wheel of foreordained history. By dying he would take upon himself the suffering destined for the elect, atone for their sins, and thus force God to inaugurate the kingdom. After his death, he believed, God would elevate him to messiahship; as messianic king, and together with the heavenly angels, he would then overthrow forever those forces that opposed God. The earliest Christians lived in the expectation that the resurrected Christ would speedily return to complete this work of redemption.

With the advent of the kingdom, the law would no longer be valid. This conviction, too, was taken over by Jesus and Paul from Jewish eschatology. For Jewish thought it was "self-evident" (69), and that for two reasons. The ethic of eschatology is "immediate and absolute" (189). Such an ethic was proclaimed by the preexilic prophets who created eschatology at a time when (according to Wellhausen's scheme) the law did not even exist. And in truth, wherever there is a pressing sense of the nearness of the kingdom, no place is left for "a meticulous observance of the last detail of the Law" (190). Second, when the coming kingdom is conceived of as transcendental, "the Law, designed for natural men, becomes purposeless" since "no longer natural but supernatural beings are in view" (191). In Jesus' teaching, too, the law is represented as valid "till heaven and earth pass away," that is, until the end of this age and the coming of God's kingdom (Matt. 5:18). Paul shares this understanding, but develops it in two important respects.

In the first place, the relationship between the law and the angels receives a novel definition from Paul. Not that Paul was alone in claiming that the law was communicated to Moses by angels (Gal. 3:19); while such a view is not found in the Old Testament, it was necessitated by the postbiblical Jewish understanding of God as so transcendent that direct contact with him becomes unthinkable. But Paul links this view of angelic mediation of the law with the Jewish eschatological worldview in an unprecedented way: "the Law was given by Angels who desired thereby to make men subservient to themselves"; hence "obedience rendered to the Law was rendered not to God but only to the Angels" (69-70; cf. Gal. 4:1-11).

Secondly, though there was nothing new in the idea that the law's validity would cease at the dawn of the messianic age, Paul declared that, with the death and resurrection of the Christ, redemption had "already begun to come into operation" (64). As a result, believers are not subject to the angelic powers to the same degree as before, and Paul can represent the law itself as already done away with by Jesus' death. In effect, Paul took the opposite course to the one ultimately chosen by Judaism: he "sacrificed the Law to eschatology; Judaism abandoned eschatology and retained the Law" (192).

Note, however, that only believers have been set free from the law. Where the natural world retains validity, the dominion of angels is still in effect. Indeed, believers themselves, if they submit to the law, return to their bondage to the world elements. This incredible situation is envisaged in Galatians 4:8-11: "Formerly, when you did not know God, you were enslaved to beings that by nature are not gods; but now when you have come to know God — or, rather, when you have come to be known by God — how is it that you are turning back again to the weak and beggarly elements, to whom you want to be enslaved again? You observe days, months, seasons, and years! I fear for you, that somehow I may have labored over you in vain."

In saying that believers have been set free from the law, we are already bordering on Paul's mystical doctrine of redemption, by which he explains how the transformation takes place. Before we deal with Paul's mystical doctrine, however, we must note Schweitzer's reaction to those who find the root of Paul's doctrine in considerations other than eschatological.

H. J. Holtzmann (*Lehrbuch der Neutestamentlichen Theologie*, 1897) is one of many to suggest that, whereas before his conversion Paul was distressed by his inability to fulfill the law, in the light of his Damascus experience he became aware of a new way to salvation apart from law. For all its popularity, this suggestion, Schweitzer believes, leads nowhere. "How do we know that Paul when he was still a persecutor of the Christians was suffering inward distress from his experiences of the powerlessness of the law? How did the vision of Christ bring about the resolution of this tension? How, exactly, did it reveal a way of salvation by which the abolition of the law was implied?" (*Interpreters*, 105). At the time of his conversion Paul became convinced that Jesus was Messiah. How did he draw from this conviction the conclusion that the law had been invalidated

— a conclusion that neither Jesus nor the primitive Christian community (which also believed Jesus was Messiah!) ever contemplated? The time has come when "there must be no more talking about the 'uniqueness of the event at Damascus' and psychologising about Paul's 'religious experience.'. . . All explanations which represent the system of doctrine as something arising subjectively in the Apostle's mind may be assumed *a priori* to be false. Only those which seek to derive it objectively from the fundamental facts of the primitive eschatological belief are to be taken into consideration" (247-48). Nor can Paul's understanding of the law be derived from the teaching of Jesus. Admittedly, Paul and Jesus shared in the common Jewish eschatological expectation. But for Paul "the hour in the world-clock" has advanced. Jesus has died and been raised. Consequently "the rule of the Angels is in process of being destroyed" and "the transformation from the earthly state of existence to the super-earthly is already going on. It is thus that [Paul] comes to regard what Jesus had said about the Law . . . as no longer authoritative. Although Jesus had recognised the Law, and had never said anything against Circumcision, both must now be regarded as no longer valid, since they presuppose that rulership of Angels which is now being destroyed" (*Mysticism*, 113-14).

Finally, the time has come to abandon all suggestions that Paul approached the law as a "purely practical question, which did not touch doctrine in the strict sense" (*Interpreters*, 246). Even Wrede is guilty on this score. It is simply inconceivable that a Paul could have rejected the law in principle because of purely practical considerations (cf. 137-38). What we find is rather that Paul reached his positions on the law "by systematically thinking out to its conclusions the primitive Christian doctrine" (83).

The Mystical Doctrine of Redemption

"We are always in presence of mysticism when we find a human being looking upon the division between earthly and super-earthly, temporal and eternal, as transcended, and feeling himself, while still externally amid the earthly and temporal, to belong to the super-earthly and eternal" (*Mysticism*, 1). Paul's mysticism consists in his conviction that "in Christ" he knows himself "as a being who is raised above this sensuous, sinful, and transient world and already belongs to the transcendent" (3).

"Being in Christ" means "having died and risen again with Him" (3), a process that begins with baptism (cf. Rom. 6:3-6). Paul's language here should not be interpreted as merely metaphorical. For Paul the references to dying and rising with Christ express "a simple reality" (15). The result is that those who are in

Christ have already begun to experience "the cessation of the natural world" through their participation in Christ's death; and by sharing in his resurrection they experience "the dawning of the supernatural world" (23).

How does this "mystical doctrine" affect Paul's understanding of the law? We have seen how Paul's *eschatological* convictions led him to believe that the law is no longer in force for the Christian, who already belongs to the messianic age. Whereas outside of Christ, in the natural world, the law retains its power, its grip on the believer has been broken. Fully consistent with this, Paul's *mysticism* explains how Christians have passed from one sphere to another: with Christ they "died to the law" (Rom. 7:4; Gal. 2:19) and were thus released from its fetters; with Christ they rose again, supernatural beings on whom the law has no claim.

What should the attitude of believers be toward the law that for them is no longer valid? Paul answers by applying here a comprehensive status quo theory: Christians are to remain in whatever external condition they were in when they became believers. This theory is stated in general terms in 1 Corinthians 7:17, 20, and is applied to circumcision in verse 18. The result is that the one who believed as a Jew must continue to live by the Jewish law (Paul himself did so), whereas the non-Jew must not submit to its regulations.

While such a position may sound like a mere expedient, a compromise arrived at under the pressures of missionary experience, in fact we are dealing once again with a logical, "necessary inference" from Paul's fundamental convictions. Here it is his mystical doctrine of the believer's existence in Christ that is decisive. "From the moment that a man is in-Christ his whole being is completely conditioned by that fact. . . . If in spite of this he begins to make alterations in his natural condition of existence, he is ignoring the fact that his being is henceforth conditioned by the being-in-Christ, and not by anything else connected with his natural existence" (194-95). The theory at least is consistent. But if Jews and non-Jews were to enjoy table fellowship together, it became clear that Jewish believers would be required to make compromises in practice (cf. Gal. 2:11-14).

The Juridical Doctrine of Redemption

Paul's juridical doctrine of salvation is the familiar one of righteousness through faith. Strictly speaking, "righteousness" in this context belongs to the future: to be "righteous" is to have "a claim to be pronounced righteous at the coming Judgment, and consequently to become a partaker in the Messianic glory" (205). Whereas in postbiblical Jewish theology such righteousness was acquired by keeping the commandments, for Paul the decisive factor was faith in the redemptive efficacy of Christ's death. But Paul's view differs in another important respect as well. Since believers are already "in Christ" (the mystical view of salvation), they possess already the state of existence that belongs to the messianic kingdom, including righteousness. "There is therefore now no condemnation for those who are *in Christ Jesus*" (Rom. 8:1).

Thus for Paul the juridical doctrine of salvation is rooted in his mystical views of the believer's being in Christ. To be sure, this is not apparent from the expression "righteousness by faith" by itself, but the phrase must be understood as a convenient shorthand, adopted in a polemical setting in which Paul had to distinguish this righteousness from that which is "by the law." But a more adequate summation of the doctrine would run "Righteousness, in consequence of faith, through the being-in-Christ" (206-7).

In Galatians the connection between the juridical view and Paul's eschatological and mystical doctrines is clear. There Paul insists that the law cannot produce righteousness since it was not even designed to do so. On the contrary, the law comes (according to Paul's eschatological doctrine) from angel powers in order to keep humanity under their dominion. The promise of righteousness is made to the "seed" (singular) of Abraham, that is, to Christ (Gal. 3:16). Hence it belongs to those who by faith are "in Christ Jesus" (the mystical doctrine of salvation; v. 26). Thus we arrive at the doctrine of "righteousness, in consequence of faith, through the being-in-Christ." At least in Galatians the argument is not that Christ's death was an atonement made to God for sins; rather, it was the means of setting free those who are subject to the angel powers (4:1-11).

In Romans, on the other hand, Paul attempts to develop the juridical doctrine of righteousness by faith in a different way. Aware that the church at Rome might have been prejudiced against him, he proceeds with great caution, exercising particular care in what he says about the law. Its connection with angel powers is not mentioned. Rather, Paul explains the need for redemption on the basis of (1) human nature, which can do no good, and (2) the nature of the law, which forbids sin but has no power to deal with it. From such a predicament redemption is secured by the atoning death of Jesus, bringing forgiveness of sin to those who believe in him (Rom. 3:21-28).

Such a view of redemption, however, must not be mistaken for the center of Paul's thought. On the contrary, it is utterly incapable of serving as a starting point for the understanding of Paul, since it is rather "a fragment from the more comprehensive mystical redemption-doctrine, which Paul has broken off and polished" to suit the needs of a particular occasion (220). If "righteousness by faith" appears to stand on its own in Romans, Galatians clearly shows its dependence on notions derived from Paul's eschatological and mystical doctrines.

In both Romans and Galatians it is mentioned only "where the controversy over the Law has to be dealt with, and — very significantly — even then only where a Scriptural argument is to be based on the as yet uncircumcised Abraham. . . . Once Paul has left behind the discussion necessitated by his Scriptural argument, about faith-righteousness and Law-righteousness, it is of no more service to him" (220-21).

Paul made no effort to base his ethics on the doctrine of justification by faith, nor could he readily have done so if he had tried. "It would have been necessary to show how the man who previously was inherently incapable of producing good works received through the act of justification the capacity to do so" (295). And how can ethics be constructed out of the "idea of a faith which rejects not only the works of the Law, but works in general" (225)? The dilemma does not concern Paul, for justification by faith is not central to his thinking. Instead he bases his ethics on what is paramount, the mystical doctrine of dying and rising with Christ. "But those who subsequently made his doctrine of justification by faith the centre of Christian belief, have had the tragic experience of finding that they were dealing with a conception of redemption, from which no ethic could logically be derived" (225).

Furthermore, freedom from the law follows naturally from Paul's mystical doctrine, since those who died "with Christ" died to the law and to sin. But no case against the law's validity can be based on the atoning death of Jesus; in fact, the other early Christians, who certainly believed that Christ's death had secured for them the forgiveness of sins, continued nonetheless to live in accordance with the law. And why not? From Christ's death for our sins we may certainly deduce the inadequacy of our attempts to observe the law; but it does not follow from the atonement that the law is no longer to be observed. Paul's convictions on that score can scarcely have been derived from the doctrine of righteousness by faith in the atoning death of Jesus. "The doctrine of righteousness by faith is therefore a subsidiary crater, which has formed within the rim of the main crater — the mystical doctrine of redemption through the being-in-Christ" (225).

And so there are three doctrines of redemption in Paul; he passes freely from one to the other. But they are not equally important. The juridical doctrine, justification by faith, is the least important of the three. The primary significance of the eschatological doctrine is that it served as the starting point from which Paul developed his theology. But it is in his mystical views that we discover the heart of his theology and personal religion.

*   *

The significance of Wrede and Schweitzer for the Pauline debate is by no means limited to their insistence that justification by faith was a peripheral concern of the apostle. The emphasis on Paul's eschatological worldview, on the "realism" of his language regarding human bondage and deliverance, on the universal aspects of his scheme of redemption, on the perils of deriving Paul's views from those of Jesus and the folly of tracing them to his preconversion psychological state: all these themes have surfaced repeatedly in the subsequent debate.

Still, the best-known phrase from Wrede's *Paul* remains his label of justification as Paul's "polemical doctrine"; and in Schweitzer's case, his description of the same doctrine as a "subsidiary crater" rivals the famous last words of *The Quest* in a bid for immortality. Perhaps it is too much, perhaps even churlish, to ask of such deathless words that they should also be true. Yet the impertinence must be permitted, for to downplay justification is to challenge cherished notions of Paul. In Part Three we will need to return to the question of the significance of Paul's doctrine of justification by faith to his thought.

But first we must turn to other attacks on "Lutheran" readings of the apostle.

Chapter 7

The Faith of Paul's Fathers:
Montefiore, Schoeps, and Sanders

According to Luther, Christianity is set apart from the world by its insistence on justification by faith, not works, and the affinities of Judaism are with the world. This simple distinction has proven attractive to many Christian scholars and theologians, not least because it has relieved them of the tedious task of examining the sources of rabbinic Judaism for themselves. From his own experience, and with considerable acumen, Luther had described a religion of works; the pattern, it was supposed, would surely serve for Judaism as well. And in fact, the correctness of the model was thought to be established by the efforts of one or two intrepid souls who culled from rabbinic writings quotations to illustrate each of its aspects. The hermeneutical circle was then made complete when these quotations were taken to provide background material for understanding Paul. The apostle was thus interpreted in contrast with Judaism, which itself was interpreted in the light of the Catholicism of Luther's day, which in turn was interpreted by Luther's reading of Paul. Until recently the cycle showed every sign of being self-perpetuating.

Such, in rough, is the genesis of the traditional view of Paul's relations with Judaism as seen by those espousing a radical revision. Their most obvious point of attack has been the understanding of Judaism imposed by the scheme. What, after all, could be more damaging than the simple demonstration that those who portrayed Judaism had very limited command of the primary sources, and that a misleading sixteenth-century analogy was the real basis for their depiction? It is not surprising, then, that the latest stage in the debate about Paul and the Jewish law has been sparked by a large-scale attack on what are taken to be Christian caricatures of Judaism. The Judaism of our hermeneutical circle proclaimed that salvation was earned by human works. Sanders denies the accuracy of that description and suggests that a Paul detached from the circle will require reinterpretation as well.

In this chapter we will review the work of three Pauline scholars who have argued that Judaism is wrongly cast as a foil for the doctrine of justification by faith, not works. Montefiore and Schoeps see Paul himself as the source of the distortion, though they explain somewhat differently how he was misled. In Sanders's work the blame rests primarily with Paul's interpreters. For all three, the traditional ("Lutheran") understanding of Paul's rejection of the Jewish law needs rethinking.

i. Claude G. Montefiore

Claude G. Montefiore is best known to students of the New Testament for his important work *The Synoptic Gospels* (1st ed., 1909). The world was young in 1909, and many Christian readers were surprised to find that a Jewish scholar was able not only to shed light on many aspects of the Gospels, but even to treat the figure of Jesus with obvious sympathy. That feat accomplished, Montefiore ventured upon the still more daunting task of understanding and fairly assessing the apostle Paul; in 1914 he published two essays under the title *Judaism and St. Paul*. Our attention will be limited to the first study, "The Genesis of the Religion of St. Paul."

Even in 1914 the questions Montefiore raised were not new. Still, he hoped that more satisfactory answers could then be given based on recent advances in the knowledge of the world in which Paul lived and — above all — on the contemporary spirit of impartiality that attempted to do justice to both Jesus and the Pharisees, Paul and the rabbis. The lack of sympathy that Christian scholars had customarily shown for rabbinic Judaism was self-evident. So, too, was their lack of firsthand knowledge. "Rabbinic Judaism seems to be the one department of learning about which many great scholars have been willing to make assertions without being able to read the original authorities, or to test the references and statements of the writers whom they quote."[1] The normal procedure had been to suppose that the Judaism Paul knew was rabbinic, to base one's understanding of rabbinic Judaism on polemical passages in Paul, and then to find support for such an understanding in quotations lifted, with no appreciation for their nature or context, from rabbinic writings. For his part Montefiore attempts to show that the Judaism with which Paul was familiar was not rabbinic; he comments on the patent injustice of basing one's view of a religion on the polemical statements of an opponent and convert; and he notes

---

1. Montefiore, *St. Paul*, 7. Parenthetical page references in the section on Montefiore are to this work.

that isolated quotations from the vast sea of rabbinic writings could be used to prove any thesis whatsoever.

The task Montefiore sets for himself is to explain "Paul's religious antecedents — his religious history and opinions before his conversion," as well as "his relation to the Judaisms of his age and time" (13). The plural ("Judaisms") is deliberate: "several Judaisms, all more or less fluid and growing, existed in the first century" (3). Though the divisions "are not water-tight or cut and dry" (5), we may nonetheless speak of rabbinic, apocalyptic, and Hellenistic Judaisms in the world of A.D. 50.

Montefiore begins with a short account of rabbinic religion. To portray first-century rabbinic Judaism is notoriously difficult, since rabbinic literature comes from a much later period and Jewish writings closer to Paul's day were produced by "writers whose relation to Rabbinic Judaism is often doubtful and disputed" (15). Montefiore adopts a curious and, at first sight, unpromising procedure. Since the rabbinic Judaism of A.D. 300 or 500 is well known, he begins by simply asking: "What was the relation of Paul's religion before his conversion to *this* Rabbinic Judaism? How far was his religion, before the event at Damascus, the same as, or different from, that of any ordinary and average representative of Rabbinic Judaism?" (16). The justification for such a procedure is that Christian scholars have traditionally characterized rabbinic Judaism on the basis of Paul's first-century writings, simply assuming that the Judaism Paul knew was essentially the same. A more accurate description of later Judaism will suffice, Montefiore believes, to show the falseness of the assumption.

Here we may note three areas in which Montefiore finds differences between rabbinic Judaism as we know it from later sources and the religion known to the apostle Paul.

1. We begin with the law. Rabbinic Jews regard the law as the gracious gift of a loving God to his people, designed to make them happy and good. Obeying God's law is the duty and the privilege that together distinguish Israel from the Gentile nations. Since the law was given for Israel's good, its observance brings life, happiness, and peace. Hence "the core and essence of the Rabbinic religion are contained in that one familiar phrase, 'the joy of the commandments'" (29-30).

The great number of commands by no means represented an intolerable burden. For one thing, the imposition of the commandments was perceived as the granting of a privilege; thus the more the commands, the greater the honor given to God's people. In an often-cited prayer, Jewish men thanked God daily that they were not women because (note the reason!) "men have more commandments to fulfill than women" (29). Actually the number of commands to which any individual was required to conform was not that large in any case.

"The compulsion of the Law was chiefly felt in two directions — the Sabbath and food. There were very many things which you might not do upon the Sabbath, but you soon learnt what they were, and if there is one thing more certain than another it is that the Sabbath was a joy. There were numerous laws about food, but some concerned the butcher, others the women who cooked; those which remained were easily acquired and remembered" (32-33).

But what happened when the laws were transgressed? Did rabbinic Jews not believe that God was angered by the violation of his commands? And since God's pleasure was thought to depend on obedience to his demands, did not the average Jew live in uncertainty and fear of the final judgment? Such dilemmas arise frequently in Christian portrayals of Judaism, but — it must be emphasized — they were not perceived as problems by the average Jew. Of course, it was recognized that no one keeps the law perfectly, and that God is angered when his commands are broken. But the Israelite remembered "that the Law was given to men, and not to angels" (40); and it was given specifically to bring about improvement, purification, and increasing holiness in God's people. Perfection was not expected. If God is angered by transgression, his compassion certainly outweighs his anger; "and by the gracious gift of repentance He helps [the Jew] both to conquer his sin and to obtain its forgiveness" (42). Counting on God's love for Israel and his willingness to forgive, the average Jew could be both "happy and hopeful: happy in the performance, within the limits of human frailty, of the divine commands in this world, hopeful in the belief of the sure inheritance hereafter of the finer and purer beatitudes of the world to come" (36-37).

All of this bears little resemblance to what we find in Paul. To be sure, Paul acknowledges that the law is holy. But whereas for rabbinic Judaism the law was always thought to bring goodness and joy, for Paul it brought neither and was not intended to do so. "The Law was a curse. It evoked the knowledge of sin. It strengthened the desire to sin. By the works of the Law no man can win God's favour or be regarded by God as righteous" (70). One could understand if a rabbinic Jew, on becoming a Christian, were to argue that the law that before Christ had divided Jew from Gentile was now done away with. It would be understandable, too, for Paul to say that the moral laws are now unnecessary, since their demands are met spontaneously by Christians who possess God's Spirit. But Paul goes much further. "The important thing is that Paul does not content himself with saying that the Law was all very well, and did very well, up to Jesus Christ's day, but need not now, (and, therefore, should not now), be observed any more, but that he actually conceived the theory that the Law did definite and positive harm. . . . It made things worse than they were, or than they would have been, without it. And all this was its intention, the purpose for which it had been given" (106-7). Montefiore finds it inconceivable that Paul could have arrived at such views after his conversion if his previous view of the law had been that of rabbinic Judaism.

2. Something has already been said of the role that repentance and divine forgiveness played in the thinking of the rabbinic Jew. Sin was taken seriously, no less seriously than by the apostle Paul; but God stood ready to forgive. "Let a man repent but a very little, and God will forgive very much. For He delights in the exercise of forgiveness far more than in the exercise of punishment" (42). Since God's mercy is so readily available, it is only "the deliberate and determined sinner" who fails to attain life. "For every decent Israelite there was a place in the future world" (44).

The contrast with Paul's position is, again, pronounced. "Nothing is more peculiar in the great Epistles than the almost complete omission of the twin Rabbinic ideas of repentance and forgiveness" (75). Had Paul been brought up in rabbinic Judaism, he would at least have argued that the standard teaching on repentance was in some way inadequate. Instead it goes unmentioned, while Paul claims on the one hand that a single offense is sufficient to cause the curse of the law and the wrath of God to descend upon us (Gal. 3:10), and on the other that "only an amazing expedient and a terrific catastrophe" (70), the death of a "sinless divine being" (78), can redeem us. The need for such "a tremendous cosmic and divine event" as the incarnation and crucifixion was simply not felt by rabbinic theology, where "God was so good and near and kind," and where "man, through the Law and through repentance, had such constant, easy and efficacious opportunities of access to him" (74). It follows, surely, that Pauline soteriology is "impossible upon a purely Rabbinic basis" (77).

3. Finally, Pauline theology proves consistently more pessimistic than rabbinic thinking. The average rabbinic Jew perceived the world as good, created and governed by a loving God. "He has never allowed its government to fall into the hands of any lesser divine being than Himself, still less into the hands of some evil spirit or demon" (45-46). But for Paul "the world is under the domination of demons and of Satan. Paul even goes so far as to call Satan the god of this world, an expression which, to the average Rabbinic Jew, would verge upon blasphemy" (69). As for the moral capacities of humanity, rabbinic Judaism was fully aware of human sin, but recognized that there was some observance of the law and righteousness in the world as well; human goodness is as real as human evil. God's help was of course thought essential, but it was "not supposed that human efforts count for nothing" (78), or that, apart from a new birth, man is completely powerless to overcome the "flesh." Hence there was no need of the cross. "Man could receive salvation, and get the better of sin, (for God was always helping and forgiving) even without so strange and won-

derful a device" (78). By way of contrast, in the world of Pauline pessimism, those "in the flesh" simply cannot do good (Rom. 7:18; 8:7).

We are faced, then, with two alternatives: "Either the Rabbinic Judaism of 50 was not the Rabbinic Judaism of 500 (or 300), or Paul at the time of his conversion was no pure Rabbinic Jew" (68); for certainly the religion of Paul before his conversion was "poorer," "more sombre and gloomy than Rabbinic Judaism" (81). Montefiore notes that there are no indications of "any great improvement in the teachings of the famous Rabbis of the fourth century over those of the first" (87). He is therefore "inclined to think that, even in 50, Rabbinic Judaism was a better, happier, and more noble religion than one might infer from the writings of the Apostle" (87). Paul's background, then, was not in rabbinic Judaism at all. We are to seek it rather in the Judaism of the Hellenistic world.

In Hellenistic Judaism, Montefiore finds a number of features that help to explain the apostle's thinking. Contact with pagan philosophy had resulted in a conception of God "more distant and less approachable, . . . more august and majestic, but less gentle and kindly" (95). And "may we not also suppose that the general spiritual anxiety which was widely diffused in the later Hellenistic world had also infected the Jews? Some of them, too, may have begun to worry about their salvation and the 'state of their soul.' And as God had become more distant, so did sin seem, not more grievous, but less eradicable, than to their 'Rabbinic' brethren" (97).

The observance of the law came naturally to rabbinic Jews, and with little need for justification. Not so for Hellenistic Jews, living in the midst of pagans. They must have wondered often about the point of prohibitions that their neighbors did not observe. They could easily have come to think of the law "as something which restrained and forbade, rather than as something through which [they] gained ineffable joys and realised the presence of God" (100). Perhaps, too, a Hellenistic Jew would more readily be struck and troubled by the condemnation of Gentiles who did not observe, because they did not possess, the Jewish law. This, too, may have led to disaffection.

Along some such lines we may explain the development of Paul's theology. In any case, the foundation was not rabbinic. Of course, a rabbinic Jew could become convinced that Jesus was the Messiah and convert to Christianity. But the Pauline theories of the law and soteriology, and the basic Pauline pessimism, cannot have grown from rabbinic soil.

ii. Hans Joachim Schoeps

Montefiore's study, stimulating though it is, remains brief and at times superficial. The task of assessing Paul's relations with the Judaism of his day was taken up again on a much larger scale by the Jewish historian of religion Hans Joachim Schoeps. His *Paul* has been widely acclaimed as one of the most significant contributions to Pauline scholarship in the twentieth century.[2] Here we can only cast a brief look at the various subjects addressed before turning to the book's best-known argument: that Paul's reduction of the law to a sum of demands that cannot be kept represents a travesty of the Jewish position.

The book begins with a survey of "the main intellectual forces in the climate" (15) of Paul's day and evaluates their impact on Paul's thinking. Schoeps first reviews the work of scholars who believed Paul's thought was heavily influenced by Hellenistic conceptions. Schweitzer, it will be remembered, attacked such a notion vigorously. For his part Schoeps is willing to concede that much in Paul's thought world was non-Jewish, and that in a number of ways Hellenistic ideas and vocabulary are evidenced in his writings. In particular, the influence of the pagan mystery cults is "unmistakable" in Pauline soteriology and "sacramental mysticism" (47). Nonetheless, "pure Hellenism" is excluded as a source for Pauline theology (23). What Paul absorbed of Hellenistic thought would have reached him through the medium of the hellenized Judaism of the Diaspora.

As we have seen, Claude Montefiore held that the Judaism Paul knew was Hellenistic, not rabbinic, and that this background explains many features of Paul's thought. Schoeps criticizes Montefiore's methodology on a number of counts. First, it is misleading to treat rabbinic Judaism as though it were a unified whole; indeed, some of the Pauline positions that Montefiore contrasts with rabbinic thought "also found exponents in Palestinian schools" (26). Second, Montefiore strictly distinguishes apocalyptic thought from rabbinic, when in fact the apocalyptic movement flourished throughout first-century Palestine. It cannot be considered a sectarian phenomenon apart from "normative Judaism." Nor, for that matter, are we to assume "an irreconcilable opposition between Hellenistic and rabbinic Judaism" (26). What we know of the former is far too inadequate in any case to be used as a basis for explaining Paul's thought. Still, whatever the flaws in Montefiore's procedure, the fact remains that Paul was a Jew from the Diaspora; and though we must bear in mind the complexity of Hellenistic Judaism, we do find many ways in which it proves an essential factor in a reconstruction of Paul's doctrine and faith.

---

2. Parenthetical page references in the section on Schoeps are to this work.

According to Acts 22:3, Paul was educated in Jerusalem by Gamaliel (Rabban Gamaliel I). Schoeps believes the influence of this school is apparent in Paul's argumentation and exegetical method. Paul was clearly a "rabbinist," and any explanation of a point in his theology that proceeds from rabbinic thought deserves from the outset "preference over all other explanations" (40). Most importantly, Paul's eschatological thought was shaped by the discussions of the Palestinian schools.

In short, none of the main intellectual forces of Paul's day can be discounted as an influence on his thought. Nor, on the other hand, should we reduce Paul's thinking to "the sum of its various component parts" (48). Paul was trying "to give expression to something quite new. This new element has dawned for him through his encounter with the risen Messiah, convincing him that the new aeon has already supervened" (40).

Schoeps's second chapter is entitled "The Position of the Apostle Paul in Primitive Christianity." Paul's Christian experience began when he met the risen Jesus on the road to Damascus. Yet the question of the significance of Jesus for Paul is a difficult one. To judge by Paul's writings, the earthly Jesus played no great role in the piety or thinking of the apostle, though an exception must of course be made for Jesus' death on the cross. Central for Paul is simply the belief *that* the Messiah has come, and thus that "the times are now post-messianic" (58). The first church was convinced that it lived at the "end of the age." Paul made this common conviction the "point of departure for the structure of his own theology" (62).

As for Paul's relations with the early church, we know that during his ministry opposition arose on two basic issues: the practice to be followed in admitting Gentiles into the church and the correct understanding of the apostolate. On the first issue the differences between Paul and the prime apostles should not be exaggerated. Peter and James adopted what amounted to a mediating position between the extreme positions of Paul, who repudiated any claim of the Mosaic law on Gentile believers, and the Judaizers, who defended its complete validity for all Christians (Acts 15:20). We may certainly conclude from Galatians 2 and from the collection Paul gathered from his churches for the Jerusalem believers that his missionary procedure met with the approval of the leading apostles. The significant difference concerned the question of apostleship. Schoeps takes the oldest view of the apostolate to be that which limited the title to the twelve who accompanied Jesus throughout his earthly ministry. For Paul, however, the criterion of apostleship was not that of "knowing Jesus after the flesh, but only of witness to the Risen Lord" (72). But in this area too it was Judaizing extremists who attacked Paul's apostleship. The circle of the Twelve was too impressed by Paul's missionary success to raise the issue.

After these introductory attempts to place Paul's work in the context of the first century, Schoeps discusses in turn Paul's eschatology (chap. 3), his soteriology (chap. 4), his teaching about the law (chap. 5), and his understanding of saving history (chap. 6). In each case he notes the roots of Paul's thinking in Jewish theology as well as areas where Paul goes beyond the bounds of what the latter could find acceptable.

Paul's *eschatology* has obvious links with the "tense Messianic expectation" (259) that pervaded Palestinian Judaism in his day. Not that there was any "unified scheme of thought about the last things" (97). Still, the notion that Messiah would come at the end of time was simply adopted by Paul from current Jewish eschatology. For Paul, however, Messiah had already come — and yet the "end" had not followed. Hence the traditional understanding required correction, and the unexpected interval before the parousia required interpretation. Paul concluded that the boundary between "this age" and "the age to come" had broken down, giving way to a brief transitional period: the messianic kingdom had begun, the age of salvation had dawned, the old aeon was in the process of passing away — and yet the old order remained somehow in place. None of these conclusions is acceptable in the eyes of Judaism, for which the world after the "transformation" that Paul purports resembles nothing so much as its old, unaltered self. It is of course the fact that Paul looks *back* on the coming of the Messiah that has led to the different perspective.

Paul's *soteriology* has roots in at least three Jewish ideas.

1. The suffering of the righteous can have an atoning value. Such an understanding grows out of biblical ideas of sacrifice as "expiatory and substitutionary" (130).

2. The "Servant of Yahweh" would suffer vicariously and surrender his life as an atoning sacrifice (Isa. 53). Schoeps believes that already in Judaism the Servant was "probably at an early period understood and personified as the Messiah" (135).

3. The "binding" of Isaac as Abraham prepared to sacrifice him (Gen. 22:9) was believed to have expiatory value. In Schoeps's opinion this belief "provided the very model for the elaboration of Pauline soteriology" (141).

Despite these Jewish roots, Pauline soteriology becomes fundamentally un-Jewish when it views Jesus as God's incarnate Son, possessing "real divinity" (149). A Jewish source for this notion is simply inconceivable. If some derivation must be suggested, we should look rather to "heathen mythological conceptions, filtered through the Hellenistic syncretism of the time" (149).

Again, Paul's view of *salvation history* grew out of Jewish convictions. Before his conversion Paul no doubt held the belief that in the messianic age the Gentiles would join Israel in worshiping Israel's God. Indeed, Paul may well have shared the missionary zeal of many Pharisees, who reasoned that they could hasten the coming of Messiah by converting the heathen. Such a task became even more urgent when Paul was convinced that Messiah had come and the messianic age had begun. Now it was crucial that the prophetic promises that had not yet come to pass should be fulfilled in as short a time as possible.

On the other hand, what the traditional understanding did not foresee was that most Jews would not recognize their Messiah but would crucify him, thereby "casting the promises to the winds" (220). Again Paul was forced to rethink the traditional view; Romans 9–11 in particular shows him grappling with the problem. He came to distinguish between the "empiric-historical Israel" and the "eschatological Israel of the promise" (238). God's election of "Israel" does not include all (physical) Israelites, but only a remnant, a chosen few. Joining them in the "true Israel" of God were Gentiles who believed in Christ. Still, in the end, when "the full number of the Gentiles come in" (Rom. 11:25), the whole of (physical) Israel will be saved as well; "as the descendants of the patriarchs," they retain a "special sanctity in election" (242). For none of these speculations are we to seek Jewish parallels, since the problems that led to the revision of traditional views were the product of Christian faith.

On *the law* as well, Paul's theology amounts to "nothing other than the rethinking of all received notions" (171) in view of the coming of the Messiah and his resurrection from the dead. Schoeps follows Schweitzer in thinking that Paul was guided by a common conviction that the law would lose its validity when the messianic kingdom began. As support he cites rabbinic traditions that saw the age of the world as predetermined at 6,000 years: 2,000 years of chaos, a 2,000-year era of the Mosaic law, then the era of the Messiah. Since for Paul the Messiah had come, it followed that the validity of the law had now passed (Rom. 10:4). What separates Paul's conviction from rabbinic views is simply the premise "that the Messianic age had begun with the death and resurrection of Jesus" (173).

Having arrived at this conclusion, however, Paul was led to reflect further about the purpose and nature of the law; and here his thinking proved in many respects incompatible with Judaism. We may note, for example, his suggestion that the law, far from limiting sinfulness (it had proven unable to do so before the coming of Messiah), must have been intended to make "sinfulness evident" and to pile "up the measure of sins" (174). Paul even views the law as leading inevitably to death, contrary to the Jewish conviction that its observance brings life. But Paul's conclusions are determined throughout by a "retrospective way of thought" (175). Starting with his faith in Jesus Christ, the Messiah and Savior, he is forced to rethink the function of the law. The result, not surprisingly, is that the law is seen as a "custodian until Christ came" (Gal. 3:24).

Other Pauline arguments share points of contact with rabbinic thought but are developed in un-Jewish ways. Like Paul (Gal. 3:10; 5:3), the rabbis were concerned that no one fulfills the whole law; yet the problem never became for them a reason to dismiss the law as the basis on which life may be conducted according to God's will. The rabbinic tradition that angels were present at Sinai when the law was given was recklessly transformed by Paul into a notion that the law was given by angels hostile to the Jewish people (Gal. 3:19). This suggestion in particular, made by Paul "in the heat of the contest" (183), would have monstrous consequences when taken up by Simon Magus, Cerinthus, and Marcion.

Paul's argument in Romans 7 has interesting rabbinic parallels. For Paul the human heart is the scene of a constant struggle between the spirit and the flesh, the human will and human moral capacities. The struggle, however, is an uneven one; actual conduct is inevitably determined by "sin" residing in the "flesh." This picture of inner moral conflict is related to the rabbinic doctrine of the struggle between the evil and the good "impulses" within us. And though usually the two are believed to have equal strength, there are certainly some rabbis who think, like Paul, that the evil impulse *(yetser hara')* dominates. And still "other voices are raised which go farther and understand the *yetser hara'* as an independently effective cosmic force, not merely as an impulse to evil but as an evil impulse conceived on almost daemonological lines, almost as an alien god dwelling in the body of man" (185). Here it is clear that Schoeps finds rabbinic parallels even to the "Pauline pessimism" that for Montefiore must have had a Hellenistic source. For Schoeps "Paul's doctrine of sin was not unusual but indeed typical of his time" (187). What Paul does not reckon with, however, is the power of repentance, "which according to Jewish belief of all ages is able to break the mastery of sin" (188).

Even this fundamental omission, however, does not mark the most radical difference between Paul and the rabbis about the law. The Septuagint (the Greek translation of the Old Testament), by rendering Hebrew *torah* as νόμος, brought about a shift in emphasis: whereas the Hebrew term "is best explained as instruction embracing both law and doctrine," the Greek equivalent comes to imply simply "a moral way of life prescribed by God" (29). Paul, whose thinking was guided by the Septuagint, understood the law as a "sum of prescriptions" to be kept (188). Righteousness and life would be granted if it was fully obeyed, but condemnation and death would follow if it was not. Here the notion of Torah has been effectively reduced to the ethical law, a body of demands that, Paul believes, have not been met because of the sinfulness of humankind. Thus righteousness cannot be attained by the works of the law, that is, by human attempts to meet God's demands. Only faith in Christ brings salvation.

But such a view represents a "fundamental misapprehension" of what Jews mean by the law. "Paul did not perceive, and for various reasons was perhaps unable to perceive, that in the Biblical view the law is integral to the covenant" (213). As the seal of God's covenant with Israel, the law is understood to bind Israel closely with its God. Through the law God intends to make his people holy.

Apart from its relation with the covenant, the law simply cannot be understood. It is not a mere "sum of prescriptions" against which human deficiencies can be measured and condemned. It is a token of God's love for his people, presupposing his relationship with them established in the covenant by his election-grace and intended to provide them with a remedy for the evil impulse within them. When Jews show a willingness to obey the law, God quickly comes to lend his aid so that sins may be overcome. That all the law's demands should be perfectly met is neither expected nor even an issue. What is important is the *intention* to obey, "because that intention is man's affirmation of the covenant, which precedes the law" (196). Israel's relationship with God is thus determined fundamentally by a covenant of divine grace. Observance of the law is not the basis but the affirmation of that relationship.

We may go further. If obedience to the law is valued primarily as an affirmation of God's covenant, then it is scarcely just to regard such works of the law as an attempt to gain righteousness by human effort and an *alternative* to faith in the pursuit of justification. After all, "faith" in the Hebrew sense "connotes trust in the sense of fidelity" (202). A contrast between faith and the works of the law is thus unthinkable, for fidelity to the covenant can only be expressed by the affirmation implied in obedience to its demands. Furthermore, even the ceremonial demands of the law can only be understood in the context of the covenant, for circumcision, Sabbath observance, and the like have value only as symbolic acts pointing to, and affirming the reality of, God's special relation with Israel. For Israel to accept the abrogation of the law would be tantamount to renouncing the covenant on which its very existence was based.

A quotation from Schoeps's final chapter provides an eloquent conclusion:

> It must ever remain thought-provoking that the Christian church has received a completely distorted view of the Jewish law at the hands of a Diaspora Jew who had become alienated from the faith-ideas of the fathers — a view which ignores that side of it connected with the *berith* [covenant] as a sanctifying ordinance and which has reduced it to a matter of ethical self-justification and ritual performance. And still more astounding is the fact that church theology throughout Christian history has imputed Paul's unacceptability to the Jews to Jewish insensitivity, and has never asked itself whether it might not be due to the fact that Paul could gain no audience with the Jews because from the start he misunderstood Jewish theology. (261-62)

iii. E. P. Sanders

Sanders's *Paul and Palestinian Judaism*[3] has had its critics, but neither timidity nor smallness of vision has ever figured among the charges. An innocuous-sounding proposal "to compare Judaism, understood on its own terms, with Paul, understood on his own terms" (xi) cloaks the ambitiousness of an undertaking whose perils are perhaps rivaled, within the purview of New Testament scholarship, only by those of comparing the historical Jesus himself with Judaism. (That, to be sure, was Sanders's next project!) We will postpone our look at Sanders's Paul until a later chapter. Here we will focus on his modest intention "to destroy the view of Rabbinic Judaism which [at the time he wrote Sanders could claim] is still prevalent in much, perhaps most, New Testament scholarship" (xii).

In comparing Paul with Palestinian Judaism, Sanders examines not individual motifs common to both, but the "patterns of religion" they represent. (The "pattern" of a religion, for Sanders, is the way it admits and retains its members, or *"how getting in and staying in are understood"* [17].) Palestinian Judaism is discussed under the headings "Tannaitic Literature," "The Dead Sea Scrolls," and "Apocrypha and Pseudepigrapha." The careful delineations betray the modern awareness of the diversity that prevailed in Palestinian Judaism at the turn of the era. Yet it is among Sanders's most important conclusions that a fundamental unity (a single "pattern of religion") underlies nearly every witness we possess to the Judaism of the period (422-23).[4] Sanders describes the unifying concept as "covenantal nomism": the notion that a Jew's standing before God is secured by God's election of Israel as his covenant people (this, then, is how "getting in" was understood in Judaism), and that obedience to the law is Israel's proper *response* to God's initial act of grace (75). While a Jew's intention to obey the law is thought necessary if the relationship with God is to be *maintained* (this, then, is how "staying in" was understood), it does not follow that salvation is "earned" or regarded as a reward for human achievements.

Sanders's portrayal of Judaism is designed to refute the notion that it was a religion of "legalistic works-righteousness" (33) in which "one must *earn* salvation by compiling more good works ('merits'), whether on his own or from the excess of someone else, than he has transgressions" (38). On the basis of an important study by G. F. Moore,[5] Sanders notes that the description of Judaism in these terms entered Christian scholarship in the nineteenth century through

---

3. Parenthetical page references in this section on Sanders are to this work.
4. In Sanders, "Covenant," that basic unity is extended to Hellenistic Judaism as well.
5. Cf. Moore, "Writers," 197-254.

the work of Ferdinand Weber. In Weber's Judaism the benefits of God's covenant with Israel were wiped out already in the wilderness when Israel worshiped the golden calf. Thereafter individual Israelites could gain acceptance before God only by compiling a list of fulfillments of the law and other good deeds that outweighed the list of their transgressions (36-38). In subsequent literature Weber's theory of Israel's fall from the covenant was ignored. Otherwise his account of Jewish soteriology was largely taken over in the work of Bousset and Schürer, Billerbeck and Bultmann. Repeatedly we find the view that in Judaism works "earn" salvation, that God "weighs" fulfillments of the law against transgressions to determine who will be saved, and that the result of such a soteriology was a despairing uncertainty of salvation on the one hand or a self-righteous boasting on the other (38-59). A better foil for the Lutheran doctrine of justification could scarcely be conceived.

In Sanders's view, only a massive misunderstanding of the nature and intent of rabbinic sources could yield such a description of Jewish soteriology. The evidence requires a different interpretation. (We will here pass over Sanders's discussions of the Dead Sea Scrolls, the Apocrypha, and the Pseudepigrapha, looking only at his treatment of the early rabbinic — or "Tannaitic" — writings.)

1. Much of rabbinic literature is "halakic" in nature; that is, it is concerned to spell out the precise application of the many provisions of divine law. Outsiders to the system, confronted and confounded by endless definitions and distinctions, are liable to conclude that rabbinic religion never rises above a peculiar brand of petty legalism. Yet behind the legal endeavor lies the conviction of the rabbis, too self-evident to require continual articulation, that obedience to the commands marks the privilege and obligation imposed on Israel by the covenant with God. Naturally it was important to define carefully Israel's covenantal responsibilities, for "Israel's situation in the covenant required the law to be obeyed as fully and completely as possible" (81). This conviction, not a belief that salvation was earned by keeping the laws, was the rabbis' motive in formulating halakah.

2. God's commitment to the covenant with Israel was believed to be unconditional: he would remain faithful to his promises even when Israel disobeyed his laws (95). Such disobedience would of course be punished, and the *individual* Israelite who repudiated the covenant would fall from the sphere of its blessings. But the rabbis never suggested that the covenant itself might be revoked. It remained the framework that determined Israel's relations with God.

3. To the question why God chose Israel and granted Israel his covenant, different answers were given (89-99). A story was sometimes told in which the covenant was actually offered to all the nations, though accepted only by Israel.

In other texts Israel was said to be chosen because of some merit of the patri-archs or of the wilderness generation. Still elsewhere the laws were said to be given with a view to the obedience that Israel would yield to them in the future. A final explanation found in the texts is that God acted simply "for his name's sake." Thus, while some explanations stress the gratuity of the election, others suggest that merit was a factor. In each case the homiletic need of the moment, not a rabbinic "systematic theology," determined the emphasis. Still, we may at least say that for the rabbis divine grace and human merit were not perceived as mutually exclusive (100; cf. 297: "I believe that it is safe to say that the notion that God's grace is in any way contradictory to human endeavour is totally for-eign to Palestinian Judaism"). At the same time, we should note that, however the rabbis may have accounted for God's election in the past, "there is no thought that subsequent Israelites must continue to earn their place in the cov-enant as individuals, or that the covenant must be re-won in each generation" (101).

4. There is in Judaism no "doctrine of original sin," no suggestion that hu-mans are born into "a state of sinfulness from which liberation is necessary" (114). "Despite the tendency to disobey, man is free to obey or disobey" (115). Firmly entrenched, moreover, in the rabbinic conception of God is the justice of his judgments: he rewards obedience and punishes transgressions (117). Nat-urally, then, for homiletic purposes, God's rewards and punishments are fre-quently stressed in the literature. Two qualifications, however, must be borne in mind. First, divine justice was meted out to Israel within the framework of the covenant. As God's people through the covenant, the people of Israel were judged by their conformity to the covenant's laws. Their obedience was thus never seen as the means by which they *became* God's people, nor did they "earn" their salvation. Second, we are not to imagine that "a man's payment" was believed to be "strictly in accordance with his deserts" (119), for many state-ments are made to the contrary. Indeed, a rabbi might choose to emphasize the importance of obedience by saying that the fulfillment of a single "light" com-mandment brings very great reward. And in general, the dominant view is not that merits and demerits are subject to strict measurement and recompense, but that God's mercy prevails and will be granted to all Israelites whose basic intent is one of obedience. "What counts is being in the covenant and intending to be obedient to the God who gave the covenant. Rejection of even one com-mandment with the intent to deny the God who gave it excludes one from the covenant, while acceptance of a fundamental commandment, such as the com-mandment not to commit idolatry, may show one's intent to be obedient" (135).

5. That rabbinic soteriology did not involve the strict weighing of fulfillments of the law against transgressions is proven by the quite different

view that is "totally pervasive" (147) in rabbinic literature. It is stated most clearly and concisely in *Mishnah Sanhedrin* 10:1: "All Israelites have a share in the world to come" (cited, 147). The only exceptions to the rule are the "worst individual sinners" and the "most unregenerate generations" (149). Not perfect, or even 51 percent, fulfillment of the law's commands, but membership in Israel, the covenant community, is the basis of the Jew's standing before God.

6. That this, and not the theory by which merits are measured, constituted rabbinic soteriology is confirmed by the frequent claims made in the literature about the efficacy of repentance and atonement. "The universally held view is this: God has appointed means of atonement for every transgression, except the intention to reject God and his covenant" (157). If repentance can bring forgiveness for any number of sins, then God does not determine human destiny by weighing merits against transgressions (176). And lest we construe repentance itself as "earning" salvation, it must be remembered that it was thought to *restore*, not establish, the Israelite's standing within the covenant (178).

7. The "righteous" Jew in rabbinic writings is thus not one who earns divine approval by compiling an impressive list of good deeds, but simply "one who accepts the covenant and remains within it" (204). Here we may anticipate our later discussion and note that, for Sanders, when Paul and Palestinian Judaism are compared as "patterns of religion," they are found to be in substantial *agreement* on the relationship between grace and works (543). In Judaism, as for Paul, salvation (or "getting in") is by divine grace, since Israel gained its status as God's people by election and the gift of the covenant. On the other hand, works are necessary, for Paul as for Judaism, if that status is to be maintained ("staying in"): "the intention and effort to be obedient constitute the *condition for remaining in the covenant*, but they do not *earn* it" (180). To be sure, Paul criticizes Judaism by saying that righteousness is by faith, not works, but the formula actually "misstates the fundamental point of disagreement" (551). When Paul talks about gaining righteousness, he refers to how one gains one's standing before God — and his contemporaries in Judaism would have agreed that this was by grace. When Palestinian Judaism talked about being righteous by obeying the law, it meant that such works are required for one to *maintain* such a standing — and Paul too, according to Sanders, required works for that purpose. Hence the essential agreement is concealed by the different senses given to "righteousness" (544).

8. Thus Pauline theology is *not* distinct from rabbinic thinking in its insistence that justification is by divine grace, not human works. The fundamental point of Paul's opposition was simply his conviction that salvation is only to be found in Jesus Christ. The inevitable consequence was that Israel's election, covenant, and law could not bring salvation (551-52). Paul's exclusive and

christocentric soteriology, not a rejection of works, is what sets his Christian faith apart from Judaism.

*   *

We are left, it seems, with the following alternatives. Either the traditional ("Lutheran") view is correct, Pauline Christianity is distinguished from rabbinic thought by its doctrine of justification by faith, not works, and scholars such as Montefiore, Schoeps, and Sanders have misinterpreted Judaism; or these latter writers are correct in their depictions of Judaism, the traditional view is correct in maintaining that Paul opposed it as a religion of works, and Paul himself is the one who (for whatever reason) misrepresented the faith of his fathers; or the traditional view is wrong on both counts, and Paul's opposition to Judaism did not lie in a rejection of works.

We will return to the issue below. But first we must note another area in which modern scholars have argued that "Lutheran" readings have distorted Paul's thought.

Chapter 8

Paul's Robust Conscience:
Kümmel and Stendahl

According to Protestant hagiography, the insights of the apostle Paul, which were hidden from ages and from generations, were discovered by Augustine and Luther. Krister Stendahl proposes a different model. The "hidden" insights were not Paul's but those of Augustine and Luther themselves. Readers of Paul in the first Christian centuries and in Eastern Christianity of all periods have read Paul very differently for the simple reason that Augustine and Luther imposed on the Pauline texts concerns of the modern West. In particular, Augustine and Luther brought keenly sensitive, introspective consciences to their reading of the apostle, whereas Paul's own conscience was robust and untroubled. Nowhere is the resultant distortion greater than in Luther's understanding of the primary function of the law.

The argument is fascinating and instructive. Before we review it, however, we need to look at what Stendahl labels the "epoch-making study" of W. G. Kümmel on which it rests. No chapter in the Pauline corpus has aroused more controversy than Romans 7, and no question in that difficult chapter is more disputed than the identity of the "I" who speaks there. The chapter appears to reveal Paul's own inner struggles and his despair of keeping the law. Kümmel denies that this is the case. Perhaps the best indication of the impact of his study is that Hübner, Sanders, and Räisänen, each of whom has written a major monograph on Paul and the law, do not feel the need to address this particular problem in depth. All refer their readers to Kümmel's work and assume that his results are fundamentally correct. This means, of course, that the current debate about the law in Paul's writings can scarcely be understood without some knowledge of Kümmel's *Römer 7*.[1]

---

1. Kümmel, *Römer 7 und die Bekehrung des Paulus* (Leipzig: J. G. Hinrichs, 1929), reprinted

i. W. G. Kümmel

The interpretation of Romans 7 advocated in Kümmel's study was not in fact new. We have already seen a similar view in Wrede's *Paul*, and Kümmel amply demonstrates that the "rhetorical" understanding of the chapter he espouses was widely held already in the patristic period and was common among scholars of the nineteenth and early twentieth centuries (87-88). Still, it is his own statement of the case that has come to be regarded by many as definitive. What follows is a restatement of Kümmel's arguments.

As noted above, a critical question for the interpretation of Romans 7 is the identity of the "I" who speaks in verses 7-25. Who is it who once "lived" without the law but died "when the commandment came" (v. 9)? Who is it who cannot carry out his own good intentions but continually finds himself doing the very evil he hates (vv. 15, 19)? Is Paul simply relating his personal experience? Or is he perhaps citing his own experience because it is typical of humanity as a whole, or of Jews outside of Christ, or, indeed, of Christians? Or is the "I" used rhetorically to portray the lot of humankind in general without necessarily reflecting the moral struggles in Paul's own life? The question is crucial, but it is best approached after the context and general trend of Paul's argument in Romans 7 have been established.

The Argument in Context

In the early chapters of Romans Paul makes frequent side remarks about the Mosaic law without pausing to support them or even, in some cases, to make them comprehensible to readers not familiar with his thought (3:20; 4:15; 5:13, 20). Particularly noteworthy in this regard is 6:14: "For sin will not rule you, since you are not under law but under grace." The first part of the verse follows from the immediate context: Christians are not to "continue in sin" since, by dying with Christ in their baptism, they "died to sin," leaving the "sphere" of sin's influence. And just as Christ was raised from the dead, so Christians are now to live a new life "for God in Christ Jesus" (6:1-13). The claim that Christians are not "under law," however, has not been demonstrated, nor how sin and the law are so closely connected that to be "under sin" is at the same time to be under law. Substantiation for these claims is first offered in chapter 7.

The opening verses of Romans 7 explain the statement in 6:14 that Chris-

---

in *Römer 7 und das Bild des Menschen im Neuen Testament.* See bibliography for details. Parenthetical page references in this section on Kümmel are to this latter work.

tians are not "under law." Only living people are subject to law — and Christians have died. In sharing Christ's death (cf. 6:2-11), they "died to the law" and may now "bear fruit for God" (7:4). This suggests, of course, that it was impossible to bear such "fruit" as long as they were "under" the law; and indeed, a close connection between sin and the law was implied in 6:14. These latter implications are developed in 7:5-6. What the law arouses are "sinful passions," and these lead to death; release from the law, by way of contrast, is followed by new and effective service of God. The objections raised to Paul's position in 6:1 and 15 have now been answered: No, Christians are not to continue in sin, for a fundamental change in their condition has taken place. They have been set free from sin and are to serve God in the Spirit (36-42).

But this answer raises new questions in turn. How can the law of God be said to arouse "sinful passions" (7:5)? Is this not tantamount to linking the divine law with sin? The suggestion is abhorrent but not self-evidently wrong. In the remainder of chapter 7 Paul must demonstrate both the law's holiness *and* its close relationship with sin.

We may begin with 7:7-13. Though the law is "by no means" sin, the fact remains nonetheless (ἀλλά, v. 7) that it is linked with sin; for apart from the law "I" would have had no personal experience ("knowledge") of sin. Consciousness of sin is only possible where law exists to be transgressed. Indeed, without law sin is "not counted" (5:13), it does not entail guilt, it has no effect on people. In the language of 7:8-9, "apart from the law sin lies dead" while "I" was truly "alive." The latter reference must mean something other than mere physical life, since the "life" here spoken of ended with the coming of the commandment (7:9), though physical life remained (cf. 7:14-25). Paul can only mean that true "life," in the full religious sense, was possible where there was no law and sin was inoperative. But all changed "when the commandment came." Sin then became active ("revived"). It incited "me" to disobedience, which was now conscious sin, entailed guilt, and brought "me" to ruin.

It is sin, not the law, that bears responsibility for what happened. The law remains "holy," its commandment "holy, righteous, and good" (7:12). The law's holiness has thus been maintained. At the same time, however, it is clear that the law has come to be linked to sin, and that God has in fact used the law "so that sin would be shown to be sin" (7:13).

The commandment Paul cites in this context is "You shall not covet" (7:7); perversely, it was when the "I" was confronted by this command that covetousness was roused and conscious sin followed. The prohibition is taken from the Decalogue (Exod. 20:17). This is confirmed by Paul's quotation of the same verse in the same abbreviated form in Romans 13:9, where there is no doubt that the Decalogue is intended. Such an understanding is clearly to be preferred to that which interprets the "commandment" in 7:7-13 as an allusion to the prohibition of eating from the "tree of the knowledge of good and evil" (Gen. 2:17). The latter makes no reference to coveting, whereas this is precisely what is prohibited in Romans 7:7. Moreover, the whole argument in 7:7-13 is a defense of the Mosaic law. A part of the Decalogue could well stand for the Mosaic law as a whole and would make understandable Paul's use in this chapter of "commandment" and "law" interchangeably, a usage that would not be appropriate if the "commandment" were the isolated prohibition given to Adam in Genesis 2:17 (42-57; cf. 85-87).

We have not yet considered the question of the identity of the subject ("I") in Romans 7:7-13. Nonetheless, even a preliminary look at the passage in its context allows us to draw the following conclusions.

1. The passage is designed to show how the law remains holy while being related to sin. Paul accomplishes his purpose by showing the effect of the law on a subject ("I"): though its command was holy, it was misused by sin and resulted in the subject's ruin. The law is not responsible, though it proves to be the means by which the horror of sin is revealed.

2. Hence, even if what is said in 7:7-13 reflects Paul's own experience, the main point of the passage *in its context* is the defense of the law, not personal confession. Further, if personal experience is being related, that experience must at least be typical if others are to see it as establishing a valid basis for a general defense of the law.

3. Without yet attempting to identify the subject, we have seen that the following conditions must be met by any identification: the "I" knew true "life" without personal experience of sin at a time when the Mosaic law either did not exist or had no bearing on him. When, however, the Mosaic law was introduced to the "I," sin and death were the result.

Paul's defense of the law continues in 7:14-25. He has described an event in which the law of God was used to bring death. He now sets out to explain how a good gift from God (7:13) could lead to such a result. He does so by establishing the nature both of the law and of the one whom the law encounters. The defense of the law thus remains the primary concern (note especially vv. 16, 22), though it must be conceded that the discord within the subject who encounters the law takes on an interest of its own as the argument develops (note, e.g., v. 18).

Paul explains that the curious process described in the preceding verses is possible because of the contrasting natures of the law and humankind. While the law is "spiritual" (i.e., it comes from God, v. 14), the "I" it encounters is "carnal" (σάρκινος, "of the flesh") and "sold under sin." "Flesh" (σάρξ) is frequently used in Paul's writings of all that resists what is Spirit (i.e., God and his activity), that is, of what is characteristic of a humanity that has turned from God. It follows, then, that a "fleshly" "I" will find it impossible to obey a "spiritual" law; what the "I" does is in fact evil (vv. 14-15). That the law is not responsible for this evil is clear from the admission that "the law is good" (v. 16). It is rather the responsibility of "sin dwelling within me" that there is a discrepancy between "the good I want" and "the evil I do" (vv. 17, 19). In the following verses, what is "within me" that vainly longs for the good is variously described as the "I" that wills, "my inner self" (v. 22), and "my mind" (vv. 23, 25). Similarly, the "law of my mind" (v. 23) is clearly the same as the "law of God" (v. 22). Ranged on the opposite side are the "I" that is said to act, the "flesh" that contains no good (vv. 18, 25), and the "sin" that dwells in the "flesh" and determines actions (vv. 17-20). This "sin" is represented in verse 23 as "another law . . . in my members . . . at war with the law of my mind." The resulting discord is summed up in the "law" (or "rule") of verse 21: "though I want to do right, evil dogs my steps."

And so the total "I," made up both of impotent willing and sin-driven action, has been made a "captive" of sin (v. 23; cf. v. 14). It cries out for a deliverer from "the body of this death" (so the phrase should be rendered, v. 24), that is, from the whole desperate situation described in these verses. This is not, of course, a desire for physical death; release from "the body of this death" no more implies physical death than does the destruction of the "sinful body" in 6:6. The plea is for deliverance, not from the physical body as such, but from the tyranny of sin over the body. Indeed, with such a deliverance the subject is already familiar, for the portrayal of the apparently hopeless dilemma is interrupted by a cry of thanks in verse 25, anticipating the victory described in 8:1-4: "Thanks be to God through Jesus Christ our Lord!" (57-68).

It is essential to see the claims of 8:1-4 in their context, where they provide the answer to the cry of 7:24: "Who will deliver me from the body of this death? . . . The law of the Spirit of life in Christ Jesus has set [you] free from the law of sin and death." (Kümmel defends the reading "you" found in the oldest manuscripts.) Curiously, however, the liberation spoken of in 8:1-2 is said to *follow* from what precedes ("There is *therefore* now no condemnation . . ."). It can hardly follow from 7:25b, which has summed up the dilemma of 7:14-24 without establishing the solution. And though the cry of 7:25a may anticipate the deliverance spoken of in 8:1-2, it is too brief, and its terms are too general, to provide a logical basis from which 8:1-2 might follow. The "therefore" of 8:1 must hark back to the whole train of thought begun in 6:1 and, in particular, to the Christian's deliverance from sin and the law spoken of in 6:14 and 7:6. The emphatic "now" of 8:1 (as in 3:21) underscores the fact that the deliverance is a feature of the new age in salvation history. Those who are "in Christ Jesus" have been delivered from the bondage to sin described in 7:14-25. They have been set free "from the law of sin and death."

How has the deliverance been made possible? Paul explains in 8:3-4. Note again that the reference in 8:3 to "what the law could not do, in that it was weakened by the flesh" echoes the situation of impotence described in 7:14-25, where the "I" that is in the "flesh" encounters the law but cannot carry it out. But God has done what the law could not do. He has condemned "sin in the flesh" by sending his Son in that very "flesh of sin" that has been described in chapter 7 (cf. 7:5, 17-20). Since God's Son has vanquished sin, Christians have been set free from its power and condemnation. They are now able to fulfill God's demands as they walk "not according to the flesh but according to the Spirit" (8:4) (68-73).

Again, without resolving the question of the subject's identity in 7:14-25, we may draw the following conclusions.

1. The logic of the passage requires that the subject ("I") of 7:7-13 be maintained in verses 14-25: the latter passage, by portraying the nature of the "I," shows how the law and sin can have had the curious effects on "me" described in 7:7-13.

2. The main purpose of 7:14-25 remains the defense of the law. Even if personal experience is being related, what is said must be capable of general application if it is to have any force in a general defense of the law.

3. We may reach the same conclusion by another route. The readers of chapter 8 are themselves said to have experienced the deliverance spoken of in 8:2. If the deliverance is thus a general one, this presupposes that the dilemma portrayed in 7:14-25 as preceding the deliverance must also be capable of general application.

4. It is clear from 7:25a and 8:1-4 that the subject of 7:14-25 knows not only the dilemma of discord within, but victory through Jesus Christ.

5. Chapter 8 returns to the perspective of chapter 6. In both chapters deliverance from the power of sin and death is described and made the basis for an appeal to let that victory have consequences in Christian living. 7:7-25 is crucial to Paul's argument, explaining the nature of the relationship between sin, the law, and the flesh that is otherwise presupposed in 6:14, 7:4-6, and 8:3. Nonetheless, in the context between Romans 6 and 8 it is a parenthesis; and it must at least be conceded that the lot of hopeless bondage to sin described in 7:14-25 is far different from the description in chapters 6 and 8 of the practical lives of Christians, over whom "sin will not rule," since they are "not under law but under grace" (6:14; cf. 6:2-4, 6, 17-18, 22; 8:4, 13).

The Subject of Romans 7:7-25

We begin with Romans 7:7-13. Since the passage is in the first-person singular, it is natural to interpret it of Paul's own experience. But such an explanation runs into difficulties (74-84).

1. Certainly Paul could never have written these verses of anything in his *Christian* experience. He did not *first* encounter the commandment against covetousness as a Christian (cf. "the commandment came," 7:9). Above all, it was not part of his Christian experience that sin first then became active through the commandment, *and he died.*

2. But it is also difficult to see how what is said in these verses could be true of Paul's life before his conversion. To be sure, many interpreters have understood the passage to refer to the transition from Paul's childhood innocence to his consciousness of the law's demands, a consciousness that was followed by lust, leading ultimately to spiritual death. But such an interpretation does not fit Paul's language.

a. How could Paul have said that he truly "*lived* without the law" if he meant the "relative innocence" of his childhood? "Alive" is here used in its full religious sense, as the contrast with (spiritual) death in 7:9 shows.

b. How could a Jew ever say that he once lived "without the law"? Paul would have learned the commandments from his earliest years. Nor can he be thinking of a period before his bar mitzvah when he was not yet responsible for obeying the commands: partly because the institution of the bar mitzvah is much later than the time of Paul, partly because even before the age of full responsibility Jewish minors are responsible for obeying some of the commands.

c. Paul speaks of a time "without the law," then of a time "when the commandment came" (7:9). The latter is surely a strange way of saying "when I became conscious of the commandment."

3. The passage is Paul's defense of the law; to relate a purely personal experience would not have served his purpose. And if we argue that Paul is citing his own experience as typical of every Jew, the problems remain: how could Paul write that he (or any Jew) once "lived" in a state "without the law," and that then "the commandment came"?

If, then, Paul is not speaking of his own experience, can he be speaking of that of Adam, understanding Adam as a representative of all humanity? After all, Adam was without sin before he encountered a divine commandment. And certainly the narrative of the "fall" in Genesis 3 is a story of "deception" (Gen. 3:13; cf. Rom. 7:11) followed by "death." The difficulty here, as we have already seen, is that the commandment that Paul quotes ("You shall not covet," 7:7; cf. 13:9) comes from the Decalogue given to Moses on Mount Sinai; it is thus not a summary of the prohibition spoken to Adam in Genesis 2:17. In fact, "commandment" is used throughout the passage interchangeably with "the (Mosaic) law," and the whole illustration is part of a defense of that law. That the "I" who encountered the Mosaic law could be Adam is thus out of the question. The fact that the subject is said to be "deceived" (Rom. 7:11) is natural enough in the context. It need hardly be an allusion to Genesis 3:13.

The only alternative to these interpretations would seem to be the "rhetorical" understanding of the "I": the first person is used, not of Paul himself, but rhetorically, as a way of depicting what happens to men and women under the law (85-89). A number of passages in the Pauline epistles illustrate such a usage (121-23). When Paul writes, for example, in 1 Corinthians 13, "If I speak in the tongues of men and of angels, but do not have love, I am a ringing gong or a clashing cymbal" (13:1; see also vv. 2-3), he is not making a statement of personal application only; the statement is general, and its meaning would not change if second-person pronouns were substituted for the first. Similarly, Paul writes in the first person, "When I was a child, I spoke like a child . . . ; when I became a man, I set aside childish ways" (13:11; see also v. 12), but his words are meant to express the common experience of humanity. Other examples may be given as well (Rom. 3:5, 7; 1 Cor. 6:12, 15; 10:29-30; 11:31-32; 14:11, 14-15; Gal. 2:18). Note especially that in Romans 3:7 a rhetorical question is put in the first person from which Paul dissociates himself in 3:8; and in 1 Corinthians 11:32 Paul makes a general statement in the first person, though he would not have thought of himself as one to whom it applied (he was not among those who came unprepared to "the Lord's supper"!). Hence the fact that Paul speaks in the first person in Romans 7:7-13 by no means proves that he is relating personal experience.

But if Paul is using the first person rhetorically to picture the lot of humanity under law, then it is clear that the portrayal has a place in a general defense of the law. Similarly, there is force in the words "I once lived without the law, but when the commandment came . . . I died" (7:9). Not that Paul is describing a specific incident; he is portraying, theoretically and pictorially, the fact that the law and sin together bring death to humankind. Apart from the law, sin would have no effective power, and people could be said to "live." When they encounter the commandments of God, however, sin becomes operative and the result is "death."

The question that remains, of course, is whether such an understanding of the "I" can be maintained in 7:14-25 as well; for, as we have seen, the logic of the passage requires that the same subject be found throughout 7:7-25.

This latter consideration in itself would seem to rule out the possibility that Paul is speaking of his own experience in 7:14-25, for we have already noted what difficulties such an interpretation of 7:7-13 encounters. Nonetheless, we will first consider whether Paul could have written 7:14-25 of his *Christian* experience (97-104). The answer must be an emphatic "No!"

1. Paul has just declared that Christians have been set free from the law, indeed, have "died to the law," in 7:1-6; as a result, they are not to be ruled by sin but are to serve God. But the law to which Christians are said to have died in 7:6 is precisely what encounters the subject of 7:7-25, and it brings the subject into that same hopeless bondage to sin from which (as Paul has just argued) Christians have been delivered.

2. According to 7:25a, 8:1-4, all who are "in Christ Jesus" have been set free from the dilemma of 7:14-24, 25b (specifically, from the "law of sin and death") in order that they may "walk not according to the flesh but according to the Spirit." How, then, could Paul describe himself as a Christian as being merely fleshly (σάρκινος), "sold under sin" (7:14), and sin's "captive" (7:23)? How could Paul say that as a Christian he *could* only do what is evil (7:18), when he will claim in 8:4 that God's Son was sent "in order that the just requirement of the law might be fulfilled in us"? And how could Paul the Christian cry out in despair, wondering *who* would deliver him from his bondage to sin and death (7:24)?

3. It is clear from Paul's letters that he reckons with the possibility of sin in his own life (Rom. 14:10; 1 Cor. 4:4; 9:26-27; 2 Cor. 5:10), though he seems not to be aware of specific sins (1 Cor. 4:4), claims that he does not live according to the flesh (2 Cor. 10:3; 13:6), and feels fit to serve as an example for others (1 Cor. 4:16; 11:1; Phil. 3:17; 4:9). All of this excludes the possibility that Romans 7:14-25 is a description of Paul's present experience. Who could set himself up as an example for others to follow, or claim "I am not aware of anything against myself," and cry out at the same time for deliverance from bondage to sin? This is not to say that Paul never experienced ethical struggles within himself. But ethical struggles are not the same thing as being hopelessly overpowered and enslaved by sin, and it is the latter of which 7:14-25 speaks.

4. Nor will it do to say that 7:14-25 is true of Paul's experience as a Christian *apart from the help of the Spirit,* or *when left to himself.* 7:25 in particular has led to such an interpretation, for αὐτὸς ἐγώ is taken to mean "I on my own" (cf. RSV, "I of myself"). But that Paul could conceive of Christian experience apart from Christ, or apart from the Spirit, is incredible. For Paul one either has the Spirit or not; and Christians do, otherwise they are not Christians (8:9). Besides, αὐτὸς ἐγώ can scarcely be translated "I on my own." The words mean "I myself" (and no other); that is, the very "I" who has been speaking throughout the passage here sums up his experience.

5. Finally, it cannot be said that the vividness of the portrayal means that

Paul must be describing his present experience. Even the dramatic question of 7:24 belongs at best to Paul's past, since what follows shows that Paul's present experience is one of deliverance, not impotence and discord.

But if the passage cannot refer to Paul's experience as a Christian, neither can the "I" be understood rhetorically of the ethical condition of Christians in general (104-9). The first, second, and fourth arguments just given exclude this possibility. Here we may add the following considerations.

1. Paul is fully aware that Christians are not sinless, that they are in need of constant admonition. But all the ethical imperatives that he writes presuppose the possibility of obedience. The norm for the Christian is to live "according to the Spirit" — the Spirit that every believer possesses (Rom. 8:9) and that makes it possible to "put to death the deeds of the body" (8:13). But the subject of 7:14-25 knows no such possibility. He is the slave of sin, and does not know who can deliver him. He is of the flesh (7:14), and nowhere is it suggested that he possesses the Spirit with which he might oppose the flesh.

2. Galatians 5:17 is often cited as a parallel description of the ethical struggles of the Christian, but it is no parallel. The whole passage in Galatians presupposes that the Christian need not give in to the flesh, that victory is possible for those who "walk in the Spirit." The opposite is true of the subject of Romans 7:14-25, who finds himself the impotent slave of the flesh. The explanation of this is simple. The Christian of Galatians 5 has the Spirit; the subject of Romans 7 does not. The point of Galatians 5:17 is not (as is supposed) that Christians are the helpless battleground of opposing forces, for verses 16 and 18 presuppose that the Spirit will enable them to triumph over the flesh. The point of the verse is simply that since the Spirit and the flesh are opposing forces, Christians may not do as they please but must obey the one or the other. Precisely this choice is not open to the subject of Romans 7:14-25.

3. Those who are anxious to preserve Romans 7:14-25 as a witness to Christian experience emphasize the inner struggle there depicted as an essential part of Christian living. But 7:14-25 speaks not merely of a struggle, but of utter helplessness, slavery to sin, and despair of deliverance. To downplay or ignore these features while emphasizing the struggle is to misrepresent the text.

4. Similarly, to object that Christians must recognize their own experience in the description of 7:14-25 is to distort the exegetical task. Exegetes may not disregard the context of a passage while interpreting it in the light of their experience. Experience must be excluded while the exegete listens to what the text is saying. Only so is the authority of the text preserved. If, after all, there is a question that needs to be asked, it is rather this: why does our Christianity depart so widely from Paul's that we recognize ourselves in his description of non-Christians?

It is thus incredible that Paul could be depicting Christian experience in the terms of Romans 7:14-25. Is he, then, rhetorically describing in the present his personal experience of moral impotence before his conversion (109-17)?

1. The possibility would seem to be excluded from the start, since the "I" of 7:7-13 did not refer to Paul and the logic of the passage requires that the same subject be maintained throughout.

2. 8:2 is intended to describe the deliverance effected by the "law of the Spirit of life" from the dilemma of 7:14-25. But the original reading of 8:2 is that this "law . . . has set *you* free from the law of sin and death." Since the deliverance is not stated of Paul himself, it is not likely that the dilemma was merely his own.

3. Above all, we have Paul's own testimony in Galatians 1:13-14 and Philippians 3:4-6 to the nature of his preconversion piety, and it tells not of moral impotence but of a "blameless" life according to the law. Paul clearly believed that he had lived up to the Pharisaic ideal — and that ideal was one of joy in the law of God. Philippians 3:6 and Romans 7:14-25 are simply irreconcilable — *if* the latter is interpreted of Paul's preconversion experience.

This leaves us, again, with the rhetorical understanding of the "I" as depicting the condition of humanity in general under the law (117-26). Paul is using first-person pronouns, as he does elsewhere, to depict the lot of humankind. The perspective from which the portrayal is drawn is that of Paul the Christian: it was first "in Christ" that Paul became convinced of the impotence of moral strivings outside of Christ, and clearly the cry for deliverance in 7:24 is placed on the lips of the sinner by one who has experienced redemption. The purpose of the passage, as our study of the context has made clear, is to show the relationship between sin and the law, and the effects that sin and the law have on those "in the flesh." That the tense shifts from the past in 7:7-13 to the present in 7:14-25 is easily explained. Paul first describes in the past tense the "event" in which sin used the law to bring death. But when he then comes to describe the nature of the law, the nature of humanity, and the state of affairs that prevails for men and women under the law, the present tense comes naturally. The passage as a whole demonstrates the utter moral impotence of humanity under the law, a gloomy contrast to the glorious picture of redemption in Romans 6 and 8.

Finally, we must note an objection that is frequently raised to such an interpretation (134-38). How can Paul ascribe to non-Christians an agreement with, and even delight in, the law of God (7:16, 22)? While it is true that such statements go beyond what Paul says elsewhere of humanity outside of Christ, in the context of Paul's argument here they are understandable. First, Paul's primary purpose in the passage is not to portray the human condition, but to defend the law; and it is clear that the statements of 7:16, 22 are meant to underline that the law itself is good and bears no responsibility for the fact that people do not obey it. Second, the lot of humanity under the law is here seen from the perspective, not of the non-Christian, but of the Christian. It is thus possible that Christian experience of the Spirit's resistance to the flesh has colored Paul's picture of the struggle between the "mind" and the flesh. But most importantly, it must be noted that the agreement between the mind and the law of God in this passage merely serves to emphasize the hopelessness of the human situation. Certainly there is discord within the subject of the passage. But it is not true that Paul is here depicting the coexistence in the Christian of a sinful flesh and a renewed mind. Such an understanding would require that the "I" who is spoken of as "fleshly" and "sold under sin" in 7:14 merely referred to one *part* of the Christian while another part represented the believer's new life in Christ apart from sin. But the "I" of verse 14 must be the whole person, for verse 15 shows that this "I" includes *both* the willing of the good and the doing of the evil. Again, in verse 23 it is the whole person who has been made sin's "captive," and it is the whole "wretched man" who cries out for deliverance from the tyranny of sin and death in verse 24. In the light of 8:2, this can only be a picture of the non-Christian.

The Conversion of Paul

Here we may be brief. If the interpretation advocated for Romans 7 is adopted, then the chapter offers no basis for speculation about Paul's psychological condition before his conversion. We cannot conclude from Romans 7 that Paul the Pharisee despaired of ever fulfilling the law; in fact, the evidence of Galatians 1 and Philippians 3 indicates the contrary. Consistent with Galatians and Philippians is the evidence of Acts, for there is no suggestion in Acts of psychological preparation preceding Paul's conversion. That he was vainly "[kicking] against the goads" (Acts 26:14) can hardly refer to a struggle on his part to repress an inner attraction to Christianity; it is simply a proverbial expression for senseless opposition. In this case, as the context makes perfectly clear, the reference is to Paul's persecution of Christians. Such opposition is useless, for Christ will direct Paul, as an ox driver an ox, where he pleases. That Acts wants to portray a Paul struggling against the attraction of Christianity is incredible in the light of 9:1-2, 22:4-5, and especially 26:9-12. It was only the appearance of Jesus to Paul near Damascus that convinced him that the Christians who proclaimed Jesus' resurrection were right, and turned the enemy of Christ into his missionary and apostle (139-60).

Such is Kümmel's argument. If true, it would mean that Romans 7 should not be read as Pauline autobiography, that it provides no evidence of inner turmoil or pangs of conscience felt by Paul. It is this conclusion that led Stendahl to distinguish sharply between what we know of the apostle's experience and that of Luther.

ii. Krister Stendahl

We may begin our summary of Stendahl's argument where it most clearly overlaps with that of Kümmel.

The Conscience of Paul

In Stendahl's view traditional pictures of Paul's inner struggle with sin are based on the misleading analogy of Luther and on faulty interpretations of Pauline texts. A fresh examination of Paul's writings shows that his conscience was remarkably "robust" both before and after his Damascus encounter with the risen Christ.

Our best evidence for Paul's piety before his Christian calling is found in Philippians 3. Nothing in the passage suggests that he had found it difficult to keep God's law — his performance, he says, was "blameless" (3:6). Clearly he suffered no pangs of conscience on that score! To be sure, his values shifted when he met Christ, but it was "his glorious achievements as a righteous Jew,"[2] not painful shortcomings and a plagued conscience, that he left behind. What once occasioned pride seemed worthless when compared with the treasure of knowing Christ. But the insight was a new one. It reflects no previous dissatisfaction.

Nor does the evidence suggest to Stendahl that Paul's Christian conscience was burdened by besetting sins. While Paul harbored no illusions that believers were without sin, he never intimated that his own conscience was troubled by personal wrongdoing. The confident assertion of Acts 23:1 ("Brethren, I have conducted myself in all good conscience before God up to this day") has a number of parallels in the epistles. According to 2 Corinthians 1:12, Paul's conscience agreed with the assessment that his conduct was marked by "holiness and godly sincerity." Paul's hope, according to 5:11, was that his conduct would

---

2. Stendahl, *Paul*, 80. Parenthetical page references in the remainder of this chapter are to Stendahl, *Paul*.

meet with the Corinthians' approval just as it met with God's. Most telling is Paul's frank confession in 1 Corinthians 4:4 that he was "not aware of anything against" himself. Though Paul was not averse to acknowledging "weakness," what he meant by the term was physical handicaps (2 Cor. 12:7; Gal. 4:13) and sufferings (2 Cor. 12:10), not sin. Thus it would be completely incompatible with the evidence elsewhere to read Romans 7 as a confession of Paul's inability to cope with sin. And in fact, Kümmel has shown that Romans 7 must not be understood as autobiography. It is a defense of the law.

The Concerns of Paul

Interpretation of Paul has gone astray because we have lost sight of his central concern: his role among Jews and Gentiles and relations between Jewish and Gentile believers. On what terms were Gentile converts to be admitted to the messianic community? How were they to be made heirs to the promises God gave to Israel? These were issues that engaged the Apostle to the Gentiles. He wrestled with the problem of Israel's law, not because his conscience was tormented by a failure to keep its commands, but because it appeared to bar the access of Gentiles to the people of God. His solution, and the central conviction of his ministry, was the doctrine of justification by faith *apart from the works of the law;* that is, that Gentiles would "become part of the people of God without having to pass through the law." This was "Paul's secret revelation and knowledge" (9).

The Distortion of Paul

But the problem that so occupied Paul's thinking was no longer an issue after the end of the first century. Christianity had become largely a Gentile faith. If the specifically Pauline teaching on faith and the law finds few echoes in Christian writings before Augustine, the reason may well be that it had lost its immediate relevance. "The early church seems to have felt that Paul spoke about what he actually spoke about, i.e. the relationship between Jews and Gentiles — and that was no problem during those centuries" (16). Paul's writings took on new importance only when they were used by Augustine to address a problem that Paul himself never faced: the "Western development" and the "Western plague" of the "introspective conscience" (17).

Augustine himself may well have been among the first to give expression to the dilemma. In a sense he may be called "the first modern man" since "his

Confessions is the first great document in the history of the introspective conscience." Paul's treatment of the Gentile question was now "applied in a consistent and grand style to a more general and timeless human problem" (85): How is a conscience tormented by its sins ever to be set free? Can we ever find assurance of salvation? The introspection that could lead to such despair became more and more refined in late medieval piety. The rigors of penance, the self-examination characteristic of monastic life, the soul-searching that followed in the dreaded path of the Black Death — all these played a role. Luther, "a truly Augustinian monk" (83), was but one of many who practiced introspection with the utmost intensity.

For Luther and subsequent Protestant tradition, Paul's doctrine of justification by faith provided solace from the tormenting question, "How can I find a gracious God?" This was not, however, the issue that the doctrine was designed to meet, and its reapplication led to distortions of Paul's meaning.

1. In his epistle to the Galatians, Paul was concerned to show that "Gentiles must not, and should not come to Christ *via* the Law" (87). The law referred to was, of course, that of Moses, given to the Jews 430 years after God's promise was made to Abraham (Gal. 3:17). Paul insists that the law cannot save, and warns the Galatians in the strongest possible terms against complying with its requirement of circumcision (5:3). As part of his argument he stresses the limitations of the law's validity and function. It was only in force until Messiah came (3:19) and faith in him was possible (3:23). The role of the law until that time was that of "Custodian for the Jews," a kind of "waiting room with strong locks" (86). In its context, then, Paul's claim that "the law was our custodian until Christ came" (3:24) is designed to show why Gentiles need not submit to its rule: the Mosaic law was intended only for Jews ("*our* custodian"), and served its purpose only until Christ came.

But the context of Paul's argument — the controversial relations between Jews and Gentiles — was later lost to view, the problem of the introspective conscience was forced upon the text, and the point of Paul's words was reversed. "Law" came to be used in a general way for the divinely imposed imperative. And whereas Paul's words were designed to *exclude* the (Mosaic) law as a path to salvation, they were read to mean that the law (now in the sense of a confrontation with God's moral demands) was a *necessary precondition* for faith: it was now our "schoolmaster [or 'tutor'] to bring us unto Christ" (KJV; ASV). Here the (redefined) law is understood as given "to make man see his desperate need for a Savior" (87). True faith is thought to be impossible unless human self-righteousness has been crushed by the law. Thus what Paul depicted as a once-for-all transition from the age of the law to that of Christ has become a necessary process in the life of each believer. "The only door into the church" becomes "that of evermore introspective awareness of sin and guilt" (96) — in spite of the fact that Paul, "a rather good Christian" (96) himself, showed little such awareness!

2. A similar transformation took place with regard to the opening chapters of Romans. Paul's concern was to place Jew and Gentile on the same footing before God. Both are equally culpable; the path to justification by faith lies equally open to both; thus Abraham "is the father of us all" (Rom. 4:16). When the first-century context was forgotten, however, Romans came to be read as "a theological tractate on the nature of faith" (5), prescribing a path through awareness of sin to faith in Jesus Christ, and thus providing a solution to the human predicament. In the same way, at a time when the status of the Mosaic law was no longer the issue as it was for Paul, his argument in defense of the law in Romans 7 became distorted and the chapter was read on the one hand as a statement of human nature and the power of sin, and on the other as a testimony that Paul himself had been "shattered" by the law before coming to faith!

3. Finally, the current emphasis on "forgiveness" is but another indication of the shift brought about by the introspective conscience. Terms related to forgiveness are "spectacularly" absent from the Pauline writings (23). Today they serve to define the sum and substance of what Jesus Christ is thought to provide. The reason is no doubt that forgiveness suits our psychological bent and the quest of the West for relief from sin and guilt. Our concern is more centered "in ourselves than in God or in the fate of his creation" (24).

For Stendahl, then, the "use" of the law as "God's mighty hammer" bringing complacent sinners to despair has little support in Paul. The roots of the notion are rather in problems peculiar to the modern West. Hence the function and indeed the definition of the law need reexamination. Does the same apply to "Lutheran" explanations of why "works" cannot justify?

Chapter 9

The "Righteousness of the Law": Bultmann, Wilckens, and Sanders

Paul's conviction *that* no one can be justified by means of the law is expressed in the epistles too frequently and too explicitly to leave any scope for argument. On the other hand, it is not so readily apparent *why* Paul finds the "righteousness of the law" inadequate, and scholars have made the most of the ambiguity. As we have seen, Luther was ready with a barrage of explanations, ranging from the belief that our best efforts are offset by transgressions to the view that our best efforts, apart from faith, are themselves misdirected, presumptuous, even blasphemous. The range of explanations represented in contemporary scholarship is equally diverse, but the debate has been enhanced immeasurably by a marked trend toward advocating one of the possibilities while downplaying or excluding the others. The juxtaposition in the present chapter of the work of three prominent scholars will give some picture of the state of the debate: it remains unresolved whether Paul saw the righteousness of the law as something good (Wilckens), bad (Bultmann), or indifferent (Sanders).

i. Rudolf Bultmann

If we are to trace Rudolf Bultmann's understanding of the righteousness of the law — or, for that matter, of most other subjects as well — we must begin with his view of Pauline anthropology.[1] For Paul, in Bultmann's view, man is fundamentally *creature,* a created being who has nothing that he has not received, who lacks any possibility of security in himself or in the transitory, visible

---

1. All the parenthetical page references in this section are to Bultmann's works, using the short titles shown in the bibliography.

world he inhabits, and who is totally dependent on his Creator. It is only as man acknowledges this that he is "at one with himself" and "achieves his authentic Being" (the phrases were current when Bultmann wrote). Thus the possibility of being good or evil, of finding life or death, confronts man in the choice whether or not he will acknowledge and obey his Creator. To fail to do so, to live as though one were independent and autonomous, is sin, rebellion against God, and at the same time a missing of man's true existence, since man is fundamentally creature (cf. *Theology,* 228-29, 232).

Man lives in the "flesh," that is, in the sphere of things visible and tangible, subject to corruption and death ("NT," 18). Life "*in* the flesh" does not in itself imply sin. On the other hand, it does open for man the possibility of living "*according to* the flesh," of trying to derive one's life from, and base one's security on, the created sphere. But this is "sin, because it is a turning away from the Creator, the giver of life, and a turning toward the creation — and to do that is to trust in one's self as being able to procure life by the use of the earthly and through one's own strength and accomplishment" (*Theology,* 239).

In principle, then, good and evil, life and death are equally options within man's reach. In fact, however, Paul is of the opinion that "*man has always already missed the existence that at heart he seeks,* his intent is basically perverse, evil" (227; cf. "Problem," 202-3). Through his self-assertion man has become a totally fallen being ("NT," 31). The perverse desire to gain recognition for one's achievement is universal and, at the same time, "the root of all other evils" (*Setting,* 183). In Judaism this common "human striving has . . . taken on its culturally . . . distinct form" in the desire to win recognition in God's sight by obedience to God's law; hence zeal in fulfilling God's law becomes the typically Jewish sin ("End," 43)! How has this paradoxical state of affairs come about?

What one encounters in the Old Testament law is of course the demand of God. The human attitude demanded by the law is that of obedience, the genuine obedience that acknowledges the Creator and refuses to seek life and security anywhere but in him. If met with such obedience, the law would lead to life. Indeed, the intent of God's commandment "is to snatch man out of his self-reliant pursuit of life, his will to rule over himself," and so set him again on the path to true life (*Theology,* 250; cf. 259, 315). But in the very fact that the law promises "life" for those who submit to God and obey his commands lies the possibility of misunderstanding. Man, knowing that to transgress God's law is sin and that life is promised to those who obey it, may conclude that he can secure his *own* life and establish his *own* righteousness by doing what the law requires. But such apparent conformity with the law is really its perversion. It is merely a refined, highly deceptive expression of the universal desire to gain recognition by one's own accomplishment. To be sure, there is an apparent renunciation of self in the willingness to do what God's law demands. In fact, however, the self has not been renounced, for it is using its very "obedience" as the basis on which to claim recognition (cf. 246, 267, 315-16). Hence, "according to Paul the person who fulfils the law needs grace as much as the one who trespasses against it — indeed it is he most of all who needs it! For in seeking to establish his own righteousness, he is acting *fundamentally* against God" ("End," 46).

Jewish zeal in fulfilling the law is thus no less an expression of life "according to the flesh" than Gentile sensuality (cf. Gal. 3:2-3). Nowhere is this more apparent than in Philippians 3, where the basis for Paul's erstwhile "confidence in the flesh" is given. The prerogatives of Israel are listed since they belong to the sphere of the earthly and visible. So, too, are Paul's efforts in fulfilling the law (Phil. 3:6). Such efforts are expressions of an attitude oriented toward the flesh, "the self-reliant attitude of the man who puts his trust in his own strength and in that which is controllable by him" (*Theology*, 240). The sin of self-reliance reaches its culmination in "boasting" — and again, both Jew and Greek are guilty. The Jew boasts of God and the Torah (Rom. 2:17, 23), the Greek of his wisdom (1 Cor. 1:19-31). Both forget that they have nothing they have not received (1 Cor. 4:7). And God for his part insists that all human pretensions must be shattered "so that no human being might boast in the presence of God" (1:29).

We are now in a position to answer why, in Bultmann's view, Paul rules out the works of the law as a path to salvation. Two reasons may be cited.

First, "there is no true fulfilment of the Law" (263). This is implicit in Galatians 3:10 and is the point of the argument in the opening chapters of Romans. No one can be justified by the works of the law because no one fulfills them in their entirety. All are transgressors (cf. "End," 50). This is as true of Jews as of Gentiles. Indeed, Romans 2:17-24 was written to remind Jews who may "suppose that in God's eyes they are superior to the Gentiles . . . that as transgressors of the law they are not a bit better" ("Anthropology," 149; cf. "End," 40).

But the fundamental reproach that Paul brings against "the way of the law" is not that it is "wrong because, by reason of transgressions, it fails to reach its goal . . . , but rather that the *direction* of this way is perverse and, to be sure, because it intends to lead to 'one's own righteousness' (Rom. 10:3; Phil. 3:9)" ("Anthropology," 149). The "real sin" of Jews is thus not their violation of God's law but their intention to become righteous in his eyes by keeping it. "*Man's effort to achieve his salvation by keeping the Law* only leads him into sin, indeed this effort itself in the end *is already sin*." This conclusion follows from "the insight which Paul has achieved into the nature of sin" as "man's self-powered striving to undergird his own existence in forgetfulness of his creaturely existence, to procure his salvation by his own strength" (*Theology*, 264). Since such striving leads to boasting, the ultimate reason why "works" do not justify is simply that "man must not have any boast before God (Rom. 3:27; 4:2)" (283).

Bultmann's understanding of what Paul means by redemption follows naturally from this interpretation of sin. The cross of Christ gives expression to God's judgment on the world and its illusions. In light of the cross, what is required of man is that he "subject himself to God's judgment, i.e., to the judgment that all of man's desires and strivings and standards of value are nothing before God, that they are all subject to death. . . . All of man's accomplishments and boasting are at an end; they are condemned as nothing by the cross" ("Jesus," 197). Faith, on this understanding, amounts to a willingness to submit to God's judgment, to renounce all boasting and every attempt to find security in oneself, and to find one's security only in God (*Mythology*, 40; cf. "NT," 19-20). The believer is one who comes to recognize that righteousness is a gift that cannot be gained by anything he does; his "achievements" establish no claim on God (*Theology*, 281). Thus the choice with which the gospel confronts the sinner with is "whether or not he is willing to understand himself anew and to receive his life from the hand of God" (269). Conversion inevitably involves the "resolve to surrender [one's] whole previous self-understanding . . . and to understand [one's] existence anew" ("Paul," 115; cf. 122; "End," 45; *Theology*, 187-88).

And what, finally, is the will of God for the believer? "Christian morality is simply the fulfilment of the Old Testament commandments (Rom. 13.8-10; Gal. 5.14)" ("End," 36; cf. *Theology*, 262). Even though the law cannot serve as the basis for gaining favor with God by one's achievements, its content remains a valid statement of God's will ("End," 60). The ethical demands placed upon believers are thus no different from those made of all persons (cf. "Problem," 213-14). Two qualifications to these statements must, however, be added.

1. Though the substance of the moral demand remains the same, the manner of its fulfillment is critical (cf. *Theology*, 283, 341). Christian "fulfilling of the law" is no longer "'work' in the sense of meritorious accomplishment" (344). The one who "works" may obey the law outwardly, but his obedience only extends to the content of what he does; he does not submit *himself* to God, but rather "stands side by side with what he does," thinking he "has a right to be proud of [his] accomplishment" (316; cf. *Setting*, 69). The believer, however, has radically renounced any claim to "accomplishment," and thus in his acts of obedience submits himself as well as his deed to the demand of God. He is set free from sin (the Pauline indicative) only as the self-renouncing decision of faith is constantly renewed in fresh acts of radical obedience to the commandment of God (the Pauline imperative) (cf. *Mythology*, 76-77; "NT," 21; "Paul," 142).

2. Though Paul does not work out the distinction, it is clear that when he

speaks of the abiding validity of the law, he is thinking of its ethical rather than its ritual or cultic commands. Thus "freedom from the law" implies the freedom to distinguish between what is valid and what is not valid within the law. Paul speaks of this task as proving "what is the good and acceptable and perfect will of God" (Rom. 12:2 RSV and NRSV mg.), as approving "what is excellent" (Phil. 1:10) (cf. *Theology*, 341).

We conclude: for Bultmann's Paul the pursuit of the righteousness of the law is the typically Jewish expression of man's universal striving for recognition on the basis of his accomplishments. Faith is the renunciation of such striving as one recognizes one's utter dependence on God. It is expressed in genuine, radical obedience to God's demand in the law.

ii. Ulrich Wilckens

Much of what Ulrich Wilckens has written about the righteousness of the law has been formulated in deliberate, at times almost diametric opposition to the views of Rudolf Bultmann. Yet the criticisms raised represent only the negative side of what is in its own right an impressive counterunderstanding of Paul. In what follows I will for the most part allow the criticism of Bultmann to remain implicit, focusing rather on Wilckens's own reading of the relevant aspects of Paul's thought.[2]

We may begin with Romans 2. Wilckens is one of the few scholars who believe Paul means what he says in Romans 2:13: "For it is not the hearers of the law who are righteous before God, but the doers of the law who will be found righteous." Admittedly, the verse restates a basic principle of Judaism. But for Wilckens this does not mean that Paul here adopts his opponents' point of view for the sake of argument, that he reasons from a position that he himself regards as inadequate, superseded, misleading, or even perverted (cf. *Römer*, 1:145). On the contrary, the radical demand for works righteousness in Romans 2:13 is precisely *Paul's* position in opposition to contemporary Jewish thought (Review, 853-54). In Jewish theology of Paul's day all sins were not equal. Heathen sins might damn, but those of Jews were countered by their membership in the covenant people of God. Hence the "righteousness" of all Jews who did not apostatize was ultimately guaranteed (*Römer*, 1:150-51). This is the position, and such is the "boasting," that Paul is opposing in Romans 2; the passage says nothing of the supposed self-righteous claims of Jews to have *kept* the law and

2. All the parenthetical page references in this section are to Wilckens's works, using the short titles shown in the bibliography.

earned their salvation. It is against Jewish boasts of salvific privileges that Paul here insists on a righteousness demonstrated in deeds, contending that the sins of Jews leave them no better off than pagans. God will judge all according to their works, with no regard for membership in the people entrusted with his law. A Paul who insists on works righteousness against Jews who rely on God's favor: the contrast with Bultmann's Paul could hardly be more dramatic (cf. 1:177)!

If Paul means what he says in Romans 2:13 — God *does* promise salvation to those whose works show them to be righteous — he also takes seriously the claim of the law that those who do its demands will live (Lev. 18:5, quoted in Rom. 10:5; Gal. 3:12). The law was given for "life" (Rom. 7:10). Paul's gospel is in no way opposed to works as such (1:145). On the contrary, the complete validity of the demand for righteous deeds in Romans 2:13 is the presupposition behind Paul's judgment in 3:9 that all are under sin, and forms the basis for the dilemma from which, according to Paul's gospel, only Christ can deliver.

For Paul, according to Wilckens, there is one reason — and one reason only — why no one can be justified by the works of the law (cf. "Werken," 79-94): all have sinned, and where works are the decisive criterion by which righteousness is assessed and humankind is judged, then the sins of *all* bring *all* humankind under the wrath of God. This is the point of Romans 1:18–3:20. The heathen are guilty of concrete sins (1:28-32) — and so are Jews (2:21-22). Throughout the passage Paul consistently maintains the position that actual deeds of righteousness are what God requires (cf. 2:14, 26-27). Nowhere does Paul suggest that Jews are wrong in attempting to keep the law; they are judged because they transgress it. Similarly, 5:12-21 is concerned to show the universality of sin as transgression. And in Romans 7 "I" am "sold under sin" (7:14), not because "I" try to keep the law (that, after all, is what "I" am supposed to do!), but because, for all my noble desires, "I" do what the law prohibits.

Such is Paul's position in Romans — and the picture is in this regard no different in Galatians. There too we read that "by works of the law shall no one be justified" (2:16) because Jews as well as pagans are found to be *sinners* (2:17); distinctions based on the privileges of salvation history have thus become irrelevant. Since, according to 3:10, the law pronounces a curse on *all who do not obey* its commands completely, those subject to the law are said to be under its curse. Salvation by keeping the law is no longer a possibility. To be sure, the law promises life for those who carry out its demands (3:12); yet it has no power to *create* life (ζωοποιῆσαι, 3:21) for transgressors, but must simply curse them ("Entwicklung," 172-73). Thus salvation can only come apart from the law; indeed, it must include the removal of the law's curse upon transgressors (3:13).

In Wilckens's view Paul's understanding of the human dilemma is thus more radical and more pessimistic than that of his Jewish contemporaries. As a result, it requires a solution quite outside the salvific institutions granted to Israel. The latter are real enough in themselves, but powerless to cope with the problem posed by human sin (*Römer*, 1:222). The sacrificial system outlined in the priestly code of the Pentateuch could atone for "unwitting" sin, but it made no provision for deliberate, radical wrongdoing (Num. 15:30-31). Justification of sinners is thus not possible by means of the Jewish cult (1:238). To agree that works of righteousness are required and conclude that therefore only a few can be saved, as the Jewish apocalyptic tradition tended to do, is again to fall short of Paul's radical view of the dilemma that *none* is righteous when deeds are the criteria (1:84, 152-53). To say that the election of Israel in itself guarantees Jewish participation in God's salvation, or that concrete observances of the law can offset transgressions, is to view the effects of sin less seriously than Paul does (cf. "Christologie," 71, 74; *Römer*, 1:240-41; 2:99-100). Thus whereas Bultmann's Paul differs from (Bultmann's) Judaism in condemning any attempt to establish one's own righteousness by fulfilling the law, according to Wilckens's understanding Paul differs by his more radical view of the consequences of transgression.

If we are to grasp Paul's thinking on sin and on how sin's consequences are canceled by the death of Christ, Wilckens believes we must reckon with Old Testament notions of sin and atonement. The Israelites shared with much of the ancient Near East the idea that what one experiences is directly related to what one does. This relationship is misunderstood when it is thought of purely in judicial terms (i.e., God the judge measures deeds by the standard of the law and rewards or punishes accordingly). Such a view of the process is too abstract, whereas the Israelites regarded deeds, once committed, as having a kind of concrete existence of their own, as creating a sphere of power about them for good or evil that then works itself out on the doer: "The one who digs a pit will fall into it; a stone will return on the one who sets it rolling" (Prov. 26:27). God is thought of not as assigning retribution but as overseeing the process, directing the consequences of deeds so that they return, for good or ill, to the doers (cf. 24:12). And atonement, properly understood, is not a human attempt to placate a God bound by his righteousness to punish, but *God's* way of delivering sinners from the consequences of their sins by providing a substitute victim on whom those consequences can work themselves out (*Römer*, 1:128, 236-38, 243; cf. *Resurrection*, 78-79). When sin and its effects are viewed so concretely, it follows that neither a simple pardoning of transgressions nor compensating for them by deeds of righteousness is adequate for solving the dilemma; both "solutions" leave untouched the pernicious process begun by sin. Only when the evil that has been set in motion has been allowed to exhaust itself, either on the doer or on a substitute provided by God, is it effectively done away with.

Concrete *sin,* then, and not a perverted self-understanding, is the cause of the human dilemma; and the solution must be suited to the dilemma. Faith per se, in the sense of a correct self-understanding, does not reverse the human predicament; the death of Christ is the atoning sacrifice for sin provided by God (*Römer,* 1:89, 200-201, 232, 247-48). If Paul contrasts the righteousness of faith with that of the law, he does so in order to make the point that *sinners* cannot be justified by works of the law and that, since all are sinners, only faith *in the crucified Christ* can avail ("Christologie," 75; "Werken," 92). It is because of its christological content that faith can be said to justify ("Werken," 108). Neither in what Paul says about the righteousness of God nor in his view of faith are *anthropological* considerations central. The decisive convictions are christological: that God has intervened in the death and resurrection of Christ for the salvation of sinners (*Römer,* 1:92, 211-12).

Hence faith per se must not be seen as opposed to works, nor does it deliver the believer from the obligation to do deeds of righteousness, to "fulfill the law." The deliverance it brings is rather from the consequences of sins committed in the past and, indeed, of the believer's failures to live up to the law in the present: all have their atonement in the death of Christ (1:145-46). The law's role of condemning the sinner is thus ended. And the law as a means to life, which, because of universal sin, was already inoperative, is now replaced by the saving act of God's righteousness in Christ (2:22; cf. "Christologie," 68). Nonetheless, the law as a statement of God's will remains, and believers are intended to fulfill it — through love ("Werken," 109).

That the law as a path to salvation has been done away with has important consequences for its adherents (*Römer,* 1:178; cf. "Werken," 98-104). Whereas for (Wilckens's) Paul the works of the law are good in themselves, and the law was originally given to be obeyed and to bring life, the latter possibility has now and forever been closed. For Jews *now,* after the crucifixion of Christ, the attempt to establish righteousness by keeping the law is a vain pursuit in defiance of the righteousness revealed in Christ and available to faith (Rom. 9:31-32; 10:3; Phil. 3:9). It must be noted, however, that such a pursuit is vain, not because there is anything inherently wrong in attempting to do what the law commands, but because, with Christ, the period in which the law could lead to righteousness reached its end (Rom. 10:4).

For the believer in Christ, on the other hand, it is important to define in what respect the law has been done away with and in what sense it remains valid. Believers are free from the *condemnation* of the law — not that the sentence of the law is evaded or that God in his mercy has decided to dispense with the law's verdict, for the curse of the law is allowed its full force; Paul means rather that since that curse has been exhausted on Christ, believers are delivered from its effects (*Römer*, 1:186; 2:70). On the other hand, they are to fulfill "the whole law" by carrying out the single command to love one's neighbor (Rom. 13:8-10; Gal. 5:14). Practically, of course, this involves a massive reduction of the law's demands. The concentration on the command to love means that, at least for Gentile Christians, even basic commandments like circumcision and, in general, the cultic and ritual demands of the law are abrogated (Gal. 2:14; 4:10). Furthermore, it should be remembered that it is as Christians are guided by the Spirit that they are able to fulfill the law ("Entwicklung," 176). But the principle of judgment by works set forth in Romans 2:5-11 remains valid for Christians. Their acquittal is assured by the death of Christ, which frees them from the consequences of their failings (*Römer*, 1:146). But the law as such is not done away with.

Finally, we may ask how Paul arrived at his views of the law. Other Jews who believed that Jesus was the Messiah still maintained their confidence in the status of Israel as God's chosen people and in the abiding, salvific force of Israel's covenant law; hence, for example, they required circumcision of non-Jewish believers. Why did Paul adopt a different position? Why did he see — from the very moment of his conversion ("Bekehrung," 14-15) — the law and Christ as exclusive alternatives?

Wilckens suggests that the pre-Christian Paul must have belonged to one of the Hellenistic synagogues in Jerusalem ("Entwicklung," 154-55). There he encountered and came to persecute Christians who claimed that the temple cult and the sacrifices prescribed in Torah were done away with by the atoning death of Christ (cf. *Römer*, 1:174, 241). Thus even before his conversion Paul would have regarded Jesus and Torah as exclusive alternatives. His conversion would have simply meant that he now championed the former alternative.

Paul's radical assessments of the universality of sin and of the law as cursing sinners are clearly the *consequences* drawn from his Christian conviction that Christ died for sins (cf. "Entwicklung," 166-67). Indeed, apart from a belief in the justification of sinners through Christ, Paul's depiction of the universality of sin and the powerlessness of the law would amount to an outright denial of God's righteousness (cf. *Römer*, 1:179-80). Only Paul's belief that the "righteousness" of God has been revealed in the atoning death of Christ can explain his depiction of the human dilemma.

As we have seen, Wilckens understands Paul's doctrine of justification as fundamentally the justification of *sinners* through the atoning death of Christ. In his early (postconversion) thinking, Paul's soteriology was founded on his

Christology in a traditional way: the forgiveness of sins, the "justifying" of sinners, was proclaimed on the basis of the atoning death of Christ (1 Cor. 1:30; 6:11; 2 Cor. 5:21) (cf. "Christologie," 69-72). The necessary human response was of course always seen as "faith in Christ," but it was first in contesting the views of his Galatian opponents that Paul used the phrase polemically, contrasting it with the works of the law. In Romans Paul attempted to work out the positions he had arrived at polemically in Galatians in a more positive, general way (69). It should be clear, however, that on Wilckens's understanding the basic christological structure of Paul's doctrine of justification remained constant throughout and, in fact, was fully consistent with traditional, pre-Pauline theology. In confronting proponents of the law, Paul drew radical consequences about the dilemma posed by human sin and the impotence of the law to save. But the basis of those consequences was the universal Christian conviction that "Christ died for our sins" (1 Cor. 15:3).

We conclude: for Wilckens's Paul the pursuit of the righteousness of the law was positively enjoined on the Jews, who, however, failed to attain their goal because they transgressed the law. Salvation is by faith in the death and resurrection of Jesus, who thus provided atonement for transgressions. But the demand to fulfill the law, now seen as summed up in the love commandment, remains valid for believers.

iii. E. P. Sanders

Even before Sanders, in *Paul and Palestinian Judaism,* begins his discussion of the apostle, his study of Palestinian Judaism (reviewed in chap. 7 above) has given reason to doubt that the "boasting" of Jews in their own righteousness can be Paul's reason for rejecting the righteousness of the law. Had that been Paul's charge, his picture of Judaism would have been a distorted one; but though the existence of such a distortion in Paul has frequently been asserted, Sanders finds no evidence to support the claim: "The supposed objection to Jewish self-righteousness is as absent from Paul's letters as self-righteousness itself is from Jewish literature" (*Law,* 156).[3] Certainly Paul opposed boasting in anything other than the cross of Christ. But there is in the epistles "no indication that Paul thought that the law had failed *because* keeping it leads to the wrong attitude or that his opposition to boasting *accounts* for his saying that righteousness is not by law" (35). Implicit in such a statement is, of course, a re-

---

3. All the parenthetical page references in this section are to Sanders's works, using the short titles shown in the bibliography.

jection of Bultmann's interpretation of key passages in Paul. Sanders's alternative interpretations are, briefly, as follows.

1. The Jewish boasting rejected in Romans 3:27 is not (Sanders believes) that which expresses pride in human achievement but rather that which assumes and relies on the special privileges granted to Jews. The term thus has the same significance as in 2:17, 23. And while the opening verses in Romans 4 establish that Abraham was justified by faith, not works, there is no hint of the view that the attempt to gain righteousness by observing the law is itself the fundamental Jewish sin and Paul's reason for objecting to the law (33). The argument of 3:27–4:25 simply does not address the attitude of self-righteousness. Its subject is God's plan of salvation announced in the Abraham story and now made available to both Jew and Gentile on the same terms: faith in Jesus Christ.

2. In its context the statement in Romans 9:32 that Israel sought righteousness not by faith but by works cannot mean that Jews failed because they observed the law in the wrong way. Their problem, as the immediate sequel shows, is their lack of faith *in Christ,* who is the "stumbling stone" over whom they "stumble" (37). Nor does the claim in 10:3 that Jews try to "establish their own" righteousness refer to a self-righteousness based on personal achievements in keeping the law. In the immediate context (10:2) Paul even commends the "zeal" of Jews. But the Jews are seen to be wrong in pursuing a kind of righteousness available only to themselves ("their own," i.e., that which follows from observing the *Jewish* law) rather than recognizing that God's righteousness is available to Jew and Gentile alike on the same basis. Not Jewish self-righteousness, but the equality of Jews and Gentiles is the point of the argument.

3. Nor does Philippians 3:9 condemn any supposed self-righteousness by Jews. Paul does reject the righteousness of the observant Jew, but again, this is not because there is anything inherently wrong in such righteousness — on the contrary, it is regarded *in itself* as "gain" (3:7). Rather, since Paul has come to believe that true righteousness is found only in Christ, he necessarily looks upon any other righteousness as "loss" *by comparison* (44-45); hence the rejection of the "righteousness of the law."

When these critical passages are interpreted in this way, we are left with no textual support for the view that Paul regarded the righteousness of the law as wrong because it leads to self-righteousness and boasting. That in itself might seem to rule out Bultmann's interpretation. Sanders notes as well the complete absence of any suggestion that law observance leads to boasting in Galatians (*Paul Pal. Jud.,* 482); and even in Romans the variety of ways Paul uses the word "faith" (πίστις) in the opening chapters suggests that his goal can hardly be to establish faith as specifically the abandonment of boasting; his concern is simply to do away with any requirement to keep the law (490-91). But the primary criticism that Sanders brings against Bultmann, the "principal fault" he finds in the latter's treatment of Paul, is that he "proceeded from plight to solution and supposed that Paul proceeded in the same way" (474). It is wrong to think that it is "Paul's analysis of the nature of sin which determines his view" (481-82). What Paul begins with is the conviction that only belonging to Christ brings salvation. "For Paul, the conviction of a universal solution preceded the conviction of a universal plight" (474). If this, as Sanders argues, is the case, then the *starting point* of Paul's thought can hardly be any sense that the effort to keep the law was misdirected. Whatever the criticisms Paul may bring against the law, they all *presuppose* his faith in Christ.

Sanders's arguments against Wilckens's position follow similar lines. Obviously "the common observation that everybody transgresses" is found in Paul as well, and, to be sure, in the opening chapters in Romans Paul uses it as an argument "to *prove* that everyone is under the lordship of sin. But this is only *an argument to prove a point*, not the way he actually reached his assessment of the plight of man" (499). Transgressions do not constitute the real plight of humankind. The problem, perceived by a Paul who is already convinced that Jesus is Savior and Lord, is that people are under a different lordship and need Christ to be their Savior (443). That we are dealing with an argument "based on the conclusion" rather than the other way around is clear from the "remarkably inconsistent" nature of Paul's "statements of universal sinfulness" (*Law*, 35). Romans 2 actually "holds out the possibility of righteousness by the law as a real one" (35), contrary to what we find elsewhere in Paul. Even the different ways in which Paul regards transgressions — as the *cause* of sin's dominion in Romans, or "as the *result* of being in the flesh (Gal. 5.19-21)" — indicate that this was not Paul's starting point (*Paul Pal. Jud.*, 501). Moreover, it is important to note "that Paul does not cite human inability to fulfill the law in his principal arguments against his opponents, Galatians 3 and Romans 4, when he undertakes to prove that righteousness *cannot* be by law." Thus, while we cannot "say that Paul never thought that everybody sins," it remains true that that "view is not put forward as the ground of his own view that righteousness must be by faith, to the exclusion of doing the law" (*Law*, 25).

Other attempts at explaining why Paul rejected the righteousness of the law may be dealt with more briefly. Some think, on the basis of Galatians 3:13, that Paul inevitably rejected the law when he came to believe that Jesus, on whom the law pronounced a curse, was really the Messiah. This seems logical, but in fact no one in the first century appears to have reasoned that way. In its context Galatians 3:13 explains why Christians are no longer under the law's curse. It is "not actually an argument against righteousness by the law," nor does Paul reason in the way suggested anywhere else when he "recounts his own rejection of the law" (26). Many scholars ("especially of an earlier period") have argued on the basis of Romans 7 "that Paul had become frustrated in his attempt to find righteousness under the law and therefore denounced it" (48 n. 2). Yet Romans 7 represents, not Paul's reason for rejecting the law, but one of his several attempts to explain the relationship between the law and sin. Paul shows elsewhere that he believes Jews can do what the law requires — and that he himself had done so (77)! Romans 7 is quite unique in Paul, suggesting as it does that "humanity without Christ cannot fulfill the law at all" (78). Thus it can scarcely be made the basis of his rejection of the law. Finally, the suggestion that Paul's views were determined by a supposedly common scheme that saw the validity of the law ending with the dawn of the messianic period may be rejected if for no other reason than that Paul "*never appeals to the fact that the Messiah has come as a reason for holding the law invalid. . . . If such reasoning governed his view, he kept it completely to himself*" (*Paul Pal. Jud.*, 479-80).

Paul's real *reason* for excluding the law has already been suggested: his exclusivist soteriology necessarily ruled out the righteousness of the law as a path to salvation. "If salvation comes only in Christ, no one may follow any other way whatsoever" (519). Admittedly, Paul produces many *arguments* against the law. He cites Scripture to prove that righteousness comes only by faith. He claims that the law provokes transgressions; or that, while good in itself, it has become an agent in the service of "Sin"; or that it is powerless to cope with the weakness of the human "flesh" (*Law*, 26, 65-76). Yet the very diversity that characterizes Paul's portrayals of the human plight under law demonstrates that he "did not begin his thinking about sin and redemption by analyzing the human condition, nor by analyzing the effect of the law on those who sought to obey it. Had he done so we should doubtless find more consistency" (81). Paul's actual thinking is more clearly reflected in 2 Corinthians 3:4-18 and Philippians 3:3-11, where the Mosaic dispensation is described in positive terms ("glorious," "gain") but abandoned because of the surpassing splendor of the new dispensation. Paul "came to relegate the Mosaic dispensation to a less glorious place *because* he found something more glorious. . . . Once a greater good appears, what was formerly good is regarded not just as second best, but as 'loss.' . . . The only thing that is wrong with the old righteousness seems to be that it is not the new one" (138, 140). "This logic — that God's action in Christ alone provides salvation and makes everything else seem, in fact actually *be* worthless — seems to dominate Paul's view of the law" (*Paul Pal. Jud.*, 485).

There is, however, another consideration, a further "primary conviction" of Paul's, that governed his thinking: Paul believed he was called to be the apostle to the Gentiles. Christ has been appointed Lord of the whole world and Savior of all believers — including Gentiles. Hence righteousness cannot come by keeping the Jewish law, because that would exclude Gentiles. "The salvation of the Gentiles is essential to Paul's preaching; and with it falls the law; for, as Paul says simply, Gentiles cannot live by the law (Gal. 2.14)" (496).

It is, then, these Christian convictions about God's solution in Christ rather than any deficiency he perceived in the law itself that, in Sanders's judgment, led Paul to reject the law. Paul's thinking was not determined by a view that the righteousness of the law is itself bad because it leads to boasting, or that it is good but unattained; it is merely indifferent when compared with God's righteousness in Christ — though, admittedly, in Paul's black-and-white thinking this led to its outright rejection as "loss" (*Law*, 137-41).

And what of the law in the life of the Christian? Here we encounter the surprising fact that when Paul "was asked, as it were, the question of what was the necessary and sufficient condition for membership in the body of Christ, he said 'not the law.' . . . When, however, he thought about behavior, he responded, 'fulfill the law'" (84)! To be sure, without making any theoretical distinction between aspects of the law that remain binding and those that do not, Paul never in fact enforced the provisions regarding circumcision, dietary restrictions, or the observance of special days and seasons (100-101). And admittedly, it is the leading of the Spirit that enables Christians to do what the law requires (105). It remains the case, however, that when Paul is not dealing with the polemical issue of the basis for membership in the people of God, he can speak quite positively of the role of the law in Christian behavior (114). This again suggests that his critique of the law is not the starting point of his thought.

*   *

The positions reviewed in this chapter demonstrate — if little else — the lack of a scholarly consensus on Paul's view of the law. Not surprisingly, some scholars have suggested that the problems of interpretation are the result of a lack of consistency or coherence in Paul's own statements on the subject. We turn now to a consideration of three forms in which this proposal has been argued.

Chapter 10

The "Hobgoblin" of Consistency:
Drane, Hübner, and Räisänen

The novice who wishes to pass unsuspected at a gathering of New Testament scholars needs only to wait for an appropriate moment to utter the axiom: "But of course, Paul was no systematic theologian!" That, with an otherwise steadfast adherence to the principle of Proverbs 17:28, should ensure acceptance.

Like a number of axioms of the discipline, this one contains a grain of truth. Paul's writings have been preserved for posterity in the Christian Bible, but this unanticipated development should not be allowed to conceal their original, occasional nature. He wrote letters, not theological treatises, designed to deal with concrete situations in contemporary Christian communities rather than as a vehicle for the ordered presentation of his thought. The epistle to the Romans has long been regarded as the exception that proves the rule; but even this concession to the devotees of system may not be necessary. Recent studies have stressed that Romans too is a response to peculiar conditions prevailing at a crucial point in the life of Paul and in the history of the early church.

Paul did not write systematic theology. Yet this in itself does not mean that such theology cannot be constructed from his piecemeal responses to particular issues. Several of the scholars we have considered have attempted to do just that, and Schweitzer's denunciation of those who refuse to admit the logic of Paul's positions was noted. Still, doubts have persisted, nourished in part by the patent discrepancies that exist between the numerous systems proposed as Pauline. Do Paul's diverse claims about the law really yield a single, coherent picture? Do we not rather find a development in his views from one epistle to the next? Or perhaps we should simply admit a total lack of coherence?

While "Lutheran" readings of Paul have served as a starting point for other chapters in our review, the perspectives on Paul discussed here represent a challenge not so much to "Lutheran" interpretations per se as to any understanding of Paul that supposes that his various statements on the law can be reduced to a coherent scheme. Drane and Hübner believe that a significant shift in Paul's thinking on the subject can be traced between the writing of Galatians and that of Romans. Räisänen maintains that Paul's thinking on the law is characterized throughout by contradictions. To many readers, such a menu no doubt portends an unpalatable meal; but the proof — one way or the other — can only be found "in the pudding."

i. John W. Drane

In the title of his monograph Drane asks whether Paul should be considered a "libertine" or a "legalist."[1] In the substance of the book he argues that the answer depends on which epistle one is considering. A libertine (of sorts) when he wrote Galatians, a legalist (of sorts) when he wrote 1 Corinthians, Paul finally developed in his thinking to the point where his views are expressed in a more balanced form in 2 Corinthians and (especially) Romans. For our purposes a brief summary of the proposed development from Galatians to Romans via 1 Corinthians will suffice.

The Galatians to whom Paul wrote were under pressure from "false teachers" to become circumcised and observe the Jewish law. Only so, it was argued, could they be "incorporated into the true People of God" (84). In responding to an insistence that the Old Testament law be observed, Paul was naturally concerned to demonstrate the inferiority of the law to the Christian gospel. The result is a series of "devastating denunciations of the Old Testament Law and all that it stood for" (5). By its very nature the law is inferior to God's promise, according to Galatians 3:18. The law's divine origin is denied in 3:19. In 3:21 Paul claims it is too weak to give life. The law does indeed serve as a revealer of sin and a "custodian" (3:19, 24), but these positive aspects of its function are stated quite baldly. No attempt is made to show the law as a benevolent gift of God.

Does the rejection of the law mean a rejection of morality? Not at all, argues the Paul of Galatians. It is only a morality of the purely external kind — the only morality that law can dictate — that has been done away with. The precepts of the Jewish law are no longer relevant, but in their place Christians have been given the Spirit of God, who provides them with sufficient guidance and strength for moral behavior. It is consistent with this conviction that Paul gives no specific instructions in Galatians on Christian conduct in particular

---

1. All parenthetical page references in this section are to Drane's *Paul: Libertine or Legalist?*

circumstances. Such instructions are unnecessary and run counter to the principle of Christian liberty, which knows no limits in this epistle.

At the time he wrote Galatians, however, Paul did not anticipate the problems to which such views could lead. His own opposition to legalism in Galatians came back to haunt him in Corinth, where he was confronted with gnosticizing libertines whose pursuit of unrestrained liberty led to intolerable consequences. And so the Paul who writes 1 Corinthians now appears in the guise of a quasi legalist. The Old Testament law as such is not a subject for discussion. But when Paul claims that "keeping the commandments" is essential (1 Cor. 7:19), "he reintroduces the *form* of legal language, which in turn leads him into an ethical position in 1 Corinthians not so very much different from the legalism he had so much deprecated in Galatians" (65). No longer does Paul simply rely on the guidance of the Holy Spirit. Rather, he "[defines] in very precise terms the ways in which the principle of Christian ethics should be applied, and by bringing in himself as an authorized example, and his own teaching as a kind of universal moral code, he moves a considerable distance in the direction of the 'law ethics' which he had so much deplored in the Galatian situation" (64). As for Christian liberty, 1 Corinthians 6:12 introduces deliberate limitations on Paul's earlier position; the rules given at various points in the epistle "constitute a substantial modification of the original principle of Christian freedom" (69); and the plea that Christian liberty should be restrained by a consideration of the needs of weaker brethren represents something of a discovery for Paul himself, who showed no compunction on that score in his encounter with Peter at Antioch, related in Galatians 2:11-14.

What we find in Romans is Paul's attempt "to give a completely balanced exposition of his theological position, which would be susceptible of misunderstanding by neither Judaizers nor Gnosticizers" (124). In essence he returns to many of the things he had said in Galatians, but with modifications necessitated by his Corinthian experience. In Romans, as in Galatians, the law cannot save, and its precepts are not binding on Christians. On the other hand, the law is no longer despised: it is described as God's law (8:7), as spiritual (7:14), holy, just, and good (7:12). Its positive role in preparing for salvation through Christ receives an emphasis lacking in Galatians (cf. Rom. 3:21), and Christians are even said to fulfill its demands (8:3-4). While the Holy Spirit's role in Christian ethics is maintained in Romans as in Galatians, in the later epistle Paul "goes on to describe in some detail the ways in which the Christian ought to behave" (134).

In the final analysis Paul should not be considered a libertine or a legalist. He was first and foremost a servant of Jesus Christ, prone to blunders "in his enthusiasm for his vocation" (135), but willing to take whatever risks seemed necessary "for the sake of the gospel" (1 Cor. 9:23).

ii. Hans Hübner[2]

Hübner's study of development in Paul's thought[3] focuses on perceived shifts between Paul's positions on the law in Galatians and those we encounter in Romans. Hübner speculates that Paul's very negative view of the law in the earlier epistle may have become known to the Jerusalem apostles, and that their severe criticisms forced him to reconsider the matter. The primary concern of *Law in Paul's Thought,* however, is not with historical reconstruction but with the interpretation of the Pauline texts. Though Hübner treats Galatians and Romans separately, the (not to be despised) voice of convenience suggests that we simply note the relevant points on which he sees significant differences between the epistles.

1. We may begin with the origin and purpose of the law. Like Drane, Hübner interprets Galatians 3:19-20 as indicating that angels were the actual source of the law, not merely its mediators. Since the purpose of these angels was "to promote transgressions" (so Hübner interprets 3:19), the character of the angels must be that of hostile demons. This interpretation allows verse 21a to appear in its full force: since the law was given by demons, the question whether such a law is "against the promises of God" becomes indeed acute! As for the law's purpose in Galatians, the discussion must be conducted on three levels (cf. "Proprium," 462-63). The "immanent purpose" of the law is found in what the law itself promises: it gives life to those who carry out its commands (3:12). The purpose of the demons who gave the law was to provoke transgressions (3:19). Overriding both is the purpose of God, who made of the law a "custodian until Christ came" (3:24).

The picture in Romans is much simpler, largely because there is no suggestion that the law came from hostile angels. Here the law is divine, its purpose that of bringing the knowledge of sin (3:20; 7:7). Whereas in Galatians the law was said to provoke transgressions, in Romans it is explicitly exonerated of any such responsibility. Sin itself is to blame — though it uses the law to achieve its ends (Rom. 7).

---

2. All the parenthetical page references in this section are to Hübner's works, using the short titles shown in the bibliography.

3. I.e., *Law,* which is the focus of our attention in this section. In subsequent publications Hübner has underlined that justification by grace and faith alone is the unchanging heart of Paul's theology: the building blocks may change, but the framework of the theological edifice remains the same (*Israel,* 10; also "Proprium"; cf. already *Law,* 7, 65, 149). The emphasis in *Law,* however, is on what *changed* in Paul's thinking between Galatians and Romans, and on this count Hübner's subsequent work repeats his earlier claims (e.g., *Israel,* 131-34, where he sees a development in Paul's thinking concerning Israel parallel to that which he traced in *Law* regarding the Mosaic law).

2. A dominant feature of Galatians first discovered by Hübner is the contrast between a quantitative and a qualitative understanding of the law (cf. *Theologie*, 102-4). The former requires obedience to each of Torah's individual demands; the law's curse is thought to strike those who transgress a single one, though (on the normal quantitative view) full compliance with the law is considered a manageable proposition. This, Hübner believes, was the view of Torah held by Beth Shammai, one of the schools within the Pharisaism of Paul's day. In Galatians Paul himself expresses such a quantitative view — a case, according to Hübner, of not yet shaken adherence to the tenets of his alma mater: "only total obedience to the Law is obedience to the Law at all. . . . If just a single prescription of the Law is transgressed against, the effect is as if the entire Torah had been disregarded" (*Law*, 24; cf. "Proprium," 462). Paul assumes, however, that no one fulfills the law in all its requirements; hence the law brings a curse to all rather than life (Gal. 3:10, 13).

But for the Christian the "law" is defined in a new, qualitative way. No longer is it a totality of individual commands; the "whole law" valid for the believer is simply the command to love (Gal. 5:14). It is crucial to Hübner's argument that this whole law is *not* to be identified with the law of Moses; rather, it represents a radical reduction of its demands to a single commandment binding on believers.

The contrast between the two views of the law is not maintained in Romans. On the one hand, Paul does not argue here, as he did on the basis of the "quantitative" view of Torah in Galatians, that a curse strikes those who do not keep *each* of Torah's precepts. On the other hand, whereas in Galatians the Christian is not bound by the Mosaic law itself but only by a radically reduced form of it (the qualitative view), in Romans the actual law of Moses (when correctly understood) remains valid for believers. The love commandment, which alone survives the radical reduction of Torah in Galatians, is seen in Romans 13:8-10 as simply a summary of the still-binding demands of the Mosaic law.

3. From the preceding distinction it follows that Romans allows for a dialectic in the Christian's relation to the law on which Galatians is silent. In Galatians Christians are "free" from the law. No limitations are placed on their freedom, though they are warned not to abuse it (5:13). In Romans, however, the law is rehabilitated, and Hübner insists that a distinction must be drawn between Torah as it has been *perverted* into a law of works and Torah as it is perceived from the standpoint of faith (cf. 3:27). Properly interpreted, the law is on the side of faith, not works: "the Law in so far as it is 'scripture' testifies of itself that in so far as it is a divine demand its intention is not to be a 'Law of works'" (*Law*, 143, emphasis removed). It is thus a distortion of the law to imagine that it demands works as the basis of righteousness; such a distortion leads one to

see one's existence as based on one's own activity, thereby forgetting that one "owes one's being to God" (121). It is from this distortion of the law, "from the dominion of the perverted Law" (135), that Christians are set free (cf. "Proprium," 464-66). They remain subject to God's law. *"Freedom from the per-verted Law is the dominion of the Law of God"* (*Law*, 135), which still states the will of God for believers (Rom. 7:12; 13:8-10). As a result, in Romans (but not in Galatians) Paul can say, "We uphold the law" (3:31); that is, we allow the law to serve its intended function by showing the misunderstanding involved in inter-preting it as a "law of works." In Galatians Christ is the end of the law. In Romans he is "the end of the misuse of the Law" (so Hübner interprets 10:4 [138]; cf. "Proprium," 466).

4. Finally, according to Hübner, Galatians lacks any prohibition of boasting in one's own works before God, a prohibition that in Romans is an essential part of the Christian's self-understanding. Indeed, Galatians 6:4 appears to al-low for Christian "boasting"; not of course for works of the law that have been performed, but for one's "work" as a Christian.

In Romans, however, such boasting is excluded, largely because Paul has now thought through the implications of a righteousness based on works.

> If the Law is defined as the sum of commandments which when complied with make man righteous, and if furthermore being righteous means being righteous in the presence of God, then the whole point for the man who un-derstands the Law in this way is that he claims recognition in the sight of God for the works he has achieved. Yet more: he is in fact dependent on so doing, he must claim recognition for them in the sight of God. But this means no more nor less than boasting in the presence of God. If *righteous-ness through works* is legitimate . . . then it *implies the legitimacy of self-glorying or boasting.* (*Law*, 116)

Such boasting, such elevating of oneself in the sight of God, Paul now perceives, is fundamentally evil. Hence the Paul of Romans is led both to denounce the view of the law (as a "law of works") that leads to such a result and to exclude boasting of one's works from Christian experience (Rom. 3:27; 4:2). In place of such boasting, Paul says in the paradoxical statement of 5:2-3 that Christians "boast in the hope of God's glory, but that this coincides with our boasting also of suffering or distress" (122).

Such, in brief, are the major developments that Hübner detects by compar-ing Galatians with Romans. The ("Lutheran") Paul who opposes human works and boasting of their performance is the Paul of Romans, not Galatians. As in Drane's study, the impressiveness of Paul's theology is granted, but its blossom is thought to be late, not perennial.

iii. Heikki Räisänen[4]

If, as Ralph Waldo Emerson would have it, "a foolish consistency is the hobgoblin of little minds," then Räisänen's *Paul and the Law* bids fair to prove that Paul was never so afflicted. For Räisänen it is not enough to say that Romans betrays shifts in Paul's thinking from what we encounter in the earlier epistles. On the one hand, the interval between the writing of Galatians and Romans was scarcely sufficient to allow major developments in Paul's thought, nor is it likely that, after twenty years of missionary work, Paul's thinking suddenly matured. On the other hand, Paul's statements about the law are not consistent even within the limits of single epistles. In short, "contradictions and tensions have to be *accepted* as *constant* features of Paul's theology of the law" (*Law,* 11); the exegete should "take them very seriously as pointers to Paul's *personal theological problems*" (12) requiring "a historical and psychological explanation" rather than resolution in terms of "theological dialectic or theories of interpolation or development" (14). Under five headings Räisänen explores Paul's thought with this agenda in mind.[5]

1. On two counts Räisänen finds inconsistencies in Paul's very concept of law. In the first place Paul sometimes speaks as though Jews alone were given the law, whereas in other texts Gentiles, too, are subject to its demands. Secondly, Paul speaks of the law as a unity and never explicitly distinguishes between its moral and ritual parts, but his argument in several places presupposes a reduction of Torah to its moral demands.

a. If "*nomos* in Paul refers to the authoritative tradition of Israel, anchored in the revelation on Sinai, which separates the Jews from the rest of mankind" (16), then there is nothing surprising in those passages that speak of Jews as liv-

---

4. All the parenthetical page references in this section are to Räisänen's works, using the short titles shown in the bibliography.

5. The summary that follows focuses on the argument of Räisänen's *Law.* In "Analyse" and "Research," Räisänen argues that Paul's argument in Rom. 9–11 is marked by similar inconsistencies. "The crucial question is the treatment of Israel, and for this question there are two sharply diverging solutions . . . : that empirical Israel is not elected but hardened and damned in advance to reprobation (9:6-29), and that empirical Israel — or most of it — will be saved because of God's loyalty to his promises and to the election of the people (11:11-36)" ("Research," 192). "Paul's wrestling points to an insoluble *heilsgeschichtlich* dilemma in his theology. He presupposes (a) that God has acted in a decisive way in the past and given his people promises that cannot change or vanish, and (b) that God has acted in a decisive way in Christ and that there can be no salvation apart from Christ. . . . It was not possible to invest Jesus Christ with exclusive soteriological significance without at the same time in effect breaking with the classical covenantal nomism. Paul will have it both ways, and this brings him into an insoluble self-contradiction as regards Israel" ("Research," 196).

ing "under law" and Gentiles as being without it (Rom. 2; 1 Cor. 9:20-21; cf. Gal. 2:15). The distinction is clear, and its basis in the traditions of God's unique revelation to Israel on Mount Sinai is obvious.

Curiously, however, when Paul speaks of the human dilemma from which Christ delivers, the power and curse of the law appear to be universal, affecting Gentiles as well as Jews. According to Galatians 3:13-14, "Christ redeemed *us* from the curse of the law . . . that *we* might receive the promise of the Spirit through faith"; the first-person pronouns can hardly refer to Jewish believers alone (cf. also 3:23-26). 4:5-6 assumes that the (Gentile) Galatians were redeemed from bondage "under the law" so that they might be "adopted" as "sons." The Roman believers addressed in Romans 7:4-6 are said to have "died to the law"; yet the Roman church included Gentiles as well as Jews. Thus, "apparently without noticing it," Paul oscillates "between the notion of a historical and particularist Torah and that of a general universal force" (21).

b. Though some scholars have suggested that Paul rejected only the ritual elements of the law, such a view does not withstand scrutiny: Paul can speak positively of Israel's cult (λατρεία, Rom. 9:4) and negatively about the moral law (4:15; 7:5, 7-11; 2 Cor. 3:6-7). Nowhere, in fact, does he consciously distinguish between the cultic and the moral aspects of the Torah.

Nonetheless, when Paul speaks in Romans 2 of Gentiles who "keep the law" (v. 27; cf. vv. 14, 26), the statement is patently untrue if Israel's ritual law is included. Paul can only be thinking of moral standards recognized by Jews and non-Jews alike. Similarly, when Paul claims that believers fulfill the law (8:4; cf. 13:8-10; Gal. 5:14), it is obvious that he has tacitly reduced Torah to its moral requirements. Paul never articulates such a distinction, and presumably he himself is unaware of the oscillation in his concept of the law; yet his argument depends upon it.

2. Räisänen finds in the apostle's writings evidence that Paul believed that the law both is and is not still valid. The force of the latter statements is sometimes evaded by claims that Paul repudiated Jewish misunderstandings of the law rather than the law itself. But Galatians 3 clearly states that the law as given on Mount Sinai was intended to be a temporary measure. Similarly in 2 Corinthians 3 Paul speaks of the Sinaitic law and the ministry of Moses as inferior and transient without suggesting that such liabilities resulted from Jewish legalistic misunderstandings. And why, if the human dilemma was one of misunderstanding the law, was the death of Christ and even of Christians to the law the necessary path of deliverance (Gal. 2:19; Rom. 7:1-6)?

Paul's sweeping statements about Christian freedom further substantiate the view that he believes the law has been set aside. No one for whom the Mosaic law remained the valid statement of God's will could claim that "nothing is unclean in itself" (Rom. 14:14), that the propriety of eating food offered to idols depends on the circumstances (1 Cor. 8:10), that "all things are lawful" when sexual license is under discussion (6:12). Passages such as Romans 12:1-2, Philippians 1:10, and 4:8 make it clear that Paul relied on no ready code for discovering the will of God. Moreover, in a context where the righteousness based on the law is contrasted with that of faith, Paul declares that Christ marks an end to the former (Rom. 10:4). Paul's varied attempts to explain how the law was set aside (it was temporary by design; believers somehow died to the law; believers have been liberated from the law through the vicarious death of Christ) at least confirm that freedom from the law was one aspect of his thought. Finally, the evidence of the epistles shows that Paul himself did not scrupulously adhere to the law. In 1 Corinthians 9:20-21 he notes that he behaves differently ("as one outside the law") in the presence of Gentiles than he does among Jews; nonobservance of the "ritual" Torah must be meant. Galatians 4:12 refers to the apostle's abandoning of ritual observance in the course of his activity among the Galatians. 2:17 indicates that Paul and, at one time, Peter lived in a way that made them "sinners" from the perspective of Torah. And how could Paul have written 4:10 if he himself had kept the Sabbath in Galatia? Is he likely to have observed Jewish dietary laws when he emphatically claims that *all* foods are clean (Rom. 14:14)?

Yet Paul was not a consistent antinomist. Occasionally he cites demands of Torah as though they were still binding (1 Cor. 9:9; 14:34 [?]; 2 Cor. 8:15). More importantly he sees the Christian's task as "fulfilling the law" (Gal. 5:14; Rom. 8:4; 13:8-10), claims that "keeping the commandments of God" is essential (1 Cor. 7:19), and insists that he himself upholds the law (Rom. 3:31). "Paul thus wants to have his cake and eat it": Christians are free from the law, yet "now as before the law is justified in putting a claim on man, even on the Christian" (*Law*, 82).

3. Is it possible to keep the law? Again Räisänen's Paul comes down hard on both sides of the issue. In Galatians 3:10 the curse of the law, which strikes "every one who does not abide by all things written in the book of the law," is said to fall on all those subject to the law: the implication, clearly, is that none of the adherents of the law abides by all its commands.

That everyone transgresses the law is Paul's explicit point in Romans 1:18–3:20: all have sinned (3:20) and are under sin's power (3:9). Yet Paul's argument in support of his point is neither convincing nor coherent. In it he accuses Jews and Gentiles alike of serious transgressions. His conclusions would follow only "if the description given of Jews and Gentiles were empirically and globally true — that is, on the impossible condition that Gentiles and Jews were, *without exception,* guilty of the vices described" (99). Even if judged by the coherence of its own statements, Paul's argument fails. In the context of his denunciation of Jews, Paul contrasts Jews with *Gentiles who keep the law* and are approved by God (2:14-15, 26-27); but Gentiles, like Jews, are universally condemned in chapters 1 and 3. The attempts that have been made to reconcile these statements are implausible. The Gentiles praised are not "casual" observers of a few commands, for 2:27 credits them with observing (the totality of) the law; in any case, "Gentiles fulfilling just a few requirements of the law could hardly condemn the Jew (as v. 27 states), for undoubtedly he has fulfilled a few things as well!" (103). Nor will hypothetical but nonexistent Gentile observers of the law serve Paul's purpose of condemning Jews! That Gentile *Christians* are meant is simply impossible. Throughout the passage (beginning with 2:9) Paul contrasts Jews with Gentiles, circumcised with uncircumcised; in this context ἔθνη (2:14) must mean simply "non-Jews." And Paul would never say that Christians do not know the law, that they keep the law "by nature" rather than by the Spirit, that they "are a law to themselves" (2:14). The contradiction must stand: "when Paul is not reflecting on the situation of the Jews from a certain theological angle he does not presuppose that it is impossible to fulfil the law" (106, emphasis removed). Paul's testimony to his own blamelessness according to the law (Phil. 3:6) supports this conclusion. Arguments for universal sinfulness occur only when Paul wants to support the position that "the death of Christ was a salvific act that was absolutely necessary for all mankind" (108).

The inadequacy and, indeed, unfairness of Paul's argument become even more apparent when we compare his statements about non-Christian behavior in Romans 7 with his claim about Christians in 8:4. According to 7:14-25, those living "under the law" are "not able to do any good at all" (110). Here Paul draws on Hellenistic traditions about the discrepancy between human intentions and actions in order to support his thesis that those living "in the flesh" and "under the law" are morally impotent and incapable of pleasing God. Christians, by way of contrast, can and do fulfill God's requirements in the law (8:4; cf. 2:29; 13:8-10; Gal. 5:14-23). They have died to sin, so that sin will not reign over them (Rom. 6:14); freedom from the law allows them to be led by the Spirit, an existence characterized by the Spirit's fruit (Gal. 5:22-23) and by the possibility of overcoming the desires of the flesh (5:16). Yet such idealized pictures of Christian behavior stand in stark contrast with the way Christians actually behaved in some of Paul's own congregations. Paul "compares Christian life at its best (if not an ideal picture of it) with Jewish life at its worst (if not a pure caricature). Paul thus uses different standards for Christians and Jews respectively" (117).

Theological theory has forced Paul into a corner. "His point of departure is the conviction that the law *must not* be fulfilled outside of the Christian community, for otherwise Christ would have died in vain. Among Christians, on the other hand, the law *must* be fulfilled; otherwise Christ would be as weak as the law was (Rom. 8.3)" (118). The actual conduct of Christians proves the "'doctrinaire' character" of Paul's assertions (118).

4. Not even about the origin of the law does Paul speak with one mind. Normally, to be sure, Paul assumes that the law is divine (Rom. 7:22; 8:7; 9:4; cf. 7:12; 1 Cor. 9:8-9). Even in Galatians it is apparent that Paul "at bottom" (132) continues to link God with the giving of the law: it is still an expression of God's will, and God's intentions with the law are still a subject for discussion. Nonetheless, Galatians 3:19 leaves open the possibility that angels were the actual originators of the law, and the context shows that Paul was indeed "toying" with the idea (133). In 3:17 he uses the bald expression "the law . . . came" with no indication of a divine source, whereas the "covenant" is explicitly said to have been "ratified by God." In Paul's analogy the law's relation to God's promise is paralleled with the additions that an outsider might want to make to the will of a testator. Finally, according to 3:20, a mediator is said to be unnecessary when God communicates with humanity, for God is "one"; that a mediator was involved at the giving of the law thus implies that "God was *not* involved" (130). Paul himself never returned to the idea. The suggestion that angels were the source of the law marks a momentary overreaction in a polemical context, revealing the "latent resentment" that Paul must have felt toward the Mosaic law (133).

Hopeless confusion results when Paul attempts to explain God's purpose with the law.

a. Was the law intended to give life to those who observe it? The answer, according to some passages in Paul, is clearly yes. The argument of Romans 3 is that God provided the free gift of salvation as a remedy after men and women had sinned; at least theoretically the law could have been observed and led to life. Similarly in Romans 7:10 Paul insists that the law was intended to give life, though, as the sequel shows, it was too "weak" to carry out this function (8:3). But this line of thought is contradicted by other passages that exclude in principle the notion that the law could convey life (cf. esp. Gal. 3:21). The first position provokes the question why God would bother giving a law too weak to serve its purpose; the second, why, if God did not intend to provide life through the law, did he give a law that promises life (Lev. 18:5; cf. Gal. 3:12; Rom. 10:5).

b. In discussing the role actually performed by the law, Paul consistently links it with sin. It is difficult, however, to be more precise. Romans 3:20 suggests that the law brings an awareness of sin. This is straightforward enough, but it is not Paul's characteristic emphasis. A second suggestion is that the law "defines sin as 'transgression,'" making "sin a conscious and wilful activity"

(141). This seems to be the argument of Romans 5:13 (cf. 4:15), where Paul says that only in the presence of law is sin "counted." The statement is strange in the light of 2:12-16 ("all who have sinned without the law will also perish without the law" [2:12]!) and in view of the actual fate of sinners between Adam and Moses: were Noah's contemporaries, for example, not held accountable for their sins?

Paul's third suggestion is both his most characteristic and most problematic. The law actually "brings about sinning" (141). This is probably the point in Galatians 3:19 (cf. also 1 Cor. 15:56) and is certainly Paul's thesis in Romans 5:20; 7:5, 7-13. At times Paul suggests that the presence of the law is actually "necessary to induce man to sin" (142, referring to 7:7-11); elsewhere sin, already present (cf. 5:20; 7:13-14), is merely the reason why the law cannot "effect what it ought to have effected" (143). At the root of this proposal is the everyday experience that "prohibitions sometimes incite people to transgress them" (149). But Paul transforms a common experience into a sweeping generalization with a "vigorous theological emphasis" (149) — an emphasis, however, that does not do justice to the empirical reality of Judaism (did the law really promote sin among Jews?) and which, if it is to be made at all, could be made equally well of Paul's own apostolic commandments (do *his* commands, like the law's, incite to sin?).

5. Finally, Räisänen discusses Paul's famous contrast between works of law and faith in Christ. For Paul the two are rival principles of salvation: the former is pursued by Jews, whereas the latter represents a new soteriological system replacing the old one.

The Pauline texts have given rise to a desolate picture of Judaism among Christian exegetes, but Räisänen follows Sanders in thinking that much of the common caricature has no real basis in Paul's words. For Paul "the Jews err in imagining that they can be saved by keeping the law rather than by believing in Christ" (176); he does not speak as though smugness, self-righteousness, and boasting in one's achievements were characteristic sins of Jews.

Nonetheless, Paul distorts Judaism by the very suggestion that the law was its "way of salvation." Again, following Sanders, Räisänen believes salvation in Judaism was perceived "as *God's* act." God had chosen his people and entered a covenant with them. "Salvation, i.e., a share in the age to come, was based on God's faithfulness in his covenant." The observance of Torah was, for the Jews, an expression of "gratitude and obedience to its Giver" (178). Thus "the theme of *gratuity* with regard to salvation is conspicuously present in Judaism" (179), and Paul's contrast between salvation by grace in Christ and the Jewish path centered on the works of the law lacks foundation.

Nor is Paul himself consistent in propounding salvation by grace. Like the rabbis, he "speaks of right behaviour as *necessary* for salvation" (184), of judgment as based on *deeds*. Grievous sins lead to condemnation even for Christians. The pattern is precisely what we find in Judaism. Paul's doctrine of grace differs only from the Judaism of his own distorted representation.

At this point a reader may be inclined to ask how a reasonably intelligent man like Paul could have managed to contradict himself on so many counts within the limits of time imposed by our common mortality. Räisänen proposes an explanation, but with some diffidence,[6] noting that it is necessarily hypothetical and warning that the analysis of the problems in the Pauline texts must not be thought to depend on the plausibility of his proposal about their origin.

Räisänen shares with Kümmel and Stendahl the conviction that Paul's critique of the law was not spawned by frustrated attempts at keeping it. Still, Paul's repeated depictions of life under the law as bondage must have some basis in his personal experience. Perhaps before his conversion Paul's compliance with Torah was marked either by fear of punishment or by doubts about the point in observing precepts for which no motive was supplied.

At his conversion Paul came in contact with Hellenistic Christians who displayed a "liberal" attitude toward the Torah, were "*somewhat* relaxed" in their "attitude to the observance of the ritual Torah," and perhaps were inclined to neglect circumcision "as part of the missionary strategy" (254). No theological foundation had yet been established for such laxity; the new way of life flowed spontaneously from the experience of ecstatic gifts and the sense of eschatological fulfillment in the community. At first Paul, too, "simply adopted this 'liberal' position" (255): the tentative, inconsistent nature of his arguments in the later epistles forbids us to think that he had reflected on the issues for twenty years or more.

When, however, a reaction came, and Jewish Christians urged that Gentile believers submit to the law, Paul was forced to defend his position. "Over the years Paul had become internally alienated from the ritual aspects of the law,"

---

6. Since the publication of the first edition of *Paul and the Law*, Räisänen has in fact proposed a second hypothetical explanation (see *Law*, xvii-xix; *Torah*, 186-97). Among Diaspora Jews there was a tendency to "spiritualize" the ritual commandments of the Mosaic law, including circumcision. Hellenist Christians may have found in this tendency a theological motivation for admitting uncircumcised Gentiles into the church: they did not see themselves as abandoning the law, but merely as giving it its true ("spiritual") meaning. Paul encountered and took over their reinterpretation of the law through his contact with the church at Antioch. His more negative statements about the law (particularly in Galatians) are the product of the controversies in which he was engaged; many of the more positive things he has to say may be traced to his Antiochian heritage.

had "fully internalized the Gentile point of view and identified himself with it" (258). Now he was not able to "retrace his steps" (261). "He thus came upon several *ad hoc* arguments for the termination of the law . . . and its allegedly sin-engendering and sin-enhancing nature etc. The numerous problems and self-contradictions in his statements expose the overall theory as more or less artificial. It would seem that the difficulties can best be explained if the whole theory owes its origin to a polemical situation" (261-62).

In his conclusions, however, Räisänen goes further: Paul's real problem is that he is attempting to defend the indefensible position "that a *divine* institution has been *abolished* through what God has done in Christ" (264-65). Either Paul "must attribute to God an unsuccessful first attempt to carry through his will . . . or else he gets involved in the cynicism that God explicitly provides men with a law 'unto life' while knowing from the start that this instrument will not work" (265). In fact, "if something is truly divine, it is hardly capable of being abrogated! . . . The only reasonable way to cope with the Torah theologically . . . is to admit that it was *not* a direct divine revelation to Moses" (265-66). But that, of course, was an option that Paul did not consider.

The problem, in short, is how Christians can justify dispensing with a law they believe to be divinely ordained. In a book which, perhaps more than any other, shows an awareness of earlier attempts to answer the question, Räisänen concludes that Paul has no satisfactory solution; indeed, in the terms in which it is posed, the question is simply unanswerable. Inevitably such conclusions will provoke further studies. Yet, if not the last word on the subject, Räisänen's work makes the task of those who would advance beyond it a daunting undertaking.[7]

---

7. Mention should be made here of the work of Kari Kuula, a student of Räisänen, who argues (as does Räisänen) that Paul necessarily rejected Judaism once he came to believe that salvation is only found in Christ, but that he also wanted to retain a measure of continuity with his Jewish past. As a result, his letters are characterized by dubious argumentative strategies, forced interpretations of Scripture, and artificial suggestions about the law's place in God's salvific plan (Kuula, *Law*, 208).

Chapter 11

Saint Paul against the Lutherans: Wright, Dunn, and Donaldson

The conviction most central to the "new perspective on Paul" pertains in the first place to Judaism, not Paul: first-century Jews, it is claimed (in dependence on E. P. Sanders's *Paul and Palestinian Judaism*), were not legalists who supposed that they *earned* their salvation (or membership in the people of God) by deeds they did in compliance with the law. Since the "Lutheran" Paul rejected his ancestral religion because it pursued salvation by "works," our better understanding of Judaism requires a revolution in our understanding of the apostle.

From this point paths diverge.[1] It is possible to hold, with the new perspectivists, that Judaism was not legalistic while still holding, with the "Lutherans," that Paul thought it was: Paul, we must then conclude, was wrong. The solution is enticingly simple, though the implication that we are in a position to correct Paul's understanding of first-century Judaism is at least startling, if not (as some would insist) grossly improbable. More commonly it is held that Judaism was not legalistic, that Paul has been misread when he has been thought to reject it in those terms, and that the error is to be attributed to Luther and his heirs, whose views of Judaism we need not scruple to amend.

Heikki Räisänen (as we have seen) believes that Paul himself misunderstood Judaism. The scholars at whom we look in this chapter follow the lead of E. P. Sanders in thinking that the misunderstanding lies rather with Paul's interpreters.

1. Cf. Matlock, "Studies," 435-36.

i. N. T. Wright[2]

Tom Wright must be reckoned among the first to espouse the new perspective on Paul. Sanders's *Paul and Palestinian Judaism* appeared in 1977. In the immediate wake of its publication, Wright declared already in 1978 that "the real Judaism was not a religion of legalistic works-righteousness," that it was "based on a clear understanding of grace," and that "good works" were meant to express "gratitude, and demonstrate that one is faithful to the covenant" ("History," 79-80). In further agreement with Sanders, Wright insisted that Pauline scholarship must use other categories to understand Paul than "the thin, tired and anachronistic ones of Lutheran polemic" (87): "the tradition of Pauline interpretation has manufactured a false Paul by manufacturing a false Judaism for him to oppose" (78). The Paul of history did not criticize Jews for using the law as a "legalist's ladder" (65) or for reliance on *"Menschenwerke"* (71). Rather (and here Wright announces something of his own agenda), Paul "mount[ed] a detailed and sensitive criticism of Judaism *as its advocates present it*" (82, emphasis Wright's).

Much of what Wright has written about Paul was anticipated already in that early article. A focus on Israel and its covenant has remained a constant feature. For our purposes we will note what Wright takes Paul to be saying about Israel's vocation, failure, and restoration, and about justification by faith.

The Story of Israel

God the creator entered a covenant with Israel, intending thereby to undo the sin of Adam and its effects: "God called Abraham to deal with the problem of Adam" ("Theology," 33). Had Israel offered the obedience that Adam refused, it would have proved not only the "true Adam, the truly human people of the creator god," but also "the light of the nations" (*People*, 265, 267). Indeed, intrinsic to the covenant was the divine promise that Israel would convey God's blessing to the Gentiles: through Abraham's "seed" the nations of the world would be blessed, and would come to be united in a "single worldwide family" (*Climax*, 150).

But Israel, the divinely appointed "physician" to the world ("Law," 147), was itself sick. No less than the other nations, Israel shared in the effects of Adam's sin: "the chosen people were as human, and fallen, as everyone else" (*Founder*,

2. All the parenthetical page references in this section are to the works of N. T. Wright, using the short titles shown in the bibliography.

130). "The problem of Israel . . . is the hidden Adam in the Jew" ("Law," 143). Adam, confronted by a divine command, disobeyed; Israel, given the commands of Torah, "recapitulated" Adam's sin (*Climax*, 197, based on Rom. 7:7-12). The sin of the covenant people threatened the very purpose of the covenant: a sinful people was in no position to bring light to the Gentiles. When Paul in Romans 2 accuses Jews of transgressing the law, his point is not that the charges are true of each individual Jew, but that the presence of such transgression in Israel prevents the people from fulfilling the task to which they were called and in which they took their pride ("Theology," 37).

Israel sinned as all people sin. But the "Adam" in Israel made Israel's singular vocation the basis for Israel's characteristic sin, the "meta-sin" (*Climax*, 240) of boasting of the nation's special place in God's plan and treating the symbols of its distinctiveness (Sabbath, circumcision, the dietary laws) as "badges of superiority" (243). Paul did not charge Jews with supposing that they could merit God's favor by keeping Torah's demands. Rather, he criticized Israel's "relentless pursuit of national, ethnic and territorial identity" (*Founder*, 84). By emphasizing its distinctiveness along national lines, Israel was, paradoxically, becoming *like* the other nations rather than serving as their light. Possessing God's law, ethnic Israel believed itself inalienably God's people and confined the bounds of God's covenant to those who displayed the external "badges" of Jewishness ("Law," 139).

Through its sin as a nation Israel incurred the curse of the covenant spelled out in Deuteronomy 27–28: the nation was subjected to the divine judgment of exile. (Galatians 3:10, Wright believes, speaks of this *national* curse rather than that of individual transgressors [*Climax*, 142, 146].) That judgment, that "exile," was believed to continue in the first century. Many Jews had returned to their homeland from Babylon, but the conditions of life they experienced fell far short of the restoration promised in Isaiah and Ezekiel. In Paul's day "Roman occupation and overlordship" represented "the mode that Israel's continuing exile had now taken" (141). To say, with Sanders, that the post-Damascus Paul devised a plight for Israel to correspond to the solution he perceived in Christ is, for Wright, not the whole story. Paul *revised* his earlier sense of Israel's plight, but in pre-Damascus days he would have shared with other Jews a yearning for Israel's redemption (260-61; cf. "Law," 141).

Israel's destiny was unique — but it was also representative. That the gift of Torah provoked Israel to sin was inevitable inasmuch as Israel was no less "flesh," no less "in Adam," than were other nations. Indeed, it was the divine plan that the sin of the world would be collected (or "heaped up") in Israel — and there dealt with decisively (*Climax*, 152, 198, 202-3; cf. "Theology," 52).

Just as Israel served as the representative of all humankind, so Jesus, as

Messiah, was Israel's representative. But whereas Israel repeated Adam's sin, Jesus "offered God the obedience and faithfulness which should have characterized Israel but did not" (*Founder,* 54). Such obedience did not, however, preclude Jesus' participation in Israel's fate. On the contrary: the curse of the covenant that found expression in Israel's exile and subjection to foreign overlordship reached its climax in the death of Israel's Messiah at the hands of Roman soldiers. Such was God's intention: in Messiah's representative death the curse of his people would be exhausted (*Climax,* 141). Beyond exile, in the divine scheme, lay redemption. And just as Jesus bore the fate of his people in his representative death, so in his representative resurrection lay Israel's deliverance from the "ultimate enemies" of sin and death (*Founder,* 51). In the resurrection of Jesus Israel's exile came to an end, Israel's promised vindication became reality, Israel's covenant was fulfilled.

Hitherto Israel's sin and the curse of its exile had prevented God's blessing from spreading, through Israel, to the Gentile nations. With the exhaustion of the covenant's curse, its promises were extended to Gentiles. Gentiles could now be summoned to join in the day of deliverance. The gift of God's Spirit was the sign that the covenant had been renewed, and that its blessings were available for all (*Climax,* 154).

In this way God's covenantal commitments were kept. Torah was not *designed* to be the means by which God's blessing would reach the nations: how could it, when God's intention was to unite people of all nations in a single family of faith, whereas the imposition of Torah created a *plurality* of peoples by dividing Gentiles from Jews? Torah, moreover, far from bringing God's blessing either to Israel *or* to the nations, had brought the curse of the exile on God's unfaithful people and on any Gentile who chose to embrace its "works" (i.e., circumcision, food laws, and the like: the boundary markers of Israel's distinctiveness).

The divine plan to unite people from all nations in a single family was evident already in the promise given to Abraham. (Wright understands Abraham's single "seed" in Galatians 3:16 to refer to the single "family" of God's people [163-64].) Habakkuk 2:4 underlines that the single family of God's people would one day be demarcated by faith, not by the boundary markers spelled out in Torah for Israel (148-49). Hence the fulfillment of God's covenant involves the redefinition of "Israel" as God's people along lines determined by grace, not race; by faith, not by the "works" (or boundary markers) of Torah. "Israel is transformed from being an ethnic people into a worldwide family" (240). Not all Jews, to be sure, are prepared to allow the transformation. Those who cling to the path of "national righteousness" and reject the gospel have both misunderstood God's intentions and perpetuated the "meta-sin" of ethnic Israel. The Israel that, according to Romans 11:26, is destined for salvation is the single family drawn from all nations and marked by its faith (249-50).

Justification by Faith

Justification by faith is not itself Paul's gospel, though it is implied by that gospel. Nor does it represent Paul's answer to the question how an individual can be "saved" or enjoy a right relationship with God (*Founder*, 116). For Wright Paul's "central belief" was "that the creator god was also the covenant god" and "that the covenant with Israel was always intended as the means of setting the entire cosmos to rights" ("Theology," 66). Justification by faith is, for Paul, the principle by which the true community of God is identified ("Synthesis," 185).

Ethnic Israel looked for the day when God would deliver them from their oppressors and so demonstrate his "righteousness," his faithfulness to the covenant. If we conceive Israel's vindication in the setting of a law court, the divine judge would pronounce in favor of his people while condemning their oppressors. When Israel looked forward to its "justification" as God's covenant people, it envisioned just such a decisive act of divine redemption (*Founder*, 33-35, 98-99). And "the all-important signs . . . that one belonged to the company who would be vindicated when the covenant god acted to redeem his people" were "the works of Torah," that is, the covenant boundary markers spelled out in Torah (circumcision, laws of Sabbath and purity observance, and the like) (*People*, 238).

For the post-Damascus Paul, God's "righteousness" — his covenant faithfulness — was climactically at work in Jesus: Israel's covenant was intended as the divine tool to free the cosmos of the effects of sin, and for this goal the representative death and resurrection of Jesus were the divinely appointed means ("Theology," 33-34). "Justification" meant for Paul what it meant for other Jews: the decisive vindication of God's people when God (as in a court of law) pronounced in their favor. ("Righteous," or "justified," here designates those in whose favor the divine judge has pronounced.) But for Paul the people of God destined for justification were not those demarcated by the "works of Torah." "Justification" — a divine verdict at the end of history, known in anticipation by God's people in the present — is for those who have *faith* in the gospel (*Founder*, 131-32).

For Paul, then, unlike Luther, the target of the doctrine of justification by faith rather than "the works of the law" was not the vain and presumptuous attempt to gain divine favor by human endeavor. What Paul was at "pains to demolish" (99) was the "national righteousness" (*Climax,* 261) pursued by those who imagined that their place in the covenant people of God was secured by their loyalty to the signs of Jewish ethnic identity.

ii. James D. G. Dunn[3]

Though the new perspective on Paul owes its origins to the labors of E. P. Sanders, it was christened by James D. G. Dunn,[4] who has subsequently proved most energetic in its promotion and defense. An imposing list of special studies and commentaries paved the way for his comprehensive monograph *The Theology of Paul the Apostle;* for a number of these studies, as for *Theology* itself, a starting point and justification are found in the need to rethink Paul's thought, or some aspect of it, in the light of the new perspective.[5] In working out the implications of Sanders's pioneering research as he sees them, Dunn has arrived at a distinctive[6] reading of the apostle that demands our attention.

Traditional interpretations of Paul are commonly accused of following Luther and imposing sixteenth-century categories on Paul's differences with Judaism: confusion with the medieval church has resulted in a portrayal of Judaism as "legalistic, dependent on human effort, and self-satisfied with the results."[7] Such misreadings are to be corrected, apparently, by retaining the categories but recognizing that, rightly understood, Jews were good Protestants and champions of grace. "Judaism is first and foremost a religion of grace," Dunn writes,

> with human obedience always understood as response to that grace. . . . Somewhat surprisingly, the picture which Sanders painted of what he called "covenantal nomism" is remarkably like the classic Reformation theology of

---

3. All the parenthetical page references in this section are to the works of James D. G. Dunn, using the short titles shown in the bibliography.

4. Cf. *Law,* 183-206, for Dunn's early article "The New Perspective on Paul."

5. E.g., "Apostate," 258; *Law,* 188; *Romans 1–8,* xiv; *Theology,* 5.

6. Cf. *Law,* 186-87, for Dunn's distancing his own interpretation from what he considers Sanders's "idiosyncratic Paul who in arbitrary and irrational manner turns his face against the glory and greatness of Judaism's covenant theology and abandons Judaism simply because it is not Christianity."

7. So Dunn ("Justice," 7; cf. *Romans 1–8,* lxv), building of course upon Sanders. Cf. also *Partings,* 14: "The obvious corollary [to Luther's assumption that Paul meant by 'justification by faith' what he himself did] was that the Judaism of Paul's day must have taught the equivalent of the Catholicism of Luther's day — Judaism as a religion of legalism, with no place for grace and free pardon."

works — that good works are the consequence and outworking of divine grace, not the means by which that grace is first attained. . . . The Judaism of what Sanders christened as "covenantal nomism" can now be seen to preach good Protestant doctrine: that grace is always prior; that human effort is ever the response to divine initiative; that good works are the fruit and not the root of salvation. ("Justice," 7-8)

"Once again, then, the degree to which Jewish covenantal theology parallels classic Protestant doctrines . . . is plain. . . . These doctrines [of perseverance and good works] follow as directly from Jewish covenantal theology as they do from classic Protestant theology of justification by faith" (18).

Clearly the *truth* of the Protestant doctrine of justification by faith and divine grace, not by anything humans can do, is not for Dunn in any question: he repeatedly asserts its importance,[8] and — most significantly — believes it was axiomatic for first-century Jews ("Ground," 327, 331-33; "Justification," 89-90; *Law,* 190-91; *Theol. Gal.,* 76; *Theology,* 345, 718). What requires rethinking, on Dunn's understanding, is the *point* of Paul's insistence that justification is "by faith" and not by "works of the law." To what in Judaism was Paul objecting if not to the belief that salvation could be earned by good deeds? For Dunn's answer to that question, we look briefly at how he believes Paul understood the human dilemma, the divine response, and the role of the law. We turn then to a summary of the misunderstandings that Paul (according to Dunn) found in contemporary Judaism and, in particular, to Dunn's much-discussed interpretation of the "works of the law."

A (Brief) History of the Work of Redemption

A humanity that has refused to acknowledge God, that has attempted "to dispense with the Creator," finds itself as a consequence subservient to sin and death (*Theology,* 96-97). The ungodliness of Gentiles — seen typically in their idolatry and sexual immorality — was a staple feature of Jewish polemics ("Works," 105). But for Paul Jews are subject to the same indictment as Gentiles; the privileges they enjoy do not exempt them from the judgment due their own

---

8. The affirmations (e.g., "Justice," 2; "Justification," 87; *Partings,* 123-24; *Theol. Gal.,* 75) must of course qualify any presentation of Dunn as an opponent of the "Lutheran" Paul. The designation remains appropriate, however, in that Dunn constantly refers in his work to perceived shortcomings in "Lutheran" interpretations and insists that the real point of Paul's disputes — and, indeed, of his doctrine of justification by faith — has been obscured in "Lutheran" tradition.

disobedience.[9] Using the "apocalyptic schema of two ages," Paul declares the present age to be "evil," the whole world — Jew as well as Greek — "under (the power of) sin" (*Ep. Gal.*, 194). Indeed, "Israel's own experience of sin and death" is "in some sense paradigmatic for humanity as a whole" (*Theology*, 97).

Subservience to sin must end in death: "there is no other end possible for all human beings" (211). To bring about salvation God "reached down to the depths of human impotence under the powers of sin and death" and "identified himself in an unprecedented way (incarnation?) with the man Jesus" (206).[10] If Adam, for Paul, represented all humankind in his death-incurring disobedience, Christ was no less a representative and epoch-launching figure (200). In his death sin's power was exhausted; in his resurrection there began a new age free from the dominion of sin and death. Since all humanity in Adam must die, even those identified with Christ cannot *escape* death (386); but they meet its claims through their share in the death of Christ: "Christ's sharing *their* death makes it possible for them to share *his* death" (223). Such a "share" (or "membership" in Christ as a representative figure) is granted to those who respond with faith to the gospel: "The summons to believe was a fundamental part of Paul's gospel. The 'call' of God must be responded to. People had to receive what God offered through him if the process of salvation was to begin" (324).

But the gospel Paul proclaimed was the "outworking" of the divine promise given already to (or the divine "covenant" made already with)[11] Abraham

---

9. So Rom. 2, where Paul is concerned to condemn "both the actual disobedience and the typical Jewish attitude to the law" ("Works," 106, where Dunn corrects the impression given by his earlier work that he thought Jewish attitudes the sole object of Paul's attacks; cf. also "Ground," 320-21). Dunn's understanding of "the typical Jewish attitude" will be dealt with below.

10. The tentativeness apparent in Dunn's formulation reflects his concern not to read later dogmatic formulations into the Pauline texts. He has no doubt that, for Paul, Jesus represented the embodiment of preexistent divine wisdom; indeed, according to Col. 1:19; 2:9, the "full presence of God" was "pleased to dwell," and could be encountered, in Christ (*Theology*, 204-5). He finds doubtful, however, that Paul understood Christ himself (i.e., as a distinct divine "Person") to be preexistent (266-93; cf. *Christology*, 176-96).

11. Dunn speaks repeatedly of "the covenant" (singular), referring to that made with Abraham (e.g., "Apostate," 263; *Ep. Gal.*, 249; *Law*, 197). When Paul speaks of two covenants in Gal. 4:24, Dunn believes he has in mind "two ways of understanding the one covenant purpose of God through Abraham and for his seed. What Paul is about to argue is that the Abraham covenant seen in terms of freedom and promise is a fuller expression of God's electing grace and a fuller embodiment of the ongoing divine will than the Abraham covenant seen in terms of law and flesh" (*Ep. Gal.*, 249; cf. *Theology*, 146 n. 94). Paul's language of a "new" covenant and an "old" (cf. esp. 2 Cor. 3) is dependent on Jer. 31, where the new covenant is not so much "different" as "a more effective version of the old one. . . . For Paul too the new covenant was all about a more effective way of fulfilling the old covenant." Moreover, the contrast of interest to Paul in

("Apostate," 262; *Ep. Gal.*, 165; "Gospel," 372, 374). The promise designated Israel in the first place as its target, but included a blessing to the nations as well. The (universal) gospel thus represents no abandoning of the covenant with Abraham, but its planned fulfillment, inasmuch as it was God's intention from the beginning that the divine blessing and saving initiative should one day be extended, from its initial restriction to Israel, to include all nations (*Law,* 197): "the gospel consists primarily or essentially in the promise to Abraham that all the nations would be blessed in him" ("Gospel," 372). The gospel's particular focus on Jesus was of course new, but represented at the same time the "foretold way of completing the old purpose" (384).

A second crucial feature in the story of Abraham for Paul was its establishment of the principle that "acceptance by God" is "a matter wholly and solely of faith on the human side" (*Theol. Gal.*, 83). Abraham was "justified" when he believed; so, presumably, were others before Christ's coming. Now that "God's purpose and promise have been realized in Christ," he is "the natural and proper focus for the promise-releasing-and-fulfilling faith" (*Ep. Gal.*, 197). Faith is the "more fundamental identity marker" of the people of God (to be "justified by faith" is in fact to be acknowledged by God as "in the covenant") (*Law,* 190), even though, in the period before Christ (and thus before the "broadening out" of God's covenant blessing to include the Gentiles), Israel was marked as well by such "narrowly nationalistic identity markers" as "circumcision, food laws and sabbath" (198; *Theol. Gal.*, 82).

For Paul, then, the promise given to Abraham and the appropriate response of faith have "precedence" over the law and the works it prescribes (*Ep. Gal.*, 195). "The primary role in first establishing the covenant relation is the initiative of God" (shown, for Paul, in the promise given to Abraham); "the corresponding response on the human side to such divine initiative is faith, the trust which Adam did not display but which Abraham supremely exemplifies. . . . Strictly speaking, the law has no role at that point. Strictly speaking, 'the law is not from faith' (Gal. 3.12)." Its role begins at a secondary phase — "to regulate life for those already chosen by God" (*Theology,* 153). The law is a "guide for living" but not, in itself, the conveyer of life (721). It "may regulate the life of righteousness," but "it is not the basis or source of that righteousness" (*Ep. Gal.*, 193).

Indeed, as we have seen, prior to the coming of Christ Jews as well as Gentiles lived "under the power of sin." The law, though neither able nor in-

---

2 Cor. 3 is not that between the old and new covenant, but that between two modes of ministry ("Covenants," 116-17). It would be fair to say that Dunn here approximates Calvin's understanding of a single divine covenant of grace operative through the ages.

tended to overthrow sin's dominion (195), found its primary function in defining what sin is and in making evident, when its commands were broken, sin's nature as transgression against God (*Theology*, 133-34). In so doing the law marked the standard of God's judgment — for Jews (to whom the law was given) and for Gentiles as well (who also had some awareness of the divine expectations) (136-37). A secondary, and temporary, function of the law featured its sacrificial cult, which provided the people of Israel with a means to cover their sin and remove their guilt until such time as transgression "could be dealt with definitively and finally in the cross of Christ" (*Ep. Gal.*, 190).[12] Yet another subordinate role of the law featured those commands that restricted Israel's contact with the Gentile nations. In this way the law protected the people of Israel, who were "like a child growing up in an evil world," from the "idolatry and the lower moral standards prevalent in the Gentile world" (199). (Admittedly the law, in keeping Israel distinct from the Gentiles, could be said at the same time to have "prevented the blessing of Abraham [from] reaching out to the Gentiles" [169].)

This latter role of the law, too, was meant as an interim measure, appropriate only until the promise given to Abraham could be fulfilled in Christ. Then barriers between Jews and Gentiles would be done away with and the divine blessing made accessible to all who responded to the gospel with faith like that of Abraham. Consequently, now that Christ has come, commandments "which, for good or ill, had come to mark out Israel and to maintain Israel's separation from the other nations (particularly circumcision, food laws, and feast days) . . . and, less explicitly, those which Christ had rendered unnecessary (Temple sacrifice)" were "devalued and discarded in Paul's theology" (*Theology*, 720).[13] Put differently — and in accordance with the teaching of Jesus — the love commandment may be said to spell out how, and which of, the commandments are to be obeyed: "where requirements of the law were being interpreted in a way which ran counter to the basic principle of the love command, Paul thought

12. Dunn suggests that this is Paul's point about the law's function in Gal. 3:19 ("Test-Case," 460; *Theol. Gal.*, 89; *Theology*, 139).

13. Dunn notes, however, that "such a gradation or hierarchy of commandments within the Torah was hardly unusual within the Judaism of Paul's time" (*Theology*, 720). Elsewhere Dunn suggests faith as the criterion by which commands to be pursued may be distinguished from those to be abandoned: "The law could only be fulfilled out of faith, that is, out of a deep-rooted consciousness of creaturely dependence on the Creator, constantly expressed and nourished in and through worship of the Creator. Where any particular command of the law in a given situation ran counter to that faith it could and perhaps should be dispensed with. . . . Where faith was expressed in and through obedience to a command, that command was still the law of faith" ("Law of Faith," 81-82; cf. *Theology*, 641).

that the requirements could and should be dispensed with" (656). The law to be fulfilled is thus the "law of Christ"; it is the old law still, but as taught and lived out by Jesus (658).

The law itself, then, has not been done away with: it remains a statement of God's will whose requirements are meant to be fulfilled, not merely formally, but "by trusting in God('s Christ), in walking by the Spirit, in loving the neighbour" ("Test-Case," 472; cf. "Law of Faith," 81; "Nomism," 137). Believers, who belong to the new age, have been given God's Spirit, whose promptings from within, rather than the externally imposed constraints of the law, are the key to their "moral effort and acceptable conduct" (*Ep. Gal.*, 296). Yet norms are still needed, lest "a too exclusively focused Spirit-ethic" degenerate into "fleshly" attitudes (324). For believers' lives must still be lived "in the flesh," inasmuch as all "human existence" has an "inescapably fleshly character": the resultant "need to satisfy appetites" leaves the individual exposed to the temptation to orient oneself toward "what is transient and perishable," thus living "solely at the animal level of satisfying merely human appetites and desires" (*Theology*, 67-68). Hence "there is no perfection for the Christian in this life; the desires of flesh as well as of Spirit characterize the ongoing process of salvation. . . . Believers (Paul states it as a general truth) experience in themselves a real unwillingness and antagonism against the Spirit as much as against the flesh" (*Ep. Gal.*, 298-99).[14] Without the Spirit's power there is no coping with the "desire of the flesh"; but the norms of the "law of Christ" are needed, too, to "provide essential guidelines and illustrations of what counts as Christian conduct" (300, 324).

The History of Redemption Misperceived

To this point we have seen nothing in Dunn's work that would perturb a proponent of the "Lutheran" Paul. That humanity's subservience to sin and death required that God take the initiative for its salvation was the view of all "Luther-

---

14. For Dunn the tension evident in Rom. 7:7-25 characterizes the life of the believer who belongs at the same time to both the old age and the new, and who can thus be said to live both "already" and "not yet" in the new age: "having emphasized the decisiveness of the 'already' (7.4-6), [Paul] thought it necessary also to acknowledge the seriousness of the 'not yet.' Notwithstanding the decisiveness of the beginning of salvation, there was still an unavoidable and marked continuity with what had gone before" (*Theology*, 476). Hence the exhortations of Rom. 8 stress that "in the tension of the between times [believers] had to be resolute in maintaining their alignment with the Spirit and in resisting the lure of sin in flesh" (480). "Luther's *simul iustus et peccator* is also *semper iustus et peccator* until God's final summons" (493).

ans." That the gospel was already announced to, and believed by, Abraham, and requires a response of faith like that of Abraham from all its hearers; that the "law" is to be fulfilled by love and in the Spirit; that believers must live "in the flesh" and contend with its "desire" all their lives: none of this takes us beyond the bounds of the "Lutheran" Paul. It is rather (if anywhere)[15] in his presentation, on the one hand, of Jewish and Jewish-Christian misunderstandings of God's purposes, and, on the other, of the origin and point of Paul's doctrine of justification by faith, that Dunn shows the impact of the new perspective.

Paul found himself confronted with a situation in which Jewish Christians demanded that all who would belong to the people of God, *including* Gentile believers in Christ, must observe the laws that set Jews apart from Gentiles (i.e., the boundary markers of circumcision and of food and festival laws). In Paul's terminology these people advocated "justification by the works of the law." In principle the latter "works" included all the law's demands; under circumstances in which specific laws distinguishing Jews from Gentiles were the issue, however, the focus was clearly on these boundary-marking ordinances (*Theology*, 358).[16] Paul's response, the assertion of justification by faith rather than by the works of the law, thus did not address the question how an individual may find peace with God, or whether salvation is to be earned by human works (to that extent the "Lutheran" tradition has misread the context and point of Paul's polemic),[17] but the terms on which Gentiles were to be admitted to the people of God, and whether *particular* "works" required of Israel in the Mosaic law are to be observed by all God's people now that the Messiah has come (355; cf. "Justice," 4-5). "What [Paul] meant was, 'Justification is not confined to Jews as marked out by their distinctive works; it is open to all, to Gentile as well as Jew, through faith'" ("Justice," 14; cf. *Theology*, 363-64).

---

15. For the view that, in spite of all the rhetoric about a new perspective, Dunn's commentary on Romans betrays numerous "Lutheran" affinities, see Deidun, "New Perspective," 79-84; cf. also Matlock, "Sins," 82-86.

16. Dunn finds the Qumran usage of the phrase "works of the law" to be parallel to the Pauline: while "in principle" the phrase meant "all that the law required," the understanding of those requirements was inevitably that of the sectarians, and focused on "loyalty to the sect's distinctive interpretations of the law on disputed points" (*Ep. Gal.*, 136; cf. "4QMMT," 147-53).

17. Cf. *Theology*, 365: "Had Paul's primary or even underlying polemic been directed against a prevalent view among Jews (and Christian Jews) that justification depended on works of achievement, he is hardly likely to have expressed himself so unguardedly as he does in commending good works to his readers. . . . Paul evidently did not associate 'works of the law' with 'good works.'" Also *Partings*, 136: "It is surely incredible that Paul should be thought to say that God does not want his human creatures to do good works. . . . There was always something odd, not to say suspect, about the assumption that Paul's polemic against 'works of the law' was a polemic against 'good works.'"

The misunderstandings that (Dunn's) Paul finds in the position of his opponents are multiple.

1. They were "behind the times" (*Theology*, 145, 160). With the coming of Christ the promise given to Abraham had been fulfilled and the divine blessing once restricted to Israel had now been extended to Gentiles (144). As a result, those aspects of the Mosaic law that created barriers between Jews and Gentiles no longer served a function. Paul's fellow Jews, in insisting that the boundary markers of the Jewish people still be respected and observed, betrayed their failure to "grasp the limited and temporary scope of the epoch represented by Moses" (149).

2. But the misunderstanding betrayed by advocates of the "works of the law" went deeper. They had allowed the law's "more fundamental role . . . in defining sin, bringing it to consciousness as transgression, and judging it" to be overshadowed by "Israel's special relation with God through the law" (155). As a result they failed to treat their own sin with sufficient seriousness ("Works," 108-9), believing that their "favoured status before God . . . would exempt them from judgment" (*Theology*, 115). This was the typical attitude that Paul attacked in Romans 2.

3. The law spelled out how those who were already God's people were to live within the covenant. Its righteousness was thus a "secondary righteousness," to be practiced by those already in possession of the "primary righteousness" based on faith. The two levels of righteousness were confused, however, by those who required that Gentile believers show both, thereby giving the righteousness of the law "a more fundamental status" than it was due (516).

4. To understand the people of God in terms of a "national identity marked out by physical kinship" and "circumcision in the flesh" is to put "confidence in the flesh," the realm of the physical and visible (69; cf. 145; *Law*, 199; "Nomism," 135; *Theol. Gal.*, 111).

5. In the course of the controversy Paul himself came to the realization that "if *entry* into the covenant is by faith, the same principle should apply to life *within* the covenant; membership of the covenant people should *not* be tied to or be made to depend on particular rulings regarding food and table-fellowship; *it should depend solely on faith*" (*Partings*, 133; cf. *Law*, 162; "Nomism," 131). "Human dependence on divine grace had to be unqualified or else it was not Abraham's faith, the faith through which God could work his own work. That was why Paul was so fiercely hostile to the qualification which he saw confronting him all the time in any attempt to insist on works of the law as a necessary accompaniment of or addition to faith. God would not justify, could not sustain in relationship with him, those who did not rely wholly on him. Justification was by faith, by faith alone." Thus the dispute whether spe-

cific "works of the law" should be imposed on Gentile believers led Paul to "a profound conception of the relation between God and humankind — a relation of utter dependence, of unconditional trust." This conception was summed up in his doctrine of justification (*Theology*, 379).[18]

Here, of course, Dunn's Paul differs little from his "Lutheran" counterpart: both stress absolute, unconditional trust in God, and exclude as a consequence any additional requirements. Dunn's affiliation with the new perspective is generally marked (at least in part) by his insistence that the conviction was equally axiomatic in first-century Judaism. Yet he is willing to grant that, to Paul's mind, those who added works of the law to the requirement of faith thereby compromised the essence of the latter. Those Jews who thought of "covenant righteousness in terms of ethnic identity and 'works'" had, in Paul's mind, departed "from the fundamental recognition that faith on man's side is the only possible and sufficient basis to sustain a relation with God, as exemplified above all in Abraham's unconditional trust and total dependence on God and his promise" (*Romans 1–8*, 43). Indeed, to believe that their "status" was "to be documented and maintained over against Gentile sinners by works of the law" was to show an attitude that "is not so very far from the attitude of the merit-earner" ("Works," 113).

"But," Dunn adds, "the two are not the same." The Jews who opposed Paul did not think the works of the law a way to *earn* salvation, and the thrust of Paul's attack was rather on "the *restrictiveness* implicit" in their emphasis on works of the law (*Theology*, 372). Still, Paul's polemic, according to Dunn, sprang in part from the perception that if justification is based on faith, it leaves no room for additional requirements.[19]

6. Those who (according to Gal. 3:10) "rely on the works of the law" are those "whose relationship with God [is] characterized and determined by works of the law, . . . who invested their identity too far in the presumption that Israel was set apart from 'the nations'" (*Ep. Gal.*, 172). They thus abused "what

18. Cf. *Theology*, 372: "Paul expounds justification by faith in a way which not only addresses the argument over the terms of Gentile acceptance, but also presses beyond to provide a fundamental statement of human dependence on God."

19. Cf. *Ep. Gal.*, 186, where, in commenting on Gal. 3:18, Dunn says: "Paul stakes his case on the theological axiom that salvation is always, first to last, a matter of divine initiative and grace." If *Paul's* case rests on that axiom, then presumably he views the position of his opponents as compromising its vital truth. Still, what Paul is attacking is not works righteousness, but a "mind-set too narrowly focused on the law and an identity too much understood in terms of the law" (187). Cf. "Justification," 94: "Israel's claim to a special relationship with God was perverting the more basic insight of God's grace: as free grace it was open to all and not restricted to Jews and their proselytes."

God demands of those in relationship with him, since that relationship is always constituted by and dependent on faith." The "covenant law" itself demanded such faith, "*not* requirements of the law understood and practised in such a way as to deny the sufficiency of the very faith on which the covenant was based" (173). Hence those who demand works of the law fail to do what the law itself requires (they fail to "abide by all that has been written in the book of the law to do it") and are subject to its curse (Deut. 27:26). Ironically enough, they thus find themselves, together with Gentiles, outside the covenant (178; cf. *Law*, 227-29; *Theol. Gal.*, 83-87).

But when the curse of the law was borne by the crucified Jesus, he too was effectively placed "outside the covenant, outside the people of God." When God then "declared himself 'for' this crucified and cursed Jesus (by resurrection), he also declared himself 'for' those affected by the curse" (*Ep. Gal.*, 178, referring to Gal. 3:13; cf. *Partings*, 123). The curse had struck both Jews who, in excluding Gentiles from the promise, had misunderstood the law *and* Gentiles, who were without it. Through Christ's death the curse was removed, barriers were broken down, and Gentiles and Jews alike could experience God's blessing (*Theology*, 375; cf. *Law*, 229-30).

Before we leave Dunn, it is worth mention that his (seemingly boundless) energy has been tapped by numerous graduate students, several of whom have published work pertinent to our theme. Here we can only note the important work of Bruce Longenecker.

Longenecker's dissertation *(Eschatology and the Covenant: A Comparison of 4 Ezra and Romans 1–11)* claims that both Paul and the author of 4 Ezra departed from the "ethnocentric covenantalism" (a designation Longenecker prefers to Sanders's "covenantal nomism") prevalent in early Judaism, believing it wrong "in the light of their respective crisis events."[20] Without successfully rebutting ethnocentric covenantalism, Paul replaced its solution to universal sinfulness with a christocentric solution (280). Longenecker stresses that ethnocentric covenantalism, not Jewish attempts to earn salvation by works, was the target of Paul's polemic. He allows, however, that Paul appears to expand his criticism in places (Rom. 4:1-5; cf. 9:11-12, 32; 11:5-6) to include a charge of legalism (213-14).[21]

---

20. B. Longenecker, *Eschatology*, 278-79. Parenthetical page references in this paragraph are to this work.

21. A similar point is made by John M. G. Barclay: in Paul's attack on Jewish national pride in Romans, he "allows himself some broader reflections on the need for mankind to recognize its insufficiency before God; and in the course of ruling out the adequacy of Jewish works of the law Paul reflects on how God's grace is highlighted and clarified when it is independent of works" (*Truth*, 246-47).

Longenecker's more recent *The Triumph of Abraham's God: The Transformation of Identity in Galatians* represents a bold attempt to mediate between different readings of Galatians: between the "apocalyptic" reading represented by Beker and Martyn and the "salvation-historical" reading found in Wright and Dunn, *and* between traditional "Lutheran" interpretations and those informed by the new perspective. On the former dispute Longenecker sees the "new creation" in Galatians as having "no organic connection to Israel's past history other than the God of that history"; in Galatians at least, Gentile believers are *not* incorporated into the "continuing story of Israel's unfolding history." On the other hand, even in Galatians Paul cannot "envisage God's eschatological redemption in Christ without also articulating how that same event has afforded the long-awaited redemption of ethnic Israel." In short, "If in Galatians Paul does not defend a line of salvation-historical continuity leading from the covenant people of Israel and culminating in Christ, neither does he intend to repudiate that a form of covenant relationship existed between God and ethnic Israel prior to Christ."[22]

Similarly, there is (Longenecker believes) truth in both new perspective and traditional "Lutheran" readings of the epistle. The former provides the basis for a truer understanding of the position of Paul's opponents and of the issues debated in Galatia. Nonetheless, a number of themes central to "Lutheran" approaches are indeed to be found in Paul's response: the view that the law cannot convey life because humans cannot obey it perfectly; that nomistic observance takes place within the framework of "fleshly" existence and continues to express human rebellion against God; that humanity's bondage is such that human activity comes to nothing and only God's invading grace can provide redemption (180-81). Moreover, Longenecker repeats his earlier claim that, "while the kind of Judaism that Paul seeks to undermine in Romans is ethnocentric . . . rather than legalistic, he nonetheless finds that, from a Christian perspective, Judaism's ethnocentric covenantalism reduces to nothing else than legalism" (140). In none of these cases does Paul portray Jewish covenantalism on its own terms. The Judaism of Paul's depiction is Judaism as it "really" is — reality being determined by Paul's reconfigured, Christian worldview (182).

---

22. B. Longenecker, *Triumph,* 175-79. Parenthetical page references in the remainder of this section are to this work.

iii. Terence Donaldson

If the new perspective is to survive its infancy, it must prove persuasive in accounting not only for Paul's discussions of "faith" and the "works of the law," but also for other aspects of Paul's thought once seen to follow from (the traditional understanding of) justification by faith. Terence Donaldson's *Paul and the Gentiles* tackles the latter challenge for Paul's Gentile mission.

That Gentiles should be evangelized was self-evident (Donaldson concedes) for older readings of Paul. If Paul's fundamental concern was with the plight and salvation of all humankind; and if, through his Damascus experience, he came to view Jewish works of the law as but one instance of the sinful attempt to claim a standing with God on the basis of human achievement, then Paul's newfound appreciation of justification *by faith* leads unproblematically to a mission to all nations.[23] If the Damascus experience meant for Paul a conversion from Jewish particularism to a universalistic understanding of salvation, and if it carried the implication that Israel as an ethnic entity has no abiding place in the divine agenda, then Paul's commitment to a Gentile mission requires no further explanation (6, 20). But the issues look very different from the new perspective. Judaism was not in fact legalistic, nor did justification by faith represent either a central Pauline conviction or a Pauline rejection of (a supposed) Jewish legalism. The Damascus experience, moreover, did not for Paul deprive the distinction between Jews and Gentiles of its fundamental significance. It did, to be sure, profoundly alter his thinking: it convinced him that God had raised Jesus from the dead, and that Jesus was, after all, God's Messiah. By themselves, however, these new convictions would not have impelled him to launch a Gentile mission. What, we must now ask, would have prompted such an endeavor?

In essential respects, then, Donaldson takes Sanders's work as a starting point from which to explore a subject he believes Sanders left unresolved. Donaldson accepts Sanders's portrayal of first-century Judaism as characterized by covenantal nomism: "election and ultimately salvation [were] considered to be by God's mercy rather than human achievement" (9, quoting Sanders). Indeed, a premise of Donaldson's study is that the pre-Damascus Paul must himself have been such a covenantal nomist (51). Methodologically Donaldson adopts and refines Sanders's distinction between Paul's "arguments" in favor of a particular position and his real "reasons" for holding it (40-41, 48). For his part Donaldson speaks of three structural levels that need to be identified in interpreting Pauline texts (46-47). The first is that of Paul's funda-

---

23. Donaldson, *Paul*, 5. Parenthetical references in this section are to Donaldson's *Paul*.

mental convictions, which provide the basic framework, or "semantic universe," for all his thought. The second is the theological thinking that Paul carried on as he worked out, for their own sake as well as for practical purposes, the implications of his core convictions. The third (and surface) level is that of Paul's actual responses to concrete situations.

Much, then, is derived from Sanders. In regard to Paul's Gentile mission, however, Donaldson finds Sanders's suggestions for its roots unconvincing (12-13). An adequate explanation for Paul's concern for the Gentiles, based on what the new perspective has taught us about Judaism and Paul, has not yet, he believes, been supplied. Hence his undertaking, not so much to explicate Paul's surface statements about the mission as to penetrate to the convictional level of Paul's thought and see both where and how a commitment to a Gentile mission found a place in his thinking.

Donaldson narrows the possible answers by a process of elimination. In each case he asks whether the notion in question, when combined with Paul's new faith in Jesus as God's Messiah, would have been sufficient to provoke Paul to embark upon a Gentile mission. We may note the most important suggestions that he considers and rejects.

1. It might be thought that Paul's native conviction that God is one, or that God is impartial, though long repressed to protect Jewish particularity, would have found gratifying expression in a Christian faith that made access to one and the same God possible on identical terms for Jews and Gentiles alike; the universalism of Paul's new faith would then have spawned a Gentile mission. But in fact, Donaldson believes, Paul's post-Damascus Christian convictions were no more universalistic than his pre-Damascus beliefs as a Pharisee: the path of Torah was itself open to Jews and Gentiles alike, provided the latter abandoned their idolatry, (in the case of males) underwent circumcision, and became a part of the people of Israel. Paul must have come to think (for a reason still to be explored) that Torah and faith in Christ were mutually exclusive paths to salvation, and that the latter but not the former is effectual for reaching that goal. By itself, his (lifelong) faith in the oneness and impartiality of God would not have combined with his new belief in the messiahship of Jesus to bring about a Gentile mission (81-106).

2. Paul's claim that salvation is by faith, not works, fails for a number of reasons to account for his Gentile mission. Here Donaldson builds on the work of Sanders and of those predecessors of the new perspective (such as Wrede and Schweitzer) who contest the traditional Lutheran reading of justification by faith and its centrality in Paul's thought (111). Paul (Donaldson observes) does not oppose faith to works, or view the latter negatively, in contexts other than those discussing Gentile entry into the community of God. Even in

the latter discussions the works Paul has in mind are the ethnic identity markers (such as circumcision and food laws) spelled out for Jews in the law, not good deeds in general done in an attempt to merit God's approval (120-21). The emphasis in Paul's antithesis between "faith in Christ" (or "the faithfulness of Christ") and "works of the law" is in each case on the second, not the first, noun in the pairing: Paul is not contrasting two subjective human attitudes, but two objective paths to righteousness (116, 119). Since (for Paul) salvation is to be found in Christ, it is not to be found in Torah; hence it follows that the ethnic identity markers required of Jews in Torah should not be demanded of Gentiles.

Even Romans 3:27–4:25 does not demonstrate a fundamental opposition between faith and works in Paul's thinking. The contrast is introduced merely as a tactical device to defend the place of uncircumcised Gentiles in the community of believers. That Paul is not contrasting faith and works in any principal way is apparent from his allowance that faith can be *combined with* works (such as circumcision and the other observances enjoined in the law) in the case of Jewish believers (Rom. 4:11-12, 16). If a proper attitude of faith in the case of Jews does not exclude their observance of Torah's demands, then the notion that faith excludes works was hardly fundamental to Paul's thinking — or the conviction that sparked his Gentile mission (123-25).

3. Nor can that spark be found in a conviction that all are sinners (131-51). Had the pre-Christian Paul been distressed by the universality of sin and found no solution for the problem in Judaism, then his Damascus experience might be thought to have revealed God's answer to humanity's plight and provoked Paul's mission to the Gentiles.

But Torah itself made provision for sin through repentance, atonement, and forgiveness. That the pre-Christian Paul was not troubled by the inadequacy of Torah to cope with human sinfulness is suggested by Philippians 3:6 (and other passages). For that matter, had Jewish transgression of the law induced Paul to see the path of the law as inadequate, then the reality of Christian transgression ought to have provoked a similar insight on Christian faith. In fact, the inconsistencies in Paul's argument for humanity's culpability before God in Romans 2–3 (Paul appears to allow, for example, for righteous Gentiles in 2:14-16, 26-27 — in the middle of his argument for universal guilt) suggest that his primary concern in the passage is to establish, not universal sinfulness per se, but that Jews and Gentiles stand on equal footing for salvation in Christ. Thus anthropological convictions about human sinfulness were scarcely the root of Paul's critique of the law — or of his Gentile mission.

4. Can one, then, account for Paul's Christian mission to the Gentiles as the offshoot of a native conviction that Jews and Gentiles are equal, and that God's

design from the beginning was to set aside Israel's distinctiveness by offering salvation to all on identical terms (151-61)?

Had such been Paul's thinking, he could not have been a covenantal nomist even before Damascus, for belief in Israel's election requires a divine differentiation between Jews and Gentiles — though not one that need exclude the latter from salvation. Indeed, covenantal nomists had no difficulty believing in a divine offer of salvation to Gentiles who, like Jews, submitted to Torah; yet they remained convinced of Israel's special place in God's plan. So too, Donaldson insists, was the apostle Paul (see, e.g., Rom. 11:1-5, 16, 25; 15:27). Indeed, the distinction between Jews and non-Jews is inherent in Paul's very conception of his apostleship (as a Jew, for whom the Servant missionary in Second Isaiah was a model) to the Gentiles. Most significantly, Paul saw the Christian gospel (in the same way covenantal nomists saw proselytism) as offering Gentiles a place in the family of *Abraham* (Gal. 3:7, 29; Rom. 4:11-12) — the founding father of a differentiated humanity! Clearly Paul's Gentile mission was not predicated on a fundamental belief in the equality of Jews and Gentiles.

5. Paul's rejection of Torah and of the boundary markers it prescribed for the people of God might itself be thought to mean the end of any significant differentiation between Jews and Gentiles and, hence, the basis for an outreach to non-Jews (165-86).

Donaldson agrees that, as a result of his Damascus experience, Paul rejected Torah. Paul clearly viewed Christ and Torah as rival ways of determining membership in the community of salvation. Such a rivalry (Donaldson argues) would not have arisen had the appearance of Messiah ushered in the age to come at once: in that case adherence to Torah would have defined the community of the righteous until Messiah came, bringing deliverance to God's people. But Christians believed that Messiah had come though the end had not; hence acceptance of Christ came to be seen as assuring salvation among his followers at the same time as adherence to Torah continued to play an identical role among non-Christian Jews. If before his Damascus experience Paul persecuted Christians because he saw their faith as incompatible with faithfulness to Torah, after Damascus the same perception of mutual exclusivity compelled him to reject Torah.

So much Donaldson grants. But for Donaldson Paul's no to Torah did *not* mean a no to Israel. The distinction between Jews and Gentiles retained significance (as we have seen). Hence the displacement of Torah by Christ as the boundary marker of the righteous could not by itself have sparked Paul's Gentile mission.

6. Many Jews, taking their cue from texts such as Isaiah 2:2-4/Micah 4:1-4, Isaiah 25:6-10a, 56:6-8, foresaw a day when Gentiles would be attracted to the

God of Israel as they witnessed the eschatological redemption of his people. Might Paul not have thought that, with the coming of Messiah, the time for such an "eschatological pilgrimage" of Gentiles had come — and that it was the task of his mission to promote it (187-97)?

Problematic for the proposal is Paul's failure to cite the key pilgrimage texts when he speaks of his mission. Fatal is the observation that the crux of the eschatological pilgrimage tradition lay in seeing Gentile faith as a *response* to Israel's restoration; Paul, who saw Israel's salvation as *following* (even provoked by) the success of the Gentile mission (Rom. 11:11-26), can hardly have conceived the latter within the framework of this tradition.

7. Might not the pre-Damascus Paul have been among those Jews who believed that, while Jews had been given Torah, Gentiles could be saved by renouncing idolatry, worshiping the God of Israel, and observing basic standards of morality? Might not, after Damascus, faith in Christ have come to occupy the place in Paul's thinking previously held by the minimum requirements for "righteous Gentiles"? Can we not thus account for his conviction that Gentiles could be saved by faith in Christ apart from the law (while, as at least some would add, he still believed Torah to be the path to salvation for Jews) (230-36)?

But when Jews speculated about "righteous Gentiles," they envisaged them remaining outside the covenant and people of Israel. Paul, in contrast, saw Gentile believers joining Jewish Christians as full members of the family of Abraham. Moreover, any suggestion that Paul entertained notions of distinct paths to salvation for Jews and Gentiles is excluded by his repeated insistence that there is "no difference" between Jews and Gentiles in their common plight under sin and in their common access to "righteousness *apart from the law*" through the faithfulness of Christ (Rom. 3:21-30).

8. Might Paul have converted to a form of Christianity already engaged in a Gentile mission? Might he not simply have adopted their practice without (initially at least) further concerning himself with its theological justification (266-69)?

It seems unlikely. The case for a pre-Pauline Christian mission to Gentiles is at best unproven. And could Paul, who had persecuted Christians because of his commitment to Torah, have casually abandoned Torah without any attempt at justifying what he was doing?

9. Perhaps Paul began his Christian activity with a mission to Jews, turning to Gentiles only when, and because, his initial endeavor had failed. To facilitate the acceptance of the Christian message by Gentiles, he might then have abandoned the requirement that they obey Torah (269-71).

The suggestion lacks textual support (1 Cor. 9:20-21 and 2 Cor. 11:24 say nothing of an initial, now abandoned mission to the Jews; and the "preaching" of "circumcision" spoken of in Gal. 5:11 can only have had Gentiles as its target: circumcised Jews did not need to have circumcision preached to them!). Had Paul begun his Christian activity by proclaiming a gospel that required circumcision, he would not have denounced (as he does in Gal. 1) such a message as a perversion of the gospel: not when any who were aware of his past could expose the hypocrisy of his denunciation. Finally, Galatians 1:17 and 2 Corinthians 11:31-32 seem to indicate that Paul engaged in the evangelization of Gentiles from the very beginning of his life as a Christian.

How, then, does Donaldson account for Paul's mission to the Gentiles? We may outline his proposal in the following steps.

1. Prior to his Damascus experience Paul was among those Jews who believed Gentiles could share in God's salvation only if, prior to the dawning of the age to come, they became proselytes, submitting to Torah and becoming incorporated in the people of Israel. Paul himself encouraged Gentiles to do so (he "preached circumcision," Gal. 5:11) (275-84).

2. Prior to his Damascus experience Paul perceived that faith in Jesus as Messiah and adherence to Torah were rival ways of defining the people of God. Such a conviction would have followed from his awareness that the community of Christian believers included some who were lax in their observance of Torah, yet excluded those who were righteous by the standards of Torah but lacked faith in Christ. Committed to the path of Torah, Paul persecuted believers in Christ (173, 284-92).

3. The Damascus experience convinced Paul that Jesus was God's Messiah, that Christ was God's way to salvation, and hence (since he continued to see Torah as an exclusive alternative) that faith in Christ, not adherence to Torah, defined the boundaries of the people of God. Still convinced that Torah was a gift from God, Paul came to see its divinely given function as preparatory to the coming of salvation in Christ (243-44).

4. Paul's perception that Torah and Christ were exclusive alternatives was reinforced by the parallel functions each was thought to perform (172, 205-7, 210-11, 242). Both were seen as divinely provided means of deliverance from the dilemma posed by human sin. Both served to determine membership in the people of God. Both were seen as paths to "righteousness." Both had come to be assigned attributes and functions associated with divine Wisdom.

5. As a Christian, Paul continued to pursue his pre-Damascus vocation to bring Gentiles into the community of God. He continued to understand God's community as Israel, the family of Abraham (Gal. 3:7; 6:16; Phil. 3:3; Rom. 4:11-12; 11:17-24). But faith in Christ, rather than adherence to Torah, now defined membership in the community (236-48).

6. The apostle Paul retained his pre-Damascus convictions that Gentiles

could be saved only if they became members of God's people before the dawning of the age to come, and that the restoration of Israel would usher in that age. Hence his belief that Israel's temporary rejection of the gospel gave Gentiles the necessary opportunity to be saved, and that the period of the Gentile mission would end with the redemption of Israel (Rom. 11:11-16, 25-26) (222-26).

7. Paul believed the end was imminent. In a brief interim period it was possible to reject the marks of ethnic identity spelled out in Torah for the people of God while still maintaining the distinct identities and roles of Jewish and Gentile believers. In time, however, a community defined by belief in Christ rather than by the boundary markers that set apart the Jewish people was unable to retain a distinctively Jewish presence (185-86, 246).

*   *

Wright, Dunn, Longenecker, and Donaldson are by no means the only scholars to adopt the new perspective on Paul.[24] They are, however, important voices in the debate, and the suggestion that what Paul found wrong with Judaism was its ethnocentricity, though linked particularly to the work of Wright and Dunn, has been adopted (with variations) by a number of scholars.[25]

Still, by no means all scholars have abandoned the "Lutheran" interpretation of the apostle. We turn now to representative critics of the critics of that reading.

---

24. Cf. my article "Perspective."
25. See, e.g., Barclay, *Truth*, 240; Boyarin, *Jew*; Garlington, *Obedience of Faith*.

Chapter 12

"Lutheran" Responses

Not all Paulinists have been convinced by the "new perspectivist" claim that first-century Judaism was "Lutheran"[1] but Paul's doctrine of justification was not.[2] The critics selected for treatment here[3] are among those who, in the course of wide-ranging studies of Paul, argue, against the new perspective[4] and (to this extent at least) in harmony with a "Lutheran" reading, that his doctrine of justification by faith, not by the works of the law, excludes human endeavor as a factor in gaining God's approval.

i. C. E. B. Cranfield[5]

Cranfield's *Romans* is a classic of British New Testament scholarship, with merits that repay both frequent consultation and extended reading: attention to the

---

1. I.e., Judaism insisted that salvation is by grace, not human achievement; cf. Dunn, "Justice," 8; Sanders, *Paul. Pal. Jud.,* 543; Wright, "History," 79-80.

2. I.e., it does not address how human beings can be found acceptable by God ("by divine grace, not human works"), but the terms of Gentile admission to the people of God (by faith in Christ *without* having to observe the boundary markers of the Jewish people); cf. Dunn, *Partings,* 124; Sanders, *Paul,* 63; Wright, *Climax,* 173.

3. Brief treatment of a number of studies not included here can be found in my article "Perspective."

4. Charles Cranfield is something of an exception, since (as noted below) his major work was written prior to the appearance of Sanders's *Paul and Palestinian Judaism.* Later articles do, however, respond to more recent debates.

5. The parenthetical page references in this section are to the works of C. E. B. Cranfield, using the short titles shown in the bibliography. Pages in the two-volume commentary on Romans *(Romans)* are numbered consecutively, the second volume beginning on p. 445.

nuances of Greek syntax, an enviable neatness in delineating and assessing alternative interpretations, and theological weight as a thoughtful, robust statement of a distinctive reading of the apostle. That Cranfield's Paul speaks Greek with a Genevan accent makes him doubly attractive for our purposes: a neglect of the Reformed perspective in an earlier incarnation of this book was perceived and deplored by several of its reviewers. As for Cranfield's relation to the present discussion, his magnum opus belongs essentially to the pre-Sanders era of Pauline scholarship. In several subsequent articles, however, he has spanked various participants in the present debate — your correspondent included — for not informing ourselves well enough, or thinking matters through with sufficient clarity, to arrive at his conclusions. His points are always backed by scholarship, and usually by a time-tested tradition; they are eminently worthy of a hearing.

The Law and Legalism

For someone who saw the same divine source behind the Mosaic law as behind his own apostolic commission, Paul seems to say surprisingly negative things about the law. By way of explanation, a number of contemporary interpreters are content to point out that Paul, believing salvation could be found in Christ alone, was bound to undercut perceived alternatives. No one would deny the element of truth in this explanation; but it leaves us to wonder why Paul said the particular things he did, and how he combined them in his own thinking with a conviction of the law's divine origin.[6]

Typical of Calvin and the Reformed tradition is the insistence that the law, when taken as a whole, is in perfect harmony with the gospel, but that the term is also used of particular aspects of the whole (in which case the law's continuity with the gospel may well be obscured) or even of a distorted understanding of the law's true nature or purpose (in which case the continuity will inevitably be lost to view).

Thus when Paul claims that Christians are not "under law" or have "died" to it, it is self-evident to those schooled in a Reformed way of thinking that "law" is being used in a limited sense: it can hardly refer to the moral order under which all human beings live and which, as set forth in the moral commands of the Mosaic code, is the subject of fervent praise in the Psalms (a sense in

---

6. That combining them was of little moment to the apostle is occasionally suggested, but highly unlikely in so fundamental an issue, and contrary to the impression shared by many readers that much in Romans reflects precisely such a concern.

which the Reformed, no less than the sweet psalmist of Israel, are wont to employ the term). Nor can it mean the Mosaic order as a whole, since the goal of that order was Christ, and it represented a renewal of the Abrahamic covenant to which believers of every age belong. Hence the context of each usage must be consulted to discover the particular aspect of the law under consideration.

It is quickly apparent how solidly Cranfield belongs to this interpretive tradition. It is a mistake, he believes, to view law and gospel as "two different modes of God's action. . . . *God's word in Scripture is one;* . . . there is but one way of God with men, and that an altogether gracious way; . . . gospel and law are essentially one, and their unity . . . has been once and for all revealed to us in that one gracious Word of God, whose name is Jesus Christ, in whom at the same time God gives Himself wholly to man, and claims man wholly for Himself" (*Romans*, 862, emphasis Cranfield's).

When, then, Paul writes that believers are justified "apart from the law" (Rom. 3:21), he means simply that they are justified apart from its works (cf. 3:28): "God's gift is not earned by man's fulfilment of His requirements" (853). That believers are not "under the law" but have "died" to it and been "released" from it (Rom. 6:14; 7:4, 6) means only that they are not subject to its condemnation (Paul's point is clear in Rom. 8:1; and the contrast between "under the law" and "under grace" in 6:14 is equivalent to that between being under God's condemnation on the one hand and enjoying his undeserved favor on the other [320, 330, 853; cf. *On Rom.,* 114]). When in 1 Corinthians 9:20 Paul says that he himself is not under the law, he means that he is not bound to observe the ceremonial law in any literal way (though even the ceremonial law is not to be dismissed, but honored by "looking steadfastly" at Christ, its goal) (114-15). The law Paul says he "died" to in Galatians 2:19-20 may be the ceremonial segments of the Mosaic code as well as the law's condemnation of sin (115-16). In such texts Paul means by the "law" one or more of its aspects.

On the other hand, in a number of texts in which Paul speaks negatively about the law, his subject is in fact the law as legalistically misconstrued. So we may conclude, though "the Greek language of Paul's day possessed no word-group corresponding to our 'legalism,' 'legalist' and 'legalistic.'" Paul was therefore "pioneering" in "very difficult terrain," and we ought to "reckon with the possibility that Pauline statements, which at first sight seem to disparage the law, were really directed not against the law itself but against that misunderstanding and misuse of it for which we now have a convenient terminology" (*Romans*, 853).

For the giving of the law itself *"establishes the possibility of legalism"* (847, emphasis Cranfield's). In the case of fallen, sinful human beings, the law, as "the revelation of God's will for men," is meant in the first place to enable them to recognize their "sin as sin" (846-47),[7] to make "objectively visible . . . the impossibility, for sinful men, of a righteousness earned by works," and so to bring to light humanity's "desperate condition" and need of the divine remedy found in Christ (850). Indeed, the law's own sacrificial order foreshadowed Christ's redemptive work (849-50). In both these respects[8] the law pointed sinners to Christ, who is thus (as Paul affirms in Rom. 10:4) the law's true "goal" (848-51). If on the other hand sinners are blind to their own sinfulness and resort to the law while failing to perceive its christological ethos and purpose,[9] then the very commandment that *ought* to prompt an awareness of their need for grace may *in fact* tempt them to think themselves able to fulfill it and thereby earn for themselves a righteous status before God (847). This is the "legalistic" misunderstanding to which the very presence of the law among sinners inevitably gives rise. It is a misunderstanding to which Paul himself was once subject when, before his encounter with Christ, he declared himself "blameless . . . as touching the righteousness which is in the law" (a judgment he recalls in Phil. 3:6 [847]). It was only enhanced by the tendency of the Jewish oral law to make of the demands of God's law "something manageable and achievable" (848).

It is of such legalists that Paul is thinking when he says that "as many as are of the works of the law are under a curse" (848, referring to Gal. 3:10). Legalism is the "slavery" binding many Jews of Paul's day to which he refers in Galatians 4:25, that from which Christians (according to 5:1) have been set free (851). When Paul distinguishes the "letter" from the "Spirit" (Rom. 7:6; 2 Cor. 3:6), he cannot mean by the former term God's law as such (it is, after all, itself "spiri-

7. That is, the character of sin as disobedience to God becomes apparent when a known divine commandment is transgressed.

8. And in other respects as well. As Scripture, the law's promises spoke of Christ and of the "righteousness of faith" (Rom. 1:1-3; 3:21; 10:6-10; Gal. 3:8 [848-49]). In outlining "perfect obedience," the law pointed to Christ as "the one and only Man who has truly and fully loved God . . . and . . . His neighbour" (849; Christ is, in Cranfield's view [following Barth], the one spoken of in Rom. 10:5 who "does the righteousness which is of the law" and so "lives" — though by so doing he also "earned a righteous status and eternal life . . . for all those who believe in Him" [521-22]). Finally, the law has Christ as "its goal and meaning" in that it "sets the necessary forensic stage on which Christ's saving work is wrought, and He is its goal, in that the justification which He achieves for us is no mere amnesty or indulgence, no caprice or sentimentality on the part of God, but acquittal 'in God's severe and true judgment which searches the hearts and is no respecter of persons.' . . . In this fact which Paul brings out so clearly is to be recognized God's respect for His creature man, His taking His creature seriously in the dignity of his moral responsibility" (850-51; the quotation within the quotation is from Barth).

9. In Rom. 9:30–10:4 legalism (seeking to come to terms with the law "on the basis of works" rather than "on the basis of faith") is shown to be "inextricably bound up" with a failure to give due recognition to Christ as the law's *"inmost meaning and goal"* (851, emphasis Cranfield's; cf. 510).

tual," Rom. 7:14), but the law as observed without reference to Christ — its ceremonies regarded as "possessed of an independent value in themselves quite apart from Him" — and thus "denatured" (851, 853-57). Similarly, the law seen as temporary in Galatians 3:19 is "not the law in the fullness and wholeness of its true character, but the law as seen apart from Christ" (859).

Once one has realized that statements declaring believers free from (or dead to) the law intend only one or more of its aspects or even a misunderstanding of its true nature, one will not be inclined to suggest (as Westerholm and others have done) that God's law has been abrogated by Christ, or that believers are not subject to it. How indeed could Paul ever envisage God's people as exempt from God's law, particularly when he affirms the latter to be "spiritual," its commandment "holy, righteous, and good"?[10] Moreover, Romans 7:14-25, correctly understood, shows the law as "guiding the obedience of the new ego which God is creating," and 8:7 implies that those guided by the Spirit (unlike those with the mind-set of the flesh) should strive to be subject to God's law (*On Rom.*, 118). The law's continuing validity for believers is apparent as well in Romans 3:31, 8:4, 13:8-10, and 1 Corinthians 7:19 (*Romans*, 861; *On Rom.*, 118-19). That believers, led by the Spirit, no longer need the guidance of the law is an illusion to which Paul had far too much experience of the frailties of his converts to succumb (*On Rom.*, 120-21).

Justification by Faith — and Works

Paul wrote to the Roman Christians in part to inform them of his intention to visit them. Most of the Romans did not know him, however, and he deemed it appropriate to introduce himself by setting before them "a serious and orderly summary of the gospel as he had come to understand it." In addition to various strategic reasons for doing so, Paul may well have been "conscious of having reached a certain maturity of experience, reflection and understanding, which made the time ripe for him to attempt, with God's help, such an orderly presentation of the gospel." And after all, apart from the gospel the apostolic commission in whose service he would be visiting the Romans had no point (*Romans*, 817).

The lengthy section from Romans 1:18 to 3:20 is misunderstood if taken as Paul's own moral evaluation of his contemporaries, or as an attempt to demonstrate empirically the sinfulness of the non-Christian world (*On Rom.*, 101). Paul presents a judgment that can be "recognized and submitted to only in the

10. *On Rom.*, 118, referring to Rom. 7:12, 14.

light of the gospel" (*Romans,* 104 n. 1): Gethsemane and Golgotha show the dreadful extent of God's "wrath" against human sin at the same time as they provide the basis for God's forgiveness (*not* his condoning) of human sin (110). Christians themselves are by no means exempt from the indictment; they, too, are surely included in what is said about humanity in general in 1:18, of "all" Jews and Greeks in 3:9, of "all" human beings in 3:23 (*On Rom.,* 101-2). Paul's statement that the "doers of the law will be justified" (2:13; cf. 2:6-11) and his references to "righteous" Gentiles in chapter 2 are by no means inconsistent with his depiction of universal sinfulness: in both cases he has in mind (though, in the unfolding logic of his argument, it would be premature to say so explicitly) the "righteousness" of believers in Christ, a righteousness marked, however, not by good works that compel divine recognition (Christians, too, are sinners) but by humble trust in divine mercy, followed by weak and faltering steps in the direction of obedience with which God is nonetheless pleased, seeing in them an expression of faith in him (*Romans,* 151-63, 171-73; *On Rom.,* 102-4).

When Paul, then, speaks of believers as "justified," he means that, though sinful, they have been acquitted of their guilt, and granted a righteous status, by God. Their own moral transformation is not included in the term, though it is true and important to say that justification cannot be separated from sanctification (*Romans,* 95).[11] Similarly, the "righteousness of God" in 1:17, 10:3 refers to the status of righteousness that God confers on believers; note that in Philippians 3:9, in an expression and context so similar to those of Romans 10:3 that the phrases must be deemed equivalent, "righteousness" is explicitly said to be "from" God; the prepositional phrase "from God" is also used of "righteousness" in 1 Corinthians 1:30, while Romans 5:17 speaks explicitly of "righteousness" as a "gift" (97-98). This understanding of "righteousness" by no means limits the gospel to "something individualistic" (the misreading that Käsemann was so anxious to avoid); but without righteousness as a gift, the gospel is no good news at all, while conversely the gift is itself the "basis and the firm assurance of the ultimate fulfilment of all God's promises for the individual, for mankind as a whole, and for the whole of God's creation" (825).

Believers are justified by faith. "It is of the very essence of faith, as Paul understands it, that it is opposed to all human deserving. . . . For Paul man's salvation is altogether . . . God's work" (90). Faith is an "openness to the gospel" brought about by God himself: God's Spirit "bring[s] home to a person the reality of God's love" and so "creates the response of faith" (90; cf. *On Rom.,* 39). The "faith" by which believers are justified is "in Jesus Christ" or "in Christ": so

---

11. In Rom. 4:6-8 it is apparent that God's reckoning righteousness to a person apart from works amounts to "His forgiving of sins" (*Romans,* 233).

πίστις Ἰησοῦ Χριστοῦ must be rendered (Rom. 3:22; Gal. 2:16; 3:22; Phil. 3:9; cf. Rom. 3:26; Gal. 2:20). Cranfield confesses bewilderment at the enthusiasm shown in recent scholarship for the interpretation that takes the phrase to refer to Christ's own faith (or his faithfulness) (*On Rom.*, 96). In addition to the overwhelming evidence of Pauline and other New Testament usage,[12] Cranfield notes that for Paul "'faith' . . . carries with it . . . a 'sinfulness-admitting' sense." Faith is "the attitude of one who knows and confesses that he is a sinner" (cf. Rom. 4:5-8). "If πίστις . . . was in Paul's mind as strongly associated with the situation of the sinner who knows that he has no ground on which to stand before God except God's own sheer grace in Jesus Christ as I think it was, then this would suggest that it would not be likely to come at all naturally to him to speak of Jesus Christ's πίστις" (96-97).[13]

"Justification" is by faith and "not by works of the law" (Rom. 3:28; Gal. 2:16; cf. Rom. 3:20); that is, "no flesh will be justified in God's sight on the ground of works," since the "perfect obedience" required is not to be found among human beings (*Romans*, 198). That Paul intends such a sweeping judgment is apparent beginning already in Romans 1:18, and made emphatic in the conclusion to his argument in 3:20, repeated in 3:23; hence it will not do to limit his target to Jewish overemphasis on, and pride in, the distinguishing markers of their covenantal status (*On Rom.*, 5-6, countering Dunn). Indeed, in Paul's references throughout Romans to those who "do" (or "fulfill" or "serve") the law or "keep" its ordinances, there is no reference to circumcision and the other boundary markers that set Jews apart from Gentiles (7). Moreover, the law is discussed in the epistle "in its fundamental theological and ethical character," not "as providing an obvious national identity-marker distinguishing Jews from Gentiles" (8). That works and boasting are ruled out in Paul's discussion

12. Cranfield notes that apart from the 7 ambiguous expressions under discussion, in none of the 84 occurrences of πίστις (faith, faithfulness) in the acknowledged Pauline epistles is there a "clear reference either to the faith or to the faithfulness of Christ"; a similar picture emerges from a look at the remaining 152 instances of πίστις in the New Testament. Of the nine occurrences of πιστός (faithful) in the acknowledged Paulines, only one (1 Thess. 5:24) might possibly refer to Christ; and only nine of the other fifty-eight New Testament occurrences of the adjective do so. As for the verb πιστεύω (believe, have faith), in none of the 42 occurrences in Paul's acknowledged writings is the reference to Jesus' faith, and the same holds true for the 243 NT usages as a whole (Jesus is the subject of the verb only in John 2:24, where his faith is not in view, and in 1 Tim. 3:16, where the verb is passive, so that Jesus is the object of the faith intended). Conversely, there are many unambiguous references to faith *in* Christ (*On Rom.*, 82-84). Cranfield provides a detailed treatment and refutation of Ian G. Wallis's *The Faith of Jesus Christ in Early Christian Traditions* in his *On Rom.* (81-97).

13. Cranfield adds: "It would also suggest that we should be wise to hesitate about trying to construct a theology in which Jesus Christ's faith has an important place" (*On Rom.*, 97).

of Abraham in Romans 4 is not because of the presumption shown in "the typical national confidence" of the Jew, based on "their election by God and privileged position under the law" (so Dunn); rather, the point is that Abraham's moral deficiencies undercut any possible claim that he fulfilled the law. This is apparent in verse 5 (Abraham believed in the one who justifies "the ungodly") and in verses 7-8, where justification "apart from works" amounts to "having sins forgiven" (*On Rom.*, 9-10). When in 9:11-12 Paul excludes as a factor in God's election anything done, "good or bad," he clearly has moral "works" in general in mind, not reliance on distinctively Jewish "works of the law" (10). In short, while some Jews may well have been "complacently reliant on their nation's privileged position," and while Paul must have disapproved of such an attitude, the apostle hardly seems preoccupied with *that* mind-set. And insofar as Dunn's interpretation "reduces Paul's argument to polemic against a misunderstanding probably not shared by the majority of those he was addressing (not to mention Christians of today), would it perhaps be fair to say that its effect is a weakening of the impact of the Epistle . . . ?" (13).

ii. Thomas Schreiner and Andrew Das[14]

Charles Cranfield's very Reformed understanding of "law" in Paul was fashioned without reference to the work of E. P. Sanders. That Thomas Schreiner's more recent reading *(The Law and Its Fulfillment: A Pauline Theology of Law)* is equally Reformed[15] in its outlook suggests that, for his part, he has not been

14. The parenthetical page references in this section are to the works of Schreiner and Das, using the short titles shown in the bibliography.

15. Of course, neither Cranfield nor Schreiner merely replicates Calvin's commentaries. The former, to cite but one notable example, departs markedly from Calvin in his reading of Rom. 9: the divine "hardening" of which Paul speaks is seen as subordinated to divine mercy, God's purpose being that the "vessels of wrath" themselves become "vessels of mercy" (*Romans*, 497). By way of contrast, Schreiner affirms a traditional Calvinist interpretation of the chapter ("Election," 89-106; cf. "Grace," 382). Conversely, to this reader at least, Cranfield's hesitation to see more in Paul's references to Christian righteousness than a trust in God's mercy accompanied by a "very weak and faltering" obedience (*Romans*, 155) seems closer to Calvin than Schreiner's much more optimistic understanding of Christian obedience to the law (see below). Note, for example, that whereas Calvin understands the reference in Rom. 2:26 to the uncircumcised who keep the law to be hypothetical ("no such can be found," *Comm.* Rom. 2:26), Schreiner believes Paul is thinking of Christians (*Law*, 196-201); and whereas for Calvin the fulfillment of the law spoken of in Rom. 8:4 cannot be that of Christians themselves ("as long as believers sojourn in the world, they do not make such progress that the righteousness of the law is full or complete in them") but must refer to the obedience of Christ that is imparted to believers, Schreiner takes Paul to mean that "those who have the Spirit actually keep the law" (*Romans*, 404-7).

persuaded by the new perspective. The inference is confirmed on the first page of his preface: "I am still convinced that the Reformers understood Paul better than those who are espousing new approaches" (*Law,* 11). Even more emphatic are his conclusions: "I believe the Reformers were profoundly correct in insisting that Paul's gospel is supremely a gospel of grace that was framed in the context of a legalistic soteriology with roots in Judaism" (243). Clearly Sanders's best efforts at banishing the term "legalism" from discussions of Judaism and Paul have found no hearing with Schreiner. We may begin our review by asking why.

To begin with, Schreiner finds evidence that Palestinian Judaism was legalistic in the same material that Sanders cites to show that it was not. Suggestive, first, are the "sheer number and detail of laws which are codified in the Mishnah" (115). Second, as Sanders himself notes, references to the covenant are few. Sanders may well be correct in thinking that the covenant was the assumed basis of all behavior. But theology may fairly be measured in part by what it stresses, and any theology (Jewish or Christian) that "claims to stress God's grace but rarely mentions it and that elaborates human responsibility in detail inevitably becomes legalistic in practice, if not theory" (116). Finally, though the rabbis were not formulating systematic theology in proposing why God elected Israel, two of the three answers they gave (as cited by Sanders)[16] "betray a legalistic mindset" (117). Very different is the thinking of Paul, who is adamant that God's election is based solely on his sovereign freedom (118).

Schreiner grants that Sanders's work should caution us against naive portrayals of Palestinian Judaism: "It is not evident that rabbis weighed merits against demerits" (115). Still, even Luther's opponents could rightly claim that, in their theology, "no good work was accomplished apart from grace. . . . One could research the Roman Catholic side in the debate thoroughly (as Sanders has examined Palestinian Judaism) and conclude that any idea of legalism or earning merit was foreign to Roman Catholicism" (119). All one would thereby prove is that "legalism" is differently construed from different perspectives. Sanders, by showing that Jews were convinced of their own dependence on divine grace, has indeed corrected certain caricatures of the Jewish position, but (Schreiner believes) he has by no means shown that what Luther and Paul deemed legalistic thinking was not to be found in Palestinian Judaism.

Legalism, as Schreiner understands the object of Luther's and Paul's protestations, means not an exclusive reliance on one's own achievements, but simply the belief that humans must contribute to their attaining of eternal life (94-

---

16. "The covenant was offered to all nations but only Israel accepted it" and "Israel was chosen because of the merit of the fathers or the generation of the exodus" (Schreiner, *Law,* 117).

95); after all, neither the "other gospel" of Paul's Galatian opponents nor the theology that provoked Luther lacked reference to Christ's redemptive work; both, however, believed it must be supplemented by human activities. As Luther correctly perceived, Paul's insistence that justification is not by the "works of the law" reflects his exclusion of any such contribution — and since Paul was hardly "articulat[ing] a theological axiom unrelated to a problem he had faced" (94), there must have been those who deemed human observance of the works of the law essential. Paul's point is missed when his formulation is thought to be directed merely against Jewish exclusivism, with its emphasis on the particular laws that defined Jewish identity (cf. *Paul*, 110-15; "Works of Law," 225-31). For one thing, Paul uses "works" to refer generally to human deeds, and "works of law" to signify deeds demanded by the Mosaic law; the terms are not limited to the peculiar marks of Jewish distinctiveness (Rom. 2:6, 9, 10; 4:1-8; 9:11-12; 11:6; etc.) (*Law*, 52-54).[17] For another, Paul's charge throughout Romans 2 is that Jews are liable for divine judgment because they have transgressed God's moral demands, not because they exclude Gentiles and trumpet Jewish prerogatives (55-56). Moreover, it is clear from the beginning of Romans 4 that Paul thinks human works in general can play no part in justification (54-55, 101). In a number of other Pauline texts, too, the alternatives of salvation by "doing" or by "believing" (without "doing") are set forth, and the latter alone deemed viable (e.g., Gal. 3:11-12, 18; Rom. 9:32; 10:3, 5-13) (60, 107, 125; cf. also "Failure," 216; "View," 129).

Not that works are themselves wrong, or that one who fulfilled all that the law requires would not be recognized as righteous in God's sight (*Law*, 44; cf. "View," 125; "Works of Law," 238-39). Perfect obedience, however, is what is demanded, as the "all" in Galatians 3:10 ("Cursed is everyone who does not abide by *all* things written in the book of the law to do them") and the reference to keeping the "whole law" in 5:3 indicate (*Law*, 45, 63-64); and that no one can obey the law perfectly was both the common Jewish understanding in Paul's day (64) and a natural conclusion to draw from the Old Testament record of Israel's persistent failure to obey God's law (49).[18] Some scholars think Paul

17. Note that in Gal. 3:10 "works of law" is equivalent to "everything written in the book of the law" (*Law*, 57).

18. That no one keeps the law perfectly is the evident assumption, Schreiner believes, in Gal. 3:10: the "for" that links the two halves of the verse "shows that Paul is explaining *why* those who are of the works of law are under a curse — *because* all are cursed who do not obey the entire law"; and if the curse can be said to strike "all" because it strikes "all who do not obey," then "all" are believed not to obey (*Law*, 44-46, emphases Schreiner's; cf. "Evaluation," 257). Moreover, the threat of Gal. 5:3 is "so ominous" precisely because Paul "thought the law unfulfillable" (*Law*, 64). The same thought is apparent in Rom. 3:9-26 (65-66) and 1:18–2:29 (66-68). Nor is it

could not have ruled out the law as a path to salvation simply because it required but never met with perfect obedience; the law itself, they point out, provided for the atonement of sins. Schreiner grants the point but dismisses the objection, for in Paul's mind the coming of Messiah had brought a new stage in salvation history. Now that "Jesus has provided definitive atonement on the cross," the Old Testament sacrifices can no longer atone (44). Indeed, the need for Christ's atoning work suggests that the Old Testament sacrifices were never more than provisional, intended to point to Christ rather than themselves provide final forgiveness (44, 62-64).

The Mosaic covenant as a whole had an interim character (124). For a time it was intended to keep Jews untainted by pagan practices and to show that without the Spirit people are powerless to observe God's law (171, 173). Now, in one sense, it has passed away — though the coming of Messiah represented the fulfillment rather than the abrogation of the Mosaic law (160). In another sense, however, the Mosaic covenant "remain[s] authoritative for the church of Christ" (160). If Lutherans stress the discontinuity between the old covenant and the new, Schreiner aligns himself with a Reformed theology that sees "the two covenants as basically continuous in principle but recogniz[es] the differences in salvation history" (244).

In what sense does the Mosaic covenant retain validity (cf. *Paul*, 307-29)? To begin with, its moral norms remain in force for believers, as Galatians 5:14 and Romans 2:26, 13:9 make clear (*Law*, 149, 154, 171; cf. "Abolition," 55-56). The common objection that Jews did not distinguish moral from ritual laws is not decisive, since a tendency to exalt the ethical rather than the ceremonial demands of the law is already attested in Judaism (*Law*, 156). Paul took the moral demands seriously, believing that people will be judged by their works: though the references in Romans 2 to such a judgment are often deemed hypothetical, they do not seem so, and other texts in Paul confirm that people's destiny will correspond with their deeds (184-86, referring to Gal. 5:21; 6:8; 1 Cor. 6:9-10; Eph. 5:5-6; etc.). Of course, the unregenerate cannot produce works that God will approve. On the other hand, believers, who have been given the Spirit, are "empowered to observe the law" (198, referring to Rom. 8:4). "The saving work of Jesus Christ radically changes people so that they now obey the law they previously disobeyed" (203). As a result, they now perform the good works "neces-

---

contradicted by Rom. 2:14-15, which speaks of "unbelieving Gentiles who occasionally observe the law" (193), or 2:7, 10, 26-29, where the obedience of believers empowered by God's Spirit is in view (189-204; cf. "Works," 139-155). Nor does Phil. 3:6 show that Paul thought he himself had perfectly fulfilled the law: "his purpose is to say that his obedience to the law was extraordinary compared to his contemporaries," but 1 Cor. 15:9 makes clear that Paul was aware of personal preconversion sin (*Law*, 70; cf. "Evaluation," 261-62; "Obedience," 157-58).

sary for salvation" — though, since these deeds *follow* the transformation wrought by Christ's salvific work, they can hardly be said to "earn salvation"; rather, they furnish evidence that salvation has indeed been granted (203; cf. *Romans*, 145).[19] Nor is the obedience even of Christians ever perfect prior to their "full redemption": it will, however, be "significant, substantial, and observable" (*Law*, 204; cf. *Romans*, 390-91).

The nonmoral laws of the Pentateuch are no longer to be observed literally, but Schreiner expends considerable effort to show how they can still function as "authoritative words." Paul thought that the Old Testament sacrificial laws are now defunct, but that they found their fulfillment in Christ's sacrifice (cf. Rom. 3:25 [*Law*, 162]). The same can be said of the Old Testament feasts, as 1 Corinthians 5:7 implies (162-63). That the food laws need no longer be observed is clear from Romans 14:14; but Paul may well have thought that the Old Testament food and purity laws pictured the holiness required to enter God's presence; now that God dwells in his people, these laws may appropriately be given ethical application (163, referring to 2 Cor. 6:14-17). In general we should not expect in Paul's "occasional letters to churches the explication of everything found in the Old Testament. What we do see in Paul, however, gives us a paradigm by which we can understand his view of the Old Testament law" (164).

In three important respects the work of Andrew Das *(Paul, the Law, and the Covenant)*[20] shares while expanding on positions taken by Schreiner.

In the first place Das, like Schreiner, believes Paul understood the law to demand perfect obedience of those who would gain life through its commands. Das goes further, however, in challenging Sanders's view that Jews thought differently: "Sanders wrongly minimized Judaism's belief that God intended the law to be obeyed strictly and in its entirety" (*Law*, 7). Das examines several pre-70 Jewish sources (*Jubilees*, the works of Philo, and Qumran literature) and concludes that God's demands are never set aside, that right conduct is always required: God is holy — and expects holiness from Israel. In Tannaitic literature, too, at least certain rabbis declared that God's judgment was strict and demanded perfect obedience, though others thought those would be approved whose good deeds outweighed their evil.[21] Not that the Judaism of these

---

19. Schreiner quotes approvingly C. F. D. Moule's distinction between the view of Palestinian Judaism (good works are the "means of 'staying in' [the community of salvation]") and that of Paul (good works are a "symptom of 'staying in'") (*Law*, 203 n. 69).

20. I am grateful to Dr. Das for supplying me with a copy of his manuscript prior to its publication.

21. Das argues, against Sanders, that when *b. Sanh.* 81a speaks of a single righteous deed as decisive for divine approval, it has in view a situation where a person's good and bad deeds are

sources was legalistic:[22] the demand for perfect obedience was made within a framework of grace marked by election and by measures that atoned for human failures (39 n. 100). Yet "the very existence of a system of atonement shows that any act contrary to God's law, even the least infraction, had to be rectified in some way; each of God's laws demands obedience" (43-44).

Secondly, Das holds, together with Schreiner, that for Paul it is unthinkable, in the light of Christ's salvific work, that the Old Testament sacrifices atone for sin. Das goes further: the whole gracious framework of Judaism (election, covenant, sacrifices of atonement) has collapsed for Paul; the apostle consistently denies "any salvific or life-giving capacity in the old/Mosaic covenant" (8). Without its gracious framework Judaism is left with a law demanding perfect obedience of its adherents, who will be judged solely by their achievements (214 n. 76). In Paul's eyes, then, Judaism is indeed legalistic — though only because he has excluded from it the framework of grace within which non-Christian Jews thought themselves to be living.[23] Yet Paul's position should not be dismissed as idiosyncratic: Das examines a series of Jewish works (4 Ezra, 2 Baruch, 3 Baruch, 2 Enoch, and Testament of Abraham) from the post-70 period in which, because of the Jewish War's catastrophic outcome and the pressures of Diaspora living, the election and covenantal framework of Judaism are similarly displaced by an accent on the law's demands and on strict judgment according to deeds. The roots of such a position are to be found in the earlier insistence on complete compliance with God's law. When the covenantal framework of that demand disappears from view, legalism is left.

Thirdly, Schreiner and Das believe Paul finds the works of the law inadequate for salvation because humans cannot measure up to the law's demand for perfect obedience. The new perspective excluded such an interpretation at the outset; after all, it was reasoned, Judaism never thought the law required perfec-

---

so evenly balanced that a solitary act can tip the scales in one direction or the other; and *m. Avot* 3:16 is only one of a number of rabbinic texts that speak of a judgment based on whether the majority of one's deeds are good or evil (*Law*, 32-36).

22. That pre-70 Judaism (as well as that reflected in Tannaitic sources) was not legalistic is an important emphasis in Das's work, and in this he differs markedly from Schreiner. It should be noted, however, that Schreiner's more expansive definition of legalism (i.e., legalism is found not simply where there is no thought of a need for divine grace, but wherever it is believed that humans must contribute to their salvation) is not taken up. Judaism was not legalistic for Das, because it did not hold that one can "gain God's favor apart from God's grace and mercy through the accomplishment of what the Law requires" (*Law*, 1 n. 1).

23. Das's position here is close to that of Schoeps, who also believed that Paul understood the law apart from its context in the covenant. For Schoeps, however, Paul's position was the result of a misunderstanding rooted in his Hellenistic Jewish background; for Das the Jewish covenant can have no salvific force for Paul in the light of the salvation brought by Christ.

tion, knowing, as it did, means to atone for the failures of repentant sinners; the point of Paul's opposition (it was thought) must therefore have been another, and Dunn (among others) has looked to Judaism's nationalistic exclusivity for the solution. Das agrees that Paul attacked a perceived Jewish preoccupation with ethnic identity, but he finds that Dunn strains unconvincingly to deny the obvious import of texts that rule out any role for human works in salvation (e.g., Rom. 4:4-5; 9:30–10:8 in the light of 9:12-16; 11:6; Gal. 3:12). The need for such exegetic contortions disappears once one realizes that for Jews the law does indeed demand full obedience, and God does indeed judge humans according to their deeds; and that these become the decisive convictions in Judaism for those who believe, like Paul, that Judaism's covenantal framework of grace has been displaced.

iii. Frank Thielman[24]

Perhaps a corner in the chutzpah hall of fame should be reserved for those of us who write about Paul. We are, after all, hardly less liable than other mortals to misconstrue the thinking of our spouses; that of our teenage offspring we have long since despaired of divining. We too contend daily with the impenetrable *other*ness of our contemporaries: any forgetfulness of our limitations incurs prompt and painful refutation. The study of the ancients, on the other hand, allows a good deal of scope for our pretensions and, best of all, immunity from instant rebuttal — and we have certainly milked its potential to the fullest. Given a first-century apostle a few of whose letters we have read, we make bold to distinguish what he said from what he really thought, and even to pontificate on why he thought the way we think he did. Indeed, as the assumptions that governed Paul's thinking become more and more remote from our own, the assurance with which we pronounce on the direction and deficiencies of his reasoning seems only to increase. Isn't America wonderful?[25]

Ed Sanders is certain that Paul's thinking proceeded from solution to plight: convinced that Christ is the solution to the human dilemma, the apostle made sundry attempts to define a plight from which Christ might be thought to have effected deliverance. The inconsistencies Sanders discerns between these various accounts betray, to his mind, their secondary nature. Paul's anthropology is thus held to be derived, not entirely satisfactorily, from his Chris-

---

24. The parenthetical page references in this section are to the works of Frank Thielman, using the short titles shown in the bibliography.

25. And, of course, other lands of limitless academic opportunity.

tology. When Frank Thielman addresses the issues Sanders raises, he keeps his readers in no protracted suspense about the target and thrust of his argument: the monograph bears the title *From Plight to Solution: A Jewish Framework for Understanding Paul's View of the Law in Galatians and Romans.*[26]

Not that Thielman represents a return to Protestant portrayals of Judaism from the pre-Sandersian era. The Reformers and their disciples were wrong, he believes, in making no attempt to understand Judaism in its own terms (*Paul,* 27); for his part Paul did not regard Judaism in general as a "legalistic religion" (239) or attribute to it "a doctrine of salvation by works" (188). Some Jews there were who, while acknowledging God's grace in the election of Israel, believed God had left to them the choice between life through obeying his commands and death should they choose disobedience (Sir. 15:15-17; *Pss. Sol.* 9:4-5; cf. Deut. 30:11-20). That such Jews were boastful of their righteousness does not follow, still less that they lived in fear lest their evil deeds should prove to outweigh their good at the final judgment. Nonetheless, they thought their efforts could (and must) be combined with God's grace if they were to obtain his favor at the last (66, 238).

Paul's understanding was different, but not for that reason un-Jewish. Though covenantal texts in Leviticus (like chap. 26) and Deuteronomy (like chaps. 28–31) do indeed speak of Israel's choice between obedience and disobedience as determinative of the people's "life" or "death," the same texts anticipate that Israel will opt for the path of disobedience and thereby bring upon itself the curse of God's covenant. Such, moreover, is the story of Israel as told in the historical books of the Jewish Scriptures and in psalms (like 78, 105, and 106) that review the nation's past. Above all, the prophets repeatedly denounce the rebelliousness that God's people show in transgressing his law, declare their sinfulness incorrigible, yet find hope for the future in a decisive divine intervention: God will one day purify his people, end the curse consequent upon their disobedience, and enable them, through the gift of his Spirit, to do his will. "I will sprinkle clean water upon you, and you shall be clean from all your uncleannesses, and from all your idols I will cleanse you. A new heart I will give you, and a new spirit I will put within you; and I will remove from your body the heart of stone and give you a heart of flesh. I will put my spirit within you and make you follow my statutes and be careful to observe my ordinances" (Ezek. 36:25-27; cf. 11:19-20; Jer. 31:31-34).

---

26. Thielman's understanding of Israel's "plight" shares much in common with that of N. T. Wright, and the two are often grouped together in the summaries and critiques of other scholars. For our purposes, however, it is important to distinguish them inasmuch as Wright makes much of the discontinuity he sees between Paul's understanding of justification and its "Lutheran" interpretation, whereas Thielman sees significant continuity.

Thus, whereas the Jewish Scriptures tell a story of "continual violation of God's law or covenant" on the part of God's people and of their suffering as a consequence, the same Scriptures point to a future in which the "vicious cycle of sin and rebellion" will be broken and God's people transformed to do his will from their hearts (49; cf. *Plight*, 36). Such a restoration, in light of the people's innate recalcitrance, will necessarily be both initiated and effected by God (*Paul*, 65).

This understanding of Israel's history and eschatological hope remained current in Paul's day. Indeed, it was commonly believed that the curses Israel was threatened with in Leviticus and Deuteronomy had not only fallen on God's people but remained in force — and would do so until the day of God's redemption: so the scattering of Jews among the nations and the dominance of Palestine by the Romans were interpreted (55; cf. *Plight*, 72). Hence, while no doubt some Jews believed they would be acquitted at God's judgment provided they freely chose to obey God's law, "others believed humanity to be so sinful that true obedience would come only as a result of God's prior work in the human heart" (*Paul*, 68).

Far from concocting an artificial dilemma to suit his Christology, then, Paul merely appropriated a "plight to solution" pattern well established in the scriptures and thinking of Second Temple Judaism. His "deeply held conviction" that the law cannot justify because, outside of the eschatological community, its demands cannot be met was in fact a common understanding among Jews of his day (239). When Paul writes in Romans 7 that one may acknowledge the goodness of God's law but be prevented by the flesh from carrying it out, he expressed a view well attested in Jewish texts with parallels even in Greek and Latin literature: "many who pondered the question of evil reflected on the inability of people to choose the good consistently" (*Plight*, 121). Paul's claim that "those who rely on works of the law are under a curse" (Gal. 3:10) was not even controversial in his day, since it was well known that "membership in the people of God, as it is defined by the Mosaic covenant, is membership in a people with a plight — they are cursed by the very law that defines them as God's people, because they, as a people and as individuals, have not kept the law" (*Paul*, 126-27). Nor would the claim that follows — "Because no one is justified before God by the law, it is obvious that 'The just shall live by faith'" (so Thielman construes Gal. 3:11 [127]) — have occasioned surprise: a humanity acknowledged to be "under sin" must inevitably trust God to provide an eschatological solution to the dilemma (*Plight*, 70-71).

Paul did, to be sure, point out to those *other* Jews who thought their obedience to God's law a factor in their approval at God's judgment that the human condition as Scripture describes it is bleaker than they imagine; God's gracious intervention alone can redeem us (*Paul*, 188). This insistence in Romans and Galatians is broadened in Ephesians and the Pastoral Epistles to a general affirmation of salvation as the gift of a gracious God in which human effort has no role (229, 234, 244). The Reformers were by no means mistaken, then, in tracing such an emphasis to Paul (26-27, 244), though it would be wrong to conclude that Jews in general ascribed salvific merit to their deeds. Rather, Paul's own position was standard in Judaism.

Paul differed, of course, from most Jews in his belief that the eschatological age had begun, that the various communities of Christian believers represented the eschatologically restored people of God whose sins had been forgiven, from whom the curse of the law had been removed, and to whom the Spirit of God had been granted to enable them to do God's will (245; cf. *Plight*, 119). The death of Christ he saw as God's expected eschatological intervention: the curse pronounced by the Mosaic law on its transgressors was borne by Christ, who thus inaugurated the period of God's redemption (*Paul*, 129; cf. Gal. 3:13-14). Now Gentiles have "joined believing Jews to constitute the eschatologically restored Israel" (138; cf. Gal. 6:16).

Yet even here a partial parallel to Paul's view can be seen in the conviction of the Qumran covenanters that they were the eschatological people of God, and that among them God's intervention to purify his people from their sin had at least been partially realized (*Plight*, 36-41). For the covenanters, as for Paul, the new age, though inaugurated, had not yet fully come, nor had temptation been banished even from the community of God's elect: not yet are God's people sinless (121). A need remained for concrete ethical guidance to be given to God's people (*Law*, 18).

According to the common Jewish expectation, the restored people of God would be enabled by God's Spirit to carry out the law of Moses. In *From Plight to Solution* Thielman interpreted Paul along similar lines: Paul's claims that believers fulfill the law (Rom. 8:4; cf. 13:8-10; Gal. 5:14) were seen as straightforward statements that the expected day had dawned. If Paul saw no place for the continuing observance of certain aspects of the Mosaic law (circumcision, the food and festival laws), Thielman took the apostle's position to be close to that of many Hellenistic Jews, who played down and considered expendable the same aspects of the law whose observance by the Galatians Paul opposed (*Plight*, 54-59). In later writings, however, Thielman concedes that for Paul the Mosaic law has completed its divinely appointed purpose and is no longer in effect ("Ethics," 64-65; *Law*, 9). Believers are nonetheless subject to an analogous "law of Christ," a "law" that absorbs some elements of the Mosaic law while excluding others, and whose basis is found in the ethical teaching of Jesus ("Ethics," 65-68). Still, a tension is apparent in Paul's own ethical teaching: Paul is convinced that the new age has begun and that God's Spirit indwells believers, rendering external instruction unnecessary (cf. Jer. 31:34; Isa. 54:13); at the same time, he is aware that the old age has not passed away, nor have believers been immunized against its influence. On the one hand, then, Paul "refuses to impose his authority in some ethical matters because to do so would violate the principle that the Spirit leads other believers into a discernment of God's will" (cf. Rom. 14:1–15:13; Phil. 3:15; Philem. 8-9; note that 1 Cor. 6:12 and 10:23 may well represent a distortion of this element in Paul's teaching); on the other hand, he "handed down to his churches a set body of moral teaching which provided a rough outline of what the Christian should look like who had been transformed by God" (65-72).

The extent to which Paul simply appropriated a common Jewish eschatological pattern forbids us to see him as a solitary figure who, either with creative genius or with "haphazard and inconsistent" ad hoc attempts, set out to formulate a uniquely Christian perspective on human nature and God's law (*Plight*, 27, 91). Others, of course, before Thielman, stressed the fundamentally Jewish framework within which Paul worked, though Thielman finds their proposals unsatisfactory. No standard doctrine prevailed among Jews — and was taken over by Paul — by which the Mosaic law was expected to end, or be significantly modified, in the messianic age (contrary to Schweitzer, Schoeps, and W. D. Davies) (11-12). Nor did Paul merely attribute to Christ the place and merits other Jews ascribed to Torah (contrary to Wilckens); he did not see Christ and Torah as alternatives (119). Rather, following a standard Jewish eschatological hope, Paul saw Christ as the divine means by which a people hitherto unable to keep God's law were freed from the curse that followed their transgressions and enabled to obey God's will.

Already in 1 Thessalonians, as in all his later epistles, Paul saw his converts as the eschatologically restored people of God (*Paul*, 75-77). Already in the Corinthian epistles, as emphatically as in Galatians and Romans, Paul can speak both positively of the goodness of God's law and negatively of the condemnation and death it deals out to those within its sphere (111-12; cf. "Coherence," 250). In Galatians no less than in Romans, the "works of the law" do not justify because no "flesh" can do them (Gal. 2:16; 3:10-14). Paul's views of the law were clearly formulated, but hardly first formed, when he wrote Galatians and Romans. Rather, they appear to have been consistent throughout the period marked by his epistles, though with a consistency largely borrowed from the Jewish pattern on which they were dependent (*Plight*, 121).

iv. Mark Seifrid[27]

Mark Seifrid has written a good deal about the new perspective on Paul. On the positive side, he notes that its effects have not been "entirely deleterious"; that it takes up the perennially necessary task of coming to terms with "the Reformers' article of justification"; that it has won a hearing for the (correct, though not original) claim that Judaism was not a religion of strict legalism, and has challenged the notion that the pre-Christian Paul was burdened by a sense of guilt; that it has called attention to the social dimension of Paul's arguments on justification; and that, while the "detour" it has induced much current study of Paul to pursue is an "unproductive" one, it is at least "interesting" ("Alleys," 73-74; *Justification,* 47; *Righteousness,* 15).

In a more negative vein (and here our list must be more selective), Seifrid laments that "a so-called 'Lutheran' reading of Paul has been dismissed" without an adequate grasp of what Luther meant by justification ("Alleys," 74).[28] "Covenantal nomism," he observes, is misleading as a designation of early Judaism's soteriology,[29] and is in any case not exempt from Luther's attack on salva-

---

27. The parenthetical page references in this section are to the works of Mark Seifrid, using the short titles shown in the bibliography.

28. Seifrid insists in particular on the error of supposing that the Reformers' reading of Paul is oriented toward a purely "individualistic" salvation. There is nothing individualistic about the view that the world's sin was condemned in Christ objectively and independently of any awareness on the part of human beings, or that, objectively and externally, the gift of justification is manifest in Jesus Christ ("Alleys," 93-95).

29. In identifying righteousness with "(Israel's) covenant status" and claiming that that status is preserved but not obtained by "righteous behavior," Sanders departs from biblical terminology (where being in the covenant signifies entrance into covenant responsibilities, not the enjoyment of saving blessings), Qumran thinking (where the covenant provides the context in which righteousness is found but "does not save as a promise prior to and independent of obedience"), and rabbinic usage (where "covenant" is used in ways too diverse to permit the simple equation of "being in the covenant" with "participating in salvation"); moreover, "righteousness" terminology "obviously can be used with reference to conformity to divine demands, and not merely membership within Israel" ("Language," 434-40). In general, Sanders imposes theological questions and concerns on the Tannaitic materials that hardly emerge from the materials themselves (*Justification,* 57); as for Jewish literature in which soteriological questions do come to the fore (Seifrid discusses at length 1QS [The Community Rule] and the *Psalms of Solomon* [*Justification,* 78-135]), Sanders "glosses over the various ways in which covenant and election, obedience and mercy were understood. . . . When such concepts are in flux, it is relatively unimportant (although correct) to say that Palestinian Judaism as a whole may be described as 'covenantal nomism'" (*Justification,* 59; cf. "Alleys," 75-76). Furthermore, Friedrich Avemarie has shown that rabbinic literature itself preserves, side by side in unresolved tension, statements attributing Israel's salvation to its unconditioned election and others insisting that salvation is contingent on obedience. "Covenantalism" and "nomism" coexist without the overarching synthesis that Sanders imposes on the sources ("Perspective," 5-6; *Righteousness,* 15-16).

tion by works.[30] Sanders provides no account of how Paul's conversion affected his prior understanding of salvation — even though the Christian Paul saw "the Christ-event as the fulfillment of the values and hopes of Judaism." He does not explain how a pious Jew like Paul could "conceive of Messiah as Savior apart from *Torah*," or conceive him as Savior of the Gentiles "apart from their incorporation into the nation of Israel" (*Justification*, 50). He misinterprets Bultmann, whose reading of Paul's conflict with Judaism is more subtle than Sanders allows (25-37, 53-55). He minimizes the importance of forensic justification to Paul's thought on inadequate grounds[31] and is wrong in claiming that notions of "guilt, repentance and forgiveness play no role in Paul's soteriology" (52 n. 172); he is wrong also in thinking that beliefs adopted by Paul subsequent to his conversion could not have become central to his theology (54). As for Dunn's attempts to build on the "new perspective," they betray further misconstructions of both Judaism and Paul. When Dunn claims Paul opposed an exclusivistic national righteousness that insisted on the observance of circumcision, food, and Sabbath laws as markers of Jewish identity, he does not duly acknowledge the religious and ethical values attached by Jews to these markers, or Jewish receptiveness toward non-Jews who adopted these practices to signal their rejection of idolatry and worship of the one true God, or the subordination (particularly apparent in Jewish texts that place some Jews "outside the boundaries") of the idea of nation to the larger one of "true religion and piety" ("Alleys," 77-80). There is, moreover, a Jewish "ethnocentrism" that is entirely biblical and paralleled in Paul's own understanding of the gospel "to the Jew

30. On the contrary, Sanders's covenantal nomism ("God gives his grace to the one who by effort and intent is faithful to the covenant") is itself "quite similar" to the medieval theology to which Luther reacted ("divine saving action is formally primary — bringing one into a state of grace and subsequently sustaining one there — but materially dependent on human response and 'maintenance of covenant status'") ("Blind Alleys," 92). After his conversion, however, Paul "no longer viewed God as cooperating with human effort within the framework of the covenant with Israel. Now for Paul, God's act in Christ effected salvation in itself" (*Justification*, 255; cf. *Righteousness*, 17).

31. Sanders suggests that forensic justification cannot have been central to Paul's thinking since it was not the root of sundry other Pauline convictions. But the same can be said of the Pauline tenets that Sanders deems fundamental; and the assumption that Paul's thought developed deductively by a process that his letters allow us to reconstruct is highly problematic (*Justification*, 51-52). Much of the argument of Seifrid's *Justification by Faith* is devoted to establishing the centrality of forensic justification to Paul's thinking (the claim is distinguished from the notion that justification represented "the logical starting point of all Paul's reflections" [270]): noting that it came to be invoked in contexts other than those involving Jew-Gentile relations, Seifrid concludes that "Paul consistently reflected upon and applied to various concrete situations his belief that deliverance from impending divine wrath was supplied on the basis of God's act in Christ alone" (255).

first." If the nationalism of some Jews had become "proud and prejudiced," there was no need for the cross of Christ to demonstrate the error of their ways: such attitudes are abundantly condemned in the Hebrew Scriptures themselves (*Righteousness*, 19-21; cf. "Perspective," 7-8). In fact, Paul never attacks Jewish observance of the law. When in Romans 2–4 he insists that "works of the law" do not justify, he was not (as Dunn would have it) using the phrase to denounce nationalistic righteousness; in Romans 4 he appears to *distinguish* circumcision, the primary mark of Jewish identity, from "works (of the law)"; and the contrast Paul draws between "works" (or "working") and "concepts such as impiety, transgression, and forgiveness indicates that he here takes up the ethical aspect of ἔργα νόμου ['works of the law'], exploring the moral dimension of covenant fidelity." The "works" the "circumcised were to perform marked the difference between the righteous and the ungodly" ("Alleys," 82-84). Nor can we say, with Wright, that Paul saw faith in Christ as the answer to Jewish yearnings for deliverance from the nation's exile. Many Jews regarded the exile as long past (*Righteousness*, 23-25; cf. "Perspective," 10-11). Paul himself, prior to his conversion, rather than "bemoaning the state of his people or their domination by Rome," seems to have "regarded himself as part of the circle of the faithful who waited in confidence for the day of judgement" ("Alleys," 90). Nor was he alone. Much of the literature of the period does not treat Israel's sin as "absolute and all-encompassing," but distinguishes groups of the Jewish "pious" from "the wicked" ("Perspective," 9). If Paul saw contemporary Israel as in any sense "in exile," their banishment represented judgment, not for a past history of "unqualified rebellion" ("they have zeal for God"), but for a failure to "submit to the righteousness of God in Christ," a failure that made them, in effect, "God's enemies," "branches" broken off from the "olive tree" of God's people. But in this respect the coming of Christ marked the new beginning, not the end, of Israel's exile ("Alleys," 91; cf. *Righteousness*, 168-69).

Such, then, are the pros and (representative) cons that Seifrid finds in the new perspective. Without tallying votes, we may safely conclude that the nays carry the day; Seifrid is among the new perspective's staunchest critics. But his overwhelmingly negative response should not be seen merely as the sum of diverse objections; it is clearly the obverse of his own reading of the apostle, a reading explicitly aligned with that of "the Reformers." To that reading we must now turn.

Of Sin and the Law

When Seifrid speaks, in the plural, of "the Reformers," he appears to be thinking of Luther and Luther. Of Calvin and the Reformed tradition, we have earlier noted their lofty notion of law as God's eternal will for humankind; of the law's condemnatory role as "accidental" rather than inherent in its nature; of the essential continuity between law and gospel; and of the law's principal function as guiding the behavior of God's people. In Seifrid's work, it is rather Luther's sharp contrast between law and gospel that finds echoes, though the former term is applied, not (as in Luther) to the demands of God in general, but (following Pauline usage) to those of the Mosaic dispensation.

Adam's transgression was the first of two acts that "determine the entire course of human history" (Righteousness, 70, referring to Rom. 5:12-21); the consequent subjection of all humanity to sin and death represents the condition "under which all sinned."[32] Romans 1 depicts somewhat generically "Adam's transgression reliving itself in all generations" (49-50 n. 46). Similarly, in 7:7-13 Paul pictures the recapitulation of Adam's transgression that occurs when a human being encounters the law: the "primal sin" is reenacted, though now, to be sure, there is no fall from a pristine state, but an establishing of the reality that sin indwells humanity (115-18; cf. 63).

To fallen human beings the divine law is given. In most instances where Paul uses the word νόμος, he refers to the law of Moses delivered to Israel.[33] To say that the Mosaic law is a law of works (so Rom. 3:27) is not to misconstrue its nature legalistically;[34] the law, precisely as law, demands deeds of obedience of those who would obtain life while condemning the transgressions of the disobedient (105).[35] Inevitably, fallen human beings prove unable to meet its demands: apparent compliance is merely external, neither altering the idolatrous human heart nor expressing true love for God or neighbor (102-4, 148-49). Still, a recognition of human waywardness marks the fulfillment of the law's very purpose. The law is misused, not when it is thought to demand deeds as its condition for life, but when the "reality of sin and guilt which it exposes" is denied (105; cf. 149).

32. So Seifrid, following Theodor Zahn, renders the conclusion of Rom. 5:12 (Righteousness, 70 n. 91).

33. Inasmuch as the law is given to Israel, it has a "particular aspect" (i.e., laws whose observance is required only of Israel); it is, however, a unit and cannot fairly be divided into moral and ceremonial components (Righteousness, 63 n. 73; 123; cf. "Revelation," 124). As for Gentiles, they have been entrusted with a knowledge of God's will (it is written in their hearts, according to Rom. 2:15) "equal to the manifestation of his will in the law of Moses" (Righteousness, 54) and rendering their disobedience, like that of the Jews, inexcusable (cf. "Revelation," 122-23). Paul also uses νόμος of Scripture when the latter "performs the functions of the law, that is, when it expresses God's demands, or testifies to divine judgment" (Righteousness, 97).

34. Seifrid rejects Cranfield's suggestion that Paul uses νόμος to mean "legalism" (Righteousness, 96 n. 12; cf. also "Approach," 13).

35. Cf. 126 n. 101: the commands given at Sinai "cannot be detached from their authority to condemn without ceasing to be 'law.'"

Jews (including the pre-Christian Paul) knew well that they fell short of full compliance with the law, yet thought the law's requirements were adequately met when their acts of piety were supplemented by attention to the law's provisions for atonement (102-3). Paul viewed human disobedience more radically. We do not fail partially, merely lacking strength to fully carry out God's law; rather, we are in outright rebellion against God (125). All are "idolaters" and "liars" (57-58; cf. Rom. 1:21-23; 3:4) who fail to give God his due; hence God has a "contention" against us.[36] The law cannot cure our fallenness. Instead it effects our transgression,[37] reveals our bondage to sin,[38] pronounces our sentence of death, demonstrates the justice of God in his contention against us — and so sets the stage for the incarnation (108-9; cf. "Declaration," 131).

It is an indispensable stage: "the law which condemns serves as the necessary counterpart to the gospel, which announces the joy of condemnation overcome" (*Righteousness*, 124). Those who would read God's law as an "offer of grace which is to be fulfilled 'in faith'" in fact rob it of its proper function; the gospel can be "properly understood only on the basis of the condemnation and death ministered by the law" (120 n. 88). The law's sentence of death is by no means to be escaped, since God's Spirit gives life only to that which has been killed, and righteousness is granted only "where the judgment of condemnation has been rendered" (112).[39]

---

36. God's "lawsuits" against his faithless people are familiar from the books of the Hebrew prophets. Seifrid prefers to designate them "contentions" since God, as the aggrieved party, contends directly with those who have wronged him rather than (as in our understanding of a lawsuit) pleading his case before an impartial judge. Still, the contention is legal in character, involving as it does a dispute about who is in the right (*Righteousness*, 43 n. 30; also 59).

37. Transgression is, after all, inevitable when rebels against God are confronted with God's demands in the law (cf. "Revelation," 128).

38. Not that the law necessarily creates a *sense* of guilt within human beings. In transgressing the law's commands, human beings *experience* sinning (the "knowledge of sin" spoken of in Rom. 3:20; 7:7-13 ["Revelation," 127]), and God's claim that they are "liars" is established: "the law establishes God's just charge against humanity in the public square, whether humanity acknowledges it or not" (128). Faith enables believers to recognize their guilt and the justice of God's claims against them, thus anticipating the final judgment when all will submit to the divine charge (*Righteousness*, 61-62).

39. Israel's destiny as outlined in Rom. 9–11 — through disobedience and judgment to mercy — corresponds precisely to this pattern: "Israel and the nations are the tools by which God the Creator establishes the ungodliness of all, and so justifies the ungodly" (*Righteousness*, 167). Paul is thus asserting fundamental convictions in these chapters, "not wrestling with a cognitive dissonance brought about by an unexpected course of events" (152-53, 158; cf. *Justification*, 245 n. 248).

Of Justification and Faith

If Adam's sin was the first of two determinative acts in human history, the obedience of Christ was the second. Not that his decisive importance lies in the model of faithfulness that he left; rather, in the death to which his faithfulness brought him, he atoned for our sins.[40] The law's condemnation of humanity's sinfulness was not set aside but carried out on the cross, and it entailed not the dismissal but the triumph of God's contention against us (66; cf. "Perspective," 17). The cross does not supplement human obedience with atonement for our partial failures, but marks the death of humanity in its radical disobedience (*Righteousness*, 103; cf. *Justification*, 178). In Christ's resurrection a new creation was brought into being, a new life beyond the domain of sin and of the law that condemns sinners.

The new creation, like the condemnation of the old, is a reality outside of us, in the person of Christ. In the death and resurrection of Christ *God* is justified — he is shown to be in the right in his contention with his sinful creatures; so, too, is sinful humanity — we are made new persons by sharing in the life of the new creation. The justification of the sinner and of God are thus inextricably bound together (*Righteousness*, 66; cf. "Declaration," 132; "Gift," 686-87). Justification involves more than a righting of our relations with God, and God's righteousness is more than his faithfulness to his covenant people in working their salvation. In the Hebrew Scriptures God acts to justify when, as king and judge of the universe, he establishes justice and restores right order in his creation. He vindicates the righteous *and* his own rightful claim to be God, bringing retribution to bear on those who oppress his people and deny him.[41] All these elements are present in the cross and resurrection of Christ: the vindication of God, the condemnation of his foes, the establishing of right order in the new creation. These — not the problems of nationalism or ethnicity — are the issues when justification is the theme (*Righteousness*, 84-85).

---

40. Those who would render πίστις Χριστοῦ "the faithfulness of Christ" and see in Christ's human faithfulness the means of our salvation emphasize the moral ideal expressed in his death "at the expense of its atoning significance" (*Righteousness*, 143). They fail, moreover, to see that, without the resurrection, Christ's (faithfulness in) death cannot justify (142-43). And they simply ignore that the New Testament authors all speak of believing *in* Jesus Christ as the means by which God grants salvation while rarely mentioning Christ's "faithfulness," still less his "faith": "in the New Testament 'faith' is based upon the work of God *in* Christ. Despite their clear affirmations of Jesus' humanity, the New Testament authors did not speak of *Jesus'* believing in God, since he himself was the object of faith" (140).

41. *Righteousness*, 38-47, drawing on "Language," 415-42; cf. also "Declaration," 124-31; "Gift," 685-86; "Perspective," 12-16.

What, then, is the role of faith?

Justification takes place wholly in Christ, yet sinners are given a share in Christ through faith (149, 176). By faith they recognize their radical disobedience, renounce all attempts at attaining a righteousness of their own, and acknowledge the justice of God's judgment against them (66, 156). By faith they have a share, here and now, in Christ's triumph over sin and death. All that God has done in Christ is grasped by faith, received by those who believe in him. It is theirs — yet not theirs, but Christ's, possessed by believers only in faith and hope (174-76). It will become theirs fully when, at the final judgment, God raises them from the dead (184).

Saving faith is not abstract, but faith *in* Jesus Christ, crucified and risen ("Gift," 682-83). Yet neither is it a mere human assent to the facts about Christ which must then be "shaped by love" before it can be "savingly effective." Faith is obedience *to* the gospel created (ex nihilo) by God's word *in* the gospel. It is God's work, not ours;[42] the gospel is faith's source as well as its object (*Righteousness*, 131-32).

In themselves believers remain sinners, a part of the fallen world and in need of the law's instruction: the "wretched persons" of Romans 7 who are subject to sin and death (124-25).[43] Yet though they remain sinners, they are also righteous, for the old reality that still dogs their existence has been defeated in Christ, and they are given, by faith, a share in Christ's resurrection life and righteousness. They know love, not as an ideal they must strive to fulfill, but as a reality in the person of Christ: Christ, present to them in faith, is necessarily active in them in love, performing his works (149; cf. "Gift," 683). Just as all sin is the reenactment of Adam's sin, so all obedience is the obedience of Christ in the humanity justified in him (*Righteousness*, 118). All that God requires of us is already reality in Christ. Any growth we make is a growth in faith, as we grasp more firmly what we have already been given in Christ (137-38). And when, at the last, we are judged by works (Rom. 2:13), it is the works of Christ, made ours through faith, that will gain God's approval (148-49).

42. The point is missed by those who claim that if πίστις Χριστοῦ means faith *in* Christ, then faith itself becomes a "bizarre sort of work": "this is to fail to see that for Paul, in the critical sense faith is decidedly not a 'work'; that is, it is not the deed or accomplishment of fallen human beings, but the work of God within us through the gospel" (*Righteousness*, 145).

43. The "wretched" existence described in Rom. 7 is not peculiarly that of believers, but it remains true of believers as they are ("intrinsically considered"; apart, that is, from the saving resources that are theirs in Christ) in this world (*Justification*, 236-37; "Subject," 326).

Chapter 13

Other Perspectives

Academic research has its rewards, but no one can deny its tedium. Like many others, I have found it important to supplement work on this project with writing of a more inspirational nature; hence my forthcoming *All I Really Need to Know I Learned at a Baseball Game*. One segment of the latter enterprise — the "Law for Attending a Baseball Game in the Company of a Child" — seems relevant to our present inquiry. Perhaps I may be permitted to quote it: "Attending a baseball game in the company of a child is a Good Thing; but the seat cannot be found from which something that a child desires to see is not obstructed from view."

This is not the place to cite further (it is in any case not finished) the profound homily that accompanies this principle, drawing out a few of its broader implications for life's journey. Here we note only its obvious applicability to our study. No one vantage point captures all that is important in Paul. The scholars whose works are summarized in this chapter see a coherence between Paul's doctrine of justification by faith, understood — along "Lutheran" lines — to exclude human endeavors from any part in salvation, and Pauline convictions in the specific areas on which they focus: Paul's anthropology, his rhetoric, his apocalyptic worldview, and his theology of the cross. If they are correct, it follows that important aspects of Paul's thought may be lost to the view of those who adopt the new perspective on the apostle.

i. Paul's Anthropology: Timo Laato

Among the topics warmly debated in the saunas of Finland is the new perspective on Paul. Heikki Räisänen's provocative work in particular has stirred up

226

controversy within his native land no less than outside it. His position has gained a sturdy proponent in the work of his student Kari Kuula, whose monograph *The Law, the Covenant, and God's Plan*[1] leaves no doubt about its academic paternity. But the "Lutheran" Paul has strong defenders in Finland as well. Two of them may be considered here.[2]

Timo Laato sees the "greatest weakness in [Sanders's] argumentation" to be his "inadequate coverage of the question of the capacity of humankind."[3] In Judaism human beings are considered to have free will: a capacity both to choose and to do good rather than evil (67, 73).[4] Admittedly they are born with a propensity to disobedience, but it falls short of a compulsion (73). The sin of Adam and Eve is not thought to have affected either their own or their descendants' subsequent ability to do good, though it exemplifies the disobedience to which humans are liable (74-75). For Paul, on the other hand, the sin of Adam introduced into the world the dominion of sin — "sin" here referring not simply to "the multitude of individual, concrete transgressions" actually committed, but to the "wretched state of calamity" in which humans find themselves unable to do, or even to choose, the good (75, referring to Rom. 5:12). Adam's sin has fixed the destiny of his descendants (105, referring to Rom. 5:18-19). In Romans 7:7-13 Paul interprets the story of Genesis 2–3, showing how the descendants of Adam and Eve each participate in the fate of their forebears (139). When Romans 7 goes on to speak of the human incapacity to do good, the point is not that people are "so depraved" that they always *do* "only evil and never good," but that no one can carry out the commandments *"from pure motives"*: the commandment cited in the passage and transgressed even in deeds of seeming piety is the prohibition of covetousness (125-26).[5] Clearly, then, the "anthropological presuppositions of the Jewish and the Pauline pattern of religion" differ markedly from each other: "the former is based on human free will, while the latter is founded on human depravity" (146).

The difference in anthropology is matched by one in soteriology (167). In Judaism "salvation requires human cooperation" (150). The generation of the

1. See chap. 10, sec. iii above.

2. The work of Lauri Thurén will be considered in sec. ii below. Cf. also Timo Eskola, *Theodicy*.

3. Laato, *Approach*, 62. Parenthetical page references in this section are to Laato's *Approach*.

4. Laato agrees with Sanders that even with the emphasis in Qumran literature on the "eternal and irresistible grace of God," the "sectarians did not understand this in such a way as to exclude man's ability to choose which of two ways he would follow" (72 n. 19).

5. Christians remain subject to this weakness. They are to "walk in the Spirit" and so avoid *carrying out* the desires of the flesh; but they continue to experience those desires and so are kept from obeying the law from their hearts as they ought (131, 144).

exodus entered the covenant by accepting the Torah of their own free will (an acceptance not matched, according to a well-known tradition, by Gentiles, who proved unwilling to part with their sins). Later generations of Jews, though born into the covenant, must subsequently — and *"consciously"* — "take up the yoke of the kingdom of heaven"; so, too, must Gentiles who become proselytes to enter the covenant (148-50). Moreover, those within the covenant must fulfill the law if they would gain a place in the future world (157) — and (this is, of course, the point) it is within their capacity adequately to do so. For Paul, however, God himself must call into being the new creation. Faith does not replace the works of the law as the required *human* contribution for salvation; rather (as 2 Cor. 4:6 shows), "God acts creatively by the Gospel and calls forth the faith" in a way that "excludes human cooperation totally" (151-52, noting also Rom. 4:17; 10:17; 1 Cor. 1:28). Elsewhere (Phil. 1:29; cf. 3:12b) Paul "classifies faith explicitly as a gift of God's grace" (152). Nor does Paul think those called to faith ever reach a stage in their "spiritual development" in which they can "fulfil the law by [their] own will power. By faith [they] have placed [themselves] completely outside the field of human action" (160). When Paul, then, criticizes Jewish soteriology, he cites its "anthropocentric" as well as its "antichristological" implications. The two belong inevitably together (198).

ii. Paul's Rhetoric: Lauri Thurén and Jean-Noël Aletti

Yet another Finnish contribution comes from Lauri Thurén, the title of whose monograph *(Derhetorizing Paul)* conveys to those who can pronounce it the book's pivotal point. Too often Paul's writings have been read in a "static" way, as though Paul wrote merely to inform his readers of his religious ideas, and what he wrote on a matter reproduced exactly what he thought.[6] This approach has led to errors by both those who want to derive from Paul's letters direct statements of timeless, universal truth and those who, finding Paul's argumentation at the surface level problematic, conclude too readily that he was an inconsistent thinker (56). Paul intended to *affect* his readers by what he wrote, to induce a desired response, to influence their thoughts and actions (24); this intention gives his letters a "dynamic" character that must dictate our reading of them. Rather than harmonizing or systematizing his various utterances (whether to discover coherence or chaos), we must "derhetorize" Paul's texts: the persuasive devices must be identified and their effects on Paul's expressed

---

6. Thurén, *Derhetorizing Paul,* 23. Parenthetical page numbers in the following text refer to this work.

ideas "filtered out" before we search for a "possible invariant system of thought" lying beneath the surface (28, 57).

On the other hand, Paul's interest in theology is not to be underestimated, and the search, beneath the rhetoric, for the theology of his letters is by no means inappropriate. "Paul really seems to have had a special interest in theological questions, and a tendency . . . to approach even practical questions from a theological point of view" (17-18; cf. 138); in fact, "his search for consistency in theology was a major reason, maybe *the* reason, for his revolt against the law" (185; cf. 163-64). It is telling that his letters have always provoked theological inquiry in a way that the letters of Peter and James have not (18).

"Derhetorizing" Paul clears up a number of problems perceived by modern students of his views of the law. A few examples may be cited. In the context of Galatians 3:19-20, Paul is establishing a "distance between God and the law" by many rhetorical means to support his rejection of the law while avoiding the appearance of criticizing God. But the notion that Paul here proposes a demonic origin of the law exceeds both what the text says and what would have been rhetorically wise for Paul to suggest (83). Galatians 5:16 ("Live by the Spirit, and you will not carry out the desires of the flesh") must not be read woodenly as a promise of complete triumph over sinful desires. It is, in its rhetorical effect, an exhortation; its point, prosaically construed, is simply that, to the extent that people live by the Spirit, they will not carry out the desires of the flesh (88). Paul does not sometimes think the law leads to life (Rom. 7:10) while at other times denying that it does so (Gal. 3:21). For the apostle, "in practice the law never gives life" (114). But "on the rhetorical level" this "idea can be expressed in many ways depending on what kind of response is sought." The fault may be seen as the sinner's, who does not meet the law's requirement for life (so Rom. 7:10; cf. 10:5; Gal. 3:12); alternatively, to discourage embracing the law Paul may choose to highlight the law's inability to secure its own obedience (Gal. 3:21). In fact, "both the seemingly contradictory sayings 'the law cannot give life' and 'the law can give life to anybody who follows it' are based on the same syllogism, by adding a premise: The law has in itself ability to give life, but since nobody complies with the law, the ability is never realized" (114). Paul never sees the law as having ultimate authority for Christians: in this he remains constant in Galatians, 1 Corinthians, and Romans. In the latter two letters, however, without contradicting the main emphasis in Galatians, Paul does occasionally cite the law as providing "supplementary support" to his own "moral principles" in a way that would have been ill advised in the context of his polemic against embracing the law in Galatians (134).

A further example of the need to "derhetorize" Paul is even more central to our discussion. When the soteriology of Judaism is derived from a static reading of Paul's letters, the results differ from what we know of the reality. But Paul was not writing a textbook on Judaism; an objective description of the faith of his opponents would not have served his purpose, and he makes no claim to have so represented it. What we have is rather a "pedagogically overstated" presentation of an alternative position to his own, not without some perceived relation to the actual thinking of his opponents (otherwise Paul's rhetorical purposes would not have been served), but theoretic to the extent that it includes what to Paul's mind were the "true nature" and possible consequences rather than the simple substance of his antagonists' views. We are left with a "legalistic" picture of a righteousness pursued through the law apart from Christ, grace, faith, and the promise only if we are guilty of a static reading of Paul's very dynamic texts (68-69, 145-46, 165-66, 177).

(On the other hand, Thurén believes, recent Pauline scholarship has correctly moved beyond Sanders's "one-sided amendment" of earlier studies on rabbinic theology to a more balanced view. Ancient Judaism was more diverse than Sanders has allowed. "Both divine grace and human obedience could be emphasized," and both are repeatedly seen to have a role in salvation. We seldom find in Jewish texts [or, for that matter, in many early Christian texts] Paul's "radical view of man's universal guilt and explicit disregard of the human contribution to salvation" [147-48, 177-78]. Paul made grace and works exclusive alternatives — in the process, giving "grace" a restricted meaning not normally borne by the term [170] — in a way that Judaism did not. Judaism did not, like Paul, emphasize grace or faith alone while "totally rejecting the role of good works for salvation" — and to that extent at least it provided a basis for Paul's rhetorical differentiation between a "righteousness of the law" and that of faith [142, 146, 178].)

Why, in the end, did Paul reject the law? Part of the answer may lie in the perception that the law constituted a barrier between Jews and Gentiles that "must be eliminated before true universal monotheism is possible." The prophets themselves had proclaimed the "religious differentiation between Jews and Gentiles as temporal" (163). Perhaps Paul simply took the further step of proclaiming that the source of the differentiation, the Torah, was transient too.

But the question then arises why universal monotheism could not have been reached by proclaiming the universal validity of the law apart from the boundaries it imposed upon Jews (166). Something deeper must be at stake — and an old, now unpopular idea may provide a glimpse of the answer. Regardless of what actually happened in first-century Judaism, those who possess a law are, in principle, susceptible to the temptation to boast not simply of its possession, but also of their compliance with it (166). It is common for scholars now to confine the boasting excluded by Romans 3:27 to the possession of the law, but the thesis there stated is expanded on and illustrated in chapter 4, where it is allowed that *if* one is justified by works, then one has reason to boast, though boasting is ruled out where there is dependence on grace. And 2:23 suggests that boasting in one's possession of the law is appropriate only *if* one complies with its commands. The boasting ruled out by the message of faith in 3:27 is thus likely both that of the possession of the law and that of one's obedience to it (169-71).

Clearly Paul thinks that where the works of the law play a role in salvation, boasting of one's righteousness is at least a theoretic possibility (Phil. 3:4-6 suggests it was not only theoretic [168-69]). Yet Paul's opposition to boasting that deprives God of his glory is expressed in different contexts and appears to be basic to his thinking (173). Undoubtedly he thought God must disapprove of such boasting (177). What, most profoundly, was wrong with the law for Paul may well have been that it provoked pride and trust in something other than God (183).

Jean-Noël Aletti's studies of Romans have culminated in two monographs designed to highlight the coherence in Paul's argumentation that becomes apparent when attention is paid to its rhetorical features.[7] Noteworthy in particular is Aletti's insistence that interpretation be guided by Paul's own *propositiones* (i.e., by Pauline affirmations, often provocatively formulated, that then become the subject of clarification and justification in an argumentative unit) (*Clefs*, 36; "Modèle," 9-10; "Romans," 1560). But Aletti's studies also show full awareness of the work of E. P. Sanders: Sanders's portrayal of Judaism as based on covenantal nomism is warmly endorsed, and Aletti agrees that Paul himself understood Judaism very much as Sanders has described it. For Aletti, however, Paul engaged covenantal nomism in ways more fundamental and forceful than Sanders would have us believe. In the epistle to the Romans Aletti sees an extended work of deconstruction in which Jewish understandings of the nature and function of the law are first undermined, then replaced by a Christian configuration (*Loi*, 292-94). Here we note only a few key illustrations of Paul's procedure as Aletti understands it.

For Aletti (as, on this point, for many others) Romans 1:16-17 represents the main *propositio* developed in the argument of the epistle ("Modèle," 15-17). The first main section that follows (1:18–4:25) elaborates on the thesis that Jews and Greeks alike are justified by faith alone. It may be divided into two subsections. The first, 1:18–3:20, deals — on the basis of expectations and ideas found within Judaism itself ("Justice," 362-63) — with the operative principles of divine retri-

---

7. The parenthetical page references that follow in this section are to the works of Jean-Noël Aletti, using the short titles shown in the bibliography.

bution, and anticipates the obvious Jewish objection to Paul's *propositio:* grace and justification, a covenantal nomist would point out, are already to be found within the Mosaic system; indeed, apart from its commands and its provisions for pardon, righteousness is unthinkable. In the second subsection (3:21–4:25) Paul develops his own thesis, on the basis of his own theology, that justification is by faith alone, apart from the works of the Mosaic law ("Romans," 1557-58).

The first subsection, Aletti believes, is much misunderstood. Paul is often thought to be bent on establishing the universal sinfulness of humankind (*Clefs,* 68-69): heedless human beings must be awakened to the reality of their sin, roused to shame and repentance, and thus prepared to receive the gospel (77-78; *Loi,* 66). Aletti notes, however, that Jews who loved the law and aimed to observe it would certainly have granted that "all have sinned"; they nonetheless drew a firm distinction between themselves and the "sinners" or "wicked" (Gentiles and apostate Jews), believing that in Torah God had provided for the atonement and forgiveness of their failings (42-43). It was thus hardly the case that Paul proposed dependence on grace to Jews relying simply on their works: the issue was rather *where* God's grace is effectively to be found (89, 293-94). Accordingly, Paul's aim in the opening chapters is, first, to undermine traditional boundaries between Jews and Gentiles, then to show that Jews not only commit *acts* of sin but that they, like Gentiles, *are* "sinners" (in the strong sense of the word), dominated by the power of "sin" and subject to God's judgment ("Cohérence," 154-55; *Loi,* 272-73). They are thus (and this, of course, is the point) in need, no less than Gentiles, and on no other terms than they, of divine justification ("Romans," 1566).

The coherence of the path by which Paul reaches this conclusion is often underestimated because insufficient attention is paid to the signposts Paul provides of the stages in his argument. Prior to Romans 3 Paul makes no attempt to establish the universality of sin; indeed, the *propositio* with which this section opens (1:18) announces God's opposition, not to the sins of *all* human beings, but to *all* ungodliness and wickedness (*Loi,* 63). The thesis is surely unexceptionable to Jewish readers, though formulated without any reference to differences between Jews and Gentiles (unlike many commentators, Paul does *not* claim that the sins enumerated in Rom. 1 are typically Gentile) in a way that contributes to the leveling of such distinctions (62; "Romans," 1558-59). In chapter 2 Paul emphasizes the well-known biblical principles that God judges all according to their works, that he is impartial, that he knows the hearts of all, and that the circumcision that matters is that of the heart (*Loi,* 273-74); but the upshot of *Paul's* restatement of these traditional themes is that, before the divine judgment seat, boundaries between Jews and Gentiles are not as clear-cut as Jews imagine them to be. In the first sixteen verses of the chapter he establishes that a decisive line cannot be drawn between those (i.e., Jews) who know God's will because they have the Mosaic law and those (i.e., Gentiles) who do not know it; the latter, without the law but through their consciences, have a conception of what is right ("Cohérence," 165-66; *Loi*, 55; cf. "Justice," 369). If God declares righteous those who obey the law (so 2:13), must he not — impartial as he is — approve as well those non-Jews who follow their conscience ("Cohérence," 166-67; *Loi*, 56)? Paul's point (nota bene!) in 2:14-15 is not to affirm that such good Gentiles exist, but to insist on the principle that a God who is impartial must judge Jews and Gentiles in the same way: doers of good (for the *principle* it makes no difference whether any such can be found) must be rewarded, while the wicked must be punished (56-57; "Romans," 1564). In 2:17-24 Paul is by no means saying that all Jews are guilty of the sins listed, but merely that some Jews are, and that they are subject to the same judgment as Gentile wrongdoers (*Loi*, 58-59, 64). By the end of chapter 2, then, Paul has established that the sole criterion for determining who is righteous is the "circumcision of the heart" — and that such a category is by no means the private preserve of Jews (60).

It is first in chapter 3 that Paul declares the universality of sin's dominion (3:4, 9, 12, 19) (cf. "Incohérence," 50-53). Given that an assessment of the human heart is at stake, Paul makes no attempt to establish the thesis on the basis of his personal experience; only God can pronounce such a verdict ("Cohérence," 174; *Loi*, 64). Hence Paul establishes the point by citing Scriptures that speak, first, of the universality of human sinfulness (3:10-12), then of the perversity of all things human (3:13-18) ("Romans," 1565). If, as Scripture insists, Jews no less than Gentiles are sinners (in the strong sense of the word) and liable to God's judgment, then the provisions of the Mosaic law for atonement and forgiveness have clearly proved ineffective (3:19-20) — and it is "apart from" them[8] that Jews no less than Gentiles must be justified (*Loi*, 60, 65).

That justification is by faith, and apart from the works of the Mosaic law, is then declared in the *propositio* of 3:21-22 and developed in the argumentative unit it introduces (3:21–4:25). The works Paul means to exclude are those demanded by the Mosaic law: Abraham was justified without them (he was, after all, uncircumcised at the time), and so must be the "children" whom he was promised and who are born as his "children" when they come to share their "fa-

---

8. The law's provisions for atonement are surely part of the law that Paul insists can have no part in justification (Rom. 3:21-22). Paul does not pause at this point in his argument to ask why these provisions were given. Nonetheless, his borrowing of terms from the Jewish sacrificial cult in 3:25 presupposes that he interpreted its rites typologically. They thus served to prefigure Christ's death on the cross and to prophesy redemption through him (*Clefs*, 237-39; cf. "Cohérence," 160-61).

ther's" faith. Arguing from Scripture, Paul thus rules out the Jewish "path to righteousness" through the law.[9] His point, however, goes still deeper. In presenting Abraham as one who was justified as a sinner and made a father beyond all human possibility, Paul insists that the work was entirely God's own. Moreover, the justification of ungodly Abraham by faith, apart from the works of the law, was paradigmatic of the justification of all sinful humanity apart from any good works of their own (100). The gratuity of justification is underlined by the *gezerah shewa* introduced in 4:3-8:[10] just as the forgiveness by which, according to Psalm 32:1-2, David's sin was not "counted" against him was an act of divine grace, so must be the justification by which Abraham was "counted" righteous in Genesis 15:6 (*Clefs*, 100-101; 91-94).

Not until Romans 7 does Paul take up in detail the divinely appointed function and, at the same time, the weakness of the Mosaic law ("Criticism," 77-95; *Loi*, 135-65). The discussion belongs to Paul's clarification of the provocative *propositio* in 5:20-21, by which the law of Moses was said to cause sin to "abound." The law is said to be holy but unable to effect a transformation of sinners (and such, as 5:19 indicates, are all the descendants of Adam) or to deliver them from the death to which sin has brought them ("Romans," 1576). Of note here is Aletti's understanding of the subject of 7:14-25. The "I" in these verses is precisely the pious Jew who knows the law and desires to practice it (though, of course, the servitude to sin which Paul attributes to faithful Jews in this best-case scenario applies to all other human beings as well). Paul is again responding to an inevitable objection of Jews who see in the law not simply a statement of the divine will, but divine protection, sustaining, and support in their moral endeavors. Using the rhetorical device of *antanaclasis* (i.e., repeating the same word in different, and even opposing, senses), Paul observes that Jews seeking to observe the law of Moses in fact find that that law puts them in contact with laws other and less benign: that of sin, and that of the flesh, which renders them prisoners of sin's law (7:21-25) (cf. "Rhétorique," 43-44). Such, Paul believes, is the situation of even pious Jews, though it is not one they themselves recognize. Paul portrays such Jews as aware of their plight and cry-

---

9. In Rom. 10:5-17 (the explanation [or *probatio*] of the *propositio* in 10:4 [*Clefs*, 123]) Paul contrasts the two economies, that of the law and that of faith (or of Christ). Paul's point in these verses is to show that the two economies are incompatible, the former based on "doing" (so 10:5), the latter on a "believing" that involves no human pursuit, but the accepting of a divine visitation and gift (10:6-8). Paul here presents the path to life prescribed by the Mosaic law in the terms in which it was understood by Jews (10:5 is a quotation of Lev. 18:5), believing that his earlier argument had already established that this path was not viable (*Clefs*, 108-9, 118; *Loi*, 218-26).

10. That is, since Gen. 15:6 and Ps. 32:1-2 (LXX 31:1-2) have in common an occurrence of the Greek word λογίζομαι, the two passages are allowed to illuminate each other.

ing for deliverance because he believes that, when those subject to the law discover the contradiction in their lives, they desire liberation from it — and the desire itself marks the beginning of the path to deliverance.

The law, then, serves to reveal both God's truth and justice and human deceit and injustice, though it offers no escape from divine wrath; that is the prerogative of faith (*Clefs*, 240; cf. "Justice," 373).

iii. Paul's Apocalyptic Worldview: J. Louis Martyn

Louis Martyn's writings on Paul must be included in our study, though one suspects they would not have been substantially different if *Paul and Palestinian Judaism* had not been written.[11] The discussion is here placed with that of critics of the new perspective, though Martyn comments on Sanders's work with respect and appreciation, adopts Sanders's understanding of first-century Judaism as marked by covenantal nomism, and agrees with Sanders that Paul's own theology proceeded from solution to plight.

But Martyn's Paul does not reject Judaism because it is not Christianity, then devise sundry and desultory arguments to rationalize his position. Rather, he is driven by a burning theological conviction: God has invaded the cosmos to set things right. Human beings can contribute not a thing to their redemption. Hence the *human* activity of law observance (the works of the law) is necessarily and emphatically rejected by Paul as a factor in the *divine* "rectification"[12] of human beings. So bald a summary conveys little of the power of Martyn's portrait of the apostle and his thought; it suffices, however, to suggest its distance from the Paul of the new perspective.

If the apostle as seen by advocates of the new perspective responds to his opponents with a (more or less nuanced) critique of Judaism as it really was, Louis Martyn's Paul dismisses *all* religion as a mere "human enterprise" while proclaiming that the old world has been done away with, the new has dawned. What Martyn misses in many contemporary treatments of Paul (those of Ernst Käsemann and J. Christiaan Beker are notable exceptions) is a grasp of the "apocalyptic" thrust of the apostle's thought. His own work focuses on the letter to the Galatians. So will our summary, though we will touch upon areas in which Martyn thinks Romans (written in part, he believes, to correct possible misinterpretations of the earlier letter) offers a somewhat different view.

---

11. The parenthetical page references in this section are to the works of J. Louis Martyn, using the short titles shown in the bibliography.

12. So Martyn renders δικαιοσύνη; traditionally, "righteousness" or "justification."

Martyn insists (following Sanders and, as he duly notes, Karl Barth) that Paul's thinking proceeded from solution to plight. Economy of presentation prescribes a departure from that order in our summary.

The Human Plight

In Galatians 1:4 Paul quotes a Jewish Christian formula that is "to a significant degree foreign to [his] own theology" (*Galatians*, 90). According to the traditional formula, "Christ died for our sins." Paul does not reject the formula: he knows that people "commit discrete transgressions" (97). But he immediately corrects it by identifying the more fundamental human need for deliverance from "the present evil age." The drama of right and wrong involves more actors than human beings and their Creator; in Paul's (apocalyptic) way of thinking, the world has fallen under the control of malevolent, anti-God powers who hold humanity in bondage. Slaves as they are, human beings are in no position to initiate their own redemption. God must invade a world turned hostile to him, vanquish the forces that tyrannize humankind, and liberate their thralls.

For Jews and Christians alike the divine response to humanity's dilemma begins to take shape with Abraham, but for Paul the divine promise to Abraham "and to his seed" (Gal. 3:16) cannot be rightly understood apart from Christ, the (singular) "seed" in which it found fulfillment. In explicitly denying that the promise was given to a plurality of people ("the text does not say, 'and to the seeds,' as though it were speaking about many people"), Paul makes it clear that the ethnic descendants (plural) of Abraham do not constitute the promised seed. No doubt the "teachers" (those whose influence on his Galatian converts Paul was writing to oppose) invited Gentiles to enter Israel, the already existing people of God, by adopting the terms of its covenant. *Their* thinking thus retained the framework of covenantal nomism found throughout first-century Judaism. Paul has at times been thought merely to have modified their position by proposing different terms for admission to the people of God. But at least for the Paul of Galatians, no people of God *existed* prior to Christ.[13] On the contrary: "prior to the coming of Christ the human race was essentially an enslaved monolith" (*Issues*, 172). The promise to Abraham "and to his seed" was in a state of suspension (it "sat out the dance" of Israel's history ["Events," 172]) until the (singular) "seed" came of whom it spoke (3:19). In Christ its nonethnic character — "both at its inception and in its fulfillment" (*Issues*, 175) — is re-

---

13. On this point Romans reflects further thinking on Paul's part, though he continued to deny that divine election functioned in an ethnic way.

vealed. The promise was based solely on God's elective grace and pointed to the day when God would incorporate human beings, regardless of race, into Christ, the "seed" of Abraham.

The Sinaitic law was undoubtedly the starting point of the teachers' theology, where it was seen as God's fundamental response to the human dilemma: Christ died to atone for transgressions against the law, but the boundaries of the people of God were still thought to be defined by the charter given on Mount Sinai. For Paul, on the other hand, the Sinaitic law must be reckoned among the *anti*-God powers holding humanity in bondage. God (at least in Galatians) had nothing to do with its origin.[14] Had God been the giver of the law, there would have been no need of Moses as mediator; as a single party, God would have acted on his own behalf. Mediation was required because the law was instituted by a *plurality* of angels — acting in the absence of God (so Martyn understands 3:19b-20).

Whereas the voice of divine *blessing* speaks in the promise to Abraham, what the law imposes on humankind is its (*not* God's) *curse*. Both Jew and Gentile are subject to that curse, for "the universal power of the Law's curse consists precisely of its act in differentiating and separating observant from non-observant, the pious from the godless, Jew from Gentile" (*Galatians*, 327). Indeed, as the ancients were inclined to understand the fundamental elements of the cosmos in opposite pairings (air versus earth, fire versus water), so for Paul the pairing of Jew and Gentile, representing the realms of law and not-law, is the most fundamental of the various pairs of opposites (or antinomies) that make up the "elements of the cosmos" and that themselves hold humanity in bondage (see 3:28; 4:3, 9). The divine blessing promised to Abraham envisaged a humanity united in Christ; on the other hand, a differentiating law can only curse, and within its "cursed realm no one is being set right" (312). Hence the law's promise that "the one who does the commandments will live by them" (3:12, quoting Lev. 18:5) is false, in flat contradiction of the *divine* promise that "the one who is rectified by faith will live" (Gal. 3:11, quoting Hab. 2:4).

To this negative depiction of the law two qualifications must be added. First, though God (in Galatians) "had no role of any kind in the genesis of the Law" (366), he was nonetheless able to use it for his purposes: "the Law was compelled to serve God's intention simply by holding all human beings in a bondage that precluded every route of deliverance except that of Christ" (363). Second, though Paul distinguishes the divine voice that communicates promise

---

14. In Romans the Sinaitic law is the law of God, not in itself an anti-God power. It has, however, been made an instrument in the hands of sin.

and blessing from the cursing, enslaving voice of the law, in Galatians 4:21 he indicates that *both* voices can be found *in* the Law. The promise to Abraham may be said to belong to the original — pre-Sinaitic — divine law, together with the single guiding sentence about divine love found in Leviticus 19:18 (cited positively in Gal. 5:14). This divine law must not be confused with the Sinaitic law that originated with angels, imposed a plurality of commands on the Jews and, on humankind, the curse of differentiation between Jew and Gentile, circumcision and uncircumcision, law and not-law. To be sure, it is only in Christ that the two voices of the law can be distinguished — as it is only in Christ that the original divine law is restored to its intended purity (and so becomes the "law of Christ" [Gal. 6:2]).

Not only did the Sinaitic law differentiate between Jew and Gentile, circumcision and uncircumcision; it also introduced the distinction between sacred and profane that is at the foundation of all religion. Religion is "the various communal, cultic means — always involving the distinction of sacred from profane — by which human beings seek to know and to be happily related to the gods or God" (*Issues*, 79). Far from being able to counteract what is wrong with the world (no "human enterprise" could serve such a purpose [79]), religion is in fact "one of the major components of the wrong" (82), partly in that it enshrines the distinction between sacred and profane that makes up one of the antinomies that enslave humanity, partly in that it represents the initiative of slaves who cannot procure their own redemption rather than of the God who must redeem them. Judaism is itself such a religion — though it must be added at once that Paul does not denigrate Judaism per se; his polemic (even in Gal. 4:21-31) is directed against the Jewish Christian mission that would impose the Sinaitic law on Gentiles. And the world that Paul sees as now passed away is not specifically that of Judaism, but "the world of *all* religious differentiation" (*Galatians*, 565).

The Divine Solution

To say that Paul's thinking is *apocalyptic* does not mean that he sees the divine solution to humanity's plight in any mere self-disclosure on God's part. When God pulls back the heavenly curtain, he does so not to reveal what is on the other side but to "step through" and "[alter] irrevocably our time and space" (*Issues*, 282). God *invades* the cosmos by sending his Son, thus declaring war against the cosmic forces of evil that enslave the human race.

The latter are vanquished — on the cross. When Christ was crucified, the Sinaitic law pronounced its curse on *him:* the Son of God thus bore (and embodied) the curse that enslaves humankind, defeated it, and so liberated human beings from their state of enslavement.

Indeed, the cosmos itself in which humanity has lived — the cosmos founded on distinctions between Jew and Gentile, circumcision and uncircumcision, law and not-law, sacred and profane — was crucified with Christ on the cross. The old antinomies were done away with (Gal. 3:28; 5:6; 6:15). In Christ there is no new *religion* opposed to other *religions* (though the imperial church came to see itself that way), but a new *creation* in which distinctions between sacred and profane, and "all forms of opposition among religions" (81), no longer exist. To see the church as a mere "holy community that stands apart from the profane orb of the world" is to understand it in religious categories that it exists to abolish. The church is rather God's new creation, "the beachhead God is planting *in* the world" (79), the ever expanding community called into being by the Spirit of God as it invades the present evil age, bringing divine liberation to captive humankind. Ultimately all humanity — indeed, the whole cosmos — is to share in the divine deliverance.

The present time may thus be seen as the "juncture of the new creation and the evil age" (*Galatians*, 102). God's war of liberation was both "commenced and decisively settled" on the cross (101): the final outcome is not in doubt. Paradoxically, however, the divine invasion that brought an end to the antinomies on which the cosmos was founded (Jew and Gentile, law and not-law, sacred and profane) introduced a *new* antinomy, for the invasion of the Spirit provoked the resistance of the Flesh. (The teachers probably spoke of the "desire of the flesh" to refer to the "evil inclination," inherent in each individual, that is to be resisted by observing the law. For Paul the term is used, not of a mere inclination within the individual, but of a cosmic, suprahuman, anti-God power.) War is waged between them as each seeks to defend and expand its communal orb of power.

The church is the community of the Spirit both in its inception (the Spirit sets free the will of captive human beings, enabling them to respond to God in faith) and in its continued life (the Spirit cries out to God in the hearts of believers, bears fruit in their corporate life, and enables them to hear God's guiding voice). What has traditionally been considered a parenetic section in Galatians (5:13-24) is better seen as a Pauline *description* of the communities living in the spheres of the Flesh and the Spirit. Those in the Spirit's realm are not summoned to practice virtue and avoid vice — the traditional stuff of ethics, which deals with the "timeless concerns among human beings in general" (*Issues*, 233 n. 1). Rather they are given an account of the character of life in the new creation brought about and sustained by the divine Spirit. For them the operative imperative is the call to be (or to "live out") what they already are.

Rectification — by Faith

"Paul's fundamental perception of δικαιοσύνη is that of God's powerfully invasive deed in making the whole of the cosmos right" ("Events," 166 n. 12). When he says that divine rectification is operative "by faith" (Gal. 2:16; etc.), he refers to the faithfulness, shown to the point of death, of Jesus Christ. The Pauline contrast between rectification by faith and by the works of the law thus follows the pattern of other antinomies in Galatians in opposing divine to human activity: as *human* activity, law observance is impotent to rectify; the faithful death of Christ, on the other hand, represents "God's active power to set things right" (165).

Paul's point is fundamentally misunderstood when the "faith" of the antinomy, and the true source of rectification, is taken to be *human* faith *in* Christ. The gospel is then thought to open up a *human* possibility for approaching God by *faith* that is preferable to a path (such as that of law observance) based on *works*. When proponents of the new perspective speak of Paul's views about "getting in" and "staying in" the community of the people of God, the issues are put in terms congenial to the "teachers" and non-Christian Jews; but such terms distort the thinking of Paul, for whom the *human* path to blessedness is neither an issue nor a possibility. "The gospel is about the divine invasion of the cosmos (theology), not about human movement into blessedness (religion)" (*Issues*, 170). For Paul God's act of rectification is "no more God's response to human faith in Christ than it is God's response to human observance of the Law. . . . It is the *first* move" (151). Like repentance, faith does not even lie within the realm of possibility for the enslaved human will. Hence "Christ's faith is not only prior to ours but also causative of it" (*Galatians*, 276). Just as God's promise preceded and "elicited" Abraham's faith ("Events," 169), so the faith of Christians is "elicited, kindled, incited by the faith of Christ, enacted in his atoning death" (*Galatians*, 314).

Clearly the agenda for Martyn's writings on Paul has not been set by the debate surrounding the new perspective. Just as clearly, if central to the new perspective is the claim that Paul's rejection of the works of the law had nothing to do with opposition to a role for human activity in justification, then Louis Martyn must be reckoned among its most forceful critics.

iv. Paul's Theology of the Cross: Jürgen Becker

For those who said it couldn't be done, Jürgen Becker has written a recent, big, and important book on Paul that makes no mention of E. P. Sanders.

Not that Sanders has been singled out for neglect. The book proceeds virtually without reference to any secondary literature — indeed, without footnotes. Becker explains that he wished to reach out beyond the guild of exegetes to others with "a general interest in Paul," readers who might have been baffled or intimidated by references to endless academic discussions; as for scholars, Becker ventures to believe that they will recognize without prompting those to whom he is indebted.[15]

The following summary, though omitting issues of Pauline chronology and biography that are treated at length in Becker's study, will retain his disposition in outlining the development of Paul's thought.[16] Important for our purposes is the path, from election theology through that of the cross, by which Becker sees Paul arriving at an understanding of justification by faith that excluded any human contribution — and, thereby, any human boasting apart from that in Christ's cross.

The Pharisaism of Paul's day, following developments in Israel's Wisdom tradition, had identified the law of Moses with "pre-existent wisdom," the "inner law of all creation and history and the life norm of every human life" (41). Though Jews, as God's elect people, had been given the law in written form so that they might follow it and achieve life, all people, as God's creatures, are obligated to observe it: Gentiles are believed to know its requirements "by nature" (46-47; also 397). Obedience, moreover, is within the power of all: "the imperative 'you shall' addresses a person whose nature includes 'you can.' . . . Freedom of the will is Pharisaic doctrine" (49). "Every individual" has been given "the opportunity and duty to fulfill the Torah" (50).

Sadducees and Essenes interpreted the law's promise of "life" to its doers to refer to God's favor in this present age; for Pharisees — and here Pharisaism was indebted to early Jewish apocalypticism — the promised life was extended to that of the world to come, an age inaugurated by divine judgment (41-42, 49). Rewards and punishments would be assigned by God as wages are by an employer:[17] God will "settle accounts," giving people "credit" for their deeds as

---

15. Becker, *Paul,* xiii. Parenthetical page numbers in this section are to Becker's *Paul.*

16. Like Drane and Hübner, Becker sees in Paul's epistles evidence of significant development in his thought. Unlike Drane and Hübner, however, Becker does not see Paul revising or rejecting earlier positions; rather, new situations drove Paul to more profound understandings of the gospel.

17. Becker here refers to *m. Avot* 2:16: "[R. Tarfon] used to say: It is not thy part to finish the task, yet thou art not free to desist from it. If thou hast studied much in the Law much reward will be given thee, and faithful is thy taskmaster who shall pay thee the reward of thy labour. And know that the recompense of the reward of the righteous is for the time to come" (Danby's translation).

these are recorded in his book (48).[18] None can escape that judgment or its fearful finality: "deeds have a fundamental significance for salvation or damnation" (48). "The gate into ultimate final salvation is divine judgment" (42).

Pagan prospects were known to be grim. The whole Gentile world was "crooked and perverse" — its idolatry and immorality were frequent subjects of synagogue fulminations — and faced certain damnation (43-44). For Jews, on the other hand, the outlook was favorable: in making them his elect people, God had singled them out for salvation. Faithful Jews would find mercy at the judgment and be deemed righteous because they "[held] to the law as a lifelong task" and fulfilled the law's prescriptions in repenting of their sins (46). But though the outcome for them was benign, the issue must still be put to the test: Jews no less than Gentiles would be judged as individuals by their deeds.

Pharisaism was also marked by its stress on the sanctification of everyday life, a program that meant observance of purity laws in the daily lives, not simply of priests, but of the people as a whole (42). Even in the Hellenistic Diaspora a degree of separation from non-Jews was required, an insistence designed to preserve the distinctiveness of God's covenant people (42). When the Jewish Christians of the Damascus synagogue accepted into their fellowship God-fearing Gentiles who had received God's Spirit, Paul, as the local "spokesman for anti-Christian Jews," "proceeded . . . aggressively" against them (42, 63-69). "Seeing in the law the all-defining norm of life mean[t] . . . distinguishing between the chosen people of God and the sinful nations, and erecting immovable boundaries" (67).

But after the resurrected Jesus appeared to Paul, the latter was quick to deduce that Christ's followers were *not* to be persecuted for the sake of the law; indeed, he himself took up a mission to Gentiles *without* regard to the law (76). "The Father-God of the law" had become for him "the Father of Jesus Christ." Faith in Christ, it followed, was sufficient for salvation. And the people of God destined for salvation were not Jews and proselytes who swelled their number, but the Christian church that was open to all people (78). All these conclusions ensued from Paul's experience of the resurrected Christ.

---

18. Among the texts to which Becker refers are *m. Avot* 2:1 ("Be heedful of a light precept as of a weighty one, for thou knowest not the recompense of reward of each precept; and reckon the loss through [the fulfilling of] a precept against its reward, and the reward [that comes] from transgression against its loss. Consider three things and thou wilt not fall into the hands of transgression: know what is above thee — a seeing eye and a hearing ear and all thy deeds written in a book") and 3:1 ("Akabya b. Mahalaleel said: Consider three things and thou wilt not fall into the hands of transgression. Know whence thou art come and whither thou art going and before whom thou art about to give account and reckoning . . . — before the King of kings of kings, the Holy One, blessed is he") (Danby's translation).

An initial Pauline mission in northern Syria and Cilicia was followed by a dozen years or so in which the apostle was active in, or served the outreach of, the church in Antioch. That church now took the lead in early Christianity's expansion among Gentiles, conveying the gospel to those who (unlike the Gentiles reached by the Damascus Christians) had no previous association with Judaism, and founding Gentile Christian churches (86). God's evident blessing on their proceedings was again perceived in the divine gifts of faith and the Spirit to uncircumcised Gentiles. That a person is not justified by works of the law but only through faith in Christ (Gal. 2:16; Rom. 3:28) was a fundamental conviction of the Antiochian church. The law whose observance was thus shunted aside amounted, of course, to the ritual and ceremonial aspects of the Mosaic code, those requirements that served to separate Jews from Gentiles (105). Still, in abandoning parts of the Mosaic law the Antiochian Christians were effectively denying to the law any soteriological function. They came to treat the law as the antithesis of faith (104).

Paul himself played such a major role in shaping developments in Antioch that his early thought cannot be distinguished from Antiochian church tradition (104). Though he wrote no letters during the period, traditional material in later letters reflects his early thinking (83). Moreover, 1 Thessalonians was written so soon after Paul left the Antiochian mission field that we can regard its statements as substantially Antiochian (130).

Both proximity to Judaism and distance from it emerge as discernible features. Jewish notions of election remain central: from a humanity that had provoked God's wrath and faced imminent judgment — Paul's expectation of an *imminent* end was taken over from the Jesus tradition (121) — God had graciously elected a people to obtain eschatological salvation (44, 132). On the other hand, Paul saw no relation between this end-time election of people from all nations and Jewish claims to be God's covenant people (138). The divine call, for Paul, was mediated by the proclamation of the gospel and the accompanying operation of the Spirit in bringing its hearers to faith (132-34). The proclamation itself issued from the one true God, the creator and eschatological judge of all humankind; in this respect, too, the Christian message had obvious links with synagogal preaching. But according to the Pauline and Antiochian gospel, God had, just before the last judgment, raised his Son from the dead to be a Savior (136). Furthermore, the gospel was distinguished by the transforming presence of the Spirit of God, a power that the law did not possess. It brought not only the responsibility but also the resources to please God, thereby rendering superfluous the requirements of the law (105-6, 135-36; also 393).

Paul never jettisoned the election theology of his early Antiochian period, but during his "Ephesian period" (so Becker labels the period reflected in the Corinthian letters, Philemon, and Philippians A [= Phil. 1:1–3:1; 4:1-7, 10-23]) the apostle "redefine[d] the nature and boundaries of Christian self-understanding through the theology of the cross and the binding of freedom to love" (163). The new emphases marked Paul's creative response to Corinthian enthusiasts of the Spirit. Other early Christians spoke of the death of Christ; Paul became the first to attach significance to the *cross* as the implement of execution. The insights gained in this period informed all Paul's subsequent writing (205-6).

To the Corinthians' way of thinking, the exalted Lord had triumphed *over* the cross. The hallmark of his followers' lives was thus to be found, not in the rigors of discipleship, but in the spiritual gifts they enjoyed: tongues, a wisdom hidden from the world, and ecstatic experiences of immediacy with the heavenly Lord (203-4). Claims of divine revelations led to divisions in the church (205). Whereas for the Paul of 1 Thessalonians the Spirit's guidance was to be evident in "the concrete everyday life of a good marriage and occupational honesty" (205), for the Corinthians it was seen rather in ecstatic experience that was *not* of this world. Moreover, the freedom brought by the Spirit to live in holiness and brotherly love was construed by the Corinthians as a freedom to maintain contact with the mores of their pagan past (211-12).

Paul's response centered on the demonstration of God's power in the weakness of the cross. In that light, human assessments must be overturned and all reality revalued: God chooses what is weak, what counts as nothing. "The crucified One makes known once and for all only the God who in the depths, in deathly misery, in lostness and nothingness intends to be God and Savior" (208). Nor is it the lot of Christians in *this* world to reign with the exalted Christ; they must rather take their stand with Christ crucified. On this side of death their knowledge is limited, their ecstasy momentary, their sins and temptations a continuing bane (210). Their only boast is in the Lord (209). The apostles themselves are not to be assessed on the basis of "present experiences of the Spirit," nor is their task to "[light] the fire of the Spirit everywhere and to promot[e] ecstatic experience" (223). Rather, it is to proclaim, in comprehensible speech and in adverse conditions, God's offer of reconciliation. The power of the Spirit on which the apostle relies is that of compelling faith in the gospel (236-38).

Paul's theology of election and that of the cross are both presupposed in the theology of justification that marked the final phase of his theology (279). For that matter, justification terminology itself was not new, though its occurrence in earlier epistles was sporadic and traditional (279). The reorientation of his message by which justification became a central theme was occasioned by the opposition Paul countered in Galatians and Philippians B (= Phil. 3:2-21 and 4:8-9). It found mature statement in Romans: "Romans develops the apostle's message of justification for the first time without direct polemics against an actual opponent and as a systematic framework for Pauline theology as a whole" (314).

Paul's language of justification was adapted from its usage in several "typical contexts" or "word fields." The first is that of traditional statements about the last judgment. From his time as a Pharisee Paul had believed in "an eschatological, forensic court scene": every individual must stand before the divine judge to have his or her works tested and a "divine authoritative judicial verdict" given. The approved would be "justified" (280-83). The Antiochian church had also used justification terminology for the present experience by which the divine Spirit, conveyed through baptism, transformed human existence, making the "unrighteous" "righteous" (283, citing 1 Cor. 1:30; 6:9-11). Nor should the contribution to Paul's terminology of such Septuagintal texts as Genesis 15:6, Psalm 143:2, and Habakkuk 2:4 be overlooked (285).

Paul's developed usage is marked by its "polemical edge regarding the law" (286). This, too, was anticipated in the Antiochian formula echoed in Galatians 2:16 and Romans 3:28: already in Antiochian theology, works of law were deprived of any salvific significance and the acceptance of the missionary message of the church, leading to baptism, was declared the source of justification (287). Paul's mature theology of justification, while preserving these Antiochian emphases, was conditioned no less by his later theology of the cross: those who regard the works of the law as requirements for salvation thereby grant their own "legal achievements" a share in the redemption that is the work of Christ alone, and for which Christ alone is due glory (289). Both the Corinthians who boasted in their spiritual gifts and the Judaizers who demanded law observance were in effect "trust[ing] increasingly in what they themselves [were] and [could] exhibit," whereas one must boast only in the Lord — that is, "glory exclusively in the 'cross of Christ'" (290).

> Paul had to make clear to the Corinthians that in the gospel a God is at work who chooses the weak of the world, so that one cannot boast before God.... The Pauline God does not confirm the strengths of humanity (1 Cor. 1:26-27) but is always occupied only with saving what counts as nothing (1 Cor. 1:18) and thus with saving all, because before him all are as nothing and sinful. This creative sole-effectiveness of God, which alone reaches into the depth of human lostness, through which, further, the gospel can exist comprehensively for all, and which, in short, offers the gospel as grace ... — this is what Paul sees in danger of being betrayed when the Judaizers in Galatia preach circumcision. Since, for them, grace alone is apparently not enough because

and inasmuch as they additionally require observance of the law, in Paul's judgment they are saying something like this: God's sole creativity is not sufficient to save people. They themselves must do something in addition: works of the law. Only the two together make up righteousness. . . . In the Pauline sense we can see something in common between the fiery virtuosos of ecstasy in 2 Corinthians and the sober preachers of the law in Galatians: neither lets God be only God, because both in their different ways want to correct God as interpreted by the cross of Christ. (292-93)

For the Paul of Galatians, then, the formula "by works of the law shall no one be justified" represents a fundamental statement of the divine intention, not merely a concession that people's perversity prevents them from satisfactorily keeping the law (298). God's purpose from the beginning was not that the law should convey life and righteousness, but merely that it would discipline sinners, enabling them to live together under somewhat regulated conditions (299). Its validity has now ended for believers in Christ, though the latter are obliged to fulfill the commandment to love (the "law of Christ") inasmuch as it expresses the pattern of Christ's life, which his followers are to share (301).

If Galatians divides the epochs of history into the age of the law and that of faith, Philippians B is more concerned with the transformation of the individual from the old way of life to the new. The old for Paul meant the righteousness of the law and involved a "confidence in the flesh" that distorted the human relationship to God. Again, what Paul opposes is not a false conviction that one is capable of keeping the whole law, but an understanding of life that has failed to be informed by the significance of Christ (328-29). Through Christ "what counts for nothing is chosen and what claims to count for something becomes nothing, in order thus to be redeemed" (327-28). In this light the righteousness based on law betrays itself as a human product opposed to the divine gift of righteousness transmitted through Christ (330). Those who have received the gift are, to be sure, obliged to do God's will by conforming in their conduct with the ethos of the Christ event. Not that Christians themselves establish a relationship with Christ by imitating him; but their "understanding of life and living of life must be Christlike," and thus appropriate to the new reality of lives that have been granted and shaped by Christ (319, here referring to Philippians A). In practice, ethical norms advocated all over the world may be drawn upon (cf. Phil. 4:8-9), but they must be tested by their congruence with this model (331; also 394-95, 431, 434).

In the opening chapters of Romans much is repeated from the election theology of 1 Thessalonians and, indeed, from the heritage of synagogue sermons. All humanity stands under God's wrath. Gentiles are condemned in traditional

Jewish terms, while the contrast between Jewish privileges and failures in Romans 2 borrows from penitential sermons of the Hellenistic synagogue (358). The universal judgment of Romans 3:20 is derived from the authoritative voice of the Scriptures cited in 3:10-18 (359).

These theological judgments, it should be noted, are necessarily preceded by the human *experience* of the difference between what should be and what is (359; also 386). "For Paul, one's own knowledge of a failed design of life and the insight of bearing the responsibility for it are basic experiences of human life" (360). This experiential knowledge takes further shape, in the light of the gospel's offer of peace to God's enemies, in an awareness of sin, not simply as one's failure to keep specific commandments, but as "planning one's life and understanding the world apart from God. This is hostility toward God, because it robs God of the honor of being what he is for all reality" (361). Sin leads one to overestimate human possibilities, no longer acknowledging one's creaturehood or expecting everything good from God alone (362). A human being is thus not to be regarded simply as "a doer alternately of good or evil," nor is the sinner simply one in whom evil deeds outweigh the good; rather, "in an unfathomable way he or she is a sinner as a person and his or her sinful deed is the consequence of this being. . . . All deeds that do not proceed from faith are now sin" (390-91).

Conversely, the gospel offer of reconciliation is received by a faith that, in Romans 3:21–4:25, is no mere acceptance of a proclaimed message, but a "fundamental and constant orientation of the individual toward the God who is near in the gospel" (367). It is exemplified by Abraham, who, in contrast to "the person who works and expects wages," relied on God's promise (369). Again Paul is drawing on the theology of the cross spelled out earlier in 1 Corinthians 1:26-31, by which God chooses the "things that are not." That earlier exclusion of human boasting had already been taken up in Galatians 6:13-14 and Philippians 3, though there with a new focus: "in Galatians and Philippians B, Paul has extended the revaluation of all human values, known from 1 and 2 Corinthians, to righteousness under the law, so that now it too is included among the worthless things that give no reason to 'boast'" (370). Behind Romans 3:27-28, 4:2-5, and 5:1-5 lies this conviction that "anyone who achieved righteousness before God from works would have his (own) support apart from God, namely, his laudable way of life. . . . The basic sense of the question in 1 Cor 4:7 (a person receives everything of value from God) has become the fundamental description of the divine relationship, which the message of justification sets forth as the only thing possible before God" (371).

From beginning to end Paul's theological development was rooted in his own experience of God's call and of "the effect of the gospel on the worldwide mission field" (373). Its key is not to be found in a posited continuity with Old Testament–Jewish tradition, as though that sacred history was simply being carried forward in the church. Paul's "pressing concern is how he can let the Christ who is near in the gospel determine and value everything" (374). In the gospel God reveals himself as no mere bookkeeper, calculating the balances of human deeds for retribution on judgment day. "Rather, according to Paul, his nature consists in re-creating the unlovely so that under his love they become lovely, in turning enemies into reconciled people, in giving worth to the worthless. This is the self-characterization of the Father of Jesus Christ. That people can live only on this basis is the meaning and purpose of Paul's message of election, reconciliation, and justification" (379).

Chapter 14

The Quotable Anti-"Lutheran" Paul

In Part Two I have attempted to summarize studies of Paul significant for our purposes, but in their own terms, without caricature, and, indeed, for their own sake rather than simply to set the stage for the argument of Part Three, where caricature will of course be indispensable. Such is the state of the industry today that even the most industrious student of Paul finds it hard to keep abreast of the latest Pauline scholarship. Surveys of parts of the field can at least convey a sense of trends and developments and may even help us decide which of the many works we are not yet acquainted with we really must read for ourselves. Along some such lines I trust that even readers who find nothing in Part Three of this book persuasive, stimulating, or diverting may find something to be gained from the book's first two installments.

Still, there *is* a Part Three, and this seems the place, not for a summary of the summaries of Part Two, but for a highlighting of the most significant claims of the critics of the "Lutheran" Paul to be addressed in what follows. It seems best to cite these claims in the words of the critics themselves. After all, if their positions will be represented in Part Three in terms required by my argument and, no doubt, with an element of caricature, then it is only fair that they first be given the opportunity to caricature their own positions in terms of their own choosing.[1]

---

1. In a few cases scholars are quoted whose work, though important, has not been treated above. I have provided brief summaries of a much more extensive list of contributors to the debate on the new perspective on Paul in my article "Perspective."

i. Judaism Preaches Grace

Various aspects of the "Lutheran" reading of Paul were questioned long before Sanders. For the past quarter-century, however, the focus of the critique has been provided by Sanders's claim that Judaism was *not*, after all, a religion of works righteousness, but rather one of grace.

> On the point at which many have found the decisive contrast between Paul and Judaism — grace and works — Paul is in agreement with Palestinian Judaism. . . . *Salvation is by grace but judgment is according to works.* . . . God *saves* by grace, but . . . *within* the framework established by grace he rewards good deeds and punishes transgression. (Sanders, *Paul Pal. Jud.,* 543)

> Salvation . . . is always by the grace of God, embodied in the covenant. (Sanders, *Paul Pal. Jud.,* 297)

> Election and ultimately salvation are considered to be by God's mercy rather than human achievement. (Sanders, *Paul Pal. Jud.,* 422)

> We have misjudged early Judaism, especially Pharisaism, if we have thought of it as an early version of Pelagianism. (Wright, *Founder,* 32)

> Second, and fundamental to Jewish self-understanding and covenant theology, was the recognition and affirmation that Israel's standing before God was due entirely to the initiative of divine grace. (Dunn, *Theology,* 345)

> The Judaism of what Sanders christened as "covenantal nomism" can now be seen to preach good Protestant doctrine: that grace is always prior; that human effort is ever the response to divine initiative; that good works are the fruit and not the root of salvation. (Dunn, "Justice," 8)

ii. What Paul Finds Wrong with Judaism

If Judaism preached good Protestant doctrine after all, then what could Paul possibly have found wrong with it? According to Räisänen, Paul wrongly attributed to Judaism the wrong of pursuing works righteousness. For Sanders's Paul, Judaism was wrong because Christianity was right, and Judaism was not Christianity (i.e., it did not accept Jesus as the Christ). Furthermore, it put Gentiles at a decided disadvantage should they want to belong to the people of God: Jews had merely to remain Jews, whereas Gentiles had to adopt Judaism. Other scholars, picking up on the latter point, have freed Judaism from the outdated (and rather uninteresting) charge of legalism in order to indict it on more state-of-the-art offenses: nationalistic pride, ethnocentrism, racism, and the like.

> Paul suggests that non-Christian Jews (and wayward Christians) agreed with him on the goal of religion, which was righteousness, but disagreed on the means of attaining it: the "non-believing" Jews tried to achieve righteousness by works, whereas Paul had realized that it could only be received by grace through faith.
>
> Precisely this, however, is the problem: *Did* the Jews really look for "righteousness" (in anything like the Pauline sense of the word) in the Torah? Here the answer must be a clear "No." (Räisänen, *Law*, 178)

> Our analysis of Rabbinic and other Palestinian Jewish literature did not reveal the kind of religion best characterized as legalistic works-righteousness. But more important for the present point is the observation that in any case that charge is not the heart of Paul's critique. . . . Doing the law, in short, is wrong only because it is not faith. In itself obedience to the law is a good thing . . . and is faulted only when it seems to threaten the exclusiveness of salvation by faith in Christ. (Sanders, *Paul Pal. Jud.*, 550)

> *This is what Paul finds wrong in Judaism: it is not Christianity.* (Sanders, *Paul Pal. Jud.*, 552)

> What is wrong with the law, and thus with Judaism, is that it does not provide for God's ultimate purpose, that of saving the entire world through faith in Christ, and without the privilege accorded to Jews through the promises, the covenants, and the law. (Sanders, *Law*, 47)

> When [Paul] criticizes Judaism, he does so in a sweeping manner, and the criticism has two focuses: the lack of faith in Christ and the lack of equality for the Gentiles. (Sanders, *Law*, 155)

> If we ask how it is that Israel has missed her vocation, Paul's answer is that she is guilty not of "legalism" or "works-righteousness" but of what I call "national righteousness," the belief that fleshly Jewish descent guarantees membership of God's true covenant people. (Wright, "History," 65)

> The classic Protestant understanding of justification . . . has missed or downplayed what was probably the most important aspect of the doctrine for Paul himself . . . , the fundamental critique of Israel's tendency to nationalist presumption, not to say racial pride. (Dunn, "Justice," 14)

Paul's criticism of Judaism was, more accurately described, a criticism of the xenophobic strand of Judaism, to which Paul himself had previously belonged. (Dunn, "Apostate," 261)

Paul's dispute with Israel over the law had to do not with "grace" as opposed to "legalism" (in the normally accepted sense of the terms) but with a more ethnically inclusive vision of God and his law as over against one which was nationalistically restrictive. (Garlington, *Obedience of Faith*, 265)

What Paul finds wrong with unbelieving Israel is not some tendency on their part to attempt to win salvation through self-achievement. . . . Israel has considered righteousness to be their own and theirs alone (ἰδίαν), as a nationalistic possession. They have defined the covenant along ethnic lines, thereby excluding others. (B. Longenecker, *Eschatology*, 218-19)

The fundamental problem with "the pious Jew" for Paul is not so much his perversity in thinking he can earn salvation through his own striving apart from God's grace but his ethnocentrism, whereby he considers himself to be righteous by reason of God's grace upon the people Israel. (B. Longenecker, *Eschatology*, 228)

Paul was . . . troubled by, critical of, the "ethnocentrism" of biblical and post-biblical religion, and particularly the way it implicitly and explicitly created hierarchies between nations, genders, social classes. (Boyarin, *Jew*, 52)

The problem is not really legalism. It is nationalism — viz., the demand that all Gentile Christians must become part of the Jewish nation before they can enjoy the full blessing of God. (Hansen, *Abraham*, 162)

iii. What "Justification by Faith" Is For, and What "Not by Works" Is Against

1. In the opinion of many recent scholars, justification by faith and not by works (of the law) can hardly represent Paul's response to a Jewish "legalism" that did not exist; nor, indeed, is it allowed to have addressed the modern, Western, individualistic, introspective, guilt-ridden inquiry to which legalism was the wrong answer: "How can I, a sinner, find a gracious God?"

The first issue at hand is whether Paul intended *his* argument about justification to answer the question: How am I, Paul, to understand the place in the plan of God of my mission to the Gentiles, and how am I to defend the rights of the Gentiles to participation in God's promises? *or,* if he intended it to answer the question, which I consider later and western: "How am I to find a gracious God?" (Stendahl, *Paul,* 131)

The subject matter [in Gal. 2–4; Rom. 3–4] is not "how can the individual be righteous in God's sight?", but rather, "on what grounds can Gentiles participate in the people of God in the last days?" (Sanders, *Paul,* 50)

"Justification by works" has nothing to do with individual Jews attempting a kind of proto-Pelagian pulling themselves up by their moral bootstraps. (Wright, *Founder,* 119)

We must see justification by faith as a polemical doctrine, whose target is not the usual Lutheran one of "nomism" or *"Menschenwerke",* but the Pauline one of Jewish national pride. (Wright, "History," 71).

The issue being debated in Galatia was not the question of more modern, individualistic forms of Christian theology: "How can I, a sinner, be saved by a just God? Is it by my works or by my faith?" Instead, the issue is one of covenant theology. (B. Longenecker, *Triumph,* 106)

2. Justification (or righteousness) is rather a matter of *belonging;* of being "in," not "out"; of having membership in the covenant. Paul's concerns in advocating justification by faith were to promote inclusiveness and egalitarianism.

The discussion of "being righteoused by faith" is substantially the same [in Romans as in Galatians]. The problem is, again, that of Gentile inclusion in the people of God. The single most important theme of Romans is equality of Jew and Gentile. (Sanders, *Paul,* 66)

The language of "justification" . . . is *covenant* language. (Wright, *Founder,* 117)

δικαιοσύνη, I suggest, can often be translated, more or less, as "covenant membership." (Wright, *Climax,* 203)

What Paul means by justification, in this context, should therefore be clear. It is not "how you become a Christian," so much as "how you can tell who is a member of the covenant family." (Wright, *Founder,* 122)

Paul has no thought in this passage [Rom. 3:27, 29] of warding off a proto-Pelagianism, of which in any case his contemporaries were not guilty. He is here, as in Galatians and Philippians, declaring that there is no road into covenant membership on the grounds of Jewish racial privilege. . . . "Justification," as seen in 3:24-26, means that those who believe in Jesus Christ are declared to be members of the true covenant family. (Wright, *Founder,* 129)

The Pauline doctrine of justification by faith strikes against all attempts to demarcate membership in the people of God by anything other than faith in Jesus Christ; particularly, of course, it rules out any claim to status before God based on race, class or gender. (Wright, *Founder,* 160)

Justification means acceptance into a relationship with God characterized by the grace of Israel's covenant. (Dunn, *Theology,* 388)

Justification by faith is a banner raised by Paul against any and all such presumption of privileged status before God by virtue of race, culture or nationality, against any and all attempts to preserve such spurious distinctions by practices that exclude and divide. (Dunn, "Justice," 15)

Righteousness is understood — both by Paul and his interlocutors — in precisely the same covenantal way, as a membership term describing the status of those who belong to the community of God's people. (Donaldson, *Paul,* 121)

Righteousness . . . is a membership term: to say that one is righteous is not, in the first instance, to say that the person conforms with some absolute standard of moral perfection, but that the person is a member in good standing of the covenant community. (Donaldson, *Paul,* 171)

"Righteousness" terminology is firmly rooted in the deep soils of Jewish covenant theology. . . . To be marked out by righteousness, or to be justified, is primarily about having membership within the covenant people of the just and sovereign God whose own covenant righteousness will be established once and for all in the eschatological in-breaking of divine sovereignty. (B. Longenecker, *Triumph,* 104)

Paul's point is that the judicial pronouncement of God that declares someone to be within the covenant people is not based on Jew-Gentile distinctions. The covenant is no longer conceived in nationalistic terms. Even though as Jews they claimed a privileged status, now as Jewish Christians they know that only those who believe in Jesus Christ are declared by God to belong to the covenant family. The main emphasis of the argument here is that faith in Christ excludes Jewishness as the determining criterion for covenantal status. (Hansen, *Abraham,* 101-2)

3. The works (of the law) that Paul rejected are not the good deeds by which some have imagined themselves acceptable to a God known for his exacting standards; they are rather the works required by the Jewish law that erected barriers between Jews and Gentiles. Against Jews who relied on such works, and against the insistence that Gentile converts must be like them, Paul raised strenuous objections.

> The question is not about how many good deeds an individual must present before God to be declared righteous at the judgment, but, to repeat, whether or not Paul's Gentile converts must accept the Jewish law in order to enter the people of God or to be counted truly members. (Sanders, *Law,* 20)

> [Israel] was determined to have her covenant membership demarcated by works of Torah, that is, by the things that kept that membership confined to Jews and Jews only. (Wright, *Founder,* 130)

> The badges of membership by which some Jews had sought to demarcate themselves in the present time, ahead of the eschatological verdict, were focused upon the works of the law — the works, that is, which marked them out as covenant-keepers, as true Israel. The "works of the law" — sabbath, food-laws, circumcision — thus enabled them to attain a measure of what scholars have called "inaugurated eschatology," the anticipation in the present of what is to come in the future. (Wright, *Founder,* 132)

> When Paul said in effect, "All are justified by faith and not by works," he meant *not* "Every individual must cease from his own efforts and simply trust in God's acceptance," however legitimate and important an interpretation of his words that is. What he meant was, "Justification is not confined to Jews as marked out by their distinctive works; it is open to all, to Gentile as well as Jew, through faith." (Dunn, "Justice," 14)

> "Works of the law" do not denote any attempt to earn favour with God. There is nothing of that in the indictment. What we *do* see, and see in plenty, is a Jewish assumption of "favoured nation" status, and the corollary assumption that even when Jews sin it is not so serious as Gentile sin. It is *this* attitude and misapprehension which Paul sums up in the confidence of justification by works of the law. The clear implication being that it is his "works of the law" (since they maintain his covenant status and document his distinctiveness from Gentile sinners) which give the "Jew" his false confidence and which cloak the seriousness of his sin. (Dunn, "Works," 109)

"Works of the law" are what distinguish Jew from Gentile. To affirm justification by works of the law is to affirm that justification is for Jews only, is to require that Gentile believers take on the persona and practices of the Jewish people. (Dunn, *Theology*, 363-64)

Paul evidently did not associate "works of the law" with "good works." The two phrases operated within different substructures of his thought. (Dunn, *Theology*, 365)

There was always something odd not to say suspect about the assumption that Paul's polemic against "works of the law" was a polemic against "good works." (Dunn, *Partings*, 136)

Paul's definition of faith in this passage does not entail a dissociation of faith from works in general. . . . Rather, faith is dissociated from a certain type of works, namely, circumcision and other such works as were used as means of gaining or maintaining Jewish identity. (Hansen, *Abraham*, 114)

4. Paul's "doctrine" of justification by faith and not by works (of the law) is thus concerned to show, not how a sinner can find favor with God (don't even ask), but on what terms Gentiles can *belong* to the people of God (i.e., by faith in Christ *without* becoming Jews).

While Paul addresses himself to the relation of Jews to Gentiles, we tend to read him as if his question was: On what grounds, on what terms, are we to be saved? . . . But Paul was chiefly concerned about the relation between Jews and Gentiles — and in the development of *this* concern he used as one of his arguments the idea of justification by faith. (Stendahl, *Paul*, 3)

In [Rom. 1–8] Paul argues that since justification is by faith it is equally possible for both Jews and Gentiles to come to Christ. . . . He does not deal with the question of how man is to be saved — be it by works of law or by anything else. (Stendahl, *Paul*, 29)

The subject of Galatians is not whether or not humans, abstractly conceived, can by good deeds earn enough merit to be declared righteous at the judgment; it is the condition on which Gentiles enter the people of God. (Sanders, *Law*, 18)

"Being righteoused by faith in Christ not by works of law," then, in Galatians means substantively that Gentiles who have faith in Christ do not need to become Jewish and that even those who are already Jews in good standing are rightly related to God only by their faith in Christ. (Sanders, *Paul*, 63)

The real problem [dealt with in Galatians] is not "legalism" as usually conceived within traditional Protestant theology, but rather the question of whether one has to become a Jew in order to belong to the people of God. (Wright, *Climax*, 173)

The problem [Paul] addresses [in Galatians] is: should his ex-pagan converts be circumcised or not? Now this question is by no means obviously to do with the questions faced by Augustine and Pelagius, or by Luther and Erasmus. On anyone's reading, but especially within its first-century context, it has to do quite obviously with the question of how you *define the people of God:* are they to be defined by the badges of Jewish race, or in some other way? (Wright, *Founder*, 120)

"Justification by faith" was Paul's answer to the question: How is it that Gentiles can be equally acceptable to God as Jews? (Dunn, *Theology*, 340)

The primary thrust and cutting edge of the doctrine of justification as it emerges in Paul's writings is as an expression of his Damascus-road-given insight that *God's covenant grace is also for the Gentiles as Gentiles, that the eschatological fulfilment of the promise through Abraham does not require Gentiles to merge their ethnic identity into that of the Jewish people.* (Dunn, *Partings*, 124)

The leading edge of Paul's theological thinking was the conviction that God's purpose embraced Gentile as well as Jew, not the question of how a guilty man might find a gracious God. (Dunn, *Law*, 232)

For Paul it was possible for people of every race to be regarded as faithful and obedient apart from the distinctive marks of Jewish identity; no longer was commitment to circumcision, food laws, sabbath and feast days the test of loyalty to God and the enduring ideals of Judaism. All of the privileges of Israel, and more especially her standing as the special possession of God, were available to the nations simply by faith in Jesus the risen Christ. (Garlington, *Obedience of Faith*, 253)

Cut to the quickest of the quick, then, the issue that divides the "Lutheran" Paul from his contemporary critics is whether "justification by faith, not by works of the law" means "sinners find God's approval by grace, through faith, not by anything they do," or whether its thrust is that "Gentiles are included in the people of God by faith without the bother of becoming Jews." In the one case justification is directly connected to the Pauline gospel summed up in the words "Christ died for our sins" (1 Cor. 15:3) and "Be reconciled to God" (2 Cor.

5:20). It promises deliverance from sin. In the other case the good news of justification is found in the best-of-both-worlds scenario that it paints for Gentiles: "You people want to become Jews, but you are afraid of the knife. Have I got an offer for you!" It promises deliverance from a good deal of hassle. For readers whose attention has (understandably) lapsed but who want to know what is essential before beginning Part Three, the former is the position of the "Lutheran" Paul and the latter isn't.

Part Three

The Historical and the "Lutheran" Paul

Chapter 15

Matters of Definition, 1: "Righteousness" in Paul

What the law was meant to do, what it does and cannot do: the debate on Paul's view of these matters is endless. Yet relatively little attention has been paid to what Paul meant by the "law." Repeatedly we are informed in an almost casual way that νόμος in the epistles refers to "the Old Testament law." The ambiguity of the phrase goes unnoticed, questions of definition are apparently thought resolved, and with little further ado, discussion is launched into the more enticing topics mentioned above.

That haste makes waste is, however, one of those rare truths equally applicable to the diverse worlds of biblical scholarship and reality. In the course of a protracted yet inconclusive debate, we constantly stumble upon reminders that our subject needs better definition. Too late we learn that νόμος sometimes means, not the Old Testament law itself, but its perversion, "legalism"; that Paul's notion of law may or may not have formed a contrast with the gospel as he saw it; that Paul's law is emphatically based on works for some, as emphatically based on faith for others, while still other scholars deny that he posed the question in these terms. Moreover, even the casual reader cannot but notice that the debate on the relation between Christian conduct and the law flounders in part because the term is used differently by the various antagonists. In short, before we tackle what Paul says about the law, we need to know what he means by the term (chap. 16 below).

No less central or better defined is the term — ubiquitous in the current debate — "grace." While one may enthusiastically endorse the "new perspective" dictum that first-century Judaism was a religion of grace and acknowledge that it represents an important corrective of earlier caricatures, it is hardly pedantic to point out that more precision is needed before such a statement can illuminate a discussion of the "Lutheran" Paul. Pelagius and Augustine — to take but the most obvious examples — *both* believed in human dependence on divine grace, but they construed that dependence very differently. The "Lutheran" reading of Paul is not simply one that values grace without further definition, but one that (as we have seen) entails a quite specific understanding of the role grace plays in human salvation; that understanding, moreover, is linked to a particular understanding of human nature, of the human dilemma, and so on. New perspective criticism of the "Lutheran" paradigm has insisted that Paul could not have advanced "Lutheran" convictions in his polemic against Judaism since — *as Sanders has shown* — Judaism did not differ from Paul in its understanding of the relation between divine grace and human works. To assess the claim we need to look carefully at Sanders's discussion (which contains more nuances than is commonly noted) of the place of grace in Judaism (chap. 17 below).

Much discussed, by way of contrast, is Paul's use of *dikaio*-terminology (i.e., "righteous," "righteousness," "justify," etc.): much discussed *and* much disputed. The topic can scarcely be evaded here, given its centrality to issues of "Lutheranism" in Paul. We may begin with it.[1]

i. Terminology

When God says "Let there be," there is. When we say "Let there be," we may, for the sake of argument, *imagine* that there is.

Let there be an (indeclinable) English adjective "dikaios" whose occurrence corresponds strictly with that of the Greek adjective δίκαιος in the letters of Paul. And let there be an English noun "dikaiosness" and an English verb "dikaiosify" (passive: "to be dikaiosified") whose occurrence corresponds precisely with that of the Greek words δικαιοσύνη and δικαιόω (passive δικαιόομαι), respectively, in Paul's writings. Greek ἄδικος will then be "undikaios"; ἀδικία, "undikaiosness."

The problems that this wretched proposal[2] attempts to cope with are well known to students of the apostle. The English equivalent most often used for

---

1. One cannot interpret passages without some understanding of the terms they contain; for that reason it is well to begin our study of Paul with matters of definition. At the same time, at least any unusual (usage of) terminology cannot be understood apart from some interpretation of passages. Inevitably, repeatedly, and unapologetically, then, I cross the line in these chapters on "matters of definition" (chaps. 15 to 17) between the definition of terms and (at least a preliminary) interpretation of passages. Later (chap. 18) we will look at the relevant passages in their epistolary contexts.

2. In fairness to me I should point out that alternative proposals — such as the use of "rightwise" or "righteous" itself as a *verb* — cannot be said to have swept the field.

Paul's δίκαιος (righteous) has, to be sure, a cognate noun ("righteousness") that, with a modicum of goodwill and a maximum of explanation, may be allowed to stand for Paul's δικαιοσύνη; but it has no cognate verb whatever to represent Paul's δικαιόω. Moreover, the standard English rendering of Paul's δικαιόω (justify) is itself not entirely felicitous, partly because it bears no apparent relation to English "righteous" or "righteousness" whereas Greek δικαιόω is transparently related to δίκαιος and δικαιοσύνη; but partly also because of the circumstance — unfortunate in a translation — that the normal English meaning of "justify" ("to give a good reason for") is not what Paul means by δικαιόω.

To these much-discussed problems no satisfactory solution has been found. Permit, then, for the sake of argument, yet another unsatisfactory one. In the end, of course, existing rather than imagined English words will have to be found to render Paul's Greek terminology; it will be wise, however, to postpone such decisions for a time lest the results of our survey be steered by provisional renderings. If the English language is stretched in the process, we may at least claim an apostolic precedent: Paul undoubtedly employed *dikaio-* terminology in ways that went beyond the limits of normal Greek usage.[3]

At the end of this chapter we will explore the implications of what we have seen for the claim that *dikaio-* language is *covenant* language[4] and for Sanders's conclusion that, in Paul but not Judaism, it is "transfer" terminology. We begin, however, with Pauline usage. For our purposes three groups of Pauline texts employing *dikaio-* terminology may be noted. In the first group, dikaiosness is ordinary; in the second, extraordinary; in the third, divine.

ii. Ordinary Dikaiosness

The simplest place to begin is with the contrast Paul frequently draws between dikaiosness (and its various cognates) and sin (and its synonyms). The claim that all are "under sin" (Rom. 3:9) is confirmed by the scriptural declaration that not a single person is dikaios (3:10); the declaration is expanded upon in the following verses by various representations of human turpitude (3:10-18). If one would scarcely die for a person who is dikaios, how much more astounding is it that Christ died for sinners (5:7-8)? Dikaios*ness*, moreover, has nothing in com-

---

3. The focus here is on *Pauline* usage of the terminology as attested in the seven New Testament letters whose Pauline authorship is all but universally acknowledged. References to non-Pauline usage will largely be limited to the footnotes. For clarity of presentation, I will also proceed, in the text of the discussion of Pauline usage, as though what I say is uncontroversial. Concessions to reality on this score will also be confined to the footnotes.

4. See chap. 14, sec. iii.2 above.

mon with lawlessness (or simply "wickedness," Gk. ἀνομία, 2 Cor. 6:14). Readers in Romans 6 are urged to devote themselves to the service of dikaiosness rather than to that of sin (or "uncleanness," "lawlessness"; 6:18, 19).[5] Paul is not aware of wrongdoing on his part (οὐδὲν γὰρ ἐμαυτῷ σύνοιδα);[6] but since the Lord, not he, is the only competent judge of such matters, he does not claim to be dikaiosified (ἀλλ' οὐκ ἐν τούτῳ δεδικαίωμαι, 1 Cor. 4:4). Clearly to "dikaiosify" here means to find (to be dikaios, or to be) innocent of wrongdoing,[7] a judg-

5. The directive in this case is of course given to believers. Though there is some ambiguity — and much controversy — whether Paul thinks Christians are obligated to keep the law, there is no ambiguity when it comes to dikaiosness: it is (by definition, one may say) what Christians, like all other human beings, are to do. (In addition to Rom. 6, note that Paul uses *dikaio-* terminology in connection with Christian behavior in 1 Cor. 15:34; 2 Cor. 6:7; Phil. 1:11 [though δικαιοσύνης here may be a genitive of source; but see Fee, *Philippians*, 103-5]; 4:8; 1 Thess. 2:10. Paul's unusual usage of the terminology [sec. iii below] must not be allowed to obscure its more conventional employment [as it tends to do in Sanders's discussion; see *Paul Pal. Jud.*, 544; also *Law*, 6].) In this respect the *dikaio-* terminology parallels that of the "good," to the practice of which all are obligated (Rom. 2:10; 12:9; 13:3-4; 16:19; etc.).

6. A particular charge brought against him by the Corinthians may be in mind; cf. 1 Cor. 4:3; 9:3.

7. In the context, a judicial (or quasi-judicial) setting is in view: "It is the least of my concerns that I should be judged by you or by any human court; I do not even judge myself. For I am not aware of any wrongdoing on my part, but I am not thereby dikaiosified; the one who judges me is the Lord. So do not judge anything ahead of time, before the Lord comes" (1 Cor. 4:3-5).

In a judicial context, to "find (to be dikaios, or to be) innocent of wrongdoing" is of course to "declare innocent," "acquit" or "clear of any charge of wrongdoing." In a number of Septuagintal texts, the importance of dikaiosifying (δικαιοῦν) the dikaios is underlined, as is the wrongfulness of dikaiosifying the ungodly (δικαιοῦν τὸν ἀσεβῆ) (Exod. 23:7; Deut. 25:1; Isa. 5:23; cf. Sir. 9:12). (In the Hebrew parent text the terms rendered in Greek by δίκαιος and its cognates are regularly *tsaddiq* and its cognates.) In these texts: (i) The dikaios is repeatedly opposed to the "ungodly" (ἀσεβής). (ii) Both the dikaios and the ungodly are seen to be such because of what they themselves have done. This remains the case even if the Greek (and the underlying Hebrew text) intends those who are innocent or guilty in particular disputes rather than those who are upright or ungodly in general; after all, innocence or guilt in particular disputes is itself a matter of what one has, or has not, done. Still, the terms of the contrast (dikaios versus ἀσεβής) invite the broader interpretation; the implication is, presumably, that the dikaios and the ungodly have acted in character in the matter in dispute, so that the one who is dikaios (in this matter, as typically) is to be acquitted and the one who is ungodly (in this matter, as characteristically) is to be condemned. Cf. Yinger, *Judgment*, 25-26. (iii) The judgment by which either the dikaios (rightly) or the ungodly (wrongly) are dikaiosified (declared innocent, cleared of any charge of wrongdoing) affects neither the dikaiosness of the former nor the ungodliness of the latter. The ungodly who are dikaiosified do not thereby become dikaios, and the dikaios do not owe their dikaiosness to the act by which it is given judicial recognition. Nor, for that matter, do the dikaios who are unjustly condemned thereby become ungodly; dikaios they remain, though their cause has been subverted (so Deut. 16:19 [also Exod. 23:8]; cf. Prov. 17:15, 26). It is thus emphatically *not* the case that "the 'righteous' one is that one in a legal action . . . who wins

ment about himself that Paul might be expected to make on the basis of his own clear conscience, though he refuses to do so.

In brief, and in the broadest of terms, then, (ordinary) dikaiosness, as contrasted with sin, must be what one *ought* to do,[8] the dikaios (in the ordinary way) is the one who does dikaiosness,[9] and to dikaiosify is to "declare (to be dikaios, or to be) innocent of wrongdoing." A quotation from the Septuagint may be allowed to illustrate the ordinary sense of all three terms: Solomon prays that when an oath of innocence is sworn at the temple, God will hear in heaven and will judge τοῦ δικαιῶσαι δίκαιον δοῦναι αὐτῷ κατὰ τὴν δικαιοσύνην αὐτοῦ — in such a way, that is, as to "dikaiosify the dikaios, and so render to him according to his dikaiosness," or (in more normal English, where cognate terms can no longer be maintained throughout) "find innocent of any wrong-

---

his case or is acquitted" (Bultmann, *Theology*, 272; also Wright, *Founder*, 97-98, 119; "Theology," 39); the dikaios are those who *ought* to prevail in court — because they *are* dikaios — whether or not this happens. If the dikaios were by definition those dikaiosified in court, then the call to "dikaiosify the dikaios" would be a summons to a tautologous rather than a just act. (iv) The rightfulness of dikaiosifying the dikaios is more transparent in the Greek (and Hebrew) than in English equivalents. The verb δικαιοῦν conveys the sense, not simply of acquitting, but of giving the legal treatment appropriate to the dikaios. Such treatment can of course be given to those to whom it is not due, as well as to those to whom it is. But the justice of the latter procedure and the injustice of the former (note ῥήματος ἀδίκου in LXX Exod. 23:7) is more self-evident in Greek than in English.

For Sanders's refutation of Bultmann's claim that "in Judaism righteousness is a forensic/ eschatological term," see *Paul Pal. Jud.*, 494; rather, in much of Palestinian Judaism the righteous were "those who obeyed the commandments and atoned for transgression. They do not wait to be declared righteous; the righteous are alive and well."

8. Paul's ordinary usage thus approximates normal Greek usage, even though the "oughtness" of one's obligations is differently conceived. Cf. Burton, *Galatians*, 460-61; Olley, *Righteousness*, 21-43; Ziesler, *Meaning*, 47-51.

9. For 1 John the truth of the tautology is too readily forgotten: "Little children, let no one deceive you: the one who does dikaiosness is dikaios (ὁ ποιῶν τὴν δικαιοσύνην δίκαιός ἐστιν)" (3:7). That the *tsaddiq*/dikaios is the one who does *tsedaqah*/dikaiosness is apparent throughout the Hebrew Bible and the LXX; nowhere is it more explicit, however, than in Ezekiel. According to LXX Ezek. 18:5, the dikaios is the one who practices judgment and dikaiosness (ὁ δὲ ἄνθρωπος, ὃς ἔσται δίκαιος, ὁ ποιῶν κρίμα καὶ δικαιοσύνην . . .). What is entailed in the practice of dikaiosness, and that by which one is shown to be dikaios (so v. 9), is then spelled out in a list of things that ought to be done (vv. 6-9). The cases of a sinful son and a dikaios grandson of one who is dikaios are then discussed, and it is insisted that the dikaios will live because of the dikaiosness that he himself has done, whereas the one who sins will die. Then the following summary statement is made: "the dikaiosness of the dikaios will be upon him (δικαιοσύνη δικαίου ἐπ' αὐτὸν ἔσται), and the lawlessness of the lawless will be upon him" (v. 20). According to LXX Ezek. 33:13, all the dikaiosnesses (δικαιοσύναι, plural) that the dikaios has done will be forgotten if he commits lawlessness (in v. 18 he is said to turn from his dikaiosness [ἐν τῷ ἀποστρέψαι δίκαιον ἀπὸ τῆς δικαιοσύνης αὐτοῦ] and commit acts of lawlessness). See also LXX Ezek. 3:20.

doing the upright person,[10] and so render to him according to his uprightness" (3 Kgdms. 8:32; cf. LXX 2 Chron. 6:23). We need only note that dikaiosness (δικαιοσύνη) here is not simply what one ought to do but also what one has ("according to *his* dikaiosness") when one has done it. Paul, too, speaks of *one's* dikaiosness (2 Cor. 9:9, 10;[11] Phil. 3:9; cf. Rom. 10:3) — and of the *un*dikaiosness (ἀδικία, Rom. 3:5) of the one who does wrong — in this sense.[12]

How does Paul conceive "what one ought to do"? His most telling discussion is found in Romans 1:18-32, where he elaborates on a charge of *un*dikaiosness (ἀδικία) brought against all humanity (1:18; see also 2:8).[13] Those who would proclaim their autonomy and trumpet their freedom from obligations they choose not to embrace are tersely dismissed: such a stance represents a willful suppression of the truth (cf. 1:18, 28). We are born into a world not of our making, and incur thereby, and in the course of living, obligations that we may shirk or defy but that no human fiat can set aside. God, *as* God, is to be worshiped by his creatures (1:19-21, 25). As the creator and benefactor of human beings, he is due their honor and thanks (1:21). Moreover, what is appropriate to human sexuality has been determined in creation and is to be respected in human behavior (1:26-27). Human beings are further bound to respect the lives of their fellows, to devise no ill against them, to speak the truth about them, to keep faith in their commitments, to show compassion where compassion is called for — and so on (1:28-32). Such obligations are clearly not a matter of living up to some abstract ideal of rightness; rather, they amount to living in recognition of and in harmony with the reality of creation's God-given order and of one's place within it. They are thus inherent in the lot of all humans as such[14]

10. Or "the innocent person," to whom should be rendered "according to his innocence." See n. 7 above.

11. Note, however, that in 2 Cor. 9:9, 10 δικαιοσύνη reflects the more specific sense that Hebrew *tsedaqah* came increasingly to bear, "generosity toward the needy." See Przybylski, *Righteousness*, 66-74; Sanders, *Paul Pal. Jud.*, 199-201.

12. We may compare what Przybylski says about Tannaitic literature: "The noun *tsedeq* is used to denote all aspects of religious teaching which are normative for man's conduct. The person who lives according to the norm of *tsedeq* not only does righteousness *(tsedeq)* but also has righteousness *(tsedeq)*" (*Righteousness*, 75).

13. According to Rom. 1:18, God's wrath is revealed against all human ἀσέβειαν καὶ ἀδικίαν. Recent commentaries seem united in the recognition that the latter two terms are not to be sharply distinguished. That humans suppress the truth ἐν ἀδικίᾳ (1:18) is shown by their refusal to acknowledge God (1:19-23), so that ἀδικία can differ little from ἀσέβεια. See, e.g., Cranfield, *Romans*, 111-12; Dunn, *Romans 1–8*, 55-56; Schlier, *Römerbrief*, 50; Wilckens, *Römer*, 1:104.

14. Herein lies the truth in what theologians have spoken of as a universal "covenant of works" (cf. McGiffert, "Grace," 463-502; Møller, "Beginnings," 46-67); the terminology, however, is un-Pauline. Clearly the pan-covenantalism rampant in pockets of our discipline today is no recent development. See further sec. v below.

— and all at some level know both what they ought to do and that God rightly condemns those who refuse to do it (1:32). He reveals his wrath against all human *un*dikaiosness (1:18).

Thus not only is the requirement of dikaiosness given with the creation of human beings; their compliance is subject to the scrutiny and, ultimately, the (dikaios) judgment of God, who is committed to upholding the goodness of creation's order (see also Rom. 2:5; 3:5, 6).[15] Both the context and the future tense of the verb indicate that the last judgment is intended in 2:13: "It is not the hearers of the law who are dikaios in God's eyes (παρὰ [τῷ] θεῷ), but the doers of the law will be dikaiosified." One will be found dikaios at the judgment if one is a "doer [rather than a mere hearer] of the law." The text presumes that one is or is not such a doer, and presumably it is a matter on which human beings may have an opinion (i.e., one may be dikaios in the eyes of people as well as those of God, since Paul here feels a need to specify the latter). In the end, however, since only God is in a position to adjudicate the question rightly, and since Paul (not uniquely, of course) believed that God *will* do so, it is crucial that one is dikaios "in God's eyes." Note, too, that those who are dikaios *in God's eyes* are *not* dikaios because God has *made* them so; rather, God has *found them to be so* — inasmuch as they themselves are doers of the law. Similarly, since to be "dikaiosified [by God]" is here synonymous with being "dikaios in God's eyes," not even the verb suggests here that God *constitutes* one as dikaios; divine *recognition* of human dikaiosness is meant.[16] Furthermore, if dikaiosness is still a

15. It should be stressed that, though divine expectations of dikaios behavior by all human beings, and divine judgment of all according to those expectations, are spelled out most fully in Romans, they are implicit in *all* Paul's letters wherever he finds human behavior sinful or anticipates divine judgment. See chap. 18 below; also Hübner, "Rechtfertigung," 82-86, where the theme of human responsibility before God is rightly found fundamental to all Paul's thought. These convictions were of course Paul's already from the time of his Jewish upbringing. Cf., e.g., *Pss. Sol.* 9:4: "Our deeds lie within the choice and capacity of our soul, to do what is right (δικαιοσύνην) and what is wrong (ἀδικίαν) with the deeds of our hands; and in your righteousness you examine human beings. The one who does what is right stores up life for himself with the Lord, and the one who does what is wrong is to blame that his life is destroyed."

16. Compare what was said in n. 7 above about Septuagintal usage of the verb. Note that δικαιοῦν here does not mean *simply* "approve (without further definition)," "declare to be on good terms with God." It indicates approval *as a person who is dikaios* — *because* one is seen to be a "doer of the law." Good standing with God is a *result* of being deemed dikaios, but one is — and is found to be — dikaios on the basis of one's deeds. Note, too, that "ordinary" dikaiosness includes both "ethical" and "juridical" texts. *All* life is lived in God's presence and is subject to his scrutiny. Behavior that is dikaios (spoken of in the ethical texts) is behavior that *ought* to be dikaiosified in any trial (n. 7 above) and that *will* be dikaiosified by God: such is the insistence of the juridical texts, in which both the matter to be resolved (i.e., who is the dikaios in the situation under review) and the judgment itself (i.e., whether the one who is

matter of doing what one ought (as we saw elsewhere in Paul), and one is dikaios in God's eyes (or "dikaiosified" by God) if one is a doer of the law (as Paul says in Rom. 2:13), then it follows that the law is understood to prescribe what people ought to do. This is not — it may fairly be said — a revolutionary conclusion.[17]

That the *doers* of the law will be deemed dikaios at the final judgment (2:13) is consistent with the principle of Romans 2:6 that God will "give back to each one according to his *deeds* (ὃς ἀποδώσει ἑκάστῳ κατὰ τὰ ἔργα αὐτοῦ)." In the intervening verses Paul writes that those who are "patient in doing good" will be granted eternal life, whereas those who "obey *un*dikaiosness (ἀδικία)" face divine wrath (2:7-8). Affliction awaits each one who *"does what is evil,"* whether Jew or Greek; glory awaits each one who *"does the good,"* whether Jew or Greek (2:9-10). Throughout these verses judgment — for Jews and Greeks alike — is based on the same criterion, whether one's deeds are "good" or "evil." Those, then, who are deemed dikaios in 2:13 parallel those who "do the good" and are granted eternal life in 2:7, 10 (just as those who serve *un*dikaiosness in 2:8 parallel those who do evil in 2:9). It follows that to be deemed dikaios is to be recognized as one who has done the good; moreover, if the doers of the law are also doers of the good, Paul must believe that the law spells out the goodness re-

---

dikaios will be duly acknowledged) entail *ethical* considerations. The (normal) linkage needs to be underlined if the *extraordinary* nature of the second group of Pauline texts (sec. iii below) is to be appreciated.

17. It was noted above that dikaiosness is not, for Paul, a matter of living up to abstract ethical ideals, but rather of recognizing, and living in harmony with, creation's — divinely given and divinely supervised — order. Clearly Paul thinks human obligation, so conceived, is capable of statement in a body of laws, and that the — divinely given — laws of Torah fulfill that function (cf. Becker, *Paul*, 397; see further below). He is here anticipated by several centuries of Jewish thought, which (since Sir. 24:23; and see already Deut. 4:6-8) had long identified the "wisdom" by which all human beings should live with the Mosaic Torah; cf. Finsterbusch, *Thora*, 31-38; Schnabel, *Law*, 89, 162. Those familiar with Greco-Roman philosophical thought stressed Torah's consonance with *nature*; so, e.g., 4 Macc. 5:25-26 and, especially, Philo (see Koester, "Concept," 533-36; Najman, "Law," 55-73; Reinhartz, "Meaning," 341-44; Wolfson, *Philo*, 2:192-94). Cf. Bockmuehl, "Law," 17-44. C. Marvin Pate notes the identification of Torah with wisdom in Jewish sources and links the identification to an attitude of Jewish particularism; if outsiders were to partake of true wisdom, they could do so only by way of the Jewish Torah (*Reverse*, 33). Pate then argues that Paul *separates* wisdom from Torah and contrasts the two in order to "overcome Jewish national exclusivism by including Gentiles in the plan of God's salvation" (9). Jewish "nomism" and "particularism" are thus replaced by Pauline "fideism" and "universalism" (247). This approach necessitates that Rom. 2:17-20 be deemed a reflection of Paul's *pre-Christian* view identifying wisdom and the law (137). But Paul (as we shall see immediately) gives ample indication that, as a Christian apostle, he continued to think Torah embodies the goodness required of all human beings.

quired by God. Thus the immediate context of 2:13 provides confirmation for the (nonrevolutionary) conclusion drawn above: the law is understood to prescribe what people ought to do, and those who behave accordingly are dikaios. Paul will later say, in support of his claim that the law is a good thing, that what the law commands is "holy, dikaios, and good" (7:12). The point — in 7:12 as well as in Romans 2 — is not that behavior otherwise neutral *becomes* good or dikaios first when, and because, the law commands it; rather, behavior that *is* good and dikaios is spelled out in the law.[18] To do what the law commands, whether one is Jew or Greek, is to do the good that God requires of all.[19] To violate its commands is to do the evil that brings condemnation on all evildoers, Jew and Greek alike.[20] The *fundamental* requirement to do the good and avoid the evil (i.e., the requirement to be dikaios) is the same for all human beings; the law for its part *enshrines that principle* and spells out its details for the benefit of those to whom it was given.

Note that the law is *not* thought here to provide Jews with a path to dikaiosness that is peculiar to themselves; it merely gives them unique *guidance* about the goodness required of all.[21] Paul goes on to justify the *universality* of

18. So also Deut. 4:8. Note, too, how the speaker of Rom. 7:16, acknowledging the desirability of what the law commands, agrees that the law *is* "good." "Goodness" is here conceived *apart* from the law (rather than simply defined *by* the law), though the law's commands are seen to conform with it. Conversely, the prohibitions of the law — "You shall not commit adultery," or murder, or steal, or covet — are cited as examples of doing "evil" to one's neighbor (Rom. 13:8-10). Again, the law's commands are thought to *spell out* (what is good, and in this case) what is evil for human beings to do; their issuing is not thought, however, to create otherwise nonexistent moral obligations.

19. Cf. Rom. 2:26-27: "If the uncircumcision (= the uncircumcised Gentile) keeps the requirements of the law, will not his uncircumcision be credited as circumcision? And will not the one who, though uncircumcised by nature, fulfills the law condemn you (the Jew) who, though you possess the law's letter and circumcision, are a transgressor of the law?"

20. We may compare the point of Rom. 4:15 and 5:13. Sin exists in the world even apart from law (e.g., murder was wrong even before the Decalogue was given); when, however, the law's demands were given (e.g., "You shall not murder!"), deeds (such as murder) that were sinful in any case became also transgressions of the law.

21. Indeed, Paul appears to be implicitly refuting, throughout Rom. 2, the assumption that Jewishness, or possession of (circumcision and) the law, gives Jews either a unique path to dikaiosness or a decisive advantage in its pursuit. Those tempted to think so are opposed in this chapter on the basis of the law's own requirement of dikaiosness, a requirement that Paul insists is only met — by Jews and non-Jews alike — through dikaios deeds. The refutation continues in Rom. 3, where, for its part, the dikaiosness of faith is shown to be equally accessible to all. Schoeps (as we saw in chap. 7, sec. ii above) thought Paul detached Torah from the covenant and reduced it to a set of demands by which human conduct can be assessed. It was *common*, however, for Jews of the Second Temple period (and earlier) to speak of *torah* in Hebrew, or of νόμος in Greek, while thinking only of the Sinaitic legislation and its sanctions (see chap. 16, sec. v be-

the obligations enshrined in the law by declaring that Gentiles, though not having the law (in its written form), nonetheless show their awareness of its demands whenever they carry them out.[22] Still, it is doubtless of benefit to have one's obligations enunciated clearly: possession of the law enables Jews to instruct Gentiles in their *mutual* responsibilities ("You, then, who [as a Jew (see v. 17)] teach another, do you not teach yourself? You who preach against stealing, do you steal?" [Rom. 2:21]).[23] That all are nonetheless subject to the same

low). It was also *common* to see Torah as the embodiment of the way of life prescribed for all human beings (indeed, as embodying the law of nature; see n. 17 above). And Paul did *not* detach the gift of the law from other privileges granted to Israel (note Rom. 3:1-2; 9:4-5), including, specifically, the Sinaitic covenant (2 Cor. 3:6-14; cf. Rom. 9:4). That Paul differed from other Jews in his understanding of the *efficacy* of Torah (and of the Sinaitic covenant) is (as we shall see) the result of distinctively Christian convictions, not of a confusion about the nature of Torah.

22. The point of Rom. 2:14-16 is that the dictum of 2:13 ("the doers of the law will be dikaiosified") is applicable even to Gentiles, who do not possess the (written) law: had dikaiosness been attributed to hearers of the law, Jews might have been its sole possessors; but since it belongs to "doers of the law (οἱ ποιηταὶ νόμου)," it may legitimately be expected of Gentiles as well. That can be the case only if Gentiles are themselves aware of at least the substance of the law's commands; such awareness, Paul argues, is apparent "whenever Gentiles do what the law requires (ὅταν γὰρ ἔθνη . . . τὰ τοῦ νόμου ποιῶσιν)." The echo of οἱ ποιηταὶ νόμου in v. 13 is deliberate (cf. Gathercole, "Law," 33), showing that Gentiles, though not hearers of the law, are not thereby kept from being its doers (since "the work of the law is written on their hearts"). To further support his claim, Paul goes on to invoke the conscience of *these same* Gentiles as well as *their* self-accusatory "or even" their self-excusatory thoughts (Paul's formulation suggests that the incidence of excusatory thoughts is less likely or less frequent than that of accusatory ones, even for the Gentiles under discussion, who at times "do what the law requires"; cf. Das, *Law,* 181). That accusatory as well as excusatory thoughts support Paul's point confirms that his intention is to show, not that there *are* righteous Gentiles (that he does *not* say), but that Gentiles are morally aware, so that the goodness embodied in the law's commands may be expected of them no less than of Jews. Cf. Bassler, *Impartiality,* 141-49; Laato, *Approach,* 80-83; Martens, "Reading," 63-64; Whiteley, *Theology,* 59.

Augustine wondered whether the Gentiles spoken of in Rom. 2:14-15 might be Gentile *Christians* (*De spir. et litt.* 26.44–27.47). But he went on: "If this interpretation is rejected, and if those who 'do by nature the things contained in the law' are not to be reckoned among those who are justified by the grace of Christ, then they must belong to the number of the heathen who worship not the true God in truth and righteousness, and yet do some things . . . which judged by the standard of right conduct call not only for the witholding of blame but even for merited and proper commendation. . . . We must remember that the image of God in the human soul has not been so completely obliterated by the stain of earthly affections, that no faint outlines of the original remain therein; and therefore it can rightly be said even in the ungodliness of its life to do or to hold some parts of the law" (27.47–28.48). Similarly, Calvin: "There is no nation so opposed to everything that is human that it does not keep within the confines of some laws" (*Comm.* Rom. 2:14).

23. It is *not* said in Rom. 2:21-24 that all Jews are guilty of the particular transgressions mentioned; Paul's point is simply that Jewish possession of the law does not excuse Jews from

basic requirements is confirmed when Romans 3 goes on to speak of the condemnation of all for the same moral failures: "for there is no difference, for all have sinned . . ." (3:22-23).[24]

In Galatians 3:12 Paul articulates the principle underlying the law in these terms: "The one who does these things [i.e., the statutes contained in the law]

---

the obligation to do its commands. Throughout Rom. 2 Paul insists on the *principle* that doing what is good (or fulfilling the law's demands), whether one is Jew or Greek, is what counts with God; doing what is evil (or violating the law's commands), whether one is Jew or Greek, brings God's condemnation. In making that claim Paul notes that Gentiles, though without the written law, show enough moral awareness to be responsible for their actions (2:14-16); that Jews, though in possession of the written law, are not thereby excused from complying with its demands (2:17-24); and that the only circumcision that counts in the end is the spiritual circumcision shown by those — whether or not they are physically circumcised — who actually *do* what the law commands (2:25-29). The latter point is made through positing, in the form of conditional sentences, the various possibilities: a circumcised Jew who keeps the law (2:25a), a circumcised Jew who transgresses the law (2:25b), and an uncircumcised non-Jew who keeps it (2:26-27). (The case of the uncircumcised non-Jew who does *not* keep the law is omitted since it is of no use to the argument.) Note that the conditional force of 2:(25 and)26 is carried over into 2:27 (the "uncircumcision by nature that fulfills the law" in 2:27 is resumptive of "the uncircumcision" that "keeps the requirements of the law" in 2:26); pressing the point that keeping the law, not physical circumcision, is what matters, Paul insists that an *un*circumcised keeper of the law would be better off than a circumcised transgressor. Thus 2:25-27 as a whole must be understood as working out, through an examination of the various possibilities, the *principle* that physical circumcision is ultimately irrelevant when God assesses human behavior; it is hardly meant as an *affirmation* that "doers of the law" are actually to be found among either Jews *or* non-Jews. Cf. Das, *Law*, 185 n. 49.

Paul thus uses the chapter to spell out, in the light of God's impartiality (2:11), the ramifications of the criterion of judgment given in (2:6-10 and) 2:13: "the doers of the law will be dikaiosified." What is said is crucial *background* for his claim in chap. 3 (anticipated in the denunciation of human "ungodliness and undikaiosness" in 1:18-32) that since all human beings "have sinned" (3:23; all are "under sin," 3:9), none can in fact be dikaiosified by the principle of 2:13: so 3:20a, which, in the context, simply means that those who are not dikaios (because they have not done what they ought) cannot be found dikaios by a law that spells out what they ought to do (i.e., by the "works of the law") (3:20). But neither the claim (advanced in chaps. 1 and 3) of universal sinfulness *nor* a claim (Paul never makes) that there are *in fact* people who will be dikaiosified because they observe the law should be read into Rom. 2; merely the enunciation of the fundamental principle that God holds Jews and non-Jews alike responsible to do the good and avoid evil. Cf. N. Elliott, *Rhetoric,* 134.

24. Again (cf. n. 15 above) it should be stressed that Paul's explicit denial in Rom. 2 and 3 that Jews possess a path to dikaiosness peculiar to themselves is implicit in all his other correspondence. The "wrath" and "condemnation" that await all the world apart from God's rescue operation in Christ (1 Thess. 1:10; 5:3; 1 Cor. 1:18; etc.) are never, for Paul, confined to the Gentile nations, nor does he ever suggest that the deliverance Christ offers Gentiles is one already enjoyed by Jews under their covenant: Jews no less than Gentiles need to be "saved" (cf. Rom. 10:1, 12-13; 11:14; 1 Cor. 9:19-22; etc.).

will live by them." Though Romans but *not* Galatians is explicit in applying the principle to Gentiles as well as to Jews, the principle itself is the same in Galatians 3:12 as in Romans 2:13 ("the doers of the law will be dikaiosified"): to be a "doer of the law" (so Rom. 2:13) is to be "one who does [its statutes]" (Gal. 3:12); such a person is promised *life* in Galatians 3:12, (deemed dikaios by God and) granted eternal *life* in Romans 2.[25] Romans 10:5 provides the missing link between the verses: the basic principle of the law is repeated in the terms of Galatians 3:12 ("the one who does these things will live by them"), but the principle itself is labeled the "dikaiosness of the law," showing (as does Rom. 2:13) that "doing" what the law commands is the path that the law prescribes to recognition as dikaios in God's eyes.[26]

To sum up what we have seen to this point. In their ordinary sense the various "dikaios" words belong to Paul's basic moral vocabulary. Dikaiosness ("righteousness," "uprightness," "rectitude"; Gk. δικαιοσύνη) is what one ought to do and what one has if one has done it; it is required of all human beings. One is dikaios ("righteous," "upright"; Gk. δίκαιος) when one does dikaiosness — when, in other words, one lives as one ought and does what one should. To be dikaiosified (δικαιοῦσθαι) is, in effect, to be given the treatment

---

25. Cf. Eckstein, *Verheissung*, 147. Dunn sees in Gal. 3:12 (as in Rom. 10:5) a reference merely to the law's role in regulating the life already enjoyed by those who, by faith (spoken of in 3:11), are *within the covenant* (*Theology*, 375, 378; cf. *Theol. Gal.*, 85). Vv. 11 and 12 are thus seen, not in contrast with each other, but as indicating the terms for entering into the covenant (by faith, 3:11) and for enjoying life within it (by doing what the law requires, 3:12): Dunn's Paul is fully aware of the creed of the covenantal nomist! But the Paul of Galatians clearly intended an antithesis. (i) The promise held out in v. 11 to those with faith and in v. 12 to those who do the things written in the law is in both cases the same: they "will live" (ζήσεται); there is no basis for finding in the repeated term quite different promises (entrance into the covenant; life within it). (ii) The issue for Paul throughout Galatians is whether one is to be dikaiosified by the law and its works or by faith (in Jesus Christ); the same alternatives remain the focus of vv. 11-12, with v. 12 spelling out (in explicit contrast with that of faith) the principle on which the law promises life. (iii) Paul contrasts the "righteousness based on the law" with that "based on faith" in Rom. 10:5-6 (cf. Phil. 3:9), citing the same text to illustrate the former in Romans as here in Gal. 3:12; it would be odd if the same contrast were not intended here. (iv) By Dunn's explanation, Gal. 3:12 must be saying something very different from Rom. 2:13, even though the wording (as shown above) is similar. According to Rom. 2:13, "doing the law" is the path by which *anyone* — Gentile (cf. 2:14) as well as Jew; no covenant is in view — can be deemed dikaios and granted life; but when, according to Gal. 3:12, the law is similarly said to promise life to its doers, Dunn would limit its offer to the *continued* enjoyment of life by Jews already *within the covenant* (a "life" of which, for that matter, Paul appears to know nothing; cf. 3:22).

26. Cf. Phil. 3:6, where Paul says he was "blameless" (ἄμεμπτος) as far as the dikaiosness based on the law is concerned. The presupposition is again that the dikaiosness required by the law pertains to human moral behavior: one may or may not be *blameless* in the matter.

appropriate to one who is dikaios; in a legal context it means to be declared innocent of wrongdoing, or acquitted. When the last judgment is in view, it means to have one's dikaiosness (rectitude) acknowledged by God. The dikaiosness of the law is spelled out in the principle that those who do what the law requires will enjoy life in God's favor. While this might be thought to pertain peculiarly to Jews (who are in unique possession of the written law), Paul insists that the good spelled out in the law is the responsibility of Jews and non-Jews alike, and that all will be judged by whether or not they have *done* this good.

Below I will argue for the conclusion (this one *is* revolutionary) that Paul meant what he said in these texts; but all will agree that the more distinctively *Pauline* usage of the terminology occurs in passages that speak — in marked contrast to the ones we have seen — of *sinners* being *made* dikaios, of *ungodly* people being dikaiosified, of people who do not have dikaiosness *receiving* it. If in the first group of Pauline texts dikaiosness is a matter of doing what one should, in the second group it is attributed to people of whom that cannot be said. To these texts we must now turn.

iii. Extraordinary Dikaiosness

That humans become attached to life and are loath to lose it becomes, for Paul in Romans 5, the starting point for a paradox central to his Christian thought. He begins with the platitudinous: "one will scarcely die for a person who is dikaios" (Rom. 5:7). That "dikaios" is here used in (what I have called) its *ordinary* sense[27] is apparent from the contrast drawn with "sinners" in the next verse: "But God demonstrates his love for us in that, while we were still [not dikaios — the morally decent sort of person for whom few would die anyway — but actually] sinners, Christ died for us" (5:8).[28] Paul then continues: having been dikaiosified by Christ's blood, we will be saved by Christ from the coming

---

27. The apparent distinction between the dikaios and one who is good ("scarcely for one who is dikaios . . . perhaps for one who is good") may suggest that the former is thought of as morally upright but lacking in the more sympathetic characteristics associated with human *goodness* (see Dunn, *Romans 1–8*, 255-56; Moo, *Romans*, 308; Sanday and Headlam, *Romans*, 127-28).

28. Winninge, *Sinners*, argues that Paul introduces something "entirely new" to Judaism when he regards "all Jews and Gentiles" as "sinners from the outset" (264). Of Rom. 5:6-10 Winninge writes: "Whereas Paul's Jewish contemporaries could admit that all human beings occasionally committed sins, they would never have thought of classifying the basically faithful as sinners (status). In fact, Rom 5:6-10 revolve around this central point" (306-7).

wrath (5:9). Whereas in 2:13 the dikaiosified are those whose dikaiosness is *recognized* by God on the basis of what they have done (they are "doers of the law"), something quite different must be meant in 5:9, where "sinners" (who have just been contrasted with the person who is dikaios, and, indeed, whose very status as sinners depends on the validity of the unmet requirement of ordinary dikaiosness) are said to be dikaiosified on the basis of *Christ's* death. Still, the *result* of being dikaiosified seems identical in the two texts: the dikaiosified are those who, at the last judgment, will be granted eternal life rather than condemned to divine wrath.[29] We may say that when the dikaios are said to be dikaiosified in 2:13, this is merely what one would expect; but when in 5:7-9 those *contrasted with* the dikaios are said to be dikaiosified, the paradox is meant to highlight the extraordinary nature of what takes place.

To be sure, what happens would not be extraordinary at all if we could ascribe it to a simple miscarriage of justice. In the Septuagint, as we have seen,[30] the wrongfulness involved when one dikaiosifies (acquits, or clears of any charge of wrongdoing) the ungodly (δικαιοῦν τὸν ἀσεβῆ) is repeatedly condemned (Exod. 23:7; Isa. 5:23; cf. Deut. 25:1; Sir. 9:12). But such an injustice, unthinkable in any case when God is the agent, is explicitly ruled out by Paul's finding, in God's dikaiosifying of sinners, a demonstration of divine *dikaiosness* (Rom. 3:25-26)! The meaning of the verb — to treat as one would appropriately treat the dikaios, to free of any charge of wrongdoing, to acquit — is the same in Paul as in these Septuagintal texts. The *object* of the verb — those who are in fact guilty of doing wrong — is also the same. But in Romans 3:25-26, as here in 5:9, what would otherwise be an act of injustice — to clear the guilty of any wrongdoing — is something very different because of the role played in the process by the death (the "blood") of Christ. That role, only alluded to in our text, will be discussed below.

Later in Romans 5 Paul speaks of people otherwise consigned to death who will reign in life *through Jesus Christ* since they are the *recipients* of an overflow of grace and of a *gift* of dikaiosness (5:17); he could scarcely signal more clearly the exceptional nature of *this* dikaiosness. Elsewhere dikaiosness was contrasted with sin, uncleanness, lawlessness, and the like. Clearly it pertained to moral goodness, to the practice of virtue — to nothing, in short, that can readily be

---

29. Gal. 5:5 speaks of believers awaiting dikaiosness in the future; but according to Rom. 5:9, they *have been* dikaiosified and *will be* saved from the coming wrath (cf. 5:1; 9:30; 1 Cor. 6:11). Just as Adam's disobedience brought death and condemnation on all human beings — a sentence under which they now live, though it will be definitively pronounced at the last judgment — so Christ's obedient death brought dikaiosness and life to all believers, a liberation they now enjoy and one that will be confirmed at the last judgment. Cf. Rom. 5:15-21.

30. See n. 7 above.

said to be "received,"[31] though it may be exemplified and said to be possessed by those who exemplify it (cf. "having my own dikaiosness, based on [observance of] the law," Phil. 3:9).[32] None of this can be meant when Paul speaks of those *(sinners)* who "*receive . . .* the gift of dikaiosness" (note that the alternative to "having my own dikaiosness" in Phil. 3:9 is "having . . . dikaiosness *from* God"): received dikaiosness cannot be one's rectitude (established by one's own doing of what is right).[33] What is it, then? If to dikaiosify (δικαιοῦν) is to (treat as dikaios, or to) clear of any charge of wrongdoing, and if such an action is *just* when the object of the verb is the dikaios, *unjust* when it is a wrongdoer, but (somehow) *just* again when it is the wrongdoer but the death of Christ is involved in the process, then the dikaiosness *received* by sinners through Jesus Christ must be not their moral rectitude but their being treated as dikaios, their being cleared from any charge of wrongdoing, their acquittal:[34] a treatment that, though otherwise wrong, is somehow just because of what Jesus Christ has done.

According to Romans 5:19, the "many" who find themselves "sinners" as a result of Adam's disobedience will, *through the obedience of Christ,* be made dikaios (δίκαιοι κατασταθήσονται). The future tense suggests that the last judgment is in view;[35] as in Romans 2:13, those who are dikaios are granted a favorable verdict at that judgment. But whereas in Romans 2 the dikaios are merely

---

31. No one has better grasped the absurdity of "receiving righteousness" than N. T. Wright: "Righteousness is not an object, a substance or a gas which can be passed across the courtroom" (*Founder,* 98). But the absurdity of it all in no way alters the fact that Paul speaks of "receiving the abundant overflow of grace and of the gift of righteousness" (Rom. 5:17); and both 1 Cor. 1:30 and Phil. 3:9 speak explicitly of a righteousness "from God." We may compare Luther's distinction between "active" and "passive" righteousness: "When I see that a man is sufficiently contrite, oppressed by the Law, terrified by sin, and thirsting for comfort, then it is time for me to take the Law and active righteousness from his sight and to set forth before him, through the Gospel, the passive righteousness which excludes Moses and the Law and shows the promise of Christ, who came for the afflicted and for sinners. This is our theology, by which we teach a precise distinction between these two kinds of righteousness, the active and the passive" (*Gal.,* 26:7).

32. We may compare Septuagintal texts where δικαιοσύνη is used with a possessive pronoun referring to those whose dikaios deeds result in their possession of δικαιοσύνη; so, e.g., 2 Kgdms. 22:21, 25 (par. Ps. 17:21, 25); 3 Kgdms. 8:32; 2 Chron. 6:23; Pss. 7:9; 36:6; 111:3; Ezek. 14:14, 20; 18:22; 33:13, 18.

33. Rom. 9:30 also speaks of Gentiles obtaining a dikaiosness that is emphatically not of their own doing (it is not "pursued" by them, ἔθνη τὰ μὴ διώκοντα δικαιοσύνην). For the notion of pursuing (i.e., following one's determination to practice) δικαιοσύνη, see LXX Ps. 37:21; Prov. 15:9; Isa. 51:1; and cf. Zeph. 2:3; Sir. 27:8, and Wagner, *Heralds,* 121-22 n. 7.

34. Cf. 2 Cor. 3:9, where dikaiosness is explicitly contrasted with "condemnation."

35. Cf. Käsemann, *Romans,* 157-58; Schlier, *Römerbrief,* 175.

recognized as such because of the good they have done (they are "doers of the law"), the "sinners" of 5:19 will actually be "*made* dikaios" through the obedience of Christ. This is, of course, consistent with the extraordinary idea that sinners can be justly dikaiosified (acquitted, cleared of any charge of wrongdoing) because of the death of Christ (5:9), or that dikaiosness (now meaning acquittal, *not* rectitude) can, through Jesus Christ, be "received" by people whose own behavior has not been good (5:17). If in 5:19 sinners are "made dikaios," the adjective can no longer mean (what it ordinarily means) "right acting," "upright"; it must mean "freed from any charge of wrongdoing" — in some extraordinary way that depends neither on the recognition nor even on the pretense that one's own deeds have been dikaios.[36]

To sum up: In its "ordinary" usage — in Paul as elsewhere — the *dikaio*-terminology may be said to take its cue[37] from the noun δικαιοσύνη, "what one ought to do," or "what the one who has done what one ought thereby possesses." The dikaios (δίκαιος) is the one who does δικαιοσύνη, and to dikaiosify (δικαιοῦν) is "to treat as one ought to treat the dikaios," "to declare innocent," "to acquit" (though the object of the verb may well be one who ought *not* to be given such treatment). The ordinary usage of all three terms is apparent in the phrase δικαιῶσαι δίκαιον δοῦναι αὐτῷ κατὰ τὴν δικαιοσύνην αὐτοῦ, "to acquit the upright, treating him according to his rectitude." The necessary point of

36. As noted above (n. 7), the *tsaddiq*/dikaios in the Hebrew and Greek (LXX) Scriptures is by no means necessarily the one who *is* acquitted in court (injustices do occur), but the one who *ought* to be acquitted. Paul, however, clearly uses "dikaios" of acquitted sinners (Rom. 1:17; 5:19), those who extraordinarily enjoy the status that would ordinarily belong only to those who had themselves *done* what is dikaios. It is thus true of Paul's *extraordinary* usage to say that dikaios and dikaiosness indicate the status enjoyed by believers as a result of a forensic declaration and that they carry no implications about the ethical conduct of the ones said to "be dikaios" (or to "receive dikaiosness"). I would only stress that (i) this is *not* a conventional usage of the terms — though it may have been anticipated in texts like LXX Isa. 46:12-13; 53:11; 1QH V, 22-23 (Sukenik XIII, 16-17), and in earlier Christian tradition (see n. 37, immediately below; on the LXX texts, see C. H. Dodd, *Bible*, 57-58); and (ii) the implication remains, even in Paul, that those who are dikaios by extraordinary means possess a dikaiosness that would ordinarily belong only to those who do what is dikaios (again, see n. 37).

37. The metaphor is introduced for its heuristic value only; nothing is implied about the history of these terms' usage. I should add that though (what I here label) Paul's extraordinary usage is particularly characteristic of the apostle, I make no claim about his originality in using it. The latter issue could not be addressed without considering (i) Septuagintal texts where dikaiosness is clearly related to "salvation" (these are touched on in sec. iv below), as well as the difficult Isa. 53:11; (ii) possible parallels among the Qumran texts, particularly in the *Hodayot*; and (iii) Paul's possible relation to earlier Christian tradition, perhaps reflected in some of his own formulas (Rom. 3:24? 1 Cor. 6:11?), and explored by (among others) Jürgen Becker, as we saw in chap. 13, sec. iv above. Cf. Dahl, *Studies*, 96-105; also Winninge, *Sinners*, 320.

continuity between Paul's extraordinary and his ordinary usages of the terminology is found in the verb; for Paul, too, it means "treat as one ought to treat the dikaios," "acquit." Paul's extraordinary usage of the noun and adjective may be said to take their cue from this meaning of the verb: δικαιοσύνη now means not rectitude but the (paradoxically just) acquittal of the heretofore sinful; δίκαιος now means not the upright but the one so acquitted.[38] To adapt our encapsulation of ordinary usage to the extraordinary, we may speak of acquitting (δικαιοῦν) the wicked, thereby granting them the gift of acquittal (δικαιοσύνη) and thus making them the acquitted (δίκαιοι).[39]

38. Sanders rightly observes the priority of the adjective in Judaism and of the verb in Paul (*Paul Pal. Jud.*, 545); I would only note that the priority of the adjective applies to Paul's understanding of ordinary dikaiosness as well as to Judaism.

39. When Sanders (following Ziesler) proposes "forgive" for δικαιόω in Rom. 4:5 (*Paul Pal. Jud.*, 492 n. 57), he captures the point inherent in Paul's usage that God is dealing graciously with human sin. What "forgive" lacks is a sense of the decisive, once-for-all character of Paul's term. "Forgiveness" is not quite (what dikaiosness in Paul can be) the opposite of "condemnation" (2 Cor. 3:9; cf. Rom. 5:18).

It has long been debated whether the claim that sinners are dikaiosified means merely that they are treated as though they were dikaios (though in themselves they are not) or whether their character is so transformed that they may now rightly be called dikaios; in this latter view, if the dikaios are people who do what God requires, then God makes sinners into that kind of people, even though in the past they were very different. Both positions capture important aspects of Pauline thought. Paul *does* think (as the latter position holds) that believers have been transformed; they belong to the "new creation" (2 Cor. 5:17); they are intended to practice dikaiosness (Rom. 6:13, 18-19; Phil. 1:11). He also speaks (as the former position insists) of believers as those who receive a δικαιοσύνη that is not inherently their own (Rom. 5:17), of their being the beneficiaries of a divine exchange between Christ's δικαιοσύνη and their own sin (2 Cor. 5:21; cf. 1 Cor. 1:30). We may say, however, that Paul's more distinctive usage of the *dikaio-* terminology pertains rather to believers' acquittal than to their transformation — while adding that the involvement of Christ (see below) makes the acquittal one of due process rather than (as *some* Protestant treatments would suggest) a kind of legal fiction. See Cranfield, *Romans*, 95; Schreiner, *Paul*, 203-9; Ziesler, *Meaning*, 1-9, 48.

The point of contention is thought to be avoided by those who claim that dikaiosness in these contexts refers *merely* to God's acknowledgment of people as being on good terms with himself (see also n. 16 above). Such an acknowledgment of believers (it is claimed) involves neither treating them as something they are not (they really *are* on good terms with God) nor the transformation of their character into something other than what it was: dikaiosness is (here at least) a relational term and carries no moral connotations (cf. Bultmann, *Theology*, 276-77; Dunn, "Justice," 17; Hill, *Words*, 152; Ziesler, *Meaning*, 8). But whether or not *dikaio-* terminology can *ever* completely lose its moral connotations, it seems clear that in Paul it has not. Paul's insistence on the extraordinary nature of the dikaiosness of faith — that paradoxically it is given freely, without works, as a gift, and to the ungodly — indicates that he is well aware that dikaiosness is normally the possession of those whose deeds are dikaios. Certainly believers are (as a result of Christ's death) now declared by God to be on good terms with himself; but when

Since our focus here is on Paul's usage of the *dikaio-* terminology, the much that *could* be said about his understanding of Christ's role in the granting of dikaiosness may be reduced to the little that is essential to our theme; still, something *must* be said, since it is Christ's involvement that renders the process one of (extraordinary) dikaiosness rather than simple injustice. No single picture emerges. In Romans 3:25-26 God's dikaiosness (see sec. iv below) is said to be demonstrated precisely when he acquits sinners: God has not overlooked human sinfulness — that *would* violate his dikaiosness — but has directed its bane, not on the heads of the sinners themselves, but on Jesus Christ, who exhausted it when he died as an atoning sacrifice. The same picture is invoked by the reference to Christ's "blood" in 5:9 (perhaps echoing 3:25). In 5:15-19 the very human beings whose sinfulness was determined by Adam's representative act of disobedience now receive dikaiosness (acquittal) thanks to Christ's representative act of obedience. In 6:7 the "dikaiosified from sin" are those who have "died"[40] *with* Christ when they were baptized "into" (i.e., so as to belong to) him (cf. 6:3). According to a striking locution in 2 Corinthians 5:21, those reconciled to God through Christ are said to "*become* dikaio*ness* in (or 'through') him." Their identification with dikaiosness takes place through a divinely negotiated "interchange":[41] Christ, who did not "know sin" (and who was thus in himself dikaios), was "made sin for us" so that we (who *did* know sin, and who were thus in ourselves *not* dikaios) might *become* dikaiosness in him (see also 1 Cor. 1:30). In various texts, then, the dikaiosness of believers is linked to Christ's atoning death, to his representative act of obedience, to the participation of believers in his death, or to the interchange God brought about between believers and Christ. The pictures differ but the effect is the same: sinners are rightfully dikaiosified by God because of what Christ has done for them.

This dikaiosness, which is contrasted with that linked to the law (Gal. 2:21; 3:11-12; 5:4; Rom. 10:5; Phil. 3:9), its works (Gal. 2:16; Rom. 3:20, 28), or works in

---

Paul says they are dikaiosified, something of the thought remains that they are declared *by extraordinary means* to be on the *same good terms with God that they would have enjoyed had they themselves done* — what Paul, in these contexts, insists that they had *not* done — *what is dikaios.*

Similarly, though "dikaiosify" may broadly be said to mean "accept" or "approve," the point should be borne in mind that the "acceptance" or "approval" spoken of is that which, in the "normal" course of things, would be granted only to *doers* of dikaiosness. Cf. Burton, *Galatians*, 468, 473.

40. Paul may here have pressed into service a proverb (meaning, in its general usage, something like "Death pays all debts") to serve his (rather different) argument. Cf. Byrne, *Romans*, 191-92; Dunn, *Romans 1–8*, 320-21; Moo, *Romans*, 376-77; Schlier, *Römerbrief*, 198-99.

41. The term is of course borrowed from a well-known article by Morna Hooker ("Interchange in Christ," now in Hooker, *Adam*, 13-25), drawing on a theme in Irenaeus: "Christ became what we are, in order that we might become what he is" (22).

general (Rom. 4:2, 5-6; cf. 2:6; 9:31-32),[42] is (in Paul's terminology) a dikaiosness of *faith* (Gk. πίστις).[43] Scriptural warrant for positing it is found in Genesis 15:6: "Abraham believed (ἐπίστευσεν) God, and it was credited to him as dikaiosness" (Rom. 4:3; Gal. 3:6).[44] What is extraordinary about it is summed up in Romans

42. Paul entertains the possibility of dikaiosness by (unspecified) works in the case of Abraham — though only to dismiss it (Rom. 4:2). Jewish tradition, taking its cue from Gen. 26:5, saw Abraham as compliant with the law's demands centuries before they were given to Moses; see B. Longenecker, *Eschatology,* 211-12. Paul for his part does not relate the deeds of Abraham to the law. He may not have *wanted* to, since he elsewhere finds it significant that Abraham lived (and received the divine promise) long before the law was given (Gal. 3:15-17; cf. Rom. 4:9-10). In any case, he did not *need* to, since he has already established that the requirement of ordinary dikaiosness is the same for those with or without the (written) law: Jews and non-Jews alike must do the good (2:6-11) that is spelled out in the law (τὰ τοῦ νόμου, 2:14). It is, no doubt, more natural to speak of the requirement of ordinary dikaiosness among those who have the law as that of doing "the works of the law," and to discuss the possibility of ordinary dikaiosness among those (like Abraham) who lack the written law as an issue of their (unspecified, though necessarily good) "works." But the essential requirement of appropriate behavior is the same for both (hence Paul can speak interchangeably of works of the law and works; cf. Rom. 3:20, 28 and 4:2, 6); and the requirement of appropriate works is the principle on which the law is based (hence Paul can speak interchangeably of "the law" and "the works of the law"; cf. Gal. 2:16 and 2:21; 5:4 [see further chap. 16, sec. ii below]). Ordinary dikaiosness, based on the kind of appropriate behavior that is spelled out in the law, is the only alternative Paul ever considers to the extraordinary dikaiosness of faith. *Tertium nihil est.*

43. According to Donaldson, it is a mistake to treat Paul's faith/works contrast as having "to do fundamentally with mutually exclusive *human* stances and dispositions. The contrast is between Christ and law, not faith and works. . . . To put it another way, [Gal.] 2:16 sets up a contrast between two objective means of righteousness — Christ or Torah — rather than between two subjective human attitudes" (*Paul,* 116). The point is well taken that faith, for Paul, is not to be detached from the kerygma to which it is a response. At the same time, it should be noted that, for Paul, (i) however "objective" the means of righteousness may have been, human *faith* remains the *necessary* response to the gospel; those who do not believe are not saved (1 Cor. 1:21; 2 Cor. 4:3-4; etc.); (ii) faith is also the *appropriate* response to the gospel: "good news" is not something to be done, but to be *received* or *believed;* (iii) obedient *deeds,* on the other hand, represent the appropriate response to the demands of a law: a command is scarcely a fit object for belief. Like soup and sandwich, then, works and the law, and faith and Christ, simply *go* together. Cf. Meyer, *Christians,* 135.

44. In the opinion of some scholars (e.g., Barrett, *Romans,* 83-84; Moo, *Romans,* 262; Moxnes, *Theology,* 109-10), the verb "credited" (ἐλογίσθη) itself suggests that there is something unusual about this dikaiosness, that it is not Abraham's in the normal way. Cf. Rom. 2:26, where it is said that the uncircumcised Gentile will be "credited" (λογισθήσεται) with circumcision if he observes the requirements of the law; that he does not possess circumcision in the normal sense of the word seems implied in the verb. Again, the sinner against whom the Lord does not "count (λογίσηται) sin" (4:8) is not without sin in the usual sense of the expression. In other contexts, however, the verb does not suggest a reckoning that is contrary to fact, appearance, or norm. Cf. Burton, *Galatians,* 154-55, 470.

In Rom. 4 Paul does not reflect explicitly on whether Christ played a role in the extraordinary dikaiosness enjoyed by Abraham and spoken of by David in the Psalms. As we saw in Part

4:6: "David speaks of the blessedness of the person to whom God credits dikaiosness *without works.*" Normally, Paul implies, one could not be credited with dikaiosness "without works." This observation, of course, corresponds with all that we have seen above: dikaiosness, by any but its most extraordinary sense, is a matter of doing what one should. Hence the works *without* which one is extraordinarily credited with dikaiosness must be the moral (dikaios!) works on which a judgment of dikaiosness is otherwise self-evidently based; and to be sure, the person lacking these works in 4:6 is the sinner who experiences the blessedness of dikaiosness only through the forgiveness of *sins* (4:7-8). Abraham might be thought to have the requisite works, but in Paul's mind a text that ascribed his dikaiosness to faith suggested otherwise[45] and made Abraham a prototype of all (cf. 4:22-24) who "do not work"[46] but "believe in the one who

---

One, Augustine, Luther, Calvin, and Wesley believed that the promise of the coming Christ was the object of the faith (however inchoate) of the Old Testament saints, and that Christ's death for sins was, proleptically, the basis for their righteousness. Paul may well have thought so too. Gal. 3:8 suggests that the promise given to, and believed by, Abraham was a preannouncement of the gospel by which God would acquit Gentiles (cf. Lambrecht, *Studies*, 287; Williams, "Righteousness," 264; *Wisdom, Blessing*, 142-43); Rom. 3:25-26 indicates that the forbearance shown by God toward sins committed before the coming of Christ was rooted in his determination to deal with sin once and for all through the atoning death of Christ; and John 8:56, 12:41 show that *similar* thoughts were entertained by another early Christian writer. The alternative, of course, is that Paul lighted on Gen. 15:6 because it spoke of a dikaiosness granted to one who believed, saw an analogy to the dikaiosness granted to believers in Christ (the analogy is developed in 4:18-25), but did not at this point reflect further on Christ's role in the crediting of dikaiosness to Abraham.

45. Paul's argument in Rom. 4:4-5 is elliptical; spelled out more fully, it would look something like this:

    i. *Positive illustration of principle:* In the case of one who works, the wage he receives is not considered a gift of beneficence, but as due compensation.

    [ii. *Negative illustration of principle:* In the case of one who does no work, anything he receives is a gift of beneficence, not due compensation.]

    [iii. *Positive statement about dikaiosness based on works:* In the case of the godly person who does the works God requires, such works are credited to him — duly, *not* as a gift of beneficence — as dikaiosness.]

    iv. *Negative statement about dikaiosness based on works:* In the case of the ungodly person who has not done the required works but who believes in the one who dikaiosifies the ungodly, his faith is credited to him — not as his due, but as a gift of divine beneficence — as dikaiosness.

Cf. Käsemann, *Romans*, 110; Schlier, *Römerbrief*, 124; Wilckens, *Römer*, 1:262-63.

46. The absence of the *moral* deeds normally requisite if one is to be deemed dikaios must be meant: partly because Paul goes on to illustrate further the dikaiosness that is "without works" by citing the psalmist's blessing of the one whose *moral* failings are forgiven (cf. Bell, *Study*, 229-30; Kruse, *Paul*, 195); partly because the "one who does not work" in 4:5 is contrasted with the "one who works" in 4:4, and the latter is one who deserves recognition for deeds that are necessarily good but otherwise unspecified; partly because 4:5 specifies the dikaiosified per-

dikaiosifies the ungodly." They are, as Paul puts it in 3:24, dikaiosified "freely by [God's] grace." When the ones dikaiosified are *sinners* (or the ungodly, or God's enemies, etc.), their dikaiosness *cannot* be the "normal" one based on God's recognition of their deeds as appropriate (dikaios). Lacking such deeds themselves, they must "receive" dikaiosness "freely" (3:24), "without works" (4:2, 5, 6), as a "gift" (5:17) — none of which can be said of those recognized as dikaios because they are doers of the law. *The contrast between the dikaiosness of the law and that of faith amounts to that between the dikaiosness of those who do the good spelled out in the law and that of sinners.*[47]

---

son "who does not work" as "ungodly," invoking an idiom (δικαιοῦν τὸν ἀσεβῆ) in which the point is always that, in explicit contrast with the dikaios, the ἀσεβής is guilty of wrongdoing (see the references in n. 7 above; Rom. 5:6-9 confirms that for Paul the dikaiosified "ungodly" include Jewish [he numbers himself among them] as well as Gentile sinners); and most importantly, because Paul is here discussing the dikaiosness of faith introduced into his argument at 3:21 precisely as the divine solution to the dilemma posed by the *moral* shortcomings of all human beings, Jews and non-Jews alike ("there *is* none dikaios," 3:10).

The issue in *these* verses, then, is not whether circumcision and other specifically Jewish works are required of Gentiles who would enter the people of God, but rather with how *sinners* may find God's favor. In what follows Paul is indeed concerned to show that Abraham was dikaiosified *before* he was circumcised (and hence, that circumcision is not a requirement for his Gentile "descendants," 4:10-12). But he raises that issue in v. 9 ("Does *this* [already defined] blessedness pertain to the circumcision [only] or also to the uncircumcision?"), only *after* he has established the reality of such a "blessedness . . . apart from works" in vv. 1-8; that is, the issue of circumcision (and presumably other distinctively Jewish practices) is quite separate from the question whether one can be dikaiosified by faith without works. Cf. Cosgrove, "Justification," 666: "The theme of justification *kata charin* occupies Paul's attention in 4:2-8, and that of its locus outside the sphere of the law forms the center of interest in 4:9-17a." Once Paul has established that *sinners* (including David, whose circumcision and "Jewishness" were not in question; cf. 4:6-8) can be dikaiosified by faith apart from works (i.e., apart from the moral behavior on which such a judgment would normally be based), he raises the question whether *this* extraordinary "blessedness" can apply to non-Jews who remain uncircumcised as well as to Jews. But Paul is clearly as intent on showing that circumcised Jews, as sinners, need the dikaiosness of faith as he is on making the point that Gentile sinners who have been granted dikaiosness through faith do not need to be circumcised. Cf. Gathercole, "Evidence."

47. Faith in God (who "dikaiosifies the ungodly," Rom. 4:5) is the only possible recourse for sinners of whom dikaiosness (which they by definition do not have) is demanded, just as it was the only recourse for a couple whose childbearing years were long past but from whom a child nonetheless *had* to be born (4:17-21). Cf. Aletti, *Loi*, 89. Paul thus underlines in Rom. 4 that the faith by which humans are dikaiosified is the faith in God shown by the helpless in an otherwise hopeless predicament. Though not in itself decisive, the observation of Cranfield seems astute that when the πίστις Χριστοῦ by which humans are justified (Rom. 3:22, 26; Gal. 2:16) is interpreted as Christ's own "faith," this dimension of justifying faith has been lost to view (*On Rom.*, 96-97). Cf. Calvin, *Comm. Rom.* 4:5: "Only those who feel in themselves that they are ungodly will attain to the righteousness of faith."

It should be apparent that the two types of dikaiosness (only two are ever in question) of which Paul speaks are not, for him, simply different options offering much the same goods on somewhat different terms.[48] Nor is it the case that the dikaiosness of faith merely offers to Gentiles what Jews already enjoyed through the dikaiosness of the law.[49] The dikaiosness based on appropriate (dikaios!) behavior as spelled out in the law is, for Paul, the more *basic*, for Jews and non-Jews alike: the gift of the law to Jews has not *fundamentally* altered the human condition. Of *course*, Paul observes, dikaiosness *would* be by the law — if God had given a law that could convey life to the dead; but no law requiring dikaios deeds (this *is* what laws do) can resuscitate the dead (Gal. 3:21). Paul repeatedly speaks of the dikaiosness of faith as an *ab*normal, emergency measure introduced for the benefit of people whose *in*appropriate behavior has closed the door to "normal" dikaiosness:[50] the language is surely strained when one speaks of sinners, the ungodly, and the like — those who by definition have *not* lived dikaiosly — "receiving" dikaiosness and being "made" dikaios. The dikaiosness of faith has "just now" been "revealed" (Rom. 3:21-22). Faith has effectively come into the world with Christ (Gal. 3:23, 25). That one may be dikai-

48. Contrast, e.g., Watson, *Paul*: "The faith-works antithesis" amounts to "an antithesis between life as a Christian, with its distinctive beliefs and practices, and life as a Jew" (65). *"Faith is incompatible with works because participation in the life of a Pauline Gentile Christian congregation is incompatible with continuing membership of the Jewish community"* (134). Paul's contrast between faith and works will be explored further in chap. 16 below.

49. Cf. the important remarks of Garlington, *Obedience of Faith*, 260-61.

50. Cf. Merklein, *Studien*, 2:306. Note that when Paul begins his account of the *need* for the dikaiosness of faith (first spoken of in Rom. 1:16-17), he immediately refers to the *un*dikaiosness of human beings apart from the gospel (ἀδικία occurs twice in 1:18, and recurs in 1:29). He returns to the dikaiosness of faith in 3:21 after having flatly declared (drawing on a quotation from the Psalms) that "there is none dikaios" (3:10), and that, for that reason, the principle that doers of the law will be dikaiosified (2:13) is without effect among human beings ("no flesh will be dikaiosified by the works of the law," 3:20).

According to Gal. 2:21, if dikaiosness were possible through the law, then Christ died to no purpose; that is, no emergency measure (such is surely the death of the Son of God [2:20]) would have been required if dikaiosness were possible in the ordinary way by keeping the law. But the latter route is clearly of no benefit to Gentile *sinners* (2:15), and Jewish Christians, by believing in Christ Jesus *in order to be dikaiosified*, express their recognition that they, too, are sinners needing to be dikaiosified (2:17). Hence the dictum of 2:16 ("*no* flesh will be dikaiosified by the works of the law") merely states the obvious (as does Rom. 3:20; see n. 23 above): none of those who have not done what they ought to do will be found innocent when judged by a law that spells out what they ought to have done. Were one, then, to *continue* to pursue dikaiosness through the law even after Christ has died, one would frustrate this supreme display of divine grace (2:21; cf. 5:4). In Gal. 3 dikaiosness by faith (3:11) is again seen as the solution to the crisis created by sin and the curse pronounced by the law (3:10, 14; cf. 3:22-23). See, further, the discussion of Galatians (and of alternative interpretations) in chap. 18 below.

os on the basis of faith is the message now being proclaimed in the gospel of which Paul is unashamed (Rom. 1:16-17); and in that it brings salvation (1:16), it represents the divine response to a crisis (introduced in 1:18).[51]

Given Paul's advocacy of the dikaiosness of faith, it is perhaps not surprising that a number of scholars dismiss what he says about the *other* dikaiosness as merely hypothetical, the adoption on Paul's part of the perspective of others for the sake of argument, if not an indication of the inconsistency of Paul's thought. Certainly we will need to explore in more detail below why he insists that dikaiosness *cannot* be attained by "the works of the law" (Rom. 3:20, 28; Gal. 2:16). What must be emphasized, however, is that far from being incompatible with Paul's claims about the dikaiosness of faith, the fundamental truths of the dikaiosness of the law represent their indispensable foundation: that human beings, Jews and non-Jews alike, are *moral* beings (the terminology is ours) who are required to do good, not evil (Paul's terminology); that God holds them responsible for their actions and judges them accordingly;[52] that doing what is good is the (normal!) path to enjoying life in God's favor. Sin represents a departure from what ought to be done; however universal it may be among human beings as we know them, it remains inexcusable (Rom. 1:20, 32; 3:19), a perversion that "entered" the world only through a particular human act of disobedience (5:12). If we may speculate (Paul in his letters does not) and imagine that human beings had always lived as they ought, the fundamental moral principle on which the world is run — those who do the good that they were made to do will enjoy life in God's favor, while those who do not are doomed — would not have been seen as problematic. It is problematic for Paul precisely because it is axiomatic. From his first letter to his last he depicts the communities to which he writes as delivered by the gospel from a world turned evil and from the divine wrath that hangs over wayward humanity: the wrath of divine *retribution,* inevitable precisely *because* God judges people according to their conformity or failure to conform to the norms of goodness inherent in his creation and spelled out in his law. Had Romans 2:6, 13; 10:5; etc., with their requirement of ordinary dikaiosness, *not* been founda-

---

51. Cf. Byrne, *Sons,* 231: "In Paul's theology God did not simply substitute a new way of salvation in place of the Law. There is an intrinsic connection between the failure of the Law way and the death of Christ. The death of Christ and the Christian's participation in that death makes possible the doing of full justice to the Law's just verdict, the operation of God's uprightness as well as his forgiveness, and the triumphant victory of his grace and love — all held together in the polyvalent concept of the 'righteousness of God' (cf. esp. Rom 3:24-26)."

52. Yinger (*Judgment,* 174-75) correctly notes that the "statement that only the doers of the law will be justified ([Rom.] 2:13) is, after all, simply the flip side of Paul's repeated insistence that those who do unrighteousness will not inherit the kingdom of God."

tional to Paul, everything he says about God's grace (or mercy), his salvific act in Christ, and the (emergency measure of the) dikaiosness of faith would be meaningless.[53]

iv. Divine Dikaiosness

Paul speaks as well of *God's* dikaiosness. In Romans 3:5 God's dikaiosness is his rightness, his truthfulness (cf. v. 4), as demonstrated in his faithfulness to his commitments (cf. v. 3): a rightness that is vindicated whenever called in question by (sinful, lying, unfaithful) human beings (cf. v. 4) and by which he (rightly) judges the world (cf. vv. 5-7). In the same vein, 2:5 indicates that the dikaios judgments of God will be revealed when, on "the day of wrath," he judges the hard-heartedness of human beings and their refusal to repent. The same divine dikaiosness appears to be referred to in 3:25 and 26 as well: God's advocacy of what is right and good seemed silent when he "passed over sins committed in the past, at the time of God's forbearance." What proves God to be dikaios after all is his putting forward of Christ Jesus as the atoning sacrifice for sins: far from overlooking human wrongdoing, God had merely postponed its decisive condemnation until it could be channeled onto the crucified Christ rather than onto the wrongdoers themselves. In this way he proved dikaios himself (his rightness and commitment to goodness were never more apparent) at the same time as he dikaiosifies (acquits) sinners who have faith in Jesus (3:26).

Elsewhere, too, God's dikaiosness is explicitly tied to the (extraordinary) dikaiosness of faith. What is not always clear is whether the reference is to his own salvific act in dikaiosifying (acquitting) sinners or whether it is to the "gift of dikaiosness (acquittal)" that he gives them.[54] The latter (referred to, as we have seen, in Rom. 5:17) is certainly intended in Philippians 3:9, where a dikaios-

---

53. Cf. Wilckens, *Römer*, 1:132.

54. According to Stuhlmacher, "Paul talks about the righteousness of God 'synthetically.' He uses it to designate God's own creative and saving activity (e.g., Rom 3:5, 25-26) as well as the grace gift of righteousness in which believers share (e.g., Rom 3:22; 2 Cor 5:21)" (*Doctrine*, 20; cf. his *Reconciliation*, 81-82; *Theologie*, 335-36). Käsemann very properly reminds us that one cannot receive God's *gift* without being claimed by the *Giver*: "When God enters the arena, our experience is, that he maintains his lordship even in his giving; indeed, it is his gifts which are the very means by which he subordinates us to his lordship and makes us responsible beings" (*Questions*, 174; cf. *Perspectives*, 74-75, 82). The observation captures a crucial aspect of Paul's thought, though it is perhaps somewhat optimistic to think that *that* point is made whenever Paul speaks of God's δικαιοσύνη.

ness that is explicitly said to be "from God" (τὴν ἐκ θεοῦ δικαιοσύνην) is contrasted with Paul's "own" dikaiosness. The same gift is presumably in view in Romans 10:3, a closely parallel text contrasting a recognition of God's dikaiosness with the attempt of Jews to "establish their own dikaiosness."[55] It *could* be meant in Romans 1:17 and 3:21-22 as well.[56] On the other hand, since God's dikaiosness is used as a parallel to his salvation in a number of Septuagintal texts,[57] many scholars read it the same way in Romans 1:17: "For in it [i.e., the gospel] the dikaiosness of God [= his *salvation*, already introduced in v. 16] is revealed [or 'operative,' 'effective'] from faith to faith, as it is written, 'The one who is dikaios by faith will live.'" This makes good sense — as far as it goes. Still, dikaiosness, though at times *parallel* to "salvation," necessarily means something more. A salvation that is *also* designated God's dikaiosness is one in which the divine endorsement of good and hostility to evil are given triumphant expression: what is right, and God's commitment to uphold the right, must be vindicated in the process. Since Romans 3:25-26 indicates clearly that for Paul such a vindication is involved in God's display of dikaiosness in Christ, we must assume that it is to be understood in 1:17 as well. But even that is not all. To render δικαιοσύνη "salvation" in 1:17 is to obscure Paul's play on words between the revelation of God's *dikaiosness* in the gospel and the reference (quoted from Habakkuk) to the human being who is *dikaios* through faith; the life of the latter must somehow illustrate the former.[58] Hence, if δικαιοσύνη is not simply God's *gift* of acquittal here, we must say it is *that salvific activity by which God's commitment to uphold the right is vindicated at the same time as sinners* (those guilty of the *un*dikaiosness of 1:18) *who believe the gospel become dikaios* (in accordance

55. Note that in Phil. 3:9 "my own dikaiosness" is that which is "based on law," whereas "the dikaiosness that is from God" is "based on faith." The distinction is repeated in Rom. 10: "their own dikaiosness" in 10:3 is the "dikaiosness based on law" in 10:5 (see also 9:31); the dikaiosness of God is that which is "based on faith" in 10:6 (compare 9:30).

56. Cf. Augustine, *De spir. et litt.* 11.18 (of Rom. 1:17): "This is the righteousness of God, which was hidden in the Old Testament and is revealed in the New: called the righteousness of God, because God by imparting it makes man righteous, even as it is 'the Lord's salvation' by which he causes men to be saved"; 9.15 (of 3:22): "the righteousness of God, not that by which God is righteous, but that wherewith he clothes man, when he justifies the ungodly."

57. E.g., LXX Pss. 30:2; 39:11; 50:16; 70:2, 15; 97:2-3; Isa. 51:5, 6, 8; 59:17; 62:1. For many, God's salvific activity is right because it represents his faithfulness to the covenant he entered with Israel; cf. Dunn, "Justice," 16-17; Hill, *Words*, 88-89; Wagner, *Heralds*, 44; Wright, *Climax*, 234; *Founder*, 113-33; Ziesler, *Meaning*, 40-42. But though God's dikaiosness requires that he be faithful to his covenants (after all, part of the dikaiosness of the dikaios is that they keep their commitments), it does not follow that God's dikaiosness can be *reduced* to covenant faithfulness; see Seifrid, "Language," 415-42, and sec. v below.

58. Cf. Seifrid, *Justification*, 215: "The δικαιοσύνη θεοῦ here is the means by which the individual becomes δίκαιος"; also Ljungman, *Pistis*, 40, 44-47.

with Habakkuk's dictum). This may seem overloaded, but each aspect of the clarification is amply attested in the chapters that follow, and Paul clearly means 1:17 to serve as a heading for his subsequent argument.

The same alternatives confront us in the references to God's dikaiosness in 3:21 and 22. The phrase *may* simply speak of the gift by which God acquits sinners.[59] But if his act of salvation is meant, then this must be understood as an act that vindicates his own patronage of the good (underlined in vv. 25 and 26) at the same time as it enables humans (none of whom is dikaios, 3:10, 20) to be "dikaiosified freely by [God's] grace" (3:24).

In short, *both* ways of understanding the term (as God's gift of acquittal, or as the salvific act by which God's support of the moral order is shown at the same time as sinners are acquitted) are true to Paul's thought; we need not here decide between them in ambiguous cases.

Finally, we may return to the question of English equivalents for Paul's *dikaio-* terminology. The adjective δίκαιος is normally rendered "righteous," the noun δικαιοσύνη (our "dikaiosness") "righteousness." These renderings, however in need of accompanying explanation, are not readily improved upon. Normally the *dikaio-* terminology, like that of "righteous(ness)" in English, pertains to moral behavior, the "oughtness" of conduct appropriate to moral agents. If, extraordinarily, sinful people may be said to "receive" δικαιοσύνη and thereby become δίκαιος in Greek, then we will have to allow that they "receive" "righteousness" and thereby become "righteous" in English: the context in which the terms occur will have to make Paul's point clear, in translation as in the original. Similarly, if God's δικαιοσύνη is either the gift of *such* "righteousness" to sinners or the act by which sinners become "righteous" in this sense, then "righteousness" may serve for it as well. The verb is more problematic, but perhaps "declare righteous" is as good a rendering as any. That (or "declare innocent") is what the verb *ordinarily* means; and if we may extend the meaning of "righteous" and "righteousness" to include Paul's extraordinary usage of δίκαιος and δικαιοσύνη, then we (presumably) ought to be prepared to allow "declare righteous" to stand for his δικαιόω.

v. Dikaiosness and "the Covenant"

1. To this point I have discussed Paul's usage of the *dikaio-* terminology with scarcely a reference to "the covenant." So astonishing an omission can only be accounted for by a narrow preoccupation with the Pauline texts, which never link

---

59. So, e.g., Bultmann, "ΔΙΚΑΙΟΣΥΝΗ," 13.

the vocabulary of "righteousness" with mention of "the" (or even *a*) covenant,[60] and a consequent neglect of recent Pauline scholarship, which connects the two constantly.[61] The oversight must now be redressed. If, after all, "justification by faith" is to mean (what critics of the "Lutheran" Paul take it to mean) that Gentiles are included together with Jews in the people of God, then it would be most convenient if "the justified" were those "declared to be members in (the covenant, or) the people of God." The customary tack to reach that desired end is to suggest that "righteousness" language itself, when understood in a "Hebrew" rather than a "Greek" way, is "covenantal."[62] With that claim we may begin.[63]

The contrast between the *tsaddiq* (LXX δίκαιος) and the "wicked," together with that between the "wise" and "fools," is perhaps the central motif of the book of Proverbs; no book in the Bible uses the language of righteousness with anything approaching comparable frequency.[64] Yet the framework of Proverbs

---

60. Paul's references to covenants of any description are few, and he never in fact speaks of "the covenant" without further definition. He knows Israel's *covenants* (plural; Rom. 9:4); an old covenant and a new (1 Cor. 11:25; 2 Cor. 3:6, 14); a covenant represented by promises made to Abraham 430 years before the law was given (the term "covenant" is chosen because, in Greek, it can also refer to a "will"; Gal. 3:15, 17); and two covenants represented by Abraham's two sons (4:22-24). Those who would make *the* covenant a central concept in Pauline thought thus distort Pauline usage of the term as well as its peripheral character in his epistles (cf. Martyn, "Events," 179); and the view that "righteousness" in Paul means "membership in the covenant" labors under the added liability that nothing in Paul's writings makes it self-evident which, of the several he mentions, he would have envisaged as "the" covenant. Perhaps I should add that nothing said in this section is meant to question the propriety of highlighting the concept of covenant in the belief that it encapsulates themes crucial to Jewish and/or Christian faith. At issue is simply the propriety of ascribing that hermeneutical move to Paul.

61. Seifrid, "Declaration," 124, speaks of the "covenant romanticism" that "has captured current study of Paul, in which 'the covenant with Israel' has become the unexamined basis for resolving all questions about his soteriology."

62. Cf. Dunn, *Law*, 190; *Theology*, 341-42.

63. For a fuller treatment, see Seifrid, "Language," 415-42, with extensive bibliography.

64. To cite evidence from two chapters only, *tsaddiq* and cognate forms are found in Prov. 10:2, 3, 6, 7, 11, 16, 20, 21, 24, 25, 28, 30, 31, 32; 11:4, 5, 6, 8, 9, 10, 18, 19, 21, 23, 28, 30, and 31; in most cases a contrast is drawn with "wickedness" or "the wicked." It should be noted that "the righteous" in Proverbs (as, generally, in biblical and postbiblical Jewish texts) are not considered to be without sin (cf. Prov. 20:9; Yinger, *Judgment,* 62). Still, it is assumed that the basic orientation of one's life (whether righteous or wicked) will be reflected in one's actions (see Yinger, 25-26). Occasional reminders in the literature that in God's eyes no one can *really* be "righteous" (e.g., Job 4:17-19; 15:14-16; 25:4-6; Ps. 143:2) obviously intend the term in a stricter sense: no one can be entirely without sin (cf. 1 Kings 8:46; Prov. 20:9; Eccles. 7:20). Such reminders do at least demonstrate that "righteousness," by definition, pertains to doing what one ought, not belonging to a covenant. The point is perhaps clearest when members of the covenant community at Qumran confess their own (together with all humanity's) lack of righteousness (cf. Sanders, *Paul Pal. Jud.,* 281).

(and of Old Testament "wisdom" literature in general) is emphatically *not* covenantal (the word "covenant" is not mentioned in Proverbs apart from a reference to marriage in 2:17): since God "by wisdom" created heaven and earth (3:19), it behooves human beings to gain "wisdom" and to govern their lives accordingly (so showing themselves "wise" and "righteous") if they would prosper. For a significant strand of Hebrew literature, then, what human beings (Israel is not specified) ought and ought not to do is discussed using the language of righteousness in a completely *non*covenantal framework.

According to Genesis 18, the judgment that loomed over Sodom would have been avoided had its people included but ten who were "righteous" (18:23-32) — inasmuch as God, the judge of all the earth, would not have destroyed the "righteous" (people of Sodom) together with their wicked neighbors (18:25). Righteousness for the people of Sodom was a life-and-death issue, but the citizens were part of no covenant. Nor, for that matter, were covenantal considerations weighed in determining the righteousness of the people of Gerar (Gen. 20:4), or that of such well-known non-Israelites as Noah (6:9; 7:1) and Job (LXX Job 1:1).[65]

Conversely, in the Hebrew and Greek (LXX) Bibles, membership in the covenant people of God carries with it no entailment of righteousness (*tsedaqah*/δικαιοσύνη). In becoming God's people Israel was certainly set apart from the nations as *"holy"* (Deut. 7:6). But their adoption into the covenant was not based on any claim on their part to "righteousness" (9:4-5), nor is it said to convey righteousness to them: they remain — even *as God's people,* and in explicit contrast with righteousness — a "stubborn [literally, 'stiff-necked'] people" (9:6). As the adopted and redeemed people of God, they can be said to have more *reason* than others to do what they ought. Moreover, the commandments given to govern their behavior are themselves righteous (4:8), so that Israel can be said to find its "righteousness" *(tsedaqah)* in *observing* them (6:25; the Greek here reads ἐλεημοσύνη). The Sinaitic covenant may thus be said to provide its members with a framework within which righteousness is to be pursued, and where unambiguous guidance is given on how to attain it. Still, not even Israelites within the covenant are righteous without doing righteousness. And though what Israelites *ought* to do — and hence what makes them righteous — is to keep the laws of the covenant, "righteousness" does not *mean* "covenant faithfulness"; otherwise (as noted above) it could not be expected of Gentiles.

---

65. Nor is covenant membership the issue when judges decide the "rightness" of particular complaints. Egregious wrongs could indeed lead to the exclusion of the wrongdoer from the community. But not all cases involved egregious wrong in which judges (and God) were to "declare the righteous to be in the right, rewarding them according to their righteousness" (1 Kings 8:32).

Throughout the Hebrew and Greek (LXX) Scriptures, "righteous" *and* "wicked" are found side by side, in Israel and other nations. The two are distinguished, in Israel as among the nations, by their deeds.[66] And whether one is one or the other matters supremely when God judges the world and *all* its peoples in *righteousness* (LXX Pss. 9:9 [also MT; English versions 9:8]; 95:13 [MT, English 96:13]; 97:9 [MT, English 98:9]).

The case is no different in postbiblical Hebrew and Jewish texts in Greek: righteousness is a matter of doing what one ought (in the case of Jews, this may well mean keeping the laws of the covenant), not belonging to a covenant per se.[67] In support we may note the following considerations.

a. It is a matter of discussion whether Gentiles — who are by definition outsiders to *any* Jewish covenant — can be righteous; some thought they could.[68]

b. Acknowledgment is repeatedly made that no human being is really "righteous"[69] (though *some* human beings were always thought to belong to God's covenant people).

c. God's people are nonetheless called upon to be righteous, as God is righteous.[70]

d. Individuals known for their peculiar piety are singled out for the label "righteous."[71]

---

66. See the references to Ezekiel in n. 9 above.

67. The breadth of our question is such that developments in the usage of the terminology (see, e.g., n. 11 above) and distinctions between its usage in different sources (cf. nn. 36 and 37 above) need not be considered. In suppport of the *broad* point being made, note the following quotations: "The division between the righteous and the wicked [in the Old Testament Pseudepigrapha and the Qumran literature] did not correspond generally to the division between Jews and non-Jews. Instead, the division was between the righteous and the wicked *within* Israel according to their deeds" (Yinger, *Judgment,* 155); "*zedek* is here [1QS] best viewed as the quality of that which is right and pleasing to God, while *tsedaqah* is an action in keeping with that quality" (Bockmuehl, "Salvation," 397); "just as [in the Damascus Document] the noun *tsedeq* is a technical term for the proper conduct of man, so the adjective *tsaddiq* is used in the Damascus Document to designate those whose conduct is in accordance with *tsedeq*" (Przybylski, *Righteousness,* 22); and in Tannaitic literature, "the righteous are those who practise the commandments. . . . Being righteous *(tsaddiq)* is the result of man's actions" (Przybylski, 52).

68. See Donaldson, *Paul,* 65-69; Przybylski, *Righteousness,* 48; Sanders, *Paul Pal. Jud.,* 206-12.

69. Cf. 11Q5 XXIV, 7: "Do not judge me according to my sin; for no one living is deemed righteous *(yitsdaq)* before you." Also 1QH XVII (Sukenik IX), 14-15; VIII (Sukenik XVI), 19; XV (Sukenik VII), 28.

70. *Sifre Deut* 49 (Finkelstein, p. 114; on 11:22). Cf. Przybylski, *Righteousness,* 43.

71. *Sifre Deut* 1 (Finkelstein, p. 5; on 1:1); 38 (Finkelstein, p. 75; on 11:10). Cf. Przybylski, *Righteousness,* 44.

e. Gradations of righteousness, depending on variations in virtue, are spoken of in several texts.[72]

f. A number of texts make apparent the particular virtue or behavior on which the designation "righteous" (or "righteousness") in a particular case is based;[73] elsewhere right action more broadly defined is meant.[74]

g. "The righteous" are treated in various texts as parallel to those who fear God,[75] those who love God,[76] the faithful,[77] those who walk in perfection,[78] those who serve God,[79] those who walk honestly,[80] and so on.

h. Everywhere we find a contrast drawn between the language of righteousness and that of wickedness.[81]

That (in the eyes of some Jews) *all* Gentiles could be dismissed as "sinners,"[82] and that the label "righteous" could be limited to faithful observers of

---

72. 1QH XVII (Sukenik IX), 15; *Sifre Deut* 10 (Finkelstein, p. 18, on 1:10); 47 (Finkelstein, pp. 104-7, on 11:21). Cf. Przybylski, *Righteousness*, 45.

73. Note *Sifre Deut* 33 (Finkelstein, pp. 59-60, on 6:6), where the righteous are distinguished from the wicked in that they bound themselves by oath *not* to yield to their evil inclination, whereas the latter bound themselves by oath to do so. See also *m. Avot* 2:2; *m. Sotah* 1:9; *Sifre Deut* 16 (Finkelstein, p. 27, on 1:16). Cf. Przybylski, *Righteousness*, 44, 61-65.

74. E.g., 4QMMT C 31-32 (4Q398 14-17 ii 7-8): "And it shall be credited to you as righteousness *(tsedaqah)* when you do what is upright and good before him." Cf. Mijoga, *Notion*, 102. According to *Sifre Deut* 47 (Finkelstein, p. 105, on 11:21), there is no "enmity, hatred, jealousy, or rivalry" among the righteous. Cf. also *Sifre Num* 133 (Horovitz, p. 176, on 27:1), quoted by Przybylski (*Righteousness*, 62): "R. Nathan says: Scripture teaches you that (with) every righteous person *(tsaddiq)* who (according to scripture) grew up in the bosom of a wicked person *(rashaʿ)* and did not do according to his deeds, (this is reported) to make known to you how great his righteousness *(tsidqo)* must have been that he grew up in the bosom of a wicked person *(rashaʿ)* and did not do according to his deeds. And every wicked person *(rashaʿ)* who (according to scripture) grew up in the bosom of a righteous person *(tsaddiq)* and did not do according to his deeds (this is reported) to make known to you how great his wickedness *(rishʿo)* must have been that he grew up in the bosom of a righteous person *(tsaddiq)* and did not do according to his deeds."

75. *Pss. Sol.* 2:33-34; 13:11-12.

76. *Pss. Sol.* 10:3; *Sifre Deut* 10 (Finkelstein, p. 18, on 1:10).

77. 4Q521 2 II, 5-6.

78. CD I, 20-21.

79. CD XX, 20-21.

80. 4Q184 1, 14-15.

81. Note *Pss. Sol.* 3:6-7: "Sin does not dwell on top of sin in the house of the righteous. The righteous is ever searching his house, to banish the unrighteousness of any false step he may have taken." Contrast v. 10: the sinner has piled up "sins upon sins." Note also *Pss. Sol.* 2:33-35; 13:6-12; 14:6-10; *m. Avot* 5:1; CD IV, 7; XX, 20-21; 1QH XII (Sukenik IV), 38; *Sifre Deut* 53 (Finkelstein, pp. 120-21, on 11:26).

82. Cf. Abegg, "Works Righteousness," 144-45.

(a particular understanding of) the laws of the covenant,[83] should not be thought to imply that "sinner" and "righteous" *mean* "outsider to" and "member of the covenant" respectively; the point is simply that only those faithful to (a particular understanding of) the laws of the covenant were thought to do what they ought and live as they should. The texts, it need hardly be said, show no reticence in remarking on the sins that *made* others "sinners."[84] Here, to be sure, the categories of "sinners" and "outsiders" on the one hand and "righteous" and "faithful members of the covenant" on the other *overlap* entirely; yet the terms (like "Cretan" and "liar") do not *mean* the same thing. If "sinner" *meant* "outsider to the covenant," then human sinfulness would have originated, not with the disobedience of Adam, but with the divine granting of the covenant to Abraham. To the best of my knowledge, evidence of such a notion is not forthcoming.

And what of Paul? In *none* of the texts cited above where the language of ordinary dikaiosness is used is the context covenantal. "There is none righteous" (Rom. 3:10) does not mean "there is no one in 'the (?) covenant'"; the point (as the context renders indubitable) is that everyone — Jew and Gentile alike — is an incorrigible sinner. Whether or not the "righteous" person for whom one would scarcely be prepared to die (5:7) is a member of some covenant was scarcely in Paul's mind when he employed the epithet. Nor is his own covenant membership the issue when he used the verb to say that, though aware of no wrongdoing on his part, he was not thereby "acquitted" (1 Cor. 4:4). Since the "doers of the law" in Romans 2:13 potentially include Gentiles (2:14), their covenant membership cannot be the point of saying that God will find them righteous; they are righteous because they have done what they ought. And so on.

What, then, of extraordinary righteousness? In the relevant texts the treatment one would expect to be accorded the righteous (those who do what is right) is extraordinarily granted to those who are *not* righteous ("sinners," the "ungodly," etc.). Since covenant membership is not the issue in the adjudication of the ordinarily righteous, it can hardly be the point where the same treatment is administered to "sinners." If further confirmation is needed, note that the negative counterpart to being granted extraordinary righteousness is being condemned (2 Cor. 3:9; cf. Rom. 5:16, 18; and see Matt. 12:37). Indeed, in 2 Corinthians 3:9 the ministry of the Sinaitic *covenant* itself is one of *condemnation*.

In short, "righteousness," by definition, represents what "sinners," as "sinners," lack and need. It is *not*, by definition, that from which Gentiles, *as* Gentiles, are excluded.

---

83. Cf. Dunn, *Law*, 73-77; Winninge, *Sinners*, 185-86.
84. E.g., *Pss. Sol.* 2:3-17, 35; 14:6.

And what of *God's* righteousness? Is it his covenant faithfulness?

Perhaps the first thing to be said is that there is no antecedent reason why it should *not* be. Part of the righteousness of the righteous is that they keep their commitments, and Paul certainly believed that God made promises to the patriarchs[85] that he kept through the servanthood of Christ (Rom. 15:8). The gospel itself, though for all people, brings salvation "first" to the Jew who believes (1:16). That it does so confirms God's faithfulness to his people. All the preconditions are in place, then, for Paul to speak of God's "covenant faithfulness" as his "righteousness."

On the other hand, "righteousness" itself does not *mean* "covenant faithfulness."[86] And — botheration! — when Paul speaks of God's promises he never speaks of God's righteousness, and when he speaks of God's righteousness he never speaks of God's promises.[87] It is true that he talks of God's "righteousness" in 1:17 immediately after saying that the gospel brings salvation "first" to the Jew; but in the context, what is righteous about God's righteousness is not that the message of salvation is directed in the first instance to Jews,[88] but that it reverses human *un*righteousness (1:18), making "righteous" all who have faith (1:17), bringing salvation to all who believe (1:16). Similarly, the "righteousness of God" in 3:22 is manifestly what overcomes the impossibility of anyone being "declared righteous" by the law (3:20), and what "freely declares righteous" those who have sinned (3:23-24). In 3:25-26 God's righteousness is shown, not because an unmentioned promise has been kept, but because Christ's atoning death makes it a "righteous" thing for God to do when he "declares righteous" those who have faith in Jesus.[89]

85. In Gal. 3:16-17 the "promises" to Abraham are even called a "covenant" in one of Paul's rare usages of the term. On the important theme of promise and fulfillment in Pauline theology, see Söding, "Verheissung," 146-70.

86. Cf. Schreiner, *Paul*, 197-99.

87. Rom. 3:5 is perhaps a partial exception, since God's righteousness here at least includes his faithfulness to Israel in spite of Israel's own *un*faithfulness (3:3). But the term even in 3:5 is broader, since it is that by which God judges the world (3:5-7).

88. Note that *judgment* is said to be "to the Jew first" in Rom. 2:9-10. The phrase underlines Israel's special place in God's dealings with humanity, but hardly in itself signals the fulfillment of particular (here unmentioned) promises.

89. The apparent challenge to God's righteousness in 3:25-26 (as noted above; and cf. Barrett, *Romans*, 75-76; Cranfield, *Romans*, 211-12; Sanday and Headlam, *Romans*, 89-91; etc.) is (very explicitly) his "overlooking of sins in the past" ("for a demonstration of his righteousness *on account of the overlooking of past sins*"); Christ's atoning death proves that God is nonetheless righteous. Hays ("Logic," 112-13; cf. *Echoes*, 52-53) finds the substance of 3:21-26, and its demonstration of divine righteousness, in the claim that "God has not abandoned his people"; this is thought to answer the questions Hays finds raised in 3:1-8: "Has God abandoned his promises to Israel? Is he inconsistent or unjust?" But (i) the question whether God

In brief, God's "righteousness" *need* not mean his "covenant faithfulness"; given Paul's general inattention to matters covenantal, it is unlikely that it would do so; and nothing in the contexts in which he uses the term requires such a sense. Links can of course be drawn (though Paul does not draw them) between God's righteousness and commitments he made to Abraham;[90] one who crosses a stream to look for water on the other side may well find it. But why ignore the stream? God's righteousness in Paul is, explicitly, the act of divine grace by which, through the sacrificial death of his Son, he declares sinners righteous — thus championing (see sec. iv above) the goodness of his creation.

2. In Sanders's *Paul and Palestinian Judaism*, the claim is made that, for Paul but *not* for Judaism, *dikaio-* terminology is "transfer" terminology; that is, it is used of the transfer by which those who are otherwise *not* God's people become the people of God (they "get in," to use Sanders's phrase).[91] Since, in Judaism, Jews can be said to "get in" by an act of God's grace (the election of Israel), and Paul says the same about Christians, "grace" effectively plays the same role in Judaism as in Pauline Christianity. The similarity, according to Sanders, is obscured by Paul's peculiar usage of the *dikaio-* terminology.

The role that Sanders assigns grace in Judaism will be explored in chapter 17 below. Here our focus must be confined to his claims about the language of righteousness.

The view that *dikaio-* terminology in Paul refers to the transfer by which "outsiders" are brought into the people of God is, of course, at best true only of his extraordinary usage; and even here, though Paul clearly believes that those who are "declared righteous" become members of God's people, being declared righteous is not the *same* as being declared such a member. That said, it is certainly worth noting that in Paul's most distinctive usage, *dikaio-* terminology is *linked* to the process by which people *become* members in the people of God,

---

has abandoned his people is at best indirectly raised in 3:1-4; the direct question is whether Jews have, or circumcision brings, any advantage. A question that is not put can scarcely be the focus of the subsequent argument. (ii) God's righteousness is indeed questioned in 3:5-8, but the point of the question in *these* verses is not whether God has abandoned Israel, but whether God can be just in judging the world whose evil brings God glory. Paul raises the objection only to dismiss it; it is in any case *not* the subject of his demonstration of God's righteousness in 3:25-26. (iii) The focus of 3:21-26 is on the divine response to the sinfulness of *all* human beings. Not only are Jews *not* singled out for special mention; Paul makes a point of insisting that, on the subject under discussion, "there is no difference" (3:22). It is hard to see how, on a subject in which "there is no difference," Paul's point can be that "God has not abandoned his people."

90. Cf. Williams, "Righteousness," 241-90.

91. *Paul Pal. Jud.*, 544-45; cf. Sanders's *Law*, 45.

whereas in Judaism the vocabulary is (largely) restricted to those already deemed to belong. Indeed, the observation appears to have a significance beyond what Sanders envisions.

For Sanders Paul uses *dikaio-* terminology in a variety of ways; the noun, for example, sometimes means (according to Sanders) simply "salvation" or "life."[92] Clearly Paul *does* employ a variety of terms — a variety of *pictures,* we may say — for the process by which outsiders become Christians. The pictures are not, however, "dead" metaphors, nor are they completely interchangeable.[93] The "saved" but not those "declared righteous" are contrasted with the "perishing" (1 Cor. 1:18; 2 Cor. 2:15). One is "saved" but not "declared righteous" from "the wrath" (Rom. 5:9; cf. 1 Thess. 5:9). "Enemies" are "reconciled," not "declared righteous" (Rom. 5:10); "sinners" (or the "ungodly") are "declared righteous," not "reconciled" (4:5; 5:8-9; Gal. 2:15-17). Righteousness but not reconciliation or salvation is contrasted with "condemnation" (Rom. 5:18; 2 Cor. 3:9; cf. Rom. 8:33-34).

Even in Paul's extraordinary usage of the vocabulary, then, the *dikaio-* terminology does not lose its (ordinary) connection to right- and wrongdoing and the adjudication of both. *God's* righteousness counters and transforms human *un*righteousness (Gk. ἀδικία, 1:17-18; cf. 3:10, 20-21). All have sinned, but they are freely declared righteous (3:23-24). David speaks of the extraordinary righteousness attributed to one whose sins were forgiven (4:6-8). Jesus was "handed over" for our transgressions and raised that we might be declared righteous (4:25). Christ died for sinners so that we would be declared righteous through his blood (5:8-9). Through the disobedience of one man many were made sinners, but through the obedience of another the many (sinners) will be made righteous (5:19). That an extraordinary acquittal of sinners is involved is the point of Paul's use of *dikaio-* language for the process by which outsiders (who, for Paul, are sinners) are transferred to the people of God (who, for Paul, are those acquitted of their sins for Christ's sake).[94]

92. *Paul Pal. Jud.,* 491-95, 501, 544-45.

93. So also Sanders: the various "transfer" terms are not all "synonymous" (*Law,* 6).

94. It is true that in Gal. 3:21 δικαιοσύνη is used as a parallel to the giving of life (as noted by Sanders, *Paul Pal. Jud.,* 495): "If a law that were able to give life had been given, then indeed dikaiosness would have been by the law." But the statement avoids a virtual tautology ("If a law that were able to convey righteousness had been given, then indeed righteousness would have been by the law") by a slight ellipsis: Paul assumes but leaves unstated that sin brings condemnation and death, whereas an acquittal *from* sin (δικαιοσύνη) brings life; cf. εἰς δικαίωσιν ζωῆς, Rom. 5:18; also 5:17, 21; 6:16. Alternatively, "lifegiving" in Gal. 3:21 ought to be interpreted, in the light of the reference to δικαιοσύνη, of an acquittal leading to life, in contrast with a condemnation that brings death; so Burton, *Galatians,* 195. The verse hardly justifies depriving δικαιοσύνη in Paul of its specific meaning.

It can hardly be an accident, then, that Paul but not Judaism relates *dikaio-* language to the "transfer" by which outsiders are brought within the people of God. (a) As Sanders notes, the rabbis had no doctrine of "the essential sinfulness of each man";[95] Paul did. Hence Paul but not Judaism (as a whole)[96] saw the process by which people "got into" the people of God as necessarily including their being acquitted ("declared righteous") of wrongdoing. (b) The divine election of Israel, though undoubtedly an act of divine grace and never even remotely "earned," *could* nonetheless be justified by the rabbis as entailing a recognition by God of some merit in Israel (or in some of its people);[97] in such contexts it could hardly be seen as involving the (extraordinary) acquittal of the "ungodly" — nor was it discussed by the rabbis in these terms. This, however, is precisely how Paul views entrance into the people of God, a process from which *any* divine recognition of human merit is programmatically excluded. (c) If one is to speak at all of "soteriology" in Judaism, it must be recognized that the term cannot mean quite what it means in discussions of Pauline Christianity. "There does appear to be in Rabbinic Judaism a coherent and all-pervasive view of what constitutes the essence of Jewish religion and of how that religion 'works,' and [Sanders notes] we shall occasionally, for the sake of convenience, call this view 'soteriology.'"[98] On the other hand, if (as in discussions of Pauline soteriology) the term is thought to "imply that all are in need of a salvation which they do not possess, thus further implying a concept of original sin," then the term should *not* be used of Judaism.[99] Again, the difference in soteriology (Jews did not think they had been saved from "lostness," whereas Paul thought Christians had) parallels the difference in usage of the *dikaio-* terminology: Jews did not (generally) think they were sinners who had become members of the covenant by being extraordinarily declared righteous, whereas for Paul such a declaration was an essential part of Christian salvation.

In short, that Paul but not Judaism connects *dikaio-* terminology with the process by which outsiders come to belong to God's people appears a curious anomaly as long as the terminology is allowed little force beyond its designation of the transfer. But when the terminology is granted its ordinary sense (those who do the right are the righteous, and God will acknowledge them as such) as well as its extraordinary sense in Paul (sinners who have not done the

---

95. *Paul Pal. Jud.,* 114. Cf. also 397: Jews had "*no* view of man's fundamental lostness."

96. Again, the Qumran *Hodayot* scroll points to the possibility of exceptions. Cf. also 1QS XI, 9-15.

97. See the discussion in chap. 17 below.

98. Sanders, *Paul Pal. Jud.,* 75.

99. Sanders, *Paul Pal. Jud.,* 17-18.

right are, through the death of Christ, declared by God to be righteous), then the difference between Paul's usage and that of Judaism becomes both intelligible and telling.[100]

---

100. In a similar vein, Sanders sees an inconsistency between Paul's willingness to speak of the "righteousness of the law" in some texts while denying elsewhere that righteousness *can* come through the law. Since, for Sanders, Paul's only reason for rejecting the righteousness of the law is that it is not the righteousness of faith, he can only suggest, on the one hand, that Paul's references to the righteousness of the law show that, dogmatic denials notwithstanding, Paul really knows that Jews have such a righteousness, and, on the other, that his dogmatic denials mean no more than that the righteousness of the law is not the right *kind* of righteousness (*Paul Pal. Jud.,* 484, 505-6, 546; also *Law,* 27, 45). The dilemma Sanders ascribes to Paul again arises from his emptying Paul's *dikaio-* terminology of its specific content. Once one recognizes that the righteousness of the law is what people should but do not do, it becomes evident why the term is *important* to Paul at the same time as he insists that the only viable righteousness for *sinners* is that of faith.

Chapter 16

Matters of Definition, 2:
The "Law" in Paul

Many Pauline interpreters think *other* Pauline interpreters misunderstand what Paul meant by the "law" and its "works." Some Pauline interpreters think Paul himself misunderstood what Judaism means by "the law." On both accounts, matters of definition require our attention.

Much of importance for Paul's understanding of law has been touched upon in the discussion of his *dikaio-* terminology. The more focused discussion of this chapter proceeds by arguing the following points.

1. Paul sometimes uses "law" (νόμος) to mean the Old Testament Scriptures, or more specifically the Pentateuch. But according to his most frequent usage, "law" refers to the Sinaitic legislation.

2. Though Paul certainly believes that the Old Testament Scriptures point to Christ and witness to the righteousness of faith, he understands the Sinaitic legislation as comprised of commandments that need "doing," and hence as based on works rather than faith.

3. It is fully consistent with this usage of "law" to see "law" and "gospel" as standing in contrast with each other. This conclusion is supported, not contradicted, by an examination of the Pauline phrase "law of faith" in Romans 3:27 and of Paul's argument in 9:30-32.

4. Paul does not use νόμος, by itself or together with ἔργα (works), to mean a *perversion* of the law held by "legalistic" Jews of his day. Indeed, the notion that the law demands works is a Pauline thesis, not a Jewish misunderstanding.

5. Paul's usage of νόμος is fully in line with Hebrew usage of *torah*.

i. The Meaning of "Law"

We begin with the uncontroversial. Both Hebrew *torah* and Greek νόμος had long been used to denote the first part of the sacred Scriptures of the Jews (the Pentateuch), and Paul uses νόμος (law) in this sense as well. The sacred writings could then be said to be made up of "the law and the prophets" (Rom. 3:21; cf. Matt. 7:12; John 1:45; Acts 13:15; etc.). Moreover, when Paul speaks of a passage in Isaiah as coming from the "law" (1 Cor. 14:21, of Isa. 28:11-12), and provides a series of quotations from the Psalms and Isaiah (Rom. 3:10-18) as evidence of what "the law says" (v. 19), his extension of the term "law" to include the sacred Scriptures as a whole can be paralleled in both Greek and Hebrew sources.[1] On this, at least, there is agreement.

In the same verse that Paul refers to the testimony of "the law (= the Pentateuch) and the prophets," he claims that the "righteousness of God has been manifested *apart from the law* (χωρὶς νόμου)" (3:21). The wordplay is no doubt deliberate: God's righteousness is both "apart from the law" and supported by "the law" (and the prophets). In the former case "law" cannot mean the Pentateuch or the sacred Scriptures as a whole. For its definition we turn to Paul's usage of the term in Romans 2, which provides the context for Paul's claim.

According to Romans 2, non-Jews do not "have" the law (v. 14), whereas Jews both have it (v. 20) and rely on it to provide instruction in God's will (vv. 17-18). So much could, of course, be said of the Jewish Scriptures. But other verses show that "law" is used here in ways inappropriate of the sacred text as a whole. The law is something that can be "done" (cf. "doers of the law [ποιηταὶ νόμου]," v. 13; πράσσειν, v. 25) or "kept" (τελεῖν, v. 27). Conversely, one may be a "transgressor" of the law (παραβάτης νόμου, vv. 25, 27; cf. v. 23). Such usages presuppose that the law in this narrower sense is made up of requirements that may be kept or broken by those subject to them. Again, in verse 14 the components of the law (τὰ τοῦ νόμου) are the object of "doing" (ποιεῖν); presumably they are equivalent to "the precepts of the law" (τὰ δικαιώματα τοῦ νόμου) that, according to verse 26, are to be "kept" (φυλάσσειν). Similarly, τὸ ἔργον τοῦ νόμου (literally, "the work of the law," v. 15) is correctly paraphrased "what the law requires" (RSV). In fact, Paul supplies in this context several examples of the law's requirements: the prohibition of stealing, adultery, and idol worship are among the demands with which Jews are familiar because they possess the law, but which, according to Paul, they nonetheless transgress, thus "breaking the law" (vv. 20-23). The particular commands listed are, of course, all taken from the Decalogue (Exod. 20:1-17).

---

1. Cf. John 10:34; 15:25; Bacher, *Terminologie,* 197.

Evidence that for Paul "law" is frequently used in this narrower sense of a particular collection of divine requirements is not confined to Romans 2. According to Galatians 6:13, Paul's opponents "do not themselves *keep* (φυ-λάσσειν) the law." If those who are circumcised are "bound to *keep* (ποιεῖν; literally 'do') the whole law" (5:3), then "the whole law" is obviously a collection of demands to be kept. Returning to Romans, we find that the introduction of the law at the time of Moses (Rom. 5:13-14; cf. Gal. 3:17) is what made "transgression" possible (Rom. 4:15): demands must be made before they can be broken! Romans 7:7-12, a most revealing passage, uses "law" and "commandment (ἐντολή)" interchangeably: "I was once alive apart from the *law,* but when the *commandment* came, sin sprang to life and I died. . . . So the *law* is holy, and the *commandment* is holy, righteous, and good." Here the prohibition of coveting (v. 7; cf. Exod. 20:17) is given as one of the law's requirements. Other commandments from the Decalogue, together with the requirement of neighbor love, are listed as demands of the law in Romans 13:9-10.

All these texts indicate that the "law" in Paul's writings frequently (indeed, most frequently) refers to the sum of specific divine requirements given to Israel through Moses.[2] This usage of the term must be carefully distinguished from instances in which the Pentateuch or the sacred Scriptures as a whole are meant. That ambiguous cases — such as the notorious Romans 3:31[3] — occur is not surprising, since the divine legislation ("law" in the narrower sense) is contained within the sacred Scriptures ("law" in the broader sense). But such instances are few and would not seem to justify the general claim that Paul normally means by νόμος "the Old Testament Law (without distinguishing between the legal parts and the rest of the Pentateuch)."[4] The law that can be kept, done, fulfilled, or transgressed is clearly "the legal parts" of the Pentateuch. The law given 430 years after the Abrahamic promise (Gal. 3:17, 19) was not the Pentateuch as a whole but the Sinaitic legislation, the substance of the νομοθεσία ("the giving of the law") mentioned in Romans 9:4.

The Sinaitic legislation was accompanied by promises and sanctions, and Paul includes these when he speaks of the law. Thus the law offers life to those who perform its commands (10:5; Gal. 3:12; cf. Rom. 2:13, 25; 7:10), while it pronounces a curse on transgressors (Gal. 3:10, 13). When the law has been transgressed, its curse becomes operative, so that the law of God, like sin and death, can be personified as a hostile power from which people need deliverance (4:5; cf. Rom. 5:20; 7:6). Later we will need to examine the passages in which Paul

---

2. Cf. Maurer, *Gesetzeslehre*, 82.

3. See the discussion of possible meanings for νόμος here in Rhyne, *Faith*, 27, 31-32, 71-74.

4. Cranfield, "Law," 44.

speaks of people being "under the law." Here we may anticipate that discussion by saying that the basic meaning of the phrase appears to be "bound by the demands of the Mosaic law code and subject to its sanctions."

ii. The Law and "Works"

That the Old Testament Scriptures predicted "the sufferings of Christ and the glories that followed" (1 Pet. 1:11) was the universal conviction of the early Christians, but Paul's use of the witness of Scripture goes much further. He finds the righteousness of faith itself to be announced in Scripture (Rom. 3:21; Gal. 3:8), noting Scripture's declaration that Abraham was justified by faith (Rom. 4:3-5), its pronouncement of blessing on those counted righteous "apart from works" (vv. 6-8), the promise it contains for Abraham and his offspring (v. 13; Gal. 3:16), and so on. In a discussion of Romans 10:4, Räisänen disputes (rightly, I believe) the view that τέλος in this verse means "goal"; he adds, however — what no one will dispute — that it is at least fully consistent with Pauline thought to say that Christ is the goal of the Old Testament law in this sense: the Scriptures point to the Savior.[5]

But, as we have seen, "law" in Paul most often means the Sinaitic legislation, and *it is not legitimate to apply what Paul says of the Scriptures in general to the Sinaitic laws without further ado*.[6] It does not follow, for example, that because Paul thought *the Scriptures* witness to faith, or contain the divine promise, he could not have contrasted *the Sinaitic legislation* with faith and God's promise. On this score the apostle proves repeatedly free of constraints that bind at least some of his interpreters.

Cranfield, for example, has argued that Paul uses "law" in Galatians 3:15-25 to mean something less than "the law in the fullness and wholeness of its true character"; it is "the law as seen apart from Christ."[7] His reason for suggesting

5. Räisänen, *Law*, 53-56; cf. Sanders, *Law*, 38-39.

6. Cf. Moo, "Law," 88.

7. Cranfield, "Law," 63; also Schnabel, *Law*, 274. Cranfield here echoes Calvin, who (see the discussion in chap. 3) believed Paul sometimes used "law" to mean the whole Mosaic religion, which was based (in Calvin's view) no less than that of Christ on the righteousness of faith: indeed, its efficacy depended on the mediating work of Christ foreshadowed in its rituals. Calvin also allowed, however, that Paul sometimes used "law" to mean only "what belonged peculiarly to the law" — its commands and prohibitions, promises and threats — *apart from Christ*. This is "the bare law in a narrow sense." Paul was compelled to adopt such a usage because others sought to attain righteousness by keeping the commandments of the law without recognizing the law's relationship to Christ. For Calvin there could be no contrast between the "law," rightly understood, and the gospel, though such a contrast clearly obtains if the law is understood

that Paul must be speaking of a distorted form of the law is that "Paul here distinguishes the promise from the law (verses 17 and 21), although the promise in question is contained in the Pentateuch."[8] Räisänen has shown that such an interpretation cannot be sustained: if Paul meant by the "law" in verses 17 and 19 what he is supposed to have meant by the "law" in 18, it would follow that 430 years after the promise was given to Abraham, the angels gave Israel a distorted form of the law on Mount Sinai; in that case one wonders when the true law arrived![9] But Cranfield's dilemma was simply not felt by Paul; certainly the Pentateuch (the law in a broader sense) contains the "promise," but Paul here means by "law" the Sinaitic legislation. And in this sense the Mosaic law and the Abrahamic promise are not only distinct, but are even said to be mutually exclusive as ways for granting the "inheritance" (v. 18). We will return to this contrast below.

George Howard argues that 3:12 cannot mean what it is usually taken to mean, that the law does not rest on faith. "Is it proper to ascribe such an argument to the apostle when it must have been clear to all that faith was the very warp and woof of the law? The whole law and the Prophets were fundamentally and primarily concerned with faith in God and all that that implied, including loyalty, trust, commitment and absolute submission to his sovereignty."[10] Howard is of course correct in insisting on the prominence of faith in *Scripture* ("the whole law and the Prophets"). But, as we have just seen, the law in the context of 3:12 is not Scripture as a whole, but the Sinaitic legislation. And what Paul says of Scripture must not be transferred automatically to "law" in this narrower sense.

To repeat: according to Paul's most frequent usage of νόμος, the term refers to the sum of specific divine requirements given to Israel through Moses. They are intended to be "done" (ποιεῖν, πράσσειν) or "kept" (φυλάσσειν, τελεῖν), though the placing of concrete demands of course makes possible the "transgression" (παράβασις) of the law as well as its obedience. With this in mind we return to the passage — 3:12 in its context — at which Howard takes offense.

---

without Christ. The point here is simply that *one* argument advanced in favor of such an interpretive scheme rests on a confusion about Paul's usage of νόμος. Cranfield has responded that Paul is not likely to have thought that the law in the narrower sense (i.e., the divine requirements given to Israel through Moses) could be "separated from its context in Scripture and assigned a value inferior to that of the rest of the Pentateuch" (*On Rom.*, 119). I am not suggesting that Paul *valued* the Mosaic legislation less than he did the Scriptures; I do think he could distinguish the two and see them serving different functions.

8. Cranfield, "Law," 62.

9. Räisänen, *Law*, 43-44.

10. Howard, *Crisis*, 63.

After citing Genesis 15:6 with its declaration that Abraham's faith was credited to him as righteousness (Gal. 3:6), Paul concludes that those who share Abraham's faith are those recognized as his children (3:7). Indeed, when Abraham was promised that all nations would be blessed in him, Scripture had in mind that God would declare Gentiles righteous through faith (3:8);[11] their faith thus brings them the same blessing (the same declaration of righteousness) that Abraham enjoyed by faith (3:9). The blessing linked to faith in 3:7-9 is then contrasted in 3:10 with the situation created for its adherents by the law: all who are "of the works of the law"[12] are (not declared righteous, but) under a curse — the curse that (according to Deut. 27:26) strikes the law's transgressors. The verse is of course intended to discourage Paul's Gentile Christian readers from adopting a Jewish way of life under the law (in the first place by being circumcised, though other Jewish observances would follow [5:2-6; 6:12; but also 4:10]); it does so by insisting that those subject to the law are the objects of its curse.[13]

11. The reference to Gentiles in v. 8 is taken over from Gen. 18:18; Paul is of course countering the insistence that Gentile believers submit to the law. Still, at this point in Paul's argument the justification of Gentiles *as such* is not Paul's focus, which is rather that *all* who are "of faith" (the phrase is hardly confined to *Gentile* believers) are thereby declared righteous just as Abraham was (Gal. 3:7, 9), whereas what the law brings to its subjects (whether they are Jews or Gentiles is not the issue here) is a curse (3:10). The question addressed throughout these verses is whether one is declared righteous by the law or by faith (in Jesus Christ); the ethnicity of the "one" to be declared righteous is irrelevant.

12. Since the quotation of Deut. 27:26 in Gal. 3:10b is meant to clarify the declaration of 3:10a, those who are "of the works of the law" and "under a curse" in 3:10a must be those obligated to do "all that is written in the book of the law" and cursed when they fail to do so in 3:10b. Those "of the works of the law" are thus those living within the sphere of the law's requirements and sanctions; they are those to whom the law's operative principle ("the one who does [its statutes] will live by them") applies (3:12). The phrase thus refers in the first place to Jews living under the Sinaitic covenant and to any Gentiles who join their number; all are said to be under the law's curse (3:10). At one point they must have included Paul himself as well as others (the "us" of 3:13) who have been redeemed by Christ *from the law's curse.* For other interpretations of the verse, see chap. 18, sec. iii.

13. The "curse" hanging over "all who are of the works of the law" in 3:10 may in fact be extended in 3:13 to include *all* sinners. In favor of such an extension we may note that (i) a redemption limited to Jewish Christians living under the Sinaitic law and to Gentiles who have joined them seems odd; (ii) the "we" in 3:14 certainly includes Gentile as well as Jewish believers, suggesting that it may do so in 3:13 as well (where "we" are the ones redeemed from the law's curse); (iii) in a similarly ambiguous passage in Gal. 4, Paul probably does include Gentiles among those redeemed "from under the law" (note that those so redeemed are said in 4:5 to have received the "adoption," and those who have received the adoption are said in 4:6 to include the Gentile Galatians). The ambiguity arises because (as we saw in our discussion of Paul's *dikaio-* terminology) Paul does not see the position of Jews under the Sinaitic covenant as *fun-*

Verse 11 follows; it is patient of at least three different interpretations.

1. After the assertion in 3:10 that "all who are of the works of the law" are subject to the law's curse against transgressors — a line of thought to which Paul will return in 3:13 — verse 11 can be seen as adducing a completely different argument in favor of the righteousness of faith. Habakkuk 2:4 affirms it and thereby — since the law is based on a different principle from that of faith (v. 12) — rules out the law as a path to justification.

2. Alternatively, 3:10 might be thought to lead directly into 3:11: the dilemma created by human transgression and the law's curse (3:10) provokes the question, How can *transgressors* who are under God's curse be found righteous (or "justified") in God's sight? Verses 11-14 then provide the answer: negatively, verses 11-12 rule out the possibility that this can take place through the law (it is clear that one cannot be found righteous in God's eyes by the law, since Habakkuk says one is righteous through faith and the law is based on a different principle); positively, verses 13-14 show that the death of Christ frees transgressors from the curse of the law, thus making it possible for Gentiles[14] to experience justification, the blessing promised to Abraham (cf. 3:8).

3. Yet another possible reading sees implicit already in the affirmation of 3:10 (all who are of the works of the law are under a curse) the conclusion that none can be justified by the law. Verse 11 is then rendered, "But *since* no one is found righteous in God's eyes by the law, it is clear that 'The righteous *through faith* shall live.'"[15] The righteousness of faith is thus seen (as in our second alternative) specifically as an emergency measure introduced to cope with the dilemma created by human transgression and the law's curse. That faith's righteousness must be distinguished from that of the law is then underscored by the declaration that the law is based on a different principle from that of faith

---

damentally different from that of Gentiles: *all* are subject to God's demands for righteous behavior (though for Jews these are spelled out in the commands of the Mosaic law); *none* in fact is righteous (Rom. 3:10; Gal. 3:22; 2:17 after v. 15), and therefore *all* are under God's wrath. That wrath, we may say, takes expression in the curse of the law for those who have been given its commands (3:10); but it seems that Paul, speaking somewhat loosely, allows that Gentiles delivered from God's wrath against sinners (Rom. 1:18; 5:9; 1 Thess. 1:10; etc.) are delivered from the (analogous) "curse of the law" in Gal. 3:13. On the ambiguity of Paul's pronouns in Galatians, see Young, "Shifts," 205-15. See further chap. 19, thesis 2 below.

14. That Gentiles ("nations") are mentioned in 3:14 as the recipients of the blessing of Abraham follows from the reference to the blessing of all the Gentiles ("nations") in 3:8. In fact, the blessing of justification of 3:14a and the promise of the Spirit of 3:14b are both the possession of all believers, Jews and Gentiles alike.

15. I.e., a comma is placed *before* δῆλον rather than after it, and the initial ὅτι is read "since." This interpretation, considered but rejected by Burton (*Galatians*, 166), is mentioned by Wright, *Climax*, 149 n. 42, and adopted by Kim, *Perspective*, 129, and Thielman, *Paul*, 127-28.

(v. 12). Paul then shows how Christ has coped with the law's curse (v. 13), opening the door to the justification of Gentiles promised to Abraham (v. 14; cf. v. 8).

Clearly the second and third interpretations allow for a smoother progression of thought than the first, which sees Paul introducing an argument in 3:11-12 unrelated to his claims in 3:10 and 14. For our purposes we need to note (1) that Jews are not faulted for trying to *do* what the law commands; on the contrary, Scripture is cited as saying that this is what the law requires; (2) that according to all three interpretations, the weight of Paul's argument falls on his insistence that the law brings a curse on its adherents (3:10) — a curse that is borne by Christ (3:13); (3) that the main thrust of the passage is thus hardly that righteousness is impossible under the law because it is based on a principle of works rather than one of faith; (4) that the latter observation is merely an aside, serving to underline why Habakkuk's claim that "the righteous *through faith* shall live" cannot have been meant to refer to the law (since the latter is based on a different principle); (5) that verse 12 is nonetheless a *telling* aside, in that it shows what for Paul is the operative principle of the law (it requires deeds in compliance with its commands) that distinguishes it from faith; (6) that, moreover, this distinction pertains directly to the relative efficacy of the two paths to righteousness. The law's basic principle ("The one [and *only* the one] who *does* these things will live by them" [3:12]) is, after all, what leads, by way of transgression, to its adherents being cursed rather than found righteous ("Cursed is every one *who does not abide* in all the things written in the book of the law *to do them*" [3:10]).[16] Conversely, the efficacy of the path of faith lies in what Christ has done *for* those cursed by the law ("Christ redeemed us from the curse of the law, having become a curse for us" [3:13]). When God offers righteousness to sinners through the curse-bearing death of Christ, those prepared to *trust* God will naturally abandon further efforts to gain righteousness by what *they* do, crediting and accepting the word of what God, in Christ, has done for them.[17]

The point is both obvious and crucial that what Paul means by "law" in Galatians 3:10-14 does not differ from his usage in the other passages we have considered: the "law" refers not to the Pentateuch, but to the divine requirements imposed upon Israel at Mount Sinai and intended (need it be said?) to be done. But whereas in other passages it was regarded as self-evident that the law

16. Cf. Wilckens, *Römer*, 1:175-76 n. 476.

17. Paul does *not* see "believing" and "doing" as opposed in *every* context; the *same* faith in God that will express itself in obedient activity where activity is called for will necessarily *abandon* further efforts to secure what God offers freely of his own initiative.

was to be done or kept, that it was not to be transgressed, here the axiom is made the basis for a fundamental claim about the nature of the law: *since* the basic principle of the law is that it requires deeds, it "does not rest on faith." Faith,[18] and deeds (or faith and the law) are seen — in this context at least — as exclusive alternatives.

18. I.e., the faith of believers. This is contested by Howard (*Crisis,* 46-65; "End," 335; "Faith," 459-65) and Hays (*Faith,* 119-96), who, wary of reading the Reformation's contrast between human faith and works into Paul, suggest that πίστις here refers to the divine "faithfulness." This interpretation is closely linked with their reading of the πίστις Χριστοῦ formulas (which are contrasted with "works of the law" in Gal. 2:16; cf. v. 20; 3:22; Rom. 3:22, 26; Phil. 3:9) as "the faithfulness of Christ" rather than (human) "faith in Christ." The debate generated by these claims has been both lively and extensive; its importance is easily exaggerated (as Hays, "Justification," 1131, rightly notes; cf. also Dunn, *Theology,* 385): both sides see human faith as the appropriate and necessary response to the gospel, and both sides agree that God declares believers righteous because of what Christ has done. For my part, I have no objection whatever to the subjective genitive reading of the πίστις Χριστοῦ formulas other than that it is wrong.

i. We may begin with Gal. 3:11-12: justification cannot be attained by the law since Habakkuk says it comes by faith ("the one who through faith is righteous shall live," v. 11) and "the law does not rest on faith" (v. 12). "Faith" in v. 12 must have the same meaning as in v. 11. Yet when Paul quotes Hab. 2:4 in Rom. 1:17, the verse is understood as referring to human faith rather than divine faithfulness (note that it is quoted to support the claim that salvation is for "every one who *believes,* for the Jew first and also for the Greek"). Presumably the verse is understood similarly when quoted in Gal. 3:11. (Note that Campbell, "Meaning," 91-103, proposes that the language of Hab. 2:4 "function[s] as the fundamental linguistic template" from which Paul derived the phrase ἐκ πίστεως and related expressions.) Moreover, the claim that one is "righteous through faith" in 3:11 is surely the same as that supported by the quotation from Gen. 15:6 in v. 6, where Abraham is credited with righteousness because *he* believed: human faith in God is meant.

ii. With regard to the πίστις Χριστοῦ formulas, the first thing to be said is that grammar cannot resolve the debate. Greek grammar allows genitives subjective *and* objective, and others that are neither. A main argument raised in support of the view that the πίστις Χριστοῦ formulas mean "the faithfulness of Christ" (subjective genitive) is that Paul's other uses of a genitive with πίστις are regularly subjective rather than objective. But this should not occasion surprise, since the list of possible objects of one's faith becomes all but depleted when "Jesus" (Rom. 3:26), "Christ" (Gal. 2:16), "Jesus Christ" (Gal. 2:16; 3:22; Rom. 3:22), and "the Son of God" (Gal. 2:20) are removed from it. "God" remains, to be sure; but in the context of Paul's mission it is natural that faith in Christ receives an emphasis that is not required for faith in God, and Mark 11:22 at least shows that "God" may stand as an objective genitive with πίστις. (Objective genitives with "faith" are also found in some if not all the following texts: Acts 3:16; Eph. 3:12; Phil. 1:27; Col. 2:12; 2 Thess. 2:13; James 2:1; and Rev. 2:13.)

iii. Against the view that the πίστις Χριστοῦ formulas refer to faith in Christ, it is frequently argued that such a reading makes Paul's language highly redundant in Gal. 2:16, 3:22, and Rom. 3:22. The argument has, however, been countered by the observation that an ambiguous phrase should be given the interpretation that imports the least new meaning into the context (cf. Silva, *Words,* 153-56; *Philippians,* 186-87, esp. n. 31); and in any case, the "redundancy" seen by some is

A contrast between faith and deeds — deeds demanded by *God's law* at that! — is so astonishing in the context of Jewish thought[19] that many have wondered whether Paul really intended it.[20] On the other hand, the two components on

---

denied by others: Gal. 2:16, after noting that one is declared righteous "by faith in Christ Jesus," emphasizes that (not only Gentile sinners [cf. 2:15] but) "we [Jews] too believed in Christ Jesus in order that *we* might be declared righteous by faith in Christ"; in any case, "faith in Christ," on the objective genitive reading of πίστις Χριστοῦ, is repeated in the verse no more than is "works of the law." An emphasis on the πάντας of Rom. 3:22 removes any redundancy in the objective genitive reading there; similarly with τοῖς πιστεύουσιν in Gal. 3:22.

iv. The issue, in the end, can only be resolved by a look at the broader context of the formulas in Pauline thought; and that context, to my mind, is decisive. Paul's thesis that one is *declared righteous* διὰ πίστεως Ἰησοῦ Χριστοῦ and *not by the works* of the law (Gal. 2:16; cf. Rom. 3:20, 28) is surely being restated in Rom. 4:5, where the "faith" is explicitly human: "To one who does *not work* but *trusts* (πιστεύοντι) him who *justifies* the ungodly, *his faith* is credited as *righteousness*." Similarly, it would be perverse to interpret "justified by faith" in Rom. 3:28 differently than in 5:1; but the latter verse is drawing a conclusion from 4:22-24, where righteousness is said to be "credited to *us who believe*" as Abraham believed. Human faith is meant. Nor should the faith that justifies according to 3:28 be different from the faith of the circumcised and the faith of the uncircumcised, the basis of justification according to v. 30 (cf. the similar insistence on the faith required of Jews and Gentiles alike in 1:16; 4:11-12; 10:11-12). And the "righteousness based on faith" (10:6) is expressed in the message "With the heart one believes and is justified" (v. 10). These references leave no doubt that when Paul speaks of faith as essential for justification, he is thinking of human faith.

On the other hand, important as Christ's "obedience" is to God's declaration of sinners as righteous (Rom. 5:19; cf. Phil. 2:8), Paul never calls *Christ's* obedience πίστις (faith, faithfulness); nor, given his association of faith in the "justification" texts with the appeal to God by the hopelessly sinful, would it have been natural for him to do so (cf. Cranfield, *On Rom.*, 96-97). The suggestion (Hays, *Faith*, 165) that Jesus Christ was "justified ἐκ πίστεως and that we, as a consequence, are justified *in* him" misconstrues the point of Paul's talk of justification as the extraordinary righteousness offered to sinners who believe (see chap. 15 above).

Readers anxious to familiarize themselves with the debate should be sure to allow sufficient time for the undertaking; they may profitably begin with the exchange between Richard Hays and James Dunn reprinted in the appendices of the second edition of Hays's *Faith*.

19. How, a Jew would wonder, is faith in God to be shown apart from obedience to his commands? Cf. Avemarie, "Werke," 291-92; Garlington, *Obedience of Faith*, 233 n. 1. But see n. 17 above.

20. In Sanders's view (*Paul Pal. Jud.*, 480, 483-84), Gal. 3:11-12 is a dogmatic declaration based on proof texts: since righteousness, according to Habakkuk, is by faith, it cannot be by law. But (i) the alternatives as such have already been clearly stated in 3:11; the point of adding v. 12 is to show that the law is based on a different *principle* from that of faith; (ii) it is (as noted above) precisely *because* the law by its very nature requires doing that it encounters transgressors as a curse (3:10, 13; cf. 4:4-5); (iii) the faith Paul has in mind is not simply *different* from law, but linked to a *redemption* from the dilemma that the law, with its requirements and curse, poses for sinners (3:10, 13; 4:4-5; cf. 2:17; 3:21-22); (iv) consistent with this difference are those noted earlier between the righteousness ("dikaiosness") granted *duly* to doers of the law and that granted freely, without works, as a gift to those who (do not work but) *believe* (cf. Rom. 4:1-8).

which the contrast rests — the gratuitousness of salvation by faith and the necessity of doing (and not merely hearing) the law — are both comprehensible enough in principle and sufficiently well attested in Paul's writings to caution against its hasty dismissal. In the end, what is decisive is not whether *non-Christian* Jews contrasted faith and deeds; we must allow for the possibility that Paul's perspective changed after his Damascus encounter with the risen Christ. The question to be asked is whether such a contrast has a basis in *his* thought.[21]

In Romans 4 Paul writes: "If it is those who adhere to the law who are to be the heirs, faith has been negated and the promise set aside. . . . That is why it depends on faith, in order that the promise may depend on grace" (vv. 14, 16). Two alternatives are envisaged: Abraham's "heirs" are either the adherents of the law or those who have faith (cf. v. 13). That Paul opts for faith should occasion no surprise. Note, however, that when Paul accounts for the viability of faith and the nonviability of the law, he *contrasts* the latter with faith, God's promise, and grace: all are excluded from a process in which obedience to the law is a requisite.[22] Granting at once that Paul's argument must incorporate premises foreign to Judaism, we may attempt to arrive at some understanding of what he meant by these crucial terms.

1. We may begin with grace. For Paul's (non-Christian) Jewish contemporaries, a contrast between law and grace would have been unthinkable: Torah, the sign of God's special favor to Israel, is scarcely to be *contrasted* with the divine grace that bestowed it.[23] Paul, too, saw the law as God's gift to Israel (cf. 3:2;

21. That the contrast *has* such a basis was shown in the discussion of Paul's usage of the *dikaio*- terminology in chap. 15 above. Here the issue is approached through what he says about the law.

22. Cf. Räisänen, "Legalism," 72: "Grace, faith, promise, and Spirit are, according to [Paul], something diametrically opposed to the law. The entirety of Paul's argument is, indeed, little more than a constant reiteration of this axiom." In the context of current discussions, it is worth noting that Paul follows up the protasis of his unreal condition in 4:14 ("if those who are of the law were heirs") by insisting that this would entail the exclusion, not of *Gentiles*, but of *faith* and the divine *promise*. And when in v. 16 Paul accounts for why the inheritance must be given by faith rather than the law, he begins, not with the inclusion of Gentiles, but with that of grace: "in order that it might be by grace." Paul then adds that because the granting of what God has promised is by grace, the inheritance is the sure possession of Jewish and Gentile believers alike. His point is not that the law would allow the promise to be given to Jews whereas faith allows it to be given to non-Jews as well, but that an inheritance granted through the law would not be secure for anyone ("for the law works wrath" on transgressors, 4:15), whereas the path of faith, dependent as it is on divine grace, makes the inheritance secure (βεβαίαν) for "all [Abraham's] seed," both Jews and non-Jews (4:16).

23. The contrast is unthinkable to a number of modern Pauline scholars as well; cf. W. D. Davies, *Studies*, 95, 117-18; Moule, "Obligation," 394-97. On the Pauline opposition between law and grace, see van Dülmen, *Theologie*, 176, 190-91.

9:4), but that conviction apparently did not prevent him from contrasting it with grace in 4:13-16 — as he manifestly does in 6:14-15 and Galatians 5:4. The "inheritance" is given either "through the law (διὰ νόμου)" or "through the righteousness of faith (διὰ δικαιοσύνης πίστεως)" (Rom. 4:13). And one of the reasons, according to Paul, that it had to be given by faith rather than the law was "in order that the promise may depend on grace" (ἵνα κατὰ χάριν, v. 16). Had the granting of the inheritance depended on law, it could not have been given κατὰ χάριν, "by grace."[24]

How are we to understand Paul's *contrast* between a path of law and one of grace? The context supplies the answer.

In 4:1-8 Paul argues that Abraham was declared righteous by faith rather than by his works. Had he been declared righteous by his works, he would have had something of which to boast and would have been credited with righteousness as his due. But since he was in fact (as Genesis attests) declared righteous by faith (and thus apart from works), he has nothing of which to boast; he was credited with righteousness by an act of grace, not in recognition of anything he had done. David (Ps. 32) attests a similar reckoning of righteousness "apart from works": so one must construe divine forgiveness of a sinner.

Such, in brief, is Paul's argument. What is important for us here is what it implies about the law. Four observations are in order.

a. The argument is conducted *without explicit reference to the law*. Paul celebrates a divine attributing of righteousness to those who show no righteous deeds, but the latter are not here linked to the law.[25]

b. Though the argument is advanced without reference to the law, its insistence that one is declared righteous by faith (4:3, 5) and "apart from works" (4:6; cf. v. 2, 5) is surely intended to paraphrase or support the thesis that "a person is declared righteous by faith apart from the works of the law" (3:28). The latter thesis, stated immediately before the argument of 4:1-8, is taken up after it as well (in 4:13-16).

c. If an argument about righteousness apart from righteous deeds (4:1-8) supports a conviction about righteousness "apart from the works of the law" (3:28), then the works that the law demands are presumably understood as righteous deeds, the kinds of deeds lacked by the "ungodly" person of 4:5 and

---

24. Sanders allows that *Paul* sees Christian faith based on grace and accuses Jews of "rejecting grace." Since, in Sanders's interpretation, the role Paul sees grace playing in Christian faith is in fact no different from what it played in Judaism, he concludes that Paul meant only that *true* grace is associated with the former but not the latter (*Law*, 157). Cf. also B. Longenecker, *Eschatology*, 213; *Triumph*, 140-41. It should be apparent from what follows, however, that for Paul a righteousness based on law cannot *by definition* be founded on grace.

25. See chap. 15, n. 42 above.

the sinner of 4:6-8. (This coheres nicely with what Paul says about the law in 2:13, 7:12, 10:5, etc., as noted in chapter 15.)

d. Such an understanding of a law that demands righteous deeds can readily be contrasted with grace, if the latter is understood (as in 4:4) as gratuitous gift. And the contrast drawn between dependence on *deeds* and dependence on grace in 4:1-8 accounts as well for the distinction drawn in 4:13-16 between the *law* and grace: an "inheritance" granted "through the law" would be one granted to those who did the law, and would be given as the recipients' due; it could not, then, be a gift of grace.

One other passage may be considered here.[26] That for Paul salvation is a gift of grace is of course not in dispute (the point is even more apparent, for example, in Rom. 5). But that, *because* salvation (or righteousness) is granted by grace, it *cannot* be granted through the law, is an (often unnoticed) emphasis in Romans 9 to 11 as well. In chapter 9 Paul is bent at all costs on making the point that God constitutes his people *without* regard to the deeds they do. As in 4:1-8, it is not *particular* works that Paul is concerned to exclude; God achieves his purposes without reference to human activity (in general). He chose Jacob, not Esau, "when they had not yet been born or done *anything good or bad,* so that God's intention of operating by means of his own election might proceed, depending not on (human) works but on the one who calls" (vv. 11-12).[27] Everything hinges "not on the one who wills or runs, but on God who shows mercy" (v. 16).[28] The insistence (again, familiar from Rom. 4) that a gift of grace excludes by definition any consideration of the works of the recipient is repeated in chapter 11: the "remnant" of God's people has come into being by a divine election of grace; "but if it is by grace, it is no longer on the basis of works; otherwise grace would no longer be grace" (11:5-6).

Paul underlines the same point in the paradoxical but programmatic formulation of 9:30-32: Gentiles have "obtained righteousness" *without* striving for ("pursuing") it, whereas Jews are engaged in a vain "pursuit" based upon works.[29] That the point is important to Paul is confirmed by its repetition: in chapter 10 he will note that God has been "found by those who did not seek

---

26. For what follows, see my articles "Romans 9–11," 215-37, and "Response," 247-49; also Smiles, *Gospel,* 238-39 n. 42.

27. Cf. G. N. Davies, *Faith,* 123.

28. Cf. Lambrecht, *Studies,* 293.

29. Cf. Luther, *Bondage,* 33:318, of Rom. 9:30: "What is this but a confirmation by the unequivocal example of the two nations and the clearest possible testimony of Paul that grace is given freely to those without merits and the most undeserving, and is not obtained by any efforts, endeavors, or works, whether small or great, even of the best and most virtuous of men, though they seek and pursue righteousness with burning zeal?"

[him]" (10:20), whereas he repeats in chapter 11 that "Israel failed to obtain *what it was seeking*" (11:7). Paradoxical though it may seem, Paul's point is precisely that the relation between pursuit and attainment, where God's righteousness is concerned, is a negative one — since (as he has just declared) everything depends, *not* on (human) running, but "on God who shows mercy" (9:16). Furthermore, the suggestion that Israel has failed to achieve its goal because it has wrongly pursued it "as though it were based on *works*" (9:32) can only be meant to suggest, after the labored insistence earlier in the chapter that God operates *apart from any consideration of human works,* that Israel's error lies (at least in part) in its failure to grasp this divine modus operandi.[30]

But the contrary path that Israel pursues is, more specifically, that of the law: "Israel, pursuing a law of righteousness [i.e., a law that demands righteousness], did not attain to the law" (9:31). Paul explains the failure of their pursuit by saying that it was based on works rather than faith; clearly he thinks the goal of righteousness that the law sets forth can only be reached by faith (in Christ, the "stone" upon which Israel has "stumbled" [9:32-33]).[31] On the other hand, he can hardly deny that the law demands deeds. Rather he concedes the point: "Moses writes concerning the righteousness that comes from the law, that 'the person who does these things will live by them'" (10:5). This path to righteousness is then contrasted with that of faith made available to people apart from any endeavor on their part; after all, no human can play any role in bringing Christ down from heaven or back from the dead (10:6-7). Israel's error lay, not in attributing to the law a demand for deeds, but in thinking that righteousness could be attained through its means: "For Christ is the end of the law, that *everyone who has faith* may be declared righteous" (10:4).

We have not yet explored in detail *why* Paul believes that a law that demands righteous deeds cannot lead to righteousness. The point for the moment is that such a law operates, for Paul, on a principle other than grace. However unthinkable a contrast between the law and divine grace might have been in the context of Second Temple Judaism, Paul clearly thought the unthinkable.

2. In Romans 4:13-16 law is contrasted not only with grace but also with *faith:* "if it is those who adhere to the law who are to be the heirs, faith has been negated. . . ." The same contrast was already noted in Galatians 3:12: "the law is not based upon faith, but 'the one who does these things will live by them.'"

---

30. Cf. Das, *Law,* 238-42.

31. Certainly Paul here attributes to Israel a *christological* error (the failure to acknowledge Christ); but this complements rather than rules out the "anthropological" error involved in Israel's pursuit of the law by means of works. It is part of the essence of faith in Christ that it accepts the "gift" (so Rom. 5:16-17; cf. 3:24) of *God's* righteousness (10:3) made available in Christ. Cf. Laato, *Approach,* 197-201; also Gundry, "Grace," 16-18.

The point is no different. The law requires that its subjects comply with its commands. And just as "faith" and "doing [the righteous deeds spelled out in the law]" are opposed as paths to justification in Galatians 3:12, so in Romans 4 faith (πίστις) is the mark of one who "*does not work* but trusts (τῷ δὲ μὴ ἐργαζομένῳ πιστεύοντι) the one who *justifies* the ungodly" (4:5; cf. 9:32). Faith, in other words, is here a trusting response to a divine initiative that, *because* it trusts God to fulfill his word, abandons further efforts ("doing") at achieving the same ends.[32] Thus, for Paul, if adherence to the law (by doing its demands) is required for justification, a faith (which abandons its own endeavors to achieve the justification that God has offered) is ruled out: "If it is those who adhere to the law who are to be the heirs, faith has been negated. . . ." And whereas a law that demands deeds stands in contrast with God's grace, a faith that credits and accepts what God offers is its natural complement: "that is why it is based on faith, in order that the promise may depend on grace" (4:16).[33]

3. The law requires that its subjects comply with its commands. *God's promise* to Abraham, however, cannot be made conditional upon what humans do. Therefore, if adherence to the law is required of Abraham's descendants, "the promise has been set aside" (4:14). The same point is made in Galatians 3:18: "If the inheritance is by the law, it is no longer by promise." For Paul God no longer acts solely to fulfill his own sovereign promise *if* his granting of the "inheritance" is dependent on human obedience to the demands of the law.[34] Thus the law, which by its very nature demands works, by that same nature excludes the promise, and vice versa. On the other hand, since faith in God for one's justification does not involve human work (Rom. 4:5), it does not compromise, but properly complements, God's sovereign promise.[35]

With this in mind, it becomes clear as well why Paul can equate the righteousness based on law with one's own righteousness, and contrast both with the righteousness of faith (Phil. 3:9; Rom. 10:3, 5-6). According to Sanders,[36] the righteousness based on law is a pursuit open only to Jews (to whom, after all, the law was given). Hence "their own" righteousness (10:3) means the righteousness available only to Jews, not Gentiles ("*my* own righteousness" in Phil. 3:9 is, of course, less congenial to this line of thought). And the point of the

32. See n. 17 above.

33. Cf. Bläser, *Gesetz*, 188-89.

34. Cf. Hays, *Echoes*, 114: "God's blessing is thus pegged securely to God's elective grace (promise) rather than conditioned on the performance of commandments (law)." Also Calvin, *Inst.* 3.11.17: "The gospel promises are free and dependent solely upon God's mercy, while the promises of the law depend upon the condition of works."

35. Cf. Bläser, *Gesetz*, 149, 167-69, 188; Schreiner, *Law*, 125.

36. Sanders, *Law*, 36-45; cf. also Dunn, *Law*, 223; Wright, "History," 82-83.

contrast with the righteousness of faith is that the latter is open to Jews and Gentiles alike. But Paul's insistence in other passages that the law is based on works as opposed to faith suggests that the usual and, I think, simpler explanation of these texts is the correct one.[37]

In Philippians 3:5-6 Paul attempts to document his protestation that he can match and even surpass the claims of those Jews whose "confidence" is "in the flesh." Some of the privileges he lists were his by birth, others by the piety of his parents. But he emphasizes in particular the evidence of his own strict compliance with the demands of the law: "in terms of the law, a Pharisee; in terms of zeal, a persecutor of the church; in terms of the righteousness based on the law, I was blameless."[38] But all these "gains" he now finds worthless; knowing Christ far outweighs them (vv. 7-8). His desire is to be found in Christ, "not having my own righteousness, based on law, but that which comes through faith in Christ, the righteousness from God that depends on faith" (v. 9).

Here Paul's "own" righteousness is "based on law," and it is contrasted with the righteousness that "depends on faith." We have already noted in other passages how Paul contrasts the law and faith, insisting that the former demands deeds of its subjects whereas the latter is the mark of those who abandon such efforts, accepting God's offer of justification in Christ. The same contrast is surely intended here. If the righteousness of the law is expressed by human deeds in compliance with the law, and *Paul has documented his claim to that righteousness* (cf. "in terms of the righteousness based on the law," v. 6) *by citing his own "blameless" conduct,* then Paul's "own" righteousness is the result of his personal zeal in fulfilling the law's demands.[39] Such righteousness is contrasted with the righteousness "from God that depends on faith": a *received* righteousness (cf. Rom. 5:17), in other words, where one's own works are not a factor.[40]

In Romans 10:3 it is non-Christian Jews who "[seek] to establish their own" righteousness, a righteousness that is again contrasted with "the righteousness of God." Without entering into the discussion of a much disputed passage at this point, we can simply note that verses 5-6 appear to carry the contrast fur-

---

37. Cf. Das, *Law,* 248-49; Heil, "Termination," 490; Hofius, *Paulusstudien II,* 164; Kim, *Perspective,* 75-81; Schreiner, *Paul,* 122-23.

38. The righteousness of the law according to which Paul was "blameless" can only have centered on his own law-compliant conduct.

39. Note that δικαιοσύνη is regularly used with a possessive pronoun in the LXX for a righteousness that results from the righteous deeds of its possessor; see chap. 15, n. 32 above.

40. Cf. Augustine, *De grat. et lib. arb.* 12.24: "Now what does he mean by 'not having my own righteousness, which is of the law,' when the law is really not his at all, but God's — except this, that he called it his own righteousness, although it was of the law, because he thought he could fulfil the law by his own will, without the aid of grace which is through faith in Christ?"

ther, now in terms of "the righteousness that is based on the law" and "the righteousness based on faith." Certainly Philippians 3:9 strongly supports the identification of "their own" righteousness (Rom. 10:3) with that "based on the law" (10:5). But Romans 10:5 in fact carries us back to the starting point of this discussion: with a paraphrase of Leviticus 18:5, it argues (as does Gal. 3:12) that the righteousness "based on the law" is one that requires "doing [the righteous deeds spelled out in the law]"; and this is then contrasted with the righteousness of faith (Rom. 10:6-13). Again we find Paul using "law" of the divine commands, and contending that its righteousness is one of "works."

Finally, we should note that this understanding of "law" confirms the traditional understanding of the Pauline phrase ἔργα νόμου ("the works of the law") as "deeds demanded by the law" (3:20, 28; Gal. 2:16; 3:2, 5, 10). The phrase is thus a close parallel to the Johannine τὰ ἔργα τοῦ θεοῦ, i.e., deeds demanded by God (John 6:28).[41] Similarly the "works of the Lord" (τὰ ἔργα κυρίου) in LXX Jeremiah 31:10 are tasks he assigns, and τὰ ἔργα αὐτοῦ in Baruch 2:9 are explicitly said to be "works that he commanded us."

But this natural reading of the phrase, which coheres perfectly with Paul's well-attested view of the law as a sum of demands for deeds to be done, is repeatedly challenged in contemporary Pauline scholarship. And, repeatedly, the challenges are accompanied by attacks on the "Lutheran" contrasts of law and gospel, works and faith. Certainly it is the task of scholars to reexamine constantly the received wisdom of the past.[42] But in this instance the alternatives proposed do not commend themselves.

1. Lloyd Gaston suggests that the only natural way to understand the phrase, according to the rules of Greek grammar, is to take νόμου as a subjective genitive: "works which the law does."[43] A number of passages in Paul refer to effects that the law is said to bring about: it brings the knowledge of sin (Rom. 3:20), deception (7:11), death (7:10-11), wrath (4:15), and so on. Thus Paul is claiming that the law itself cannot effect salvation in stating that "by the works of the law shall no one be justified" (Gal. 2:16).

But the parallels cited above demonstrate that ἔργα νόμου can mean "works demanded by the law." And though Gaston's proposal is an interesting one, it does not explain why Paul supports his claim that one cannot be justified by the works of the law (Rom. 3:28) by showing that Abraham was not justified by "works" (4:2), where Abraham's own deeds are meant. Paul then proceeds with a reference to the "one who works" and receives his due (4:4) and the

---

41. Cf. John 6:29; also 4:34; 9:4. See von Wahlde, "Faith," 304-15.
42. Cf. the remarks of Kuss, "Nomos," 173-75.
43. Gaston, *Paul,* 100-106.

"one who does not work" but believes (4:5). If his argument has any relevance for the claim that justification is by faith, not by the works of the law, then the latter must refer, not to the law's effects — the illustration of Abraham says nothing on that score — but to deeds done by humans.

2. A second counter to the traditional understanding is advocated by James D. G. Dunn. While conceding that "works of the law" refers in a general way to "what the law requires, the 'deeds' which the law makes obligatory,"[44] Dunn argues that in a context where "God's saving righteousness" was believed to be "restricted to Israel" and where, as a result, Jews had become preoccupied with maintaining their distinctness from Gentiles, certain laws (i.e., those that served to differentiate Israel from other nations, "circumcision and food laws in particular") naturally came "more into focus than others."[45] For Paul, then, "works of the law" stood for Israel's attempts to protect its "privileged status and restricted prerogative"[46] by insisting on the observance of these boundary-marking requirements of the Mosaic law. The works of the law against which Paul "consistently warns" thus amounted to "Israel's misunderstanding of what her covenant law required. That misunderstanding focused most sharply on Jewish attempts to maintain their covenant distinctiveness from Gentiles and on Christian Jews' attempts to require Christian Gentiles to adopt such covenant distinctives." The "misunderstanding" involved Israel's failure to take into account God's "promised (covenanted) intention to bless also the nations."[47]

But whether or not Paul thought Jews had misunderstood the law, a phrase that means "what the law requires"[48] is curiously chosen if it is intended to convey the sense of "a distortion of what the law requires."[49] And in fact, Paul uses "the works of the law" and "the law" interchangeably — as he could hardly have done if the former expression meant a misunderstanding of the latter. In Galatians 2:16 he denies that one can be declared righteous by "the works of the

44. Dunn, *Theology*, 355.

45. Dunn, *Theology*, 355, 358. Cf. *Law*, 223: "'Works of the law' denote all that the law requires of the devout Jew, but precisely because it is the law as identity and boundary marker which is in view, the law as Israel's law focuses on these rites which express Jewish distinctiveness most clearly. . . . 'Works of the law' refer not exclusively but particularly to those requirements which bring to sharp focus the distinctiveness of Israel's identity."

46. Dunn, *Theology*, 355.

47. Dunn, *Theology*, 366.

48. Jacqueline C. R. de Roo ("Concept," 116-47) has demonstrated that at Qumran, "works of the law" included "ethical" as well as "ritual" deeds (137). Cf. also Mijoga, *Notion*, 113. Broadly supportive of Dunn's reading is Abegg, "Works Righteousness," 139-47.

49. Cf. Matlock, "Sins," 78: "How exactly can Dunn have 'works of the law' signify *both* 'what(ever) the law requires' *and* a particular perversion of the law, the 'misunderstanding' and its characteristic emphases and effects ([Dunn, *Theology*,] pp. 354-59)?"

law"; in 2:21 he clinches his argument for that claim by noting that if one *could* be declared righteous "through the law," Christ would have died to no purpose. The thesis of 2:16 is repeated in 3:11, though here "law" replaces "works of the law": "that no one is declared righteous by the law is obvious." Those who think differently are said in 5:4 to "strive to be declared righteous by the law"; it is surely for their benefit that Paul insists in 2:16 that "no one will be declared righteous by the works of the law." In Romans, too, the phrases are used with no apparent differentiation. "Apart from the law" in 3:20 is hardly to be distinguished from "apart from the works of the law" in 3:28. Indeed, Paul's assertion in 3:20a that no one is declared righteous by "the works of the law" is supported in 20b by a statement of what the "law" *does* accomplish (it brings "knowledge of sin").[50] "Works of the law" and "law" are clearly coterminous here. And Paul's insistence in 3:31 that he does not "overthrow the law" is intended to counter an objection to his claim that justification takes place "apart from the works of the law" (3:28).[51] Had it been self-evident to all that Paul was rejecting a Jewish *distortion* of the law when he ruled out righteousness through its works, he would not have been suspected of overthrowing the law itself in the process.

But there is more to be said: Paul uses "works of the law" and "law" interchangeably *because he sees the very essence of the law in its requirement of works.*[52] The point is confirmed (as we have seen) when Paul supports his claim that "(the works of) the law" cannot convey righteousness (3:20, 28) by showing that Scripture speaks of a righteousness "apart from (righteous) works" in 4:1-8. Not particular works that set Jews apart, but works in general — anything "done" that might deserve a recompense (μισθός, 4:4) or justify pride (καύ-χημα, 4:2) — are here meant,[53] and that in contrast with the "faith" of one who "does not work" but benefits by divine grace without any consideration of personal merit.[54] Since the issue (the works of the law versus faith in Jesus Christ) permits restatement in terms of a general distinction between works and faith, it is the law that demands deeds, not the law as misconstrued by Jews, that is at issue in Paul's references to its works.[55]

---

50. Cf. G. N. Davies, *Faith*, 118; Thielman, *Plight*, 24.

51. Cf. Rhyne, *Faith*, 59.

52. Dahl (*Studies*, 169) suggests that when Paul contrasts "by faith" with "by works of the law," the "formulas are best understood as abbreviations for 'The righteous shall live by faith' and 'He who does them shall live by them.'"

53. Cf. Moo, "Law," 97.

54. Cf. (as noted above) Rom. 9:11-12, 16; 11:6, where Paul is similarly concerned to exclude *any* role for human works in divine election, but where law observance is not explicitly in view.

55. Cf. Schreiner, *Paul*, 110-15.

It is of course true that the letter to the Galatians represents Paul's response to the demand that his Gentile converts be circumcised. But Paul responded to that issue, *not* by saying that the true purpose of a law that required circumcision was distorted by Jews who required circumcision,[56] but by insisting that the law *as such* cannot convey righteousness,[57] so that Gentiles should *not* submit to its regimen: if one could be declared righteous on the basis of the law, then Christ would have died to no purpose (2:21); the law cannot convey righteousness because it "does not rest on faith" (3:12); it was merely "added for the sake of transgressions" (3:19); it served as a "pedagogue" until Christ came (3:24); the Sinaitic covenant was one of slavery (4:24);[58] and so on. Throughout the letter it is Paul's thesis that the very nature of the law is such that it cannot justify, that its function is more limited; why, then, see his claim that "the works of the law" do not convey righteousness (2:16) as meaning anything different, or take the phrase to denote a drastic misunderstanding of the law?[59]

The point of Romans 3:20 is no different. In the preceding argument the assumption that Jews possess a peculiar path to righteousness, or peculiar advantages in its pursuit, is clearly under attack (2:17-29; 3:9, 19). But the assumption of privilege on the part of (some?) Jews is not what is said to condemn them. *That* distinction is reserved for actual *transgressions* of the law's very concrete demands (2:12, 25, 27; cf. vv. 21-23). The "works of the law" that do not justify are the demands of the law that are not met, not those observed for wrong reasons by (purportedly) nationalistic Jews.[60]

---

56. Cf. Matlock, "Sins," 77: "An Israel that understood the law as enjoining its separate existence would *seem* to have understood the law rather well."

57. Cf. Calvin, *Comm.* Gal. 2:15: "[Others] hold that this [i.e., 'works of the law'] does not refer to moral works. But the context shows clearly that the moral law is also comprehended in these words, for almost everything that Paul adds relates to the moral rather than the ceremonial law."

58. Paul speaks explicitly of "two covenants" in 4:24, and identifies one as "from Mount Sinai." In saying that the covenant of Sinai leads to "slavery," he is warning his readers of what it means to live "under the law" (4:21), a condition from which Christ has provided redemption (4:5; cf. 5:1). Nothing suggests that only those who *misunderstood* the law were slaves in need of redemption. Dunn, however, is consistent with his position when he claims that, in spite of the reference to two covenants, Paul really means that there is *one* (the promise to Abraham); the "covenant from Mount Sinai" he takes to represent that single covenant "misconceived" (*Ep. Gal.*, 249; *Theology*, 146 n. 94).

59. Cf. Hong, *Law*, 146.

60. Noting what Paul goes on to say about the law in Romans, Kim comments: "To me, it would be an amazing feat if [Dunn] can account for Paul's associating the law with sin and death with his view that the issues of the law outstanding between Paul and the Judaizers were focused only on circumcision, food laws, and the sabbath, rather than concerned with the general and fundamental problems of the law" (*Perspective*, 41).

Dunn carries the logic of his interpretation to its curious conclusion in a novel reading of Galatians 3:10: "For as many as are of the works of the law are under a curse; for it is written, 'Cursed is every one who does not abide by all the things written in the book of the law, to do them.'" From this curse of the law Christ is said in verse 13 to provide redemption. The verses have long been read as indicating that the law demands righteous deeds and condemns ("curses") those who fail to do them, but that Christ took the law's condemnation on himself, thus freeing transgressors from its bane. Whatever else may be said for such an interpretation, its elements are unexceptionably Pauline.

For Dunn, however, those "of the works of the law" must be Jews who misconstrue the law's true purpose by insisting on the observance of its boundary-marking prescriptions, thus effectively limiting God's salvific purposes to their own people.[61] The law's curse is thus directed at Jewish *misunderstandings* of the law,[62] and it is from the effects of such *misunderstandings* that Christ's death brings deliverance:[63] his death was in fact a kind of object lesson in that when Christ died as one cursed by the law and thus outside the covenant, God was *showing* that he is *for* outsiders to the covenant; hence Jews should not be restrictive in their claims on its blessings.[64] So limited a view of the atonement

61. Dunn, *Law,* 227: "Those who are ἐξ ἔργων νόμου are those who have understood the scope of God's covenant people as Israel *per se,* as that people who are defined by the law and marked out by its distinctive requirements." Also *Theology,* 375.

62. "To thus misunderstand the law by giving primacy to matters of at best secondary importance was to fall short of what the law required and thus to fall under the law's own curse" (Dunn, *Law,* 227). "The curse of the law is not simply the condemnation which falls on any transgression and on all who fall short of the law's requirements. Paul has in mind the specific short-fall of his typical Jewish contemporary, the curse which falls on all who restrict the grace and promise of God in nationalistic terms, who treat the law as a boundary to mark the people of God off from the Gentiles, who give a false priority to ritual markers. The curse of the law here has to do primarily with that attitude which confines the covenant promise to Jews as Jews: it falls on those who live within the law in such a way as to exclude the Gentile as Gentile from the promise" (228-29).

63. Dunn, *Law,* 229-30: "The curse which was removed by Christ's death therefore was the curse which had previously prevented that blessing from reaching the Gentiles, the curse of a wrong understanding of the law. . . . As soon as we recall that 'those under the law' are under the curse of the law (v. 10), the purpose of Christ's redemptive work can be specified quite properly as the removal of *that* curse, as the deliverance of the heirs of the covenant promise from the ill effects of the too narrow understanding of covenant and law held by most of Paul's Jewish contemporaries." Also *Theology,* 375: "The curse of the law, however, has been absorbed by Christ (3.13). So the curse has been removed. And with it both the misunderstanding of the law's role and its effect in excluding Gentiles from the promise, which had brought the curse into effect, have been declared null and void."

64. Dunn, *Law,* 230: "Christ in his death had put himself under the curse and outside the covenant blessing (cf. Deut. 11.26; 30.19-20) — that is, put himself in the place of the Gentile! Yet

would have astonished even the most dogmatic TULIP theologian. According to Paul, Jews before Christ lived "under sin" no less than did the Gentiles (Gal. 3:22); they lived in the "flesh" — a flesh for whose typical expressions Paul has a handy list (5:19-21), none of whose items is readily rendered "ethnocentrism." How is it, then, that their failure to "abide by all the things written in the book of the law" can be limited to their claims of racial privileges? Did the Sinaitic covenant itself provide atonement for all transgressions *except* this one? For that matter, were *all* Jews guilty of racism — or were the select few who escaped *this* sin in no need of Christ's death? Was the death of Christ the only way Jews could be disabused of their misunderstanding? Had it no broader function?[65]

We may be grateful to Dunn for following the logic of his new perspective to its extraordinary conclusion. Rightly noting that Paul's language of justification by faith was provoked by the insistence that Gentile believers submit to the requirements of the Sinaitic law, scholars since Stendahl have proceeded by limiting *Paul's* concern in formulating the doctrine to the terms by which *Gentiles* can be admitted to the people of God. If *that* is the focus of the doctrine, then

---

God vindicated him! Therefore, God is *for* the Gentiles; and consequently the law could no longer serve as a boundary dividing Jew from Gentile. . . . Christ's death was effective, in Paul's view, precisely because it broke through the restrictiveness of the typical Jewish understanding of God's righteousness." Also *Ep. Gal.*, 178; *Law*, 257; *Theol. Gal.*, 86-87.

65. Cf. Dunn, *Law*, 229: "The curse which was removed by Christ's death therefore was the curse . . . of a wrong understanding of the law. . . . This may seem at first a surprisingly narrow understanding of the redemptive effect of Christ's death. . . . But Paul's meaning and intention here is in fact quite narrow and specific." *Theol. Gal.*, 86: "Paul understood the significance of the cross and its curse primarily in terms of its significance for the Gentile question." Luther presses a line of argument similar to that above in rejecting the notion that Paul's critique of the law was restricted to its ceremonial aspects: "Christ died for the sins of the whole world from the beginning of the world before there was any ceremonial law. Consequently Paul must be understood as speaking about the law and sins of the whole world from the beginning on. Those who really continue to understand him only with reference to the ceremonial law must necessarily concede that he must be understood as speaking only of sin against the ceremonial law, when he refers to law and sin by turns. . . . It follows, therefore, that Christ achieved nothing by his death except that he redeemed the Jews alone from the ceremonial law or only abrogated the ceremonies. And he died in vain also for the Jews, since he did not die for the sins against the moral law" (*Faith and Law*, 34:115). Cf. also *Bondage*, 33:302-3: "[Some] are in the habit of trying to get round Paul here, by making out that what he calls works of the law are the ceremonial works. . . . Even if there had never been any other error in the Church, this one alone was pestilent and potent enough to make havoc of the gospel. . . . It is not true that Paul is speaking only about ceremonial laws; otherwise, how can the argument be sustained by which he concludes that all men are wicked and in need of grace? . . . What is the use of a grace that liberates us only from ceremonial works, which are the easiest of all?" See also *Gal.*, 26:123, 180-81, 203. Calvin is no less forthright; see, e.g., *Inst.* 3.11.19-20. For Augustine's response to Dunn, see chap. 1, n. 18 above.

Jews themselves either have no need of it[66] or their need must be the product of their unwillingness to extend the blessings of their covenant to Gentiles. Dunn's limitation of the law's curse to Jews guilty of racism is thus consistent with a limited understanding of what Paul meant by "justification by faith"; but it coheres ill with Pauline claims that all the world is "under sin" and culpable before God, that Jews no less than Gentiles are "sinners," God's "enemies," the "ungodly," who need to be declared righteous by faith. Paul, it appears, did *not* think Jews lived happily and blessedly under the law's rule as long as they did not become too insistent on its boundary-marking requirements; nor was "justification" of possible benefit only to Gentiles and Jews of a xenophobic cast.

3. Finally, a number of scholars, convinced that Paul could not have said that the law in any proper sense rests on works, contend that the phrase "works of law" denotes deeds that spring from a Jewish distortion of the law into legalism. "The works of the law" are then "deeds of obedience to formal statutes done in the legalistic spirit, with the expectation of thereby meriting and securing divine approval and award, such obedience, in other words, as the legalists rendered to the law of the O.T. as expanded and interpreted by them."[67] The phrase thus takes on a decidedly negative tone: "the works of the law" are themselves sinful. Fuller thinks they amount to "the sin of bribing God,"[68] and thus represent "a gross rebellion against the law, instead of compliance with it."[69]

Paul himself is by no means so negative.[70]

a. As we noted above, Paul uses "the works of the law" and "law" interchangeably. He would not have done so if "the works of the law" were tantamount to the law's perversion. And — to repeat again — *since Paul's thesis throughout Galatians is that the nature of the Mosaic law is such that it cannot justify, that the law's function is more limited, there is no reason to claim that the parallel statements about the "works of the law" in Galatians 2:16 (= Rom. 3:20, 28) concern a perversion of the law.*

b. The contrast between the works of the law and faith in Jesus Christ is de-

---

66. So, e.g., Gager, *Origins*, 247; Gaston, *Paul*, 122, 136; Stowers, *Rereading*, 128-29, 189-90. The suggestion leads Kim (*Perspective*, 20) to ask pointedly: "If a Messiah did not benefit Israel, what kind of messiah would he be?"

67. Burton, *Galatians*, 120; cf. Moule, "Obligation," 393.

68. Fuller, "Works," 33.

69. Fuller, *Gospel*, 95.

70. Cf. already Grafe, *Lehre*, 10, where the idea that "the works of the law" are themselves imperfect is rejected. In Grafe's day, however, the suggestion countered was that the phrase denoted a purely external, formal righteousness lacking a true (inner) morality. See also Bläser, *Gesetz*, 96-97.

veloped in Romans 4:1-6 in terms simply of faith and works.[71] And there it is clear that the works are not themselves sinful; rather, the distinction is drawn between one who believes but does not work and one who works and receives "his wages . . . as his due" (vv. 4-5). Similarly, in 9:11-12 Paul insists that God's election depends on his call, not on human works, *whether those deeds are "good or bad."* Paul's point is that human works — good or bad — are not a factor in salvation, not that works in themselves are sinful.

c. Paul's usage of "work(s)" (ἔργον/ἔργα) shows that the term for him is neutral, applicable to good as well as evil deeds (2:6-7; 9:11-12; 13:3; 15:18; 1 Cor. 3:13-15; 15:58; etc.). Nothing in his normal usage prepares us for the claim that the connotations of "the works of the law" are pejorative.[72]

d. Paul's declaration in Romans 3:20 that "no human being will be declared righteous in his sight by the works of the law" concludes an argument that began at 1:18. But one searches the argument in vain for the notion that Jewish obedience to the law's statutes is marked by a "legalistic spirit." Paul contends rather that people will be judged *according to their "works"* (2:6; the term is neutral, cf. vv. 7-8); that Jews will need to be "doers" of the law, not simply hearers, if they are to be justified (v. 13); that their transgressions lead to condemnation (vv. 17-27); and that they, like the Gentiles, find themselves "under the power of sin" (3:9). In the conclusion to this argument, the "works of the law" can only be understood positively. That such works do not lead to justification follows simply from Paul's judgment that Jews do not do them.[73]

e. The point of Galatians 3:10 is no different. Those who are "of the works of the law" are the same as those "under the law" in 4:5. Of the former we are told that they are under a curse from which Christ redeems (3:10, 13); of the latter we are told that Christ came to redeem them (4:4-5). Since the redemption is for all those "born under the law," the dilemma is equally universal. The Jew's personal understanding, interpretation, or even distortion of the law does not enter the picture.[74] The point of 3:10 is not what happens to those who distort the law, but the effect of the law on all those within its sphere: it brings a curse, not life (cf. the similar point in Rom. 4:15). Thus to be "of the works of the law," as to be "under the law," means that one is subject both to the law's demands and to its sanctions.[75]

---

71. For the following, cf. Moo, "Law," 95-96.

72. Cf. Yinger, *Judgment,* 158-59.

73. Rightly, Cranfield, *Romans,* 198. Cf. also Gutbrod and Kleinknecht, "νόμος," 1072: "Nevertheless, Paul says of the Law that it cannot give life, Gl. 3:21. This is because no one keeps it, not because Paul regards the works of the Law as sin. When Gentiles do by nature the works of the Law, these are acknowledged by Paul to be good works, R. 2:14."

74. The NRSV rendering of 3:10 ("all who rely on the works of the law") is thus misleading.

75. Similarly τῷ ἐκ τοῦ νόμου in Rom. 4:16 means "the one who is subject to the law," "the Jew."

Why are all those subject to the demands of the law under its curse? In Galatians 3:10b Paul supplies an explanation: the curse strikes "every one who does not abide by all things written in the book of the law, to do them." In other words, transgression of the law draws upon the transgressor the law's condemnation — a point Paul makes abundantly clear elsewhere (Rom. 2:12, 27; 4:15; 5:13; etc.).[76] As in Romans 3:20, it is failure to do the works of the law that is condemned, not the works themselves.

We are thus left with the view that the "works of the law" are the deeds demanded by the Sinaitic law code, a law that rests on works.

iii. The Law and Faith

As we noted in chapter 2, Luther used "law" to refer to "whatever is not grace." All of Scripture could then be divided between the categories of law and gospel. Pauline usage, as we have outlined it, does not generalize in this way: Paul's "law" does not, for example, include the demands of Jesus! Nonetheless, Luther has captured an essential aspect of Pauline thought. Though Paul's "law" refers specifically to the Mosaic code, he does view it as demand, and distinguish it from grace and the path of faith. To this extent the contrast between "law" and "gospel," though never explicit in the epistles, does not distort Paul's point.

But such a contrast has come under increasing attack in recent literature. In part, the point of the attack is the simple reminder that the gospel, too, is accompanied by obligations[77] — a point that neither Paul nor his "Lutheran" interpreters would have denied. In part, the attack is theologically motivated by a concern for the unity of Scripture,[78] or by a fear that the contrast between law and gospel implies "that the law was an unsuccessful first attempt on God's part at dealing with man's unhappy state, which had to be followed later by a second (more successful) attempt (a view which is theologically grotesque, for the God of the unsuccessful first attempt is hardly a God to be taken seriously)."[79] If, however, we confine our attention here to the basis of the attack in Pauline exe-

---

76. Cf. Räisänen, *Law*, 94-96, where the weaknesses of other readings of Gal. 3:10b are shown.

77. E.g., Barth, "Gospel," 3-27; Moule, "Obligation," 389-406.

78. I.e., the unity of Scripture is thought to be threatened when law and gospel are opposed. Here the distinction between law in the sense of the sacred (Old Testament) Scriptures and law as the Sinaitic legislation is important: the claim that the Sinaitic code demands deeds does not (for Paul at least) compromise the witness of the Scriptures to the righteousness of faith.

79. Cranfield, "Law," 68. Comments on this point will be offered at the end of sec. iv below.

gesis, two areas need consideration. Positively, it is claimed that in two crucial texts (Rom. 3:27 and 9:30-32)[80] Paul indicates that the law, properly understood, demands faith, and that the law's nature is distorted when it is seen as demanding works. Negatively, it is claimed that νόμος in a number of Pauline texts (particularly where it is linked with "works") means not "law," but "legalism." We will take up the positive challenge first.

1. After showing that God's "righteousness" is available "through faith in Jesus Christ" (3:21-26), Paul continues: "Then what becomes of our boasting? It is excluded. On what principle? On the principle of works? No, but on the principle of faith." So, at least, the RSV renders 3:27. But the Greek word translated "principle" is νόμος, and though "principle" is certainly a possible meaning for the term in other contexts, a number of recent scholars have argued that the term must refer here, as it does in the preceding verses, to the law of Moses. Paul is thought to be saying that the law of Moses, correctly understood, is a law of faith, and that, as such, it excludes the boasting that accompanies its perversion into a law of works.

The current debate takes as its starting point an article by Friedrich from 1954.[81] Few scholars before that time thought Paul's "law of faith" referred to the law of Moses; those who since 1954 have espoused that view have appealed almost invariably to Friedrich's argumentation. Friedrich pointed out that the phrase "law of faith" was not introduced in a casual, unreflective way. After all, it is preceded by the question: "By what sort of *law* (is boasting excluded)?" Paul has thus deliberately prepared for an answer using *law* (νόμος). And though νόμος may mean "rule," "principle," or "order" elsewhere (e.g., 7:21), it is unlikely to have that meaning in 3:27, since in 3:19-31 the word consistently refers to the Mosaic law.

In Friedrich's view 3:21 provides the key to the interpretation of 3:27. In the earlier verse Paul speaks of the law in two ways: righteousness appears apart from the law, yet it is witnessed to by the law. "Apart from the law" means, clearly, apart from the law's works (cf. v. 20), while the righteousness to which the law bears witness is that "through faith in Jesus Christ" (v. 22). Thus the law is seen from two perspectives: on the one hand it demands deeds; on the other it witnesses to faith. Similarly in verse 27 Paul is speaking of the dual nature of the Mosaic law. Boasting is made impossible, not by the Mosaic law in its role of demanding works, but by the Mosaic law as a witness to faith. Verses 27-28 de-

---

80. From Rom. 3:31 we may deduce only that, according to Paul, the *true* nature and purpose of the law come to light when it is viewed from the perspective of justification by faith. A more specific definition of the law's nature and purpose must be derived from other texts.

81. Friedrich, "Gesetz," 401-17.

liberately echo 21-22: "apart from the works of the law" (v. 28) parallels "apart from the law" (v. 21), the "law of faith" (v. 27) reminds us of the witness of the law (v. 21), and "by faith" (v. 28) parallels "through faith" (v. 22). It is this role of the law as a witness to faith that Paul claims to establish in verse 31 and that he elaborates in Romans 4. There, however, he drops the term "law of faith," using as its equivalent the word "promise."

In an article from 1973 E. Lohse broadly accepted Friedrich's understanding of 3:27: the "law of faith" is the Old Testament law, which provides testimony to faith in a number of crucial texts.[82] But whereas Friedrich finds in 3:27 a dual function of the law and assumes the legitimacy of both aspects, for Lohse the law becomes a sum of demands ("law of works") only in its Jewish misinterpretation. God's law properly understood is a witness to the liberating promise experienced by those who show the faith of Abraham. This becomes, for Lohse's Paul, the valid and only true meaning of the Mosaic law.

The view that Paul here refers to the Mosaic law as a "law of faith" as opposed to works has become, almost "overnight,"[83] crucial to a number of presentations of Paul's understanding of the law.[84] But Räisänen has argued forcibly and, I believe, decisively against it.[85]

a. In an important lexicographic study,[86] Räisänen has amply demonstrated that Greek usage of νόμος offers many parallels to a broader understanding of the term ("principle," "rule," "order"), so that such a rendering in 3:27 (and in 8:2) cannot be excluded on lexical grounds. In fact, few would contest that, at least in 7:21, νόμος must mean something like "principle" ("a νόμος· that, when I desire to do what is good, evil dogs my steps"). Yet the collection of evidence is welcome and should lay to rest any suspicion that the use of νόμος to mean "principle" in 3:27 is an unnatural rendering of the Greek.

b. Friedrich is correct in saying that Paul's usage of the phrase "νόμος of faith" is deliberate. On the other hand, the deliberate use of νόμος does not in itself prove that we are dealing with a statement about the Mosaic law, since the word could have been chosen deliberately but polemically as a contrast to the "law of works."

c. The fact that νόμος in the immediate context does refer to the Mosaic law is a serious consideration, but hardly decisive, since Paul uses the word with other meanings elsewhere, and even plays on different meanings in 7:21-25.

d. The most important argument raised by Friedrich is the parallel be-

---

82. Lohse, "νόμος," 279-87.

83. Räisänen, *Torah*, 53.

84. This includes the presentation of Hübner, summarized in sec. ii of chap. 10 above. For further bibliography, see Räisänen, *Torah*, 48-68.

85. Räisänen, *Torah*, 48-68.

86. Räisänen, *Torah*, 69-94.

tween 3:21-22 and 27-28. Both refer to a justification that is by "faith" and "apart from (the works of) the law." The parallel between the "witness" of "the law and the prophets" (v. 21) and the "νόμος of faith" (v. 27) is, however, less clear, and certainly not compelling enough to determine the sense of the latter phrase.

e. If 3:27 is a programmatic statement about the dual nature of the law, and "law of faith" expresses the positive aspect of the law's function, then the sequel is hard to explain. The crucial phrase "law of faith" is not repeated, verse 31 speaks of the law as a unity, and chapter 4 speaks of the law as something negative (4:13-15). Friedrich suggests that "promise" is introduced in Romans 4 as the equivalent of the "law of faith" in 3:27. But are we really to assume that Paul thought his readers would identify "promise" and "law of faith" with the Mosaic law when he explicitly contrasts the "promise" with the "law" in 4:13-14?

The context tells against Lohse's reading of 3:27 as well, by which the law, properly understood, is a "law of faith," becoming a "law of works" only when it has been distorted by Jews. Throughout the passage (3:20-31) Paul uses the "works of the law" and "law" interchangeably. Indeed, the climax of the argument of 1:18–3:20 is reached in the declaration that righteousness is operative "apart from the law" — by faith (3:21-22). Chapter 4 continues the contrast between law and faith, and rejects the claim that righteousness can come through the law by showing that Abraham was justified, not by works, but by faith. Immediately before *and* after 3:27, then, Paul links the law with a demand for works and distinguishes it from the path of faith. The point of 3:27, then, can hardly be that the law, rightly understood, is a matter of faith, not works.

Moreover, 3:27 itself is introduced as a claim, not about the law, but about boasting. In what follows, too, it is clear that Paul's focus is on the "boasting" of the Jews. Nothing suggests that he is attempting to introduce — in the latter half of the verse — an important distinction about the nature of the law that then drops out of view in verse 28 and in the negative discussion of the law in chapter 4.

f. Still more decisive, however, is the fact that the "νόμος of faith" in 3:27 is *the effective means by which boasting is once and for all excluded.* It will not do to paraphrase the verse as though it said that the law's true meaning is revealed by faith. The text tells us, not what has happened to the law, but what the "νόμος of faith" itself has accomplished. Since a single event is referred to, surely God's act of salvation in Christ, which Paul has just finished expounding in 3:21-26, is what is meant. This act of salvation, creating the new "order of faith," is what excludes boasting.[87]

---

87. Michael Winger ("Meaning," 108; cf. *Law,* 91-92) comments on the "unusual" use of the genitive case by which νόμου πίστεως is construed as "a way of understanding" νόμος. Though

Understood thus, 3:28 follows 3:27 naturally, whereas if the earlier verse is speaking of the Mosaic law as a "law of faith," the claim is no sooner made than it is dropped. Certainly the γάρ (for) of 28 leads us to expect a further reference to the two νόμοι of 27 — and that, in fact, is what we find. The "law of works" that is said not to exclude boasting is picked up in the reference to the "works of the law" that are said not to justify in 28. The Mosaic code is intended. The "principle" or "order" of faith mentioned in 27 is spelled out in the thesis of 28, "one is justified by faith." This latter righteousness is indeed witnessed to by "the law and the prophets" (i.e., the sacred Scriptures, v. 21); but the "law" in the narrower sense, the Sinaitic legislation, is spoken of, here as elsewhere, as a "law of works."

2. And what of 9:30-32? Here Paul says that Gentiles have "attained" righteousness without even "pursuing" it, "that is, righteousness based on faith." Israel, on the other hand, was actively engaged in pursuing the "law of righteousness" (so, literally, νόμον δικαιοσύνης) but did not "attain to the law" (so, literally, εἰς νόμον οὐκ ἔφθασεν). The reason given is that they did not carry on their pursuit (the verb διώκειν is apparently to be understood in v. 32)[88] "by faith, but as though (they could reach that goal, the law of righteousness) by works" (so we may fill out Paul's elliptical language). Does this not indicate that Israel had distorted the law's true nature in pursuing it by works rather than faith? Does it not imply that the law, properly understood, is based on faith?

a. It is important that we define the law of which Paul is speaking. Cranfield, here as elsewhere, does not distinguish between the Old Testament Scriptures ("law" in a broad sense) and the Sinaitic legislation, but seems to think the former is intended. At any rate, Paul's reference to the "law of righteousness" is interpreted of the law's (= Scripture's) witness to the righteousness of faith: 3:21-22 and 10:6-13 are cited as support.[89] For Badenas, too, "νόμος in this context (9.31; 10.4, 5) . . . refers to the general concept of 'Torah' as it was

---

νόμος by itself may serve as a name for the Jewish law, it does not do so when it is part of a larger noun phrase; in such a case, one expects the other words of the phrase to define which of the many νόμοι is in view.

88. Cf., however, Gordon, "Israel," 163-66, who argues that it is the copula that is omitted and that the clause should be rendered, "Because the Sinai covenant [νόμος] is not identified/characterized by faith." This brings the statement strictly in line with Gal. 3:12 and Rom. 10:5. "When Paul asks 'why' the Jews did not attain unto the Torah, his answer addresses the *nature* of the covenant recorded in the Torah (that it demands perfect obedience), not the nature of the *pursuit* of the Torah" (165). Gordon is followed by Kruse, *Paul,* 224. Note, however, Moo, *Romans,* 626 n. 41: "Gordon's suggestion is intriguing, considering the parallel with Gal. 3:12a, but has difficulty accounting for the ὡς."

89. Cranfield, *Romans,* 508.

understood in Paul's contemporary Judaism, and designates the OT, perhaps mainly in its revelatory aspects."[90]

But the Old Testament Scriptures, and especially their "revelatory aspects," make a strange object for verbs of pursuing (διώκειν) and attaining (φθάνειν, 9:31). The verse reads more naturally if the demands of the Mosaic legislation are meant. No doubt, with a little goodwill, a satisfactory sense of Paul's "law of righteousness" can be devised if the Old Testament Scriptures are meant (e.g., "the Torah viewed from the perspective of the δικαιοσύνη it promises, aims at, or bears witness to").[91] But since the "righteousness that is based on the law" in 10:5 is that which is required by the Mosaic code (note the quotation from Lev. 18:5), the "law of righteousness" in 9:31 is again more naturally understood as the Mosaic law code that demands righteousness. The appropriateness of the comparison with 10:5 is confirmed by the fact that Israel's pursuit of the "law of righteousness" in 9:31 is set against the "righteousness through faith" of verse 30, just as the "righteousness that is based on the law" in 10:5 is contrasted with the "righteousness based on faith" in verses 6-13 (see the discussion below). Finally, we should note that Paul elsewhere speaks of Jewish zeal — indeed, his own former zeal — not for the Old Testament Scriptures as such, but for meeting the standards of the Mosaic law code (Phil. 3:6, 9; Rom. 10:3, 5). The law pursued by Israel in Romans 9:31, then, is the Mosaic legislation.

b. But to say that the Mosaic code is based on faith, not works, is blatantly incompatible with what Paul says elsewhere. In Philippians 3:6, 9 he contrasts the righteousness based on law (ἐν νόμῳ, ἐκ νόμου) with that of faith; there is no hint that the former designations refer to a *distortion* of the law. He could not be more explicit than he is in Galatians 3:12 in stating that the "law does not rest on faith"; he uses that claim as a crucial step in his argument that justification must be by faith, not by law, and supports it with a quotation from Scripture. Nor does the evidence in Romans suggest that, at the time of its writing, Paul had changed his mind. Here, too, the righteousness of faith is emphatically set in contrast with the law (cf. Rom. 3:21-22: "But now the righteousness of God has been revealed *apart from the law,* . . . the righteousness of God through faith in Jesus Christ"; 4:13: "The promise to Abraham and his descendants . . . did not come through the law but through the righteousness of faith").

Most importantly, the righteousness of law and that of faith are contrasted in 10:5-6, in the immediate context of 9:30-32. It has, to be sure, been argued

---

90. Badenas, *End,* 143.
91. Badenas, *End,* 104.

that Paul identifies rather than contrasts the two phrases here.[92] But this requires us to believe

i. that whereas he quotes Leviticus 18:5 without elaborating on it as a self-evident demonstration that "the law does *not* rest on faith" in Galatians 3:12, he quotes the same verse without elaboration as a self-evident demonstration that the law *does* rest on faith in Romans 10:5;[93]

ii. that whereas Paul contrasts the righteousness of the law and that of faith in Philippians 3:9, he identifies them here;[94]

92. E.g., Badenas, *End*, 118-25; Fuller, *Gospel*, 66-88; Hays, *Echoes*, 75-77; Howard, "End," 336-37; Wagner, *Heralds*, 160. Contrast Calvin, *Inst.* 3.11.17, on Rom. 10:5-6 (though in other contexts Calvin is careful *not* to contrast "law" and "gospel"): "Do you not see how [Paul] makes this the distinction between law and gospel: that the former attributes righteousness to works, the latter bestows free righteousness apart from the help of works? This is an important passage, and one that can extricate us from many difficulties if we understand that that righteousness which is given us through the gospel has been freed of all conditions of the law."

93. Hays, *Echoes*, 109, notes that in Gal. 3:10-12 Paul employs scriptural citations "to drive a wedge between Law and Faith as means to righteousness and life." When, however, one of the same quotations appears in Rom. 10:5 (Lev. 18:5), Hays simply notes that "Paul argues very differently in Romans from the way that he had argued earlier in Galatians" (208 n. 87). Similarly, Wagner, *Heralds*, 158 n. 121. See the following note.

94. Again, Hays notes the divergence between Philippians and his reading of Rom. 10, but insists that "the harmonizing impulse must not override the internal logic of the argument in Romans 10" (*Echoes*, 208 n. 87). Perhaps not; but to my mind the more natural reading of Rom. 10 itself has the added advantage of being quite in line with what Paul says about the law and faith in Gal. 3:11-12 and Phil. 3:9.

i. In order to avoid the apparent contrast between vv. 5 and 6 ("Moses writes *x* of the righteousness that is based on the law . . . but the righteousness that is based on faith says *y*"), Hays must read vv. 6-11 as spelling out the content of the αὐτά in v. 5 ("the one who does *these things* will live by them"); Paul indicates nothing of the sort. Cf. Dunn, *Romans 9–16*, 602: "When Paul sets righteousness ἐκ πίστεως alongside righteousness ἐκ something else, with δέ as the linking word, he obviously intends his readers to understand a contrast between the two phrases (4:16; 9:30, 32; as well as Gal 2:16 and 3:21-22)." See also Vos, "Antinomie," 258-60.

ii. To support his claim that what Paul says about the righteousness based on faith (10:6-11) is merely a clarification of what is meant by the righteousness of the law (10:5), Hays cites Rom. 3:21 and Rom. 4 as demonstrating that "the sum and substance of the Torah, according to the whole argument of this letter, is righteousness through faith" (76). The claim overlooks the importance to Paul's argument in Romans that righteousness through faith is "apart from law" in 3:21 and contrasted with the law in 4:14.

iii. Hays finds Paul's argument in Rom. 10:6-8 to be that "the real meaning of Deuteronomy 30 is disclosed not in lawkeeping but in Christian preaching" (82). It is not clear why the distinction between "lawkeeping" and "Christian preaching" that Hays finds in vv. 6-8 cannot be allowed between vv. 5 (the "righteousness of the law") and 6 (the "righteousness of faith") — especially since that distinction brings the verses in line with Gal. 3:11-12; Phil. 3:9; Rom. 3:21; and 4:14.

Hays concludes that those who read Rom. 10 as I do have made a "tragic error": thinking that

iii. that whereas in Philippians 3:9 Paul identifies his own righteousness with that based on law, here he distinguishes between Israel's own righteousness (Rom. 10:3) and the righteousness based on the law (v. 5); and

iv. that whereas in Romans itself the righteousness of faith is emphatically set in contrast with law, Paul here equates it with the law's righteousness.

The faith that can banish all these anomalies from sight is certainly of the mountain-moving variety!

c. We return, then, to Romans 9:30-32, aware that Paul in the immediate context, as well as elsewhere in his writings, contrasts the law's righteousness with that of faith. Are we to believe that he reverses himself here? Verses 31 and 32 make the following points:

i. Israel pursued a "law of righteousness."

ii. Israel did not attain to this law.

iii. The reason for the failure is that Israel pursued its goal not by faith, but as though it could be attained by works.

Each of these three statements is consistent with Pauline arguments elsewhere. None of them implies that the law itself is based on faith rather than works.

i. That the Sinaitic law code requires righteousness, and that Israel strives to attain that righteousness, is (as we have seen) self-evident to Paul.

ii. It is equally self-evident (from the perspective of Christian faith) that Israel has not attained to the righteousness required by the law. Paul here simply restates the thesis of 3:20: "no flesh will be justified before God by the works of the law." In Romans 2–3 the argument was that, though the law promises righteousness and life to those who "do" its commands (2:13), Jews (like Gentiles) are under sin and so cannot be justified by the works of the law; they have not attained that goal. The point of 9:31 seems identical. Though the righteousness of the law is indeed a matter of works, and life is promised to those who perform the works (10:5 restates the principle of 2:13), Jews do not achieve that goal — they do not "attain to the law (that requires righteousness)."

iii. Jewish failure to attain to the law (that requires righteousness) can be explained at two stages. In the first place transgressions of the law prevent those who are subject to the law from obtaining the life it promises. This is Paul's

---

"Torah and Christ are antithetical," we have failed "to acknowledge that the Law and the Prophets bear witness to the righteousness of God" (77). On this count at least I can offer some reassurance. I confess to thinking that Paul contrasts the ordinary righteousness required by the law with that offered, extraordinarily and through Christ, to those who believe; but I am fully prepared to acknowledge that Paul finds a witness to the latter "righteousness" in "the Law and the Prophets." The difference (noted in sec. ii above) between law as Scripture and law as "the sum of the commandments given to Israel through Moses on Mount Sinai, with the accompanying sanctions," is helpful here.

point in Romans 1–3; moreover, the transgressions and consequent condemnation to which the law leads are touched upon in chapter 5 and developed at length in chapter 7. If Paul does not repeat in 9:32 what he has said in chapters 1–3, 5, 7, and 8:3, the reason, presumably, is that he feels no need "to say everything every time he opens his mouth,"[95] not that he has changed his mind about human transgressions. Since, however, life under the law inevitably leads (by way of transgressions) to death, the righteousness and life that the law promises are in fact only obtainable by faith in Christ apart from the law and its "works" (3:20-22).[96] On a second level, then, the Jewish failure to arrive at the goal to which the law pointed can be ascribed to their persistence in the path of works rather than submitting to the righteousness based on faith; for, paradoxically, the *goal of the law* can only be attained *apart from the law*, by faith.

Paul's point here may be compared with his statements about the law's fulfillment (8:4; 13:8-10; Gal. 5:14). In Paul's view those under the law do not fulfill it. The law is even said to be too "weak" to bring about its own fulfillment (Rom. 8:3-4). Paradoxically, however, those who are not under the law but are "led by the Spirit" (Gal. 5:18) produce righteousness that the law cannot condemn (vv. 22-23), righteousness that in fact amounts to the law's fulfillment (Rom. 8:4; Gal 5:14). Just as the law is fulfilled by those free from the law who live by the Spirit, so, in Romans 9:30-32, the law can only be "attained" by those who do not pursue the law but live by faith. But this does not contradict Paul's claim that the law itself rests on works, not faith.

In the verses that follow, Paul faults the Jews with failing to submit to the righteousness of God as they seek to "establish their own" righteousness (10:3). And, as we have seen, their own righteousness is equivalent to that of the law (10:5; cf. Phil. 3:9). The curious result, according to both Philippians 3:9 and Romans 10:3-5, is that the righteousness of God's law is opposed to that of God. But 10:4 is intended to resolve the conundrum: "Christ is the end of the law, that every one who believes may be declared righteous." God's law promised righteousness to those who did its commands (10:5; cf. 2:13), though righteousness was in fact never achieved that way.[97] With Christ the righteousness of

---

95. Deidun, "Cake," 48; cf. Aletti, *Loi*, 225-26.

96. Laato, *Approach*, 198, emphasizes that Rom. 9:30–10:3 criticizes the soteriology of non-Christian Jews both because it is "anthropocentric" ("Jews stumble on the stone of stumbling *because* they are supposedly able to live by works") and "for its antichristological implication. It is not a matter of either-or."

97. Of course Paul did not believe that God condemned all those who lived "under law" before Christ; on the contrary, God "passed over" sins committed before the revelation of his righteousness in Christ (Rom. 3:25); and both Abraham and the psalmist give testimony *before Christ* to the righteousness of faith (Rom. 4:1-8). The point remains, however, that the law itself justifies no one.

faith has "now" been "revealed" (3:21), "faith" has "come" (Gal. 3:23), and the righteousness of the law has once and for all been set aside.[98] Indeed, the Sinaitic economy, as Paul indicates elsewhere, was *temporary by design* (2 Cor. 3:7, 11; Gal. 3:23-25; 4:1-5). Its role was negative and preparatory: it "consigned all things to sin," acting as a "pedagogue until Christ came" (3:23-24); it "increased" sin, so that grace might abound (Rom. 5:20); for all its glory, its "ministry" was one of death and condemnation (2 Cor. 3:7, 9). But now that the "new covenant" has come (v. 6), the "*old* covenant" (v. 14) (in the nature of the case) has come to its end. To pursue the righteousness of God's law after God has revealed its end in Christ (Rom. 10:4) is to defy the righteousness of God (v. 3).

iv. The Law and Legalism

Those who deny that Paul views the law as based on works frequently claim that he uses the term νόμος at times for God's law itself but at other times for its perversion into "legalism."[99] The attractiveness of the proposal is not hard to explain: it allows scholars to attribute to legalism any statement in Paul about the law that resists assimilation to a preferred reconstruction of his views. If, for example, one is convinced that the law has not been done away, one can always suggest that Romans 10:4 refers to the "end" of the "misused" law,[100] or that 7:4 may mean that Christians have died to the "legalistic misunderstanding and misuse of the law."[101] That Christians are not "under law" (6:14) can be explained by saying that they have been freed from the illusions about the law held by Paul's Jewish contemporaries.[102] The law that is curiously linked with the "elemental spirits" in Galatians 4:1-10 can, again, be identified with "the legalistic misunderstanding and misuse" of God's law.[103] Obviously the possibilities opened by this hermeneutical device are endless.

Most significant for our purposes here is the claim that it is legalism, not

---

98. Cf. Räisänen, *Law,* 54, on Rom. 10:4: "Bearing in mind that v. 5 is connected with an explanatory γάρ to the previous verse, the nomos in v. 4 must be associated with the righteousness from the law disqualified in v. 5. It must then belong together with the 'own' righteousness which the Jews try to establish (v. 3). With regard to such a law Christ can only be its end!" Cf. also Hahn, "Gesetzesverständnis," 50.

99. Cf. the discussion of the "works of the law" in sec. ii above, where the view was rejected that the term "works" signified a legalistic distortion of the law for Paul. Here the issue is whether "law" itself can mean "legalism."

100. Hübner, *Law,* 138; cf. W. D. Davies, *Studies,* 106; Moule, "Obligation," 402-3.

101. Cranfield, "Law," 56.

102. Cranfield, *Romans,* 320; Hübner, *Law,* 135; Moule, "Obligation," 394-95.

103. Cranfield, "Law," 63-64.

God's law, that Paul depicts as incompatible with faith in texts like Galatians 3:12,[104] and with God's promise in verse 18.[105] Why would Paul use the same word to mean both the God-given law and its distortion without indicating to his readers which he meant? Cranfield notes that "the Greek language used by Paul had no word-group to denote 'legalism,' 'legalist,' and 'legalistic.' . . . This means, surely, that he was at a very considerable disadvantage. . . . We should, I think, be ready to reckon with the possibility that sometimes, when he appears to be disparaging the law, what he really has in mind may be not the law itself but the misunderstanding and misuse of it for which *we* have a convenient term."[106]

The argument tantalizes but does not compel.

1. Whether or not the Greek language possessed a suitable single word for "legalism," it surely provided, and Paul's vocabulary included, sufficient resources for indicating whether he was speaking of the law as intended by God or in the (allegedly) perverted form in which it was understood by Jews.[107]

2. A study of the passages in question shows that no such distinction is intended. How can the law in Galatians 3:18 (a text where its perversion is purportedly found) be any different from the law in verses 17 and 19, where the giving of the law (doubtless in its intended form) is mentioned? How can the law of 4:1-10 refer to a "misunderstanding" of what God meant when Christ himself is said to have been subject to it (v. 4)? How can the death of Christians *with Christ* have been to a misunderstanding of the law that Christ cannot have shared (Rom. 7:4)? How can Paul have intended Galatians 3:12 to state his opponents' view of the law when, rather than correcting it, he cites Scripture in its support, and incorporates it into his argument that justification cannot come from the law? How can "under the law" mean "subject to an illusion about its nature" when Paul claims that he himself lives at times "as one under the law" (1 Cor. 9:20)?

3. As was shown above, the views that the law, in the sense of the Sinaitic legislation, rests on works (Gal. 3:12) and is distinct from God's promise (v. 18) are fully consistent with Paul's language elsewhere. We are dealing with fundamental Pauline theses, not Jewish misunderstandings.[108]

---

104. Cf. Fuller, "Works," 41, who suggests that the verse means that "legalism is an attitude of heart which cannot coexist with the attitude of faith."

105. Fuller, *Gospel*, 199-204. That theological convictions underlie such exegesis is noted by Moo, "Law," 87-88. They are spelled out by Cranfield, "Law," 67-68. Cf. also Fuller, *Gospel*, 99, 103-5; "Works," 30.

106. Cranfield, "Law," 55.

107. Cf. Moo, "Law," 86; Räisänen, *Law*, 43.

108. Cf. Ebeling, *Word*, 266.

4. The term "legalism" itself needs definition[109] — and here Räisänen has proposed a helpful distinction.[110] He notes that while legalism involves the view that "salvation consists of the observance of precepts," boasting and self-righteousness may, but do not always, accompany this notion. When they do not, we may speak of "a 'soft' or 'torah-centric' form of legalism";[111] when they do, we have a "hard" or "anthropocentric" legalism. To this we may add that soft legalists, who try to obey God's law because they believe God has commanded them to do so, may not believe they are thereby earning their salvation, still less establishing a claim on God based on their own merit. Surely love for God, or even fear of his judgment, is an adequate motive for obeying his commands. No such explanation as hypocrisy, self-seeking, merit mongering, and outright rebellion against God need be invoked to explain why religious people would attempt to do what they believe their God has commanded them. To think otherwise is to insist, for example, that Psalm 119 expresses the religion of a sham, and that Deuteronomy 30:16 commands it.

Unfortunately, in many discussions of legalism by New Testament scholars, the possibility of soft legalism is not even considered. The legalist, for Cranfield, is the one who tries to use the law "as a means to the establishment of a claim upon God, and so to the defence of his self-centredness and the assertion of a measure of independence over against God. He imagines that he can put God under an obligation to himself, that he will be able so adequately to fulfil the law's demands that he will earn for himself a righteous status before God."[112] For Moule legalism is "the intention to claim God's favour by establishing one's own rightness."[113] For Hübner those who see righteousness as based on works define their existence in terms of their own activities, leave God out of consideration, and in effect "see themselves as their own creator."[114] For Fuller legalism "presumes that the Lord, who is not 'served by human hands, as though he needed anything' (Acts 17:25), can nevertheless be bribed and obligated to bestow blessing by the way men distinguish themselves."[115]

Such definitions would be innocent enough if accompanied by an aware-

---

109. Cf. Jackson, "Legalism," 2. Dr. Sanders (in conversation) questions the wisdom of attempts to define "legalism" as a neutral term, given its almost universally accepted pejorative connotations; hence his use of "nomism."

110. Räisänen, "Legalism," 63-83.

111. Räisänen, "Legalism," 64. Cf. also R. Longenecker's distinction between "nomism" and "legalism," in *Paul*, 78-83.

112. Cranfield, "Law," 47.

113. Moule, "Obligation," 393.

114. Hübner, *Law*, 120-21.

115. Fuller, "Works," 36-37.

ness that legalists of this kind represent only some of those who interpreted Deuteronomy 30:16 as saying that obedience to God's law was the path to life. But all too frequently there is no such awareness. The — apparently inevitable — alternative to faith is the sinful, self-seeking, merit-claiming works of the (necessarily "hard") legalist. Whereas Paul can contrast faith in Christ with the works of the law, and mean by the latter no more than the deeds demanded by the law, the very notion of works is so inextricably linked in the minds of some scholars with self-righteousness and pride that (as we have seen) the works of the law can only be conceived as sinful. It is not surprising that for such scholars the law whose works are viewed as sinful cannot be seen as divine, but inevitably becomes the legalistically distorted form of God's law that prevailed (we are assured) among the Jews of Paul's day.[116] But — it must be emphasized — in Paul's argument it is human deeds of any kind that cannot justify, not simply deeds done in a spirit of legalism. *Paul's very point is lost to view when his statements excluding the law and its works from justification are applied only to the law's perversion.*

5. Finally, a few comments on the theological problem posed by Cranfield are in order. Does the law represent an unsuccessful first attempt on God's part? Is the gospel God's remedy for an initial plan that has gone wrong?[117]

a. For Paul the Mosaic legislation was God's gift to his people, Israel's righteousness and path to life — provided its commands were heeded. Such a view follows naturally, even inevitably, from a reading of Deuteronomy (4:1; 5:33; 6:24-25; 8:1; 11:26-28; etc.). As a Christian, however, Paul was convinced that the death of God's Son was essential to salvation; and this could only mean that the Mosaic law does not itself lead to the life it promises,[118] and hence (if one chooses to use the term) that the Sinaitic covenant was "unsuccessful" (cf. Jer. 31:32!). As Paul sees the matter, the Jews who have been given the law are simply a paradigm case[119] of what has happened with all human beings: made (and re-

---

116. Cf. Bultmann, "Anthropology," 148-49; Fuller, *Gospel*, 87 n. 33; Käsemann, *Perspectives*, 146-47.

117. For Räisänen (*Law*, 150-54) the problem is, again, Pauline inconsistency: the apostle claims *both* that God gave a law that promised life to its doers (cf. Rom. 10:5; Gal. 3:12) *and* that God never intended to provide life through the law (cf. Gal. 3:21). Note, however, the comments of Thurén, *Derhetorizing Paul*, 112-14, who observes that "the seemingly contradictory sayings 'the law cannot give life' and 'the law can give life to anybody who follows it' are based on the same syllogism, by adding a premise: The law has in itself ability to give life, but since nobody complies with the law, the ability is never realized." "In practice the law never gives life," though the idea, on the rhetorical level, can be expressed in different ways.

118. Cf. Grafe, *Lehre*, 11; Kuss, "Nomos," 211-13.

119. Cf. Dunn, *Theology*, 97; Wright, *Founder*, 130.

quired) to do good, they have chosen to do evil, and thus forfeited their right to the life for which they were intended.

b. But of course, that human beings in general, and Jews in particular, fall short of the goodness required of them cannot be the whole story — *especially* for Paul. God *must* have known what would happen. And, God being God, he must have planned from the beginning that justification would be found through Christ and by faith, not by the works of the law (cf. Gal. 3:8-9).[120] From this it follows that, while the law promises life, God must have designed it with other purposes in mind (see chap. 19 below). The result is that God's dealings can no longer be considered unsuccessful; the problem remains, however, that the law promises a life that, in God's plan, it would not give.

c. But the dilemma, thus put, is simply a variant of the issue faced by any who would believe in an omniscient Creator whose will has been transgressed by his creatures. In Genesis 2:17 God gives a command that is broken in chapter 3: those who accept the story must either believe that God did *not* know what his creatures would do *or* that he gave a command that he knew would be transgressed. The latter position alone is consistent with divine omniscience. Indeed, Christian readers (as a rule) go further still, believing that God gave a command both knowing it would be broken *and* having in mind the remedy to follow: Christ's death for sin was part of God's plan "before the foundation of the world" (1 Pet. 1:20). Hence sin entered the world both *contrary* to God's will (God never "wills" sin) and *according to God's plan* (which included, from the beginning, sin's remedy).[121] Paul's view of God's designs with the law conforms to this pattern: God promises life to those who obey his commands, but has planned from the beginning his remedy for transgressors. In each case we may (if we like) speak of a God of "unsuccessful" first attempts and find such a view of the deity "theologically grotesque." It is a charge to which a faith in a God who is both creator and redeemer is inevitably susceptible.

d. The issue, then, is one that lies at the roots of Christian theology; and to it, of course, there are classic responses.[122] That God placed requirements on

---

120. Cf. Bultmann, *Theology*, 1:263.

121. Cf. Augustine, *Ench.* 28.104: "Since [God] did foreknow that man would make bad use of his free will — that is, that he would sin — God prearranged his own purpose so that he could do good to man, even in man's doing evil, and so that the good will of the Omnipotent should be nullified by the bad will of men, but should nonetheless be fulfilled."

122. To my suggestion that there are parallels to Paul's notion that God promised life to the doers of the law while knowing that none would so attain it, Räisänen has responded (quite rightly) that "one person's problems cannot be solved by referring to others involved in analogous difficulties" (Review, 271). The issues — as hinted above, they are anything but new — go beyond the scope of this book; but see, e.g., the discussion of Augustine in chap. 1.

human beings was necessary if they were to act as *moral* beings, choosing between good and evil. God's knowledge of what human beings would do, it is insisted, did not compel them to act in ways contrary to their own will. Furthermore, the potential for moral goodness and the goodness of divine redemption are thought to outweigh the evil brought into the world by human beings and so to justify God in creating them and giving them commands — though knowing they would not do as he commanded.[123]

v. The Law and Torah

To this point we have seen how Paul uses "law" (νόμος) most frequently to mean the demands placed upon Israel at Mount Sinai, with the accompanying sanctions. The law demands deeds and is thus contrasted with faith, God's promise, and grace.

But such an understanding of Pauline usage exposes the apostle to attack on a different front: that Paul's νόμος represents a gross distortion of the Hebrew word *torah*, which cannot be reduced to a "sum of prescriptions."[124] By way of response to this now common critique, the following considerations may be raised.[125]

1. The claim that Hebrew *torah* is incorrectly rendered νόμος appears to have been introduced to the apologist's arsenal by Solomon Schechter.[126] In arguing that legalism has never "constituted the whole religion of the Jew, as declared by most modern critics," Schechter made the following claims:[127]

> It must first be stated that the term *Law* or *Nomos* is not a correct rendering of the Hebrew word *Torah*. The legalistic element, which might rightly be called the Law, represents only one side of the Torah. To the Jew the word Torah means a teaching or an instruction of any kind. (117)

> It is true that in Rabbinic literature the term *Torah* is often applied to the Pentateuch to the exclusion of the Prophets and the Hagiographa. . . . But even the Pentateuch is no mere legal code, without edifying elements in it.

---

123. Cf. Augustine, *Ench.* 26.100: "Nor would he who is good allow the evil to be done, unless in his own omnipotence he could bring good even out of evil."

124. Schoeps, *Paul*, 188.

125. The argument that follows represents a summary of my article "Meaning." For a more extended treatment of the views of Solomon Schechter, C. H. Dodd, Hans Joachim Schoeps, Samuel Sandmel, and W. D. Davies, see my "Nomos," 45-56.

126. Schechter, *Aspects*, 116-26.

127. The page numbers in the following text are from Schechter, *Aspects*.

The Book of Genesis, the greater part of Exodus, and even a part of Numbers are simple history. (118-19)

Thus *Torah*, even as represented by the Pentateuch, is not mere Law, the Rabbis having discerned and appreciated in it other than merely legal elements. Moreover, the term *Torah* is not always confined to the Pentateuch. It also extends, as already indicated, to the whole of the Scriptures. . . . To the Jew, as already pointed out, the term *Torah* implied a teaching or instruction, and was therefore wide enough to embrace the whole of the Scriptures. (121, 125)

It is the Torah as the sum total of the contents of revelation, without special regard to any particular element in it, the Torah as a faith, that is so dear to the Rabbi. (127)

Schechter's argument here shows an ambiguity that has dogged the debate ever since. He appears to be discussing the meaning of the word *torah* in general (note the first and third sentences of the first excerpt above); yet most of his attention focuses rather on the contents of "*the* Torah," now a technical term for the Pentateuch, or all of the sacred Scriptures, or even the "sum total of the contents of revelation." But the issues need to be kept separate. The variety of traditional materials that have come to be called "the Torah" may justly form the basis for an argument that legalism is not "the whole religion of the Jew"; this does not, however, mean that the word *torah* itself cannot mean "law." After all, just as "Exodus" has come to be the title of a book of Scripture because it contains (together with other materials) the story of the exodus from Egypt, so "Torah" may have become the designation of a collection of materials because it contains (together with other materials) the laws known as the *torah* (in a narrower sense). But the ambiguity in the argument has largely gone unnoticed. It has become all too common to make categorical statements about what *torah* can and cannot mean on the basis of the contents of "the Torah":

In Jewish usage these five books were and still are known by the collective name of the Torah. This alone shows that Torah is wrongly translated by "Law," because there is a great deal in the Pentateuch which is not law at all.[128]

The word Torah is only very imperfectly translated by "Law." . . . It contained far more than mere "precept" or laws.[129]

128. Herford, *Judaism*, 31.
129. Parkes, *Conflict*, 35-36.

And when the Torah is called "the Law," the error is that only the Halachah is Law; the Haggadah is not Law.[130]

2. The widespread acceptance of the notion that *torah* does not mean νόμος owes much to the belief that C. H. Dodd substantiated it. He did not. On the contrary, Dodd noted that the Hebrew *torah* "could be used collectively both of the priestly code of ceremonial observance . . . and also, by an extension of meaning, of the code of commandments, statutes and judgments contained in Deuteronomy. . . . It is in this sense that *torah* can fairly be regarded as equivalent to νόμος."[131] Dodd's complaint was rather that the Septuagint continued to use νόμος where *torah* means something quite different from "law." His charge is justified, though it is occasioned rather by the Septuagint's propensity for stereotyped renderings[132] than by the excessive legalism of Hellenistic Judaism. But what Dodd actually said has become less important than what he has been perceived to have said. Since the publication of his study, it has become axiomatic for many that the Septuagint is to blame for the misunderstanding of *torah* as "law," and that the distortion introduced by the Septuagint is responsible for countless woes. For some authors Paul is himself a victim of the distortion; for others he is an accomplice in the crime.

> Nothing has contributed more to the misunderstanding between the two religions [Judaism and Christianity] than the fact that the Septuagint translated the word "Torah" by the narrower word *nomos* and the English still further reduced the meaning by rendering *nomos* as *law*.[133]

> In the LXX there takes place with the translation *torah* — *nomos* — a shift of emphasis towards legalism. . . . The source of many Pauline misunderstandings with regard to the evaluation of the law and covenant is to be sought in the legalistic distortion of the perspective for which Hellenistic Judaism was responsible.[134]

> Torah does not mean Law, and never did, and the example of Paul, who did most to perpetuate the mischievous error, does not justify either himself or those who have imitated him.[135]

---

130. Herford, *Judaism*, 58. Similarly misguided are claims that *torah* "properly" or "basically" has a given meaning that is derived from its (proposed) etymology. See Barr, *Semantics*, 107-60, for the fallacy involved.

131. C. H. Dodd, *Bible*, 30-31.

132. Cf. Tov, *Use*, 55.

133. Parkes, *Foundations*, xv.

134. Schoeps, *Paul*, 29.

135. Herford, *Judaism*, 30-31.

To debase divine *instruction* (a concept which linguistically as well as regarding content, corresponds to Torah) by equating it with the narrow-minded word *nomos* (the law) — all of this is an absurd caricature which finds its source in Paul.[136]

3. There are, however, any number of cases in the Old Testament where *torah* is (or where *toroth* are) said to be "commanded" to be "done" or "kept" and not "transgressed." In such cases "law" (or "laws") would seem a more adequate rendering than "instruction," "teaching," or "revelation."

> . . . because Abraham heeded my voice and kept my charge, my commandments, my statutes, and my *laws*. (Gen. 26:5)

> And the Lord said to Moses, "How long do you refuse to keep my commandments and my *laws?*" (Exod. 16:28)

> These are the statutes, the ordinances, and the *laws* that the Lord made between himself and the people of Israel on Mount Sinai through Moses. (Lev. 26:46)

> They have transgressed the *laws*, altered the statutes. (Isa. 24:5)

> They did not heed your voice or walk in your *law*; all that you commanded them to do they did not do. (Jer. 32:23)

> . . . in order that they should keep his statutes and observe his *laws*. (Ps. 105:45)

Most importantly, in the Deuteronomistic literature "this *torah*" (or "the *torah* of Moses," or "this book of the *torah*," or "the book of the *torah* of Moses," etc.) is used of the substance of the Deuteronomic code, the sum of the commandments imposed upon Israel at Mount Sinai and accompanied by sanctions. Again, "law" is surely the most adequate rendering.

> And what great nation is there that has statutes and ordinances as all this *law* that I put before you today? (Deut. 4:8)

> Take to heart all the words with which I charge you today, that you may command your children to be careful to do all the words of this *law*. (Deut. 32:46)

---

136. Lapide and Stuhlmacher, *Paul*, 39.

Only show strength and great courage in your care to act according to all the *law* that Moses my servant commanded you. (Josh. 1:7)

Keep the charge of the Lord your God to walk in his ways, to keep his statutes, his commandments, his ordinances, and his testimonies, according to what is written in the *law* of Moses. (1 Kings 2:3)

Yet the Lord warned Israel and Judah by every prophet and every seer, saying, "Turn from your evil ways and keep my commandments and my statutes, according to all the *law* that I commanded your fathers." (2 Kings 17:13)

This Deuteronomistic usage of *torah* to designate the requirements imposed upon Israel is taken up in the later literature of the Old Testament as well, though now extended to include, for example, the priestly code.[137]

All Israel has transgressed your *law* and turned away, not heeding your voice. (Dan. 9:11)

And they found it written in the *law* that the Lord had commanded through Moses that the people of Israel should dwell in booths during the feast of the seventh month. (Neh. 8:14)

Our kings, our princes, our priests, and our fathers have not done your *law* or paid heed to your commandments. (Neh. 9:34)[138]

4. By a natural development, the scope of "the *torah* of Moses" was later extended to include the whole of the Pentateuch;[139] and naturally the Greek followed suit and spoke of the Pentateuch as ὁ νόμος. While a reminder of the scope of "the Torah" may well be in order, Hellenistic Judaism can scarcely be

---

137. Cf. Lindars, "Torah," 120-21.

138. Perhaps the most interesting passage in this regard is Ezra 7:12-26. The passage, in Aramaic, refers to "the law of the God of heaven" (v. 12), "the law of your God" (vv. 14, 26); Ezra is referred to as "the scribe of the law of the God of heaven" (v. 21). The Aramaic word used *(dāth)* is well attested as meaning "decree," "law" (cf. Dan. 6:9, 13, 16 [vv. 8, 12, 15 in English versions]: "the *law* of the Medes and the Persians," etc.). In Ezra 7 it is clearly used as the equivalent of the Hebrew *torah*: in the immediate context, Ezra is called "a scribe skilled in the law *(torah)* of Moses that the Lord the God of Israel had given" (v. 6; cf. v. 21) and as one who "prepared his heart to study the law *(torah)* of the Lord, to do it, and to teach in Israel its statutes and ordinances" (v. 10). Clearly the Septuagint was not original in translating *torah* with a word meaning "law"; those who condemn the Septuagint version and Hellenistic Jewry for rendering *torah* with νόμος ought to apply the same judgment to the author and community of Ezra!

139. Cf. Clements, *Theology,* 110-20.

faulted for designating it "the law"; the title, in both Hebrew and Greek, has grown out of its Deuteronomistic usage, where it means "law."

5. It follows that when Paul uses νόμος to mean the sum of obligations imposed upon Israel at Mount Sinai with the accompanying sanctions, such usage is a precise equivalent of what Deuteronomistic and later Old Testament literature meant by *torah*. That Paul's view of the role of the "law" in the divine scheme differs radically from that of the rabbis is only to be expected. It is not a consequence of his use of Greek νόμος.

Chapter 17

Matters of Definition, 3:
Grace in Sanders's Judaism[1]

According to Sanders's *Paul and Palestinian Judaism,* the positions of Paul and Palestinian Judaism on "grace" and "works" were identical: "getting in" to the people of God was by grace, whereas works were the condition of "staying in."[2] The enormous impact of Sanders's work is in part the result of his unique ability to sum up pithily his principal claims (e.g., that the solution precedes the plight [442], or that what Paul finds wrong with Judaism is that *"it is not Christianity"* [552]). On the other hand, nuances (often found in Sanders's own discussion) are inevitably left unstated in slogans like these — and easily go unnoted. On this crucial issue of our study, then, it will be worth our while to look closely at the fine print behind Sanders's memorable claim.

There is, at least to my mind, an immediate plausibility in the thesis that scholars who say Jews sought to "earn" salvation by their works have imposed "Lutheran" categories on Judaism that are foreign to its ethos. Something of that initial plausibility is forfeited, however, to my mind at least, when the refutation is formulated in the same ("Lutheran") terms, and first-century Jews are said, in effect, to have been good Protestants all along and champions of grace.

---

1. The aim in this chapter is simply to clarify Sanders's claims about grace in Judaism in order that fair comparisons can be made with Paul. Questions have, of course, been raised about various aspects of Sanders's presentation, and a few of these will be noted in footnotes; but a fresh study of the place of grace in Judaism cannot be undertaken here.

2. Cf. Sanders, *Paul Pal. Jud.,* 543: "On the point at which many have found the decisive contrast between Paul and Judaism — grace and works — Paul is in agreement with Palestinian Judaism. . . . Salvation is by grace but judgment is according to works; works are the condition of remaining 'in,' but they do not earn salvation." See also *Law,* 105-6; *Paul Pal. Jud.,* 517, 548. In the discussion that follows, page references to Sanders's work in the body of the text are to his *Paul and Palestinian Judaism.*

Yet such a claim is attributed to Sanders by supporters[3] and critics[4] alike. Clearly Sanders's slogans have been heeded; it is worth asking whether subtleties in his text have been missed.

In fact, Sanders makes the point, explicitly and repeatedly, that a contrast between works or merit on the one hand and faith or grace on the other is *not* native to Judaism. New Testament scholars may think Judaism teaches salvation by works rather than faith, but "the antithetical contrast, not by works but by faith, is Paul's own. . . . Paul's own polemic against Judaism serves to define the Judaism which is then contrasted with Paul's thought" (4). "The Rabbis did not have the Pauline/Lutheran problem of 'works-righteousness,' and so felt no embarrassment at saying that the exodus was earned; yet that it was earned is certainly not a Rabbinic doctrine. It is only an explanatory device. One might have expected the Rabbis to develop a clear doctrine of prevenient grace, but grace and merit did not seem to them to be in contradiction to each other" (100). "Grace and works were not considered as opposed to each other in any way. I believe it is safe to say that the notion that God's grace is in any way contradictory to human endeavour is totally foreign to Palestinian Judaism. The reason for this is that grace and works were not considered alternative roads to salvation" (297).

One may well wonder how a Judaism that, according to Sanders, did not consider "grace and works" to be "opposed to each other in any way," and that did not see "grace and works" as "alternative roads to salvation," is widely believed, on the basis of Sanders's work, to preach good Protestant doctrine that salvation is by grace, not works. Why, for that matter, does Sanders himself say that for Judaism "salvation is always by the grace of God" (297)?

---

3. Cf. Dunn, "Justice," 7-8: "Judaism is first and foremost a religion of grace. . . . Somewhat surprisingly, the picture which Sanders painted of what he called 'covenantal nomism' is remarkably like the classic Reformation theology of works — that good works are the consequence and outworking of divine grace, not the means by which that grace is first attained. . . . The Judaism of what Sanders christened as 'covenantal nomism' can now be seen to preach good Protestant doctrine: that grace is always prior; that human effort is ever the response to divine initiative; that good works are the fruit and not the root of salvation."

4. Cf. Alexander, Review, 105: "Perhaps Sanders has not identified the point at issue here with total accuracy. His answer to the charge of 'legalism' seems, in effect, to be that Rabbinic Judaism, despite appearances, is really a religion of 'grace.' But does this not involve a tacit acceptance of a major element in his opponents' position — the assumption that 'grace' is superior to 'law'? The correct response to the charge must surely be: And what is wrong with 'legalism,' once we have got rid of abusive language about 'hypocrisy' and 'mere externalism'? . . . If we fail to take a firm stand on this point we run the risk of seriously misdescribing Pharisaic and Rabbinic Judaism, and of trying to make it over into a pale reflection of Protestant Christianity."

The claim is, of course, conditioned by the polemical purpose for which Sanders wrote. He set out, he tells us, "to destroy the view of Rabbinic Judaism which is still prevalent in much, perhaps most, New Testament scholarship" (xii). On the nature of that erroneous but "prevalent" view, Sanders is very clear: "Judaism is [seen as] a religion in which one must *earn* salvation by compiling more good works ('merits'), whether on his own or from the excess of someone else, than he has transgressions" (38). "At the judgment all of one's works would be counted and weighed, the verdict on a man's fate being determined by the balance of merits and demerits" (45). "Salvation is earned by the merit of good works" (51). "The principal element is the theory that works *earn* salvation" (54). "Christian scholars" have "conclude[d] that the Rabbinic view of religion is that the covenant (and salvation) are earned and that the grace of God plays no substantial part" (97). When Sanders insists that salvation in Judaism is "by grace," he merely adopts the terms of an existing debate, arguing *against* the widespread notion that for Jews salvation was earned by those whose good works, strictly measured, outweighed their transgressions.

The refutation, as we have seen, is energetically pursued on several fronts. Rabbinic literature does admittedly speak of a judgment where good deeds are weighed against bad[5] and even, on occasion, of participation in the "age to come" as "merited" by actions in the present (133-34, 141, 189). Such statements, Sanders insists, serve homiletic purposes (129-30, 139, 141, etc.);[6] they do not represent the substance of a rabbinic soteriology (139-40, 143, 146, etc.).[7] The

---

5. The relevant texts are discussed by Sanders, *Paul Pal. Jud.*, 128-47.

6. One may perhaps wonder how the rabbis could have used for pedagogic purposes statements that the last judgment would be based on the majority of one's deeds if everyone knew that salvation depended on nothing but election and repentance (cf. Avemarie, *Tora*, 40 n. 96).

7. Not all scholars, of course, have been persuaded. Some continue to cite the legalistic-looking texts as evidence that Judaism was indeed legalistic; cf. the early response of Gundry, "Grace," 1-38; and more recently, Talbert, "Paul," 1-22. Stanton ("Law," 104-6) points to the possible relevance of Justin, *Dialogue* 8.4, in which "a learned Jew expresses the view that one's standing with God is dependent on carrying out the whole law." Friedrich Avemarie (*Tora;* "Erwählung," 108-26) argues that in the end we simply have to say that rabbinic literature shows two different ways of thinking about participation in the world to come. One is the principle of retribution: whoever obediently fulfills what Torah requires is rewarded with eternal life. The other follows the principle of election: whoever belongs to Israel has a share in all that has been promised to Israel, including a part in the world to come. Both ways of thinking are abundantly attested. Whereas Sanders's model requires the subordination of the retribution texts to the election texts, and whereas earlier scholars (such as Billerbeck) subordinated election texts to the retribution ones, both stand side by side in the literature, functioning autonomously; and both have to be given due weight. There was no single, coherent soteriology in rabbinic literature. Cf. also Alexander, "Torah," 270-71; Quarles, "Soteriology," 185-95; Snodgrass, "Justification," 77-79.

rabbis *could* not have really thought that salvation was based on a strict measurement of one's deeds, since they manifestly believed God to be merciful toward all those within the covenant who "basically intended to obey, even though their performance might have been a long way from perfect" (125); moreover, God "has appointed [again, for those within the covenant] means of atonement for every transgression, except the intention to reject God and his covenant" (157).

God would be merciful to those within the covenant who had signaled their intention to live by its laws. Still, the heart of Sanders's claim that in Judaism salvation is by grace lies a step further back: God's *election* of Israel *as his covenant people* provided the basis for Israel's "salvation";[8] and that *election* was an act of divine grace. Again Sanders could not be more explicit: "covenantal nomism is the view that one's place in God's plan is established on the basis of the covenant" (75). "The all pervasive view is this: all Israelites have a share in the world to come unless they renounce it by renouncing God and his covenant" (147). "The fundamental basis of [Rabbinic] religion [is] God's election of Israel. The theme of repentance and forgiveness functions within a larger structure which is founded on the understanding that 'All Israelites have a share in the world to come.' This view, it is clear, is based on an understanding of the

---

8. This claim has been contested on several grounds. "Staying in" the covenant through obedience, Sanders agrees, is an essential condition for salvation; this suggests to some scholars that salvation can hardly be based solely on the grace of election. Cf. Rieger, "Religion," 150-52; also Enns, "Expansions," 97-98: "Despite Sanders's arguments, it is still not entirely clear how 'salvation' can be by grace but 'staying saved' is a matter of strict obedience. If salvation can be lost by disobedience — i.e., if obedience is necessary to 'preserve' salvation — in what sense can we say with Sanders that 'salvation *depends* on the grace of God'? How can there be sins unto death when *election* is the basis of salvation? . . . I wonder, too, whether we should equate salvation with election, as Sanders seems to do. Is salvation the best word to describe one's *initiation* into the covenant wholly apart from the final outcome? . . . It might be less confusing to say that *election* is by grace but *salvation* is by obedience." Others insist that Israel's covenant does not play the role Sanders assigns it in particular bodies of Jewish literature (so Collins, *Athens*, 14, of apocalyptic [cf. also Bauckham, "Apocalypses," 148-49] and Wisdom literature, and 244, of Hellenistic Judaism in general; Spilsbury, "Josephus," 241-60, of Josephus; Hay, "Philo," 357-79, etc.). In a massive study of the Pseudepigrapha and Dead Sea Scrolls, Mark Adam Elliott argues that there was within Second Temple Judaism a substantial dissent movement that saw Israel living in a time of apostasy. The covenant had been broken, and a large part of Israel was now "effectively disqualified from the benefits of that covenant and of membership in God's chosen people" (*Survivors,* 115). By far the dominant view of the covenant among these groups was not that of an unconditional, irrevocable, national covenant, but of a conditional, individual, dynamic, and dualistic covenant — "dualistic" in the sense that the division between those inside and outside the covenant lay, not at the boundaries between Israel and the Gentiles, but within Israel itself (248-50, 307).

grace of God" (177). "Election and ultimately salvation are considered to be by God's mercy rather than human achievement" (422).

The conclusion is clear. So, too, are the premises on which it rests: belonging to the people God had chosen was tantamount to possessing salvation, and Israel's election as God's covenant people was perceived to be an act of grace. To readers schooled in "Lutheran" ways of thinking, the latter supposition no doubt seems intuitively true. Yet its substantiation from a literature that did not see grace and works as opposed to each other in any way can at best be oblique. And so, indeed, it proves.

We may begin where the rabbis are most unobliging. Blithely unaware of "the Pauline/Lutheran problem of 'works-righteousness,'" they repeatedly affirmed that God "chose Israel because of some merit found either in the patriarchs or in the exodus generation or on the condition of future obedience" (87).[9] The theme is a common one in the literature, and is of course flatly contradictory of the notion that the election of Israel was "totally gratuitous, without prior cause in those being elected" (87).[10] Before too much is made of these statements, however, the following observations should be noted. (1) The motive behind each of these texts, according to Sanders, is to "mak[e] God's choice seem non-arbitrary" (91). In electing Israel God must be shown to have been neither capricious nor unjust; hence merits were ascribed to Israel to justify God's choice (cf. 98).[11] (2) The fact that different explanations are given for the election shows that no *one* explanation represented rabbinic "doctrine" on the subject (100). (3) Even where some "merit" is cited as justifying God's election of Israel, it is not thought that the election was (strictly speaking) "earned": God's love can never be earned, and his blessings are out of all proportion to any merits that may be attributed to their recipients (101, 422). (4) "Even if the

9. The texts cited by Sanders as illustrating this theme in fact deal largely with Israel's deliverance from Egypt: the "merits" God perceives in the patriarchs, the exodus generation, or future generations of Israelites are cited as the reason God redeemed Israel, *not* the reason why he chose Israel in the first place to be his people. Cf. Avemarie, *Tora*, 40-42. Sanders explains: "We have focused primarily on the election as exemplified by the redemption from Egypt, leaving aside the question of *when* God's decisive choice of Israel was made" (*Paul Pal. Jud.*, 92 n. 27).

10. That the two types of texts are in "direct conflict" is noted by Sanders (*Paul Pal. Jud.*, 90). The texts in which he finds the theme of "total gratuity" will be treated below.

11. The underlying premise, that "one cannot obtain reward except for deeds," is spelled out in *Mekilta* Pisha 5 (Lauterbach 1.33-34; on 12:6), where the "reward" "merited" by Israel was specifically its redemption: the time had come "for the fulfilment of the oath which the Holy One had sworn unto Abraham, to deliver his children. But as yet they had no religious duties *(mitsvot)* to perform by which to merit redemption. . . . Therefore the Holy One, blessed be He, assigned them two duties which they should perform so as to be worthy of redemption. . . . For one cannot obtain rewards except for deeds" (quoted in Sanders, *Paul Pal. Jud.*, 89).

election had been earned in the past, there is no thought that subsequent Israel-ites must continue to earn their place in the covenant as individuals, or that the covenant must be re-won in each generation" (101; cf. 92 n. 27; also 104).

That Israelites (of one generation or another) merited the election is, how-ever, only one of the explanations given in rabbinic literature for God's choice of this particular people. Sanders notes two others as well. According to one, "God offered the covenant (and the commandments attached to it) to all, but only Israel accepted it" (87). Again, it must be said that the rabbis who thus at-tributed God's selection to "Israel's moral superiority to other nations" (88) be-tray a blithe insensitivity to "Lutheran" concerns. The third explanation is that "God chose Israel for his name's sake" (88). The texts cited (99) echo Ezekiel 20:9 and stress (as does Ezekiel) that Israel in Egypt deserved extinction and was unworthy of the benefits God was about to confer upon them; yet he showed them mercy "for the sake of his name." In other words, because God had made commitments to Israel's forefathers, he would jeopardize the honor of his name were he to treat the Israelites now as their deeds deserved; hence, "for the sake of his name," he dealt with them in mercy. These texts, it should be noted, do not in fact claim that God elected Israel as an act of sheer divine mercy; rather, having *already* made commitments to Israel's forefathers, *and with the merits of those forefathers explicitly in view,*[12] God treated their descen-dants more mercifully than they deserved.

In short, the basis of Sanders's claim that salvation in Judaism is "by grace" is the claim that salvation is rooted in God's election of Israel and that election was an act of divine grace. Yet none of the explanations given for the election in rabbinic sources suggests the utter gratuity of God's choice; indeed, two of the three speak to contrary effect. For the theme of gratuity we must look else-where.

Sanders finds it in passages in which the Israelites are said to have entered the covenant *before* they obeyed its commandments. Here there can have been no thought that such acts of obedience *earned* the election or the covenant.[13] The texts Sanders cites[14] are as follows (the enumeration, intended to facilitate the discussion below, is my own).

---

12. See *Mekhilta of R. Simeon b. Yohai* on Exod. 6:2 (Epstein, p. 5), quoted by Sanders, *Paul Pal. Jud.,* 99.

13. Sanders, *Paul Pal. Jud.,* 85: "We may begin by noting several passages in which a Rabbi explicitly states that entrance into the covenant was prior to the fulfilment of commandments; in other words, that the covenant was not earned, but that obedience to the commandments is the consequence of the prior election of Israel by God."

14. See the section headed "The Theme of Gratuity" in Sanders, *Paul Pal. Jud.,* 85-87.

1. "R. Joshua b. Karha said: Why does the section *Hear, O Israel* (Deut. 6.4-9) precede [the section] *And it shall come to pass if ye shall hearken [diligently to my commandments]*? — so that a man may first take upon him the yoke of the kingdom of heaven and afterward take upon him the yoke of the commandments." (*m. Ber.* 2:2)

2. "When it says 'I am the Lord thy God,' it means this: Am I not he whose kingship you took upon yourselves at Sinai? [When the Israelites answer affirmatively, God replies] 'You have accepted my kingship, accept my ordinances.'" (Somewhat paraphrastically, *Sifra* Ahare pereq 13.3 [to 18.1f.])

3. "*I Am the Lord Thy God* (Ex. 20.2). Why were the Ten Commandments not said at the beginning of the torah? They give a parable. To what may this be compared? To the following: A king who entered a province said to the people: May I be your king? But the people said to him: Have you done anything good for us that you should rule over us? What did he do then? He built the city wall for them, he brought in the water supply for them, and he fought their battles. Then when he said to them: May I be your king? they said to him: Yes, yes. Likewise, God. He brought the Israelites out of Egypt, divided the sea for them, sent down the manna for them, brought up the well for them, brought the quails for them. He fought for them the battle with Amalek. Then He said to them: I am to be your king. And they said to Him: Yes, yes." (*Mekilta* Bahodesh 5 [Lauterbach 2.229-230; on 20:2])

4. "Likewise, God said to Israel: 'I am the Lord thy God, thou shalt not have other gods — I am He whose reign you have taken upon yourselves in Egypt.' And when they said to Him: 'Yes, yes,' He continued: 'Now, just as you accepted My reign, you must also accept My decrees: "Thou shalt not have other gods before Me."'" (*Mekilta* Bahodesh 6 [Lauterbach 2.238; on 20:3])

5. "Thou hast shown us mercy, for we had no meritorious deeds." (*Mekilta* Shirata 9 [Lauterbach 2.69; on 15:13])

6. "Already before I (God) gave them the commandments [concerning the Sabbath] I advanced them the rewards [the granting of manna] for them." (*Mekilta* Bahodesh 1 [Lauterbach 2.199; on 19:2])

7. "R. Joshua says: The Holy One, blessed be He, said to Moses: Say to the Israelites: I have brought you out of Egypt, I have divided the Red Sea for you [a list is given] — how long will you refuse to observe My commandments and My laws?" (*Mekilta* Vayassa' 6 [Lauterbach 2.121; on 16:28])

That God has been good to Israel is clearly an emphasis in the third, fifth, sixth, and seventh quotations. That Israel accepted the covenant *before* God spelled out his commandments is stressed in the first four. That the Israelites *earned* the covenant *by obeying its commandments* is clearly excluded by the same quotations, and is contrary to the tone of quotations 5 to 7 (in which, however, neither the election nor the covenant is in view).[15] All of this strongly supports Sanders's claim that Israel was not thought to have earned the covenant apart from divine grace. On the other hand, none of these quotations says that the election or the granting of the covenant was itself an act of divine grace. To say that Israel's "acceptance of God's kingship always precedes the enjoining of the commandments" (86) is not the same as saying that God gave his covenant and commandments to Israel as an act of unmerited favor.[16] Indeed, the insistence that Israel had to accept God's rule (the same passages in *Mekilta* note that other nations, given the opportunity, refused to do so) before he would give them his commands appears to confirm rather than contradict the other rabbinic statements cited by Sanders in which the election was justified in terms of some merit attributed to Israel.

We may say that in a literature that does not see grace and works opposed in any way, one should not *expect* direct declarations that salvation, or even election, is *simply* a matter of grace. If for polemical purposes one wants to establish the importance of grace in Judaism, then statements like those just cited must serve the purpose. And indeed, it is to precisely *these* texts that Sanders refers when he goes on immediately to say, "We have already seen passages in which God's election was thought of as being totally gratuitous, without prior cause in those being elected" (87). But here Sanders's polemical purposes have surely imposed a "Lutheran" construction on the texts: neither the "total" gratuity of the election nor, indeed, any exclusion of human contributions is in view.

One other group of texts cited by Sanders requires attention. Sanders grants (as we have seen) that the distinction between works and grace is not native to Judaism; he nonetheless employs it (as we have also seen) in his claim that, for Judaism as for Paul, salvation is by grace, whereas works are the condition of "staying in" the people of God. His justification for doing so is partly

---

15. Quotation 5 appears close to contradicting Sanders's claim that Judaism did not see "grace and works" as "opposed to each other in any way"; still, mercy is cited as characterizing the way God has dealt with his people; it is *not* given as the explanation for election. Quotation 6 shows God's goodness in advancing a "reward" that was yet to be "merited," though the principle that rewards are merited is presupposed. Quotation 7 picks up the scriptural themes of divine patience and Israel's stubborn disobedience, though without claiming that Israel was first chosen as an act of unmerited divine favor.

16. Cf. Rieger, "Religion," 133.

polemical. But Sanders also believes his slogan is justified because Judaism, studied on its own terms, *does* distinguish between grace (as expressed in the election or covenant) as the cause of salvation and human obedience as the *condition* for retaining it (141, 146-47, 180, etc.). Presupposed is the notion that the election is an act of divine grace; as we have just seen, this was hardly rabbinic doctrine, or even (if "grace" is understood to exclude merit) a rabbinic theme. We may now turn to the texts on which Sanders bases his distinction between divine grace as the *source* of salvation and human obedience as its *"condition."*

The texts are found in the midst of Sanders's discussion of rabbinic statements that "God chose Israel . . . on the condition of future obedience" (87). In support, he cites the following passages (92-93):

> "I am the Lord thy God who brought thee out of the land of Egypt." — On this condition I brought you out of the land of Egypt: on the condition that you take upon yourselves the commandment concerning just measures *(mitsvat middot);* for everyone who confesses to (i.e. agrees to) the commandment concerning just measures confesses to (confirms) the exodus from Egypt; but anyone who denies the commandment concerning just measures denies the exodus from Egypt. (*Sifra* Qedoshim pereq 8.10 [on 19:36b])

> "I am the Lord your God who brought you up from the land of Egypt" (Lev 11.45). For this purpose *('al ken)* I brought you up from the land of Egypt: on the condition that you take upon yourselves the yoke of the commandments; for everyone who confesses the yoke of the commandments confesses the exodus from Egypt, etc. (*Sifra* Shemini pereq 12.4 [on 11:45])

From these texts[17] Sanders concludes: "The point is not that obeying a commandment, or even all the commandments, *earned* the exodus, but that God accomplished the exodus so that Israel might obey the commandments and that God *made the condition for remaining in the covenant* the free intent to obey the commandments, not their successful fulfilment" (93).

The progression of the argument bears attention. Sanders initially cites these texts because they illustrate how God's election was "explained by actions yet to be performed. God foresees that Israel will fulfil the Torah and therefore chooses Israel to receive it" (92). Among the texts that make that point, several are noted in which God is said to deliver Israel from Egypt "on the condition

---

17. Sanders notes other texts as well, but the point is the same: "the exodus was accomplished by God *on the condition that* Israel would take upon itself some commandment or other" (*Paul Pal. Jud.,* 92).

that" Israel would accept his commandments in the future; that is, Israel's future submission to the commandments is the "condition" God had in mind *before redeeming them and granting them his covenant.* But the same texts serve (quite rightly) as evidence for Sanders that obedience was also the *"condition for remaining in the covenant";* after all, later generations of Israelites are in view when the text goes on to claim that "everyone who confesses the yoke of the commandments confesses the exodus from Egypt [i.e., affirms the covenant]." In short, these texts treat Israel's willingness to submit to the laws of the covenant as *both* the condition that had to be met before God would grant them the covenant in the first place *and* as the condition that had to be met if later Israelites were to retain their place within it.

When Sanders later insists that obedience was a condition for a salvation that was grounded in the divine grace of the election, it is precisely *these* texts that provide the basis for the distinction.[18] But such a distinction must be read into them. The texts attribute *both* the original election itself *and* the continued place of Jews within the covenant to the *same* willingness by Israel to submit to God's commandments.

What, then, may we say about grace and works in Judaism on the basis of Sanders's discussion of rabbinic sources? Certainly he has assembled abundant evidence from rabbinic literature in which it is clear that salvation was not believed to be earned by individual Israelites apart from divine grace. If by "legalism" we mean the conviction that it was, then Judaism was not legalistic. The view that Sanders has discredited frequently led in earlier literature to a depiction of Jews either as living in terror that at the last judgment their sins would outweigh their good deeds, *or* as self-righteous boasters in the good deeds by which they earned their salvation. That kind of portrayal appears to have virtually disappeared from the scholarly literature of the last two decades. It has been replaced by a real desire to depict Judaism sympathetically and in its own terms. Much of the credit must be given to Sanders's *Paul and Palestinian Judaism.*

Whether, apart from its polemical context, the claim that Palestinian Judaism and Paul viewed the relation between grace and works in the same terms is more dubious. If Judaism did indeed preach that salvation is by grace, it is remarkable that the rabbis seldom, if ever, got around to saying anything of the kind; remarkable that — no doubt for homiletic purposes — they kept saying things very dif-

18. Note how, in the index to *Paul and Palestinian Judaism,* under "Obedience, . . . as *condition* of staying in covenant or of being saved," pp. 92-97 are first cited. These are the pages in which the texts that speak of Israel's future obedience as the condition for their redemption from Egypt are discussed. Other page references follow, but they refer the reader back to the earlier discussion; no other texts are cited as speaking of obedience as the "*condition* of staying in covenant or of being saved."

ferent. The frustration that a number of scholars[19] have felt with the current debate is that Sanders is widely believed to have refuted a "Lutheran" understanding of Judaism when, to their minds, the position of Judaism on the relation between grace and works *as Sanders himself portrays it* seems to differ little from that of Pelagius, against whom Augustine railed, or that of the sixteenth-century church, upon which Luther called down heaven's thunder. Sanders has shown that Judaism did not generally believe that salvation was earned from scratch by human deeds of righteousness; the point is well taken, but it by no means differentiates Judaism from the classical opponents of "Lutheran" thought. Each acknowledged human need of divine grace. What the opponents of "Lutheranism" emphatically did *not* do, however — what they indeed regarded as morally disastrous to do — was to suggest that humans can contribute *nothing* to their salvation. *That* insistence is, as we have seen, the very essence of "Lutheranism." It seems fair to say that it is not to be found in Judaism as depicted by Sanders.

The rabbinic texts, as Sanders has stated, do not envisage grace and works as "alternative paths to salvation"; in this they diverge markedly from the "Lutheran" Paul. Rabbinic texts can speak without embarrassment or qualifications, as Sanders has shown, of a judgment determined by whether good deeds or bad weighed heavier, and even of the age to come as merited by particular deeds; here their sensibilities are demonstrably "*un*-Lutheran."[20] When, moreover, they ascribe God's election of Israel to merits perceived in those he elected, the suggestion, however undogmatically propounded, must be acknowledged to be simply unthinkable to any adherent of the "Lutheran" Paul. In rabbinic texts it is remarked (no doubt undogmatically) that the reward of redemption could not be granted apart from some merit on the part of the redeemed: a remark, it is fair to say, that would have confirmed the worst suspicions of at least the "Lutheran" Paul. The rabbis — we may repeat Sanders's words — were untroubled by "the Pauline/Lutheran problem of 'works-righteousness,'" and, moreover, by any notion of an "original sin" that renders human beings incapable of fulfilling God's commands (18, 114-15). The observation that the rabbis were not "Lutherans" after all is not meant to reflect either well or poorly on their thinking. The point to be made is that we do Judaism neither justice nor favor when we claim that it preached "good" Protestant doctrine on the subject of grace and works.[21]

19. See, e.g., Schreiner, *Law*, 119; Seifrid, "Alleys," 92; Silva, "Synthesis," 347-50, esp. n. 21.

20. That the rabbis spoke homiletically rather than dogmatically does not alter the difference between what *they*, unburdened by "Lutheran" sensibilities, could say to achieve homiletic ends and what a "Lutheran," constrained by "Lutheran" doctrine, could say for the same purpose. See also n. 6 above.

21. Cf. Matlock, "Sins," 83-84 n. 40; "Studies," 444.

Chapter 18

"Justification by Faith" in Paul's Thought: The Evidence in Review

To those of us engrossed in the study of the law and justification in Paul's thought, it is a cause of fleeting mortification that the apostle dispatched a letter of five chapters with nary an allusion to our preoccupations. Disconcerted though hardly daunted, we may pause briefly to wonder why the Thessalonian Paul so little resembles his real self, but we quickly move on to writings in which he proves more obliging. Alas, it soon becomes apparent that the apostle had not yet hit his stride at the time of his Corinthian correspondence either, though a few promising signs are not to be neglected. In Galatians, Romans, and Philippians we bask, and there we are wont to end our review. Ephesians and the Pastorals, as doubtfully Pauline, are not likely to attract any attention. As for the epistle of James, if Luther has not banished it from our Bibles, its pages may nonetheless be the last to which we would turn for an illumination of Paul's thought.

Yet relevance for our themes has recently been argued for each of the above-mentioned epistles, including those presumed most irrelevant. Each merits at least a look, and a review of the argument of each will minimize the risk that we ignore the contexts in which Paul discusses justification, or impose a pattern from one letter on his writings as a whole.

i. 1 Thessalonians[1]

Of the extant Pauline epistles, 1 Thessalonians was likely the first to be written,[2] though the significance of its anteriority is a matter of dispute. A number of themes prominent in later Pauline letters seem absent from the first.[3] For some scholars this means that these notions had not yet taken shape in Paul's thinking;[4] other scholars, however, track elusive evidence even in 1 Thessalonians of the themes that are later more conspicuous, or insist that, where nothing in the situation of the Thessalonians prompted the mention of a topic, we may conclude nothing about the maturity of Paul's thought.[5] Aspects of the discussion will be taken up below.

Less attention has been paid to a different Thessalonian distinctive: no extant Pauline letter was written more immediately after the founding of the Christian community to which it was addressed than 1 Thessalonians. Should we be interested in the content of Paul's initial proclamation to a non-Christian audience, no other evidence approximates the value of 1 Thessalonians. Other letters are dominated by issues that arose after Paul's initial visit.[6] In 1 Thessalonians, however, Paul's immediate worry was simply whether, in his absence, his readers were holding fast to the faith they had shown before he left them. Expressions of his concern give him ample opportunity to indicate the substance of their faith and of the proclamation that had aroused it. The fervor with which Paul reiterates these themes can be little different from that which imbued his message on its first delivery. One important issue *had* arisen after his departure; yet it, too, clearly reflects the thrust of his initial message.

At any moment,[7] Paul had warned his listeners, an outpouring of divine

1. 2 Thessalonians adds little of importance for our theme, so the debate about its authenticity need not be entered here. In the body of the text I will provide references to 2 Thessalonians only for the sake of comparison. Brief comments will be confined to the footnotes.

2. This conviction is held by the majority of scholars, though rejected by those (e.g., Bruce, *Galatians*, 3-18, 43-56; R. Longenecker, *Galatians*, lxi-lxxxviii) who believe the Jerusalem council described in Gal. 2 was distinct from, and preceded, that of Acts 15, and that Galatians was written between the two events.

3. Marshall provides a helpful summary of characteristic Pauline themes that are missing, and of others that are present, in the Thessalonian correspondence ("Theology," 173-83).

4. So, e.g., Donfried, with regard to the law and justification; cf. Donfried and Marshall, *Theology*, 64-65.

5. E.g., Riesner, *Period*, 394-403.

6. Romans is an obvious exception; but since Paul had *not* been to Rome, the epistle can have nothing to say of an earlier Pauline proclamation to its addressees.

7. So, at least, it seems in 1 Thessalonians. That 2 Thessalonians, in apparent contrast, insists that a number of events must precede Christ's return is for many scholars the prime reason for doubting its authenticity.

wrath would engulf an unsuspecting humanity and bring it sudden destruction (1:10; 5:3; cf. 2 Thess. 1:5-10). Human sinfulness had all but reached its limit.[8] Gentiles for their part had paid no heed to the true and living God while serving idols; their immorality was notorious and their conduct in general befitted darkness, not light (cf. 1 Thess. 1:9; 4:4-5; 5:6-7). As for Jews, estrangement from God was signified by their no less notorious history of rejecting his messengers: the prophets of old, the Lord Jesus but recently, and now his apostolic witnesses (2:14-16). Retribution for all would be swift and inescapable (5:3).[9] Assumed throughout is the divine demand of (what I have earlier labeled) *ordinary* "dikaiosness": human beings — Jews *and* Gentiles — are required to do what is right, and God will judge them by whether or not they have done it. A second assumption, operative throughout the epistle, is that nobody has; hence the imminent expectation of judgment for all.

Yet Paul had been entrusted by God to deliver to the Thessalonians a message of "good news" about "salvation" (2:4, 16; 5:9) — a salvation that, in the light of humanity's pending doom, was of a very specific sort. In Jesus, God's Son, there is rescue from the coming wrath (1:10; 5:9).[10] Paul does not spell out

8. Note how 1 Thess. 2:16 suggests a "measure" of sinfulness, the "filling" of which precipitates judgment ("wrath"); cf. Malherbe, *Thessalonians*, 176; Marshall, *Thessalonians*, 80. That Jews have *already* reached their "limit" and experienced the consequent wrath (note that the wrath "has overtaken" [ἔφθασεν, aorist tense] them, 2:16) is certainly a claim easier to credit in the period immediately after 70 C.E. than in Paul's lifetime; but the aorist tense may well be proleptic (or "prophetic"; so, e.g., Malherbe, 177), or the verb itself may signify the proximity rather than the actual occurrence of the doom (cf. Marshall, 80-81). The case for the inauthenticity of 2:13-16 (or of parts thereof) is not, in my judgment, a compelling one. Cf. Bockmuehl, "Church," 1-31; Das, *Jews*, chap. 5.

9. Satan is mentioned a couple times in the letter (2:18; 3:5), not as the source of the human predicament — neither he nor any demonic forces are here said to hold humanity in bondage — but as a kind of third party bent on frustrating God's plans and human salvation. Humanity's plight, however, is the direct consequence of its estranged relationship with God. In 2 Thessalonians God himself uses the deceitfulness of Satan to effect the punishment of those who have rejected the truth (2:9-12).

10. Note that, though the message Paul had been entrusted to deliver was "good news" (2:4), it had clearly (and, given the specific nature of the good news, necessarily) been accompanied by a dire portrayal of humanity's plight. Sanders rightly notes that when Paul sums up what he preached and what his listeners were to believe, he speaks of "the action of God in Christ" rather than of the "plight of man" (*Paul Pal. Jud.,* 444). It does not, however, follow that the latter was excluded from his message. Faith leading to *salvation* was the explicit goal of Paul's preaching (Rom. 1:16; 10:9-10; 1 Cor. 1:21; 9:22; 15:2; etc.); but that such faith could ever have been roused in practice without a compelling account of that from which "salvation" is needed is hard to imagine (and certainly at odds with the evidence of 1 Thessalonians) — even though, in Paul's summaries of his message (as, indeed, in later Christian creeds), it is God's saving activity rather than a particular delineation of humanity's prior condition or peril that is the focus of faith.

Similarly, though one can conceive of Christ in many ways (Son of God, Lord, divine Wis-

precisely how Jesus, or the gospel, effects salvation. It is clear, however, that the faith of believers included the conviction that Jesus had died and risen again (4:14). The Lord's death, moreover, was "for us": the language is already traditional[11] but here left undeveloped. In some unspecified way the death of Christ made it possible for those who believe to be "with him" (rather than the objects of his wrath) forever (5:10).

So intensive was the Thessalonians' expectation of both promise and threat that they were taken aback when some of their number found sufficient leisure to die in the interval (4:13-18). Such perturbation is scarcely perplexing. Whether or not Paul himself possessed the exalted spirituality of interpreters for whom the ultimate triumph of God and the restoration of the corrupted cosmos are matters of far greater moment than the salvation of the (now hardly to be considered) individual sinner,[12] 1 Thessalonians indicates that he found an immediate point of contact with listeners in Thessalonica by discussing their own prospects of escaping God's wrath. Should a neophyte in the guild of Pauline scholars, or a dotard who learned the trade half a century ago, gauchely suggest today that the topic of Paul's missionary preaching was how sinners might find a gracious God, it would be difficult to base a refutation on the text of our epistle.[13]

The answer Paul obviously gave to the question he is no longer allowed to have asked is that humans facing God's wrath must respond to the "gospel of God" (2:2; or "of Christ," 3:2) by "receiving" it (1:6), recognizing it to be, not the word of human beings, but that of God (2:13). Such a response to the word of God signifies a "turning to" (the true and living) God (1:9) and "faith" in him (1:8). Faith in God is not conceived in 1 Thessalonians apart from an acceptance of the *word* of God proclaimed by the apostles: if God's word is not believed, faith in God is — by definition, we may say — not to be found.[14] More specifi-

---

dom, etc.) that do not entail a human dilemma, it would not (and could not) occur even to an apostle to ascribe *salvation* exclusively to Christ without a sense that in some way humanity needs to be saved. An "exclusive soteriology" is by definition the one conviction that cannot be entertained prior to, and independently of, any conception of a human plight. To borrow Sanders's terms, if the solution entails *salvation,* it cannot have preceded *a* plight — though Paul's epistolary depictions of *the* human plight are in many respects undoubtedly a product of his postconversion thinking.

11. Cf. Hultgren, *Benefits,* 48-49.

12. But see the balanced comments of Sanders, *Paul Pal. Jud.,* 446.

13. Cf. Becker, *Paul,* 133, who claims that the "basic question" answered by Paul's theology in this period is this: "In view of the lostness of humanity and the imminence of final judgment, how can a person be saved? The final answer always concerns the eschatological destiny of the individual, whose disastrous prospect is overcome by the granting of a new destiny through the gospel."

14. Cf. Ljungman, *Pistis,* 89-91, 100-102.

cally (as noted above), the "word of God" that must be received included the declaration that the Lord Jesus had died "for us" and risen again, and that he is the means of God's salvation.

Those bound for salvation are thus distinguished from those doomed to wrath (cf. 5:9) by their response of faith to the gospel. The former are repeatedly identified simply as "the believing ones": the stock designation does not require that the content of their faith be spelled out (1:7; 2:10, 13; cf. 2 Thess. 1:10). In the Thessalonian correspondence a distinction is not drawn between "righteous" and "sinners" (or "the wicked"); the negative counterparts of "believers" are simply those who do not believe (or obey) the truth of the gospel (cf. 2 Thess. 1:8; 2:10, 12; 3:2). They may indeed show their hostility to it by persecuting its adherents (1 Thess. 2:14-16; cf. 2 Thess. 1:6-8).

On one level, then, (human) faith in the gospel separates those headed for salvation from those who are "perishing";[15] on another level, however, it may be said that God has "appointed" the former group to obtain salvation (1 Thess. 5:9). They are the object of God's "calling" (2:12; cf. 2 Thess. 1:11; 2:13) or "election" (1 Thess. 1:4).[16] The divine election took effect through the proclamation of the gospel[17] and the Thessalonians' response of faith. This is clearly the point of 1:4-6, whether Paul is saying that the election meant that,[18] or became obvious to the missionaries because,[19] the gospel was communicated to the Thessa-

---

15. For the latter term, see 2 Thess. 2:10.

16. Note that Jürgen Becker labels Paul's early (Antiochian) theology "election theology" (see chap. 13, sec. iv above). The explicit reference to "your" election would seem to rule out Wesley's understanding of the subject (i.e., that God has predetermined *that* those who believe in Christ will be saved, but not *who* will so believe; cf. chap. 4 above). It does not follow, however, that Paul held the Calvinist notion that God has predetermined the acts of all human beings, from Adam's sin to the faith of believers and the unbelief of others — and thus the eternal destiny of each individual. However the texts that speak of universal salvation (see n. 125 below) are to be interpreted, they are hardly compatible with a conviction that the eternal reprobation of many human beings has been divinely predetermined. Nor does Paul ever qualify his exhortations or his warnings (e.g., not to receive the grace of God in vain, 2 Cor. 6:1!) with an indication that the obedience or disobedience of his readers simply puts into effect God's predetermined plan. (On Rom. 9–11 see my article "Romans 9–11.") In Paul's day it was common to combine belief in the notions of divine predestination *and* human free will, however incompatible these have come to be seen. Paul himself shows every sign of having done so. Cf. Sanders, *Paul Pal. Jud.,* 257-70, 446-47.

17. Note that, according to 2 Thess. 2:14, the Thessalonians had been (divinely) called "through [the proclamation of] our gospel."

18. The ὅτι introducing v. 5 is here read epexegetically: vv. 5 and 6 spell out that the "election" of v. 4 entailed the effectiveness of the gospel's proclamation and the believing response of its hearers. Cf. Malherbe, *Thessalonians,* 110.

19. The ὅτι introducing v. 5 is here taken to be causal: vv. 5 and 6 spell out why the missionaries were convinced that the Thessalonian believers were the objects of God's election. Bruce,

lonians with power and received by them with joyful faith. In 2:13 Paul notes that the word of God "works effectively in you who believe": that "working" surely began (though it did not end) with the initial proclamation of the divine "word."[20]

Yet the Thessalonian believers were "called" to more than a destiny of "salvation": they were to live a life here and now of holiness, consistent with (and made possible by) the holiness of the Spirit whom God had given them (4:7-8). Salvation from God's wrath means a place in God's kingdom, and it is important that the objects of so glorious a calling should prove "worthy" of it (2:12; cf. 2 Thess. 1:11). They are "children of light" rather than of darkness; their behavior must suit the "day" (1 Thess. 5:4-8). Paul had already given the Thessalonian believers some guidance in "how [they] ought to live and please God" (4:1); in his letter he expands upon those beginnings (4:1–5:22).

The obligations he mentions are by no means to be distinguished from their faith. Both acceptance and rejection of the truth are all-encompassing: life is lived either in the acknowledgment *and* service of the true and living God or in defiance of the truth. Those who reject the truth of the gospel act entirely in character when they do so: they are, in effect, refusing to abandon the life they have already adopted, in which neither acknowledging nor pleasing God plays a role (4:5; 5:7). Their unbelief is itself disobedience, and the disobedience shown in their actions is merely an expression of their unbelief (cf. 2 Thess. 1:8; 2:10, 12). Conversely, those who respond in faith to the gospel are thereby turning *away* from a life of disobedience *to* one oriented around service to God (1 Thess. 1:8-9). Living in a way that pleases God is a natural and, in the end, inevitable expression of such faith: Paul rejoices when he sees the Thessalonians' *faith* in *action* (1:3; cf. 2 Thess. 1:11). That their faith remains deficient (1 Thess. 3:10) and has room to grow (3:2; cf. 2 Thess. 1:3) does not imply that they harbor doubts of the truth of their convictions; rather, there is still — and throughout their earthly lives there will be (cf. 1 Thess. 3:12-13; 4:1, 10; 5:23) — a need to express more consistently and completely the practical implications of their faith.

More could of course be said by way of summary of 1 Thessalonians, but enough has been said to provide a basis for addressing questions crucial to our theme: Was it a *Lutheran* congregation that Paul established in Thessalonica?

Thessalonians, 13, and Marshall, *Thessalonians*, 53, note the two possibilities without indicating a preference.

20. This Pauline theme is, as we have seen, a favorite of the "Lutherans": every Christian is "begotten" "through the Word of God. The Holy Spirit reveals and preaches that Word, and by it he illumines and kindles hearts so that they grasp and accept it, cling to it, and persevere in it" (Luther, *Large Cat.*, 60). So also Augustine, *De civ. Dei* 15.6: "If [God] does not by His own inward grace sway and act upon the mind, no preaching of the truth is of any avail."

Was he himself, at the time he wrote the letter, a *Lutheran* apostle?[21] We may take up these questions by looking at what is said both of the human plight and of salvation.

Critical to "Lutheran" doctrine is the conviction that humanity has earned God's condemnation and — it is of the essence of "Lutheranism" to underline the point — that human beings can of themselves do nothing to avert it. With a pinch of goodwill we may well conclude that the Thessalonian Paul thought no differently, though, to be sure, he was not as explicit about human impotence as he might have been.

Certainly he saw humanity's plight as desperate: divine judgment looms over wayward humankind. Here there is nothing original to Paul — or even to early Christianity.[22] No pious Jew could believe that things are as they ought in a world in which the creator is widely unacknowledged, his passion for justice and compassion widely disregarded, his will defied. And though God's patience and mercy were affirmed and celebrated, it was inconceivable that in the end he would let mortals prevail or contempt for goodness and truth go unpunished.[23] Jews commonly viewed the Gentile world as headed for warranted perdition,[24] though they saw themselves (or at least Jews of their persuasion) as God's people, the objects of God's favor in this age and the next. Paul has clearly adopted this traditional understanding — at least as far as Gentiles are concerned.

With Jewish election and covenant theology he was of course familiar; indeed, in speaking of believers as an "assembly" (ἐκκλησία) and the object of God's "election" (ἐκλογή), he applies to them Jewish terminology for the people of God (1:1, 4).[25] But 1 Thessalonians gives no hint that Paul thought loyalty to the Jewish covenant provided a viable alternative to salvation offered in Christ, or even that he considered it an option sufficiently enticing to his readers to

21. I.e., did Paul himself hold the convictions and maintain the emphases that a number of modern interpreters think have been misleadingly imposed on his letters by "Lutheran" tradition? That Paul's denominational affiliation was Baptist is, of course, not in doubt.

22. The (very traditional) understanding of humanity's plight in Paul's earliest epistles itself suggests that Paul did not first devise a dilemma on the basis of Christian convictions. It is clear, however, that Christian convictions came increasingly to shape Paul's more mature anthropology.

23. The terminology is, of course, borrowed from Ps. 9:19-20 (MT 20-21). Pss. 9 and 10 invite, though they do not themselves yet attest, notions of an *eschatological* judgment. In Paul's day such a judgment was expected by most pious Jews. Cf. Reiser, *Judgment*, 19-163.

24. *Some* Jews allowed that *some* Gentiles were righteous and would meet God's approval, but the bleaker outlook is well attested; see Donaldson, *Paul*, 51-74; Sanders, *Paul Pal. Jud.*, 206-12. 1 Thessalonians does not envisage the possibility of "righteous Gentiles" who are "saved" apart from the gospel; only those whom God has "called" through the gospel are destined for salvation.

25. Cf. Thielman, *Paul*, 73.

warrant refutation.[26] The message conveyed to the Thessalonians pertained to a salvation but recently inaugurated for *all* who believe, not to the means by which Gentiles could enter an existing people of God.[27] If — as we may assume — Paul had once embraced Jewish covenant theology, his "Damascus" encounter with the risen Christ had led him to see that Jews no less than Gentiles needed a savior from the wrath to come. In this respect we may say that Paul's Christian perception of the divine solution preceded his *reconfiguration* of the traditional plight.[28]

The depiction we find in 1 Thessalonians of the plight of humankind apart from the gospel conforms, we may fairly say, to "Lutheran" expectations. And though Paul makes no point of saying that human beings cannot extricate themselves from the condemnation they have earned, it would be absurd to

26. Still less, to judge by his letter, did Paul inform the Thessalonians that God's remedy for the sin of the world was to be found in a promise he once made to Abraham, or in a covenant he once entered with the patriarch. Paul's Galatian and Roman readers would have wondered at the emphasis, but they would probably have understood the claim that "the gospel consists primarily or essentially in the promise to Abraham that all the nations would be blessed in him," or that "the gospel itself could only be adequately understood by Paul as the outworking of the promises to Abraham" (Dunn, "Gospel," 372, 374; cf. Gager, *Origins,* 240); the Thessalonians (and, I suspect, the Corinthians; see below), bless their hearts, would have been clueless.

27. Cf. Becker, *Paul,* 138-40.

28. This is, of course, the fundamental point behind Sanders's slogan that "the solution preceded the plight." Cf. Sanders, *Paul Pal. Jud.,* 443: "Paul did not, while 'under the law,' perceive himself to have a 'plight' from which he needed salvation. If he were so zealous as to persecute the church, he may well have thought that those who were not properly Jewish would be damned, but the solution to such a plight would be simply to become properly Jewish. It appears that the conclusion that all the world — both Jew and Greek — equally stands in need of a saviour *springs from* the prior conviction that God had provided such a saviour." Also 499: "It was only the revelation of Christ as the saviour of all that convinced him that all men, both Jew and Gentile, were enslaved to sin. Before then, he must have distinguished between Jews, who were righteous (despite occasional transgressions), and 'Gentile sinners' (Gal 2:15). But once he came to the conclusion that all men were enslaved to sin and could be saved only by Christ, he could then readily relate the transgressions which he must previously have supposed were atoned for by the means provided by Judaism to the all-encompassing power of sin, and in fact use the former to prove the latter." Cf. also Donaldson, *Paul,* 144.

This seems right when it comes to the progression of *Paul's* thought (though Sanders also correctly allows that Paul's preconversion thinking remains a matter of speculation [*Law* 152-53]); it is worth remembering, however, that Paul had his predecessors. The early Jewish Christians (following, according to the synoptic Gospels, the lead of both John the Baptist and Jesus) had already declared that divine judgment awaited their compatriots should the latter not respond with faith to the gospel. Nor, of course, was it a Christian innovation to suggest that Israel's election was not to be trusted as a ticket to divine blessing; cf. Deut. 11:26-28; Amos 3:2; etc.; also M. A. Elliott, *Survivors* (see chap. 17, n. 8 above).

think he thought they could. Salvation is offered only through the "gospel of God."

But is salvation itself conceived in "Lutheran" terms?

The formula "justification by faith" does not occur. We may suspect that justification by some *other* means must be under consideration before Paul would articulate his own position so concisely as its antithesis: "we know that a person is declared righteous not by the works of the law but through faith in Jesus Christ" (Gal. 2:16).[29] Paul would later stress the gratuity of salvation[30] and deny that human works play any role when God constitutes his people.[31] Nothing in 1 Thessalonians would need to be revoked by a Paul emphatic in these convictions; yet they cannot be said to be matters of emphasis here. We may well suspect, again, that an alternative understanding of the composition of God's people must be in view — one that, in Paul's view, compromised these basic truths — before Paul would formulate his convictions in these terms.

On the other hand, if justification entails a divine initiative by which sinners meriting condemnation are reprieved and granted a place in God's kingdom, then we may fairly say that the *essence* of the concept lies at the core of Paul's message to the Thessalonians. A pronouncement of acquittal (δικαιο-σύνη) at the last judgment (or in anticipation of that judgment) is not mentioned in 1 Thessalonians, but the salvific *effect* of such a pronouncement is a central theme.[32]

The saved are (as we have seen) those called by God and rescued by God's Son. But salvation becomes theirs (as we have also seen) when they receive the word (or gospel) of God: they are "the believers." Should Paul ever be required to sum up the appropriate and essential human response to God's offered salvation in antithesis to some proposed alternative, we can only imagine the Paul of 1 Thessalonians responding, "by faith."[33]

Yet, just as the gratuity of salvation, though assumed, is not highlighted in the letter, so the faith required of those who hear the gospel is not contrasted with a path involving the "doing" of righteous deeds (or of what the law demands). Indeed, faith itself *works* in 1 Thessalonians. Only one who has not read their writings could ever imagine such a statement to be abhorrent to the

---

29. Note, however, that Paul introduces the formula in Galatians as a matter of common knowledge ("we know that . . ."). That Paul is here building on Antiochian tradition is argued by Becker, *Paul*, 96, 287. Cf. also Stuhlmacher, *Doctrine*, 20-24 (and the literature he cites, 23 n. 12).

30. Rom. 3:24; 4:4-5, 16; 5:6-10, 15-21; etc. The subject is explored in Eastman, *Grace*.

31. Cf. esp. Rom. 9:9-18; 11:5-6.

32. Cf. Hübner, "Proprium," 454-58; Kim, *Perspective*, 85-99; Pfleiderer, *Paulinism*, 1:30.

33. Cf. Hübner, *Theologie*, 51-52.

Reformers;[34] still, the Thessalonian Paul never does stress — what the Reformers never failed to stress — that salvation is the lot of believers because of their faith in what *Christ* did, *not* because of anything they might do.

Whenever Paul has been read in a distinctively "Lutheran" way, it has been in response to the perception that human works were being given a place that neither the apostle nor the Christian gospel can allow them. The Paul of Thessalonians says nothing to offend his "Lutheran" readers, but neither does he articulate a distinctively "Lutheran" position. No rival to his message of faith is combated. Whether, when a rival appears, Paul responds along "Lutheran" lines must await our review of later epistles.

ii. 1 and 2 Corinthians[35]

If 1 Thessalonians is the Pauline letter in which the fewest issues had arisen since the apostle's initial visit, then the Corinthian correspondence lies at the other extreme. Whatever the Corinthians touched turned complicated. Discussions of factions and fornication, of lawsuits and asceticism, of food offered to idols and speech intelligible to none but God preempt any reveries over the days when the church was young, its faith a story to be told. Only passing hints in these letters suggest the substance of Paul's initial proclamation.

The hints suffice to show, however, that the trip from Macedonia to Achaia had not altered Paul's message of salvation. His efforts were focused on "saving" all he could (1 Cor. 9:22; 10:33; cf. 7:16) in view of the judgment that looms for all (4:5; 2 Cor. 5:10) and the condemnation that awaits the "world" "outside" the church (1 Cor. 5:13; 11:32). Its people are "the perishing" (1:18; 2 Cor. 2:15; 4:3), and that on two counts: "unrighteous" to begin with (thus, in effect, failing the test of *ordinary* "dikaiosness," and thereby meriting their perdition; see 1 Cor. 6:1, 9-10; and cf. 2 Cor. 6:14), they remained "unbelieving" at a time when the gospel was being preached (thus, in effect, failing to avail themselves of *extraordinary* "dikaiosness"; see 1 Cor. 6:6; 7:12-15; 10:27; 14:22; 2 Cor. 4:4; 6:14). Conversely, "those who are being saved" (1 Cor. 1:18), though themselves once "unrighteous" (6:9-11), are now "the believers" (1:21; 2 Cor. 6:15). The object of their faith was the apostolic kerygma (1 Cor. 1:21; 2:4-5; 15:1-2, 11, 14): "Christ died for our sins according to the scriptures; he was buried, and he was raised again on

---

34. Cf. Luther, *Freedom,* 31:372-73: "Our faith in Christ does not free us from works but from false opinions concerning works, that is, from the foolish presumption that justification is acquired by works."

35. It will be convenient to treat the Corinthian epistles as a unit, and prior to the discussion of Galatians, though the relative dating of these epistles remains a matter of controversy.

the third day, according to the scriptures" (15:3-4). What they were saved *from* (apart from destruction) becomes clear when Paul says that, should their faith prove vain, they would be yet "in their sins" (15:17). Had billboards blotted the landscape on the road to Cenchreae, a Paul who exploited every available means in his efforts to "save some" (9:19-22) might well have proposed the pregnant text, "Now is the day of salvation" (2 Cor. 6:2).

The plight, then, for which the gospel provided the solution was posed by people's sins (1 Cor. 15:3, 17). Paul was prompt with illustrative lists of the sorts of misdeeds that made people "unrighteous" and excluded them from God's kingdom (6:9-10; cf. 5:10): misdeeds characteristic of the Corinthians themselves before they were "washed," "sanctified," and "justified in the name of the Lord Jesus Christ and by the Spirit of our God" (6:11). But the Corinthian Paul could also capture the woefulness of humanity in the doleful words "In Adam all die" (15:22). This is hardly an alternative account of the human dilemma to that which attributes it to human sin. Adam, after all, is the original and prototypical *sinner:* knowing what he ought to do, he was tempted and chose to do differently, thereby destroying his own and marring creation's integrity. Human sinfulness remains at the heart of human misery, but to trace its roots to Adam is to indicate both its universality and its inescapability: what Adam did is what all human beings, in Adam, continue to do. Furthermore, to see Adam's sin as the source of *death* ("Since by man [Adam] came death"; "in Adam all die" [15:21-22]) is to sum up the biblical vision that sees life lived in denial of its Creator as out of step with reality and, in the end, unsustainable.[36] It is already a kind of death, and the death to which it leads is both its divine judgment and its inevitable outcome. If "the sting of death is sin" (15:56), sin is that which makes death not the normal, natural, not-to-be-regretted ending of a terrestrial life, but the *un*natural, *un*necessary termination of a life lived — unnaturally — in rebellion against its Maker.

But there is more to be said. Powers of darkness are by no means prominent in the Corinthian correspondence,[37] but Satan *is* called the "god of this age" (2 Cor. 4:4); the supernatural powers served by pagans are in fact "demons" (1 Cor. 10:20-21); and on a standard interpretation, the "rulers of this age" in 2:6, 8 are angelic but evil forces.[38] Clearly Paul saw human deeds of unrighteousness not simply as a falling short of divine expectations (though they were emphatically that), but also as deeds serving the unrighteous ends of powers themselves hostile to God. If sinfulness has become inherent in humanity as

---

36. See my *Preface,* 76-78.
37. Cf. 1 Cor. 5:5; 7:5; 10:20-21; 15:24; 2 Cor. 2:11; 4:4; 11:14.
38. Cf., e.g., Barrett, *Corinthians,* 70; Conzelmann, *1 Corinthians,* 61.

a species, then the powers of evil may surely be said to prevail in "this age" — even if Paul, monotheist that he was, thought they, in the end, served divine purposes (5:4-5; cf. 2 Thess. 2:9-12). That said, it should be added that the Corinthian Paul depicts salvation as a deliverance from sins and from perdition, but not from satanic powers.

1 Thessalonians conveyed no hint that salvation might even be imagined anywhere but in Christ. 1 Corinthians 11:25, with its reference to a "new covenant" (quoted from the Last Supper tradition), at least implies the existence of an *older* covenant; and indeed, the old and the new are explicitly contrasted in 2 Corinthians 3:6-14. Still, glorious though the old (Sinaitic) covenant is said to have been, no salvific potential is ascribed to it. Its essence is found in the commandments of the Decalogue engraved on tablets of stone (thus making it a covenant "of the letter," as opposed to the new covenant "of the Spirit" [3:6]). Its "ministry" was one of death (3:7; cf. "the letter kills," 3:6) and condemnation (3:9). Since humanity in Adam is already subject to death (1 Cor. 15:21-22) and condemnation (11:32; cf. 5:13), the Sinaitic covenant, as portrayed in 2 Corinthians, did nothing to alter in any fundamental way the human condition — not even for the people to whom it was given. With or without the Sinaitic covenant, "in Adam all die."[39]

In the Corinthian epistles, then, as in 1 Thessalonians, the *only* option considered for salvation is the apostolic kerygma. Several features of the Corinthian discussion merit attention here.

1. Though there is nothing new in the creedal formula "Christ died for our sins" (1 Cor. 15:3), the emphasis in the opening chapters of 1 Corinthians on the *cross* of Christ is striking and original (1:13, 17, 18, 23; 2:2, 8). Paul's transparent aim with these references is to puncture the pretensions of his readers, reminding them that through the scandal and foolishness of the cross God had overturned human values, demonstrated the futility of human "wisdom," and left human beings with nothing of which to boast (1:18-29).[40] The issue that pro-

---

39. Rightly, Wright, "Law," 143: "the problem of Israel . . . is the hidden Adam in the Jew." Also Cummins, *Crucified Christ*, 198. Note that in 1 Cor. 15:56 the "strength of sin" is said to be "the law"; i.e., the law provokes the rebellion of the willful and condemns it as transgression. So, presumably, we may interpret a cryptic text, drawing on the evidence of Romans (4:15; 5:13; 7:7-11). In its context in Corinthians, however, the verse appears as something of a thunderbolt from a Romans sky. Hahn ("Entwicklung," 355) concludes that Paul must have communicated to the Corinthians while in their city his understanding of sin, the law, death, and — because it is so closely linked to these themes — justification.

40. As we saw in chap. 13, sec. iv, Jürgen Becker sees here the distinctive feature of the second period in Paul's theological development. Certainly the mind-set of 1 Cor. 1:18-31 pervades the Corinthian epistles, with their insistence on the display of divine strength in human weakness (2 Cor. 4:7, 10-11; 12:9-10) and reminders of human dependency on divine grace (1 Cor. 15:10; 2 Cor. 1:9, 12; 3:5-6; 12:9).

voked one of the most memorable passages in all of Paul's writings had nothing to do with works righteousness: the Corinthians were *not* attempting to gain God's favor by good works of their own. Nonetheless, as many scholars have pointed out, the Paul who wrote this passage could *not* have conceived of salvation as a cooperative enterprise for which human beings could claim any credit. He proceeds immediately to say as much (1:30-31; see below).

2. As in 1 Thessalonians, God "elects" (1:27, 28) and "calls" (1:9, 24, 26; 7:17-24) his people; and as in 1 Thessalonians, God's call is extended and his election made effective through the proclamation of the gospel and the human response of faith. The "called" in 1:24 are the same as "those who believe" in 1:21; that they are called becomes apparent in their recognition of the power and wisdom of God in the kerygma of Christ crucified (1:23-24).[41] In keeping with the emphasis running throughout the passage, Paul goes on to stress that God focused his election and calling on those who have no claims to earthly attention, thereby exposing the emptiness of all that humans esteem (1:26-29).

3. The language of justification is not prominent in the Corinthian epistles, but it is present. Inasmuch as it appears unannounced, it was presumably familiar to Paul's readers.

In any ordinary sense of the word, "righteousness" (δικαιοσύνη) is what people ought to do, or what they have when they have done it. It is not apparent how righteousness in this sense can be conveyed from one moral being to another, still less how one can *be* another's righteousness. Hence the extraordinary element in Paul's declaration of 1:30-31: it is "thanks to God" that the Corinthians "are in Christ Jesus, who became for us, by the gift of God, wisdom, righteousness (δικαιοσύνη), holiness, and redemption, in order that it might be true, as the Scripture says, 'Let the one who boasts boast in the Lord.'" Whether Paul's curious wording indicates merely that Christ became the means by which the Corinthians were justified (i.e., declared innocent, cleared of wrongdoing), or whether it refers to something like the "interchange" envisaged in 2 Corinthians 5:21[42] — we *became* the righteousness that Christ represents because God made him the sin that we know but he does not — is not clear. Paul's point here is that this extraordinary attribution of Christ's righteousness to others leaves them with nothing of which to boast. That alternative understandings of the path to righteousness leave open the door to boasting is a possible but by no means necessary implication; no other path is considered. That *this* path deliberately excludes human grounds for boasting is not implied but stated.

---

41. Note how human faith is pictured as the product of a divine work of creation in 2 Cor. 4:6; cf. also how God is thought to put in place the conditions for human faith in 1 Cor. 8:3; 12:3.

42. Cf. Hooker, *Adam*, 13-25.

In 1 Corinthians 6:8 Paul accuses the Corinthians of wronging (ἀδικεῖτε) their own "brothers"; he then reminds them that wrongdoers (ἄδικοι, the *un*-righteous) will be excluded from God's kingdom. There follows a list of doers of various wrongs of which some of the Corinthians themselves had once been guilty — before they were "washed," "sanctified," and "justified (ἐδικαιώθητε) in the name of the Lord Jesus Christ and by the Spirit of our God" (6:11). That (to reflect the play on words in the Greek) the "*un*dikaios" were "dikaiosified" — the unrighteous were declared righteous — points (as in Rom. 5:7-9) to the extraordinary nature of the transaction. The parallel with the metaphor of washing suggests that one has to be cleansed of guilt to be cleared of it; that is, the act by which God declares sinners righteous gets rid of sin rather than simply overlooks it (the point becomes important when Paul insists that God's own righteousness is vindicated in the procedure [Rom. 3:25-26]). Probably Paul is thinking of the Corinthians' baptism (the phrases with which he ends v. 11 may well echo baptismal formulas) as representing the washing that made justification possible.

In 2 Corinthians 3:9 δικαιοσύνη refers to the acquittal, the clearing of any charges of wrongdoing, that the ministry of the new covenant brings to its adherents, thereby distinguishing it from the condemning ministry of the old.

Finally, in 5:21 Paul speaks of the divine exchange between Christ's righteousness and the sin of human beings. The point in the context is that human sin had led to estrangement from God; only by not counting their sins against them could God be reconciled to sinners (5:18-20). Through Christ God made such reconciliation possible: God made the sin-free Christ the sin that humans know so that they might become righteousness "in" (or "through") him. Such is the message of reconciliation (5:20), grace (6:1), and salvation (6:2) that Paul and his coworkers proclaimed.

Is justification in *Corinthians*, then, by faith and apart from works? Essentially, yes; formulaically, no. The human response of faith to the gospel kerygma (it is *such* faith that is in view, not faith as the characteristic attitude shown by particularly trusting souls) is what is said to distinguish the "saved" from the "perishing" (1 Cor. 1:18, 21; cf. 2 Cor. 2:15-16); it follows that it separates the justified from the unrighteous. And certainly the justification of the unrighteous who believe, like the salvation of the otherwise perishing, is represented as a divine initiative for which humans — as Paul programmatically insists — can claim no credit. On this basis the "Lutheran" establishment may well choose to declare the Paul of Corinthians an *honorary* member of their fold. On the other hand, he has not yet declared his *own* membership or recited their creed.

To sum up: in Paul's references to the "world" "outside" the Christian community as made up of ἄδικοι (the "*un*righteous") and ἀπολλύμενοι (the "per-

ishing") and to the divine judgment that hangs over them are implicit the unmet, universal demands of ordinary "dikaiosness." Here lies the essence of the
human plight as depicted in Corinthians (and 1 Thessalonians). No alternative
to the cross of Christ is considered as a path to righteousness. The Sinaitic covenant, though divine and glorious, found its essence in divine commands, its
function in highlighting the condemnation and death that follow human sin.
Paul did not go to Corinth to invite the local Gentiles to share in a salvation already enjoyed by their Jewish neighbors under the Jewish covenant: those under the Sinaitic covenant were themselves "in Adam," and as such, under sentence of death. With no other option in view, and with no apparent emphasis or
programmatic purpose, Paul nonetheless uses the language of (extraordinary)
righteousness as *one* way to depict the salvation he proclaimed: through Christ
God declares the guilty innocent, clearing while cleansing them of their sins,
thereby initiating a reconciliation with sinners. Those who respond to this
kerygma with faith enter the community of the saved. The mode of their salvation, including specifically that of their justification, leaves them with no
grounds for boasting.

iii. Galatians

That God *requires* righteousness of all human beings is presupposed whenever
Paul insists that the world, unless it responds to the apostolic kerygma, faces
wrath and condemnation. That God, through the apostolic kerygma, *offers*
righteousness (now in the sense of an acquittal from wrongdoing) to sinners
may be said to be implicit in 1 Thessalonians, explicit but not prominent in the
Corinthians writings. No alternative path to righteousness is considered in
these letters. It is in the epistle to the Galatians, written specifically to combat
the attraction felt by Paul's converts to a rival understanding of the route to
righteousness, that "righteousness" language first becomes prominent.

The controversy arose over circumcision: Paul's opponents[43] were trying
to "compel [the Galatians] to be circumcised" (Gal. 6:12). Itself an indifferent
act (5:6; 6:15), circumcision found its significance in signaling the adoption of
a Jewish way of life. Paul sees the Galatians already beginning to "observe days,

---

43. Paul's insistence in Gal. 1–2 on the genuineness of his apostleship, the divine source of
his message, and the recognition he received from the "pillars" of the church in Jerusalem was
undoubtedly in response to charges made by the advocates of circumcision in Galatia: disputing
aspects of Paul's message, they found it important to undermine his authority in the eyes of the
Galatians. To call them Paul's "opponents" fairly captures this aspect of their activity in
Galatians even if it leaves unstated the views they intended to promote. Cf. Smiles, *Gospel*, 31-50.

months, seasonal festivals, and years" (4:10); *Jewish* Sabbath and festival practices must have been in view. He tells them of a departure from "the truth of the gospel" (2:14) in Antioch similar to that which now threatens them (1:6-9) — and it, too, involved Jewish observances: Peter and other Jewish Christians, anxious not to violate Jewish dietary restrictions, had withdrawn from table fellowship with Gentile believers (2:11-14). Paul recalls the terms with which he rebuked them by saying that they were "compelling the Gentiles to live as Jews" (2:14). As a response to Peter's actions the words are barely comprehensible. Perhaps Paul uttered them in Antioch with an explanation he does not now report: "what your actions say to Gentiles is that Jewish food laws are important and that they should adopt them too." But quite possibly Paul paraphrases what he originally said in these terms to highlight the similarity between the advocacy of Jewish food laws in Antioch and that of circumcision in Galatia; in both cases, Paul is saying, Gentiles are being told that they must live as Jews.[44]

Circumcision has its pains, and Jewish Sabbath and dietary laws their restrictions; in themselves they would have enticed no one. Moreover, in themselves they were believed by no one to be the path to righteousness.[45] The only grounds by which they could have been effectively urged upon the Galatians was the claim that the God whom the Galatians had come to know through Jesus Christ had commanded that these observances, too, be kept by his worshipers. One could not belong to God's people (the Galatians must have been told) and remain uncircumcised, or dismissive of Jewish food and festival laws.

Such an insistence, in the view of Paul's opponents (though not of Paul), was by no means inconsistent with faith in Jesus as the Christ who died and rose again. Paul calls those who advocated a similar position in Jerusalem "false brothers" (2:4): "false" because, to Paul's mind, they did not uphold the truth of the gospel; but looking like "brothers," presumably because they accepted the messiahship of Jesus. The advocates of circumcision in Galatia, too, appeared as Christians; so much we may infer from Paul's charge that they advanced a different (and perverted) *gospel* (1:6-9) and promoted circumcision to avoid being persecuted for the cross of Christ (6:12) — a risk that would not have arisen had they not believed Jesus to be the Messiah. Untenable though their position was deemed by Paul, they would undoubtedly have maintained that the coming of

---

44. Cf. Eckstein, *Verheissung*, 4.

45. Thus when Paul contests the view that one can be declared righteous "by the works of the law" (Gal. 2:16), he does not mean simply, "One is not declared righteous by [observing] circumcision and the food and festival laws" — even though these issues provoked the current crisis. What he is rejecting is the view that one can be declared righteous on the basis of (one's observance of) the Jewish law (cf. 2:21), of which these requirements were a part.

Messiah (a hope long entertained by Jews!) by no means canceled God's covenant with his people or invalidated its laws.

For the Jewish Christian advocates of circumcision, then, the Jewish covenant[46] and laws still provided the framework within which God's people must live. This was, moreover, the position attributed to them by Paul. When in chapter 1 Paul introduced his own past "in Judaism" (1:13-14), his immediate point was to underline that only through a divine revelation had he come to preach his present message (1:11-12, 15-16); but no doubt he also wanted to say that the way of life that the Galatians were tempted to adopt was one he knew well but had — in the light of God's revelation of his Son — abandoned.[47] They wanted to be "under the law" (4:21), to be "declared righteous by the law" (5:4; cf. 2:21; 3:21) and its "works" (2:16). Paul believed they needed to be told the conditions under which those who "are of the works of the law" really live (3:10), the slavery to which the covenant of Sinai in fact gives birth (4:21-31; cf. 3:23-24; 4:1-3), the limited purpose for which the law was given (3:19-25). Though the question that provoked the controversy was whether the Galatian believers should submit to distinctively Jewish practices, Paul has little to say about those practices per se. Everything in his response indicates that, to his mind, the issue could only be addressed by assessing the adequacy of the Sinaitic covenant to provide a framework within which its adherents could enjoy God's blessing, inherit God's promises, and be found righteous before God.[48] From all of this it follows that,

46. Presumably Paul's opponents drew no distinction between the divine commitments to Abraham and the covenant between God and Israel entered at Mount Sinai. Paul (as we shall see) did.

47. We may compare Phil. 3:2-6, where, again, in dismissing Jewish Christian advocates of circumcision, Paul equates their position with that of his *pre*-Christian past.

48. Cf. Calvin, *Comm.* Gal. 2:15: Our opponents object "that the problem was only about ceremonies. This we allow. Why then, they say, should Paul pass from a particular to the whole? This was the sole cause of the mistake of Origen and Jerome. They did not think it consonant that, while the false apostles were contending about ceremonies alone, Paul should cover a wider field. But they did not consider that the very reason for his disputing so keenly was that the doctrine had more serious consequences than at first appeared. Paul was worried not so much about ceremonies being observed as that the confidence and glory of salvation should be transferred to works. . . . Paul therefore is not wandering from the point when he begins a disputation on the law as a whole, whereas the false apostles were arguing only about ceremonies." Also *Inst.* 3.19.3: "Of course I admit that Paul is there [in Galatians] discussing ceremonies, for his quarrel is with false apostles who were trying to reintroduce into the Christian church the old shadows of the law that had been abolished by Christ's coming. But for the discussion of this question, the higher topics upon which the whole controversy rested had to be considered." Stanton ("Law," 103-4) makes a similar point: "I concede that Paul's first use of the phrase 'works of the law' in 2:16a is triggered by the issues which dominate the preceding discussion in Gal 2, circumcision and food laws. But as the initial listeners heard the argument of the follow-

for Paul, the position of the Jewish Christian advocates of circumcision departed in no essential respect from that of non-Christian Jews (and thus that of his own past). Both took the stance that God's favor was to be found within the confines, and among the practitioners, of the Jewish (Sinaitic) law. This position, and not circumcision or other Jewish boundary markers per se (see 5:6; 6:15!), provoked Paul's passionate opposition.

To judge from the quandary of Paul's converts and the contents of his other writings, Paul had not complicated his missionary proclamation in Galatia by raising issues related to the Jewish law. The age in which his hearers lived and themselves participated — he had told them — was evil, a condition reflected in the sins they committed (1:4) and entailing their slavery to powers other than God (4:8). Christ's death for their sins made possible their deliverance from the evil age, their freedom from the enslaving powers, and their knowledge of the true God (1:4; 4:8-9). Quite possibly, since Paul introduces the terminology in his letter without explanation, Paul had used the language of "righteousness," too, in his account of the difference Christ made: those who believe in Jesus Christ, though otherwise condemned as sinners, are declared righteous by God (cf. 2:15-17). A former Pharisee, Paul could not but have realized that he was attributing to Christ benefits he had once associated with life under the Jewish law; he must also have concluded long since that the Jewish law could not supply them. Yet he seems not to have troubled his converts with consideration of (what he saw as) an inadequate alternative to[49] his message. If we bear in mind, further, that the Galatian believers were confronted with advocates of the Jewish law who presented it *not* as an alternative to faith in Jesus Christ but as the framework within which such faith was to be lived, and that the Galatians themselves would have recalled Paul's Jewish background, his service of the God Jews worshiped, and his reliance on their Scriptures, we will perhaps find their confusion less astounding than did Paul (1:6; cf. 3:1).

For Paul, on the other hand, the alternatives were to be weighed not simply as potential paths to a proper religious life but as potential solutions to the human dilemma — the dilemma posed by human sins and their pending judgment, by human participation in an evil age and its pending dissolution, by human alignment with supernatural powers whose day had passed and whose doom was imminent. All these aspects of humanity's plight as Paul saw it are

---

ing verses unfold, they were left in no doubt that Paul was concerned about far more than these 'test cases of Jewish distinctiveness over against Gentiles.' Paul rejects the agitators' claim that one's standing before God (past, present, and future) is determined by carrying out the requirements of the law."

49. Instead of "an inadequate alternative to," we ought perhaps to say "the divine preparation for"; see the discussion below.

well attested in non-Christian Jewish writings of his day; none, then, is the creation of his Christian imagination. Nor was it first Christian Jews who thought the majority of their Jewish contemporaries were numbered with the Gentile wicked: *correct* observance of the law had become a divisive issue among Jews, causing the line between righteous and wicked to be differently drawn in different Jewish circles. What *was* new with Paul and his like-minded Christians was the conviction that life under the Jewish law, *however* interpreted, was subject to the same condemnation that threatened the Gentile world. It was this conviction that Paul used his letter to press upon his Galatian converts. The law consigned its subjects to slavery and sin; why should they adopt it now?

Paul's argument begins in 2:15. Several of its aspects have been highlighted in earlier chapters; here it will be helpful if we review its progression in context.[50] To appreciate its force we must recall that, though Paul's contention was that life under the Jewish law cannot convey God's blessing, those for whom the thesis was to be proven — in Antioch (as reported, beginning in 2:11) as well as Galatia — were themselves Christians; hence the implications of Christian faith and the experiences it had brought are fairly invoked in the argumentation.

Paul begins, however, by articulating (not without irony, in view of v. 17)[51] a standard Jewish view: "we" (Paul is purportedly reporting his speech to Jewish Christians at Antioch) may take as given that Gentiles are sinners whose way of life God condemns (2:15).[52] The normal Jewish view was that the case

50. Though all scholars agree with some of what follows, and some scholars may even agree with everything that follows, it is certain that not all scholars will agree with everything that follows. This is not a Bad Thing, still less a Cause for Deep Regret. Nonetheless, to achieve the good of an uncluttered reading of Paul in the text, I will, in what follows, confine the good of scholarly exchange to the footnotes.

51. Cf. Holmberg, "Identity," 406-7.

52. Gentiles were, proverbially, "sinners," and they were also outside the covenant, but they were not proverbially sinners *because* they were outside the covenant but because they, proverbially, sinned; cf. Rom. 1:18-32; 1 Thess. 4:5; and chap. 15, sec. v above. From some recent accounts one could be excused for concluding that Paul thought the sinfulness of humankind to be traced, not to the disobedience of Adam, but to the grace of God in choosing, and entering a covenant with, Israel: Gentiles thereby *became* sinners (they were "outside the covenant"); and the possibility was opened for Jews to *become* sinners (they promptly obliged) by presumptuously thinking that God's blessings were reserved for those who observed the covenantal boundary markers. But — the point is important, its subtlety notwithstanding — righteousness is a matter of what one ought to do, and sin, of what one ought not. And though many Jews certainly believed that the laws of the covenant were what all people ought to do, and thus that all who were outside the covenant and did not keep its laws were sinners, the point of calling them sinners was that they did not do what they ought, not that they did not belong to the covenant. Paul's point in 2:15 is no different. For the Paul of Galatians all human beings (apart from those who had received the Spirit) live in the realm of the flesh and produce its works. Paul's illustra-

with Jews was different: to be sure, Jews dismissive of the law were no better than Gentiles, but from such "sinners" those committed to the law's observance were to be distinguished — and would be distinguished by God — as "righteous."[53] For Paul, however, this standard distinction cannot be maintained (or, better, is seen no longer to be true) by those who hold that one must believe in Jesus Christ[54] to be declared righteous by God. For them it follows that Jews living under the law[55] are no more "the righteous" than are Gentiles.[56] When Jews — like Paul, Peter, and Barnabas — believed in Jesus Christ so that God would declare them righteous, the obvious implication was that the life they hitherto had lived under the law had not sufficed for the purpose (2:16a, b). Indeed, if Gentile *sinners* need to believe in Jesus Christ to be declared righteous, and "we too" believed to achieve the same end, then "we too" were found to be[57] "sinners" (2:17a). The Jewish law has not fundamentally altered the human condition.[58] And Scripture itself says as much: in

---

tive list of such misdeeds (5:19-21) is neither reducible to nor indeed inclusive of the "vices" of being outside the covenant or excluding from the current people of God those not showing the boundary markers of the erstwhile people of God. Human sinfulness antedated the Jewish covenant, and found typical expressions among both Jews and Gentiles that are quite independent of covenantal considerations.

53. They were not, however, thought to be sinless. Winninge (*Sinners,* 333) makes the point by distinguishing between "sinners" and the "sinfully [but *basically*] righteous." Cf. Aletti, *Loi,* 42-43.

54. On the phrase διὰ πίστεως Ἰησοῦ Χριστοῦ, see chap. 16, n. 18. Since — apart from the verses in dispute — Paul never uses πίστις or its cognates of Christ's act of obedience; since the latter, in any case, is not under discussion here; and since human faith is persistently contrasted with alternatives (involving the law [Rom. 10:5-6, with the "faith" of v. 6 expanded on in vv. 9-10; Gal. 3:11-12], or works [Rom. 4:2-3; 9:32], or works of the law [Gal. 2:16]) in justification texts, it seems to me self-evident that διὰ πίστεως Ἰησοῦ Χριστοῦ, which is here contrasted with "by the works of the law" as a possible means of justification, should be read "faith in Jesus Christ."

55. To be "declared righteous by the works of the law" (2:16) is to be "declared righteous by the law" (5:4; cf. 2:21): Paul uses "law" and "the works of the law" interchangeably in dismissing the possibility that one can, by doing the works required by the law, be found righteous before God. Cf. n. 45 above, and chap. 16, sec. ii. Those "under the law" (3:23; 4:5, 21), or those "of the works of the law" (3:10), are those whose righteousness is assessed by their conformity with the works demanded by the law.

56. Cf. Winninge, *Sinners,* 264.

57. "We" were found to be so "*when* we sought to be declared righteous through Christ." "Paul still has in mind the event of coming to faith" (Smiles, *Gospel,* 153). Cf. Eckstein, *Verheissung,* 31-32; Lambrecht, "Reasoning," 56-58.

58. Implicit already in 2:15-17 are claims that Paul will develop in chap. 3: the law brings no alleviation to the condition of sinners, but curses them and keeps them confined under the power of sin; yet it is precisely the subjects of sin who are declared righteous by faith in Jesus Christ (3:10, 21-25). Note that the declaration of righteousness through Jesus Christ is character-

God's eyes no one alive can be deemed righteous (LXX Ps. 142:2; MT 143:2).[59] The global statement permits no exception for Jews living under the law; hence, applied to this issue, it becomes "by the works of the law no flesh will be declared righteous" (2:16d).[60]

At this point Paul anticipates — he had no doubt repeatedly encountered — a vehement protest; its formulation is no less revealing of Paul's thought than its refutation. Those who brought the charge may well have thought Christ's death provided for the atonement and forgiveness of the inevitable sins that Christians, like all human beings, have committed; they did *not* think it did away with the fundamental distinction between the "righteous" (those committed to serving God and obeying his commands) and "sinners" (who show no such inclination). To say that Jews who believe in Christ prove ("we too") to be "sinners" is to erase that distinction, to disregard the law, and to discount

istically one offered to sinners, in both 2:15-17 and 3:22. *Such* a declaration, to Paul's mind, is precisely what the law — whose commands provide a basis for distinguishing sinners from the righteous, and for condemning the former while approving the latter — cannot supply.

59. "No one alive" becomes "[not] all flesh" in Paul's paraphrase. He introduces a term ("flesh") that traditionally marked the unbridgeable gap between humanity and God and that, in his usage, spoke of humanity in its untransformed condition of alienation from, and rebellion against, God. Cf. Barclay, *Truth*, 178-215. The verse Paul paraphrases was cited also at Qumran: "Do not judge me according to my sin; for no one living is deemed righteous (*yitsdaq*) before you" (11Q5 XXIV, 7); cf. 1QH XVII (Sukenik IX), 14-15; also VIII (Sukenik XVI), 19; XV (Sukenik VII), 28. In both cases (as in the original psalm) the point is that, judged strictly by their deeds, sinful human beings cannot possibly measure up to divine standards of righteousness. Cf. Hübner, *Theologie*, 65-67; Thielman, *Law*, 37; also Hays, "Logic," 114-15, who makes the same point about the quotation of the psalm in Rom. 3. Needless to say, the terms of membership in "the" covenant are not in view in the claim that *no* human being is righteous in God's eyes. Dahl rightly notes, "Some of the Scrolls from Qumran speak of the sin of man and of God's righteousness in a manner that sounds strikingly Pauline, not to say Lutheran" (*Studies*, 97). "The beliefs voiced by members of the Qumran community correspond to a number of the classical formulations of the doctrine of justification. The ungodly is righteous only through grace. A man is saved not by his own righteousness but by God's saving righteousness. Man is at the same time sinful and righteous" (99). The routes by which Paul and the Qumran writers reached their sense of a pervasive human sinfulness were presumably quite different, but that sense roused in both a conviction of the radical need for divine grace if any human being is to be deemed righteous.

60. Cf. Eckstein, *Verheissung*, 28-29. The question might be raised why the global statement of Ps. 143:2 is thought to rule out righteousness by the works of the law but not that granted by faith in Jesus Christ. But the point of the text (in Ps. 143 as well as in its Pauline paraphrase) is that human conduct per se — Paul notes that this includes the doing of works demanded by the law — cannot measure up to divine standards of righteousness (cf. the similar statements in Job 4:17-19; 15:14-16; 25:4-6); in neither the psalm nor in Paul are the words meant to exclude God's dealing in grace with creatures he must find sinful.

any moral efforts devoted to its fulfillment. It is, in effect, to make Christ a "promoter of sin" (2:17).[61]

Such was Paul's gospel when seen from the perspective of those who believed the Jewish covenant and law still provided the framework within which God's people must live.

To Paul's mind they had not rightly grasped the significance of Christ's death. That death was not to be understood as atoning for the inevitable shortcomings of those who, because of their basic commitment to observe the law, were otherwise righteous; rather, it showed that there can *be* no righteousness based on the law's observance — for otherwise Christ would not have had to die (2:21).[62] Apart from the divine provision made in the death of Christ, all human beings — including those "under the law" — live effectively in the service, not of God, but of sin. Their need is not for the forgiveness of incidental sins, but for an (apocalyptic!)[63] transformation of the conditions of human existence: their life in sin's service must end, preferably in something other than their own (final) death. For believers in Christ this has happened: they have been (like Paul) "crucified with Christ," "dying" because of the death sentence that the law pronounces on their life in sin ("I died by the law," 2:19; cf. 3:10),[64] but in the process experiencing the end of their old existence, regulated

---

61. Cf. Pfleiderer, *Paulinism,* 1:5. According to Smiles (*Gospel,* 153 n. 108), Paul always uses μὴ γένοιτο to deny "an improper conclusion drawn from a *true* ('fulfilled') premise." It is the conclusion (Christ is a promoter of sin), *not* the premise (we proved to be sinners), that is emphatically excluded. Paul's gospel proved peculiarly liable to this charge in his day: cf. Rom. 3:8 ("Some claim that we say, 'Let's do evil so that good may come of it'"); 6:1 ("Shall we go on living in sin so that there may be more and more grace?"). Cf. Eckstein, *Verheissung,* 40-41; Smiles, 148-49. In its day, then, the distinctive (and, for some, damnable) feature of Paul's gospel was held to be that it promoted sin by discounting the law and moral efforts devoted to its fulfillment. This suggests that Paul was too "Lutheran" for his contemporaries' liking.

62. Sanders, who treats "righteousness by the law" and "righteousness by faith (in Christ)" merely as alternative means to the same end, sees in Gal. 2:21 nothing more than a dogmatic declaration that since righteousness *is* by faith, it cannot be by the law (*Law,* 27; *Paul Pal. Jud.,* 484). In effect, this means that the coming of Christ made the righteousness of the law unviable rather than that the unviability of the righteousness of the law is what necessitated the coming of Christ. But for Paul the death of Christ (2:21) and "righteousness by faith (in Christ)" represent the divine possibility offered to *sinners* who *cannot* be found righteous under the law. Apart from the problem of sin, a solution involving Christ's *death* (cf. "for our sins," 1:4) makes little sense. Note also the connection between a dilemma *created under the law* and the solution offered through Christ in 3:13, 22-25; 4:4-5. Cf. chap. 15, sec. iii above.

63. To use Louis Martyn's terminology (see chap. 13 above) — which captures an essential aspect of Paul's thought, even if the word is used somewhat loosely. See also B. Longenecker, *Triumph,* 35-67.

64. Cf. Smiles, *Gospel,* 171-72.

by the law,[65] in sin's service ("I died to the law," 2:19). Now they may indeed live for God ("that I might live for God"), but only inasmuch as Christ, in whose crucifixion they have shared, is now the effective force in their lives ("I no longer live, but Christ lives in me" [2:20]). To return to the old, untransformed life that was ended at the cross ("If I were to build up again that which I destroyed") would be to prove oneself a wrongdoer (2:18) — both because it would be the wrong thing to do and because it would be to revert to the kind of existence in which wrong things were inevitably done. And it would be to frustrate the grace of God (2:21).

The movement of Paul's argument to this point should be noted. Nowhere has Paul suggested that the Christian gospel was needed if Gentiles were to enjoy blessings already experienced by Jews under their law (or covenant); it was needed, Paul indicates, not so Gentiles might become like Jews, but because in essential respects Jews under the law did not differ from Gentiles. Gentiles apart from the law are sinners; under the law Jews are sinners too. Gentiles apart from the law are only declared righteous by faith in Jesus Christ; the same path to righteousness must be taken by Jews. Gentiles apart from the law do not live for God, but Jews under the law must first *die* to the law before they can live for God themselves. Christ died for Jews under the law (like Paul) no less than for Gentile sinners, and both alike must die *with* him. Should Gentile believers, then, be circumcised and adopt other distinctively Jewish practices? No, because such practices mark life under the Jewish law — and Christ, not the Jewish law, is the solution to the human dilemma.

It was, moreover, by faith in Christ, and quite apart from any practices prescribed by the law, that the Galatians had come to experience the blessings of the new age marked by God's Spirit; for their part the subjects of the law remain in the realm of the "flesh" (i.e., the sphere of untransformed humanity). What, then, could possibly move the Galatians to want to return to the realm of the law and flesh (3:1-5)? Besides, Scripture itself shows that faith, not the Jewish law, is the basis on which God pronounces people righteous: "Abraham believed God, and it was credited to him as righteousness" (3:6, citing Gen. 15:6).

That Abraham's route to righteousness was not peculiar to himself is apparent from the promise that in him all nations would be blessed: God would declare all righteous (Scripture was announcing in advance) who shared Abraham's faith (3:7-9, with a citation conflating Gen. 12:3 and 18:18). Far from a blessing, the law brings a curse on those for whom it prescribes the path to righteousness (3:10a), since it anathematizes all who "do not continue in all the

---

65. That the law was introduced to regulate life under sin will be spelled out in 3:21-25.

things written in the book of the law, to do them" (3:10b, citing Deut. 27:26).[66] Scripture itself confirms that no one can be found righteous "by" (or "under") the law (ἐν νόμῳ): "the righteous by *faith* will live" (3:11, citing Hab. 2:4). The route of faith (in the apostolic kerygma) here announced is of course very different from that prescribed by the law: "The one who does these things[67] will

---

66. The implication on which the argument is based — that none of the adherents of the law "continues in" and "does" all that the law requires — is one the sympathetic reader of Galatians will instinctively make, knowing that Jews under the law no less than Gentiles apart from it belong to the present evil age because of their sins (1:4); that Jews no less than Gentiles have been found sinners who can only be declared righteous by faith in Jesus Christ (2:15-17); that life under the law is marked by transgression, not service of God (2:18-19); that the sphere of the law is that of the flesh, untransformed by God's Spirit (3:2-3), and therefore characterized by the "works of the flesh" (5:19-21); and that the subjects of the law are all confined "under sin" (3:23), with even its staunch advocates failing to keep its statutes (6:13). Das (*Law*, 155) plausibly explains why Paul did *not* more straightforwardly write "All who do *not* comply with the law's demands are under a curse" as follows: "How would the Galatians have taken that? Surely Paul's wording would have appeared to be a challenge to observe the law more scrupulously." The wording Paul chose stresses that *all* who embark on the law's path to righteousness end up (because they transgress the law, as Paul's argument throughout the letter makes clear) under its curse.

That the argument of 3:10 is built on the presupposed premise that no one satisfactorily keeps the law remains the interpretation of most scholars, with the variant that some place great emphasis on the requirement that "all" that is written in the book of the law must be observed: 100 percent fulfillment is needed if one is to be found righteous (see the summaries of Hübner, Schreiner, and Das in Part Two of this book). The debate on this issue seems moot: since Paul claims that "all" are "under sin," he presumably thought no human being would succeed no matter how low the passing grade of righteousness was set. A plethora of alternative interpretations has been proposed in recent years, though none, to my mind, is either necessary or persuasive: e.g., that the curse of 3:10 is conditional (Stanley, "Curse," 481-511; Young, "Cursed," 79-92; but given that Paul sees all humanity under sin, a curse conditional upon the transgression of the law would have long since become actual — and v. 13 indicates that it had done so); that the curse of 3:10 is national and remains in effect on the people of Israel, whose "exile" is thought to be continuing (Scott, "Works," 187-221; Wright, *Climax*, 137-56; cf. Thielman, *Paul*, 126-27; but the notion of a continuing exile was hardly so universally held that it could be assumed without argument [or even mention!], and Paul's statement in 3:10 seems general [ὅσοι hardly introduces so defined a curse] [see Carson, "Summaries," 546-47 n. 158; Dunn, *Theology*, 362 n. 117; Kim, *Perspective*, 136-41; B. Longenecker, *Triumph*, 137-39; Seifrid, *Righteousness*, 21-25; Wisdom, *Blessing*, 7-10, 157-58]). For Dunn's interpretation of the verse, see chap. 16, sec. ii above.

67. The antecedent for "these things" in LXX Lev. 18:5 is "all my commandments and all my judgments." Paul may think the referent apparent from the context; or he may assume that his readers will identify the "things" that the law requires to be done (3:12) with "all the things written in the book of the law," which people were to "continue in" and "do," in 3:10. Though Paul uses the phrase "works of the law" interchangeably with "the law" (compare 2:16 with 2:21; 5:4), the term "works" does show wherein, in Paul's understanding, the characteristic emphasis of the law lies. Cf. Smiles, *Gospel*, 119-20.

live by them" (3:12, citing Lev. 18:5). Faith trusts God to provide what the law requires human beings to do. Yet (Christian) faith is not a simple alternative to the law, nor is it dismissive of it; on the contrary, assuming the validity of the law's requirement of righteousness and the reality of its curse on those who fail to meet it, the righteousness offered by Christ is marked by the *redemption* it brings *from the curse of the law* on transgressors.[68] Christ, in his crucifixion, was himself the object of the law's curse ("Cursed is everyone who hangs on a tree" [Gal. 3:13, citing Deut. 21:23]); thereby he exhausted its force for those otherwise cursed who believe in him. (Indeed, the curse that the law pronounces on transgressors is hardly to be distinguished[69] from the divine condemnation that looms over all who fall short of God's required righteousness — a condemnation that can also be said to have been absorbed by Christ's death.) Hence Abraham's blessing — that is, that all nations would be blessed in Abraham, in that they are declared righteous, as he was declared righteous, by faith[70] — has now, in Christ Jesus, become a reality (3:14, referring back to 3:8). And the promised divine Spirit,[71] which could hardly be bestowed upon those still subject to the curse, has now been given to believers (3:14).

Two notes are again worth underlining here. First, the problem that the law poses for "all" who are "of its works" is that they (all) incur its curse on transgressors. Nothing different is to be expected of the denizens of an "evil age" who remain in the realm of the "flesh" (1:4; 3:3). Second, Paul sees a difference in essence between the faith by which sinners are declared righteous and the law that demands righteous deeds of its adherents (3:11-12). It is the difference, we may say, between ordinary and extraordinary "dikaiosness," between the universal requirement of righteous behavior enshrined in the law and the extraordinary divine offer of righteousness to *un*righteous people through the death of Jesus Christ. Paul's contrast between faith and the doing of the law's demands is, to be sure, not that between trusting passivity — as a general approach to life — and energetic activity. But Paul *is* saying that the deeds of sinners cannot make them righteous, though God will declare them so if they credit and accept his offer of righteousness in Christ Jesus.

---

68. Cf. Beker, *Paul*, 187; Hübner, "Proprium," 462; *Theologie*, 76-77.

69. See the discussion of thesis 2 in chap. 19 below.

70. Cf. Williams, "Justification," 92.

71. Paul has not referred to a promise of the Spirit earlier in Galatians. Perhaps he assumes familiarity with the (abundantly attested) tradition that the coming of the Spirit was a matter of divine promise; cf. Burton, *Galatians*, 176-77. Possibly he links the gift of the Spirit (as well as God's declaring Gentiles righteous) to the promise given to Abraham that in him "all nations" would be "blessed" (3:8, 14a). Deidun, *Morality*, 48-49, sees a reference to the promise of the Spirit that was to accompany the new covenant. Cf. also Hays, *Echoes*, 110; Williams, "Justification," 91-100.

By introducing Abraham into his argument, Paul makes clear that the salvation God has provided in Christ takes up a story begun in the Old Testament Scriptures; it is not, however, a story in which the law plays the protagonist's role. Paul proceeds by sharply distinguishing the promise[72] God gave Abraham from the law delivered at Mount Sinai, seeing the two (as he has just depicted faith and the law) as operating on mutually exclusive principles:[73] what God graciously offers through his promise[74] cannot be contingent on (the observance of) the law (3:18). And since the promise came first — "to Abraham and to his seed" (= Christ and, as Paul will later show, all who are "in Christ Jesus" [3:16, 26-29]) — the law must serve a different purpose.

It was a temporary purpose at that, lasting only until Christ, the seed of whom the promise spoke, should appear (3:19). From Moses until Christ, then, the law dealt with transgressions, confining its subjects under sin, restricting their movements just as "pedagogues" do those of children committed to their charge (3:22-25).[75] Had the law been able to transform[76] rather than merely regulate human life under sin, then, indeed, sinners could have been declared righ-

72. Or "covenant"; the term is introduced because of the analogy Paul draws between a will (Gk. διαθήκη) that cannot be set aside and God's unalterable promise (3:15-17).

73. See the discussion in chap. 16, sec. ii. Note, however, that just as faith and the law, though based on different principles (3:11-12), are not seen as simple alternatives competing with each other (rather, faith brings redemption to those rightly cursed by the law, 3:13), so Paul insists that the promise and the law, though operating on different principles (3:18), do not oppose each other (3:21); rather, the law confines its subjects under sin *in order that* they may obtain the promise of righteousness by faith (3:22). In spite of the sharp distinction that Paul (but not Jewish tradition) drew between God's promise and law, Paul insisted on finding for both a place in the divine scheme. It is true, however, that Paul sees the "Judaism" of his day as continuing to live under the Sinaitic covenant, whereas believers in Christ are the heirs of the Abrahamic promise.

74. "What God promised" was of course that all nations would be "blessed" in Abraham when they are declared righteous, as Abraham was declared righteous, by faith (3:8). In 3:18 it is summed up as the "inheritance," i.e., the possession of the promised righteousness.

75. Possibly Paul thinks that the law, by restricting Israel's contact with pagan nations, kept Israel from the worst excesses of pagan sin (so Dunn, *Theology*, 140-43); but Galatians contains no hint of such a role. Possibly he thinks that fear of the law's sanctions had a restraining influence on human sinfulness: Rom. 13:3-4 assigns such a function to governing authorities, 1 Tim. 1:8-11 appears to attribute it to the law, and "Lutheran" tradition (as we have seen) views this as one of the law's subsidiary functions. But nothing in Galatians supports the suggestion. In Galatians the law's "confining" of sinners most likely refers to its role in prescribing what sinners *ought* to do (3:12) and cursing their transgressions (3:10, 13), thereby accentuating their service of sin, bondage to beings that are not God (4:3), and lack of freedom to live for God (cf. 2:19). More will be said in chap. 19 about Paul's view, as expressed here and elsewhere, of the origin and purpose of the law.

76. To "give life"; see chap. 15, n. 94 above.

teous by the law (3:21). But that was not its purpose.[77] Hence the law, in the divine plan, is not an alternative competing with the promise that God would justify the nations by faith (3:21a); still less does it set that promise aside (3:17-18). Rather, it sets the stage for the promise's fulfillment: it is precisely those confined by the law[78] to the rule of sin who are to be declared righteous by faith in Jesus Christ (3:22). Extraordinary righteousness, made possible through the death of God's Son, comes into play where ordinary righteousness, demanded by the law, is demonstrably absent.

Before we move on to the argument of Galatians 4, we should recall that throughout Galatians Paul depicts the condition of Jews and Gentiles as — in the end — indistinguishable. Both belong to the "present evil age" (1:4). Jews, who think of Gentiles as sinners, prove to be sinners themselves (2:15-17). All humanity is "under sin" (3:22). All, because they participate in untransformed humanity, remain in the flesh and do the kinds of works that reflect the bent of the flesh (5:19-21; cf. 3:3; 5:24). The curse hanging over those (presumably Jews) who are "of the works of the law" (3:10) can be little different from the condemnation that awaits all sinners — and Paul appears, in 3:13-14, to think of Jewish and Gentile believers alike as delivered from its bane.[79]

The parallel is carried further in Galatians 4. Gentiles, thinking themselves to be worshiping the gods, in fact serve beings that are no gods; yet, since they are unable to come to the knowledge of the true God, their service of lesser beings amounts to an enslavement (4:8). For their part Jews, thinking themselves to be worshiping God, are actually living a life "under sin" administered by the law. Under the law they, too, are unable to live for God (cf. 2:19); thus their service, too, amounts to slavery. Both Gentiles and Jews, thinking themselves to be serving the divine, in fact are confined to the service of lesser entities, the "weak and beggarly elements" (4:9; cf. v. 3) that include the false gods of the Gentiles and the Jewish law. From such slavery the Galatian believers have been deliv-

---

77. Cf. Luther, *Gal.*, 26:91: "Let the Law have its glory. . . . I will grant that it can teach me that I should love God and my neighbor, and live in chastity, patience, etc.; but it is in no position to show me how to be delivered from sin, the devil, death, and hell."

78. According to 3:22, "the *Scripture* confined all under sin." Since the statement is introduced as a sharp antithesis (ἀλλά) to the notion that the law could bring righteousness (3:21), one would expect it to be made of the law rather than of Scripture. Presumably "Scripture" in 3:22 means something like "the law in the role that Scripture assigns it," perhaps with a reference to a specific text (such as Deut. 27:26, cited in 3:10). Cf. Burton, *Galatians*, 195-96; Lightfoot, *Galatians*, 147-48. The reference to Scripture of course ensures the understanding that human confinement by the law under sin has a place in the divine plan. Cf. B. Longenecker, *Triumph*, 125.

79. Paul's apparent extension of the domain of the law to include Gentiles is discussed under the second thesis of chap. 19.

ered. For them *now* to take up the law would be to revert to the bondage they experienced before they came to a knowledge of the true God (4:1-11). Conversely, the redemption that Christ brought those "under the law" may be said to have brought Gentiles the same freedom, the same adoption as God's *"sons,"* and the same presence of the Spirit of God's *Son* in their hearts (4:4-6).

After a personal appeal to the Galatians based on the good relations he had enjoyed with them in the past (4:12-20), Paul sums up life under the law and that of faith in a striking allegory (4:21–5:1). Abraham had two sons, Ishmael and Isaac. What distinguished them, for the purposes of this allegory, was that Ishmael was the son of a slave woman and born "according to the flesh" (i.e., in a normal, human way), whereas Isaac was the son of a free woman and born "according to promise" (i.e., extraordinarily, in fulfillment of a divine promise when his parents were too old to have children). When *these* features are singled out as the significant differences (it is the prerogative of the allegorist to choose the aspects of a story to which importance is attached), then the parallels between Ishmael and life under the Jewish law, as Paul sees it, and between Isaac and the life of faith become evident. The Jewish (Sinaitic) law regulates the untransformed human life of the flesh, and it is a life of slavery inasmuch as its adherents, bound by sin and the law, are not free to serve God. Conversely, the life of faith begins in fulfillment of the divine promise (all nations would be blessed in Abraham, inasmuch as they, too, are declared righteous by faith), and it is a life of freedom to live for God. All this is (explicitly) allegorical (see 4:24), and yet consistent with the notion in Galatians 3 that believers in Christ are the true descendants of Abraham, the true heirs of the Abrahamic promise.

Galatians 5 begins with a reminder that the merits of circumcision cannot be considered on their own, since to be circumcised is to take on the obligation to keep the whole Jewish law (5:3). From the curse to which such a way of life inevitably leads Christ has redeemed those who believe in him; to revert to the law, then, is to derive no benefit from Christ (5:2, 4); falling from the grace by which God has declared them righteous, those who would be "declared righteous on the basis of the law" can only seek that end by keeping its commandments (5:3-4).

Paul concludes his letter by depicting the life Christians are to live; aspects of his account will be discussed in chapter 19 below. Here we need only note that it is a life directed by the Spirit who opposes the flesh, and that Paul again identifies life under the law with that in the flesh (5:17-19), contrasting both with the new life in the Spirit.

By way of summary, then, we note that Galatians implies that God requires (ordinary) righteousness of Gentiles as well as Jews (note that both are responsible for their sins [1:4], and both need to be declared righteous by faith in Christ Jesus [2:16]). Yet Jews no more than Gentiles are deemed to have produced it, and life under the Jewish law differs in no essential respect from Gentile life without it. Moreover, the human dilemma goes beyond the concrete sins that humans commit; such sins reflect their belonging to an age gone wrong, dominated by sin and, indeed, by powers that are not God.[80] The law was given to regulate, not transform, this life of sin: it informs its subjects — Jews in the first place, though at times all humanity, itself required to do what is right and condemned for failing to do so, seems loosely included (3:10-14, 22-25; 4:1-7) — of what they ought to do and curses their transgressions; but it cannot introduce them to a new and different way of life. Such life is only to be found in Christ. Those who believe in him are declared righteous and given the Spirit, the mark of the new age. They have *died* with Christ to the old way of life and now live, with Christ *in* them, in God's service.

The new perspective on Paul (which is in fact rooted in a new perspective on Judaism) has raised anew the issue of what (if anything) Paul finds wrong with Judaism. Sanders's slogan "It is not Christianity"[81] has been deemed arbitrary and unsatisfactory by Dunn, who finds Judaism's shortcoming in its limitation of God's covenant blessings to those who observe the boundary markers that define a distinctively Jewish lifestyle.[82] But the question itself, though not without an answer, may be misleading. Judaism in Galatians is life lived under the Sinaitic law. As a present manifestation of that life, it is in error, Paul implies, in fostering the belief that people can be declared righteous on the basis of their faithfulness to the Sinaitic law; moreover, though Paul voices no criticism of *Jews* on this score, one may wonder what point he would see in continuing to observe the distinctively Jewish practices prescribed by the Sinaitic law now that its mission has been accomplished, its validity ended. But he does not fault the Sinaitic law per se. Its operating principle — that life is theirs who do what the law commands — is found articulated in Scripture itself. And though that principle is different from that of faith, it is not *wrong* for that reason (or any other). After all, *that* God places demands for righteous behavior on his

---

80. Is sin itself understood by Paul as such a power (i.e., a supernatural being holding human beings in thralldom)? Possibly, though the evidence for such a view in Galatians is confined to the phrase ὑπὸ ἁμαρτίαν in 3:22, which may be simply metaphorical. Note that "under law" appears to be the equivalent of "subject to the law's curse on transgressors": redemption from the law (4:5) and from its curse (3:13) was accomplished by Christ's bearing that curse (3:13), not by his overcoming of a supernatural power ("law") and setting its captives free. No *such* freeing from "sin" is depicted either.

81. To be sure, this is not the whole story, even in Sanders; see chap. 9, sec. iii above.

82. See chap. 11, sec. ii above.

moral creatures is presupposed in everything Paul writes; the law, in spelling them out, performs a divine function. Paul's point is not that people are not required to do what is right or that the law is wrong in telling them to do so, but that only faith in Jesus Christ provides a solution for humanity's captivity to sin. The fundamental question addressed by Galatians thus is not "What is wrong with Judaism (or the Sinaitic law)?" but "What is wrong with humanity that Judaism (and the Sinaitic law) cannot remedy?"[83]

On the other hand, students of Judaism rightly insist that Judaism — and indeed, the Sinaitic covenant — was *more* than a collection of demands by which human righteousness was to be assessed. The covenant was given to those chosen by God to be his people, and included provisions of atonement through which their transgressions could be forgiven. Has Paul not overlooked these essential features?

He has — and he has not. Paul has much to say about Israel's election in Romans; but it is not mentioned in Galatians,[84] and the heirs of the promise to Abraham are those who have faith in Jesus Christ, not the physical descendants (born "according to the flesh," to use the language of 4:23) of the patriarchs. And certainly he never mentions the rites of atonement that were a part of the Sinaitic covenant.

But Paul sums up the conditions of life and blessing under the Sinaitic covenant with a quotation that captures as well as any the spirit of the covenant as reflected, for example, in the book of Deuteronomy:[85] "The one who does these things [what the law requires] will live by them" (Gal. 3:12, citing Lev. 18:5). Repeatedly Deuteronomy portrays the people of Israel — chosen, to be sure, by God (Deut. 10:14-15) — *not* as already righteous ("you are a stiffnecked people" [9:6]), but as come to a crossroads where decisive choices have to be made: life and blessing await them if they obey God's commandments, a curse and death if they do not (cf. 11:26-28; 30:15-20). None of these texts speaks (nor does Deuteronomy as a whole) of rites of atonement available for those who transgress.

---

83. Cf. B. Longenecker, *Triumph*, 120-21.

84. It might, however, be implicit in Gal. 6:16, if the phrase "Israel of God" has not simply been co-opted to designate the Christian church (so Kuula, *Law*, 88, noting that by qualifying "Israel" with "of God," Paul suggests that there is a distinction between the true or real Israel — that "of God" — and the false or nominal people so designated). See Richardson, *Israel*, 74-84, and on the issue more broadly, the thoughtful comments of B. Longenecker, *Triumph*, 174-79.

85. Deuteronomy is, moreover, hardly an isolated book in the Hebrew canon: the Deuteronomistic history is of course stamped throughout by its spirit, and modern scholars seem bent on finding evidence of Deuteronomistic editing in the least suspected parts of the canonical Scriptures. Alexander ("Torah," 299) suggests that the best way to sum up the religion of the rabbis is to say that it was the religion of Deuteronomy.

It does not follow that such rites were not a staple feature of Jewish religion; clearly they were (whether or not they figured in the thinking of Deuteronomy). But such rites atoned for the inevitable sins — and even the very great sins — of people who had taken up (what would later be called) the "yoke" of God's rule and who were committed to the faithful observance of God's law. The message of Deuteronomy addresses the more fundamental issue: it summons Israel *to* that crucial commitment, by which the faithful could be distinguished from the wicked.[86] What, under the Sinaitic covenant as portrayed in Deuteronomy, decisively separates the blessed from the cursed is *not* that the former have found atonement for their sins whereas the latter have not, but that the former, though not the latter, have committed themselves to, and shown themselves faithful in, *doing* what God commands. Obedience per se was not difficult (10:12-13; 30:11-14) — though, to be sure, Deuteronomy expresses grave doubts whether Israel has the *will* to show it (9:4-29; 31:16-21, 27-29; 32:5; etc.).[87]

When it comes to the conditions prescribed by the Sinaitic covenant for enjoying life under God's blessing, there is, it seems, no essential difference between Paul's understanding as attested in Galatians and that spelled out in Deuteronomy — and, indeed, current among Paul's Jewish contemporaries. Nor is Paul's bleak appraisal of life under that covenant to be attributed merely to his omission of any reference to Jewish rites of atonement for the sins of the (otherwise) righteous.[88] More to the point is Paul's (post-Damascus) assessment of the human condition: whereas the *normal* assumption of Second Temple Jews (and presumably, of the pre-Damascus Paul) was that they could and in many cases *did* live up to the basic requirements of the covenant, the Paul of Galatians insisted that they had not and — captives of sin that they were — *could* not do so.[89] For Jews (and

---

86. For the wicked there could be no atonement *until* they repented and were prepared to submit to God's law. Paul clearly thought "sinners" lacked the capacity and even the inclination to so repent; cf. Rom. 8:7-8.

87. Cf. Thielman, *Paul*, 65, 173.

88. According to Schreiner and Das (see chap. 12, sec. ii above), Judaism emphasized both the need for observance of the law *and* the availability of atonement for transgressions; but Paul, discounting (in the light of Christ's death) the efficacy of Jewish rites of atonement, saw in Judaism simply the legalism that demanded perfect obedience to the law. But in Galatians Paul differed from Jewish *Christians* who no doubt themselves believed that the death of Jesus Christ replaced the Old Testament sacrifices in providing atonement for the failures of the otherwise righteous. In their case it is self-evident that Paul did not discount the efficacy of the act to which they attributed atonement. What he refused to accept was the notion of Jews and certain Jewish Christians alike that the law served to distinguish the righteous (those committed to, and faithful in, its observance, though perhaps needing atonement for their incidental trespasses) from sinners. His anthropology (*all* are "under sin") was more pessimistic.

89. Cf. Becker, *Paul*, 396.

Paul's Jewish Christian opponents) the law provided a basis on which the "righteous" could be distinguished from "sinners"; for the Galatian Paul it showed what its subjects ought to have done and cursed their failures. In an evil world ruled by sin, *all* are sinners, and only those who believe in Christ can be found — by divine and extraordinary means — to be righteous.[90] The more pessimistic anthropology of Galatians, and the need there shown for an apocalyptic transformation of the conditions of human existence, are reflected in its distinctive understanding of life under the Sinaitic law.

Is the Galatian Paul, then, a "Lutheran"?

The mantra in recent studies bent on refuting a "Lutheran" reading of the epistle is that the issue it addresses was *not* whether one could *earn* salvation by one's good works, but on what terms Gentiles were to be admitted to the people of God.[91] This is true and even important, but not quite the discussion stopper it is sometimes taken to be. Paul's opponents believed the Jewish covenant[92] provided the framework by which God's people are defined and within which they must live; the issue for *them* was, very naturally, on what terms Gentiles could be included in the blessings of the covenant. What they had in mind more specifically was certainly *not* whether Gentiles (or Jews) could earn salvation by accumulating good works, but whether Gentiles needed to observe the boundary markers by which those under the Sinaitic covenant were set apart from those outside it. It is also true that Paul thought Gentiles did *not* need to observe them whereas his opponents thought they did. And it is important to note that, understood on their own premises, neither Paul's Jewish Christian opponents nor Judaism as a whole thought salvation was earned by doing what was right more often than what was not.

But Galatians is misunderstood unless we realize that Paul attacked more than the notion that Jewish boundary markers needed to be observed by Gentiles.[93] The Jewish law itself — of which the prescriptions of boundary markers were a small though contentious part — did not provide a basis by which *sinners* could be declared righteous; and Jews, for all their observance of boundary markers, were no less sinners than Gentiles. Paul does not fault the law for inviting self-reliance, self-righteousness, or boasting. He does, however, observe that its operative principle demands works: people must do what it

90. Cf. Winninge, *Sinners*, 306: "Whereas Paul's Jewish contemporaries could admit that all human beings occasionally committed sins, they would never have thought of classifying the basically faithful as sinners."

91. See the quotations in chap. 14, sec. iii above.

92. As noted above, *they* drew no sharp distinction between the promise to Abraham and the legislation of Mount Sinai.

93. Cf. Räisänen, *Torah*, 121-22; Zeller, "Diskussion," 488-89.

commands if they are to enjoy life in God's favor. With that demand — which human beings are in no position to meet — he contrasts the path of *faith* by which the *un*righteous (i.e., sinners) are declared righteous because of Jesus Christ: a path for which the word "grace" suffices as a summative term (1:6; 2:21; 5:4). Paul was not addressing Pelagianism or sixteenth-century disputes over works. But he responded to the insistence that Gentiles be circumcised by taking up the fundamental issue of how human beings, in spite of their sin, can experience life in God's favor. The "Lutherans" were not mistaken in finding an answer to that question in the epistle. Nor, in ascribing salvation to an initiative of divine grace that excludes any contribution from sinful human beings, did they misconstrue its terms.[94]

iv. Romans

Much good can be derived from critical reviews — provided, of course, that one is prepared to listen to what they say. From critics who are sure to point out that the discussion of "'Righteousness' in Paul" in chapter 15 ought really to be entitled "'Righteousness' in Romans," I draw the useful conclusion that no extended treatment of justification by faith in Romans is now needed. Whole sections of the epistle critical to our theme require little further treatment. Still, the progression of Paul's argument should be noted and relevant aspects not yet considered should here be taken up.

To the Thessalonians and the Corinthians Paul proclaimed a message of salvation from the divine judgment that awaited wayward humanity. Assumed throughout — it may well have been explicit in his proclamation — was the divine requirement of righteousness: without it the "wrath" and "condemnation" of the biblical God are inexplicable. Issues related to the Jewish law do not, however, appear to have been addressed. In Paul's letter to the Galatians, on the other hand, the law *and* righteousness are central themes: Paul argues that,

---

94. Cf. B. Longenecker, *Triumph*, 179-83. Note that there is even a precedent in Galatians — where the law and its curse seem in places to include all humanity within their sphere — for Luther's broadening of the term "law" beyond the commands of the Sinaitic covenant to include the righteousness that God requires of all human beings. And in Paul's distinction between the operative principle of the law — it demands deeds — and faith, we may see the roots of Luther's hermeneutic of "the law and the gospel." That said, Galatians does *not* portray the role of the law as one of rousing in sinners a sense of guilt and despair that would drive them to the gospel: its role as a "pedagogue" (3:23-25) was very different, and lasted only until Christ ("faith") came. That Paul's missionary proclamation must nonetheless have included an *equivalent* to this role of the law was suggested above, n. 10.

though requiring obedience to its commands, the law provides no basis by which sinners may be declared righteous. This response was provoked by the insistence of Jewish Christian teachers that the Galatian believers should be circumcised and take up a Jewish way of life under the Sinaitic law. Among the *Roman* Christians — to judge by the letter Paul sent them — circumcision does not seem to have been a subject of contention. Nonetheless, the letter reveals how Paul has assimilated themes first elicited by the Galatian crisis into his basic repertoire. His gospel remains one of salvation (cf. 1:16, where the language is reminiscent of 1 Cor. 1:18, 21) from the wrath of God that looms over a wicked world (cf. 1:18; 5:9, reminiscent of the language, in particular, of 1 Thessalonians). But here, as in Galatians, the message of salvation is explicitly one of righteousness, appropriated by faith (1:17),[95] and it represents a divine response to a crisis defined but not remedied by the law (3:20).[96]

Paul's opening summary of the message he proclaims (1:16-17) is followed by a statement of the condition of humankind that prompted God's intervention. That human beings are moral creatures held responsible by God for their conduct is assumed in everything Paul wrote; here it becomes the main theme of the argument. The argument itself is advanced in a narrative mode — not for the only time in the epistle. In Romans 7 Paul will present in story form what happens when the rebellious human being ("Everyman") meets the righteous divine law: a "story" informed by more than one story from the Bible (primarily that of Adam and Eve, but with elements taken from Israel's experience under the law as well), and one from which aspects of Paul's personal experience can hardly be excluded (it is related in the first person); but it is a story to whose characters and events no names or dates can be strictly applied. The same is true of the "story" of human depravity in 1:18-32. Here the subject is the deeds of "people" (ἄνθρωποι, 1:18) and the response of God. Aorist tenses abound in the account, suggesting specific times and happenings. But no

---

95. Hahn ("Entwicklung," 342-66) rightly insists that Paul's *Rechtfertigungslehre* represents an explication of his gospel (noting, in particular, Rom. 1:16-17); he adds (357 n. 3) that it is the gratuitous character of God's salvation that the language of justification is intended to highlight.

96. On one level Paul's delineating of the gospel in Romans serves to replace its oral proclamation to an audience he had not been able to visit but to whom he felt an obligation (1:13-15; cf. Jervis, *Purpose,* 158-64; N. Elliott, *Rhetoric,* 84-87). Paul was also writing, however, to prepare the Romans for an expected visit and to garner their support for a proposed mission to Spain (15:22-29). Some introduction of himself and what he stood for would have been in order in any case; but the care and energy he devotes to the purpose reflect his awareness that he was by now a controversial figure; it was important, then, that the Romans base their understanding of his stance, not on reports they may have heard from sources of dubious sympathy, but on his own presentation of it.

names or dates can be supplied: at what particular point did humanity "exchange" God's glory for images (1:23), or God abandon humanity to the lusts of human hearts (1:24)? This is a dramatized depiction of the human condition,[97] recalling many a biblical account (and prophetic denunciation) and no doubt informed by personal observation as well; but it is not the retelling of any *one* story that Paul has read or seen. The points to be made are that human beings (the species as such is under indictment) are in a position where they *ought* to recognize God and give him honor and thanks;[98] honoring their Creator, they *ought* to live in accordance with their nature as divinely created and act decently toward each other. But they do not, and their failure is both inexcusable and provocative of divine judgment. Of course Paul, in telling the story of humankind, does not mean that every individual human being is guilty of each of the wrongs he lists; nor is the truth of his story thought to be established by empirical observation (of *every* human being?). Egregious wrongs empirically observed may illustrate the truth of the indictment, but its basic truth has been absorbed by Paul from the biblical tradition — and given shape by what faith in the cross of Christ says about the situation it redeems.[99]

Since the indictment in 1:18-32 proceeds without reference to the Jewish law, and since the idolatry and immorality that it details figure largely in Jewish accounts of Gentile vices, it has often been thought that the passage condemns the latter, leaving the judgment of Jews for chapter 2. On the other hand, the story of humankind (ἄνθρωποι) can hardly *exclude* Jews,[100] and biblical passages condemning Israel's unfaithfulness are clearly echoed even in chapter 1.[101] Moreover, the "wherefore" with which chapter 2 begins requires that the human judge of other human beings in 2:1-6 is included in the general condemnation of 1:18-32: in the light of 2:17-24, Jews who condemn Gentile depravity must be primarily, if not exclusively, in mind.[102] 1:18-32 thus portrays the sinful-

---

97. Cf. Seifrid, *Righteousness*, 50 n. 46: "There is something of a generic sense to his description; it is Adam's transgression reliving itself in all generations."

98. Cf. Schreiner, *Paul*, 106: "The fundamental problem is not that people have committed 'sins'; it is that they have committed 'sin,' that is, they repudiated the worship of God and embraced worship of the creature. This is borne out by Romans 1:24, 26, 28. Three times Paul says that God 'handed over' (*paredōken*) people to sin. In each instance the reason for his handing them over is attributed to their rejection of God. All human sins, in other words, have their fountainhead in idolatry. The degradation and blight of sin are a consequence of the failure to honor and praise God."

99. Cf. Byrne, "Need," 126.

100. Cf. Dunn, *Theology*, 93; Garlington, *Aspects*, 34-35.

101. Cf. Bassler, *Impartiality*, 122, 195-97; Das, *Law*, 172-77.

102. Note, too, that in 2:1 the one who condemns the presence in others of the vices listed in the preceding verses is said to be guilty of "the same things."

ness and liability to judgment of *all* human beings, with 2:1-6 pointing out that condemning the sins of others is no replacement for doing right oneself.

The remainder of chapter 2 is meant to demonstrate, not the *guilt* of Jews (their guilt, together with that of other people, is the subject of the denunciation beginning in 1:18), but that God's requirement of righteous behavior applies equally to Jews (who have the law in which the requirement is spelled out)[103] and to Gentiles (who do not have the written law but who are deemed nonetheless to be sufficiently aware of what they ought to do to be responsible for doing it). That God judges all according to their works and approves only the righteous who do what is good (2:6-13) means that Gentiles who are not circumcised are not *thereby* condemned, nor are Jews, who have been circumcised, *thereby* approved. Righteous conduct, not physical circumcision, is what matters.[104]

That circumcised Jews may not sin with impunity does not mean that they have not been the recipients of significant divine blessings, including the "oracles" of God. Nor does their unfaithfulness, though leading to divine judgment, mean that God for his part has not been true to his word. On the contrary, God's righteousness and truth emerge all the more clearly when juxtaposed with human unrighteousness and falsehood, though the good of their so appearing does not justify humans in doing what is wrong. God rightly judges them when they do so (3:1-8).

All, Jews and Gentiles alike, have been shown to be[105] "under sin" (3:9).[106] Scripture supports the indictment (3:10-18). As a result, the whole world —

---

103. Dunn (*Theology,* 115, 118) rightly emphasizes that Paul here attacks the notion that privileges granted to Jews include their exemption from punishment for their sins. It is worth remembering, however, that the sinfulness of Jews, for Paul, is not restricted to the sin of thinking themselves exempt from punishment for their sins, but includes those sins from whose punishment some may sinfully have thought themselves exempt. For Dunn's clarification to this effect of earlier statements, see "Works," 106. Cf. Byrne, "Problem," 302: "In Dunn's treatment, Israel's sinfulness tends to slide very quickly in the direction of national pride. The notion that Paul operated with a two-edged view of Israel's sinfulness — sinning by transgression, and national pride — may indeed have some validity, but too great a stress upon the latter fails to do full justice to the radicality of Paul's critique of human sinfulness, which Luther, with unparalleled interpretive perceptiveness, discerned."

104. For the argument of Rom. 2, see chap. 15, nn. 22 and 23 above.

105. The indictment of "humankind" in 1:18-32 is intended.

106. As in Gal. 3:22 (see n. 80 above), the phrase clearly means more than that human beings commit concrete sins; sinfulness is, inescapably, part of their nature. On the other hand, the temptation to believe that ὑπό is used by Paul either with a genitive of agent or an accusative of demonic power should be resisted. In three chapters that have said nothing of demonic powers, Jews and Gentiles have, according to Paul, been shown to be "under sin"; the same charge is now said by Paul to be supported by a catena of quotations that say nothing of demonic powers and much about the incorrigibility of human behavior. Cf. Räisänen, *Law,* 99-100 n. 29; Winger, "Grace," 169.

those "under the law" are singled out for special mention, presumably because they might well have thought differently — finds itself culpable before God with nothing to say in its defense (3:19). Human beings are required to do the "good" (2:7, 10), to be "doers of [the good spelled out in] the law" (2:13). But none is "righteous," all have "gone astray," none does what is good (3:10-12); as a result, no human being can be declared righteous because he or she has actually *done* the good defined by "the works of the law."[107] The law provides no basis by which a human being (*any* human being) can be found righteous, but it allows human sinfulness to be recognized for what it is (3:20). So far, the argument of Romans 1:18–3:20.

If Paul's "real" goal in the passage is to show on what terms Gentiles may enter the people of God, his method of launching the discussion is passing strange. To tell readers that all the world is guilty before God is hardly designed to whet their appetite for joining a particular community of the condemned, or for discovering by what terms they may do so. On the surface at least, Paul's argument has a different focus: having announced his gospel in 1:16-17, and preparing for his presentation of the extraordinary righteousness it offers in 3:21-26, Paul is showing in 1:18–3:20 why extraordinary righteousness is needed: neither Jews nor Gentiles measure up to God's demand of ordinary righteousness.

---

107. The "deeds of the law" by which one might be thought to be "declared righteous" in 3:20 are surely what the "doers of the law" do in order to be "declared righteous" in 2:13. If 2:13 sums up God's requirement of ordinary righteousness ("the doers of the law will be declared righteous"), 3:10 and 20 assert that no human being meets the requirement: "none is righteous," "by the deeds of the law no flesh will be declared righteous before God." The truth of the principle of 2:13 is not denied in 3:20, *nor are there any negative connotations to the phrase "the doers of the law" in 2:13 or "the works of the law" in 3:20.* If people cannot be declared righteous by doing good, it is not because doing good is bad, but because bad people do not do good. The offer of life to those who do the law in 2:13 is said in 3:20 to lack application in a world of sinners. This is the point of 3:20, summing up the indictment of 1:18–3:20 and preparing for the introduction of the "extraordinary righteousness" of faith in 3:21-26.

In this passage, then, the "works of the law" by which no human being can be declared righteous (3:20) are hardly the boundary markers of the Jewish people (cf. Das, *Law,* 190: "In Rom 2:17-29, however, Paul sees absolutely no problem with Jewish ethnic identity markers as long as they are accompanied by full observance of the law"; also Martin, *Law,* 146-47). They are rather the good deeds that God requires of all human beings (2:7, 10), that God has spelled out for the benefit of Jews in the Mosaic law (2:13, 18), but that human beings — all of whom are "under sin," none of whom is righteous (3:9, 10) — have not done. Dunn's observation that "there was always something odd not to say suspect about the assumption that Paul's polemic against 'works of the law' was a polemic against 'good works'" (*Partings,* 136) misses the point, as I read both Paul and his "Lutheran" interpreters. Neither Paul *nor* the "Lutherans" ever opposed good works, though Paul *and* the Lutherans were sure that sinners are in no position to be declared righteous for having done them.

The pressing question invited by 1:18–3:20 is the same as that addressed in 1 Thessalonians: how are sinners (for such are all human beings) to encounter God other than in his sin-provoked wrath? It is a question Paul *had* to raise, for without it a gospel of *salvation* had no point. It is, moreover, the question to which Paul responds in 3:21-26.

On the other hand, it remains true, as recent Pauline scholarship has emphasized, that Paul presents his gospel in the opening chapters in Romans in terms ("declared righteous by faith," "not by the works of the law") that he adopted in response to a message requiring circumcision of his Gentile converts. Nor is Paul likely to have been oblivious to that issue when he came to write Romans — and 4:9-12 proves that, in fact, he was not. And although, in the argument of 2:1–3:20, Paul's claim that physical circumcision and Jewishness are of no decisive advantage seems intended rather to disabuse Jews of the notion that they were than to discourage Gentiles from becoming Jews, it is likely enough that the controversy over Gentile participation in the church remained a factor in Paul's thinking here as well. However theological Paul's reasoning may have been, very practical questions, with obvious social implications, were at stake when Paul argued that no one could be declared righteous by the works of the law.

Still, it is remarkable the extent to which Paul's argument in the opening chapters of Romans, however informed by the Galatian controversy, merely spells out fundamental features of Paul's missionary message to the Thessalonians and Corinthians — when circumcision and other Jewish boundary markers were not an issue. It was (as we have seen) a message of salvation from divine wrath for all the world through faith in Jesus Christ. Once the issue arose whether his converts should submit to circumcision and other Jewish boundary markers, Paul made more explicit that Jews under the law no less than Gentiles without it could only be saved through faith in Jesus Christ; there was, then, no reason for Gentiles to submit to a divine law that could not, and was not meant to, provide the means by which human beings could be declared righteous. That the issue of boundary markers compelled Paul to formulate the thesis that one is declared righteous by faith in Jesus Christ, not by the works of the law, is the entirely appropriate emphasis of recent scholarship. That the point of the thesis was merely that Gentiles did not need to be circumcised, and not that all human beings, sinners that they are, can only be declared righteous extraordinarily through the death of Christ Jesus, represents the shortsightedness of which some recent scholarship is guilty.

With "But now . . ." Paul introduces God's response to the dilemma posed, not by the exclusion of Gentiles from the blessings of earlier covenants, but by the incorrigible sinfulness of Jews and Gentiles alike. Since the key term in the verses that follow (3:21-26) is "righteousness," their substance has been discussed in chapter 15 above. Here we need note only the following points.

1. God responds to the "unrighteousness" of human beings (1:18; cf. 3:10, 20) with an effective demonstration of his own "righteousness" (3:21). If the term does not refer to his own gift of (extraordinary) righteousness to sinners (cf. Phil. 3:9; also Rom. 5:17; 10:3), it speaks of the salvific *act* by which God declares sinners righteous. That God is righteous in doing so, in this context, is not because he thereby keeps promises made earlier to Abraham (no such promises are here in view), but because he promotes what is good and right in his creation *without* overlooking the sinfulness of sinners (such a violation of the moral order *would* have called in question God's righteousness); rather, he provides atonement for their sins through the sacrificial death of Jesus Christ (3:25-26).[108]

2. The effective demonstration of God's righteousness in Christ was announced in "the law and the prophets" (i.e., the sacred Scriptures), but is (necessarily) operative "apart from the law" (3:21; i.e., the sum of divine commandments given to Israel on Mount Sinai, with the accompanying sanctions).[109] Why must the law be excluded? In this context the problem with the law is not that it does not pertain to Gentiles; on the contrary, Paul has just insisted that Gentiles, too, know its essential requirements (2:14-15) and need to be its "doers" (2:13; cf. 2:26-27). But a law that requires conformity with its commandments cannot provide the basis by which sinners (cf. 3:23) can be declared righteous.

3. Paul stresses the gratuitousness of the righteousness God offers, through Christ, to sinners who believe in Jesus Christ: they are "*freely* declared righteous *by his grace* through the redemption brought about by Christ Jesus" (3:24). The emphasis itself suggests that the righteousness of faith differs from that of the law in this regard; the point is confirmed in chapter 4. The law recognizes the righteousness of those whose works fulfill its demands; such a recognition is granted to achievement rather than given by grace (cf. 4:2-5, 14-16; 11:6). Paul does not deny that the guidance of the law was itself a gift of God's goodness (cf. 2:18; 3:1-2; 9:4). Still less does he suggest that the law was wrong in demanding that people do what is right. It remains the case, however, and of significance to Paul, that a law that demands deeds is not based on grace, whereas the faith by which sinners are declared righteous is.[110]

---

108. See chap. 15, sec. iv and v.
109. On the different uses of "law" in 3:21, see chap. 16, sec. i.
110. See chap. 16, sec. ii above.

Nor is a law that demands deeds one that excludes human "boasting"; to this subject, first prominent in Paul's writings in 1 Corinthians 1, Paul turns in Romans 3:27. The term was introduced already, though without particular emphasis, in 2:17-18: "If you call yourself a Jew, and rely on the law and *boast* in God and know his will. . . ." Boasting is hardly singled out in chapter 2 as the tragic flaw of the Jew, though in the context the pride of Jews in their special relationship with God is thought to be misplaced when they transgress his law.[111] Such pride is at least part of what Paul has in mind in 3:27 as well, as his follow-up question in 3:29 suggests: "Or is God (the God) only of the Jews?"[112] But a law that demands works can excite the boasting, not simply of those to whom it has been entrusted, but more particularly of those who believe themselves to have fulfilled its commands: "For if Abraham was declared righteous because of what he did, he has occasion to boast" (4:2).[113] In short, a law that demands works leaves the door open for human boasting; a "righteousness"[114] granted "freely," "by [God's] grace," "apart from (the) works (of the law)," does not. The exclusion of boasting, first introduced in 3:27, is scarcely the *primary* point Paul makes when he affirms that justification is by faith rather than by the works of the law; it remains nonetheless *a* point that he links to that affirmation here.

The "righteousness of faith" is operative "apart from the law" (3:21). Yet Paul would not be thought to have disregarded or dismissed God's law; he declares rather that he "establishes" it by attributing to it its real function (3:31). Whether he means that the law (in the sense of the divine commandments)

111. Cf. Thompson, "Critique," 525-27.

112. Of course, Jews would not have *said* that God, who is one, is God only of their people: Paul means to show the absurdity of any presumption based on Jewish privileges by pushing such an attitude to its extreme conclusion.

It is, I believe, a mistake to distinguish sharply between a purported Jewish boasting in Israel's election and possession of the covenant and its law (the only boasting that the "new perspective" will allow to be an issue) and boasting in one's fulfillment of the law's commands. After all, being uniquely in possession of the law easily leads to a belief that one is uniquely positioned to please God by obeying the law's commands. Paul has opposed both notions already in 1:18–3:20: Gentiles, too, are aware of God's demands (2:14-15); Jews and Gentiles are under the *same* obligation to do what is right (2:1-29); Jews have fared no better than Gentiles in measuring up to the requirement (3:1-20); hence "*no* flesh (i.e., *no* human being, Jew or Gentile) will be declared righteous by the works of the law" (3:20). In 3:29-30, Paul adds that it is absurd in any case to think that the God of all the nations would provide only for the salvation of one people ("Or is God the God only of the Jews?"); on the contrary, he had proved himself to be God of the Gentiles as well as of the Jews by declaring circumcised and uncircumcised alike to be righteous by faith. See now also Gathercole, *Boasting.*

113. Cf. Thurén, *Derhetorizing Paul,* 169-70, 176-78.

114. I.e., that represented by the "law of faith" (3:27). On the phrase see chap. 16, sec. iii above.

finds its true purpose, not in providing the basis by which sinners can be declared righteous, but in bringing recognition of sin (3:20; 7:7) and defining, highlighting, and condemning transgressions (4:15; 5:13; cf. 5:20; 7:13); or whether, playing on the double sense of "the law," he means that the Scriptures ("the law and the prophets") themselves witness to the righteousness of faith (as he will demonstrate in 4:3), is left unclear.

It is in any case with the example of Abraham, as attested in the Scriptures, that Paul proceeds: the patriarch himself was credited with a righteousness based, not on deeds that would have given him cause for boasting (4:1-2), but on faith in a God who declares the ungodly righteous (4:3-5). David, too, referred to the blessedness of those to whom God credits righteousness apart from their deeds: that, after all, is what he meant when he spoke of the "blessed" whose sins are forgiven (4:6-8). Worth noting — the issue of circumcision had arisen in Galatia and could well arise elsewhere — is that Abraham was credited with righteousness before he was told to be circumcised (4:9-10). Crucial to righteousness was Abraham's faith; that he was found righteous before as well as after he was circumcised makes him a fit "father" of both uncircumcised and circumcised who share his faith (4:11-12).

In Galatians Paul had declared that God made promises to "Abraham and to his [singular] seed," and that that seed was Christ; believers become the "seed of Abraham, heirs in accordance with the promise," only because they "belong to Christ" (Gal. 3:16, 29). In Romans Paul makes the point more directly: a promise was given to Abraham and to "all his seed" — that is, to all, Jews and Gentiles alike, who share in the "righteousness of faith" (4:13, 16). What is important, in Romans as in Galatians, is that the enjoyment of God's promise is not deemed dependent on observance of the law; otherwise the law would preempt both faith and God's promise and would be given a role it cannot perform; rather, the law, by spelling out what should and should not be done, makes wrongdoing the unambiguous violation (the *transgression*) of a divine command and thereby provides an explicit basis for its divine prosecution (4:15).[115] If the divine promise was to find fulfillment (if it was to be secure) among those who so provoke divine wrath, it had to be "according to grace" (4:16), granted to those who, like Abraham, trust in God to transform situations otherwise hopeless (4:17-25). Those so "declared righteous by faith" (5:1) are in good standing with God and can take joy, whatever their present circumstances, in their certain hope of future glory. God proved his love for them when Christ died for them while they were still "ungodly," "sinners," God's declared "ene-

---

115. Cf. Cranfield, *Romans*, 242. Paul's understanding of the function of the law will be discussed in more detail in chap. 19.

mies." That those whom God has now both declared righteous and reconciled will find salvation on the day of his wrath is thus certain (5:1-11).

To this point in the letter Paul has summarized the "gospel" that brings "salvation to every one who believes" (cf. 1:16). The Galatian controversy has remained sufficiently in his mind for him to include the note that physical circumcision is *not* required for God's approval (2:25-29; 4:9-12), nor is observance of the Jewish law a condition if one would share the blessings promised to Abraham (4:13-16). Reference to the latter promise, found in both Romans and Galatians (though not in the Thessalonian or Corinthian correspondence), proves the importance to Paul of showing continuity between his message and the witness and story of the Jewish Scriptures. Still, the central issue in the argument of these chapters, from the declaration of the outpouring of God's wrath in 1:18 to the assurance of salvation from that wrath in 5:9, parallels the thrust of Paul's missionary proclamation as reflected in his other letters: how are human beings to be saved from the judgment that their deeds merit? The focus of his answer, here as elsewhere, is on Christ and on the need to respond with faith to the proclamation of the gospel. Abraham (it may or may not be pointed out) was a model of such faith, and the promise to which he responded was in effect an advance announcement of the gospel (Gal. 3:8; cf. Rom. 4:17-25). Moses (it may but need not be said) was given the law that brought clarity to the human dilemma. But the turning point in human history came, not with Abraham or Moses, but with Christ. The only rival who approximates his importance — though in a negative way — was Adam. Adam[116] was both the first human to be created and the one with whom the corruption of the old creation began; Christ inaugurated the new. To their respective roles Paul now turns.

With Adam sin entered the world, and death and condemnation became the lot of all human beings. So much is clear; to be more specific is to invite controversy.

1. On a minimalist interpretation Adam's concrete sin was the first such sin to be committed (in this sense sin can be said, metaphorically, to have "entered the world"). His example was followed by other human beings, who likewise committed concrete sins. For the sins they commit, all die ("death became the lot of all human beings, inasmuch as all sinned"). Some of what Paul says here is patient of such an interpretation; much, however, is not. If *because of* Adam many died (5:15), were brought under condemnation (5:16), and were made

116. Paul was certainly aware of Eve's presence in the Genesis narrative (cf. 2 Cor. 11:3); his focus on Adam in Rom. 5:12-21 (as in 1 Cor. 15:20-49) follows from his desire to find a single counterpart to Christ. It is of course true that the story of human responsibility and sin can be told without reference to Adam (Paul does so in Rom. 1:18–3:20 and elsewhere), just as the story of redemption can be told without reference to Abraham. The essential figure is Christ.

"sinners" (5:19), then the effects of his sin went far beyond that of setting a bad example for his descendants.[117]

2. At the other extreme, Adam's sin may be thought to have allowed a demonic power ("Sin") to gain a foothold in the world (5:12) and, indeed, to "rule" over its inhabitants (5:21). Paul's references to sin in these terms are thus construed, not as metaphors, but as pointing to a reality in which supernatural forces of evil dominate human affairs. Such a construction of the human plight is often contrasted with its portrayal in Romans 1–3, where Paul speaks only of the concrete sins that people commit.

But such a contrast both *under*interprets Romans 1–3 and *over*interprets Romans 5. Romans 1–3 speaks of the concrete sins that humans commit as illustrative of the "ungodliness and unrighteousness" that prevail among human beings, who "suppress the truth with their unrighteousness" (1:18). Human sin has led to a situation in which humans are incorrigibly sinful: their thoughts have been reduced to futility, their uncomprehending heart has been darkened, they have become foolish, they have been left the hopeless prey of their passions (1:21-24). That humans universally commit sins is a reflection of the universal corruption of human nature: all are "under sin" (3:9).[118] Conversely, in Romans 5 the reading of "Sin" as demonic power, though attractive in places, simply cannot be sustained. Conceivably a demonic power might have gained a foothold in the world through Adam's disobedience ("By one man Sin entered the world" [5:12]), but what would be the point of specifying that such a power was active *before the law was given* ("Before the law Sin [?] was in the world" [5:13a]), and what could it mean to say that a demonic power (Sin) was not "counted" when there was no law (5:13b)? Conceivably a demonic power (Sin), on entering the world, might have brought along with it another such power ("and by Sin [came also] Death" [5:12]); but elsewhere in the passage the presence of death is attributed, not to the power of "Sin," but to the concrete *sins* that Adam and his descendants commit: does "through sin came death" in 5:12 really mean anything more than "by the transgression of one many died" in 5:15? The "sin" that is said to "reign" in 5:21 is the same sin that "increased" with the coming of the law in 5:20b — and that sin is clearly the equivalent of "transgression (παράπτωμα)" in 5:20a. Demonic forces play no part in Paul's argument here.[119]

---

117. Cf. Augustine, *De nupt. et conc.* 2.27.45-46.

118. Cf. Hofius, *Paulusstudien II*, 156: "Seit Adam und von Adam her sind ausnahmslos *alle* Menschen, Juden wie Heiden, unentrinnbar der Sünde verfallen, und zwar nich bloss in ihrem bösen *Tun*, sondern ganz umfassend in ihrem gottfernen und gottfeindlichen *Sein*. Sie sind ἀσεβεῖς — 'Gottlose.'" See also Hofius, *Paulusstudien*, 127.

119. The personification of sin is carried further in Rom. 6, where the Roman believers are urged not to let sin "rule" them (6:12, 14) or to serve any longer as its "slaves" (6:6, 16, etc.). If

3. That sin entered and rules the world means more than that people sin, though it does not refer to the dominance of humans by demonic powers. We ought rather to think (as in Rom. 1–3) of the corruption of human nature[120] from what it was created to be, the sin*fulness* that marks humanity since (and because of) Adam, making human beings "sinners" (5:19) who themselves "commit sins" (5:12). That condemnation and death are the lot of all human beings is thus a consequence of Adam's misdeed while, at the same time, those so afflicted are not innocent.[121] We are all, thought Paul, in this together.[122] The old creation of which we are a part has itself been marred.[123] The coming of the law exacerbated rather than reversed the human condition (5:20).[124]

But Adam's disobedience was offset — and more than offset — by Christ's obedience: if the former deed subjected the old humanity to condemnation and death, the righteous deed of Christ has brought into being a new humanity,[125] the objects of God's grace,[126] whom God finds righteous (5:16, 17, 18, 19, 21) and to whom he grants life (5:17, 18, 21).

After Romans 5 justification does not become a theme in Romans again until chapter 9. On the intervening chapters two observations seem germane.

1. If it was typical for Jews of Paul's day to hold that salvation was by grace; if, in fact, Paul's position on the relation between grace and works was identical

---

such expressions are taken to mean that "Sin" is a demonic power, then the same, presumably, must be said of the "Uncleanness" and "Lawlessness" to which the Roman believers had once given service (6:19). And what supernatural force is meant by the "Obedience" and "Righteousness" to which (to whom?) the believers *are* to yield (6:16, 18, 19)? Cf. Winger, "Grace," 168-74, and esp. Röhser, *Metaphorik*, 103-29.

120. Cf. Becker, *Paul*, 390; Whiteley, *Theology*, 53.

121. Cf. Laato, *Approach*, 100.

122. Cf. Hofius, "Antithesis," 191: "We all of us stand in the shadow of Adam. None of us can go back before Adam."

123. Cf. Hübner, *Theologie*, 270. According to Rom. 8:19-23, even the nonhuman world has been subjected to a corruption from which it will only be delivered when the children of God experience the redemption of their bodies.

124. Paul will expand on this latter point in Rom. 7.

125. "The many" who were affected by Adam's transgression and "the many" who benefit from Christ's righteousness (5:15, 19) refer respectively to the old and the new humanity: God has restored his human creation. Cf. 11:32; 1 Cor. 15:22; and note the universal perspective of Eph. 1:10; Col. 1:20. That Paul here means that all humanity affected by Adam's sin is destined for salvation through Christ's obedience is argued by (among others) Hultgren (*Gospel*, 82-124) and Bell, "Salvation," 417-32; Schreiner is among those who think not (*Paul*, 182-88).

126. Nowhere in Paul's letters does divine grace receive greater emphasis than here; note τὸ χάρισμα, ἡ χάρις, and ἡ δωρεά all in 5:15 alone, τὸ δώρημα and τὸ χάρισμα in 5:16, οἱ τὴν περισσείαν τῆς χάριτος καὶ τῆς δωρεᾶς τῆς δικαιοσύνης in 5:17, and the "superabundance" and "reign" of "grace" in 5:20 and 21.

with that held by many of his contemporaries; and if his rejection of the works of the law from any part in justification meant no more than that Gentiles did not need to observe Jewish boundary markers, then it is curious that *he* was repeatedly called upon to quiet the suspicion that believers, by his gospel, could continue to sin with impunity. That, at least, is the suggestion he emphatically denies in Romans 6. The denial revokes nothing of what was said earlier about grace; rather, it draws out the implications of belonging, with Christ, to the new humanity. Christ shared the conditions of the *old* humanity, though without himself succumbing to sin (cf. 8:3). But he died to the way of life dominated by sin and death, and now lives for God (6:9-10). Believers in Christ are not simply freed from the *condemnation* of their sins (though deliverance from the judgment that looms over sinners is an obvious precondition for enjoying life with God). Their baptism represents the death, with Christ, of a life "serving" sin and the opening up of a new life in God's service (6:11).[127] One cannot in fact be a part of the new humanity and continue to "obey" sin: Paul puts the alternatives starkly (6:16-23), knowing that as long as believers continue in this life, temptations to sin will remain.

2. The several links Paul has drawn in the early chapters of Romans between the law and sin (3:20; 4:15; 5:13, 20; 6:14-15; 7:1-6) demand some clarification of their relation to each other; it is given in 7:7-25. The law itself is holy, its commandments holy, righteous, and good. But when rebellious human beings are confronted by a righteous law, their innate rebellion springs to life and expresses itself in a fatal disobedience (7:7-13).[128]

Paul dramatizes the encounter in a first-person narrative, drawing its substance from a variety of biblical narratives (that telling of Adam and Eve's disobedience in particular, as well as others relating Israel's experience under the Sinaitic law) and, no doubt, from personal observation and experience;[129] but

127. Both Judaism and Paul attempt to motivate right behavior on the part of God's people by noting that it is the only fitting response to what God has already done for them. In spite of some prophetic precedents (cf. Jer. 31:33-34; Ezek. 11:19-20; 36:26-27), however, it was not *typical* of Judaism to see right behavior as first made *possible* by a divine transformation of human beings; rather, the ability to do what God has commanded was generally presupposed. Paul, clearly, thought differently. Cf. Laato, *Approach*, 67-146.

128. More will be said about Paul's understanding of the purpose of the law in chap. 19.

129. Kim, *Origin*, 53, rightly warns us against denying that Paul shared something of the human experiences portrayed in Rom. 7 (i.e., the arousal of desire for what is forbidden in response to its prohibition, and the conflict between the desire to do good and the act of evil): "To deny to Paul these human, all too human, experiences is to make him twice divine. For it would imply that Paul was a superhuman being who was exempted from such experiences as are common to man, and yet that without having suffered them, he could still describe them as vividly as he does in Rom 7. Furthermore, it is to rob Paul's statements about the freedom in Christ

his depiction does not correspond strictly with *any* one story, including his own.[130] His essential point is that the law is not to be confused with sin, though it provokes a sinful response in sinful human beings.

Nonetheless, we may at least see underlying his depiction the same understanding of human depravity as reflected in 1:18–3:20 and 5:12-21: Adamic humanity does not, and — in its present state of corruption — *cannot,* do good.[131] That impotence is depicted in 7:14-25. Yet even here Paul's *point* is that the law must be acknowledged to be good even by those who do not do it. To seek to define whether he has in mind the Christian or the pre-Christian struggle with sin is probably to ask a question he did not intend to answer; indeed, his account seems to mix elements from both.[132] Most of what he says clearly reflects his Christian perception of life lived under the law, but modern scholarship has perhaps too quickly banished *every* suggestion of Christian experience from the passage. 7:24-25, if reflective of *any* experience, would seem to reflect his continuing awareness of the struggle between a mind devoted to God's service and a "flesh" drawn toward sin. Galatians 5:17 speaks of the same conflict, and there the life of believers is undoubtedly in view. To be sure, in the case of

---

from the law of their empirical reality. For he who has had no experience of the bondage of the law (of sin) cannot know freedom from it, either." Cf. also Barrett, "Conscience," 36-48; Beker, *Paul,* 240-43; W. D. Davies, *Studies,* 94; and the balanced comments of Sanders, *Paul Pal. Jud.,* 443-44 n. 5; also Sanders, *Law,* 152-53. Kim goes on to say, however, that other passages in Paul (Gal. 1:14; Phil. 3:4-6) make it clear that before his conversion he did not regard such common experiences as problematic, and that he was "rather satisfied with his achievement in Judaism" (54).

130. Rightly, B. Dodd, *Example,* 230. Cf. what was said earlier in this section about Rom. 1:18-32.

131. Neither of the earlier passages is as explicit about the *inability* of humans to do good as Rom. 7; but the point is consistent with what is said about the corruption of human nature in 1:21-24 and of human beings as "made sinners" through Adam's disobedience in 5:19. On 2:14-15, 26-27 see chap. 15, nn. 22 and 23 above. Rom. 2:14-15 does indeed allow that Gentiles show, whenever they do what the law commands, that they are aware of the requirement to do right. Only a wooden reading of Rom. 7 would find it contradictory of that point: Paul surely does not mean, even in Rom. 7, that human beings (even *unredeemed* human beings) never give to the poor, or that they do not do what is right when they do so. The "Lutheran" tradition, as summarized in Part One of our study, doubtless represents Paul's thinking: it allows that human beings have moral sensibilities (this is Paul's point in 2:14-15; cf. also 12:17; 1 Cor. 5:1; etc.) and do many acts of *relative* goodness while insisting that nothing done by those not rightly related to God can, in any ultimate sense, be God-pleasing or good (cf. Rom. 8:7-8; 14:23). That a bad tree bears bad fruit may not have been said by Paul, but Luther quite rightly (and very frequently) quotes the saying in commenting on Pauline texts. On Phil. 3:6 see sec. v below.

132. "Sold under sin" in 7:14 seems impossible as a Pauline description of the Christian (cf. 6:7, 11); yet the delight in God's law and the fervent desire to do what is right of which Paul speaks in 7:15-25 seem impossible in a Pauline description of the *non*-Christian (cf. 8:5-8).

believers it was not, for Paul, a hopeless struggle: a love that "fulfills the law" is expected of those who "conduct themselves in accordance with God's Spirit" (Rom. 8:4; Gal. 5:14). But the Paul who in *this* context longs for deliverance from "the body of this death" (Rom. 7:24; cf. 8:23) undoubtedly had in mind its ever present propensities toward sin as well as its physical weaknesses.[133]

The challenges presented by Romans 9–11 go far beyond what can — or needs to be — covered here;[134] but neither can they be totally ignored. For our purposes the following comments must suffice.

1. That human beings can only be declared righteous by faith and because of Jesus Christ is emphatically reaffirmed in these chapters. The righteousness of faith is for Jews and Gentiles alike, and only through it can they be saved (10:6-13). The pathos and point of this section in Romans have their roots in that conviction — and in the observation that most Jews, to date, have rejected the gospel. They are wrongly pursuing righteousness through keeping the law's commands (through works) rather than through faith.[135] Paul can only pray for their salvation (10:1) and do whatever he can, however indirect (11:13-14), to promote it. But even the eventual salvation of "all Israel" — in which Paul fervently believes — will only take place when Israel as a whole abandons its unbelief (11:26-27 cannot be detached from vv. 23-24).

2. Paul affirms that *Israel* is the object of God's election and will one day (necessarily through faith) find salvation (11:26-29). That many Jews do not now believe does not mean that God's purposes for his people have failed — and that for three reasons. (a) Not every descendant of Abraham need belong to the Israel whom God has elected: God's call, not physical descent, is decisive (9:6-13). (b) Moreover, the unbelief of the majority of Israel is a temporary thing: a divine hardening that serves divine purposes, but lasting only until the full complement of Gentiles has believed. (c) In the meantime there are Jews even now who believe, thus making up the present "remnant" that testifies to God's continuing relations with his people (9:27-29; 11:1-6).

3. Paul's depiction of the *nature* of Israel's sin and redemption is shaped by his Christian convictions; but the pattern itself of sin, judgment, and ultimate redemption is completely traditional. Every crisis in Israel's history provoked

133. Ziesler ("Role," 41-56; cf. also Laato, *Approach,* 125-26) suggests that, throughout Rom. 7, Paul has in mind the inability of humans to control their desires as the respect in which they *cannot* keep the law (i.e., the prohibition of coveting); the suggestion echoes Augustine's reading of the chapter, which focuses on the "concupiscence" (the "hankering for sin," also seen as a violation of the tenth commandment) that is never fully overcome in this life, even by the believer; cf. *De spir. et litt.* 4.6; 36.65; *C. duas epp. Pel.* 1.10.18–1.11.24.

134. Cf., more substantially, my article "Romans 9–11."

135. On Rom. 9:30–10:13, see chap. 16, sec. iii.

reflection on the sin that had brought divine judgment. Beyond crime and punishment lay redemption — inevitably, given God's commitment to his people. From that redemption and the ultimate salvation of "Israel" certain incorrigible Jews would be excluded (cf. Ezek. 11:21, qualifying 11:17-20; *m. Sanh.* 10:1-4, qualifying the introductory statement of 10:1). The notion that these chapters betray the hopeless contradiction between Paul's conviction that salvation is only to be found in Christ and his continuing commitment to his compatriots fails to recognize how worn is the path Paul treads.

4. Paul's insistence that God calls his people by an act of grace without regard for their works (9:11-16; 11:5-6) coheres nicely with his insistence that righteousness is attained through faith, not works (9:30-32; 10:5-13; earlier, 4:1-8).[136] His claim that the objects of salvation are the disobedient who find mercy (11:30-32) parallels what he says about the justification of sinners in the opening chapters of the epistle. And his observation that Jews, failing to submit to the righteousness God offers, continue trying to establish their "own" (10:3), means that they are still attempting, by doing what they should, to gain recognition for "ordinary" righteousness rather than recognizing the need of all for God's extraordinary gift. They have not misconstrued the law in thinking that it demands works (cf. 10:5); they have, however, failed to see that the righteousness demanded by the law can only be attained by faith in Christ (9:30-32), whose coming marks the "end of the law" as a path to righteousness (10:4).

5. What, in the Pauline corpus, is *new* in Romans 9–11 is the insistence that Israel's election and the commitments God made to the patriarchs will eventuate in the future salvation of (*now* unbelieving) Israel (11:25-32).[137] Elsewhere Paul typically appropriates Israel's prerogatives for the church (e.g., Phil. 3:3); he confines the "seed" of Abraham to whom promises have been made to Christ and those who belong to him (Gal. 3:16, 29), or to those who show Christian faith (Rom. 4:11-16); or he insists that, though God has been good to Israel, the privileges they have received carry with them no presumption of approval on the day when God judges all people without partiality (2:1–3:20). The blessing invoked on the "Israel of God" in Galatians 6:16 might conceivably be a harbinger of Romans 11:26; in the context of Galatians, however, it seems more likely to be another instance where the language of God's people is applied to the church.[138] The notion that unbelieving Israel — as a whole, though not necessarily every individual Jew, and not without coming to faith in Christ — is, because of its election, destined for salvation is unique to these chapters.

---

136. Cf. Hübner, *Theologie,* 316.
137. Cf. Becker, *Paul,* 469.
138. Cf. n. 84 above.

It is in these chapters (11:16-24), too, that we find the people of God pictured as a single olive tree whose branches, to start with, were the Jews. Gentile believers have been grafted into that tree, and, to be sure, unbelieving Jews have (at least temporarily) been broken off. But here Paul indicates — what, to judge by his epistles, he had not said to the Thessalonians, Corinthians, and even the Galatians — that believing Gentiles gain admission to a people of God constituted already *before Christ came*.[139]

The novelty of the indication should not be exaggerated: one cannot imagine Paul ever denying that David, the prophets, and the seven thousand who were faithful in Elijah's day (11:2-4) were recognized by God as his people.[140] On the other hand, it should not be underestimated either. That a covenant with *Israel* as such remains in force and will lead to that people's salvation, its present *un*belief notwithstanding, is a *mystery* that Paul discloses here to the Roman Christians (11:25-29). Paul's Gentile mission was *not* predicated all along on the conviction that Christ brought blessings to Gentiles already enjoyed — *apart* from Christ — by Jews under their "covenant." Rather, Paul was bringing to Gentiles the same gospel that other apostles took to Jews — because *both* needed to be saved (Gal. 2:7-9; cf. 1 Cor. 15:11).

With the parenesis of Romans 12–16 we need not concern ourselves here.

How "Lutheran" is Romans? It seems fair to say that all the essential features of the "Lutheran" Paul find support in Romans, though the emphases of the Reformer are not always those of the apostle. The doctrine of justification by faith is indeed the divine response to the dilemma posed, not by the earlier exclusion of Gentiles from the covenant, but by God's demand of righteousness from all human beings, none of whom is righteous (2:6-13; 3:9-20). The works (or works of the law) by which no flesh can be declared righteous (3:20, 28) are not the boundary markers that distinguish Jews from Gentiles, but the righteous deeds that God requires of all human beings. Jews continue to pursue righteousness through such works (9:32); this pursuit Paul finds misguided, not because the law does not demand works (cf. 2:13; 10:5), but because no one *is* righteous, and God has provided for the righteousness of sinners, through Christ, by faith. Justification is thus a gift of grace, received through faith, not gained by works. Received in this way, it excludes the possibility of human boasting (3:27; 4:2) — an observation that receives less emphasis in Romans than in Luther's writings, but is undeniably Pauline. Paul says, too, that the law brings recognition of sin (3:20); according to Romans 7, it provokes dormant

---

139. In Galatians Paul sees believers, through Christ, as the seed of Abraham (3:16, 29); it is *not* said, however, that Abraham had "children" in this sense before Christ.

140. On the place of "Old Testament saints" in Paul's thought, see chap. 15, n. 44.

sin into rebellious expression and makes its sinfulness apparent (7:7-13). If Paul's focus here (unlike that of Luther's primary purpose of the law) is not on the sense of guilt and dismay that the law brings to individual sinners, 1:18–3:20 surely supports the conclusion drawn above from 1 Thessalonians that Paul's missionary preaching included reference to humanity's failure to meet divine requirements and consequent expectation of judgment.

That — as the new perspective on Paul emphasizes — Gentiles need not be circumcised is certainly part of what Paul says in Romans, as he did in Galatians. But in both letters the reason given is not that blessings already enjoyed by Jews are available now for Gentiles as well, but that sinners are justified, apart from the law, by faith in Jesus Christ.

v. Philippians[141]

Our interest in Philippians here is largely confined to 3:2-11, where Paul warns his converts about those who advocate circumcision and tells of his own rejection of the "righteousness of the law" in order to embrace the "righteousness of faith." Otherwise we need only note the following.

1. In Philippians, as in the other letters we have looked at, it is clear that the message Paul originally proclaimed to his readers was one of salvation from the perdition otherwise facing the world (here the "crooked and perverted generation" of 2:15; cf. 1:28).

2. The salvation of Paul's converts, here as elsewhere, is attributed to God (1:28), who "began a good work in them" (1:6) by granting them the privilege to believe in Christ (1:29) as preached by Paul in the gospel (cf. 1:5, 7, 12; 2:22; 4:3, 15).

3. The good that believers are now able (and expected) to do is itself the work of God through Jesus Christ (1:11), in that God both directs their will so that they desire what pleases him and enables them to do it (2:13).[142]

---

141. Philippians was written *after* Romans if it was written from Rome, *before* Romans if written from Ephesus. I treat the letter here since I think the evidence slightly favors the former alternative; but nothing in my reading of Philippians depends on the chronology — nor would it be affected if the letter, as we have it, includes parts of two or three letters from Paul to Philippi.

142. Cf. Augustine, *De grat. et lib. arb.* 16.32: "It is certain that it is we that *will* when we will, but it is He who makes us will what is good, of whom it is said . . . , 'The will is prepared by the Lord' [Prov 8:35 LXX]. . . . It is certain that it is we that act when we act; but it is He who makes us act, by applying efficacious powers to our will, who has said, 'I will make you to walk in my statutes, and to observe my judgments, and to do them' [Ezek 36:27]."

4. The "good work" that God has begun in them is one that God will bring to completion (1:6; cf. 1 Thess. 5:23-24). That he must do so follows from the nature of salvation as a future hope (cf. Rom. 5:9; 8:24; 13:11) to be attained by those who maintain their initial faith throughout their lives (cf. 11:22; 1 Cor. 15:2; Gal. 4:11; Phil. 2:16; 1 Thess. 3:5). On one level, then, it is crucial that the Philippians themselves continue in the path that leads to their salvation (which they thus "work out," 2:12).[143] As they do so, however, they need to recognize that God himself, working in and through them, brings about whatever they do (2:13).

Nothing Paul writes in Philippians 3 suggests that advocates of circumcision were present in Philippi; he seems rather to be writing as a precautionary measure against the possibility of their arrival. Perhaps because of the lack of a present threat, perhaps also because his good relations with the Philippians lead him to believe that his mere warning will suffice, he deals with the matter briefly and without any of the theological argumentation invoked especially in Galatians, but also in Romans. For his friends in Philippi, Paul believed, he needed only to say that from his own experience he knew all about the "righteousness of the law" — and he had rejected it.

As in Galatians, Paul identifies his own pre-Christian experience with the position of those who would impose circumcision on his Gentile converts; in both cases the Sinaitic law was thought to provide the framework within which the people of God must live. Any who thought they measured up well by its standards should know that Paul had done even better (3:4): not only was his heritage impeccable, but he himself had observed the law according to the strict and expert interpretation of the Pharisees,[144] and he had proven his zeal by per-

---

143. Does Paul then think, after all, that believers must contribute to their own salvation? The anxiety he more than once betrays to qualify statements of what believers achieve with an assurance that God (or God's grace, or Christ) is the effective agent suggests that he does not see it that way; see Eastman, *Grace,* 44 (of 1 Cor. 15:10; 2 Cor. 3:5), 86 (of Gal. 4:9), 89 (of 2:20), 195-96, 198 (of Phil. 2:13); and note Augustine, *De gest. Pel.* 14.36: "O mighty teacher, confessor, and preacher of grace! What meaneth this: 'I laboured more, yet not I?' Where the will exalted itself ever so little, there piety was instantly on the watch, and humility trembled, because weakness recognised itself." Clearly Paul did *not* think that an act of grace brought those who believe *into* the people of God but that they now must maintain their status by their *own* deeds; he could not be more emphatic that anything they do even as believers remains a product of divine grace. Note, too, that it is frequently the necessity of persisting in *faith* that Paul stresses (Rom. 11:22; 1 Cor. 15:2; 1 Thess. 3:5). It is nonetheless true that he expects the faith of believers to be expressed in appropriate actions and denies a place in God's kingdom to those of whom this is not true (cf. Rom. 8:13; 1 Cor. 6:9-10; Gal. 5:19-21). As Calvin put it, "we are justified not without works yet not through works" (*Inst.* 3.16.1).

144. Cf. Baumgarten, "Name," 411-28.

secuting the church. In short, his performance, as he judged it by the righteousness of the law, was "blameless" (3:4-6). On the claims Paul here makes, the following observations should be borne in mind.

1. The righteousness of the law for Paul included both his Jewish heritage (the Israelite family into which he was born, his circumcision as an infant) and the conformity of his own behavior with the requirements of the law. For a Gentile convert to Judaism, only the latter could come in question. Paul seems, however, to regard native Jewishness as preferable.

2. Both the Jewishness of one's heritage and one's conformity with the law invite comparison with the claims of others: Paul, indeed, boasts of his superior merits on both counts. Here we may recall that, according to Romans 3:27, "boasting" (in the privileges enjoyed by Jews and in deeds done in fulfillment of the law) is *not* excluded by the "law of works."

3. The point Paul is making is that he knows the righteousness of the law as well as any and surpassed others in its performance, so that the Philippians may safely trust his judgment, follow his example, and reject the advocates of the law: that is his *point*.[145] From what he says one may also *infer* that he did not suffer from poor self-esteem, nor was his conscience of an introspective, troubled sort.[146] On the other hand, it would be wrong to conclude from what Paul says here that he saw nothing unsatisfactory in the righteousness of the law and only opted for faith in Christ because it somehow seemed even better. Though "blameless" from his former perspective, his persecution of the church (3:6) could only have appeared to him, from the moment he encountered the risen Christ, as a bad thing to have done (cf. 1 Cor. 15:9).[147] And all his merits under the law he characterizes as belonging to the realm of the flesh (Phil. 3:3-4). For Paul that means that they could not please God (cf. Gal. 3:3; Rom. 8:7-8); true service is carried out by the *Spirit* of God (Phil. 3:3).

Nonetheless, the dramatic change in the direction of Paul's life can be explained by the glories of Christ that he embraced at least as well as by the limitations of the law that he left behind; and here Paul focuses on the former (3:8-

---

145. Cf. Thielman, *Plight*, 110.

146. Cf. the summary of Stendahl in chap. 8, sec. ii above. Note, however, the qualifications of Espy, "Conscience," 161-88.

147. Cf. Deidun, "Cake," 51: "In [Phil. 3] v. 6 [Paul] recalls a fact which . . . Paul never allows his readers to forget (but which Sanders never mentions): that his former righteousness, seemingly at the very point of its perfection, made him a zealous persecutor of the Church. His mention of it here makes it difficult to understand Sanders' inferences from this passage, namely, that Paul considered his former righteousness to be '*in and of itself a good thing.*' . . . It is surely not too much to suppose that Paul could never have considered to be intrinsically good the righteousness which drove him to do what he was most to regret."

11). Knowing Christ, and having the righteousness God offers through faith in him[148] rather than that based on his own conformity with the law, are now his goals. He pursues them, fully aware that to share in the power of Christ's resurrection entails a share in his sufferings and death.

vi. Ephesians, the Pastorals — and James?

According to Romans 3:20, 28, no human being is declared righteous by the works of the law. In the context, Paul's argument makes clear that these works amount to the doing of good that God requires of all human beings, Gentiles and Jews alike (2:7, 10; cf. "doers of the law," 2:13). Hence the same point is made when Paul says that one is declared righteous "apart from [unspecified] works" (4:2, 5-6; cf. 9:32): apart, that is, from the good works of which one might boast (4:2) or by which one might be thought to have earned recognition as righteous; rather, such recognition is granted paradoxically to the "ungodly" as a gift of grace (4:4-5).

The same Pauline themes find restatement in Ephesians and the Pastorals: human beings are sinners and, as such, destined for wrath rather than salvation; but God offers to them salvation quite apart from the "deeds of righteousness" he otherwise requires, as an act of divine grace.[149] We may add that both Ephesians and the Pastorals insist that, though not saved *by* good works, believers have been saved *for* them.

The readers of Ephesians are described as having been "dead in their trespasses and sins,"[150] misdeeds that are seen as characteristic of "the age of this world" and in keeping with the nature and desires of its satanic ruler (2:1-2). Human beings follow the desires of their "flesh" and "thinking," but these have been so corrupted[151] that all are "by *nature* children of wrath" (2:3). But though such was the readers' past, they have been brought to life, together with Christ, in a demonstration of the extraordinary opulence of divine grace (2:4-7). "For

---

148. To "have righteousness" from another — even when the other is God — remains a curious locution; cf. the discussion of "extraordinary righteousness" in chap. 15, sec. iii above. For the reading "through faith *in* Christ" for διὰ πίστεως Χριστοῦ in Phil. 3:9, see Koperski, "Meaning," 198-216.

149. Cf. Marshall, "Salvation," 339-58. Marshall's article provides a counterbalance to Luz, "Rechtfertigung," which maximizes perceived differences between Paul on the one hand and Ephesians and the Pastorals on the other.

150. "Trespasses" and "sins" here seem synonymous; the heaping up of synonymous terms is typical of the letter. Cf. Best, *Essays*, 74-75.

151. Cf. 4:17-18. The corruption of the "old" humanity requires that it be replaced by a new, "created *according to God* [= in the divine image, from which the old humanity had fallen? cf. Col. 3:10] in righteousness and holiness of the truth" (4:22-24).

you have been saved by grace, through faith. This does not come from you, but is the gift of God; it is not of works, lest anyone should boast. For we are God's workmanship; we have been created in Christ Jesus for good works, which God prepared beforehand in order that we should live in them" (2:8-10).

"Saved," "by grace," "through faith,"[152] "not of works," "lest anyone should boast":[153] it is hard to imagine a more compact yet comprehensive statement of the themes we have seen in Paul. The formulation itself departs in certain respects from its Pauline predecessors. In Galatians and Romans one is "declared righteous" rather than "saved" by "faith" — though, to be sure, Romans 5:9 assures us that those who have been "declared righteous" *will* be "saved," and "salvation" is indeed the general Pauline term for the good offered in the gospel.[154] Salvation itself is generally a future hope — a *certain* hope, to be sure, for those who believe — in the acknowledged Pauline epistles rather than, as in Ephesians 2:8, something already possessed. Variations in detail there are; but 2:8-10 remains as fine a statement as any of Paul's "Lutheranism."[155]

Its closest rival in that regard is perhaps Titus 3:4-7. "We" were once "unintelligent, disobedient, lost in error, slaves of lusts and sundry pleasures, living in malice and envy, hateful and hating one another" (3:3). Clearly "we" were not the sort of people who could be saved by "works done in righteousness that we performed" (3:5)[156] — though our author makes *very* clear that he has no objections to such works in principle, and indeed expects them to be done by believers (3:1, 8, 14; cf. 2:7, 14). "Our" salvation was rather brought about "according to his mercy through the cleansing of our rebirth and the renewing work of the Holy Spirit, whom God poured lavishly upon us through Jesus Christ our Savior so that, having been *justified by his grace,* we might become heirs in our

---

152. "Faith" here is the response shown by people who "heard the word of truth, the gospel of [their] salvation" (1:13; cf. 1:15, 19).

153. Speaking of Eph. 2:8-9, Barclay (*Truth,* 251) notes: "This passage is proof that an aversion to individual self-righteous attitudes is not an invention of the Reformation, or even of Augustine!"

154. Note, too, that "those who are being saved" in 1 Cor. 1:18 are the same as "the believers" (whom God "saves" through the apostolic kerygma) in 1:21. It is, of course, the "believers" in Thessalonica (1 Thess. 1:7) who are "delivered" from the "wrath to come" (1:10).

155. Lincoln, "Summary," 617-30, concludes that "the sort of generalization of justification and focus on grace found in Augustine has a precedent within the canonical Paul of Ephesians where works represent human effort and performance which can obscure the gracious activity of God in providing a complete salvation" (628).

156. Marshall, "Salvation," 350, esp. n. 34, notes that 3:5 could be interpreted as saying that, though the readers "had done some righteous deeds, nevertheless God took no account of these in showing pure mercy to them"; but the context strongly suggests that the point is rather that they "had not done any righteous deeds on the basis of which they might conceivably have been saved."

hope of eternal life" (3:5-7). 2 Timothy 1:9 stresses, too, that God saved us, "not according to our works, but according to his own purpose and grace, given to us in Christ Jesus before times eternal" — though but recently revealed. In each of these cases, Ephesians and the Pastorals echo Paul's own insistence that God saves sinners by his grace, through Christ, apart from the righteous deeds he requires but does not find in fallen humanity.[157]

On page 449 of Sanders's *Paul and Palestinian Judaism* there is a one-line footnote (n. 9) in which the perfect tense of σεσωσμένοι in Ephesians 2:5, 8 is said to represent "a distinct theological development" (Paul generally spoke of salvation in the present or future). There is no other reference to Ephesians 2:8-10, 2 Timothy 1:9, or Titus 3:4-7 in either *Paul and Palestinian Judaism* or *Paul, the Law, and the Jewish People* — or for that matter in Dunn's *Jesus, Paul, and the Law*[158] or Wright's *The Climax of the Covenant*. The omission is of course not unjustifiable: these letters, for a variety of reasons, are widely considered to have been written by someone *other* than Paul and are therefore commonly disregarded in studies of Paul's thought.[159] One cannot but feel, however, that the omission, in this case at least, is unfortunate. No study that took Ephesians and the Pastorals into account could conclude, what proponents of the new perspective have sometimes claimed, that the Pelagian crisis or sixteenth-century controversies are the source of the "misreading" of Paul that sees him excluding human works from salvation rather than particular works from the terms for Gentile admission to the people of God.[160]

---

157. Cf. Kruse, *Paul,* 270.

158. Dunn's *Theology* does, however, cite these texts, though with the insistence that the perspective is no longer that of Paul: "in Eph. 2.8-9, . . . the issue does seem to have moved from one of works of law to one of human effort. But when the texts in the undisputed Pauline letters are read within the context of Paul's mission emerging from its Jewish matrix, the resulting picture is rather different. Within that context we gain a clear picture of Paul fiercely resisting his own earlier pre-Christian assumption that God's righteousness was only for Israel, and only for Gentiles if they became Jews and took on the distinctive obligations of God's covenant with Israel. . . . The danger which he particularly confronted was that ethnic identity would in the event count for more than the gracious call of God or significantly determine and qualify that call" (371).

159. I myself devoted only a footnote to them in *Israel's Law and the Church's Faith* (166 n. 64), though one that makes the same point I argue here: "Such texts ought at least to warn us that 'Reformation spectacles' are not required to read Paul as denying that human 'works' are a factor in salvation."

160. Cf. Marshall, "Salvation," 358: "The earliest interpretation of the Pauline *Hauptbriefe* in Ephesians and the Pastoral Epistles understands Paul to be denying that God acted in Christ on the basis of human works that might have predisposed him to favour humankind. . . . A question mark is thus placed against the view that Paul was opposed to 'works of the law' simply as the symbols of a Judaism which excluded the Gentiles. Rather, Paul was opposed to any view that regards works as something on which people may depend for salvation rather than purely

Nor was it only first-century "friends" (or disciples) who so construed the apostle. We have already noted in Paul's letters his response to those who thought his emphasis on grace, or his exclusion of the law, permitted (or even promoted) moral license (cf. Rom. 3:8; 6:1, 15; 1 Cor. 6:12; 10:23; Gal. 2:17; 5:13). To their voices we should add that of James, for it is hard to see anyone other than Paul as the (ultimate) *source* behind the view, opposed by James, that one can be justified or saved by faith apart from works — with Abraham as the test case (James 2:14-26);[161] and the works at the center of the controversy are not the distinctively Jewish requirements of the law, but works in general in which obedience to God, or even basic human decency, is shown: the clothing and feeding of the needy, Abraham's willingness to sacrifice his son, and Rahab's preservation of the Israelite spies are cited as examples (2:14-17, 21-25). Here we have, in the words of Friedrich Avemarie, "a very old perspective on Paul."[162] It suggests that by first-century critics, as by Augustine, Luther, and many others, Paul was deemed to have dismissed any role for (good) works in answering the perennial religious question of how a human being can be found acceptable by God.[163] It makes very clear that an insistence that salvation is by faith and grace, not (good) works, was anything but self-evident and uncontroversial in Paul's day. And it underlines the novelty of the new perspective that would limit his concerns to issues deemed more pressing by the modern mind: ethnocentrism, racism, and nationalistic pride.[164]

---

upon divine grace." Avemarie, "Werke," 304-5, cites also Polycarp, *Letter to the Philippians* 1.3 and *1 Clement* 32.4 as examples of post-Pauline texts that understood the thesis of justification apart from works in a "quasi-Reformational" way.

161. Cf. Penna, *Paul*, 93-94. Avemarie, "Werke," 289, shows the astonishing degree of verbal correspondence between James and Paul in these verses. We need not concern ourselves here with whether the target of James's polemic was Paul himself or his interpreters. For Augustine's insistence that there is no true contradiction between James's point and the writings of Paul, see the discussion in chap. 1 above; Luther, famously, was dubious about their possible harmonization (see, e.g., *Pref. James*, 35:395-96). In addition to Avemarie's discussion of the relation between Paul and James, cf., recently, Laato, "Justification," 43-84.

162. Such is the subtitle of Avemarie's "Werke."

163. Cf. Penna, *Paul*, 113.

164. Cf. Matlock, "Studies," 439 (responding to the insistence of Stendahl, Sanders, and Dunn that Paul's thought must be reconstructed in categories of his own time and place, not those of a later age): "The susceptibility of the . . . axioms of the new perspective to analysis as arising from, or at least as being in keeping with, contemporary concerns makes the stance of objectivity look immediately suspect. . . . For indeed, we moderns are not typically concerned so much about sin and guilt and forgiveness as we are about notions of community, so that *our* theological climate is reflected here." Also 442-43: In "new perspective" writings, Paul at times sounds "surprisingly liberal, Western and pluralist — and that after all the warnings of his *distance* from us (leaving us to ask once more whether Luther's Paul comes to grief more for his failure to fit the twentieth century than the first)."

Chapter 19

The Law in God's Scheme

As readers of mysteries make their way through a book, they tend to match wits with the author. From the opening pages they begin formulating their own ideas of what has taken place, or will take place, and of who is responsible for what. Approaching the end of a novel, they like to think they have figured things out; they read on, anxious to confirm their suspicions.

The end is the supreme test of the author's mettle: in a well-crafted mystery it will both surprise readers and at the same time compel their admission that it makes perfect sense in the light of what preceded it. Details overlooked in a first reading of the book now prove significant. The perfection of the "perfect ending" lies partly in its capacity to release whatever emotional tensions the novel may have roused in its readers, but partly also in the sense of appropriateness with which it leaves them. Rightly understood, they feel, the book *could* not have ended in any other way.

The revelation that Paul received of God's Son (Gal. 1:15-16) provided just such a surprising climax to the drama of divine redemption, requiring him to reassess and reconstrue a story he thought he had understood. The earlier protagonists in the story remained the same: Adam, Abraham, Moses. . . . What he understood them to have said and done did not change: after all, *that* part of the story had long since been fixed in Holy Writ. But his understanding of their roles and significance needed rethinking now that the mystery of redemptive history had been resolved and Jesus was seen as its climax. When the spotlight shifted to Christ, then Adam, Abraham, and Moses necessarily looked very different.

So, too, did the Mosaic law. Prior to Damascus Paul was as fervent as any Jew in his pursuit of its righteousness. *After* Damascus he was convinced that the only viable path to righteousness, for Jew and Gentile alike, was by faith in Christ. In important respects Christ took the place once occupied by the law in

Paul's thinking. Yet the law remained divine, its commands "holy, righteous, and good" (Rom. 7:12). Paul's Christian convictions compelled him to rethink what God's purpose for the law might have been.

"Lutheran" tradition is united in thinking that the law was meant to bring sinners to see their need for the Savior. That the claim derives from a reading of Paul is self-evident; whether the claim construes him correctly will be explored below. The "Lutheran" interpreters of Paul at whom we looked in Part One also agreed in thinking that, though Christians are not justified by the Mosaic law and are not bound by its ceremonial regulations, their conduct ought nonetheless to conform to its moral commands. The adequacy of this interpretation, too, will be tested.

In what follows I will attempt to sum up Paul's *Christian* understanding of the Mosaic law in a series of theses and to say something about the origin of each in his pre- or post-Damascus thinking.[1] Much has been said about the law in earlier chapters and requires only brief recapitulation here. A few of the theses represent restatements of positions I advanced in the tenth chapter of *Israel's Law and the Church's Faith* — a chapter that attracted more critique by itself than the rest of the book put together. In the present monograph I have done what I could to distribute objectionable material more equitably among the chapters of Part Three, but it is perhaps inevitable that an imbalance remains. Paul has not made things easy for us, insisting as he does that believers are not "under the law" while maintaining that they nonetheless "fulfill" it. One is an antinomian if one highlights the former declaration, a legalist if one focuses on the latter, and a hopeless harmonizer (perhaps in combination with one of the other two epithets) if one attempts to do justice to both. You pay your money and you make your choice.

> Thesis 1: Human beings find themselves in an ordered world not of their making, with the capacity to acknowledge or deny their dependence on the Creator, to conform to or defy the wise ordering of his creation. Life and divine favor are enjoyed by those who fear the Lord and do good. Those who reject what is good and do what is "wise in their own eyes" court disaster.[2]

There is nothing distinctively Pauline in the notions that human beings are accountable to their Maker and that their deeds bear consequences; indeed, my

---

1. The theses are largely taken over from my article "Sinai," 147-65. Material from my *Law*, 174-218, has also been incorporated.

2. Cf. what was said about "ordinary dikaiosness" in chap. 15, sec. ii.

formulation of the thesis owes more to the language of Proverbs than to that of Paul. But its substance finds articulation in Romans 1:18–2:29 and is presupposed wherever Paul condemns human *un*righteousness and anticipates divine judgment. The eternal power and deity of God, Paul argues in Romans 1, may be inferred from his created order. When, therefore, people refuse to acknowledge him or give him thanks — when they focus their devotion on creatures rather than the Creator — their conduct is both willful and inexcusable. Divine judgment is at work when those who thus close their minds to the most basic truth about their existence proceed to further violations of nature's order: they must live with the consequences of their deeds in a world marred by human violence, insolence, and irresponsibility. Nor is judgment confined to the bane of sin in this world. Still to come (Paul maintains in Rom. 2) is the day of God's righteous judgment, when life everlasting will be bestowed on all who do what is good, but wrath poured out on those who do evil. The principle applies, Paul insists, to Jews and Gentiles alike.

For our purposes the absence of any reference to the law in Romans 1:18–2:11 is significant. Merely to be a moral creature in God's world, Paul believes, is to be bound to do what is good and to avoid evil (cf. 2:6-10). Most fundamental is the duty to give God his due; those who receive life from the hands of God respond appropriately with thanks and praise. To refuse to do so, and thereby to suppress knowledge of human dependence on God, is senseless, perverse — and the precursor of other acts that are "contrary to nature (παρὰ φύσιν)" and "unfitting (τὰ μὴ καθήκοντα)" (cf. 1:26-28).

The expressions "fitting" and "unfitting," as well as "according to nature" and "contrary to nature," were used by many in antiquity. For Paul in Romans 1 they serve to define the good to be pursued and the evil to be shunned. Human beings are born into an already ordered cosmos. Nonhuman creation instinctively conforms to its order. For their part humans are faced with the moral choice of patterning their behavior in accordance with nature's order, thus doing what "befits" them, or of defying it. Since even the defiant inevitably participate in, and depend on, the wise ordering of the cosmos, such would-be declarations of independence are both preposterous and highly "unfitting."

They are also, Paul maintains, inexcusable. Those who act perversely and applaud the perverse do so, he claims, in deliberate defiance of the judgment of God (1:32). Those who do what is right, he goes on to say, thereby show their awareness of its claims upon them (2:14-15). *All* are subject to the demands of the good, demands inherent in their status as moral creatures in God's world. And their waywardness cannot be excused by ignorance.

This first thesis, though fundamental to Paul's thinking as a Christian, he doubtless picked up in Tarsus or Jerusalem rather than on the road to Damascus. Its clearest expression in the Jewish Scriptures (as suggested above) is to be found in the book of Proverbs: "The fear of the Lord is the beginning of wisdom" (9:10); "Do not be wise in your own eyes; fear the Lord and turn from evil" (3:7); "The one who finds [wisdom] finds life and gains favor from the Lord; the one who misses [wisdom] harms his own soul; all who hate [wisdom] love death" (8:35-36).

Indeed, as suggested above, the perspective in Romans 1 has close parallels in pagan thought as well. The language of "fitting" and "unfitting" behavior, of conduct "according to nature" or "contrary to nature," echoes Stoic formulations. A major difference between the thinking of most ancients and that of many in the modern West is that whereas the former saw it as a human responsibility to *discover* what is good, many moderns think they must themselves *decide* what is good. The shift is fundamental. Implicit in the ancient posture is the perception that humans are not the source of the order of the cosmos, though it is their vocation to discern and affirm it. Implicit in the modern posture is the notion that the nonhuman creation has no inherent goodness of its own, that value and meaningful order were not introduced to the cosmos prior to the (rather tardy) appearance of Homo sapiens, and that humans are free to impose whatever shape they please on their lives and environment. The ancient perspective is demonstrably that of Paul.

Thesis 2: The law of Moses articulates the appropriate human response to life in God's creation. It is a divine gift to Israel, a signal token of God's favor to his people.[3]

If our first thesis is most explicit in Romans 1:18–2:11, the second finds its primary expression in 2:12-29. The underlying assumption of the passage appears to be that though all people possess some nagging awareness of the demand to do good and avoid evil, their moral perceptions have been clouded by their predilection for evil (cf. 1:21). As a result, human beings are thought to be well served by a law that reminds them of their fundamental responsibilities. Such a reminder, providing plain guidance of what is at the same time God's will and appropriate behavior for all human beings, has been given to Jews in the law of Moses. So favored, Jews are in a position to instruct Gentiles of things that Gentiles, too, need to know — to be "guide[s] for the blind, light[s] for those in darkness, instructor[s] of fools, teacher[s] of the young." Thus the "knowledge and truth" that Paul sees embodied in the Mosaic law (2:19-20) are manifestly

---

3. Again, see the discussion of "ordinary dikaiosness" in chap. 15, sec. ii.

thought to be of universal application, though Jewish apprehension of the truth has been facilitated by the gift of the law.

From Romans 2 alone, no reader would suspect that the Mosaic law contains precepts peculiar to Israel. All people, Paul insists, will be judged by whether their deeds are good or evil. Nothing in the passage suggests that "good" and "evil" have different contents for different people. In this passage, at least, it is primarily the form in which people encounter the universal moral demands that separates Jews from Gentiles. Jews learn them from the law of Moses.[4]

In this second thesis, too, there is nothing specifically Christian. Already in Deuteronomy the "statutes and ordinances" given to Israel were thought to be recognizably righteous in the eyes of other nations (Deut. 4:5-8).[5] If Proverbs prescribes the pursuit of wisdom for all people without reference to the Mosaic law, later Wisdom literature identified Torah with the wisdom of the created order; in Sirach 24, for example, as in Romans 2, Jews are seen as having privileged access to universal norms. And Philo repeatedly makes the claim that the "law of nature," which is binding on all people, finds perfect expression in the laws of the Jews (e.g., *Creation* 3; *Moses* 2.52). Not yet, then, do we see signs of Paul's *Christian* reevaluation of the law.

Some scholars indeed suggest that in Paul's Christian reevaluation of the law he may have *departed* from this thesis: they believe that in the heat of the Galatian controversy he denied the divine origin of the law. A second problem relating to this thesis should also be considered here: whereas in certain passages Paul maintains that the law was a peculiar gift to Israel, in others its domain appears to be universal. How are we to account for the inconsistency?

1. As noted in Part Two, Albert Schweitzer interpreted Galatians as indicating that "the Law was given by Angels who desired thereby to make men subservient to themselves."[6] Schoeps understood Galatians 3:19 in a similar way: "In the last analysis this means that the law springs not from God but from the angels."[7] Drane and Hübner agree, and find here one of the ways Paul's position in the earlier epistle differs from his stance in Romans.[8] For Räisänen Paul at least "toys" with the idea of angels as the source of the law in Galatians; that he entertains the notion reflects again the inconsistency of his thought.[9]

---

4. Other passages in which Paul speaks of the Mosaic law but has in mind moral demands thought to be binding on all people are noted in chap. 15, sec. ii above.

5. See chap. 15, n. 17 above.

6. Schweitzer, *Mysticism*, 69.

7. Schoeps, *Paul*, 183.

8. See above, chap. 10, sec. i and ii.

9. Räisänen, *Law*, 133.

What can be known about the background to Galatians 3:19 has been assembled in many places;[10] our summary here may be brief. According to the Old Testament narrative, the Israelites as a whole heard God's voice utter the Decalogue, though Moses met with God to receive the remainder of the law (Deut. 5:4-31). Tradition allowed, however, that angels were present when God gave the law, and the notion that an angel actually delivered God's law to Moses (perhaps based on Moses' conversation with the "angel of the Lord" in Exod. 3) was not uncommon in Paul's day (cf. Acts 7:38, 53; Heb. 2:2; *Jub.* 1:29–2:1; etc.). The tradition, then, was a common one. But Paul's use of the tradition, on any reading, is radical.

For the Paul of Galatians the giving of the law through angels is a dramatic indication of the law's inferiority to God's promise. To be sure, even Hebrews compares "the word spoken by angels" with that "spoken by the Lord" (2:2-3) and concludes that the latter must be treated with greater solemnity. Still, no denigration of the law is intended. But in Galatians 3 Paul seems bent on showing the law's limitations on all counts: chronologically later than the divine promise (3:15-17), valid only "until the offspring should come to whom the promise had been made" (v. 19), unable to impart life (v. 21), but given "because of transgressions" (v. 19), the law, moreover, was "ordained by angels by means of an intermediary" whose presence excludes the possibility of a direct revelation by God (vv. 19-20). For the moment, at least, Paul appears to have nothing good to say about the law.

But does he intend to say more than that God allowed angels to pass on his law to Moses?[11] Is he suggesting that angels created the Mosaic code? The participle διαταγείς (rendered "ordained" by RSV, NRSV; "promulgated" by NEB) indicates that the Israelites received their orders from angels but does not make evident whether the angels were the source or the mediators of the commands. The preposition διά is ambiguous in the same way. Only context can determine which is meant — hardly an unusual situation in the interpretation of texts! Yet the context shows clearly enough that Paul is speaking of the communication by angels of a law divine in its origin.

a. Admittedly Paul speaks of the Abrahamic covenant as "ratified by God" in 3:17, but says of the law quite baldly that it "came" (430 years later). Still, the failure to stress the divine origin of the law should occasion no surprise in a passage not concerned to balance the law's credits with its debits but concentrating exclusively on the latter. In such a context an argument from silence means little.

---

10. E.g., Callan, "Midrash," 549-67.
11. Cf. my Review, 195-96.

b. Admittedly again, Paul's analogy comparing God's promise to Abraham to a will that cannot be altered by outsiders perhaps suggests that Paul is thinking of the law as coming from outsiders (angels) who are unable (though not unwilling) to alter the conditions of God's promise. But analogies are never perfect, and Paul's, as a rule, less so than most. A detail Paul himself does not press in an illustration that shares the limitations of the species is a dubious base for a challenge to the fundamental conviction that God gave the law.[12]

c. Without affirming the divine origin of the law, Paul assumes the traditional view throughout Galatians.[13] The law contains the will of God that believers fulfill (5:14). Transgression of the law involves sin (cf. 2:17-18) and draws down upon sinners the divine curse (i.e., that cited from *Scripture* in 3:10). God's purposes for the law are, moreover, a subject for discussion (3:19-24). That a law that states the divine will, invokes the divine curse, and was designed to serve divine purposes had its origin in the independent — even hostile — activity of angels is scarcely conceivable.[14] It could not in any case be advanced without a clarification lacking in Galatians.

d. It is the purpose not of hostile angels but of God that is intended with the phrase "because of transgressions" (3:19). The point of the enigmatic phrase is developed in verse 22 and, presumably, in Romans 5:20, 7:7-13, always with God's intentions in view. In Galatians 3:19 itself the adjacent phrase ("until the offspring should come to whom the promise had been made") refers to God's design with the law, thus precluding the possibility that the preceding words reflect demonic purposes.

e. If the argument throughout Galatians, including 3:19a, implies the normal view that the Mosaic law is divine, then the ambiguous expression of 3:19b ("ordained by angels") should be interpreted in a way consistent with this implication.

Our thesis claims that the law is a divine gift to Israel. That it is *divine* seems true for Paul, even in Galatians. But was he always clear that it was given *to Israel?*

2. According to Psalm 147, God "makes his word known to Jacob, his statutes and ordinances to Israel. He has not done so for any other nation; they do not know his ordinances. Praise the Lord!" (vv. 19-20). The distinction is at times just as clear in Paul: Jews who "are instructed in the law" (Rom. 2:18; cf. 9:4) are contrasted with Gentiles "who do not have the law" (2:14). Paul behaves one way in the presence of Jews, who are "under the law," but in another when

---

12. Cf. Bläser, *Gesetz*, 53.
13. Cf. Sanders, *Law,* 67-68.
14. Cf. Bläser, *Gesetz*, 51-53.

among Gentiles, who are "outside the law" (1 Cor. 9:20-21). Yet Räisänen is among the many scholars who have pointed out that when Paul depicts the human dilemma apart from Christ, he at times appears to treat Jew and Gentile alike as subjects *of the law*.[15] We may begin with the relevant texts in Romans.

In Romans 6:14-15 Paul declares that the Roman believers (Gentiles presumably included!) are "not under law but under grace"; the implication would seem to be that prior to their experience of grace, they were in bondage to the law. Still clearer is 7:4-6: those to whom Paul writes have "died to the law"; in the process they were "discharged" from it. Donaldson attempts to resolve the difficulty, suggesting that "on the basis of such verses as 2.12, 14; 7.1 and 9.4 an argument could be constructed that in Rom 5-8 Paul is speaking of the law from an exclusively Jewish Christian perspective"; if, on the other hand, we assume that Gentiles *are* included among those "under the law," then "it is not because Paul takes this for granted, but rather because he has already laid the groundwork in chapters 1 and 2."[16] There Paul argued that Gentiles may be led by conscience to conform to the law's requirements, thus becoming a "law to themselves" (2:14). As a result, Gentiles, like Jews, can be spoken of as "under the law."

Neither of these proposals can be excluded as impossible; neither commends itself as likely. Much of Romans does deal with problems of special concern to Jewish Christians; furthermore, the constituency of the Roman church included Jews as well as Gentiles,[17] and Paul at times directs his remarks exclusively to one of these groups (e.g., 11:13-32). But to read Paul's statements of bondage and deliverance in Romans 5 through 8 as limited to *Jewish* Christian experience requires such prodigious concentration that one may doubt whether Paul's intentions were so narrow. Romans 7:1 ("I am speaking to those who know the law") is sometimes taken as an indication that Jews are addressed, but Paul's detailed usage of the Old Testament in his letter to the Galatians shows that he did not think Jews alone were competent to understand an argument based on the law.[18] And there simply are no other hints in these chapters that the encouragement, admonitions, and arguments offered are intended for but a segment of the Roman church.

Does Paul, then, deliberately speak of all nations as "under law" on the basis of his argument that Gentiles may be a "law to themselves"? It seems unlikely. The point of the argument in Romans 1 and 2 is that Gentiles are respon-

---

15. Räisänen, *Law*, 18-23, with ample bibliography.

16. Donaldson, "Curse," 95-96.

17. Cf. Cranfield, *Romans*, 16-22.

18. Whether the Galatians themselves shared his optimism remains one of history's unanswered questions.

sible before God even though *they do not have the law;* the knowledge they have is a sufficient basis for judgment. Their sins are said to be committed "without the law." Their judgment will take place "without the law" (2:12). Though their moral awareness is sufficient to enable them at times to do "things required by the law" (2:14) and so to be "doers of the law" (2:13), the argument that follows continues to assume that possession of the law is a prerogative of the Jews (2:17-24; 4:14, 16). Those who are "under the law" according to 3:19 are undoubtedly Jews.[19] Thus the argument of Romans 1 and 2 can hardly have been intended to pave the way for a description of Jews and Gentiles alike as under the law.

The most likely explanation remains that of Sanders.[20] Paul's own presuppositions are Jewish. He speaks naturally, and probably without reflection, of Abraham as "our forefather according to the flesh" (4:1), or of the wilderness generation as "our fathers" (1 Cor. 10:1), even when he is writing to churches predominantly Gentile. Similarly, he at times depicts the plight of all humanity in terms borrowed from, and (strictly speaking) appropriate only to, the Jewish situation ("under the law"). Quite likely the generalization took place unconsciously. Paul *could,* no doubt, have defended his usage with a simple reminder that Gentile awareness of God's demand for righteousness creates at least an analogous situation to that of Jews. But he does not do so, and his argument in Romans 7:7-13 shows that the bondage of which he is thinking in verses 4-6 results from an encounter between the individual and the explicit demands of the Mosaic code. The Jewish situation is in mind, but Paul treats it as though it were universal.

The references in Galatians are more difficult, but may be dealt with briefly here since a precedent for imprecise usage has already been established. Donaldson finds an interesting pattern in 3:13-14, 23-29, and 4:3-7: in each case (a) a plight is described of which the law is a part, and to which a group referred to with first-person plural pronouns is subject; (b) Christ is then said to identify himself with the plight and (c) to provide redemption for those under it, so that (d) saving blessings might be made available to all believers. Donaldson believes Jews are the subject of the plight *(a)* and the objects of Christ's redemption *(c);* the progression from the redemption of Jews to blessing for all believers is thought to follow a pattern well attested in Jewish eschatological expectation, where Israel's redemption paves the way for salvation to be extended to the Gentiles.

But the passages in Galatians give us little reason to believe that Paul had such a progression in mind here. On the contrary, both 3:26 and 4:6 seem sim-

---

19. Cf. Cranfield, *Romans,* 195-96.
20. Sanders, *Law,* 82.

ply to apply to the Galatian Christians the blessings referred to in the preceding verses — they, too, have been set free and adopted as sons — without a hint that Gentiles participated on terms that differed from those of Jews (cf. 1:4; 5:1, 13). 3:13-14, too, can be read as saying that Christ's death for all brings blessings to all: if the "we" who have received the Spirit in 3:14 must include all believers, is the same not to be said of the "we" redeemed from the law's curse in 3:13?

It seems safest to conclude that Paul does picture Gentiles as sharing the Jewish dilemma; he has not systematically maintained the distinction between Jews who are under the law and Gentiles who are not. His primary concern in the passages in question is to show that God's law fulfilled a divine function, though it did not lead to life. In outlining that function for Gentile readers, he sometimes speaks as though they, too, have felt its effects. That their situation, in Paul's mind, was analogous to that of Jews is clear enough (cf. Rom. 1:18–3:20; Gal. 4:1-11). Still, since Paul raises no argument in its defense, his usage of the phrase "under the law" to include Gentiles was likely an unconscious generalization.

Thesis 3: The law of Moses contains ordinances binding only on Jews; their observance has marked Jews off from other nations as God's people.

Though Paul, like many Jews, could speak of Torah as embodying what is God's will and appropriate behavior for all people, he could also insist, as did other Jews, that it contained precepts required only of Israel. In 1 Corinthians 9:20-21 he claims that he lives among Jews, who are "under the law," as though he himself were "under the law," whereas when he is among Gentiles, who are "outside the law," he lives as one "outside the law." In this passage Jews but not Gentiles are thought to be subject to demands contained in the law: demands whose observance or nonobservance is for Paul a matter of effective missionary strategy rather than moral right or wrong. Food laws and the observance of Sabbaths and festivals must be in mind.

Similarly, the Galatians to whom Paul writes have betrayed an eagerness to be "under law" (4:21; cf. 3:2) by observing "days, months, seasonal festivals, and years" (4:10). Elsewhere Paul insists that Gentiles ought not be compelled to "live as Jews" (2:14); they are not, in other words, to be forced to adopt Jewish food laws.

Nowhere in his extant letters does Paul explain that the Mosaic law combines[21] demands binding on all humankind with other precepts required

---

21. Augustine, however, notes the combination; see, e.g., *C. Faust.* 6.2; 10.2.

only of Israel.[22] The absence of such a clarification is presumably to be attributed to the nonsystematic character of his writings. Both halves of the conviction are amply attested in his letters. And both halves are traditional.

Thesis 4: Adamic humanity does not, and cannot, submit to God's law.[23]

In Romans 1:18–3:20 Paul declares that all humanity is culpable before God for wrongdoing that begins with the refusal of creatures to give their Creator due glory and thanks and comes to include violations of creation's order and of the norms of decency toward each other. Human thinking has been reduced to futility, human understanding darkened.[24] All, in Paul's terms, are "under sin" (3:9) and liable to divine judgment (3:19-20). In Romans 5 Paul traces human sinfulness back to Adam, whose descendants were "made sinners" by his disobedience (v. 19). They live "in sin" (Rom. 6), expressing in concrete acts of sin the pretensions of autonomy and the underlying hostility toward God that Paul sums up in the term "flesh" and sees as endemic in Adam's race. When flesh that is hostile to God encounters the wisdom of God in his created order or in the Mosaic law, the issue is inevitable: human rebelliousness is provoked into sinful actions (7:7-13). Flesh does not find within itself a capacity to submit to God's law (8:7-8; cf. 7:14-25).

Such is the argument of Romans. Paul's anthropology elsewhere is less explicit but hardly more optimistic. In 1 Thessalonians Gentiles do not know God and are the prey of their sinful passions (4:5), while Jews reject God's messengers (2:14-16); apart from God's salvific work in Christ, all belong to the "darkness" that can expect divine wrath (5:3, 7-10). In the Corinthian correspondence the world outside the church is made up of the "unrighteous" (1 Cor. 6:1) who will have no share in God's kingdom (6:9). The Mosaic law may be glorious, but

---

22. They were, however, binding on Israel only until Christ came; cf. Gal. 3:19, 23-25. Continued observance was for Paul a matter of personal indifference — though missionary strategy determined his own behavior (1 Cor. 9:19-23), and one should in any case avoid giving needless offense to others (Rom. 14:1–15:6). Paul's policy as advocated in Rom. 14, though tolerant of Jewish Christians who wanted to continue traditional observances, could, if adopted, only lead in time to the loss of Jewish distinctiveness; cf. Barclay, "Law," 287-308.

23. This thesis summarizes briefly a number of the anthropological considerations noted in our review of Paul's letters in chap. 18.

24. Cf. Augustine, *De lib. arb.* 3.18.178: "It is an absolutely just punishment for sin that each man loses what he is unwilling to use rightly, when he could without any difficulty use it if he willed. Thus the man who does not act rightly although he knows what he ought to do, loses the power to know what is right; and whoever is unwilling to do right when he can, loses the power to do it when he wills to. In fact, two penalties — ignorance and difficulty — beset every sinful soul."

to sinners it can only bring "condemnation" and "death" (2 Cor. 3:7-9; cf. 1 Cor. 15:56). According to Galatians, all humanity is "under sin" unless justified through faith (3:22-24). Jews who have received the law and Gentiles who have not both live in the realm of the flesh (cf. 3:2-3); its wicked deeds are notorious (5:19-21). In Philippians, too, Paul sees humanity as "crooked," "perverse" (2:15), and headed for perdition (cf. 1:28).[25]

Thesis 5: For Adamic human beings the law cannot serve as the path to righteousness and life.

This thesis appears to run counter to several texts in Paul's letters that speak of the "righteousness of the law" or of the law as given with the promise of life for its adherents (Rom. 2:13; 7:10; Phil. 3:6, 9). Leviticus 18:5 is twice quoted to this effect by Paul, in Romans 10:5 and Galatians 3:12. Numerous parallels from Deuteronomy could also have been cited. There is no reason to suspect that Paul differed in his understanding of these texts from his Jewish contemporaries: God had chosen and redeemed Israel as his "peculiar" people, had granted them the gift of Torah, and had promised life in his favor if they kept its "statutes and ordinances."

Still, it is important to note that for Paul, however favored Jews may have been, and whatever additional motivation they may have had to do what is right, the same basic conditions apply for them as for Gentiles if they would be found righteous by God: God will judge all, without partiality, by their deeds, and approve only those who do the good (Rom. 2:6-13).[26] Jews need to be "doers," not mere "hearers," of the law that spells out the "good"; yet (as we have seen) for Paul, humanity *in Adam* does not — and effectively cannot — submit to the law. Even from Adam's most favored descendants, the gift of the law elicits only stiff-necked rebellion, not humble submission. The institution of the law may have been accompanied by the promise of life and blessing for those who obey its precepts no less than by the threat of cursing and death for those who defy them. Only the threat, however, can be operative among those in the flesh.[27] So Paul says that *all* who are "of the works of the law" are subject to the curse it pronounces on transgressors (Gal. 3:10).

25. Discussion of the roots of thesis 4 will be postponed until we have considered thesis 5.

26. This, of course, is the requirement of "ordinary dikaiosness" discussed in chap. 15, sec. ii.

27. Cf. Calvin, *Comm.* Gal. 3:10: "It is accidental that the law should curse, though at the same time perpetual and inseparable. The blessing which it offers us is excluded by our depravity, so that only the curse remains." Also *Comm.* Rom. 7:10: "It is an accident that the law inflicts a mortal wound on us, just as if an incurable disease were rendered more acute by a healing

What are the roots of Paul's anthropological pessimism? A number of texts from the Jewish Scriptures can be cited that speak of the universality of human sin. In Genesis 3 Adam and Eve are undoubtedly thought to be representative of all humankind. The chapters that immediately follow are designed to show how sin intrudes upon and corrupts all interhuman relations, as well as those between humans and the nonhuman creation and those between humans and God.

From among the nations, the Scriptures go on to say, Israel has been sovereignly chosen and redeemed to be God's covenant people. But neither before nor after Israel's election is it suggested that Israel is more *righteous* than other nations (cf. Deut. 9:4-6). On the contrary, the Pentateuch,[28] Deuteronomistic history, and prophetic literature uniformly depict the nation as stubbornly resisting God's demands in spite of extraordinary displays of God's goodness on its behalf. Prophetic texts view Israel's recalcitrance as so deeply rooted that only a divine transformation of Israel's heart — a heart transplant, as Ezekiel 36:26-27 puts it — could render the people submissive to God's ways (cf. Jer. 13:23; 31:31-34). There are, in short, numerous texts in the Hebrew Scriptures that could be cited in support of this fifth Pauline thesis.[29]

That being said, it must also be conceded that most Jews did not construe the human predicament — or at least the predicament of Israel — in terms as bleak as Paul's. The gift of Torah was commonly seen as the linchpin in God's dealings with humanity's weakness and propensity for sin. Its laws, marking out the path by which Israel could enjoy life and divine blessing, were not considered beyond human capacities to fulfill. In any case, its institutions provided atonement for those who repented of their shortcomings.

That Paul does not mention Jewish understandings of repentance and restoration is often thought remarkable. From his own perspective, however, effective repentance must surely lie beyond the capacities of a flesh that "does not, and cannot, submit to God's law" (Rom. 8:7). Paul's exclusion of Jewish notions of repentance is therefore quite consistent with his anthropology, as sketched

---

remedy. The accident, I admit, is inseparable from the law, and for this reason the law, as compared with the Gospel, is elsewhere referred to as 'the ministration of death' [2 Cor. 3:7]. The point, however, holds good, that the law is not injurious to us by its own nature, but because our corruption provokes and draws upon us its curse."

28. Cf. the comments of Luther on the book of Numbers: "laws are quickly given, but when they are to go into effect and become operative, they meet with nothing but hindrance; nothing goes as the law demands. This book is a notable example of how vacuous it is to make people righteous with laws; rather, as St Paul says, laws cause only sin and wrath" (*Pref. OT*, 35:238).

29. Cf. Thielman, *Plight*, 36.

above. Still, the source of so pessimistic a judgment demands explanation, for it remains unusual in the context of Jewish thought.

To be sure, Paul's pessimism is not unprecedented. Some interpreters have traced it to the more pessimistic strands of rabbinic teaching[30] or, perhaps, to Hellenistic Jewish thought.[31] The difficulty with such views is that, to judge from his own testimony about his pre-Christian experience, Paul must have been among the more optimistic Jews in his assessment of at least his own capacity to meet the standards required by the "righteousness of the law" (Phil. 3:4-6). The evidence for Paul's "robust conscience" to which Krister Stendahl has drawn attention[32] does not suggest a mind schooled to doubt humanity's capacity to please God.

Here, then, it seems we must speak of a postconversion reevaluation. If the crucifixion of God's Son was required to redeem humankind — a conclusion that Paul could not doubt once Jesus had been "revealed" to him as "God's Son" (Gal. 1:15-16) — then the sinfulness of humankind must be both radical in itself and beyond the capacity of existing (and less drastic) measures to overcome. To this extent E. P. Sanders is certainly correct in insisting on the movement of Paul's thought "from solution to plight." The notion that in Adam all die may well have become fundamental to Paul's thinking first when he saw it as presupposed in the affirmation that "in Christ shall all be made alive" (1 Cor. 15:22).

Not that Paul, the Christian apostle, had to create a crisis ex nihilo to correspond to and legitimate his understanding of redemption in Christ. The positing of a relationship between Adam's sin and human death was no Pauline innovation. The Jewish Scriptures (as we have noted) are replete with denunciations of human waywardness. And Frank Thielman has quite properly reminded us that the movement from plight to solution is repeatedly traced in both biblical and postbiblical Jewish tradition.[33] Nonetheless, it seems likely that Paul was first moved to draw extensively on that tradition, and to mold it in the way he did, by reflecting on the disclosure of the human predicament implicit in the cross of Christ. Like the reader of a novel with an unanticipated ending, Paul may well have felt that he first grasped the seriousness of scriptural appraisals of human sinfulness when he returned to ponder them in the light of the story's climax.

---

30. Cf. the summary of Schoeps in chap. 7, sec. ii above.
31. See the summary of Montefiore in chap. 7, sec. i above. Also Sandmel, *Genius.*
32. See the summary of Stendahl in chap. 8, sec. ii above.
33. See chap. 12, sec. iii above.

Thesis 6: The giving of the law served to highlight, at the same time as it exacerbated, human bondage to sin.

Why did God institute a law that, on Paul's reading, people would not and could not keep? The question may be asked; it is worth noting, however, that, as formulated, it seems completely detached from reality as Paul saw it. For Paul the law merely spells out the moral requirements inherent in the terms of human existence in God's world.[34] If moral creatures are completely dependent on God for their life and well-being, then they cannot live rightly without acknowledging God and giving him his due. This is not an arbitrary decree permitting adjustment to human predilections or capacities any more than solutions to mathematical problems can be altered to suit students' inclinations or abilities to deduce them. The occurrence of murder, adultery, theft, and false witness has doubtless been a feature of human society ever since humans were banished from Eden; Paul could not deem them, for that reason, morally acceptable. That humans do not — and even *cannot* — live up to moral standards that they themselves must acknowledge was a truth to be confronted, not clouded over by the suppression or falsification of the standards. Ezekiel was to bear witness to the truth whether or not Israel heeded him (Ezek. 2:3-5). In the same vein, Paul clearly believed, the law rightly attests to what is required of humankind, whether or not it is obeyed.

Whenever Paul explains God's purposes for the law, a link with sin is posited. The complex relationship he sees can perhaps be summarized in the following series of statements, each to be developed below.

1. Sin precedes the law and exists where there is no law. Even apart from the law, sinners are culpable for their misdeeds and face divine judgment.
2. The coming of the law transforms sinful acts into violations of God's commands, subject to stated sanctions.
3. Moreover, the coming of the law creates a situation in which "sin" can tempt the law's subjects to disobey its commands. In this way the actual number of sins committed is increased.
4. The law also serves to bring sinners some awareness of their dilemma.

1. That, in the checkered history of humanity, wrongdoing preceded the formulation of law codes is a proposition that few would challenge though none, perhaps, could prove. For Paul the matter was decided by comparing the relative positions of Adam and Moses in Scripture's genealogical tree: "Sin

---

34. See the first two theses of this chapter.

came into the world through one man [Adam]. . . . Sin was in the world before the law was given" (Rom. 5:12, 13). It follows, then, that the definition of sin as "the transgression of the law"[35] is not quite adequate — if we may speak legitimately of sin before the law was given.

Paul at least does so, with good biblical precedent. He also presupposes — again, with scriptural justification — the existence of sin among Gentiles who do not have the law: "All who have sinned without the law will also perish without the law" (Rom. 2:12). Throughout Romans 1–3 Paul argues not only that Gentiles sin but also that they are responsible for their wrongdoing and liable to judgment: Paul knows no guiltless sinners. Gentiles are "without excuse" (1:20); God's wrath falls upon them as well as upon Jews (1:18), though the law will play a role only in the assessment of the latter (2:12).

Räisänen is among those who find Romans 5:12-14 inconsistent with the earlier passage.[36] Romans 2 declares judgment for those who sin without the law, whereas in Romans 5 we are told that "sin is not counted where there is no law." The critical words, of course, are οὐκ ἐλλογεῖται, "is not counted" (5:13). The words perhaps suggest that sin is somehow not treated as sin or held against the sinner in the absence of law, a conclusion that does not mesh with 2:12. One might, of course, argue that Paul can hardly have forgotten in Romans 5 what he wrote in Romans 2, and hence that the context within which Romans 5 is to be interpreted must include the earlier chapter; a weakening of the force of οὐκ ἐλλογεῖται would naturally follow. But such a procedure, though normal enough in the interpretation of texts, will hardly do when Paul's consistency of thought is the point in question. If, however, the immediate context of 5:12-14 shows that Paul is still bent on maintaining the position he argued in chapter 2, then we can hardly deny the appropriateness of a weaker reading of 5:13b.

According to 5:12, sin and death entered the world through Adam's transgression of a specific commandment (παράβασις); death then became the lot of all, "inasmuch as all sinned." However we define the relation between Adam's sin and that of his offspring, πάντες ἥμαρτον most naturally means that all committed concrete sins;[37] moreover, the words are part of a phrase (introduced by ἐφ' ᾧ, "inasmuch as")[38] affirming that people's sins led to their death. The same point is made in verse 14: Paul stresses both the guilt and the punishment of all, though noting, significantly enough, that later sins were not of the same character as Adam's ("death reigned from Adam until Moses, even over

---

35. That the KJV misreads 1 John 3:4 is generally agreed; cf. Marshall, *Epistles*, 176-77.
36. Räisänen, *Law*, 145-47.
37. Cf. Cranfield, *Romans*, 279.
38. Lyonnet, "Sens," 436-56; Meyer, *Christians*, 122 n. 3.

those who did not sin in the same way that Adam transgressed"). The law, by implication, effects a change from sin to transgression, but hardly one from innocence to guilt. Between these two verses we find yet another statement that sin was "in the world" (i.e., sins were committed) even before the law was given. Since the closing words of verse 12, the first half of 13, and the opening of 14 are devoted to an insistence that those living before Moses did sin, and that death resulted from their sin, there appears to be little warrant for reading 13b as though Paul (for this half-verse?) meant that sins committed in the absence of law were not quite worthy of the name or held against the sinners. To repeat, Paul knows no innocent sinners.[39] Whatever his precise point in 13b may be, the culpability of sins committed prior to the giving of the law is not in question. οὐκ ἐλλογεῖται must refer, not to an absence of guilt or punishment, but to a difference in the way sins are prosecuted. What is that difference?

2. According to Räisänen, Paul "tries to show that, as regards man and sin, the coming of the law makes a difference," but "what he actually shows is that there is none."[40] At best Paul can point to "a technical trifle": "until the law sin had been punished because it was sin; since the law, the very same punishments are imposed because of 'transgression.'" The technicality of the change thus "would seem to be a matter of no consequence whatsoever."[41] Paul's dilemma, according to Räisänen, is that, having rejected the law by an "aprioristic theological thesis (Christ has superseded the law)," he is now forced to "undergird his thesis" by showing "that the effects of the law are negative, and only negative"; such a thesis can only be "carried through . . . with violence."[42]

But is Paul's procedure as arbitrary as Räisänen suggests? Paul believes that adultery, murder, stealing, and coveting (the four examples cited from the Decalogue in Rom. 13:9) are wrong: those who love their "neighbor" as they ought will not commit adultery with their neighbor's spouse, murder, steal from their neighbor, or even covet for themselves what their neighbor possesses. This seems a comprehensible position to hold. Paul believes, moreover, that even apart from the law people are aware at some level that such deeds are wrong; God, then, is right to punish those who commit them. These convictions, too, seem intelligible; certainly they have been held by many. Paul nonetheless believes there is a point in God telling people explicitly that they must not commit adultery, that they must not murder, steal, or covet ("whether they will hear, or whether they will forbear"); furthermore, he believes the rebel-

---

39. Cranfield, *Romans*, 282.
40. Räisänen, *Law*, 146 n. 91.
41. Räisänen, *Law*, 146.
42. Räisänen, *Law*, 149-50.

liousness of those who proceed nonetheless to commit such acts is still more apparent, and the wrongful acts more flagrantly wrong, because God has given his law: the coming of the law transforms the evil deeds of its subjects into blatant transgressions of God's revealed commands. And though a sovereign God is always free (and always right) to punish sin, there is both an appropriateness and an inexorability about God's wrath when it becomes operative as the stated sanction attached to a given law.

The transformation of sin into a more clearly defined act of rebellion, subject to the defined sanctions of the law, is the point of 5:13b (cf. 4:15). The term used — ἐλλογεῖν — "has here to do with heavenly book-keeping."[43] That sin "is not counted" in the absence of law does not mean that it goes unpunished — the immediate context affirms the opposite — but simply that God cannot judge "according to the book." Ample power to punish sin is ever at his disposal: forty days of uninterrupted rain are more than adequate for the task. But for the due registration of wrongs committed, and the consequent demonstration both of human culpability and of the divine justice that punishes sin, the institution of the law serves an important function.

3. But Paul goes further still. Not only does the law transform sin into acts of flagrant defiance against God's explicit commands; in a sense it actually *provokes* transgressions. This is Paul's point in 7:7-13. By itself verse 7 is ambiguous: "But for the law, I would not have known sin. I would not have known what it means to covet if the law had not said, 'You shall not covet.'" Paul's words here are certainly susceptible of interpretation along lines suggested by 4:15 and 5:13; though no doubt an "I" who lived before the commandment came might have longed for what belonged to someone else, such an "I" might not have *recognized* the longing as the sin of "coveting" had the law not prohibited it in those terms. The stress here, not found in chapters 4 and 5, would then be that sinners themselves gain a "knowledge" of sin — a recognition that they are acting in defiance of God's law — through the coming of the command.

But Paul goes on to say that "sin, taking the opportunity given by the com-

---

43. Räisänen, *Law*, 145. Cf., however, Hofius, "Antithesis," 195-96, who sees the verb pointing, not to an activity in the heavenly world, but to that by which knowledge of a charge is conveyed to the one accused. It indicates "that the Torah first brings to expression and to knowledge that which has already been the reality for all of us from the days of Adam, namely, that we are sinners, and that under the condemnation of God, death is the consequence of our sins. . . . The Torah does not initiate the combination of sin and death. It finds it already there. But it shows that it is really there. It brings it to inevitable expression. It objectively clarifies that *each of us* is *homo peccator,* the one who has fallen victim to death as the κατάκριμα imposed by God. Without the law we cannot know the fact that we are sinners standing under the divine sentence and justly condemned to eternal death."

mandment, produced in me all kinds of covetousness" (7:8).[44] Humanity's sin-fulness — its insistence on choosing its own path, even in defiance of its Cre-ator — springs to life and concrete expression when humans are told what they ought and ought not to do. Told not to covet, they will flaunt their presumed autonomy by coveting. In effect, then, the coming of the law served to *worsen* the human dilemma — partly because it brought definition (as "transgres-sion") to wrongs that would have been committed in any case, but partly also because it increased the actual number of sins committed. There are "sinful passions" that, among those bent on rebellion, are themselves "aroused" by a law that prohibits their expression (7:5; cf. 5:20). The cryptic claim of Galatians 3:19 — the law "was added because of transgressions" — is presumably an ab-breviated way of making the same point we find in Romans: through the law human bondage to sin is defined and increased — in order that deliverance may be found through faith in Christ (Gal. 3:22).

4. What, finally, are we to make of Romans 3:20? Here Paul concludes his lengthy indictment of humanity (1:18–3:20) with these words: "For no flesh will be declared righteous in God's sight by the works of the law, since through the law comes knowledge of sin." If the opening words of the verse are taken by themselves as the conclusion to the preceding argument, then the final phrase ("through the law comes knowledge of sin") may introduce a new point to be developed in a later context.[45] In this case, and in the light of 4:15 and 5:13, the "knowledge of sin" brought by the law might refer to the recognition roused in sinners that the wrongs they commit are violations of God's stated will for which they are liable for punishment. Less likely, perhaps, is the suggestion that "knowledge of sin" means the practical experience of sin depicted in 7:7-11: without the law, one would not "know" (i.e., experience) the sin of suc-cumbing to the temptation to disobey a divine command with which one is confronted. Paul's words are ambiguous enough, however, to allow either in-terpretation.

---

44. Bultmann found here confirmation for his thesis that the fundamental sin of Jews is their attempt to establish their own righteousness by fulfilling the law, suggesting that the "de-sire" to do so is at least included in the πᾶσαν ἐπιθυμίαν of 7:8 ("Anthropology," 154) — as though the Decalogue concludes with a command to people not to want to do what they have just been commanded to do! But the desires aroused according to v. 8 are clearly understood as violations of the law's command cited in v. 7, and that command prohibits the coveting of what belongs to another. Hence πᾶσαν ἐπιθυμίαν means "covetousness for all manner of things," in *defiance* of the command; a "desire" to *fulfill* the command is hardly in view. See my "Letter," 237-38; also Räisänen, *Torah*, 95-111.

45. Cf. Rom. 6:14, where Paul introduces a notion ("not under law") that he does not de-velop until 7:1-6.

On the other hand, we may well feel that the bringing of a knowledge of sin corresponds very nicely with the concerns of the first three chapters of Romans, and that 3:20b, as well as 3:20a, should be seen as a summary of the preceding argument. How does the argument of 1:18–3:20 relate the law to the knowledge of sin?

Certainly the law is not thought to bring such knowledge to Gentiles. They "do not have the law" (2:14), sin "without the law," and perish "without the law" (2:12). Paul's indictment in chapter 1 is directed to all humanity (1:18), but is stated in terms that leave Gentiles "without excuse" (2:20) even though they do not have God's law: "What can be known about God is there for them to see. . . . Although they knew God they did not honor him as God. . . . They exchanged the truth about God for a lie" (1:19, 21, 25). Paul seems deliberately to avoid using the law of Moses to convict Gentiles of sin.

On the other hand, "as many as have sinned under the law will be judged by the law" (2:12). Paul insists that Jews are required to obey the law's commands and will be condemned for their transgressions. Thus the law effects the conviction of Jews before the divine tribunal.

But is a demonstration of guilt at the divine tribunal what Paul means by the "knowledge of sin" in 3:20? Surely human, not divine, knowledge is intended; and if the knowledge of sin that the law brings to men and women becomes theirs first on the day of judgment, its appearance is too tardy to be of use. 3:20, then, appears to be saying that the law brings to Jews an awareness[46] that they, too, are sinners and will be judged as such. Two possibilities from the preceding argument suggest themselves.

a. In 3:19 Paul concludes on the basis of a number of quotations from "the law" (i.e., the Scriptures) that those who live under the law are guilty before God. This may be Paul's point in verse 20: Jews should learn from Scripture's testimony that "no one does good" (v. 12), and hence that they too are sinners. Note, however, that the law that brings this knowledge is Scripture as a whole, not specifically the Mosaic law code. Since the "works of the law" that do not justify, according to 20a, are the deeds demanded by the Mosaic code, one would expect Paul's explanation of what the law does accomplish, in 20b, to refer to the same body of commands.

b. In 2:17-24 Paul probes his imagined Jewish interlocutor on the subject of personal obedience to the specific commands of the law: "Do you steal? . . . Do you commit adultery? . . . Do you rob temples? . . . Do you dishonor God by breaking the law?" Perhaps, then, Paul means that reflection on the commands

---

46. Note that, according to Rom. 3:19, "what the law says it says to those [Jews] who live under the law."

of the law should arouse in Jews an awareness of their transgressions, thus leading to a knowledge of sin.[47]

Such a reading roughly corresponds with Luther's understanding of the "principal use" of the law: confronted with the law's demands, sinners are convinced of their guilt, tremble at the thought of God's judgment, and grasp at God's mercy offered in Christ. Luther, to be sure, does not restrict "law" to the Mosaic code, nor on his understanding are the sinners whose pangs of conscience the law awakens limited to Jews. The question remains: does Paul believe the Mosaic code functions among Jews in a way comparable to Luther's principal use of the law?

The suggestion is routinely rejected by many. We may recall Stendahl's argument.[48] Paul was not himself given to introspection, nor does he give any indication of having suffered from a troubled conscience; at least in his case, then, the law did not serve its "principal function"! Moreover, that the law served as a pedagogue εἰς Χριστόν (Gal. 3:24) means that it performed its task "until Christ came," not that it leads sinners through remorse for transgressions to a merciful Savior.

The case is a forceful one, but it may have been overstated. Certainly Galatians 3:24 does not speak of the way the law prepares sinners psychologically for the reception of the gospel, but rather of the temporal limitations placed on the law's validity. Yet (as I argued in the discussion of 1 Thessalonians above)[49] Paul's message of salvation in Christ demands a negative complement, a dilemma from which Christ delivers. Paul's missionary preaching certainly included warnings to Gentiles of the wrath to come, even if the Mosaic law was not proclaimed as the basis of their condemnation. Is it unlikely, then, that Jews were threatened with the same wrath, told that election was no substitute for obedience, and that transgressions of the law would lead to their condemnation? In the present context the argument of Romans 2 is addressed to Christian readers; but may it not reflect at least the general pattern of Paul's message in the synagogues?[50] Such a proclamation would, after all, be entirely in line with the message of the prophets, of John the Baptist, and indeed of Jesus himself.

Nor are we entirely dependent on conjectures. Romans 3:20 and 7:7[51] both speak of a "knowledge of sin" conveyed to sinners through the law. Naturally, for Paul, such knowledge could not be an end in itself, but must be meant to in-

47. Cf. Beker, *Paul*, 107; Wilckens, *Römer*, 1:180.
48. See chap. 8, sec. ii above.
49. See chap. 18, sec. i.
50. Cf. Meyer, *Christians*, 138 n. 14.
51. Even if the "knowledge" of Rom. 7:7 is primarily experiential, an awareness of the experience by the subject can scarcely be excluded.

duce a cry like that of 7:24 ("Who will deliver . . . ?"), to be answered with a recognition of God's promise of redemption (cf. v. 25). Luther's principal function
of the law gives its pedagogical role an emphasis that towers out of all proportion to the few allusive references in the Pauline texts; but Paul does appear to
provide its foundation.[52]

> Thesis 7: The righteousness of God revealed in Christ Jesus is operative
> apart from law. Those who continue to pursue the righteousness
> of the law mistakenly attribute to the works of their unredeemed
> flesh a role in securing divine approval.

A law that accentuates but cannot overcome human sinfulness can play no role
in humanity's redemption. It rightly demands compliance with God's will, but
places its demands on creatures who are hostile to God and incapable of pleasing him. Their transformation must be brought about by other means to which
they themselves, the "weak" and "ungodly" (Rom. 5:6), are in no position to
contribute.

Of the nature of divine redemption as Paul perceives it, we need only recall
here its utter *dependence* on divine grace and its *independence* from the law and
its works. After depicting humanity in Romans 3 as "under sin" (3:9), culpable
and without excuse before God (3:19), Paul then underlines the gratuitousness
of redemption: those who believe "are freely declared righteous by [God's]
grace through the redemption provided in Christ Jesus" (3:24). The "ungodly"
are approved, not because of anything they do, but by believing in the one who
"declares the ungodly righteous" (4:5). 5:12-21 is a paean of praise of the "grace
of God and the gift made abundantly available to many through the grace of
the one man, Jesus Christ" (5:15). The "free gift" or "grace" is operative to secure
divine approval in a situation where "many transgressions" prevail (5:16). Death
reigns until people are enabled to "reign in life" by "receiving the overflow of
grace and of the gift of righteousness" (5:17).

Nonetheless, there are those (Paul declares) who ignore *God's* righteousness and continue to try to establish their own. They seek to attain the righteousness that the law demands by doing the works it prescribes rather than realizing that God's approval can only be gained by responding in faith to what
God has done in Christ Jesus (9:30-32). In earlier chapters I have argued at
length that the works that according to Paul can play no role in attaining righteousness are the righteous deeds by which one might imagine oneself to be so

---

52. Cf. Weima, "Function," 223-27. The roots of this thesis will be noted after the discussion
of the next.

deemed rather than the boundary markers that distinguished the Jewish people from Gentiles.[53] Here we need only note that the latter suggestion fails to do justice to the clear relation between, on the one hand, Paul's exclusion of human works and, on the other, (1) the Pauline anthropology that insists that flesh cannot please God; (2) the Pauline soteriology that insists on the gratuitousness of salvation; (3) the Pauline understanding of redemptive history (see Rom. 9–11) that insists that God always operates on his own initiative without considering anything humans might do; and (4) the Pauline moral vision that insists that humans have no grounds for boasting before God (3:27–4:5; 1 Cor. 1:26-31; Gal. 6:14). The pendulum of academic fashion has of late swung far away from systematic portrayals of Pauline theology; one result has been that even the obvious relation between these fundamental features of his thought has been lost to view.

Two objections to this reading of Paul may be briefly noted here. First, is not human faith itself a "work" that contributes to the process of justification? To this objection the obvious answer must be that Paul does not see it so. The very texts in Romans that insist on the gratuitousness of God's gift of righteousness also insist that it is credited to those who believe (3:22-24; 4:1-5; 5:1-11). If that crediting were in response to some work, Paul reasons, it would be a wage, not a gift of grace. But it is clearly the latter, he claims, in that it is granted to those who "do not work but *believe* on him who declares the ungodly righteous" (4:4-5). This text, in particular, presupposes a fundamental distinction between "working" (i.e., performing deeds that merit recognition) and "believing." Later in Romans Gentiles who obtain the "righteousness of *faith*" are explicitly said *not* to be active in pursuit of righteousness — unlike Jews who pursue it but do not obtain it, thinking it a matter of works, not faith (9:30-32). That the law demands works is precisely what shows, for Paul, that its operative principle is not that of faith (Gal. 3:12; cf. Rom. 4:16; 10:5-8).

Why does Paul distinguish in this way between the faith that is necessarily involved in justification and the works that are necessarily excluded? Again we need to turn to Paul's anthropology. No product of Adamic humanity can be pleasing to God, since the underlying orientation of Adamic humanity is hostility toward God. Even deeds that outwardly conform to the law's commands can only be acceptable as expressions of faith in God, and the mind-set of the flesh is the opposite to that of faith. The human faith essential to justification cannot, then, be a characteristic or product of the flesh. Rather, it is for Paul a response to the divine word of salvation (10:17) first aroused by God himself through an act of divine illumination parallel to that by which the old creation

---

53. See particularly chap. 16, sec. ii.

came into being: "The God who said, 'Let light shine out of darkness,' has shone in our hearts to bring the light of the knowledge that the glory of God is displayed in the person of Jesus Christ" (2 Cor. 4:6). Thus faith for Paul does not — as indeed it cannot — originate in a movement of the flesh. Rather, it is a gift of God that is effective in bringing about a new, and necessarily divine, creation (Phil. 1:27; cf. 2 Cor. 5:17-18; 1 Thess. 2:13).

But (a second objection is raised) does Paul not himself require "works" of believers? Indubitably he does. Yet such works for Paul are not to be confused with the products of the unredeemed flesh. Those restored by grace to a right relationship with God and granted his Spirit to empower their living must express the reality of their new life in suitable behavior. They are to live in a manner worthy of the God who has called them to be his own (Phil. 1:27; 1 Thess. 2:12). Their faith is to be active in love (Gal. 5:6). At the same time, Paul believes, they will sense, as he did, that God is "at work" within them, granting both the desire and the ability to do what he approves (Phil. 2:13; cf. 1 Cor. 15:10; 2 Cor. 12:9; Gal. 2:20). The presence of God's Spirit *must* bear fruit in the lives of believers who are redeemed by divine grace. But this Pauline conviction hardly contradicts the thesis that no flesh can be declared righteous by its works.

Paul cites Scripture in support of each component of this thesis: that the righteousness of God revealed in Christ Jesus is operative by faith and apart from the law (cf. 3:11-12; Rom. 10:5-13); that righteousness is credited to those who "have faith . . . without works" (4:1-8); and that God operates at the initiative of his sovereign and gracious will without regard to human actions (9:10-18; 11:4-6). But Paul himself, by his own testimony, once pursued the "righteousness of the law" (Phil. 3:6). Hence the distinction between such righteousness and that of faith, as well as the conviction that righteousness is ultimately a gift granted quite apart from the works of the law, can only have been the product of his Christian reevaluation. Scripture, when reconsidered from his Christian perspective, was found to support these convictions. But the convictions impressed themselves on Paul only when the crucifixion and resurrection of God's Son were believed to be both efficacious for human redemption and revelatory of the inadequacy of earlier institutions — even *divine* institutions — to achieve such an end.

And yet the divine law must have had a divine purpose. The thesis that the Mosaic law served merely to highlight human bondage to sin (thesis 6) must also, then, have been the product of Christian considerations.

Thesis 8: Believers in Christ are not under law.

Bearing in mind that this thesis represents only the first half of the paradoxical relationship, as Paul portrays it, between Christians and the law, we may begin with statements in which Paul relegates that relationship to the past.[54] Paul can say that believers have been "redeemed" (Gal. 4:5) or "set free" (Rom. 7:6) from the law, or even that they have "died" to it (7:4, 6; cf. Gal. 2:19). The upshot is that they are not "under law" (Rom. 6:14-15; cf. 1 Cor. 9:20).

Part of Paul's point is clearly that the curse that the law pronounces on its transgressors does not threaten believers. Christ absorbed that curse on their behalf, thereby freeing them from its effects (Gal. 3:13, presumably reflected in 4:5). But Paul's language implies freedom as well from the law's demands. At times the law's ritual demands are specifically in mind (cf. 1 Cor. 9:20-21; Gal. 4:21). The Paul who insisted that neither circumcision nor uncircumcision amounts to anything (6:15; cf. 5:6), that no food need be avoided as "unclean" (Rom. 14:14), and that, in the observance of holy days, the dictates of individual consciences may be followed (14:5-6) cannot have thought Christians obligated to observe the ritual demands of the law.[55]

But when, as in Romans 6:15, Paul is concerned that Christian freedom from the law might be misconstrued as a license to sin, freedom from the law's ritual commands cannot be in view. A similar concern is addressed following declarations of freedom from the law in Galatians 5:13-26. Indeed, none of the declarations of Christian freedom suggests a limitation of that deliverance to ritual demands.[56] Nor when Paul insists that the law was a temporary imposition, confining people under sin *until* the coming of Christ and faith, can the law of which he speaks be restricted to its ritual aspects (3:19–4:7). In Romans 7:4-6 Paul says flatly that because believers have "died" to the law, they now serve God not in the old way of the letter but in the new way of the Spirit. The point is not that Christians are relieved from the obligation to observe a few ritual demands, but that theirs is a whole new way of life and mode of divine service. It is, moreover, striking (and has struck many) that Paul repeatedly refrains from citing prohibitions from the law even when dealing with basic issues related to idolatry or sexual morality, opting instead to argue from Christian principles (e.g., 1 Cor. 6:12-20; 10:14-22; 1 Thess. 4:3-8). And when Paul speaks of the need for Christians to discern the will of God, he does not refer

54. In a number of these statements, the law appears to have been a factor in the pre-Christian lives of all believers, Gentiles as well as Jews. See the discussion of thesis 2 above.

55. Barclay ("Law," 300-301) rightly notes that Rom. 14 shows Paul's "fundamental rejection of the Jewish law in one of its most sensitive dimensions." Paul makes judgments relating to the food laws and those pertaining to special days, but in a manner that is "unashamedly non-legal" and based on no "appeal to a 'higher principle' in the law or . . . allegorical interpretation of the law." Paul "makes no effort to explain or excuse himself"; it is "as if the relationship between his convictions and the law is no longer of central concern."

56. Cf. Bläser, *Gesetz*, 41-44, 228-29.

them to the law (though, according to Rom. 2:18, the law provided Jews with guidance about God's will), but speaks rather of presenting themselves to God, of refusing to pattern their way of life after that of this age, of being "transformed by the renewal of [their] mind[s]" (12:2). They "approve what is excellent" (the same phrase as in 2:18 is used of Christians in Phil. 1:9-10) when their love grows in knowledge and judgment. The fact that Jews had to discover the will of God in the statutes of Torah but Christians must discover it as their minds are "renewed" and they grow in insight shows clearly that the will of God is no longer defined as an obligation to observe the statutes of the Mosaic law.[57]

Thesis 9: Christian righteousness nonetheless fulfills the law.

This is the other half of the paradox. Enough has been said already, however, to suggest that the paradox is not as paradoxical as it is sometimes made to appear.[58]

After all, Paul never confused Christian freedom with notions of autonomy (as though those who are indebted to their Creator for their share in both his old *and* his new creation could ignore their dependence on him) or with suggestions that believers were free to pursue whatever desires they please (cf. Rom. 8:13; Gal. 5:17; 6:7). We noted above (thesis 1) that in the divinely ordered cosmos certain human activities are fitting and others unfitting; some types of conduct are according to nature whereas others defy it. Inherent in the human condition is the demand of (ordinary) righteousness: there is a goodness humans *ought* to pursue and an evil they *ought* to shun. Christians have, to be sure, been (extraordinarily) declared righteous *apart* from deeds of righteousness — but *not* so that they can subsequently ignore them! Sharing the cosmos with others, they are hardly exempt from its inbuilt expectations:[59] Paul tells his readers to "abhor what is evil and cleave to what is good" (Rom. 12:9), to "over-

---

57. The roots of Paul's thinking in theses 8 and 9 will be considered together below.

58. For Räisänen the combination in Paul's letters of declarations of Christian freedom from the law and the insistence that they nonetheless fulfill it is but another instance of Paul "want[ing] to have his cake and eat it" (*Law*, 82). In Sanders's view Paul in effect gives different answers to different questions: "Sometimes he says that the Law is, for Christians at least, at an end, while at other times he urges fulfillment of it. . . . When he was asked, as it were, the question of what was the necessary and sufficient condition for membership in the body of Christ, he said 'not the law.' . . . When, however, he thought about behavior, he responded, 'fulfill the law'" (84).

59. Indeed, for Christians the service of God involves responding "in a worthy manner" (Phil. 1:27; 1 Thess. 2:12) not only to the wise ordering of the old creation but also to the grace of God in the new.

come evil with good" (12:21), to be "wise when it comes to the good, innocent when it comes to evil" (16:19). If, then, as our second thesis maintains, "the law of Moses articulates the appropriate human response to life in God's creation," there is nothing surprising in the expectation that Christians, through love, will fulfill the law (8:4; 13:8-10; Gal. 5:14).

But what, then, is the point in saying that they are not under the law?

1. "Law" in these contexts stands not simply for the concrete commands and prohibitions of Torah, but also for the mode in which these obligations encounter rebellious humanity: as commands that are externally imposed (their inscription on tablets of stone is in marked contrast with demands recognized and endorsed within human hearts; cf. 2 Cor. 3:3, 7) upon a will bent on its self-assertion, gaining compliance (if at all) only through the sanctions with which it threatens disobedience.[60] Those who live under the law do not *really* live for God, whatever statutes they may observe (cf. Gal. 2:19; Rom. 7:4); and those who "die" to God's law die, not to the service of God, but to an unsatisfactory way of serving him. No longer is their service to be experienced as an obligation to observe demands externally imposed.[61] God's Spirit makes God's love a reality in their hearts (5:5) and enables them to serve God in the new way, filled with the fruits of the Spirit that no law condemns (Gal. 5:22-23). Without faith those under law cannot measure up to its commands. With faith that is active in love, believers not under law may in fact fulfill the righteousness that the law requires.[62]

2. Still, it is worth noting that when Paul speaks of Christians "fulfilling" the law, he is describing, not prescribing, their behavior.[63] When Paul *prescribes* what Christians are to do, the language used is not that of fulfilling the Mosaic

60. So, at least, Augustine; cf. *De nat. et grat.* 57.67: "That man is under the law, who, from fear of the punishment which the law threatens, and not from any love for righteousness, obliges himself to abstain from the work of sin, without being as yet free and removed from the desire of sinning." Rom. 13:3-4 might be cited as providing a parallel to the notion that the law has an inhibiting effect on the *expression* of evil. In any case, Augustine captures well Paul's emphasis that the flesh does not, and cannot, *(really)* submit to God's law (Rom. 8:7).

61. Cf. Augustine, *De spir. et litt.* 14.26: "The man in whom is the faith that works through love, begins to delight in the law of God after the inward man; and that delight is a gift not of the letter but of the spirit."

62. Cf. Luther, *Pref. Rom.*, 35:375-76: "To be without the law is not the same thing as to have no laws and to be able to do what one pleases. Rather we are under the law when, without grace, we occupy ourselves with the works of the law. Then sin certainly rules [us] through the law, for no one loves the law by nature; and that is great sin. Grace, however, makes the law dear to us; then sin is no longer present, and the law is no longer against us but one with us. This is the true freedom from sin and from the law."

63. Cf. Barclay, *Truth*, 142. For what follows, see my article "Fulfilling."

law:[64] "Walk by the Spirit, and do not gratify the desires of the flesh" (5:16; cf. Rom. 8:12-13). Naturally, it is from Paul's *prescriptions* that we must derive his view of the basis for Christian obligation. When, on the other hand, Christian ethics is related to the Mosaic law in the fulfillment passages, the view is retrospective.[65] Paul's purpose is to provide assurance of the quality of Christian conduct, not to define its several duties.[66]

Note, too, that Paul speaks of a Christian "fulfilling," not "doing," of the law. The verb ποιεῖν is of course very general and may occur in any context, including where the Christian practice of righteousness is the topic (cf. 13:3; 1 Cor. 9:23; 10:31; Gal. 6:9). Yet, in Paul, Christians are never said to "do" (ποιεῖν) the law,[67] though those under the law are seen as obligated to "do" its commands (Rom. 10:5; Gal. 3:10, 12; 5:3); indeed, as we have seen, the law itself, in Paul's mind, rests on the principle of "doing" as opposed to "believing" (3:12; Rom. 10:5-6). If, then, the essence of life under the law is the requirement to *do* its commands, it is not strange that Paul avoids the term in contexts where he relates Christian behavior to the law. On the other hand,

---

64. 1 Cor. 7:19 might be cited to the contrary; the Mosaic law is not, however, in view in this chapter (the only "commandments" mentioned are Pauline and dominical; cf. vv. 10, 17, 25, and the frequent Pauline imperatives), and the statement need mean no more than that submitting to God's will is essential. On two (!) occasions in the acknowledged epistles, Paul apparently draws from a *precept* in Torah additional support for his position on a matter of behavior: Deut. 25:4 is cited and interpreted allegorically (its literal force is rejected) in the midst of a lengthy justification of Paul's right to be supported by his churches (1 Cor. 9:8-10); and in 1 Cor. 14:34 (the authenticity of which has been questioned) the command that women are to be silent in church is said to be "also" found in Torah (though, presumably, as an implication of its narrative rather than an explicit demand). In neither case is Torah treated as the direct source of Christian duty. Cf. Deidun, *Morality,* 157-60.

65. Cf. Betz, *Galatians,* 275; van Dülmen, *Theologie,* 229-30; Gerhardsson, *Ethos,* 66-67.

66. The Galatians needed to be assured that the conduct produced by the Spirit *apart* from the law (cf. 5:18) was better, not worse, than that produced by those living as subjects of its demands (5:14; cf. v. 13; 6:13). After Paul's dramatic portrayal in Rom. 7 of the impotence of those living under the law to obey it, he clinches his argument by claiming that God's Son succeeds where the law proved weak: the possibility has been opened "that the just requirement of the law might be fulfilled in us, who walk not according to the flesh but according to the Spirit" (8:4). In 13:9 as well, Paul is claiming that Christian love inevitably meets the standards set by the law.

67. Cf. Barclay, *Truth,* 139. I assume that Christians are not in view in Rom. 2:13-14. Räisänen (*Law,* 63-64 n. 104) uses this passage as evidence against the view that Paul distinguished between "doing" and "fulfilling" the law, since "the Gentiles Paul had in mind could not 'do' the law (or its ἔργον) in any other sense than the Christians 'fulfilled' it, i.e. by living according to its central principle(s)." But Rom. 2 is speaking merely of deeds that comply with particular commands of the law (as opposed to its transgression); much more is meant when Paul speaks of Christian "fulfillment" of the law. See below.

where specifically Christian behavior is related positively to the Mosaic law, the verb πληροῦν or a cognate inevitably occurs (8:4; 13:8, 10; Gal. 5:14); yet these terms are *never* used where the requirements or achievements of those living under the law are in view. Given the occasional nature of Paul's correspondence, such a consistent distinction in usage is striking indeed and demands some explanation.

What Paul means by "doing" the law is clear enough: those under the law are obligated to carry out, to perform, its individual and specific requirements (5:3). Certainly the verb πληροῦν can also mean "to perform" (cf. Col. 4:17), but there are nuances to its usage that should not be overlooked. The verb "is used . . . with an impersonal object, originally at least pictured to the mind as a receptacle to be filled, an empty form to be filled with reality; thus of a promise, prophecy, or statement of fact, 'to satisfy the purport of,' 'to fit the terms of' . . . ; of commands and laws, 'to satisfy the requirements of,' 'to obey fully.'"[68] To "fulfill" the law thus implies that the obedience offered *completely satisfies* what is required. But this in turn means that πληροῦν is specially suited, whereas ποιεῖν is not, for use by an author who claims to have superior insight into what is required to satisfy the "true" intention of the lawgiver or the "real" demand of the law. Matthew 5:17 is a perfect illustration: πλρηῶσαι says something different from, something more than, what ποιῆσαι would say in the context.[69] The meaning must not be reduced to the bald claim that Jesus "does" the law (and the prophets?) by carrying out each of its specific requirements; rather, in some not clearly defined way (the verb πληροῦν has the advantage of positive connotations but not the liability of excessive specificity)[70] the "true" meaning of the Old Testament Scriptures is satisfied, and they reach their intended goal, in Jesus' ministry.

Paul's usage seems similar. He would scarcely have been content with the bald claim that those who love their neighbors have "done" the law (contrast Rom. 13:8). On the one hand, so prosaic an assertion would be too blatantly open to the objection that circumcision and food laws need to be "done" as well; on the other hand, the term would give no expression to Paul's implicit claim that those who have believed in Christ and been filled with his love fully satisfy the "real" purport of the law while allowing the ambiguity of the term to blunt the force of the objection that certain individual requirements (with

---

68. Burton, *Galatians*, 295.

69. Cf. Luz, "Erfüllung," 416. According to Luz, *Matthew*, 179, Matthew uses ποιέω (+ τὸ θέλημα) or τηρέω (+ τὰς ἐντολάς) for the disciples but reserves πληρόω for Jesus, with the nuance "that Jesus has done the will of God completely."

70. Cf. Barclay, *Truth*, 140-41; Luz, "Erfüllung," 413; Räisänen, *Law*, 87-88; Trilling, *Israel*, 178-79.

which, Paul would maintain, Christian behavior was never meant to conform) have not been done.[71]

Thus statements of the law's "fulfillment" should not be thought to compromise Paul's claim that the law does not bind believers. Christians serve God, he declares, not in the old way where conduct is prescribed by the law's "letter," but in the new way of those who have "died" to the law but live through God's Spirit (Rom. 7:6). Paradoxically the *results* of the old way under the law are said to be sinful passions, transgressions of the law, and death (7:5; 2 Cor. 3:6; Gal. 3:19). Paradoxically again, the "fruit" borne in the lives of those who have "died" to the law amounts to the law's fulfillment. The righteousness that divine commands could not elicit from a rebellious humanity becomes a possibility first for those transformed through the drama of divine redemption and the gift of the divine Spirit (Rom. 8:3-4).

3. The traditional interpretation that sees believers free from the "ceremonial" but not the "moral" demands of the law is not quite Pauline, but at the same time it is not without a point. Paul himself never makes such a distinction; his declarations of freedom from the law include all its demands without further specification; they mean, not simply that believers are delivered from the obligation to observe particular (ceremonial) statutes, but that they serve God in a new way, not "by the letter" but "by the Spirit." On the other hand, the distinction between ceremonial and moral is not without a point, since Paul does think the (moral, patently *not* the ceremonial) commands of the Mosaic law embody the expectations of goodness inherent in the human condition. And Christians, too, are to do the "good." Their doing so, however, should be very different from a formal compliance with requirements externally imposed; rather, it should represent an expression of their submission and devotion to God and of the fruit his Spirit bears in their lives.

It is in this sense (and therefore, I believe, correctly) that our "Lutherans" distinguished the moral from the ceremonial demands of the law and saw Christians as bound to fulfill the former. For Augustine the law fulfilled by those whose will has been transformed by divine grace is the law of love; its various works were written on tablets of stone for the Israelites, whereas love itself is "shed abroad in the hearts of believers" by the Holy Spirit.[72] For Luther the

---

71. Cf. Luther, *Pref. Rom.*, 35:367-68: "Accustom yourself, then, to this language, that doing the works of the law and fulfilling the law are two very different things. The work of the law is everything that one does, or can do, toward keeping the law of his own free will or by his own powers. . . . To fulfil the law, however, is to do its works with pleasure and love, to live a godly and good life of one's own accord, without the compulsion of the law. This pleasure and love for the law is put into the heart by the Holy Spirit."

72. *De spir. et litt.* 17.29.

Mosaic law as such binds only Israel, but the law of nature contained *within* the Mosaic law is to be observed by all.[73] In Calvin's view the moral law (spelled out in the Decalogue) is "the true and eternal rule of righteousness, prescribed for men of all nations and times, who wish to conform their lives to God's will."[74] Wesley believed the moral law to be "coeval with [human] nature" and written by the Creator on the human heart. "More perfect knowledge" of the law was made possible when it was inscribed on tablets of stone and given to the Israelites.[75] But it "must remain in force, upon all mankind, and in all ages; as not depending either on time or place, or any other circumstances liable to change, but on the nature of God and the nature of man, and their unchangeable relation to each other."[76]

What, finally, are the roots of these last Pauline theses? The hypothesis that Paul, already in his pre-Christian days, shared with other Jews a belief that Torah's validity would end with the coming of the Messiah has been tested and found untenable. W. D. Davies searched valiantly for Jewish sources suggesting such an understanding.[77] H. J. Schoeps proposed that Paul's views were so determined.[78] But the parallels discovered are scanty and remote. The evidence that most Jews believed Torah's laws to be eternal is so overwhelming that Paul could not have simply assumed a contrary position. Furthermore, Paul's arguments bear all the marks of a Christian reevaluation.

The belief that Messiah had come would not itself have forced Paul to reassess the validity of Torah. Reevaluation, however, was required by the belief that in order to fulfill God's redemptive purposes the Messiah had been crucified. It followed that neither the Torah, nor the Sinaitic covenant of which it was a part, nor the institutions it ordained could cope with human sin. Their role could only be seen as preparatory.

To be sure, Paul would have already read in the Scriptures that true obedience to God will be forthcoming only when God writes his laws on people's hearts, replaces their hearts of stone with hearts made pliable to his purposes, and imparts to them his Spirit (so Jer. 31:33 and Ezek. 11:19-20; 36:26-27). Such texts may well have influenced the formulation of his Christian thought. But the notion that a preparatory age characterized by the service of the letter had given way to the age of the Spirit seems, again, Christian in its origins — its inspiration lying in the conviction that God's Son has died and risen, and his

---

73. Cf. Luther, *Gal.*, 27:53; *Moses*, 35:172-73.
74. Calvin, *Inst.* 4.20.15.
75. Wesley, *Sermons*, 2:6-8.
76. Wesley, *Sermons*, 1:552.
77. Cf. W. D. Davies, *Torah*.
78. See chap. 7, sec. ii above.

Spirit has been poured out, to bring about a new creation ruled by righteousness. The message of the cross was for Paul first and foremost redemptive. But it was also revelatory of God's purposes in the time of "the law and the prophets" as well as in the present "day of salvation" (2 Cor. 6:2).

Chapter 20

Grace Abounding to Sinners
or Erasing Ethnic Boundaries?

To all but the partisans in the "new perspective" debate, it will be apparent that the alternatives of our title are falsely put. For Paul the apostolic kerygma offered salvation to sinners; the offer was needed, and could be embraced, by Jews and Gentiles alike.[1]

Paul's own vocation, he believed, was to take the gospel to Gentiles. The gospel was not *intended* only for Gentiles; it offered salvation to *all* — Jews *and* "Greeks" — who believed (Rom. 1:16). But the Gentiles were *his* mission field; others would take it to Jews (Gal. 2:7-9). For the success of the church's *Gentile* mission, however, Paul's importance — both theoretical and practical — can scarcely be exaggerated.

Paul did not himself *launch* the mission, nor was he likely the first to fail to require circumcision and the observance of other distinctively Jewish practices of his converts. Nonetheless, to judge from the opening of Galatians, the absence of any such requirement was at least characteristic of Paul's outreach from the beginning. (Though the issue is not raised in the Thessalonian and Corinthian correspondence, its very absence is telling.) At what point in his career the omission became controversial depends on the dating of Galatians and the relation between events it mentions and the narrative of Acts. What seems

1. Equally artificial is the choice occasionally urged between Paul's concern for the salvation of individuals and that for the redemption of the cosmos. Creation itself, Paul declared, will be freed from its corruption when the new humanity (the "sons of God") enters the glory for which God has prepared it (Rom. 8:18-25); the new humanity is now being constituted as sinners, one by one, respond to the invitation, "Be reconciled to God" (2 Cor. 5:17–6:2). Christ "died for *all*," Paul believed (5:15); but he was also convinced that the Son of God "loved *me* and gave himself for *me*" (Gal. 2:20). If we are to be true to Paul, neither emphasis may be denied or forgotten.

evident from Acts as well as Galatians is that the dispute marked a watershed both in the career of Paul and in the history of the early church. Paul's stance brought him enemies who dogged his steps the rest of his life and continued to malign him long after his death; at the same time, it is to his response to this crisis that we owe a number of the emphases in his theology that we recognize as distinctively Pauline. The dispute represented the gravest first-century threat to the early church's unity, while its resolution transformed the movement from a sect within Judaism to a faith destined to be embraced throughout (and by) the Roman Empire. The controversy thus marked a crucial development for Paul as for the nascent church. Moreover, recent scholarship has rightly underlined that it was in the context of *this* dispute, *not* a debate whether one is saved by human effort or divine grace, that Paul formulated the doctrine of justification "by faith, apart from the works of the law."

And there is more to be said. The same scholarship has rightly stressed that the question whether Christians must live as Jews had enormous implications for the success and strategy of the Christian mission and the day-to-day life of believers: the *realities* of life in the first century must not be forgotten in any discussion of Paul's thought! Still, such a requirement, however diverse its implications, could be *urged* only on "theological" grounds; that is, the laws that defined Jewish existence could be *required* of Gentiles only if the laws themselves were held to be divine in origin and meant to be obeyed by all. Conversely, such a claim could be *rejected* only by a "theological" counterargument, denying either that God gave the law or that the law was meant to be practiced by all God's people. In effect, then, the first-century issue for both Paul and his opponents — one that was crucial for all manner of social and strategic reasons — was reducible to the theoretical question whether the Sinaitic law provided the framework within which God's people were obligated to live. Those who believed it did not, if still convinced of the law's divine origin, were bound to construe the law's validity and purpose as limited.

Paul certainly did so. And he based his case not on the impracticability of imposing Jewish practices on Gentiles, nor indeed on a charge of ethnocentricity brought against Jews who thought Gentiles ought to live as they did, but on the inability of the law to cope with human sin. *All* human beings are bound to do what is right and good; the law spells out those obligations and requires that they be *done;* but human beings do not do them. Nor will Paul allow a distinction between "sinners" who flaunt their disobedience and the "righteous" whose basic commitment is to do what is right and whose shortcomings are atoned for by provisions within the Mosaic law (so non-Christian Jews believed) or the death of Jesus Christ (so Paul's Jewish Christian opponents apparently believed). Since Adam, Paul insisted, all human beings *are* sinners who are neither able nor inclined to submit to God's law. If sinners are to be found righteous in God's eyes, it must be apart from the works of righteousness required by God and spelled out in the law. For Paul, then, it is wrong to impose peculiarly Jewish aspects of the Sinaitic law on Gentile believers when it is clear that the law cannot provide the basis on which sinners may find favor with God. Rather, Gentiles (like Jews) are declared righteous by faith in Jesus Christ, *apart from* the law (cf. Gal. 2:21; 5:4; Rom. 3:21) and its works (Gal. 2:16; Rom. 3:20, 28).

It is thus both true and important to say that the Pauline gospel will not allow that the distinctively Jewish practices of the law be imposed on Gentiles; and it is true and important to note that it was in response to such an insistence that Paul formulated his doctrine of "justification by faith, apart from the works of the law." On the other hand, it is also important to recognize that the latter formulation merely restates in terms required by the dispute what was in effect Paul's "gospel" all along: a gospel of salvation for sinners facing God's wrath, but graciously offered through Jesus Christ to all who believed in him. The "works" that the Christian gospel (as proclaimed by Paul) excluded as the path to righteousness were by no means confined to Jewish boundary markers; they included the righteous works on the basis of which people were (ordinarily) thought to be righteous. Paul did not think it wrong to strive to do them: God himself requires righteous deeds; indeed, the requirement is the essence of God's law. Paul's point in ruling out the works of the law as the path to righteousness is based on the same perception as that expressed in the ancient dictum that he paraphrases in support: no human being (no "flesh") *can* be righteous in God's sight (Ps. 143:2); Paul adds, significantly, that the declaration applies even to those "under the law" and bound to do its works (Rom. 3:19-20; cf. Gal. 2:16).

The substance of Paul's doctrine of justification is reflected throughout Paul's letters. To the Thessalonians, the Corinthians, the Galatians, and the Philippians Paul had communicated the gospel of salvation, through Christ, from the wrath that awaits the ungodly. Neither in his initial proclamation nor in his Thessalonian correspondence did Paul concern himself with the relation between the Christian gospel and God's dealings with Israel. To correct Corinthian misunderstandings of the apostolic calling, Paul contrasted its glory and effects with those of Moses' ministry (2 Cor. 3). It was, however, when his Galatian converts were told to get circumcised and submit to the Mosaic law that Paul first clarified the relationship between Israel's law and the church's faith. All human beings, Paul insisted, are the subjects of sin (Gal. 3:22). The law God gave to Israel, though offering life to its doers (3:12), can only curse its transgressors (3:10) and consign sinners to their doom (3:21-23). But Christ bore the curse of the law (3:13). Now God will declare righteous those who put their faith in him (2:16; 3:24). Indeed, the promise of the gospel had long since been conveyed to Abraham (3:8);[2] he, too, had been declared righteous by faith (3:6). All who now believe thus share in the promises given to Abraham and his "seed" (3:7, 29). On the other hand, should those redeemed from their bondage to sin now submit to the law's regime, it would signal a return to their old enslavement (5:1-4).

In his letter to the Romans Paul repeated the basic content of the kerygma he had proclaimed from the beginning of his work as an apostle: by the grace of God and through the death of Jesus Christ, sinners who believe can be saved. But the issues raised by the Galatian controversy were still on his mind and receive further clarification. Even before the Galatian controversy Paul (and, apparently, pre-Pauline tradition) had occasionally claimed that sinners could be "declared righteous" in Christ (cf. 1 Cor. 1:30; 6:11); still, it was through that controversy that the formulation "righteousness by faith, not by the (works of the) law" became thematic, in part because an antithetic response was first now required, in part because of the role Genesis 15:6 (Abraham, too, was declared righteous because of faith) played in Paul's argument.

What did Paul find wrong with Judaism? The answer is routinely found in his rejection of the "works of the law": Jewish reliance on "works," it has been argued, entails a distortion of the law's true nature. The old view that the distortion was a matter of Jewish legalism has of late been replaced with the charge that it pertained to Jewish ethnocentrism. Neither charge is without a basis in Paul's writings. Yet neither charge captures the essence of Paul's denial that one can be declared righteous by the works of the law.

The most important and salutary emphasis of the new perspective on Paul is the insistence that Judaism was not "legalistic": Jews did not think they "earned" their salvation; they acknowledged God's goodness in granting Israel his covenant and strove to respond to that goodness by fulfilling its requirements. Admittedly, refutations of "Lutheran" readings of Judaism as a religion of works-righteousness at times owe more of their terminology to "Lutheranism" itself than to Jewish ways of seeing things. Judaism did not, after all, distinguish grace or faith from works done in obedience to God, nor did it thematically attribute salvation, the election of Israel, or the granting of the covenant to God's unmerited favor. To say that salvation in Judaism was "by grace" and im-

---

2. Paul refers to the promise as a "covenant" in Gal. 3:16-17. There is thus an unambiguous Pauline basis for speaking of Christ as the fulfillment of the covenant made with Abraham. The terminology, however, is not prominent in Paul's writings (as noted above, chap. 15, sec. v), nor did the point figure in his missionary proclamation of the gospel.

ply that "works" (in the "Lutheran" sense) were excluded is simply not true to Judaism; nor should one expect that a Judaism that did not see humanity as fundamentally "lost" nor requiring the death of God's Son for its redemption would construe the relation between divine grace and human works in the same way Paul did. Furthermore, the question has been raised whether the notion of covenant was itself as fundamental in all branches of Judaism as Sanders's argument claims; and in any case, a number of Jews in the Second Temple period saw the majority of their compatriots as apostates, *outside* the covenant, whose blessings they reserved for the few who rightly understood and observed its requirements. But none of these qualifications should obscure the fundamental truth that Judaism, described in its own terms, knew and depended on God's grace and did not promote a self-righteous pursuit of salvation by works.

As for Paul, the "works" he rejected were not simply those characterized by legalistic distortions of the law; otherwise he would not have used "works of the law" and "law" itself interchangeably. The operative principle of the law, for Paul, *was* its demand for works; a principle that merely made explicit God's requirement of all human beings to *do* what is good and right. Paul's point is that sinners cannot be declared righteous on the basis of a law whose requirement to do what is right they have not met. That said, Paul does recognize that a righteousness based on human works is one that leaves open the possibility of human boasting in its fulfillment (cf. Rom. 4:2).[3] Since one should boast only in the Lord, he adds — *after* completing his argument that sinners cannot be declared righteous by the works of the law — that a righteousness based on faith excludes inappropriate boasting (3:27). The point is generalized in Ephesians 2:8-9 and becomes prominent in "Lutheran" thinking. But Paul's primary objection to the notion that those who would be declared righteous must submit to the Sinaitic regime lies in his insistence that human beings are sinners who do not, and cannot, do the good that the law demands of its subjects. It may fairly be said that Augustine, Luther, Calvin, and Wesley all saw that point and gave it due emphasis.

Was Judaism "ethnocentric"? The argument of Romans 2 would not have been made had Paul not believed that some Jews presumed, on the basis of God's goodness to Israel, that they were exempt from punishment for wrongdoing. If the "boasting" that Paul excludes in 3:27 included that of any who might claim to have fulfilled the law (cf. 4:2), it also included that of Jews who

---

3. Note, too, the contrast in Phil. 3:3 between "boasting in Christ Jesus" and "putting confidence in the flesh." Paul clearly saw a misplaced self-assurance in at least some of those who pursued the "righteousness of the law" by fulfilling its demands punctiliously.

acted as though God were God of their people alone (cf. 3:29). Clearly, then, Paul saw evidence of ethnocentrism in some Jews. But again, it must be said that the "works of the law" that do not lead to righteousness are the deeds of righteousness not done by sinners; the phrase does not stand for the ethnocentric distortion of God's demands by some Jews.

At the end of Part Two I summed up the issue that divides the "Lutheran" Paul from his contemporary critics as "whether 'justification by faith, not by works of the law' means 'Sinners find God's approval by grace, through faith, not by anything they do,' or whether its thrust is that 'Gentiles are included in the people of God by faith without the bother of becoming Jews.'" As I see things, the critics have rightly defined the occasion that elicited the formulation of Paul's doctrine and have reminded us of its first-century social and strategic significance; the "Lutherans," for their part, rightly captured Paul's rationale and basic point. For those (like Augustine, Luther, Calvin, and Wesley) bent on applying Paul's words to contemporary situations, it is the point rather than the historical occasion of the formulation that is crucial. Students of early Christianity must attempt to do justice to both.

Bibliography

A. Texts and Translations

The Dead Sea Scrolls: Study Edition. 1-2. Edited by Florentino García Martínez and Eibert J. C. Tigchelaar. Leiden: Brill; Grand Rapids: Eerdmans, 1997-98.

Mekilta de-Rabbi Ishmael. 1-3. Edited and translated by Jacob Z. Lauterbach. 1933. Philadelphia: Jewish Publication Society of America, 1976.

The Mishnah. Translated by Herbert Danby. Oxford: Oxford University Press, 1933.

Septuaginta. Edited by Alfred Rahlfs. Stuttgart: Deutsche Bibelgesellschaft, 1935.

Siphre d'Be Rab. Fasciculus primus: *Siphre ad Numeros adjecto Siphre zutta.* Edited by H. S. Horovitz. 1917. Jerusalem: Wahrmann Books, 1966.

Sifre on Deuteronomy. Edited by Louis Finkelstein and H. S. Horovitz. 1939. New York: Jewish Theological Seminary of America, 1969.

Sifre: A Tannaitic Commentary on the Book of Deuteronomy. Translated with introduction and notes by Reuven Hammer. New Haven: Yale University Press, 1986.

B. Literature

Abegg, Martin G., Jr.

"Works Righteousness" — "4QMMT C 27, 31 and 'Works Righteousness.'" *Dead Sea Discoveries* 6 (1999): 139-47.

Aletti, Jean-Noël

Clefs — *Comment Dieu est-il juste? Clefs pour interpréter l'épître aux Romains.* Paris: Seuil, 1991.

"Cohérence" — "Romains 2. Sa cohérence et sa fonction." *Biblica* 77 (1996): 153-77.

"Criticism" — "Romans 7,7-25: Rhetorical Criticism and Its Usefulness." *Svensk Exegetisk Årsbok* 61 (1996): 77-95.

446

"Incohérence"   "Rm 1,18–3,20. Incohérence ou cohérence de l'argumentation paulinienne?" *Biblica* 69 (1988): 47-62.

"Justice"   "Comment Paul voit la justice de Dieu en Rm. Enjeux d'une absence de définition." *Biblica* 73 (1992): 359-75.

Loi   *Israël et la Loi dans la lettre aux Romains.* Paris: Cerf, 1998.

"Modèle"   "La présence d'un modèle rhétorique en Romains. Son rôle et son importance." *Biblica* 71 (1990): 1-24.

"Rhétorique"   "Paul et la rhétorique." In *Paul de Tarse,* edited by Jacques Schlosser, 27-50. Paris: Cerf, 1996.

"Romans"   "Romans." In *International Bible Commentary,* edited by William R. Farmer, 1553-1600. Collegeville, Minn.: Liturgical Press, 1998.

Alexander, Philip S.

Review   Review of *Jesus and Judaism,* by E. P. Sanders. *Journal of Jewish Studies* 37 (1986): 103-6.

"Torah"   "Torah and Salvation in Tannaitic Literature." In *Justification and Variegated Nomism,* vol. 1, edited by D. A. Carson, Peter T. O'Brien, and Mark A. Seifrid, 261-301. Tübingen: Mohr-Siebeck, 2001.

Augustine

    (In the listings for Augustine *AEW* = *Augustine: Earlier Writings,* trans. John H. S. Burleigh [Philadelphia: Westminster, n.d.], and SLNPF = Select Library of the Nicene and Post-Nicene Fathers of the Christian Church, 1st ser., ed. Philip Schaff [reprint, Peabody, Mass.: Hendrickson, 1995])

Ad Simpl.   *To Simplician — on Various Questions.* In *AEW,* 370-406.

C. duas epp. Pel.   *Against Two Letters of the Pelagians.* In SLNPF, 5:373-434.

C. Faust.   *Reply to Faustus the Manichaean.* In SLNPF, 4:151-345.

Conf.   *Confessions.* Translated by Henry Chadwick. Oxford: Oxford University Press, 1992.

De cat. rud.   *The First Catechetical Instruction.* Translated by Joseph P. Christopher. Westminster, Md.: Newman; London: Longman, Green and Co., 1946.

De civ. Dei   *The City of God.* In SLNPF, 2:1-511.

De corr. et grat.   *On Rebuke and Grace.* In SLNPF, 5:467-91.

De div. quaest.   *Eighty-Three Different Questions.* Translated by David L. Mosher. Washington, D.C.: Catholic University of America Press, 1982.

De doctr. Chr.   *On Christian Teaching.* Translated by R. P. H. Green. Oxford: Oxford University Press, 1997.

De don. pers.   *On the Gift of Perseverance.* In SLNPF, 5:521-52.

De fid. et op.   *On Faith and Works.* Translated by Gregory J. Lombardo. New York: Newman, 1988.

De gest. Pel.   *On the Proceedings of Pelagius.* In SLNPF, 5:177-212.

De grat. Chr.   *On the Grace of Christ, and on Original Sin.* In SLNPF, 5:213-55.

De grat. et lib. arb.   *On Grace and Free Will.* In SLNPF, 5:435-65.

De lib. arb.   *On Free Choice of the Will.* Translated by Anna S. Benjamin and L. H. Hackstaff. Indianapolis: Bobbs-Merrill, 1964.

De nat. bon.   *The Nature of the Good.* In *AEW,* 324-48.

De nat. et grat.   *On Nature and Grace.* In SLNPF, 5:115-51.

De nupt. et conc.   *On Marriage and Concupiscence.* In SLNPF, 5:257-308.

De pecc. mer.   *On the Merits and Remission of Sins, and on the Baptism of Infants.* In SLNPF, 5:11-78.

De perf. just. hom.   *On Man's Perfection in Righteousness.* In SLNPF, 5:153-76.

De praed. sanct.   *On the Predestination of the Saints.* In SLNPF, 5:493-519.

De spir. et litt.   *The Spirit and the Letter.* In *Augustine: Later Works,* translated by John Burnaby, 182-250. Philadelphia: Westminster, 1955.

De Trin.   *The Trinity.* Translated by Edmund Hill. Brooklyn: New City Press, 1991.

De util. cred.   *The Usefulness of Belief.* In *AEW,* 284-323.

De ver. rel.   *Of True Religion.* In *AEW,* 218-83.

Ench.   *Enchiridion.* In *Augustine: Confessions and Enchiridion,* translated by Albert C. Outler, 335-412. Philadelphia: Westminster, 1955.

Ep.   *Letters.* In SLNPF, 1:209-593.

Retr.   *The Retractations.* Translated by Sister Mary Inez Bogan. Washington D.C.: Catholic University of America Press, 1968.

Serm.   *Sermons.* Part III. Vols. 1-11 of *The Works of Saint Augustine: A Translation for the Twenty-First Century.* Translated by Edmund Hill. Brooklyn (New Rochelle, Hyde Park), N.Y.: New City Press, 1990-97.

Avemarie, Friedrich

"Erwählung"   "Erwählung und Vergeltung. Zur optionalen Struktur rabbinischer Soteriologie." *New Testament Studies* 45 (1999): 108-26.

Tora   *Tora und Leben: Untersuchungen zur Heilsbedeutung der Tora in der frühen rabbinischen Literatur.* Tübingen: J. C. B. Mohr (Paul Siebeck), 1996.

"Werke"   "Die Werke des Gesetzes im Spiegel des Jakobusbriefs: A Very Old Perspective on Paul." *Zeitschrift für Theologie und Kirche* 98 (2001): 282-309.

Bacher, Wilhelm

Terminologie   *Die exegetische Terminologie der jüdischen Traditionsliteratur.* 1899, 1905. Hildesheim: G. Olms, 1965.

Badenas, Robert

End   *Christ the End of the Law: Romans 10.4 in Pauline Perspective.* Sheffield: JSOT Press, 1985.

Barclay, John M. G.

"Law"   "'Do We Undermine the Law?' A Study of Romans 14.1–15.6." In *Paul and the Mosaic Law,* edited by James D. G. Dunn, 287-308. Grand Rapids: Eerdmans, 2001.

Truth   *Obeying the Truth: Paul's Ethics in Galatians.* Minneapolis: Fortress, 1991.

Bibliography

Barr, James
Semantics   *The Semantics of Biblical Language.* Oxford: Oxford University Press, 1961.

Barrett, C. K.
"Conscience"   "Paul and the Introspective Conscience." In *The Bible, the Reformation, and the Church: Essays in Honour of James Atkinson,* edited by W. P. Stephens, 36-48. Sheffield: Sheffield Academic Press, 1995.
Corinthians   *A Commentary on the First Epistle to the Corinthians.* 2nd ed. London: Adam and Charles Black, 1971.
Romans   *A Commentary on the Epistle to the Romans.* 2nd ed. London: A. & C. Black, 1991.

Barth, Karl
"Gospel"   "Gospel and Law." *Scottish Journal of Theology Occasional Papers* 8 (1959): 3-27.

Bassler, Jouette M.
Impartiality   *Divine Impartiality: Paul and a Theological Axiom.* Chico, Calif.: Scholars, 1982.

Bauckham, Richard
"Apocalypses"   "Apocalypses." In *Justification and Variegated Nomism,* vol. 1, edited by D. A. Carson, Peter T. O'Brien, and Mark A. Seifrid, 135-87. Tübingen: Mohr-Siebeck, 2001.

Baumgarten, A. I.
"Name"   "The Name of the Pharisees." *Journal of Biblical Literature* 102 (1983): 411-28.

Becker, Jürgen
Paul   *Paul: Apostle to the Gentiles.* Louisville: Westminster/John Knox, 1993.

Beker, J. Christiaan
Paul   *Paul the Apostle: The Triumph of God in Life and Thought.* Philadelphia: Fortress, 1984.

Bell, Richard H.
"Salvation"   "Rom 5.18-19 and Universal Salvation." *New Testament Studies* 48 (2002): 417-32.
Study   *No One Seeks for God: An Exegetical and Theological Study of Romans 1.18–3.20.* Tübingen: Mohr Siebeck, 1998.

Best, Ernest
Essays   *Essays on Ephesians.* Edinburgh: T. & T. Clark, 1997.

Betz, Hans Dieter
Galatians   *Galatians.* Philadelphia: Fortress, 1979.

Bläser, Peter
Gesetz   *Das Gesetz bei Paulus.* Münster: Aschendorff, 1941.

449

Bockmuehl, Markus

"Church" "1 Thessalonians 2:14-16 and the Church in Jerusalem." *Tyndale Bulletin* 52 (2001): 1-31.

"Law" "Natural Law in Second Temple Judaism." *Vetus Testamentum* 45 (1995): 17-44.

"Salvation" "1QS and Salvation at Qumran." In *Justification and Variegated Nomism*, vol. 1, edited by D. A. Carson, Peter T. O'Brien, and Mark A. Seifrid, 381-414. Tübingen: Mohr-Siebeck, 2001.

Boyarin, Daniel

Jew *A Radical Jew: Paul and the Politics of Identity.* Berkeley: University of California Press, 1994.

Bruce, F. F.

Galatians *The Epistle to the Galatians: A Commentary on the Greek Text.* Grand Rapids: Eerdmans, 1982.

Thessalonians *1 and 2 Thessalonians.* Dallas: Word, 1982.

Bultmann, Rudolf

"Anthropology" "Romans 7 and the Anthropology of Paul." In *Existence and Faith: Shorter Writings of Rudolf Bultmann*, 147-57. Cleveland: World, 1960.

"ΔΙΚΑΙΟΣΥΝΗ" "ΔΙΚΑΙΟΣΥΝΗ ΘΕΟΥ." *Journal of Biblical Literature* 83 (1964): 12-16.

"End" "Christ the End of the Law." In *Essays, Philosophical and Theological*, 36-66. London: SCM Press, 1955.

"Jesus" "Jesus and Paul." In *Existence and Faith: Shorter Writings of Rudolf Bultmann*, 183-201. Cleveland: World, 1960.

Mythology *Jesus Christ and Mythology.* New York: Charles Scribner's Sons, 1958.

"NT" "New Testament and Mythology." In *Kerygma and Myth*, edited by H. W. Bartsch, 1-44. London: SPCK, 1953.

"Paul" "Paul." In *Existence and Faith: Shorter Writings of Rudolf Bultmann*, 111-46. Cleveland: World, 1960.

"Problem" "The Problem of Ethics in Paul." In *Understanding Paul's Ethics: Twentieth Century Approaches*, edited by B. S. Rosner, 195-216. Grand Rapids: Eerdmans, 1995.

Setting *Primitive Christianity in Its Contemporary Setting.* New York: New American Library, 1974.

Theology *Theology of the New Testament.* Vol. 1. New York: Charles Scribner's Sons, 1951.

Burton, Ernest de Witt

Galatians *A Critical and Exegetical Commentary on the Epistle to the Galatians.* Edinburgh: T. & T. Clark, 1921.

Byrne, Brendan

"Need" "Universal Need of Salvation and Universal Salvation by Faith in the Letter to the Romans." *Pacifica* 8 (1995): 123-39.

"Problem" "The Problem of Νόμος and the Relationship with Judaism in Romans." *Catholic Biblical Quarterly* 62 (2000): 294-309.

Romans   *Romans.* Collegeville, Minn.: Liturgical Press, 1996.

Sons   *"Sons of God" — "Seed of Abraham."* Rome: Pontifical Biblical Institute, 1979.

Callan, Terrance

"Midrash"   "Pauline Midrash: The Exegetical Background of Gal 3:19b." *Journal of Biblical Literature* 99 (1980): 549-67.

Calvin, John

BLW   *The Bondage and Liberation of the Will.* Edited by A. N. S. Lane. Translated by G. I. Davies. Grand Rapids: Baker, 1996.

Cat. Gen.   *The Catechism of the Church of Geneva.* In *Calvin: Theological Treatises,* translated by J. K. S. Reid, 83-139. Philadelphia: Westminster, 1954.

Comm. ad loc. *The Epistles of Paul the Apostle to the Galatians, Ephesians, Philippians, and Colossians.* Edited by David W. Torrance and Thomas F. Torrance. Translated by T. H. L. Parker. Grand Rapids: Eerdmans; Carlisle: Paternoster, 1965.

      The Epistles of Paul the Apostle to the Romans and to the Thessalonians. Edited by David W. Torrance and Thomas F. Torrance. Translated by Ross Mackenzie. Edinburgh: Oliver and Boyd, 1960.

Defence   *A Defence of the Secret Providence of God.* In *Calvin's Calvinism,* translated by Henry Cole, 207-350. Grand Rapids: Eerdmans, 1956.

Inst.   *Institutes of the Christian Religion.* 1-2. Edited by John T. McNeill. Translated by Ford Lewis Battles. Philadelphia: Westminster, 1960.

Sadolet   *Reply to Sadolet.* In *Calvin: Theological Treatises,* translated by J. K. S. Reid, 219-56. Philadelphia: Westminster, 1954.

Campbell, D. A.

"Meaning"   "The Meaning of Πίστις and Νόμος in Paul: A Linguistic and Structural Perspective." *Journal of Biblical Literature* 111 (1992): 91-103.

Carson, D. A.

"Summaries" "Summaries and Conclusions." In *Justification and Variegated Nomism,* vol. 1, edited by D. A. Carson, Peter T. O'Brien, and Mark A. Seifrid, 505-48. Tübingen: Mohr-Siebeck, 2001.

Clements, Ronald E.

Theology   *Old Testament Theology.* Atlanta: John Knox, 1978.

Collins, John J.

Athens   *Between Athens and Jerusalem: Jewish Identity in the Hellenistic Diaspora.* New York: Crossroad, 1986.

Conzelmann, Hans

1 Corinthians *1 Corinthians.* Philadelphia: Fortress, 1975.

Cosgrove, Charles H.

"Justification" "Justification in Paul: A Linguistic and Theological Reflection." *Journal of Biblical Literature* 106 (1987): 653-70.

Cranfield, C. E. B.
"Law"   "St. Paul and the Law." *Scottish Journal of Theology* 17 (1964): 43-68.
On Rom.   *On Romans and Other New Testament Essays*. Edinburgh: T. & T. Clark, 1998.
Romans   *A Critical and Exegetical Commentary on the Epistle to the Romans*. 1-2. Edinburgh: T. & T. Clark, 1975, 1979.

Cummins, Stephen Anthony
Crucified Christ   *Paul and the Crucified Christ in Antioch: Maccabean Martyrdom and Galatians 1 and 2*. Cambridge: Cambridge University Press, 2001.

Dahl, Nils Alstrup
Studies   *Studies in Paul: Theology for the Early Christian Mission*. Minneapolis: Augsburg, 1977.

Das, A. Andrew
Jews   *Paul and the Jews*. Peabody, Mass.: Hendrickson. Forthcoming.
Law   *Paul, the Law, and the Covenant*. Peabody, Mass.: Hendrickson, 2001.

Davies, Glenn N.
Faith   *Faith and Obedience in Romans: A Study in Romans 1–4*. Sheffield: Sheffield Academic Press, 1990.

Davies, W. D.
Studies   *Jewish and Pauline Studies*. Philadelphia: Fortress, 1984.
Torah   *Torah in the Messianic Age and/or the Age to Come*. Philadelphia: Society of Biblical Literature, 1952.

Deidun, Tom
"Cake"   "'Having His Cake and Eating It': Paul on the Law." *Heythrop Journal* 27 (1986): 43-52.
Morality   *New Covenant Morality in Paul*. Rome: Pontifical Biblical Institute, 1981.
"New Perspective" "James Dunn and John Ziesler on Romans in New Perspective." *Heythrop Journal* 33 (1992): 79-84.

Dodd, Brian
Example   *Paul's Paradigmatic "I": Personal Example as Literary Strategy*. Sheffield: Sheffield Academic Press, 1999.

Dodd, C. H.
Bible   *The Bible and the Greeks*. London: Hodder and Stoughton, 1935.

Donaldson, Terence L.
"Curse"   "The 'Curse of the Law' and the Inclusion of the Gentiles: Galatians 3.13-14." *New Testament Studies* 32 (1986): 94-112.
Paul   *Paul and the Gentiles: Remapping the Apostle's Convictional World*. Minneapolis: Fortress, 1997.

Donfried, Karl P., and I. Howard Marshall
Theology   *The Theology of the Shorter Pauline Letters*. Cambridge: Cambridge University Press, 1993.

Drane, John W.

Paul   *Paul: Libertine or Legalist? A Study in the Theology of the Major Pauline Epistles.* London: SPCK, 1975.

Dülmen, Andrea van

Theologie   *Die Theologie des Gesetzes bei Paulus.* Stuttgart: Katholisches Bibelwerk, 1968.

Dunn, James D. G.

"Apostate"   "Paul: Apostate or Apostle of Israel?" *Zeitschrift für die neutestamentliche Wissenschaft* 89 (1998): 256-71.

Christology   *Christology in the Making: A New Testament Inquiry into the Origins of the Doctrine of the Incarnation.* 2nd ed. London: SCM Press; Philadelphia: Westminster, 1989.

"Covenants"   "Two Covenants or One? The Interdependence of Jewish and Christian Identity." In *Geschichte — Tradition — Reflexion. Festschrift für Martin Hengel zum 70. Geburtsdag*, vol. 3, edited by Hermann Lichtenberger, 97-122. Tübingen: J. C. B. Mohr (Paul Siebeck), 1996.

Ep. Gal.   *The Epistle to the Galatians.* Peabody, Mass.: Hendrickson, 1993.

"4QMMT"   "4QMMT and Galatians." *New Testament Studies* 43 (1997): 147-53.

"Gospel"   "How New Was Paul's Gospel? The Problem of Continuity and Discontinuity." In *Gospel in Paul: Studies on Corinthians, Galatians, and Romans for Richard N. Longenecker*, edited by L. Ann Jervis and Peter Richardson, 367-88. Sheffield: Sheffield Academic Press, 1994.

"Ground"   "In Search of Common Ground." In *Paul and the Mosaic Law*, edited by James D. G. Dunn, 309-34. Grand Rapids: Eerdmans, 2001.

"Justice"   "The Justice of God: A Renewed Perspective on Justification by Faith." *Journal of Theological Studies* 43 (1992): 1-22.

"Justification"   "Paul and Justification by Faith." In *The Road from Damascus: The Impact of Paul's Conversion on His Life, Thought, and Ministry*, edited by Richard N. Longenecker, 85-101. Grand Rapids: Eerdmans, 1997.

Law   *Jesus, Paul, and the Law: Studies in Mark and Galatians.* Louisville: Westminster/John Knox, 1990.

"Law of Faith"   "'The Law of Faith,' 'the Law of the Spirit' and 'the Law of Christ.'" In *Theology and Ethics in Paul and His Interpreters: Essays in Honor of Victor Paul Furnish*, edited by Eugene H. Lovering, Jr., and Jerry L. Sumney, 62-82. Nashville: Abingdon, 1996.

"Nomism"   "The Theology of Galatians: The Issue of Covenantal Nomism." In *Pauline Theology I: Thessalonians, Philippians, Galatians, Philemon*, edited by Jouette M. Bassler, 125-46. Minneapolis: Fortress, 1991.

Partings   *The Partings of the Ways between Christianity and Judaism and Their Significance for the Character of Christianity.* London: SCM Press; Philadelphia: Trinity Press International, 1991.

Romans 1–8   *Romans 1–8.* Word Biblical Commentary 38A. Dallas: Word, 1988.

Romans 9–16   *Romans 9–16.* Word Biblical Commentary 38B. Dallas: Word, 1988.

"Test-Case"   "Was Paul against the Law? The Law in Galatians and Romans: A Test-

	Case of Text in Context." In *Biblical Texts in Their Textual and Situational Contexts: Essays in Honor of Lars Hartman,* edited by Tord Fornberg and David Hellholm, 455-75. Oslo: Scandinavian University Press, 1995.
Theol. Gal.	*The Theology of Paul's Letter to the Galatians.* Cambridge: Cambridge University Press, 1993.
Theology	*The Theology of Paul the Apostle.* Grand Rapids: Eerdmans, 1998.
"Works"	"Yet Once More — 'The Works of the Law': A Response." *Journal for the Study of the New Testament* 46 (1992): 99-117.

Dunn, James D. G., and Alan M. Suggate

Justice   *The Justice of God: A Fresh Look at the Old Doctrine of Justification by Faith.* Carlisle, Cumbria: Paternoster, 1993; Grand Rapids: Eerdmans, 1994.

Eastman, Brad

Grace   *The Significance of Grace in the Letters of Paul.* New York: Peter Lang, 1999.

Ebeling, Gerhard

Word   *Word and Faith.* Philadelphia: Fortress, 1963.

Eckstein, Hans-Joachim

Verheissung   *Verheissung und Gesetz: Eine exegetische Untersuchung zu Galater 2,15– 4,7.* Tübingen: J. C. B. Mohr (Paul Siebeck), 1996.

Elliott, Mark Adam

Survivors   *The Survivors of Israel: A Reconsideration of the Theology of Pre-Christian Judaism.* Grand Rapids: Eerdmans, 2000.

Elliott, Neil

Rhetoric   *The Rhetoric of Romans: Argumentative Constraint and Strategy and Paul's Dialogue with Judaism.* Sheffield: Sheffield Academic Press, 1990.

Enns, Peter

"Expansions"   "Expansions of Scripture." In *Justification and Variegated Nomism,* vol. 1, edited by D. A. Carson, Peter T. O'Brien, and Mark A. Seifrid, 73-98. Tübingen: Mohr-Siebeck, 2001.

Eskola, Timo

Theodicy   *Theodicy and Predestination in Pauline Soteriology.* Tübingen: Mohr Siebeck, 1998.

Espy, John M.

"Conscience"   "Paul's 'Robust Conscience' Re-examined." *New Testament Studies* 31 (1985): 161-88.

Fee, Gordon D.

Philippians   *Paul's Letter to the Philippians.* Grand Rapids: Eerdmans, 1995.

Bibliography

Finsterbusch, Karin
Thora   *Die Thora als Lebensweisung für Heidenchristen: Studien zur Bedeutung der Thora für die paulinische Ethik.* Göttingen: Vandenhoeck & Ruprecht, 1996.

Friedrich, Gerhard
"Gesetz"   "Das Gesetz des Glaubens Röm. 3,27." *Theologisches Zeitschrift* 10 (1954): 401-17.

Fuller, Daniel P.
Gospel   *Gospel and Law: Contrast or Continuum?* Grand Rapids: Eerdmans, 1980.
"Works"   "Paul and 'The Works of the Law.'" *Westminster Theological Journal* 38 (1975-76): 28-42.

Gager, John G.
Origins   *The Origins of Anti-Semitism: Attitudes toward Judaism in Pagan and Christian Antiquity.* New York: Oxford University Press, 1983.

Garlington, Don B.
Aspects   *Faith, Obedience, and Perseverance: Aspects of Paul's Letter to the Romans.* Tübingen: J. C. B. Mohr (Paul Siebeck), 1994.
Obedience of Faith "The Obedience of Faith": A Pauline Phrase in Historical Context. Tübingen: J. C. B. Mohr (Paul Siebeck), 1991.

Gaston, Lloyd
Paul   *Paul and the Torah.* Vancouver: University of British Columbia Press, 1987.

Gathercole, S. J.
Boasting   *Where Is Boasting? Early Jewish Soteriology and Paul's Response in Romans 1–5.* Grand Rapids: Eerdmans, 2002.
"Evidence"   "Justified by Faith, Justified by His Blood: The Evidence of Rom 3.21–4.25." In *Justification and Variegated Nomism*, vol. 2. Forthcoming.
"Law"   "A Law unto Themselves: The Gentiles in Romans 2.14-15 Revisited." *Journal for the Study of the New Testament* 85 (2002): 27-49.

Gerhardsson, Birger
Ethos   *The Ethos of the Bible.* Philadelphia: Fortress, 1981.

Gordon, T. David
"Israel"   "Why Israel Did Not Obtain Torah-Righteousness: A Translation Note on Rom 9:32." *Westminster Theological Journal* 54 (1992): 163-66.

Grafe, Eduard
Lehre   *Die paulinische Lehre vom Gesetz nach den vier Hauptbriefen.* Freiburg and Tübingen: J. C. B. Mohr, 1884.

Gundry, R. H.
"Grace"   "Grace, Works, and Staying Saved in Paul." *Biblica* 66 (1985): 1-38.

Gutbrod, W., and H. Kleinknecht
"νόμος"   "νόμος, etc." In *Theological Dictionary of the New Testament,* edited by
                   Gerhard Kittel, 4:1022-91. Grand Rapids: Eerdmans, 1967.

Hahn, Ferdinand
"Entwicklung"   "Gibt es eine Entwicklung in den Aussagen über die Rechtfertigung
                   bei Paulus?" *Evangelische Theologie* 53 (1993): 342-66.
"Gesetzes-   "Das Gesetzesverständnis im Römer- und Galaterbrief." *Zeitschrift für*
verständnis"   *die neutestamentliche Wissenschaft* 67 (1976): 29-63.

Hansen, G. Walter
Abraham   *Abraham in Galatians: Epistolary and Rhetorical Contexts.* Sheffield:
                   Sheffield Academic Press, 1989.

Hay, David M.
"Philo"   "Philo of Alexandria." In *Justification and Variegated Nomism,* vol. 1,
                   edited by D. A. Carson, Peter T. O'Brien, and Mark A. Seifrid, 357-79.
                   Tübingen: Mohr-Siebeck, 2001.

Hays, Richard B.
Echoes   *Echoes of Scripture in the Letters of Paul.* New Haven: Yale University
                   Press, 1989.
Faith   *The Faith of Jesus Christ: The Narrative Substructure of Galatians 3:1–*
                   4:11. 2nd ed. Grand Rapids: Eerdmans, 2002.
"Justification"   "Justification." In *Anchor Bible Dictionary,* edited by David Noel
                   Freedman, 3:1129-33. New York: Doubleday, 1992.
"Logic"   "Psalm 143 and the Logic of Romans 3." *Journal of Biblical Literature* 99
                   (1980): 107-15.

Heil, John Paul
"Termination"   "Christ, the Termination of the Law (Romans 9:30–10:8)." *Catholic*
                   Biblical Quarterly 63 (2001): 484-98.

Herford, Robert Travers
Judaism   *Judaism in the New Testament Period.* London: Lindsey, 1928.

Hill, David
Words   *Greek Words and Hebrew Meanings: Studies in the Semantics of*
                   Soteriological Terms. Cambridge: University Press, 1967.

Hofius, Otfried
"Antithesis"   "The Adam-Christ Antithesis and the Law: Reflections on Romans
                   5:12-21." In *Paul and the Mosaic Law,* edited by James D. G. Dunn, 165-
                   205. Grand Rapids: Eerdmans, 2001.
Paulusstudien   *Paulusstudien.* Tübingen: J. C. B. Mohr (Paul Siebeck), 1989.
Paulusstudien II *Paulusstudien II.* Tübingen: Mohr Siebeck, 2002.

Holmberg, Bengt
"Identity"   "Jewish versus Christian Identity in the Early Church?" *Revue biblique*
                   105 (1998): 397-425.

Hong, In-Gyu
Law The Law in Galatians. Sheffield: Sheffield Academic Press, 1993.

Hooker, Morna D.
Adam From Adam to Christ: Essays on Paul. Cambridge: Cambridge University Press, 1990.

Howard, George E.
Crisis Paul: Crisis in Galatia: A Study in Early Christian Theology. Cambridge: Cambridge University Press, 1979.
"End" "Christ the End of the Law: The Meaning of Romans 10.4ff." *Journal of Biblical Literature* 88 (1969): 331-37.
"Faith" "On the 'Faith of Christ.'" *Harvard Theological Review* 60 (1967): 459-65.

Hübner, Hans
Israel Gottes Ich und Israel: Zum Schriftgebrauch des Paulus in Römer 9–11. Göttingen: Vandenhoeck & Ruprecht, 1984.
Law Law in Paul's Thought. Edinburgh: T. & T. Clark, 1984.
"Proprium" "Pauli Theologiae Proprium." *New Testament Studies* 26 (1980): 445-73.
"Rechtfertigung" "Rechtfertigung und Sühne bei Paulus: Eine hermeneutische und theologische Besinnung." *New Testament Studies* 39 (1993): 80-93.
Theologie Biblische Theologie des Neuen Testaments. Vol. 2, Die Theologie des Paulus und ihre neutestamentliche Wirkungsgeschichte. Göttingen: Vandenhoeck & Ruprecht, 1993.

Hultgren, Arland J.
Benefits Christ and His Benefits: Christology and Redemption in the New Testament. Philadelphia: Fortress, 1987.
Gospel Paul's Gospel and Mission: The Outlook from His Letter to the Romans. Philadelphia: Fortress, 1985.

Jackson, Bernard S.
"Legalism" "Legalism." *Journal of Jewish Studies* 30 (1979): 1-22.

Jervis, L. Ann
Purpose The Purpose of Romans: A Comparative Letter Structure Investigation. Sheffield: Sheffield Academic Press, 1991.

Käsemann, Ernst
Perspectives Perspectives on Paul. Philadelphia: Fortress, 1971.
Questions New Testament Questions of Today. London: SCM Press, 1969.
Romans Commentary on Romans. Grand Rapids: Eerdmans, 1980.

Kim, Seyoon
Origin The Origin of Paul's Gospel. 2nd ed. Tübingen: J. C. B. Mohr, 1984.
Perspective Paul and the New Perspective: Second Thoughts on the Origin of Paul's Gospel. Grand Rapids: Eerdmans, 2002.

Koester, H.
"Concept" "ΝΟΜΟΣ ΦΥΣΕΩΣ: The Concept of Natural Law in Greek Thought." In *Religions in Antiquity: Essays in Memory of Erwin Ramsdell Goodenough*, edited by Jacob Neusner, 521-41. Leiden: Brill, 1968.

Koperski, Veronica
"Meaning" "The Meaning of *Pistis Christou* in Philippians 3:9." *Louvain Studies* 18 (1993): 198-216.

Kruse, Colin G.
Paul *Paul, the Law, and Justification*. Peabody, Mass.: Hendrickson, 1997.

Kümmel, W. G.
Bild *Römer 7 und das Bild des Menschen im Neuen Testament*. Munich: Christian Kaiser, 1974.

Kuss, Otto
"Nomos" "Nomos bei Paulus." *Münchener theologische Zeitschrift* 17 (1966): 173-227.

Kuula, Kari
Law *The Law, the Covenant, and God's Plan*. Vol. 1, *Paul's Polemical Treatment of the Law in Galatians*. Helsinki: Finnish Exegetical Society; Göttingen: Vandenhoeck & Ruprecht, 1999.

Laato, Timo
Approach *Paul and Judaism: An Anthropological Approach*. Atlanta: Scholars, 1995.
"Justification" "Justification according to James: A Comparison with Paul." *Trinity Journal* 18 (1997): 43-84.

Lambrecht, Jan
"Reasoning" "Paul's Reasoning in Galatians 2:11-21." In *Paul and the Mosaic Law*, edited by James D. G. Dunn, 53-74. Grand Rapids: Eerdmans, 2001.
Studies *Pauline Studies: Collected Essays*. Leuven: Leuven University Press, 1994.

Lapide, Pinchas, and Peter Stuhlmacher
Paul *Paul: Rabbi and Apostle*. Minneapolis: Augsburg, 1984.

Lightfoot, J. B.
Galatians *The Epistle of St. Paul to the Galatians*. 1865. Grand Rapids: Zondervan, 1957.

Lincoln, Andrew T.
"Summary" "Ephesians 2:8-10: A Summary of Paul's Gospel?" *Catholic Biblical Quarterly* 45 (1983): 617-30.

Lindars, Barnabas
"Torah" "Torah in Deuteronomy." In *Words and Meanings: Essays Presented to*

Bibliography

David Winton Thomas, edited by Peter R. Ackroyd and Barnabas Lindars, 117-36. Cambridge: Cambridge University Press, 1968.

Ljungman, Henrik
Pistis   *Pistis: A Study of Its Presuppositions and Its Meaning in Pauline Use.* Lund: C. W. K. Gleerup, 1964.

Lohse, Eduard
"νόμος"   "ὁ νόμος τοῦ πνεύματος τῆς ζωῆς: Exegetische Anmerkungen zu Röm 8,2." In *Neues Testament und christliche Existenz. Festschrift H. Braun,* 279-87. Tübingen: J. C. B. Mohr, 1973.

Longenecker, Bruce W.
Eschatology   *Eschatology and the Covenant: A Comparison of 4 Ezra and Romans 1– 11.* Sheffield: Sheffield Academic Press, 1991.
Triumph   *The Triumph of Abraham's God: The Transformation of Identity in Galatians.* Nashville: Abingdon, 1998.

Longenecker, Richard N.
Galatians   *Galatians.* Dallas: Word, 1990.
Paul   *Paul, Apostle of Liberty.* 1964. Grand Rapids: Baker, 1976.

Luther, Martin
Bondage   *The Bondage of the Will.* In *Luther's Works,* vol. 33, edited by Philip S. Watson. Philadelphia: Fortress, 1972.
Faith and Law *Theses concerning Faith and Law.* In *Luther's Works,* vol. 34, edited by Lewis W. Spitz, 105-32. Philadelphia: Muhlenberg, 1960.
Freedom   *The Freedom of a Christian.* In *Luther's Works,* vol. 31, edited by Harold J. Grimm, 327-77. Philadelphia: Muhlenberg, 1957.
Gal.   *Lectures on Galatians.* 1535. In *Luther's Works,* vol. 26-27, edited by Jaroslav Pelikan. Saint Louis: Concordia, 1963-64.
Good Works   *Treatise on Good Works.* In *Luther's Works,* vol. 44, edited by James Atkinson, 15-114. Philadelphia: Fortress, 1966.
Large Cat.   *The Large Catechism of Martin Luther.* Translated by Robert H. Fischer. Philadelphia: Fortress, 1959.
Moses   *How Christians Should Regard Moses.* In *Luther's Works,* vol. 35, edited by E. Theodore Bachmann, 155-74. Philadelphia: Muhlenberg, 1960.
Pref. Ep. John *Preface to the Three Epistles of St. John.* In *Luther's Works,* vol. 35, edited by E. Theodore Bachmann, 393. Philadelphia: Muhlenberg, 1960.
Pref. James   *Preface to the Epistles of St. James and St. Jude.* In *Luther's Works,* vol. 35, edited by E. Theodore Bachmann, 395-98. Philadelphia: Muhlenberg, 1960.
Pref. Lat. Writ. *Preface to the Complete Edition of Luther's Latin Writings.* In *Luther's Works,* vol. 34, edited by Lewis W. Spitz, 323-38. Philadelphia: Muhlenberg, 1960.
Pref. OT   *Preface to the Old Testament.* In *Luther's Works,* vol. 35, edited by E. Theodore Bachmann, 235-51. Philadelphia: Muhlenberg, 1960.
Pref. Rom.   *Preface to the Epistle of St. Paul to the Romans.* In *Luther's Works,* vol. 35,

edited by E. Theodore Bachmann, 365-80. Philadelphia: Muhlenberg, 1960.

Small Cat. *The Small Catechism.* Minneapolis: Augsburg; Philadelphia: Fortress, 1979.

Table Talk *Table Talk.* In *Luther's Works,* vol. 54, edited and translated by Theodore G. Tappert. Philadelphia: Fortress, 1967.

Temp. Auth. *Temporal Authority: To What Extent It Should Be Obeyed.* In *Luther's Works,* vol. 45, edited by Walther I. Brandt, 75-129. Philadelphia: Muhlenberg, 1962.

Two Kinds *Two Kinds of Righteousness.* In *Luther's Works,* vol. 31, edited by Harold J. Grimm, 293-306. Philadelphia: Muhlenberg, 1957.

Luz, Ulrich
"Erfüllung" "Die Erfüllung des Gesetzes bei Matthäus (Mt 5, 17-20)." *Zeitschrift für Theologie und Kirche* 75 (1978): 398-435.

Matthew *Matthew 1–7: A Commentary.* Minneapolis: Augsburg, 1989.

"Rechtfertigung" "Rechtfertigung bei den Paulusschülern." In *Rechtfertigung: Festschrift für Ernst Käsemann zum 70. Geburtstag,* edited by Johannes Friedrich, Wolfgang Pöhlmann, and Peter Stuhlmacher, 365-83. Tübingen: J. C. B. Mohr (Paul Siebeck); Göttingen: Vandenhoeck & Ruprecht, 1976.

Lyonnet, S.
"Sens" "Le sens de ἐφ' ᾧ en Rom 5, 12 et l'exégèse des pères grecs." *Biblica* 36 (1955): 436-56.

Malherbe, Abraham J.
Thessalonians *The Letters to the Thessalonians.* New York: Doubleday, 2000.

Marshall, I. Howard
Epistles *The Epistles of John.* Grand Rapids: Eerdmans, 1978.

"Salvation" "Salvation, Grace and Works in the Later Writings in the Pauline Corpus." *New Testament Studies* 42 (1996): 339-58.

"Theology" "Pauline Theology in the Thessalonian Correspondence." In *Paul and Paulinism: Essays in Honour of C. K. Barrett,* edited by M. D. Hooker and S. G. Wilson, 173-83. London: SPCK, 1982.

Thessalonians *1 and 2 Thessalonians.* Grand Rapids: Eerdmans, 1983.

Martens, John W.
"Reading" "Romans 2.14-16: A Stoic Reading." *New Testament Studies* 40 (1994): 55-67.

Martin, Brice L.
Law *Christ and the Law in Paul.* Leiden: Brill, 1989.

Martyn, J. Louis
"Events" "Events in Galatia: Modified Covenantal Nomism versus God's Invasion of the Cosmos in the Singular Gospel: A Response to J. D. G. Dunn and B. R. Gaventa." In *Pauline Theology,* vol. 1, *Thessalonians,*

	Philippians, Galatians, Philemon, edited by Jouette M. Bassler, 160-79. Minneapolis: Fortress, 1991.
Galatians	*Galatians: A New Translation with Introduction and Commentary.* New York: Doubleday, 1997.
Issues	*Theological Issues in the Letters of Paul.* Nashville: Abingdon, 1997.

Matlock, R. Barry

| "Sins" | "Sins of the Flesh and Suspicious Minds: Dunn's New Theology of Paul." *Journal for the Study of the New Testament* 72 (1998): 67-90. |
| "Studies" | "Almost Cultural Studies? Reflections on the 'New Perspective' on Paul." In *Biblical Studies/Cultural Studies: The Third Sheffield Colloquium,* edited by J. Cheryl Exum and Stephen D. Moore, 433-59. Sheffield: Sheffield Academic Press, 1998. |

Maurer, Christian

| *Gesetzeslehre* | *Die Gesetzeslehre des Paulus.* Zürich: Evangelischer Verlag A. G. Zollikon, 1941. |

McGiffert, Michael

| "Grace" | "Grace and Works: The Rise and Division of Covenant Divinity in Elizabethan Puritanism." *Harvard Theological Review* 75 (1982): 463-502. |

Merklein, Helmut

| *Studien* | *Studien zu Jesus und Paulus.* 2. Tübingen: J. C. B. Mohr (Paul Siebeck), 1998. |

Meyer, Ben F.

| *Christians* | *The Early Christians: Their World Mission and Self-Discovery.* Wilmington, Del.: Michael Glazier, 1986. |

Mijoga, Hilary B. P.

| *Notion* | *The Pauline Notion of Deeds of the Law.* San Francisco: International Scholars Publications, 1999. |

Møller, Jens G.

| "Beginnings" | "The Beginnings of Puritan Covenant Theology." *Journal of Ecclesiastical History* 14 (1963): 46-67. |

Montefiore, Claude G.

| *St. Paul* | *Judaism and St. Paul.* London: Max Goschen, 1914. |

Moo, Douglas J.

| "Law" | "'Law,' 'Works of the Law,' and Legalism in Paul." *Westminster Theological Journal* 45 (1983): 73-100. |
| *Romans* | *The Epistle to the Romans.* Grand Rapids: Eerdmans, 1996. |

Moore, George Foot

| "Writers" | "Christian Writers on Judaism." *Harvard Theological Review* 14 (1921): 197-254. |

Moule, C. F. D.
"Obligation"   "Obligation in the Ethic of Paul." In *Christian History and Interpretation: Studies Presented to John Knox,* edited by W. R. Farmer, C. F. D. Moule, and R. R. Niebuhr, 389-406. Cambridge: Cambridge University Press, 1967.

Moxnes, Halvor
Theology   *Theology in Conflict: Studies in Paul's Understanding of God in Romans.* Leiden: Brill, 1980.

Najman, Hindy
"Law"   "The Law of Nature and the Authority of Mosaic Law." *Studia Philonica Annual* 11 (1999): 55-73.

Olley, John W.
Righteousness   *"Righteousness" in the Septuagint of Isaiah: A Contextual Study.* Missoula: Scholars, 1979.

Parkes, James
Conflict   *The Conflict of the Church and the Synagogue.* 1934. New York: Atheneum, 1969.
Foundations   *The Foundations of Judaism and Christianity.* Chicago: Quadrangle, 1960.

Pate, C. Marvin
Reverse   *The Reverse of the Curse: Paul, Wisdom, and the Law.* Tübingen: Mohr Siebeck, 2000.

Penna, Romano
Paul   *Paul the Apostle: Wisdom and Folly of the Cross.* Vol. 2. Collegeville, Minn.: Liturgical Press, 1996.

Pfleiderer, Otto
Paulinism   *Paulinism: A Contribution to the History of Primitive Christian Theology.* 1-2. London: Williams and Norgate, 1877.

Przybylski, Benno
Righteousness   *Righteousness in Matthew and His World of Thought.* Cambridge: Cambridge University Press, 1980.

Quarles, Charles L.
"Soteriology"   "The Soteriology of R. Akiba and E. P. Sanders' *Paul and Palestinian Judaism." New Testament Studies* 42 (1996): 185-95.

Räisänen, Heikki
"Analyse"   "Römer 9-11: Analyse eines geistigen Ringens." *Aufstieg und Niedergang der römischen Welt: Geschichte und Kultur Roms im Spiegel der neueren Forschung* II, 25, 4 (1987), 2891-2939.
Law   *Paul and the Law.* 2nd ed. Tübingen: J. C. B. Mohr (Paul Siebeck) 1987.

"Legalism"   "Legalism and Salvation by the Law." In *Die paulinische Literatur und Theologie,* edited by S. Pedersen, 63-83. Aarhus: Aros, 1980.

"Research"   "Paul, God, and Israel: Romans 9–11 in Recent Research." In *The Social World of Formative Christianity and Judaism,* edited by Jacob Neusner, Peder Borgen, Ernest S. Frerichs, and Richard Horsley, 178-206. Philadelphia: Fortress, 1988.

Review   Review of *Israel's Law and the Church's Faith,* by Stephen Westerholm. *Biblica* 71 (1990): 269-72.

Torah   *Jesus, Paul, and Torah: Collected Essays.* Sheffield: Sheffield Academic Press, 1992.

Reinhartz, Adele

"Meaning"   "The Meaning of *Nomos* in Philo's *Exposition of the Law.*" *Studies in Religion/Sciences Religieuses* 15 (1986): 337-45.

Reiser, Marius

Judgment   *Jesus and Judgment: The Eschatological Proclamation in Its Jewish Context.* Minneapolis: Fortress, 1997.

Rhyne, C. Thomas

Faith   *Faith Establishes the Law.* Chico, Calif.: Scholars, 1981.

Richardson, Peter

Israel   *Israel in the Apostolic Church.* Cambridge: Cambridge University Press, 1969.

Ridderbos, Herman

Paul   *Paul: An Outline of His Theology.* Grand Rapids: Eerdmans, 1975.

Rieger, Hans-Martin

"Religion"   "Eine Religion der Gnade: Zur 'Bundesnomismus'-Theorie von E. P. Sanders." In *Bund und Tora: Zur theologischen Begriffsgeschichte in alttestamentlicher, frühjüdischer und urchristlicher Tradition,* edited by Friedrich Avemarie and Hermann Lichtenberger, 129-61. Tübingen: J. C. B. Mohr (Paul Siebeck), 1996.

Riesner, Rainer

Period   *Paul's Early Period: Chronology, Mission Strategy, Theology.* Grand Rapids: Eerdmans, 1998.

Röhser, Günter

Metaphorik   *Metaphorik und Personifikation der Sünde: Antike Sündenvorstellungen und paulinische Hamartia.* Tübingen: J. C. B. Mohr (Paul Siebeck), 1987.

Roo, Jacqueline C. R. de

"Concept"   "The Concept of 'Works of the Law' in Jewish and Christian Literature." In *Christian-Jewish Relations through the Centuries,* edited by Stanley E. Porter and Brook W. R. Pearson, 116-47. Sheffield: Sheffield Academic Press, 2000.

Sanday, William, and Arthur C. Headlam

Romans   *A Critical and Exegetical Commentary on the Epistle to the Romans.* 5th ed. Edinburgh: T. & T. Clark, 1902.

Sanders, E. P.

"Covenant"   "The Covenant as a Soteriological Category and the Nature of Salvation in Palestinian and Hellenistic Judaism." In *Jews, Greeks, and Christians: Studies in Honor of W. D. Davies,* edited by Robert Hamerton-Kelly and Robin Scroggs, 11-44. Leiden: Brill, 1976.

Law   *Paul, the Law, and the Jewish People.* Philadelphia: Fortress, 1983.

Paul   *Paul.* Oxford: Oxford University Press, 1991.

Paul Pal. Jud.   *Paul and Palestinian Judaism.* Philadelphia: Fortress, 1977.

Sandmel, Samuel

Genius   *The Genius of Paul.* 3rd ed. Philadelphia: Fortress, 1979.

Schechter, Solomon

Aspects   *Aspects of Rabbinic Theology.* 1909. New York: Schocken Books, 1961.

Schlier, Heinrich

Römerbrief   *Der Römerbrief.* Freiburg: Herder, 1977.

Schnabel, Eckhard J.

Law   *Law and Wisdom from Ben Sira to Paul: A Tradition Historical Enquiry into the Relation of Law, Wisdom, and Ethics.* Tübingen: J. C. B. Mohr (Paul Siebeck), 1985.

Schoeps, Hans Joachim

Argument   *The Jewish-Christian Argument.* London: Faber and Faber, 1965.

Paul   *Paul: The Theology of the Apostle in the Light of Jewish Religious History.* Philadelphia: Westminster, 1961.

Schreiner, Thomas R.

"Abolition"   "The Abolition and Fulfillment of the Law in Paul." *Journal for the Study of the New Testament* 35 (1989): 47-74.

"Election"   "Does Romans 9 Teach Individual Election unto Salvation?" In *The Grace of God, the Bondage of the Will,* vol. 1, edited by Thomas R. Schreiner and Bruce A. Ware, 89-106. Grand Rapids: Baker, 1995.

"Evaluation"   "Paul and Perfect Obedience to the Law: An Evaluation of the View of E. P. Sanders." *Westminster Theological Journal* 47 (1985): 245-78.

"Failure"   "Israel's Failure to Attain Righteousness in Romans 9:30–10:3." *Trinity Journal* 12 (1991): 209-20.

"Grace"   "Does Scripture Treach Prevenient Grace in the Wesleyan Sense?" In *The Grace of God, the Bondage of the Will,* vol. 2, edited by Thomas R. Schreiner and Bruce A. Ware, 365-82. Grand Rapids: Baker, 1995.

Law   *The Law and Its Fulfillment: A Pauline Theology of Law.* Grand Rapids: Baker, 1993.

"Obedience"   "Is Perfect Obedience to the Law Possible? A Re-examination of

	Galatians 3:10." *Journal of the Evangelical Theological Society* 27 (1984): 151-60.
Paul	*Paul, Apostle of God's Glory in Christ: A Pauline Theology.* Downers Grove, Ill.: InterVarsity, 2001.
Romans	*Romans.* Grand Rapids: Baker, 1998.
"View"	"Paul's View of the Law in Romans 10:4-5." *Westminster Theological Journal* 55 (1993): 113-35.
"Works"	"Did Paul Believe in Justification by Works? Another Look at Romans 2." *Bulletin for Biblical Research* 3 (1993): 131-58.
"Works of Law"	"'Works of Law' in Paul." *Novum Testamentum* 33 (1991): 217-44.

Schweitzer, Albert

Interpreters	*Paul and His Interpreters.* 1912. London: Adam and Charles Black, 1950.
Mysticism	*The Mysticism of Paul the Apostle.* New York: Seabury Press, 1931.
Quest	*The Quest of the Historical Jesus.* New York: Macmillan, 1968.

Scott, James M.

| "Works" | "'For as Many as Are of Works of the Law Are under a Curse' (Galatians 3.10)." In *Paul and the Scriptures of Israel,* edited by Craig A. Evans and James A. Sanders, 187-221. Sheffield: Sheffield Academic Press, 1993. |

Seifrid, Mark A.

"Alleys"	"Blind Alleys in the Controversy over the Paul of History." *Tyndale Bulletin* 45 (1994): 73-95.
"Approach"	"Paul's Approach to the Old Testament in Rom 10:6-8." *Trinity Journal* 6 (1985): 6-37.
"Declaration"	"In What Sense Is 'Justification' a Declaration?" *Churchman* 114 (2000): 123-36.
"Gift"	"'The Gift of Salvation': Its Failure to Address the Crux of Justification." *Journal of the Evangelical Theological Society* 42 (1999): 679-88.
Justification	*Justification by Faith: The Origin and Development of a Central Pauline Theme.* Leiden: Brill, 1992.
"Language"	"Righteousness Language in the Hebrew Scriptures and Early Judaism." In *Justification and Variegated Nomism,* vol. 1, edited by D. A. Carson, Peter T. O'Brien, and Mark A. Seifrid, 415-42. Tübingen: Mohr-Siebeck, 2001.
"Perspective"	"The 'New Perspective' on Paul and Its Problems." *Themelios* 25 (2000): 4-18.
"Revelation"	"Natural Revelation and the Purpose of the Law in Romans." *Tyndale Bulletin* 49 (1999): 115-29.
Righteousness	*Christ, Our Righteousness: Paul's Theology of Justification.* Downers Grove, Ill.: InterVarsity, 2000.
"Subject"	"The Subject of Rom 7:14-25." *Novum Testamentum* 34 (1992): 313-33.

Silva, Moisés

| Philippians | *Philippians.* Grand Rapids: Baker, 1992. |

"Synthesis"   "The Law and Christianity: Dunn's New Synthesis." *Westminster Theological Journal* 53 (1991): 339-53.

Words   *Biblical Words and Their Meaning: An Introduction to Lexical Semantics.* Revised and expanded edition. Grand Rapids: Zondervan, 1994.

Smiles, Vincent M.

Gospel   *The Gospel and the Law in Galatia: Paul's Response to Jewish-Christian Separatism and the Threat of Galatian Apostasy.* Collegeville, Minn.: Liturgical Press, 1998.

Snodgrass, Klyne R.

"Justification"   "Justification by Grace — to the Doers: An Analysis of the Place of Romans 2 in the Theology of Paul." *New Testament Studies* 32 (1986): 72-93.

Söding, Thomas

"Verheissung"   "Verheissung und Erfüllung im Lichte paulinischer Theologie." *New Testament Studies* 47 (2001): 146-70.

Spilsbury, Paul

"Josephus"   "Josephus." In *Justification and Variegated Nomism*, vol. 1, edited by D. A. Carson, Peter T. O'Brien, and Mark A. Seifrid, 241-60. Tübingen: Mohr-Siebeck, 2001.

Stanley, Christopher D.

"Curse"   "'Under a Curse': A Fresh Reading of Galatians 3.10-14." *New Testament Studies* 36 (1990): 481-511.

Stanton, Graham

"Law"   "The Law of Moses and the Law of Christ." In *Paul and the Mosaic Law*, edited by James D. G. Dunn, 99-116. Grand Rapids: Eerdmans, 2001.

Stendahl, Krister

Paul   *Paul among Jews and Gentiles.* Philadelphia: Fortress, 1976.

Stowers, Stanley K.

Rereading   *A Rereading of Romans: Justice, Jews, and Gentiles.* New Haven: Yale University Press, 1994.

Stuhlmacher, Peter

Doctrine   *Revisiting Paul's Doctrine of Justification: A Challenge to the New Perspective.* With an essay by Donald A. Hagner. Downers Grove, Ill.: InterVarsity, 2001.

Reconciliation   *Reconciliation, Law, and Righteousness: Essays in Biblical Theology.* Philadelphia: Fortress, 1986.

Theologie   *Biblische Theologie des Neuen Testaments.* Vol. 1, *Grundlegung. Von Jesus zu Paulus.* Göttingen: Vandenhoeck & Ruprecht, 1992.

Bibliography

Talbert, Charles H.

"Paul" "Paul, Judaism, and the Revisionists." *Catholic Biblical Quarterly* 63 (2001): 1-22.

Thielman, Frank

"Coherence" "The Coherence of Paul's View of the Law: The Evidence of First Corinthians." *New Testament Studies* 38 (1992): 235-53.

"Ethics" "Law and Liberty in the Ethics of Paul." *Ex Auditu* 11 (1995): 63-75.

Law *The Law and the New Testament: The Question of Continuity.* New York: Crossroad, 1999.

Paul *Paul and the Law: A Contextual Approach.* Downers Grove, Ill.: InterVarsity, 1994.

Plight *From Plight to Solution: A Jewish Framework for Understanding Paul's View of the Law in Galatians and Romans.* Leiden: Brill, 1989.

Thompson, Richard W.

"Critique" "Paul's Double Critique of Jewish Boasting: A Study of Rom 3,27 in Its Context." *Biblica* 67 (1986): 520-31.

Thurén, Lauri

Derhetorizing Paul *Derhetorizing Paul: A Dynamic Perspective on Pauline Theology and the Law.* Tübingen: Mohr Siebeck, 2000.

Tov, Emanuel

Use *The Text-Critical Use of the Septuagint in Biblical Research.* Jerusalem: Simor, 1981.

Trilling, Wolfgang

Israel *Das wahre Israel.* 3rd ed. Munich: Kösel, 1964.

Vos, J. S.

"Antinomie" "Die hermeneutische Antinomie bei Paulus (Galater 3.11-12; Römer 10.5-10)." *New Testament Studies* 38 (1992): 254-70.

Wagner, J. Ross

Heralds *Heralds of the Good News: Isaiah and Paul "In Concert" in the Letter to the Romans.* Leiden: Brill, 2002.

Wahlde, Urban C. von

"Faith" "Faith and Works in Jn VI 28-29." *Novum Testamentum* 22 (1980): 304-15.

Watson, Francis

Paul *Paul, Judaism, and the Gentiles: A Sociological Approach.* Cambridge: Cambridge University Press, 1986.

Weima, Jeffrey A. D.

"Function" "The Function of the Law in Relation to Sin: An Evaluation of the View of H. Räisänen." *Novum Testamentum* 32 (1990): 219-35.

Wesley, John

"Bishop of London" "A Letter to the Right Reverend the Lord Bishop of London." In *The Works of John Wesley*, vol. 11, edited by Gerald R. Cragg, 327-51. Oxford: Clarendon, 1975.

Earnest Appeal *An Earnest Appeal to Men of Reason and Religion*. In *The Works of John Wesley*, vol. 11, edited by Gerald R. Cragg, 37-94. Oxford: Clarendon, 1975.

Farther Appeal *A Farther Appeal to Men of Reason and Religion*. In *The Works of John Wesley*, vol. 11, edited by Gerald R. Cragg, 95-325. Oxford: Clarendon, 1975.

JWJ *Journal and Diaries*. In *The Works of John Wesley*, vols. 18-24, edited by W. Reginald Ward and Richard P. Heitzenrater. Nashville: Abingdon, 1988-97.

Letters *Letters*. 1-2. In *The Works of John Wesley*, vols. 25-26, edited by Frank Baker. Oxford: Clarendon, 1980-82.

"Moravian Brethren" "An Extract from 'A Short View of the Difference between the Moravian Brethren (so called), and the Rev. Mr. John and Charles Wesley." In *The Works of John Wesley*, 10:201-4. London, 1872; Grand Rapids: Zondervan, n.d.

"Mr. Downes" "A Letter to the Reverend Mr. Downes." In *The Works of John Wesley*, vol. 9, edited by Rupert E. Davies, 350-66. Nashville: Abingdon, 1989.

"Mr. Potter" "A Letter to the Reverend Mr. Potter." In *The Works of John Wesley*, 9:89-96. London, 1872; Grand Rapids: Zondervan, n.d.

Necessity *Thoughts upon Necessity*. In *The Works of John Wesley*, 10:457-74. London, 1872; Grand Rapids: Zondervan, n.d.

Notes *Wesley's Notes on the Bible*. Grand Rapids: Francis Asbury Press (Zondervan), 1987.

Perfection *A Plain Account of Christian Perfection*. In *The Works of John Wesley*, 11:366-446. London, 1872; Grand Rapids: Zondervan, n.d.

Predestination *Predestination Calmly Considered*. In *The Works of John Wesley*, 10:204-59. London, 1872; Grand Rapids: Zondervan, n.d.

"Protestant" "A Word to a Protestant." In *The Works of John Wesley*, 11:187-95. London, 1872; Grand Rapids: Zondervan, n.d.

"Quaker" "A Letter to a Person lately joined with the people called Quakers." In *The Works of John Wesley*, 10:177-88. London, 1872; Grand Rapids: Zondervan, n.d.

"Sabbath-Breaker" "A Word to a Sabbath-Breaker." In *The Works of John Wesley*, 11:164-66. London, 1872; Grand Rapids: Zondervan, n.d.

Sermons *Sermons*. In *The Works of John Wesley*, vols. 1-4, edited by Albert C. Outler. Nashville: Abingdon, 1984-87.

Westerholm, Stephen

"Fulfilling" "On Fulfilling the Whole Law (Gal 5.14)." *Svensk exegetisk årsbok* 51-52 (1986-87): 229-37.

Law   *Israel's Law and the Church's Faith: Paul and His Recent Interpreters.*
                        Grand Rapids: Eerdmans, 1988.
"Letter"   "Letter and Spirit: The Foundation of Pauline *Ethics.*" *New Testament*
                        Studies 30 (1984): 229-48.
"Meaning"   "*Torah, Nomos,* and Law: A Question of 'Meaning.'" *Studies in Reli-*
                        gion/Sciences Religieuses 15 (1986): 327-36.
"Nomos"   "Torah, *Nomos* and Law." In Peter Richardson and Stephen
                        Westerholm (with others), *Law in Religious Communities in the Ro-*
                        man Period: The Debate over Torah *and* Nomos *in Post-biblical Juda-*
                        ism and Early Christianity, 45-56. Waterloo, Ontario: Wilfrid Laurier
                        University Press, 1991.
"Perspective"   "The 'New Perspective' at Twenty-Five." In *Justification and Variegated*
                        Nomism, vol. 2, edited by D. A. Carson, Peter T. O'Brien, and Mark A.
                        Seifrid. Tübingen: Mohr-Siebeck. Forthcoming.
Preface   *Preface to the Study of Paul.* Grand Rapids: Eerdmans, 1997.
"Response"   "Response to Heikki Räisänen." In *Paul and the Mosaic Law,* edited by
                        James D. G. Dunn, 247-49. Grand Rapids: Eerdmans, 2001.
Review   Review of *Das Gesetz bei Paulus,* by Hans Hübner. *Svensk exegetisk*
                        årsbok 44 (1979): 194-99.
"Romans 9–11"   "Paul and the Law in Romans 9–11." In *Paul and the Mosaic Law,* edited
                        by James D. G. Dunn, 215-37. Grand Rapids: Eerdmans, 2001.
"Sinai"   "Sinai as Viewed from Damascus: Paul's Reevaluation of the Mosaic
                        Law." In *The Road from Damascus: The Impact of Paul's Conversion on*
                        His Life, Thought, and Ministry, edited by Richard N. Longenecker,
                        147-65. Grand Rapids: Eerdmans, 1997.

Whiteley, D. E. H.
Theology   *The Theology of St. Paul.* 2nd ed. Oxford: Basil Blackwell, 1974.

Wilckens, Ulrich
"Bekehrung"   "Die Bekehrung des Paulus als religionsgeschichtliches Problem." In
                        Rechtfertigung als Freiheit, 11-32. Neukirchen-Vluyn: Neukirchener,
                        1974.
"Christologie"   "Christologie und Anthropologie im Zusammenhang der paulin-
                        ischen Rechtfertigungslehre." *Zeitschrift für die neutestamentliche*
                        Wissenschaft 67 (1976): 64-82.
"Entwicklung"   "Zur Entwicklung des paulinischen Gesetzesverständnisses." *New Tes-*
                        tament Studies 28 (1982): 154-90.
Resurrection   *Resurrection.* Atlanta: John Knox, 1978.
Review   "Zum Römerbriefkommentar von Heinrich Schlier." *Theologische*
                        Literaturzeitung 103 (1978): 849-56.
Römer   *Der Brief an die Römer.* 1-3. Cologne: Benziger; Neukirchen-Vluyn:
                        Neukirchener, 1978-82.
"Werken"   "Was heisst bei Paulus: 'Aus Werken des Gesetzes wird kein Mensch
                        gerecht'?" In *Rechtfertigung als Freiheit,* 77-109. Neukirchen-Vluyn:
                        Neukirchener, 1974.

Williams, Sam K.

"Justification"   "Justification and the Spirit in Galatians." *Journal for the Study of the New Testament* 29 (1987): 91-100.

"Righteousness"   "The 'Righteousness of God' in Romans." *Journal of Biblical Literature* 99 (1980): 241-90.

Winger, Michael

"Grace"   "From Grace to Sin: Names and Abstractions in Paul's Letters." *Novum Testamentum* 41 (1999): 145-75.

Law   *By What Law? The Meaning of Νόμος in the Letters of Paul.* Atlanta: Scholars, 1992.

"Meaning"   "Meaning and Law." *Journal of Biblical Literature* 117 (1998): 105-10.

Winninge, Mikael

Sinners   *Sinners and the Righteous: A Comparative Study of the Psalms of Solomon and Paul's Letters.* Stockholm: Almqvist & Wiksell International, 1995.

Wisdom, Jeffrey R.

Blessing   *Blessing for the Nations and the Curse of the Law: Paul's Citation of Genesis and Deuteronomy in Gal 3.8-10.* Tübingen: Mohr Siebeck, 2001.

Wolfson, Harry Austryn

Philo   *Philo: Foundations of Religious Philosophy in Judaism, Christianity, and Islam.* 1-2. 4th ed. Cambridge: Harvard University Press, 1968.

Wrede, W.

Paul   *Paul.* 1908. Lexington, Ky.: American Library Association Committee on Reprinting, 1962.

Wright, N. T.

Climax   *The Climax of the Covenant: Christ and the Law in Pauline Theology.* Minneapolis: Fortress, 1991.

Founder   *What Saint Paul Really Said: Was Paul of Tarsus the Real Founder of Christianity?* Grand Rapids: Eerdmans, 1997.

"History"   "The Paul of History and the Apostle of Faith." *Tyndale Bulletin* 29 (1978): 61-88.

"Law"   "The Law in Romans 2." In *Paul and the Mosaic Law,* edited by James D. G. Dunn, 131-50. Grand Rapids: Eerdmans, 2001.

People   *The New Testament and the People of God.* Minneapolis: Fortress, 1992.

"Synthesis"   "Putting Paul Together Again: Toward a Synthesis of Pauline Theology (1 and 2 Thessalonians, Philippians, and Philemon)." In *Pauline Theology I: Thessalonians, Philippians, Galatians, Philemon,* edited by Jouette M. Bassler, 183-211. Minneapolis: Fortress, 1991.

"Theology"   "Romans and the Theology of Paul." In *Pauline Theology III: Romans,* edited by David M. Hay and E. Elizabeth Johnson, 30-67. Minneapolis: Fortress, 1995.

Yinger, Kent L.

Judgment   *Paul, Judaism, and Judgment according to Deeds.* Cambridge: Cambridge University Press, 1999.

Young, Norman H.

"Cursed"   "Who's Cursed — and Why? (Galatians 3:10-14)." *Journal of Biblical Literature* 117 (1998): 79-92.

"Shifts"   "Pronominal Shifts in Paul's Argument to the Galatians." In *Ancient History in a Modern University,* vol. 2, *Early Christianity, Late Antiquity, and Beyond,* edited by T. W. Hillard, R. A. Kearsley, C. E. V. Nixon, and A. M. Nobbs, 205-15. Grand Rapids: Eerdmans, 1998.

Zeller, Dieter

"Diskussion"   "Zur neueren Diskussion über das Gesetz bei Paulus." *Theologie und Philosophie* 62 (1987): 481-99.

Ziesler, J. A.

Meaning   *The Meaning of Righteousness in Paul: A Linguistic and Theological Enquiry.* Cambridge: Cambridge University Press, 1972.

"Role"   "The Role of the Tenth Commandment in Romans 7." *Journal for the Study of the New Testament* 33 (1988): 41-56.

Index of Authors

472

Index of Scripture and Other Ancient Literature